Design Strategy

T0323338

Design Thinking, Design Theory

Ken Friedman and Erik Stolterman, editors

Design Strategy

Challenges in Wicked Problem Territory

Nancy C. Roberts

The MIT Press
Cambridge, Massachusetts
London, England

The MIT Press would like to thank the anonymous peer reviewers who provided comments on drafts of this book. The generous work of academic experts is essential for establishing the authority and quality of our publications. We acknowledge with gratitude the contributions of these otherwise uncredited readers.

This book was set in Stone Serif and Stone Sans by Westchester Publishing Services. Printed and bound in the United States of America.

Library of Congress Cataloging-in-Publication Data

Names: Roberts, Nancy Charlotte, author.
Title: Design strategy : challenges in wicked problem territory / Nancy C. Roberts.
Description: Cambridge, Massachusetts : The MIT Press, [2023] | Series: Design thinking, design theory | Includes bibliographical references and index.
Identifiers: LCCN 2022057279 (print) | LCCN 2022057280 (ebook) | ISBN 9780262546812 (paperback) | ISBN 9780262376594 (epub) | ISBN 9780262376587 (pdf)
Subjects: LCSH: Design—Philosophy. | Problem solving.
Classification: LCC NK1505 .R63 2023 (print) | LCC NK1505 (ebook) | DDC 744.01—dc23/eng /20230412
LC record available at https://lccn.loc.gov/2022057279
LC ebook record available at https://lccn.loc.gov/2022057280

10 9 8 7 6 5 4 3 2 1

To Dr. John Arquilla, my deep appreciation for your unwavering support of the design way,
and
To my students who asked for "more please," my heartfelt thanks for being my best teachers.

Contents

Series Foreword

As professions go, design is relatively young. The practice of design predates professions. In fact, the practice of design—making things to serve a useful goal, making tools—predates the human race. Making tools is one of the attributes that made us human in the first place.

Design, in the most generic sense of the word, began over 2.5 million years ago when *Homo habilis* manufactured the first tools. Human beings were designing well before we began to walk upright. Four hundred thousand years ago, we began to manufacture spears. By forty thousand years ago, we had moved up to specialized tools.

Urban design and architecture came along ten thousand years ago in Mesopotamia. Interior architecture and furniture design probably emerged with them. It was another five thousand years before graphic design and typography got their start in Sumeria with the development of cuneiform. After that, things picked up speed.

All goods and services are designed. The urge to design—to consider a situation, imagine a better situation, and act to create that improved situation—goes back to our prehuman ancestors. Making tools helped us to become what we are: design helped to make us human.

Today, the word *design* means many things. The common factor linking them is service, and designers are engaged in a service profession in which the results of their work meet human needs.

Design is first of all a process. The word *design* entered the English language in the 1500s as a verb, with the first written citation of the verb dated to the year 1548. *Merriam-Webster's Collegiate Dictionary* defines the verb *design* as "to conceive and plan out in the mind; to have as a specific purpose; to devise for a specific function or end." Related to these is the act of drawing, with an emphasis on the nature of the drawing as a plan or map, as well as "to draw plans for; to create, fashion, execute or construct according to plan."

Half a century later, the word began to be used as a noun, with the first cited use of the noun *design* occurring in 1588. *Merriam-Webster's* defines the noun as "a particular purpose held in view by an individual or group; deliberate, purposive planning; a mental project or scheme in which means to an end are laid down." Here, too, purpose and planning toward desired outcomes are central. Among these are "a preliminary sketch or outline showing the main features of something to be executed; an underlying scheme that governs functioning, developing or unfolding; a plan or protocol for carrying out or accomplishing something; the arrangement of elements or details in a product or work of art." Today, we design large, complex process, systems, and services, and we design organizations and structures to produce them. Design has changed considerably since our remote ancestors made the first stone tools.

At a highly abstract level, Herbert Simon's definition covers nearly all imaginable instances of design. To design, Simon writes, is to "[devise] courses of action aimed at changing existing situations into preferred ones" (Simon, 1982, 129). Design, properly defined, is the entire process across the full range of domains required for any given outcome.

But the design process is always more than a general, abstract way of working. Design takes concrete form in the work of the service professions that meet human needs, a broad range of making and planning disciplines. These include industrial design, graphic design, textile design, furniture design, information design, process design, product design, interaction design, transportation design, educational design, systems design, urban design, design leadership, and design management, as well as architecture, engineering, information technology, and computer science.

These fields focus on different subjects and objects. They have distinct traditions, methods, and vocabularies, used and put into practice by distinct and often dissimilar professional groups. Although the traditions dividing these groups are distinct, common boundaries sometimes form a border. Where this happens, they serve as meeting points where common concerns build bridges. Today, ten challenges uniting the design professions form such a set of common concerns.

Three performance challenges, four substantive challenges, and three contextual challenges bind the design disciplines and professions together as a common field. The performance challenges arise because all design professions

1. act on the physical world,
2. address human needs, and
3. generate the built environment.

In the past, these common attributes were not sufficient to transcend the boundaries of tradition. Today, objective changes in the larger world give rise to four substantive challenges that are driving convergence in design practice and research. These substantive challenges are

1. increasingly ambiguous boundaries between artifacts, structure, and process;
2. increasingly large-scale social, economic, and industrial frames;
3. an increasingly complex environment of needs, requirements, and constraints; and
4. information content that often exceeds the value of physical substance.

These challenges require new frameworks of theory and research to address contemporary problem areas while solving specific cases and problems. In professional design practice, we often find that solving design problems requires interdisciplinary teams with a transdisciplinary focus. Fifty years ago, a sole practitioner and an assistant or two might have solved most design problems. Today, we need groups of people with skills across several disciplines and the additional skills that enable professionals to work with, listen to, and learn from each other as they solve problems.

Three contextual challenges define the nature of many design problems today. While many design problems function at a simpler level, these issues affect many of the major design problems that challenge us, and these challenges also affect simple design problems linked to complex social, mechanical, or technical systems. These issues are

1. a complex environment in which many projects or products cross the boundaries of several organizations, stakeholder, producer, and user groups;

2. projects or products that must meet the expectations of many organizations, stakeholders, producers, and users; and

3. demands at every level of production, distribution, reception, and control.

These ten challenges require a qualitatively different approach to professional design practice than was the case in earlier times. Past environments were simpler. They made simpler demands. Individual experience and personal development were sufficient for depth and substance in professional practice. While experience and development are still necessary, they are no longer sufficient. Most of today's design challenges require analytic and synthetic planning skills that cannot be developed through practice alone.

Professional design practice today involves advanced knowledge. This knowledge is not solely a higher level of professional practice. It is also a qualitatively different form of professional practice that emerges in response to the demands of the information society and the knowledge economy to which it gives rise.

In his essay "Why Design Education Must Change" (from *Core77*, November 26, 2010), Donald Norman challenges the premises and practices of the design profession. In the past, designers operated on the belief that talent and a willingness to jump into problems with both feet gives them an edge in solving problems. Norman writes:

> In the early days of industrial design, the work was primarily focused upon physical products. Today, however, designers work on organizational structure and social problems, on interaction, service, and experience design. Many problems involve complex social and political issues. As a result, designers have become applied behavioral scientists, but they are woefully undereducated for the task. Designers often fail to understand the complexity of the issues and the depth of knowledge already known. They claim that fresh eyes can produce novel solutions, but then they wonder why these solutions are seldom implemented, or if implemented, why they fail. Fresh eyes can indeed produce insightful results, but the eyes must also be educated and knowledgeable. Designers often lack the requisite understanding. Design schools do not train students about these complex issues, about the interlocking complexities of human and social behavior, about the behavioral sciences, technology, and business. There is little or no training in science, the scientific method, and experimental design.

This is not industrial design in the sense of designing products, but industry-related design, design as thought and action for solving problems and imagining new futures.

This MIT Press series of books emphasizes strategic design to create value through innovative products and services, and it emphasizes design as service through rigorous creativity, critical inquiry, and an ethics of respectful design. This rests on a sense of understanding, empathy, and appreciation for people, for nature, and for the world we shape through design. Our goal as editors is to develop a series of vital conversations that help designers and researchers to serve business, industry, and the public sector for positive social and economic outcomes.

We will present books that bring a new sense of inquiry to the design, helping to shape a more reflective and stable design discipline able to support a stronger profession grounded in empirical research, generative concepts, and the solid theory that gives rise to what W. Edwards Deming (1993) described as profound knowledge. For Deming, a physicist, engineer, and designer, profound knowledge comprised systems thinking and the understanding of processes embedded in systems, an understanding of variation and the tools we need to understand variation, a theory of knowledge, and a foundation in human psychology. This is the beginning of "deep design"—the union of deep practice with robust intellectual inquiry.

A series on design thinking and theory faces the same challenges that we face as a profession. On one level, design is a general human process that we use to understand and to shape our world. Nevertheless, we cannot address this process or the world in its general, abstract form. Rather, we meet the challenges of design in specific challenges, addressing problems or ideas in a situated context. The challenges we face as designers today are as diverse as the problems clients bring us. We are involved in design for economic anchors, economic continuity, and economic growth. We design for urban needs and rural needs, for social development and creative communities. We are involved with environmental sustainability and economic policy, agriculture competitive crafts for export, competitive products and brands for micro-enterprises, developing new products for bottom-of-pyramid markets and redeveloping old products for mature or wealthy markets. Within the framework of design, we are also challenged to design for extreme situations; for biotech, nanotech, and new materials; for social business; as well as for conceptual challenges for worlds that do not yet exist (such as the world beyond the Kurzweil singularity) and for new visions of the world that does exist.

The Design Thinking, Design Theory series from the MIT Press will explore these issues and more—meeting them, examining them, and helping designers to address them.

Join us in this journey.

Ken Friedman
Erik Stolterman

Editors, Design Thinking, Design Theory Series

Preface

My interest in "wicked problems" began in the late 1990s. By 1996, the Taliban, an Islamic militia led by the Muslim cleric Mullah Mohammed Omar, controlled most of Afghanistan. It promised to uphold traditional Islamic values and deliver peace to the country. The United Nations (UN), involved in Afghanistan since the early 1980s, was working to find a political settlement, generate and distribute international aid for refugees, and protect human rights. Anticipating that the Taliban would win the civil war that had been raging for close to twenty years, the UN began preparations to deal with the Taliban's control over the country and its expected participation in postconflict reconstruction efforts.

Acknowledging that it had not been particularly successful in supporting postconflict reconstruction efforts, the UN included an experimental project in its preparations. The project's goal was to bring together the major stakeholders—the Taliban, UN agency representatives, nongovernmental organizations (NGOs), donors, and military organizations—to inform the creation of a strategic framework for the reconstruction of Afghanistan. My assignment, as a member of the mission team from the UN Staff College in Torino, Italy, was to work with the Staff College team members and the UN in-country staff to organize, design, and facilitate an in-country, five-day collaborative stakeholder workshop.

Returning home after the stakeholder collaboration, I searched the literature to help me describe and characterize the experience. My reading of Horst Rittel and Melvin Webber's influential article "Dilemmas in a Theory of Planning,"[1] in which they introduced the concept of "wicked problems," convinced me that what the United Nations and the mission team undertook in Afghanistan was truly in "wicked problem territory." The problems there were so intractable that no one could agree on what they were, much less their solutions, although the workshop attendees had some success in identifying a list of priorities that should be included in the Afghan framework. Unfortunately, the workshop's prioritized list of strategic issues was only dimly recognizable compared to the final document, which took a year to wind its way through the UN approval process. Collaborations launched with all good intentions could successfully kick off a discovery process to inform the strategic framework, but follow-on activities and downstream negotiations with hundreds of organizations, social actors, political authorities, and "warring bureaucracies" illustrated the challenges faced by the collaborative strategy in wicked problem territory. Above all, I came to understand that wicked problems like those in postconflict Afghanistan, if they can be solved at all, will be handled in the long run—the *very* long run—and one has to be prepared for all sorts of twists and turns along the way.[2]

In reading Rittel and Webber's article, I also learned of their search for problem-solving strategies that might be more viable and effective in highly contested arenas. In their view, current strategies had their limitations: the rational-analytic model of problem solving (which they referred to as the "scientific approach") was a poor fit in high-conflict environments; competition reinforced zero-sum games of winners and losers;[3] authority had its challenges in entrusting "de facto decision-making to the wise and knowledgeable professional experts and politicians";[4] and "taming" was limited when "'carving off' a piece of the problem and finding a rational and feasible solution to this piece."[5] Instead, they proposed "an argumentation process in the course of which an image of the problem and of the solution emerges gradually among the participants, as a product of incessant judgment, subjected to critical argument."[6]

Was this it? Were no other problem-solving strategies viable in wicked problem territory? Others, I learned, were asking similar questions. As Kees Dorst wisely observed:

> the inability of conventional problem-solving to deal with the new open, complex, dynamic, and networked problems is reaching a crisis point. And these types of problems will not go away. On the contrary, we will have more of these problem situations to deal with in the future. . . . We have an unprecedented need to extend our problem-solving repertoire.[7]

My efforts to expand my problem-solving repertoire took me on quite an adventure, both as a researcher and a practitioner. Reviewing case studies of change opened up intriguing possibilities. People called "social entrepreneurs" and "policy entrepreneurs" were tackling some of the toughest problems around—poverty, health care, education, homelessness—and with some degree of success. Perhaps their strategies for change and transformation could offer insights into how to maneuver in wicked problem territory. I also visited the Hasso Plattner Institute of Design at Stanford University and IDEO in Palo Alto, California, mined their websites, read their recommended books, and took their online design courses. I also learned that design had moved well beyond product and process designs. It had entered the "C suite" of innovative companies that were using design not only to create new products and deliver better customer service, but as a vehicle to envision the organization's future and its redesign.

My aperture on design widened even more, and I remember quite vividly the moment it happened. Willie Smits's TED talk[8] described his efforts to save the orangutan, an endangered species in Borneo. To protect the orangutan, which some consider a wicked problem, he had to provide temporary facilities to house animals who were ill and abused so that they could regain their health. Then he had to set up a school to teach those who had been in captivity most of their lives how to be orangutans before they could be returned to their habitat in central Borneo's dense, first-growth forests. Smits' solution was to create a second-growth rain forest on denuded land ravaged by deforestation and fire where *nothing* lived. It would serve as a temporary shelter where the orangutan could live, recuperate, and learn. But to protect the regenerated rain forest from fires and deforestation that continually plagued the region, he had to help redesign the surrounding community's social and economic system to protect the people, who would protect the forest that would protect the orangutan. In that moment, design got very big for me. The design field wasn't just about product, process, service, or organizational designs. It was also about social innovations, the redesign of social systems, and even the regeneration of the physical and social world.

Having reservations about standard problem-solving strategies in wicked problem territory, I therefore asked two questions: Was it possible to characterize design as a strategy? And if so, to what extent might the design strategy have advantages in wicked problem territory that would enable it to overcome some the disadvantages of other problem-solving strategies? The purpose in writing this book is to answer these two questions.

Following Rittel and Webber's lead in emphasizing the importance of context, the introduction explores some of the general forces of our VUCA world that appear to be driving us deeper and deeper into wicked problem territory. "VUCA" stands for: "volatility"—the exponential changes and the pace of twenty-first-century changes that are expected to see almost a thousand times greater technological change than its predecessor; "uncertainty"—the vague and blurred future, which makes it difficult to anticipate the consequences of exponential changes and the "unknown unknowns" heading our way; "complexity"—systems that are composed of many interconnected parts that are so closely intertwined and interconnected that it is difficult when problem solving to identify causes from their effects; and "ambiguity"—competing, unclear, or confusing future alternatives, each of which is plausible, but with no clear guidance on which path to pursue.

Building on this backdrop, chapter 1, "From Wicked Problems to Wicked Problem Territory," summarizes Rittel and Webber's view of wicked problems and their characteristics, compares tame and wicked problems, and introduces other problem typologies in the literature. Due to the lack of agreement in the literature on what wicked problems are and how to characterize them, I therefore recommend that we stop labeling and categorizing problems on which we cannot agree. Instead, I suggest we refer to problems as existing in certain problem-solving "spaces" that depend on the level of conflict surrounding problems and solutions. The problem "space" with the highest levels of conflict over problems and solutions then becomes wicked problem territory.

Chapter 2 completes part I with a review of five traditional problem-solving strategies (e.g., competitive strategy; authority/authoritative strategy; rational-analytic strategy; taming strategy; and collaborative strategy). Although all of these have advantages, they also have substantive limitations in wicked problem territory.

Part II then turns to the design strategy, which is the focus for the remainder of the book. The concept of strategy is well known among those who work in private- and public-sector organizations, including military organizations. We find countries with a "grand strategy," militaries with a "national security strategy," businesses with "competitive strategies," and public-sector organizations and nonprofits with missions and purposes they want to achieve. As Lawrence Freedman describes it, strategy involves the mobilization of resources and actions to bring about a desired outcome.[9] Thus, central to any strategy are its three parts—there is a goal or outcome that is pursued, an approach that mobilizes resources, and actions that attempt to achieve the goal or outcome. We can describe these three parts as the *what* of a strategy, or its intent or purpose; the *how* of a strategy, or its general approach; and the *means* of a strategy, or its methods, techniques, tools, and other elements used to execute the general approach.

Design also has a three-part story. The *what* of design is the goal or purpose that designers want to achieve—the creation of a world that could be. The *how* of design is the process that designers use to achieve their goal—variously described as "reflection-in-action," "the designerly way of knowing, thinking, and acting" and "design thinking." The *means* of design are its skill sets, toolkits, methods, and techniques central to design practice. So when we combine the details of the what, the how, and the means of design, the design strategy comes into bold relief as a "strategy to effect change," and "impact the world."[10]

Part II offers a general overview of the design strategy. Chapter 3 begins with a review of the *what* of design—its long history, discourse, landscape, growing disciplinary design fields and subfields, and design principles. The convergence between design and innovation is noted, as well as design's distinguishing features compared to art and science. The chapter ends with an overview of the *how* of design—the different ways in which designers characterize the design process.

Chapter 4 ventures beyond the exterior world of design to probe more deeply into the *how* of design, with special attention to designers' mindsets that guide design practice: the growth mindset, benefit mindset, hyperattuned mindset, imaginative mindset, analytical mindset, maker mindset, and change-agent mindset. The assumption is that mindsets inform designers' values and beliefs and attitudes, which in turn shape the external material world. Drawing from developmental theory, I also link designers' consciousness to the generation of physical material forms. Here, we learn that consciousness can evolve from a system driven by a mindset of "me," which only cares for one's own well-being, to a system driven by the concern for the well-being of the whole, including oneself. And finally, the chapter revisits the *what* of design to introduce the concept of *meta design*—designers' intentional interventions that attempt to alter people's cultural values, beliefs, and consciousness.

Finally, chapter 5 completes part II's introduction to the design strategy. I review some of design's basic *means*—the skill sets and toolkits employed in design practice that are key to delivering results in wicked problem territory. They are organized into seven general categories: designers' self-assessment; discovery process; data analytics; perspective taking, problem finding/framing, and solution generation; prototyping, evaluating, storytelling, and advocacy; change and transformation; and design project management. The underlying assumption that informs the seven categories of skill sets and toolkits is that in designing a world that could be, designers are taking on the role of creative change agent, a role that has not been fully appreciated by either designers or change agents.

Part III explores design's growing landscape into the following arenas where analysts and problem solvers warn that wicked problems lurk:

- The *strategic design* of private and public organizations, especially when an organization's future direction and strategy are anticipated to be very different from its past (chapter 6)

- The *systemic design* of multiple interconnected and overlapping economic, technical, and political subsystems and networks that make up a whole social system, such as those that exist in education, health care, and megacity planning and management, all of which are noted for their social complexity, transboundary interactions, and wide-ranging scale (chapter 7)

- The *regenerative design*, the coevolution and partnered relationship between humans and nature that involves the process of restoring, renewing, realigning, and revitalizing our social and natural world so humans and the built environment can coexist in a way that maintains the integrity of both society and nature (chapter 8)

Part IV assesses the design strategy. Chapter 9 summarizes the critiques of design and design thinking and the empirical research on strategic design that pinpoints both its limitations and its advantages. Noting some perplexing discrepancies and research results, I conclude that formative and summative evaluation techniques used in these assessments are not well suited to capturing the complexities and dynamics of design interventions in wicked problem territory. I thus recommend developmental evaluation that is highly attuned to what is being designed, how it is being designed, what learning is captured along the way, and what adaptations are necessary to improve the success rate of design interventions.

Chapter 10 offers my overall assessment of the design strategy and its comparative advantages vis-à-vis the other problem-solving strategies. I note its reliance on exploration, creativity, and learning; use of social technology; responsiveness to tensions and contradictions; and willingness to address ethical and moral issues in design. Although I am careful to treat competitive, authoritative, rational-analytic, taming, and collaborative strategies as conceptually separate and distinct since their purposes, intended results, and processes are different, chapter 10 also identifies one of the advantages of the design strategy. To be successful, it draws on some elements from all these strategies, a conclusion consistent with cultural theorists' recommendations when dealing with wicked problems. They believe, and I concur, that it is this mixing and "messy pluralism" that lie at the heart of the design strategy's power and potential in wicked problem territory.[11] Thus, the fundamental issue in this overall assessment of the design strategy is not whether it is a perfect problem-solving process. It isn't. The issue has been and continues to be whether the design strategy positions us to be better problem solvers compared to the other options currently available in wicked problem territory. I believe that the evidence to date demonstrates that it does.

Who Will Benefit from Reading This Book?

Design Strategy: Challenges in Wicked Problem Territory will appeal to practitioners and researchers who find themselves deep in wicked problem territory—whether they work in business or nonprofit organizations; deal with large-scale systems such as education, health care, policy making, and megacity planning; or conduct research on wicked problems. They will find, as I have, that the design approach to problem solving excels at generating creative ideas and transforming those ideas into innovations regardless of the domain, offering some hope that we can tackle the existential challenges facing us in the twenty-first century.

The book also will appeal to activists, change agents, leaders, policy professionals and entrepreneurs, and innovators, as well as those in transition communities interested in the strategic, systemic, and regenerative designs of governmental, economic, and ecological systems. What is of particular interest will be the design strategy's problem-solving process, which goes well beyond traditional approaches of problem solving to break the logjam of opposition and avoid traps that lock problem solvers into a never-ending cycle of conflict. As the noted systems thinker and designer Bela Banathy advised us, we "cannot take charge of [our] future—unless [we] also develop competence to take part directly and authentically in the design of systems in which [we] live and work and reclaim [our] right to do so. This is what true empowerment is about."[12]

Educators and students of design are a primary audience for this book. They will find the book's case studies that integrate theory and practice across diverse fields (e.g., human development, business and management, social systems, policy studies, and ecology) to be refreshingly interdisciplinary. Moreover, the book serves as a guide to appreciate design's evolution and its creative problem-solving approach, which is applicable no matter the context in which they work. Equally important, it signals the potential for partnerships and collaborations with change agents in the pursuit of transformational change. Beginning my professional career in change agentry and moving into design as I searched for greater creativity and innovation in the change process, I appreciate the synergy that is possible between the two fields. So whether you begin with design or change agentry, these areas of expertise are natural allies and need to inform each other as we seek to create a world that could be.

So which educators and students would find this book valuable? This is a hard question to answer, given the tremendous diversity of design courses, curricula, stand-alone design programs, and university-based design departments and schools. Some who have read the manuscript think that it is well suited for design students at the master's level, possibly those in upper-division courses at the undergraduate level, and even maybe for nondesign students with limited experience who are entering PhD design programs that are casting a large net to attract nondesign students from wide-ranging disciplines to increase student diversity. My original intention in writing this book was to aim it at nondesigners like my master's-level students, who were in an interdisciplinary program and had some exposure to design in design thinking workshops but wanted to know more about design. "More, please" was the way they put it. So for those out there who want "more, please," I hope you will find this book of value. The fun will be discovering where it will lead you.

Acknowledgments

This book has been a twenty-five-year journey. It began in the late 1990s with a United Nations (UN) mission team tasked with the creation of a strategic framework for the reconstruction of Afghanistan. Hugh Cholmondeley's invitation to join the team, for which I remain truly grateful, sent me on a path of discovery deep into wicked problem territory. Based on an article that I wrote about my experiences, Captain Frank Petho, chair of the Department of National Security at the Naval Postgraduate School (NPS), invited me to join the department and teach a course entitled "Coping with Wicked Problems." Thanks to his encouragement and the students' enthusiasm for the course, I came to appreciate how deeply people resonate with the topic of wicked problems. I also learned that it wasn't enough to tell people what wicked problems were, but it was incumbent on me to give them some change strategies to deal with them. If I didn't, by the end of the course, I had some very unhappy students who felt even more discouraged and depressed going back to work facing a barrage of wicked problems that they couldn't define or resolve.

Those lessons learned led me to the Department of Defense Analysis at NPS. I am extremely grateful to the then-chairman, Gordon McCormick, and the faculty, whose invitation to join the department changed the trajectory of my work and my life. It was in Defense Analysis where I began bringing design cases and readings into my "wicked problems" course. My students immediately resonated with design and design thinking. Trusting their advice and experiences, I expanded the content on design, which included tours and presentations at IDEO and the Hasso Plattner Institute School of Design at Stanford University, opportunities for which we all remain truly appreciative. Closing my course on the last day of my "wicked problems" course, one of my students asked if there were other courses in design at the university that they could take. I didn't like my answer—there were no more courses, at least not at our university. Saying "no" to students who were returning to the field for their fourth and fifth tours in Afghanistan and Iraq was not acceptable to me. So with the backing of the department chair, Dr. John Arquilla, I started teaching design workshops and short courses for the university, and eventually courses on design and design thinking, both in the Department of Defense Analysis and the Department of Systems Engineering. The university and I owe John Arquilla our deepest gratitude. None of these endeavors would have been possible without his guidance and financial support. Others to whom I am truly grateful are colleagues who helped launch a bottom-up design program at NPS and whose challenges helped me think through some of the questions that I had about design and design thinking. My thanks to:

- Peter Denning and Sue Higgins of the Cebrowski Institute, who opened up space for our first design challenges

- Cliff Whitcom of the Systems Engineering Department, who sponsored the first course on design thinking in systems engineering and the creation of a design lab for engineering students

- Eleanor Unlinger, head librarian, who set up a design lab in the basement of the library and served as a facilitator for design challenges

- John Arquilla, who established a design lab for the Department of Defense Analysis and encouraged my work with a visiting scholar from Norway, Espen Berg-Knutsen

- Espen Berg-Knutsen who was a wonderful collaborator on the NORSOCOM project featured in chapter 6

- Ann Gallenson, Frank Barrett, Anita Salem, and Lyla Englehorn, who were skillful facilitators for our design challenges and enthusiastic sponsors of design research throughout the campus

My design students, many not mentioned by name due to the sensitivity of their work, have my deepest respect and thanks for the exemplary research that they contributed to our design program, some of which appears in this book. So, to the team of five and the team of ten (you know who you are), thank you for the privilege of working and learning with you. I also am grateful to Sam Hayes for the use of his images of geospatial and social network analyses from his award-winning design thesis as seen in chapter 4. I also want to acknowledge and thank three former students from the Monterey Institute of International Studies (now the Middlebury Institute of International Studies in Monterey) who attended my courses: Celina Aponte; Danielle Razo (who also was my teaching assistant for the Systems Engineering design course), and Ryann Hoffman. As engaging and creative participants in my courses, they always could be counted on to offer fresh perspectives and points of views. I am happy to report that they are now successful designers whom I now call colleagues and friends.

I also am indebted to Sandra Bichl and the Career Angels HR Team for their permission to use their imagery in Figure Intro.1 that creatively depicts a VUCA world. My thanks also go to Raymond Trevor Bradley for his suggestions on how to visualize a Complex Adaptive System in Figure Intro.4 and to Dan Cunningham who graciously offered his time, not only to construct the social network in Figure 2.1, but to describe the assumptions that he had to make to generate it.

The publication of this book is cause for celebration, but it would not have been possible were it not for the professional staff at the MIT Press. A special thanks to Ken Friedman and Erik Stolterman, the general editors of Design Thinking, Design Theory, who selected this book for their series. I also owe a special debt of gratitude to Noah Springer, my acquisitions editor, for steering me with equanimity through the publication process and selecting excellent outside reviewers whose insightful feedback helped make this a better book. I'd also like to thank Megha at Westchester Publishing services. She did a superb job and even found a workaround when the California floods and blackouts made answering queries almost impossible. My thanks also go to Linda Hallinger, my indexer, and all of the staff at the MIT Press who helped bring this book to life.

Introduction

Headlines around the world alert us to some very challenging problems:

- Extreme weather events
- Droughts and their attendant problems in India, North Korea, and China; East and South Africa; Brazil; the Middle East; the Caribbean; and the American West
- Mass extinctions of animal and plant species
- Environmental degradation, pollution of the air, water, and soil
- The spread of infectious disease and pandemics
- Racism, sexism, religious intolerance, fundamentalism, and hatred of the "other"
- Genocide in Africa, Indo-China, Tibet, Europe, and the Americas
- The proliferation of nuclear weapons
- Cybercrime, cyber warfare, and cyberattacks on elections
- "Dark money" and extremist groups that influence elections around the world
- The refugee crisis and its impact on Europe, the Middle East, Asia, Canada, and the Americas
- Territorial conflicts in Europe, the Middle East, Africa, Asia, and Central and South America
- Terrorism as a weapon of war and deadly attacks worldwide
- Russia's expansion into Ukraine and eastern Europe and China's land reclamation in the South China Seas and its conflicts with Taiwan, Japan, the Philippines, and Vietnam
- Failure of national governance and state collapses when nation-states transition from authoritarian regimes to new models of governance
- Population growth projected to get to near ten billion people by 2050, outstripping resources to support them
- Fiscal crises in key economies throughout the world
- The overwhelming power of multinational corporations over governments
- Structurally high unemployment and underemployment in developing countries
- Massive income disparity, the disappearing middle class, and class conflict

- Poverty, hunger, and food crises
- Homelessness
- A worldwide epidemic of drug abuse
- Authoritarian threats to democracies worldwide

These problems are often described as "wicked," a concept first introduced in the problem-solving literature by Horst Rittel and Melvin Webber in 1973.[1] Wicked problems have:

- no definitive formulation since the problem is understood only as solutions are developed
- no stopping rule since no criteria exist to determine when problems are adequately defined and solved
- no solutions are true or false but they are assessed to be good or bad, or even more likely to be judged better or worse, satisfying, or good enough
- no exhaustive set of solutions nor any ultimate test of a solution exists
- no opportunity to learn by trial and error since the consequences of the solutions can extend across time in a number of unanticipated ways, and thus every solution is a one-shot operation and counts significantly
- no enumerable or exhaustively describable set of potential solutions, nor a well-described set of permissible operations (rules), only the judgment to determine which solutions should be pursued and incorporated into a plan for resolution
- no classes of problems that fit all members of a class since every situation is essentially one of a kind, with unique characteristics
- no natural level of problems exists since every problem can be a symptom of a higher-level problem
- no rule or procedure to determine the supposedly correct causal explanation of a problem, leaving the choice of an explanation arbitrary depending on stakeholder attitudinal criteria to determine problem resolution
- no immunity—no right to be wrong since the human costs of poor resolution are so high that people should be liable for the consequences of the solutions they generate

Thus, wicked problems are viewed as persistent, undefined, and unresolved, with severe consequences for people and the entire planet if they are not addressed.

Despite their characteristics, why have problem solvers been unable to find ways to deal with them? We have been in a constant state of problem solving throughout our evolution—figuring out how to find food and shelter, battle the elements, protect and rear our young, escape predators, respond to threats, build communities, and enrich our lives. No matter the region, country, political philosophy, or cultural tradition, historical records document our constant search for new ideas and solutions to ensure our ability to survive, and even thrive. We are hard-wired for problem solving, and our problem-solving ability is legendary. We invented a vaccine that cured smallpox, which had been the scourge of humanity for centuries. Traces of smallpox pustules were found on the 3,000-year-old, mummified body of Pharaoh Ramses V of Egypt. Its lethal worldwide transmission was estimated to have caused the deaths of 300–500 million people in the twentieth century alone. Yet on May 8, 1980, the 33rd World Health Assembly declared the disease eradicated. Geonomics and precision medicine now use patients' genetic information to identify health issues and the most suitable treatment options for illness. Gene editing—the editing of portions of deoxyribonucleic acid (DNA) that presents health risks using the CRISPR-Cas9 approach—has introduced new efficient and reliable ways to make precise, targeted changes to the genome of living cells. We invented computers, the Internet, and digital technology that make communication easier, quicker, and more efficient. We collect energy from renewable resources—sunlight, wind, rain, tides, waves, and geothermal heat—that are naturally replenished on a human time scale. We landed on the moon on July 31, 1969, and Commander Neil Armstrong of the *Apollo* mission declared the accomplishment to be "one small step for man, one giant leap for mankind." Other extraterrestrial accomplishments followed: the International Space Station, which supports a human crew for an extended period of time; operational rovers on the surface of Mars, probes of Jupiter and its moons; and probes that have left or are expected to leave the solar system and enter interstellar space, including *Voyager* 1, *Voyager* 2, *Pioneer* 10, *Pioneer* 11, and *New Horizons*. And on December 25, 2021, the National Aeronautics and Space Administration (NASA) launched the James Webb Space Telescope, which will travel 1 million miles from Earth, scan the cosmos for light streaming from stars and galaxies formed 13.7 billion years ago, and allow us to view within 100 million years of the universe-forming Big Bang.

It would appear from these monumental efforts (and they are only a small subset of human achievements throughout history) that humankind is very good at problem solving. So why do we have a growing list of unresolved wicked problems? The short answer is VUCA—the *volatility* and *complexity* that characterizes the dramatic changes in our general environment in the twentieth and twenty-first centuries and the *uncertainty* and *ambiguity* that humankind faces when trying to address these challenges.[2] We begin this overview with figure 0.1, which represents the four vectors in our VUCA world.[3]

Volatility

In figure 0.1, volatility (V) is portrayed with a jagged, erratic line facing north. It is about change. Change can be *linear*—when two things are proportional to each other, such as when one thing doubles, so does the other. If the relationship between production hours and output in a factory is linear, then a 10 percent increase or decrease in hours results in a 10 percent increase or decrease in output, respectively. Change also can be *exponential,* such that the growth rate becomes ever more rapid in proportion to the growing

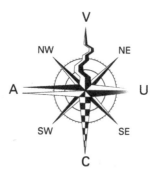

Figure 0.1
Vectors in a VUCA world

total number of size of things. An often-told tale provides an example of such growth. According to legend, the vizier Sissa Ben Dahir presented the Indian king Sharim with his new invention—a chess set. Pleased with the beautiful, handmade gift, the ruler offered the vizier a gift in return. The vizier asked for rice. He put a single grain of rice on the first square of the chessboard and asked that the rice double for each square—two grains for the second square, four grains on the third square, and so on. Believing the request was harmless enough, the king readily agreed. He turned out to be wrong. The net result for the final square alone was 2^{64}, or 18,446,744,073,709,551,616—18 million trillion grains of rice. One version of the story is the kingdom's entire wealth had to be forfeited to repay the vizier's gift.[4] The other version had him losing his head.

A graph of linear, cubic, and exponential growth is shown in figure 0.2. Linear growth is a steady line, cubic growth is a polynomial x^2 line, and the exponential growth line is explosive, like the number of pieces of rice on the chessboard. The computer scientist, inventor, and futurist Ray Kurzweil introduced the "Law of Accelerating Returns" in his 1999 book *The Age of Spiritual Machines*,[5] in which he describes exponential growth as being nearly flat for a long period until it hits the "knee in the curve," and the growth rises almost vertically from there. His assessment is that the pace of technological change has advanced at least exponentially, not linearly, and has been doing so since the advent of evolution on Earth.

Kurzweil further developed the concept of accelerating returns in 2001[6] and used the exponential growth curve to demonstrate the evolutionary process of information technologies. The often-referenced Moore's Law of Integrated Circuits, narrowly defined as the number of transistors in an integrated circuit of fixed size, was the fifth in a series of paradigms that marked the exponential growth of computer processing. The first paradigm was the creation of the mechanical calculating devices used in the 1890 US Census. The second was Alan Turing's relay-based Robinson machine, which cracked the Nazi Enigma code. The third was the vacuum tube computer that CBS used to predict President Dwight Eisenhower's election. The fourth was the transistor-based machines used in the first space launches in the 1950s. The sixth paradigm, when

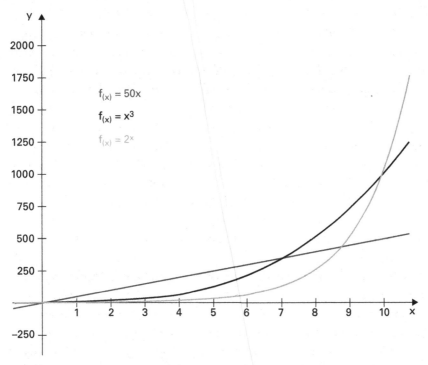

Figure 0.2
Linear versus cubic versus exponential growth
Wikimedia Commons, "linear, cubic, and exponential growth," last modified December 2014, 19:17, https://commons.wikimedia.org/wiki/File:Exponential.png.

Moore's Law is expected to reach its natural limits during the second decade of the twenty-first century, is likely to be replaced by technologies that build circuitry in three rather than two dimensions, such as nanotubes, three-dimensional (3D) silicon chips, optical computing, crystalline computing, DNA computing, and quantum computing, which will sustain the law of accelerating returns in the context of computation for some time.

Kurzweil reports that the nineteenth century saw more technological change than in the nine centuries preceding it. And then the first twenty years of the twentieth century saw more advancement than were seen in the entire nineteenth century. Now paradigm shifts (fundamental changes in approach) occur in only a few years' time. Currently, the paradigm shift rate (i.e., the overall rate of technical progress) doubles approximately every decade, which means that paradigm shift times are halving every decade and the rate of acceleration is growing exponentially. At this pace, the twenty-first century is expected to see almost a thousand times more technological change than its predecessor in the twentieth century. These same dramatic increases are expected in other fields that depend on information technology.

Here are some of Kurzweil's predictions:[7] The *genetics revolution* will enable us to reprogram our own biology. Based on major innovations in biotechnology such as human genome editing, 3D bioprinting, and the $1,000 genome,[8] we have accumulated enough knowledge of our bodies and how they work to attack the genetic and cellular roots of disease and aging. The *nanotechnology revolution*—the intersection of information and the physical world—will give us the tools to manipulate matter at the molecular and atomic scales of our brains, bodies, and world. Products from nanotech research already are appearing: sunscreen, clothing, paints, cars, and more. Currently under testing are smart contact lenses, tiny, 3D-printed batteries; cancer-killing nanoparticles; and DNA-based computing. The *robotics revolution*—embodied artificial intelligence (AI)—will enable us to create nonbiological intelligence. Today, we use forms of AI on a regular basis: Alexa, Siri, Google Now, and IBM's Watson are only a few examples. Other forms include speech and image recognition software, pattern recognition software for autonomous weapons, fraud-detecting programs for use in financial transactions, and Google's AI based statistical learning methods of ranking search results.

The next step in AI will be machines that will learn without being programmed or fed information by humans. Referred to as "deep learning," it is a powerful new mode of machine learning currently being researched. There also are predictions that the use of AI in agriculture will help humans address the issue of food scarcity with exponential technologies such as drought-detecting satellites, sensor-enabled tractors that selectively remove sick plants, AI-powered apps that identify crop disease in seconds, and robots that apply herbicides only to weeds, not to healthy plants. The idea is to hack the traditional growing processes and supercharge farmers' efficiency.

As fields that employ information technology undergo exponential growth, so does our knowledge. Buckminster Fuller, the futurist and inventor, introduced the concept of "knowledge curve" in his book *Critical Path*.[9] He estimated that if we took the stockpile of human knowledge at AD 1 as a benchmark (which equaled one unit of information and took 198,000 years to accumulate), then it took another 1,500 years to double human knowledge. The pace of knowledge accelerated thanks to the printing press, so by 1750, human knowledge had doubled again, this time over 250 years. Only 150 years later, in 1900, it had doubled yet again. By 1945, the end of World War II, knowledge was doubling every 25 years. When *Critical Path* was published in 1981, Fuller estimated that the knowledge-doubling time was 18 months. Others have used Fuller's reasoning and analysis to extrapolate that by 2000, collective human knowledge was doubling every year.[10]

Despite the positive news stories about information technology and knowledge, exponential change has another, more negative side. The International Union of Geological Sciences (IUGS), the professional society that defines the Earth's time scale, describes our current age as the Holocene and says that it began 11,700 years ago, after the last major ice age. Other experts argue for a different term for a new geological epoch—Anthropocene—meaning "man" making his mark on the scale of the planet as a whole. According to Paul Crutzen,[11] vice chair of the International Geosphere-Biosphere Programme (IGBP), the Earth entered the Anthropocene era near the end of the eighteenth century, about the time when the Industrial Revolution began. The IGBP has generated a picture and trajectory of the "human enterprise," describing it as "the Great Acceleration."[12] Originally published in 2004 and updated in 2010, the research on the structure and functioning of the Earth system provides data on *socio-economic* and *Earth trends*. Since 1950, these trends have increased significantly, many of them even exponentially, as illustrated in figure 0.3.[13]

The growing human imprint was expected, but not the dramatic change in magnitude and rate from 1950 onward. One feature stood out. The second half of the twentieth century is unique in the entire history of human existence on Earth. The last fifty years of the twentieth century have seen the most rapid transformation of the human relationship with the natural world in the history of humankind.[14] Thus the term "Great Acceleration" is used to describe the comprehensive and interlinked post-1950 changes that were simultaneously affecting socioeconomic and biological Earth systems. The most recent graphs (from 2010) led to the conclusion that human activity is now the prime driver of the Earth's physical, chemical, biological, and human processes. The global population has almost tripled in size, freshwater use has more than tripled, energy use has increased fourfold, fertilizer has risen over tenfold, and world gross domestic product (GDP) has increased sevenfold. Human activities in the past were insignificant compared to the biophysical Earth system. The two operated independently, but now it is impossible to separate them from each other. As Will Steffen and colleagues remind us:

> [T]he Great Acceleration marks the phenomenal growth of the global socio-economic system, the human part of the Earth System. It is difficult to overestimate the scale and speed of change. In little over two generations—or a single lifetime—humanity (or until very recently a small fraction of it) has become a planetary-scale geological force. . . . We are now living in a no-analogue world.[15]

Complexity

Complexity (C), facing south in figure 0.1, comes from the Latin word *commplexus*, which means entwined, "twisted together."[16] This definition suggests that for something to be complex, it must have two aspects—it has to be composed of several parts, and these parts have to be closely connected. By extension, for something to be more complex, it has to have more parts, greater diversity among the parts, and more connections between and among the parts.

Many parts   The US Census Bureau estimates that the current world population is over 7,676,613,300 billion, with one birth every eight seconds.[17] The population is expected to reach 8.5 billion by 2030, and 9.7 billion in 2050.[18] Among this population, there are debates on how many countries, territories, and dependencies people call home. The United Nations (UN) recognizes 193 member-countries and two nonmember observer-states (Vatican City and Palestine). It gives partial recognition to six other entities: Taiwan, Western Sahara, Kosovo, South Ossetia, Abkhazia, and Northern Cyprus. Two, the

Socio-economic trends

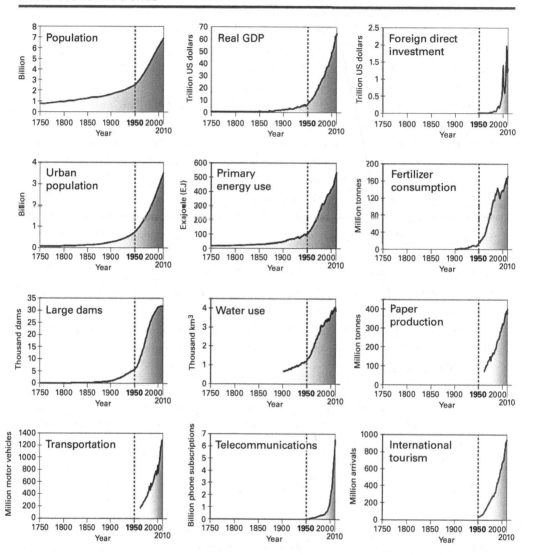

Figure 0.3

The trajectory of the Anthropocene: The Great Acceleration

Cook Islands and Niue, are considered to be self-governing overseas territories of New Zealand. Depending on who is counting, three to five de facto sovereign states (independent in actual fact but not on paper) may include Transnistria and Somaliland, as well as entities in active war zones, such as the Islamic State,[19] the Donetsk People's Republic, and the Lugansk People's Republic. So according to the United Nations, there are 195 sovereign states, 201 states that are acknowledged by at least one UN member, and 204–207 de facto sovereign states (self-declared countries). On the other hand, the Olympic Organizing Committee recognizes 206 nations, Fédération Internationale de

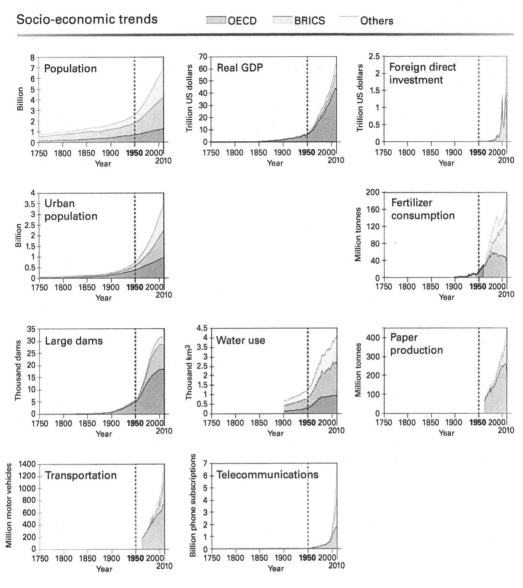

Figure 0.3
(continued)

Football Association (FIFA) identifies 211 countries eligible for the World Cup, and the International Organization for Standardization (ISO) list has 249 country codes.[20]

Diversity among the parts   The diversity among these billions of people is staggering. We speak 7,111 distinct languages, although a fifth of them only have fewer than 1,000 speakers and 23 account for more than half of the world's population.[21] We profess belief in 10,000 distinct religions, 150 of which have 1 million or more followers.[22] Although ethnicity is a slippery concept, James Fearon[23] identified 822 ethnic groups in the early 1990s that made up at least 1 percent of 160 countries. And in terms of the

Earth system trends

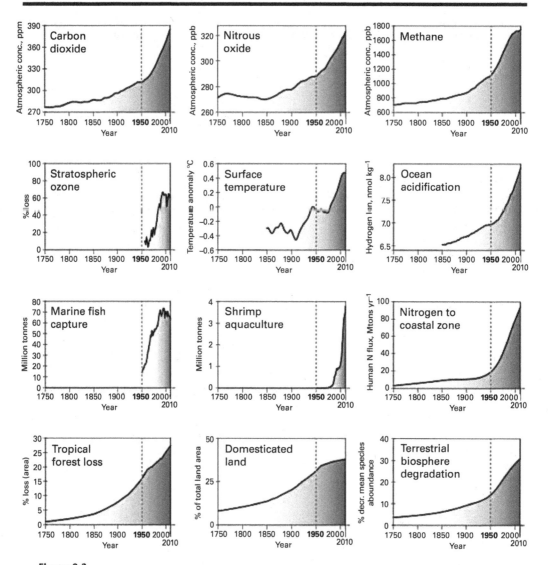

Figure 0.3
(continued)

world's population, people subscribe to various ideologies that include nationalism, liberal democracy and capitalism, anarchism, socialism, fascism, Islamism, feminism, and environmentalism.[24] These ideologies in turn produce a divergent set of economic and political policies.

Increasing connections among the parts   James Burke, in his television series *Connections* in 1978[25] and its sequels in 1994 and 1997, illustrated how unrelated events can produce achievements and scientific discoveries. These events are the result of people or groups acting in their own self-interest (e.g., profit, curiosity, religious beliefs, etc.), with no concept where their actions will lead. Yet their interplay over time produces strange but important connections, as Burke summarizes in his first episode in the series. There are links between a sixteenth-century doctor in Queen Elizabeth's court and being able to watch a computer screen; between eighteenth-century merchants concerned about ship bottoms and our wearing of nylon; between sheep-rearing French monks and the modern world's computer; and between medieval Europeans' use of fire in winter and automobile manufacture.[26]

Where connections between people and groups will lead us in the future as a result of the COVID-19 pandemic remains to be seen. But prior to 2020, we knew that people were on the move, making connections at an increasingly rapid rate. The number of international students went from 0.8 million in 1975 to 4.3 million in 2011, with a projected 8 million by 2025.[27] According to the UN World Tourism Organization, international tourist arrivals (overnight visitors) increased to 1.4 billion two years ahead of the long-term forecast issued in 2010. The growth represents the second-strongest year since 2010 and consolidates the results from 2017 (7 percent). Based on previous trends, the World Tourism Organization expects a 3–4 percent growth in international tourism worldwide in 2019.[28] Migration[29] presented an even more striking picture. Only 92 million people lived outside their country of origin in 1960.[30] The number reached 173 million by 2000, 220 million in 2010, and 272 million in 2019.[31] By 2022, the foreign-born population in the United States was a record 46.6 million and represented 14.27 percent of the total US population.[32]

Transportation technology has enabled people's movement, and new technologies have transformed the transportation industry in the twentieth and twenty-first centuries, making connections faster and cheaper. As for air travel, there were an estimated 9.38 million international passengers in 2019, which was a 3.5 percent increase from 9.06 million in January 2018.[33] Although these connections decreased dramatically due to the COVID pandemic, with a 60 percent decline in total passengers worldwide from 2019 to 2020,[34] the international transport association expects to recover to 2019 levels by 2024.[35]

The connections that are the result of these major transportation technologies can be found in the *Connectivity Atlas*,[36] a project that represents a mapping collaboration between DevelopmentSeed, the University of Wisconsin–Madison Cartography Lab, and Dr. Parag Khanna, the author of *Connectography: Mapping the Future of Global Civilization*.[37] The Harvard Map of Connectography,[38] a joint collaboration between Parag Khanna and Jeff Blossom of the Harvard University Center of Geographic Analysis,[39] offers a website of interactive maps for download, including maps of worldwide airports, flight paths, ports, and major rivers, as well as existing and proposed high-speed rail, canals, and roads. Pablo Kaluza and his colleagues also provide a dramatic visualization of the complex transportation network of global cargo ship movements and ports.[40]

Other key enablers of connections include the Internet, the World Wide Web, satellites, cloud computing, wireless connectivity, social networking sites, and smartphones, all of which have built a global, distributed communication network. The *Connectivity Atlas* displays a visual image of extensive undersea cables—a physical layer of fiber optics and high-speed, integrated circuits—that enable the web.[41] Visually portraying the entire Internet flow in 2020 would be a very difficult task. According to Cisco's Visual Networking Index, the Internet will reach 4.8 zettabytes[42] per year in 2022.[43]

This planetwide electronic grid connects nearly instantaneously and, at relatively low cost, enables users to share their ideas, knowledge, and skills. From December 1995 to December 2011, there were 2,267 million Internet users, which represented 32.7 percent of the world's population. As of June 2020, there were 4,833 million Internet users representing 62 percent of the world's population.[44] In addition, 49 percent of the population is connected on a mobile device, with 1.8 billion expected to be connected with 5G by 2025.[45]

The increasing number of people and their connections is creating a complex world. But there is more to this story. As people's connections deepen, they find value in building commitments that last longer and form interdependencies—reciprocal relations for mutual benefit. At the international level, countries trade with each other to sell what they produce and acquire what they lack. Their specialization in goods and services creates mutual benefits, and in sustaining these benefits, trading partners become dependent. They need each other—one to sell the goods and services, and the other to buy them. The networks of worldwide interdependencies that arise from the integration of economic, cultural, and political activities have come to be known as "globalization." Although globalization has been traced to early periods of history, large-scale globalization grew quickly in the nineteenth and twentieth centuries with advances in transportation (e.g., the steam locomotive, steamship, jet engines, and container ships) and telecommunications (e.g., telegraph, telephone, the Internet, fiber optics, broadband, and mobile phones). The actual term "globalization" was first employed in 1930, but economists and social scientists began to use it in the 1960s. Following the fall of the Berlin Wall in 1989, the concept of globalization "provided oxygen across a number of fields" and has come to mean intensifying global connections.[46] And now, by definition, anything can be globalized—culture, ideas, beliefs, goods, services, capital, labor, markets, and other information.[47]

Globalization, as well as the interdependencies among people and countries that it creates, are facilitated by global networks of communication, transportation, and trade; the opening of borders to allow the increased flow of goods, services, finance, people, and ideas across international boundaries; and the changes in institutional and policy regimes at the international and national levels to facilitate or promote such flows. The reach and density of this global interconnectedness create complex networks among communities, states, international institutions, nongovernmental organizations (NGOs), and multinational corporations that make up the global order. The McKinsey Global Institute created a Connectedness Index in 2014 to capture this reach and diversity. It ranks 131 countries on a number of critieria, including total flows of goods, services, finance, people, data, and communication, adjusting for country size.[48] Singapore is the most connected country in terms of flow intensity, defined as the total value of goods, services, and financial flows as a share of the country's GDP. The United States is the most connected country in terms of flow value, defined as the total goods, services, and financial inflows and outflows.

DHL, the world's leading postal and logistics company, offers the most recent view of global connectedness based on data covering 169 countries and territories.[49] Its DHL Global Connectedness Index (GCI), measured in terms of flows of trade, capital, information, and people across national borders, reached a record high in 2017 despite the growing antiglobalization tensions in some countries. In 2017, the most globally connected countries (from most connected to least) were the Netherlands, Singapore, Switzerland, Belgium, the United Arab Emirates, Ireland, Luxembourg, Denmark, the United Kingdom, and Germany, and the most connected region is Europe. In terms of capital and information flow, North America ranks second overall.[50] However, comparing domestic and international data, most trade, capital, information, and people flows are domestic rather than international,[51] and most international activity tends to be more intense among countries in close proximity.[52] Although the world is more globalized than ever before and international interactions rose to a new peak in 2017,[53] the data also reveal that it is less globalized that most people perceive it to be,[54] especially with the recent shocks of COVID-19 and Russia's invasion of Ukraine, which have created serious disruptions in supply chains.

Uncertainty

Uncertainty (U), the east-facing vector in figure 0.1, represents a vague and blurred future with unknown unknowns. Not only do we lack adequate information, awareness, and understanding of our current situation, we have difficulty anticipating the consequences of the exponential changes that are underway. One of the best ways to understand uncertainty is to introduce the concept of the *complex adaptive system (CAS)*. "Complex" refers to the many different things or parts of a system (e.g., the number of neurons in the human brain). "System" means a set of interconnected things that produce a distinctive pattern of behavior (e.g., neurons and their connections are integrated into a whole that we call the "brain"). "Adaptive" means that out of the collective firings of several billion neurons in the brain, the conscious mind emerges and enables us to learn and adapt. As John H. Holland defines the term, "CASs" are "systems that have a large numbers of components, often called agents, that interact and adapt or learn."[55]

Examples of CASs abound: the European Union (EU), the stock market, ant colonies, organizations, cities, the immune system, the cell and the developing embryo, war, networks (especially terror networks), and the World Wide Web, among others. They all have the following features, which are central to their ability to adapt, interact, and learn:

- All elements of the system are affected by and affect other system elements. Changing one system element has a ripple effect throughout the whole system. Thus, we describe it as a *dynamic interaction* among the elements, which can be physical or involve the exchange of information. So, for example, when one airline hub grounds its planes, it affects airline travel throughout the transportation system.

- The system operates under *far from equilibrium conditions,* which means that there has to be a constant flow of energy from the system's environment into the system to maintain its integrity and order. Without energy, the system dies. Equilibrium is death.[56] Food is the body's energy source that keeps it alive, and raw materials and information are businesses' lifelines to keep their products flowing into the hands of consumers.

- The absorption of energy into a system produces *fluctuations* or *perturbations* in the system since not all system elements absorb energy in same way at the same time. When energy absorption varies, the different rates can have destabilizing effects for the system as a whole.

- When a system is *destabilized* by the flux and perturbations of energy from its environment, often amplified by positive feedback in the system that increases the effect, there are a number of possibilities, *none of which is predictable*: various efforts for self-repair and maintenance of the current order; creation of new orders; and system devolution and disorder. The point at which a system evolves or devolves is called the *bifurcation point*[57] or in common parlance, "the tipping point,"[58] as seen in figure 0.4.[59]

The visualization in figure 0.4 characterizes what happens when energy is pumped into a system. Take the example of Iraq. It had an infusion of money, material, and people during the Iraq war. This infustion of energy so destabilized Iraq as a system

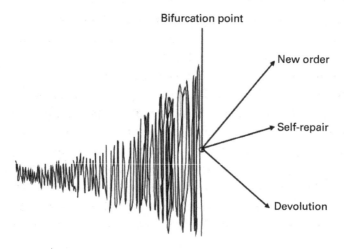

Figure 0.4
Visualizing the dynamics of CAS

that it produced larger and larger system perturbations due to infighting amoung rival groups and terrorist networks, a breakdown of policing and governance, and dramatic increases in inflation, to name only a few factors. As the perturbations got larger and larger (with greater swings and extremes, as seen in figure 0.4), Iraq became so destabilized at some point that it no could longer maintain its coherence and structure as a whole system. It reached a bifurcation or tipping point with three options. Iraq could devolve into disorder (which it did in the midst of tribal conflicts that took over a large swath of territory from Mosul to Fallujah by the Islamic State; it could attempt to resestablish its previous structure and order (which was attempted but difficult to do after Saddam's death); or it could evolve an entirely new order (which has been attempted, but between the parliamentary election in October 2021 and October 2022, Iraq has faced a political crisis, with members of the Council of Representatives unable to form a stable coalition government or elect a new president).

Other examples of these options include the following:

- *Self-repair* and *maintenance,* evident in the self-organization of cars, bicycles, motorcycles, and pedestrians weaving their way through a street corner in Hanoi that, when repeated at other street corners, ultimately keeps traffic flowing in the city as a whole.[60] I witnessed another example in Jakarta, Indonesia. When traffic became jammed up during rush hour, self-appointed citizens positioned themselves at street corners, directed traffic and got it flowing again, and received tips from drivers who were grateful for their services. In the case of drug-trafficking networks, if one link is broken, traffickers create other connections. The Colombian drug cartels, for example, have used submarines instead of overland routes when their supply lines to North America are disrupted.

- *System evolution* and *the creation of new orders,* evident in the Articles of Confederation, which eventually led to a new US Constitution in 1789 and the federal form of government that emerged from the British Empire.

- *System devolution,* evident in the invasion of Iraq and its aftermath in 2003, as noted previously. Other examples of devolution can be found in Joseph Tainter's *The Collapse of Complex Societies.*[61] Tainter, an anthropologist and historian, warned that a recurrent theme in human history is the collapse of complex societies. Using historical cases such as the Western Chou Empire, the Harappan civilization, Mesopotamia, the Egyptian Old Kingdom, the Hittite Empire, Minoan civilization, Mycenaean civilization, the Western Roman Empire, the Lowland Classic Maya, and many others, he finds that complex societies are vulnerable to collapse—"a rapid, significant loss of an established level of sociopolitical complexity."[62] This collapse has four underpinnings. First, human societies establish institutions and organizations with specialized roles and responsibilities to address and solve their problems. Second, these institutions and organizations and their roles require energy to maintain. Third, as the complexity increases, so do the energy requirements to maintain these societies, which increase their per capita costs. And fourth, when these costs for maintaining complexity reach a point of declining marginal returns (e.g., when it takes more investments and those investments yield proportionally less), then societies are in danger of collapse from either decomposition or by external threat when there is a power vacuum with "no competitor to fill the political vacuum of disintegration."[63] Societies then become smaller, less stratified, less socially differentiated, and less specialized, with less centralized control, less trade and interaction, and lower coordination and information sharing, and often are accompanied by drops in population, economic activity, and a decline in art and literature. For those remaining, "the world shrinks."[64] Jared Diamond, a geographer, anthropologist, and historian, writing in *Collapse: How Societies Choose to Fail or Succeed*,[65] identifies five interconnected forces that reinforce each other and lead to collapse: nonsustainable exploitation of resources, climate change, diminishing support from friendly societies, hostile neighbors, and inappropriate attitudes toward change. Based on these factors in the past, societies have destroyed themselves one by one. William Ophuls, a political scientist and ecologist, examines the same themes in *Immoderate Greatness: Why Civilizations Fail*. He concludes that "civilization is effectively hardwired for self-destruction."[66] His analysis suggests that very little can be done to counter it. From the inexorable trends of ecological exhaustion, exponential growth, expedited entropy, excessive complexity, moral decay, and practical failure, a civilization eventually exceeds the limits of what is physically possible. Its hubris ultimately generates a complex nexus of social, economic, fiscal, and political problems with no feasible solution. Ultimately, he concludes, CASs are unmanageable.[67]

• Central to the creation of a new order is the concept of *self-organization*—"the spontaneous appearance of order or global coordination out of local level interactions." It starts with an "attractor" in the system that brings together and aligns other local elements to a particular configuration. And through a positive feedback loop that cascades throughout the system, eventually all system elements can become aligned, making them "more than the sum of all the parts." [68] An ant colony illustrates this decentralized structure of *self-organizing systems*. The queen does not tell the worker ants what to do. Instead, each ant reacts to chemical scents and interactions that are governed by very simple rules and local connections. As the ants continue to work together, they eventually generate complex structures that become a whole colony, some of which can contain more than 300 million ants. This self-organizing process is referred to as *emergence*. Hurricanes offer another demonstration of emergence. They self-organize from a small atmospheric disturbance whirling around in a section of the warm, tropical ocean waters. The area of the ocean has to be at least 80 degrees Fahrenheit and 300 miles or more from the equator for the Earth's rotation to stir up the water. This area also has to have evaporating seawater, which condenses when it rises high enough into the atmosphere, and atmospheric pressure that is reduced near the water's surface. When these conditions occur, a hurricane emerges, defined as winds of at least seventy-four miles per hour, which can alter and change its course. Cities offer another example of emergence. Neighborhoods of like-minded people self-organize and organically form businesses and cultural sites from the bottom up. Thus, New York has Chinatown, Little Italy, the Garment District, and the Flower District, which appear without any top-down planning commissions or zoning laws.[69]

- Changes to a CAS are *nonlinear*. For example, small changes in inputs, physical interactions, and stimuli to the system can cause large effects or very significant changes in output. This is known in popular culture as the "butterfly effect"—to wit, a butterfly flapping its wings in Asia can set off perturbations that over time ultimately result in a hurricane off the East Coast of the United States. The sociologist Charles Perrow[70] also warned of cascading impacts of small system failures that can produce major failures in large, complex systems (e.g., nuclear power plants, missile warning systems, and space exploration missions). Two aspects of a system make it vulnerable to these kinds of failure. The first is complexity—a web of interconnected parts, many of which are not visible to the naked eye. Perrow refers to this as *interactive complexity*—the degree to which we are unable to foresee all the ways that things can go wrong due to the many interactions that we cannot anticipate, understand, or manage. The second is *tight coupling* among the system's parts, defined as the degree to which elements are so closely connected that we cannot stop a disaster once it starts due to lack of time, knowledge, resources, or technologies. Thus the greater the degree of interactive complexity and coupling, the greater the potential for system breakdowns with unknown, unanticipated, or unimagined outcomes. In other words, tightly coupled complex systems have little slack and a slim margin of error. If something goes wrong, complex and tightly coupled systems are unforgiving. Errors can very quickly cascade into a massive meltdown. They can produce what Homer-Dixon calls "synchronous failure." [71] The failure in one area can set off unpredictable cascades or a swarm of simultaneous failures in another area. So, for example, a sharp shift in climate could cripple food production and lead to massive protests, state crises, and destabilized regimes, which in turn could lead to interstate conflicts that could spark a major financial crisis in markets around the world. A convergence of risks—climate, geopolitical, and financial—could overwhelm the adaptive capacity and resilience of even the richest and most powerful societies. And eventually, failures could trigger a general collapse that propagates across the globe.

- Some system changes that are improbably rare events, either positive or negative, such as "black swans," can cause massive consequences.[72] These random, nonlinear, outlier events are outside the boundaries of our individual and collective knowledge. We are limited in our ability to understand them, let alone predict them. Instead, we rely on retrospective sense-making to explain them after the fact. Examples include the stock market crash of 1987, the dissolution of the Soviet Union, the Internet, and the terrorist attack of 9/11. Black swans have occurred throughout our history, but they started accelerating during the Industrial Revolution, when the world became more complex. Their appearance and consequences are increasing, due in no small measure to globalization and the growing size of our organizations and institutions. According to Nassim Taleb, we appear to have an ingrained tendency to underestimate them and now require new tools to navigate and exploit a black swan world.

- It is difficult to predict when the perturbations in a system will set off irreversible changes at the bifurcation or tipping point. When does a system reach a point of no return when system repair is no longer feasible? When does a new order surface? When does devolution occur? When is a species close to extinction? When will the stock market crash? Has the Earth's climate reached a point of no return, where no matter what corrective action is taken, the planet's climate will be irreversibly changed? Recently, scientists analyzed the climate model simulations on which the 5th Intergovernmental Panel on Climate Change (IPCC) report in 2014 is based. They found evidence of forty-one cases of abrupt regional changes in the ocean, sea ice, snow cover, permafrost, and terrestrial biosphere. Many of these events occur for global warming levels of less than 2 degrees Fahrenheit, a threshold sometimes presented as a safe limit. The scientists warn that abrupt changes are likely, but they also admit there is high uncertainty in predicting when and where these tipping points will occur. As the lead author of their report, Professor Sybren Drijfhout in the Ocean and Earth Science department at the University of Southampton, concludes, "[O]ur results show that no safe limit exists and that many abrupt shifts already occur for global warming levels much lower than two degrees."[73] Scientists have been on a quest to predict tipping for many decades, but "our track record is weak" says Rob Jackson at Duke University. "We missed the ozone hole, we missed the rapid melting of the North Pole in the last few years, and we missed last year's stock market crash. So I can't help but wonder, what will we miss this year?"[74]

Ambiguity

Ambiguity (A), the west-facing vector in figure 0.1, offers competing alternatives for a direction that we might take, each of which is plausible. The term also can mean that something is unclear or confusing. Both aspects of ambiguity characterize challenges that we currently face. Some examples are illustrative.

Efforts to lay out our options for the future has led Earth system and environmental scientists, led by Johan Rockström from the Stockholm Resilience Centre and Will Steffen from the Australian National University, to create a planetary boundary framework that signals the magnitude and direction of change and the safe operating space for humanity.[75] The framework identifies nine boundaries (climate change, biodiversity integrity [functional and genetic diversity], biogeochemical flows [phosphorus and nitrogen], ocean acidification, land system change, freshwater use, ozone depletion, atmospheric aerosol loading, and novel entities). Each boundary is marked by zones,

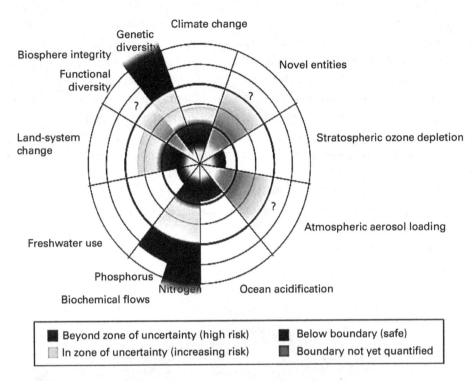

Figure 0.5
Planetary boundaries

as illustrated in figure 0.5.[76] The first circle around the center is a safe operating zone below the boundary. The next two circles constitute the zone of uncertainty or increasing risk, where we find climate change and land-system change. And the last two circles going out from the center and beyond represent the zone of high risk for biosphere integrity (specifically genetic diversity) and biochemical flows (specifically nitrogen), each moving beyond the fifth zone or circle. Only ocean acidification, stratospheric ozone depletion, and freshwater uses are in the safe zones. The zones with a question mark are not yet quantified.

The planetary framework is an important first step toward providing some guidance to problem solvers and decision makers. However, it leaves some unanswered questions. We know that the Earth is a single, complex system and the nine boundaries are interdependent. Yet the study was unable to do any systematic quantitative analysis of their interactions due to limits on current modeling and observational capabilities. Future research will need to address the multiple interacting environmental boundaries that are desirable, but that also may be difficult to achieve at the same time (e.g., water resources may decline if deforestation continues, and lands could become arid and unavailable for agriculture if the freshwater boundary is breached).[77] Stabilization of the climate requires both sustainable forests and ocean ecosystems,[78] but it is unclear how decision makers can pursue both concurrently.

The planetary boundaries framework also opens up additional questions about humanity's safe space since humanity's needs for food, health, education, income, peace and justice, housing, energy, water, and other resources are not taken into account. The economist Kate Raworth's research bridges that divide, demonstrating how to bring planetary boundaries together with social boundaries (as shown in figure 0.6).[79] The visual represents sustainable development in the shape of a doughnut that measures the extent to which people's needs are being met *without overshooting the Earth ecological limits*. The doughnut hole depicts the social foundation and includes the many dimensions of human deprivation, measured in terms of the proportion of people who lack access to life's essentials. The environment ceiling forms the outer circle or the crust that represents the planetary boundaries that life depends upon and must not be

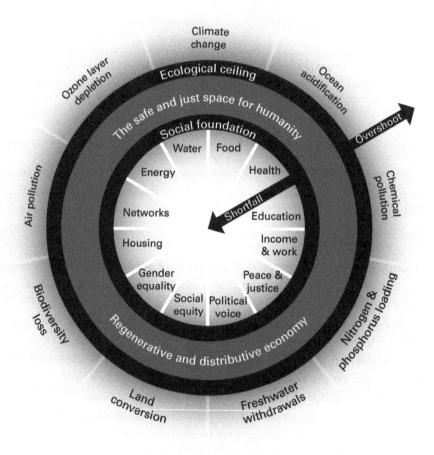

Figure 0.6
Raworth's doughnut economic model

overshot. *Between the two boundaries is an area that represents an environmentally safe and socially just space in which humanity can survive.* A prosperous economy would be one that met all twelve social foundations without overshooting any of the nine ecological limits.

Figure 0.7 builds out the model in an attempt to quantify and visually represent both the social and planetary boundaries and problem areas.[80] It depicts humanity as far from living in a safe space: one person in nine doesn't have enough to eat; one in four lives on less than three dollars a day; one in eight young people cannot find work; one in eleven has no source of safe drinking water; one child in six aged twelve to fifteen years old is not in school, the vast majority of whom are girls; almost 40 percent of people live in countries where incomes are unequally distributed; and more than half of the world's population live in countries where they lack a political voice.[81] It also shows that the ecological ceiling has already been crossed for at least four of the nine dimensions: climate change, nitrogen and phosphorous loading, land conversion, and biodiversity loss. The concentration of carbon dioxide (CO_2) is over 400 ppm and still rising, exceeding the boundary of 350 ppm, which is creating a hotter, drier climate and forcing a sea rise that threatens islands and coastal cities worldwide. Nitrogen and

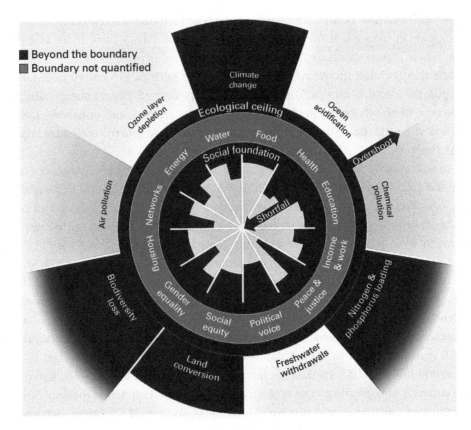

Figure 0.7
Raworth's doughnut model with boundary shortfalls and overshoots

phosphorus in synthetic fertilizers are being added to the Earth's soil at more than twice their safe levels, and their toxic runoff has resulted in the collapse of aquatic life in many lakes, rivers, and oceans and the creation of dead zones worldwide. Forested land continues to shrink, reducing its capacity to act as a carbon sink. Species extinction is occurring ten times faster than is considered safe, and freshwater withdrawal and ocean acidification are creating local and regional ecological crises.[82]

Moving humanity into the safe space is complex, since the social and planetary boundaries are interdependent and decision makers need to consider how a decision affects both. For example, the increased demand for food is closely connected to increased demands for sufficient water and energy to meet food requirements, and all three have implications for climate change. The interconnection and interdependence among the three subsystems—known as the "food-energy-water nexus"[83]—is evident in large-scale infrastructure projects that produce hydropower and provide storage for irrigation and urban uses. These projects can occur with serious downstream consequences for agroecological systems and resettlements. And while growing irrigated bioenergy crops may improve the energy supply and generate employment, it also may result in increased competition for water resources and land and detrimental impacts on local food security.[84]

Another example of this interdependence is when affordable electrical groundwater pumps are introduced, as they are in irrigated economies like China, India, and Pakistan. These pumps accelerate the depletion of water resources and aquifers, while food production becomes increasingly vulnerable to the price of the energy necessary to support the electrical pumps. This results in farmers' dependency on energy subsidies. However, when services by public irrigation agencies are poor and unreliable, farmers are left with little choice but to return to pumping water despite the ecological impacts of doing so.[85]

So when poorly designed, policies to move us within planetary boundaries can backfire and push people into shortfalls further below the social foundation or beyond the ecological ceiling into overshoot. The question is how to design policies and make trade-offs that promote both social goals and environmental sustainability. We are, says Raworth, in search of a twenty-first-century compass that can guide our way.[86]

Unfortunately, our current compass is seriously flawed. According to Joseph Stiglitz and colleagues, "those attempting to guide the economy and our societies are like a pilot trying to steer without a reliable compass."[87] Our compass is driving us to earlier calendar "overshoot days," when humanity's demand for ecological resources and services in a given year exceed what the Earth can generate in that year. December 19, 1970 marked the first overshoot day when we exhausted the Earth's budget for the year, and July 29, 2021, marked the latest overshoot day. As illustrated in figure 0.8, we currently are operating in an ecological deficit. We are liquidating the Earth's natural capital to such an extent that we require the equivalent of 1.7 Earths each year to meet our current demands for ecological resources.[88] The only drop in the rate of this resource use was in 2020 due to COVID-induced lockdowns.

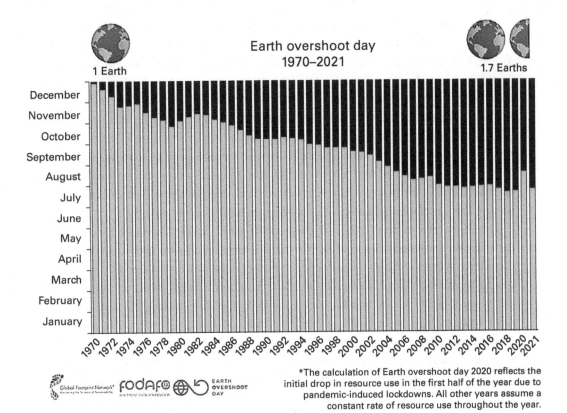

Earth overshoot day
1970–2021

1 Earth

1.7 Earths

*The calculation of Earth overshoot day 2020 reflects the initial drop in resource use in the first half of the year due to pandemic-induced lockdowns. All other years assume a constant rate of resource use throughout the year.

Source: National footprint and biocapacity accounts 2021 edition data.footprintnetwork.org

Figure 0.8
Humanity's ecological footprint versus the Earth's carrying capacity

Responses to our VUCA World

People have different reactions to our VUCA world. Let's first hear what the optimists have to say. According to Peter Diamandis and Steven Kotler, we are within reach of the "Age of Abundance."[89] "Using almost any metric currently available, quality of life has improved more in the past century than ever before". . . . and global living standards will continue to improve regardless of the horrors that dominate the headlines."[90] Over the past century, the average human life has more than doubled, the average per capita income (adjusted for inflation) has more than tripled, and maternal mortality has decreased by 90 percent and child mortality by 99 percent. The cost of food has decreased by 10 times, the cost of electricity by 20 times, transportation by 100 times, and communication by 1,000 times. Global literacy has gone from 25 percent to over 80 percent in the last 130 years.[91] And technological acceleration has produced exponential progress in communication, information technologies, and worldwide connectivity via the Internet, AI, robotics, digital manufacturing, nanomaterials, and synthetic biology.[92]

Hans Rosling, an internationally renowned physician and statistician, also offered an optimistic view. Summarizing the data in his widely viewed TED talk "The Best Stats You've Ever Seen," he concluded that "we have seen 200 years of enormous progress. That huge historical gap between the West and the rest is now closing. We have become an entirely new, converging world."[93] Max Roser's website, Our World in Data,[94] adds to the good news in terms of health, food, energy, work and life, human rights, and education. And the World Bank's most recent data on poverty track a sharp decline from 37 percent of the world's population living in extreme poverty (on less than $1.90 a day) in 2011 to 9.6 percent in 2015. As the World Bank Group president Jim Kin proclaimed: "This is the best story in the world today—these projections show us that we are the first generation in human history that can end extreme poverty."[95]

Bill Gates, as the guest editor of *Time*'s cover story called "The Optimists," added other positive reactions. Since 1990, the number of children who die before their fifth birthday has been reduced by half and the number of countries where is it legal to be gay has increased from 20 to more than 100.[96] And from Steven Pinker, we learn in *The Better Angels of Our Nature* that life is globally safer, healthier, longer, more prosperous, more tolerant, and more fulfilling, with a decline of violence in all forms, from war to treatment of children across time and geography.[97] And even with the "tectonic stresses" on humanity and the planet, such as environmental degradation, inequality generated by global capitalism, and global warming, Homer-Dixon reminds us there is an "upside of down." From growth, complexification, rigidification, and eventual breakdown come rebirth, renewal, and regrowth—assuming, of course, that there will be creativity after the breakdown.[98]

The pessimists (they would say "realists") offer a much more sobering view. In 1972, Donella Meadows and her colleagues cautioned there are "limits to growth."[99] By 1992, having found evidence that humanity was moving into overshoot, the team issued warnings in a book called *Beyond the Limit*.[100] The main challenge, as they saw it, was how to move the world back into sustainability territory. A decade later, they published a third book, *Limits to Growth: The 30-Year Update*.[101] They acknowledged that there had been progress over the years, with new technologies and new awareness of environmental problems. However, they viewed humanity as being in a dangerous state of overshoot. They pointed to examples such as the 2002 UN Food and Agricultural Organization (FAO) estimates that 75 percent of the world's ocean fisheries had been fished beyond capacity; the North Atlantic cod fishery that collapsed, with speculation that the cod species was at the point of biological extinction; and the first global assessment based on hundreds of experts' studies of soil loss that 38 percent of the currently used agricultural land (nearly 1.4 billion acres) had been degraded.

Michael Huesemann, a chemical engineer who has researched environmental biotechnology, and Joyce Huesemann, a statistician, warn us in their book *Techno-Fix*[102] that technology alone won't be able to rescue us from an ever-increasing burden of social, environmental, and economic ills. Despite the promises, technology has serious negative and irreversible effects: the inherent unavoidability and unpredictability of unintended consequences; the exploitation of nature and workers; and undemocratic controls. They describe the uncritical acceptance of technology as "techno-optimism"— the myth of technology's value-neutrality, the biases in technology assessments, the profit motive, and the main driver of technological development, which they believe has increased consumerism and materialism but failed to increase happiness. Moreover, the countertechnologies that offer efficiency improvements do not offer lasting solutions, nor do they improve sustainability. They contend that, as currently practiced, technology is unable to solve the many serious problems that we face. Indeed, if left unchecked, it will ultimately hasten social and environmental collapse. To address this existential crisis, the authors call for a shift in worldview, from separateness to interconnectedness and from a growth economy to a steady-state economy. They also call for the design of environmentally sustainable and socially appropriate technologies based on the precautionary principle that is geared to preventing unintended consequences and ensuring democratic control of technology. They also propose changes in how science is performed and technology is applied and medicine is practiced to reorient science, technology, and medicine in a more socially responsible and environmentally sustainable direction.

Peter Turchin, an evolutionary anthropologist and former evolutionary biologist, is one of the founders of "cliodynamics," a new field of historical social science that uses the tools of complexity science and cultural evolution to study the dynamics of empires and modern nation-states, as well as how societies evolve. His empirical results reveal that all large-scale, state-level historical societies experience waves of political instability roughly every fifty years, interposed by longer secular cycles. His structural-demographic analysis of American history reveals the same pattern—long periods of equitable prosperity and internal peace succeeded by periods of protracted inequity, political instability, and increasing misery. With the publication of his book *Ages of Discord* in 2016, he predicted that the United States would experience a period of heightened political and socal instability in the near future—the 2020s.[103]

Others sounded the alarm about the VUCA-world transformations on the people who were experiencing them. George Packer[104] details a single-generation "unwinding" in the United States from 1978 to 2012 that created a country of winners and losers and drove the political system, dominated by special interest lobbies, into political chaos. The grand forces and trends are in the background: the outsourcing and loss of manufacturing jobs, the decline of unions, the changing nature of the labor market, the stagnation of middle-class wages, the widening inequality and value disparities between the haves and the have-nots, the deregulation of the financial sector and the crushing recession of 2008, where governments bailed out banks but not homeowners, and the unraveling of the social fabric, with changing family structures, rising healthcare costs, and the inability of education to keep up with technological changes.

But in the foreground, Packer tells the story by presenting short biographical sketches of people who benefited from the transformations, including Newt Gingrich, Oprah Winfrey, Raymond Carver, Sam Walton, Colin Powell, Alice Waters, Jay-Z, Andrew

Breitbart, and Peter Thiel, interspersed with more detailed stories of those who struggled to deal with them.

Dean Price, the son of a long line of poor tobacco farmers in rural North Carolina, witnessed three main industries of his area (tobacco, furniture, and manufacturing) dry up. After graduating from college in 1989, he worked as a pharmaceutical representative, but he hated the work. He decided to start over and become an entrepreneur. Moving back to his hometown, he opened a convenience store, a fast-food restaurant, and a gas station and eventually expanded to a number of them along US Route 220. His strategy to stay competitive with larger companies was to introduce "discount gasoline" to the Southeast, making five cents a gallon of profit to his rivals' fifteen cents a gallon. Just as these businesses were taking off, Hurricane Katrina hit New Orleans and shut down diesel delivery, spiking diesel prices from $2.25 to $3.50 per gallon. Raising prices to protect the few supplies he had, and accused of "price gouging," his business was almost decimated by Katrina. Realizing that he had to do something different to survive, he decided to make his truck stops energy independent. Frustrated that the government enabled the United States to become dependent on foreign oil, he decided to pursue a new business—a biofuel company that eventually became the first Biodiesel truck stop in the country. However, amid the Great Recession, gas prices dropped, his company struggled, his partners bought him out, and he was forced to declare bankruptcy for his other businesses. Price then began a new venture—the recycling of used cooking oil from restaurants to provide fuel for local school buses.

Tammy Thomas, an African American woman, grew up in Youngstown, Ohio, just when the steel mills were closing down in the late 1970s and early 1980s and the population was dropping, going from 140,000 to 95,000 by 1990, and eventually to 67,000 in 2010. A child of a heroin addict, she was raised by her grandmother, who worked as a maid. She became a teenage mother and moved frequently to flee Youngtown's deteriorating neighborhoods, devastated by crime, poverty, and drugs. Determined not to become dependent on welfare, she eventually became the first member of her family to graduate from high school. In 1988, she got a union job at a Packard Electric plant that made automotive parts for General Electric, enabling her to purchase a home and send her three children to college. But by 2006, Delphi Automotive, a successor to Packard Electric, announced that it would close most of its American plants, including those in Youngstown, and shift production to Mexican duty-free and tariff-free factories established to encourage rapid industry growth in Mexico. Although the company bought out her contract, Thomas lost both her job and her pension after working there for years. She eventually found a new job as a community organizer in Youngstown, where she found a new identity recruiting local residents to advocate for neighborhood improvement, map the city's many abandoned properties, battle blight, and figure out ways to revitalize a shrinking Youngstown. Becoming very excited about the election of President Barack Obama in 2008, she empowered and trained more leaders to find their voice and organized actions to help reelect the president in 2012.

Jeff Connaughton began a decades-long interest in politics in 1979 while a student at the University of Alabama. After earning his MBA with honors from the University of Chicago, he worked for four years as an investment banker at Smith Barney, and then at E. F. Hutton. In 1987, he became a special assistant to the Senate Judiciary Committee when Senator Joe Biden served as the chair. After graduating with a JD from the Stanford Law School, Connaughton then clerked for Chief Judge Abner Mikva of the US Court of Appeals for the DC Circuit, and followed him as his special assistant when Mikva was appointed as counsel to President Bill Clinton. After leaving the White House, Connaughton drew on his connections and built a career as a lobbyist for the firm Quinn Gillespie & Associates, representing clients such as the Ivory Coast president Laurent Gbagbo, and holding frequent fundraisers for politicians, which gained him access to them. For twelve years as a lobbyist, he developed legislative and regulatory campaign strategies for corporate clients, banks, insurance companies, and Silicon Valley firms, making a great deal of money in the process.

Then, on September 15, 2008, Lehman Brothers declared bankruptcy, the Dow plunged, and Merrill Lynch and Lehman Brothers were technically insolvent—a catastrophe for the country and for Connaughton. The economy was imploding, which he attributed to Wall Street excesses (and likely malfeasance as well), while the ruling class in Washington, D.C., was doing nothing to stop it. Although he had made a good deal of money going along with corporate lobbying and tipping the scales in the interest of clients, the market crash and subsequent recession shattered his faith in the law and US institutions. So when Ted Kaufman was appointed to fill Biden's Senate seat when he became Obama's vice president, Connaughton went to work for Kaufman. Together, they sought the prosecution of financial fraudsters, prodded the Securities and Exchange Commission (SEC) to do something about the high-frequency trading and market swings, and pushed reform of the financial services industry in response to the Great Recession. However, they met with little success in either pursuing the criminal prosecutions of financial fraud cases or limiting the size of banks. As Connaughton described their efforts, lobbyists overwhelmed advocates for reform of the US financial system. They had better information and more input on financial reform legislation than he had as a Senate aide. After Kaufman's term ended, Connaughton, disillusioned with Washington, moved to Savannah, Georgia. He published a memoir of his experiences, *Payoff: Why Wall Street Always Wins*,[105] concluding that the system is rigged and the establishment can fail and still thrive, while struggling American families have to contend with a system that is rigged against them.

The underlying question that Packer asks, although he doesn't answer, concerns what common bonds and values holds Americans together after all the disorder and disillusion. Others, like Dale Maharidge and Michael Williamson in *Someplace Like America: Tales from a New Great Depression*, leave us with a similar question.[106] By 2021, the common bond appears to be anger, as Evan Osnos chronicles in *Wildland*,[107] a period from 2001 to 2021 when Americans replaced their vision for the common good with a fury and rage that, as Steven Webster documents in *American Rage: How Anger Shapes Our Politics*,[108] undermined Americans' trust in government and weakened their commitment to democratic norms and values.

In Summary

Our VUCA world has generated a whole host of wicked problems—those listed at the beginning of this chapter are just on the short list. Everything is changing so quickly—new technologies, new ways of communicating and connecting, new ways of working, and new identities, such that we now are asking questions of how to differentiate between human, humanoids, cyborgs, and AI robots. It even leaves us uncertain about what questions we should ask and what and whose answers we should trust. And gone are the days when we could isolate ourselves from others. Whether we talk about the international markets, global pandemics, or worldwide terrorism, what happens "over there" eventually affects us "over here," and vice versa. Observing the paroxysms in China and the world's financial, energy, and commodity markets in January 2016, Tom Ashbrook of NPR's *On Point* asked: "Do we now live in the shadow of Shanghai" when attempting to decide what to do with our retirement investments?[109] Or, as Justin Lahart noted in the *Wall Street Journal*, we want to chart our own course, "but the world keeps getting in the way."[110]

The interdependencies of nations and our economies give richness to our lives, but the complexities that they create and the sense of frustration and loss that they can engender have convinced some that erecting boundaries is the only option to regain a sense of order and control. But our boundary choices can put us on very ambiguous footing, as we are challenged to decide what is good, right, and just when dealing with dictators and tyrants, helping people seek safety from disasters and crises, and responding to genocides, invasions, and pandemics—sometimes all at the same time. In the almost fifty years since Rittel and Webber warned of our growing number of wicked problems, people have been actively seeking ways to deal with them. Their steadfast efforts are the subject of chapter 1.

Landing in Wicked Problem Territory

1 From Wicked Problems to Wicked Problem Territory

The massive global changes of the twenty-first century and the seismic shifts and fault lines that they have generated make problem solving and decision making difficult. As described in the introduction of this book, we have a name for the particular brand of problems they generate—they are "wicked" due to our inability to agree on the problem, much less its solution. Conversations about wicked problems have a very distinctive character and tenor. Eavesdropping on a hypothetical group of problem solvers, we hear the following exchange among people who are becoming increasingly agitated and antagonistic.

> One group member categorically insists what "the problem is." "No" says a second member with great irritation, "that isn't the problem; it is only a *symptom* of the problem." "You are both wrong" counters a third with even more heat. "You are focusing on the *consequences* of a problem and you need to focus on its *cause*. The *real problem* is. . . ."

Nassim Taleb neatly captures this type of discussion when he concludes that "the center of the problem is that none of them [know] the center of the problem."[1]

Professor Horst Rittel is credited with the first reference to "wicked problems," in a 1967 seminar in the Architecture Department of the University of California, Berkeley.[2] C. West Churchman later introduced the topic in a guest editorial he wrote for the journal *Management Science* in 1967. He attributed the term "wicked problem" to Rittel, who reportedly stated during the seminar that the term refers to a class of ill-formulated social problems with confusing information, conflicting values among clients and decision makers, and unknown implications for the whole system. Indeed, "the adjective 'wicked' is supposed to describe the mischievous and evil quality of these problems, where proposed 'solutions' often turn out to be worse than the symptoms."[3]

Rittel and Melvin Webber then published the first major formulation of wicked problems in a 1973 article entitled "Dilemmas in a General Theory of Planning" in *Policy Sciences*.[4] Their article began with an excellent summary of the conflict-ridden context in the United States, which even then was experiencing serious challenges for policy planning and goal setting. The picture that they painted, was stark:

- The nation was reeling from the revolt of Blacks, the revolt of students, and then the widespread revolt against the Vietnam War, along with the advocacy of conservationism: "Participants in these revolts were seeking to restructure the value and goal systems that affect the distribution of social product and shape the directions of national policy."[5]

- The Western world was becoming increasingly heterogeneous, differentiated into thousands of minority groups with their own common interests, value systems, and stylistic preferences. A result of this diversity was "a politicization of subpublics" that could yield "large political influence."[6] Moreover, the Industrial Age greatly expanded cultural diversity: "Post-industrial society [was] likely to be far more differentiated than any in all of past history."[7]

- There were multiple causes for variations and deviations from homogeneously shared cultural values and beliefs. The volume of information and knowledge was increasing, and technological developments were expanding the range of options that people had. Rising affluence and a growing subcultural identity encouraged groups to exploit their options and invent new ones. As awareness of the liberty to deviate and differentiate spread, more variations became possible. The unitary conception of the "American way of life" was giving way to a recognition that there are numerous American ways of life.[8]

- The nation's pluralism and the differentiation of values that accompany the differentiation of publics raised equity issues.[9] Efforts at system realignment and change (e.g., systems analysis, goals commissions, the US Department of Defense's Planning, Programming, and Budgeting System, the poverty program, model cities, and standards for environmental quality and urban life) all appeared to be driven by a common quest—"a clarification of purposes," "a redefinition of problems," a "reordering of priorities" to guide goal-directed actions, and "a redistribution of the outputs of governmental programs among the competing publics."[10]

In concluding that a unitary conception of "public welfare" was anachronistic, Rittel and Webber asked a key question. In a setting in which a plurality of publics is politically pursuing a diverse range of goals, how is the larger society to frame its problems, set its goals, and plan in a meaningful way "when the valuative bases are so diverse? From a policy design and planning perspective,

> we do not even have a theory that tells us how to find out what might be considered a societally best state. We have no theory that tells us what distribution of the social product is best—whether those outputs are expressed in the coinage of money income, information income, cultural opportunities, or whatever. We have come to realize that *the* concept of the social product is not very meaningful; possibly there is no aggregate measure for the welfare of a highly diversified society, if this measure is claimed to be objective and non-partisan. Social science has simply been unable to uncover a social-welfare function that would suggest which decisions would contribute to a societally best state.[11]

Instead, policy designers and planners relied on the beliefs of individualism that were fundamental to economic and political theory, assuming that public welfare derived from the summation of individualistic choices. And yet they knew that this was not necessarily so, as their experiences with air pollution dramatized. Ultimately, policy designers and planners were forced to recognize that an increasingly pluralistic population with intergroup differences had the potential to devolve into zero-sum inter-group rivalries. And when this occurred, creating non-zero-sum development strategies would become increasingly difficult. "What was once a clear-cut win-win strategy, that had the status of a near-truism, has now become a source of contentious differences among subpublics," as exemplified in the "inter-group conflicts imbedded in urban renewal, roadway construction, or curriculum design in the public schools."[12] So they concluded that not only are values changing with different groups of individuals holding diverse values, but there is no overriding theory or social ethic to ascertain which group is right and which should have its ends served. "What satisfies one may be abhorrent to another," and "what comprises problem-solution for one is problem-generation for another."[13] These words are remarkably prescient and descriptive of 2023 value conflicts in the American context, as well as those that have erupted throughout the world.

Rittel and Webber took two pathways to answer these questions in "Dilemmas in a General Theory of Planning." This chapter examines the first. It offers a more detailed explanation of wicked problems and their properties, compares wicked and tame problems, and includes a review of the subsequent literature on wicked problems and other problem types. Chapter 2 examines the second. Rittel and Webber ended "Dilemmas in a General Theory of Planning" by signaling a search for an alternative to the scientific approach (which I refer to as the "rational-analytic strategy" to problem solving), which they deemed a poor fit for the conflict-ridden policy and planning process. They very briefly dismissed the problem-solving strategies of competition and authority and only fleetingly suggested argumentation as a possible substitute—a problem-solving approach that Rittel had been independently exploring in his research for some time. Unfortunately, their anticipated follow-up article for a general, English-speaking audience that offered argumentation as an alternative to the scientific approach was never written. Thus, chapter 2 picks up where Rittel and Webber left off. It elaborates on the advantages and disadvantages of the rational-analytic strategy, the competitive and authoritative strategies, and includes additional reviews of subsequent strategies such as taming and collaboration (which includes argumentation) as options for dealing with wicked problems. Thus, these chapters summarize the key aspects of Rittel and Webber's work on wicked problems—what they are (chapter 1) and what problem-solving strategies are used when dealing with them (chapter 2).[14]

Rittel and Webber's Formulation of Wicked Problems

Rittel and Webber identified ten properties of wicked policy making and planning problems. They are organized into two general categories: properties concerning problem formulation and properties concerning solution generation and selection.

Properties Concerning Problem Formulation

Wicked policy and planning problems have no definitive formulation. There is no correct formulation of a wicked problem. How we frame issues depends on our values, assumptions, interests, and preferences, as well as information that we have available at any one point in time. We have no overarching social theory or ethic to determine the "right" problem frame as opposed to the "wrong" one. Wicked problems also are indeterminate; they can't be objectively known, defined, or bounded. They are subjective statements that exist because someone says they do. Moreover, we can and do change our minds about what constitutes a problem. Interfaith marriages are now commonplace in the Western world, while they still are death sentences in other areas. Marriage equality (i.e., choice of marriage partner regardless of gender) is the law in most Western countries, but other countries roundly denounce it. Problem formulation gets even fuzzier when we slip our preferred solution into a problem statement. When the problem is stated as "global warming," stopping the warming becomes the solution. It led Rittel and Webber to caution that finding a problem is often the same thing as finding a solution: "the problem can't be defined until the solution has been found." Thus they conclude that "the formulation of the wicked problem *is* the problem!"[15]

Every wicked policy and planning problem can be considered a symptom of another problem. Wicked problems are nested within an interconnected network of issues, all of which are embedded in a social context that shifts and changes over time. Is the unemployment rate the problem, or is people's lack of the requisite education for the available jobs the problem? We know that unemployment is linked to job automation, lack of education and training, globalization, and the state of the international and national economies. So what is the problem? Or to offer another example, is terrorism the problem, the symptom, the cause, or the consequence of territorial conflicts, religious differences, identity politics, or a fight over resources? In a vast network of issues, it is difficult to separate a problem, from its symptoms, causes, and consequences: "There is nothing like a natural level of a wicked problem."[16] So the first challenge in wicked problem territory is not so much problem framing as it is problem *finding*—bounding the problem space to locate the problem in the complex network of issues in which it lies. In his proposal to the Club of Rome, Hasan Özbekhan cautioned that treating individual problems in isolation was doomed to failure. Instead, he recommended viewing problems as one generalized metaproblem or metasystem of problems that needed to be addressed as a whole.[17]

Whether addressing a single problem or a system of problems, people have different and changing ideas about problems and their causes. Poverty, for example, is viewed differently by the political left and the political right. From the perspective of the left, poverty is caused by factors beyond the poor's control: globalization, automation and the loss of good jobs, poor education due to segregation by race and class, lack of parental resources, and other elements of society. From the perspective of the right, poverty is caused by the poor's lack of personal responsibility, poor choices, and government support that has left them in a cycle of dependency.[18] As Rittel and Webber cautioned, "the choice of explanation is arbitrary in the logical sense. In actuality, attitudinal criteria guide the choice. People choose those explanations which are most plausible to them"[19] and their worldviews. Thus, the causes of problems become as unbounded and indeterminate as the problem itself.

Every wicked policy and planning problem is essentially unique. By "essentially unique," Rittel and Webber meant that despite similarities among some problems, they can have additional distinguishing features that require further consideration when framing them. Take the example of deforestation. Deforestation in Borneo, which occurs due to the introduction of oil palms, differs from the unique properties of deforestation in the Brazilian Amazon, which is the result of international beef and leather trading. Thus, Rittel and Webber maintained that there were "no *classes* of wicked problems in the sense that principles of solution can be developed to fit *all* members of a class."[20] Despite the apparent similiaries among wicked problems, such as deforestation, their paricularieties may override their commonalities. As each wicked problem is unique, so will be its solutions.

Characteristics concerning solution formulation and selection. There are no definitive solution formulations, an enumerable or exhaustively describable set of potential solutions, or classes of solutions to apply to a wicked policy and planning problem. Wicked problems do not have a well-understood set of potential solutions. We have no criteria or means to identify solutions and ensure that a complete set of solutions exists and will be factored into the solution-generation process. Instead, when we formulate solutions, we make a judgment when enough alternatives have been identified. What follows is a debate over which solution in our limited and bounded solution set should be selected and pursued. For example, how should we address economic inequality? Should we offer better education and social services to low-income people? Should we make changes in the tax code to increase taxes on the wealthy and redistribute the money to those in need? Should we erect trade barriers to protect domestic workers from loss of jobs and income due to international competition? What solutions should we pursue to deal with East Saint Louis, Illinois, which as of 2019 had the highest murder rate in the nation?[21] Should we increase restrictions on gun ownership? Should we give police more powerful weapons to fight crime? Should we increase the penalties for murder? Should we attempt to change the norms and values of communities to substitute ethical self-control for police and court control? Our choice of which solutions to consider and our preference for one solution over others becomes a matter of values and judgment. Or, as Wildavsky reminded us, "problems are not so much solved as alleviated, superseded, transformed, and otherwise dropped from view."[22]

Solutions to wicked policy and planning problems are not true or false, but better or worse. People's judgments about solutions differ and vary widely depending on their personal interests, ideological preferences, and worldviews. There are no set formal criteria or decision rules to determine whether true or false solutions exist. Among economists, for example, there are wide-ranging views on income disparity and how to address it. Some don't see this as a problem but rather as a necessary evil of a dynamic society. Others are adamant that it is never acceptable. The varying solutions range from moderate changes to radical shifts in the status quo depending on the economists' worldviews.[23] And these are just economists. Throw in views from other professionals, such as social workers, educators, and the general public, and we can generate many more solutions. Ultimately, problem solvers propose a range of solutions that they judge to be at least better than or at least good enough, in contrast to current arrangements.

There is no immediate and no ultimate test of a solution to a wicked policy and planning problem.   Solutions to wicked problems generate waves of consequences. Within an unbounded time period, there are first-order, second-order, third-order, and even more downstream consequences that are impossible to predict. We can't select solutions based on their consequences because we can't anticipate what the consequences will be. For example, counterinsurgency operations can inadvertently produce "accidental guerrillas"—neutral local populations who ally with insurgents against the outsiders who come to protect or free them.[24] Moreover, although first-order consequences may yield intended advantages, downstream consequences may yield undesirable repercussions that outweigh the advantages. One example is the "cobra effect" during the British rule of colonial India.[25] The government, concerned about the number of venomous snakes in Delhi, offered a bounty for every dead cobra. Initially, the solution had its intended effect; people killed a large number of snakes to get the reward. Over time, though, enterprising individuals began to breed cobras to earn additional income. When the government realized what was happening, it scrapped the reward program. The cobra breeders then released the now-worthless snakes, which ended up increasing the wild cobra population. The solution ultimately made the situation worse. Thus, the full assessment of the consequences can't occur until the waves of repercussions have run their course. Unfortunately, as Rittel and Webber argued, "we have no way of tracing *all* the waves through *all* the affected lives ahead of time or within a limited time span."[26]

Wicked policy and planning problems have no stopping rule.   A problem solver has criteria that establish when a mathematical equation is solved. In contrast, wicked problems have no criteria to guide a search for solutions, much less an algorithm that tells the problem solver which of the many available solutions to choose. Instead, for reasons tangential to the wicked problem, the problem solver redirects his interests not because he has solved the problem, but because he "runs out of time, or money, or patience. He finally says, 'That's good enough,' or 'This is the best I can do within the limitations of the project,' or 'I like this solution'."[27] Wicked problems test our dedication, stamina, and courage to stay with problems and their solutions, no matter how frustratingly difficult and impossible they may seem. Despite the lure of "good-enough" solutions, problem solvers know that they are in it for the long haul. There is always the possibility that their efforts "might increase the chances of finding a better solution."[28] Attempting to solve wicked problems is not for the faint of heart.

Every solution to a wicked policy and planning problem is a one-shot operation. Because there is no opportunity to learn by trial and error, every attempt counts significantly. Problem solving in wicked problem territory carries a risk. Whatever solutions we attempt are consequential; each "leaves 'traces' that cannot be undone."[29] Their effects are irreversible in terms of the impact on people's lives and the resources that we allocate to address them. As of June 28, 2022, the UN Human Rights Office estimated that there were 306,000 civilians who were killed over the ten years of the Syrian war so far.[30] There is no redo button we can push to change those statistics. "Whenever actions are effectively irreversible and whenever the half-lives of the consequences are long, *every trial counts significantly*."[31] And even when we attempt to reverse a decision or correct for undesired consequences, we set off another chain of wicked problems, as we have seen when Syrian migrations to other countries have generated not only humanitarian support, but anti-immigration and populist movements in Europe and the United States.

The policy planner has no right to be wrong. Given the tremendous impact and consequence of solutions in wicked problem territory, the goal is to find at least some solutions that improve conditions. But when solutions are viewed as having failed, problems solvers who advocate and drive particular solutions cannot escape responsibility and accountability. Failure is public and carries little to no immunity from unsuccessful efforts. If weapons of mass destruction constituted the wicked problem, and the solution from the perspective of the George W. Bush administration included the war in Iraq, the overthrow of Saddam Hussein, and his replacement with a government that was sympathetic to the US, then the resultant instability in Iraq and throughout the Middle East, as well as the rise of Daesh and other terrorist groups, were some of the consequences. Problem solvers are not just liable for the solutions they propose and defend, they also are responsible in the court of public opinion and the historical record for the consequences of the decisions they make.

On top of this foundation laid by Rittel and Webber, scholars have added other layers that have broadened our understanding of wicked problems. Table 1.1 summarizes some of the major attempts to broaden wicked problem properties.

For example, Russell Ackoff, in *Redesigning the Future*, wrote about "messes" as follows:

> We have also come to realize that no problem ever exists in complete isolation. Every problem interacts with other problems and is therefore part of a set of interrelated problems, a system of problems. . . . I choose to call such a system a mess. . . . The solution to a mess can seldom be obtained by independently solving each of the problems of which it is composed. . . . Efforts to deal separately with such aspects of urban life as transportation, health, crime, and education seem to aggravate the total situation.[32]

Robert Horn and Robert Weber elaborated on "social messes," noting their ambiguity, complexity, uncertainty, intractability, and tight interconnections among economic,

Table 1.1
Broadening wicked problem properties

Source	Problem Definition	Solution Generation and Selection
Rittel and Webber (1973)	1. Wicked problems have no definitive formulation.	1. There are no definitive solution formulations, nor is there an "enumerable (or exhaustively describable) set of potential solutions," or classes of solutions to apply to a wicked problem.
	2. "Every wicked problem can be considered a symptom of another problem."	2. "Solutions to wicked problems are not true-or-false, but good-or-bad."
	3. "The existence of a discrepancy representing a wicked problem can be explained in numerous ways. The choice of explanation determines the nature of the problem resolution."	3. "There is no immediate and ultimate test of a solution to a wicked problem."
	4. "Every wicked problem is essentially unique."	4. "Wicked problems have no stopping rule."
		5. "Every solution to a wicked problem is a 'one-shot operation'; because there is no opportunity to learn by trial and error; every attempt counts significantly."
		6. Planners have "no right to be wrong."
Ackoff (1974)	5. "Messes"—"no problem ever exists in complete isolation;" "every problem interacts with other problems, a system of problems."	
Horn and Weber (2007)	6. Competing views of the problem; value conflicts.	7. Value conflicts produce contradictory solutions.
	7. Data about the problems are uncertain or missing.	8. Data about the solutions are uncertain or missing.
	8. Problems are constrained ideologically, politically, and economically	9. Solutions are constrained ideologically, politically, and economically.
	9. Problem framing involves alogical, illogical, or multivalued thinking	10. Solutions involve alogical, illogical, or multivalued thinking
	10. Considerable complexity, uncertainty, or ambiguity.	11. Solutions can involve numerous possible intervention points in a system.
		12. Problem solvers are out of touch with problems and potential solutions.
		13. Solutions face great resistance to resolution.

Table 1.1
(continued)

Source	Problem Definition	Solution Generation and Selection
Australian Public Service Commission (2017)	11. Responsibility for problems stretch across many organizations.	14. Solutions require (but lack) coordinated action by a range of stakeholders, including government at all levels, nonprofits, and private businesses and individuals.
	12. Problems have many "interdependencies and are often multi-causal."	15. Solutions lack holistic, nonlinear thinking; flexibility, toleration of ambiguity, and long-term focus.
	13. Problems "are often not stable;" they often are a moving target.	16. Traditional solutions (levers to change behavior) do not work; they lack innovative, personalized approaches that citizens may use to generate their own solutions.
	14. Problems are intractable.	17. Solutions have failed.
Lazarus (2009)	15. Time is running out to address "super wicked problems."	18. Solutions are time sensitive; the longer we wait, the more difficult the solutions will be.
	16. Those seeking to solve super wicked problems are also causing them.	19. Short-term interests and solutions trump long-term needs and gains.
	17. People have cognitive tendencies and limitations that make it difficult to identify problems and their causes.	20. Solutions lack institutional frameworks to develop, implement, and maintain laws to deal with wicked problems.
Levin et al. (2012)	19. We lack the analytical tools to deal with wicked problems.	21. There is "hyperbolic discounting" in solutions: a preference for rewards/ solutions that are received sooner rather than later and irrationally discount the future.
	20. We lack "applied-forward reasoning" about wicked problems.	22. Solutions lack "path-dependent," incremental policy interventions to "constrain our future collective selves."
Ansell and Bartenberger (2016)	21. "Unruly problems often arise in turbulent consitions or they themselves produce turbulence."	23. It is difficult to "develop a standardized response strategy and when we do . . . the results may themselves be highly variable."
	22. Unruly problems often create simultaneous demands that raise vexing trade-offs in an atmosphere of time compression and urgency."	24. "Decision makers under these conditions can easily produce outputs that amplify inconsistencies."
	23. Unruly problems "unfold in *unpredictable* ways. We may expect the problem, but be uable to predict how or where it will manifest itself."	25. Solutions produce unintended consequences.
	24. Unruly problems are "hard to fathom" We may not predict how the situation will react when we intervene to to sove it.	26. When we intervene to solve an unruly problem, we are unable to predict how upstream conditions will affect downstream conditions.

social, political, and technological factors that bound the formulation of problems and their solutions with often alogical or illogical reasoning. These interrelated and interconnected social messes are at multiple levels of society, economy, and governance—systems of systems—that make wicked problems resilient to analysis and resolution.[33]

The Australian Public Service Commission extended the properties of wicked problems by alerting us to the limitations of any single organization attempting to deal with them. Wicked problems cross organizational and national boundaries and attract a range of citizens and stakeholders in the problem-solving process. Feedback is needed from all participants, along with holistic (as opposed to linear) thinking, a toleration of ambiguity, and a long-term focus, to generate innovative solutions. Needless to say, these requirements will pose challenges to traditional approaches to problem solving that themselves need to be changed to deal with intractable problems that have an unfortunate history of failure.[34]

Richard Lazarus identified climate change as a "super wicked problem" and added three properties to table 1.1. First, "time is not costless."[35] We need to act quickly because the longer we take to tackle a wicked problem, the greater the challenge it will present in the future (e.g., climate change can cause serious economic disruption that will slow the global growth rate and make it harder to deal with it). Second, those who are in the best position to address wicked problems are the ones who likely caused them, and they are also the ones with the least immediate incentive to act within a shorter time frame. People also are caught in a "massive social trap."[36] If they can't imagine the future, they can't prepare for it. If they "discount future utility," they put off long-term investments in favor of short-term returns.[37] Thus, short-term returns trump the realization of benefits decades (and sometimes centuries) in the future. Third, we lack an existing institutional framework of government that is empowered to develop, implement, and maintain the laws necessary to address a super wicked problem like climate change. Super wicked problems have vast spatial and temporal scope. New laws and careful oversight of their implementation and updates are necessary to build this institutional framework.[38]

Kelly Levin and colleagues added to the "super wicked problem" properties. From their perspective, the lack of interest in them is not the issue. It is the tendency of our institutions and our individual proclivities as consumers and voters to make choices that give weight to our immediate interests and delay making changes in our behaviors and institutions that are clearly in our own long-term best interest. In addition to the three properties cited by Lazarus, they emphasize a fourth—the hyperbolic discounting that push solutions and policies to irrationally discount the future. They posit that the current "super wicked problem of climate change" is driven in part, by policies, technologies, and discourse that have created "a path-dependent reliance" on "high carbon" fossil fuels. Countervailing policies to trigger path-dependent "low carbon" trajectories are needed in the future. The first challenge is to identify the causal logics of path-dependent processes. Then we need to create forward-reasoning strategies and interventions that might "stick," gain "durability," expand to larger populations, and change behavior through largely unexplored and progressively small changes. Taken together, these small incremental changes pursued along a path-dependent trajectory have potential to trigger large transformative efforts. In contrast, "one-shot," "big bang" policies often fail to garner adequate support, or worse, they produce "shocks" that hamper implementation and compliance and ultimately derail policy no matter how well designed. Consequently, the researchers believe that ratcheted up, path-dependent policies, especially those that bind us to our collective selves, have a greater chance of creating behavioral change.[39]

Chris Ansell and Martin Bartenberger reinforced the temporal dynamics of problems and introduced the concept of "unruly problems"—problems that "often arise in turbulent conditions or they themselves produce turbulence."[40] They identify six broad temporal characteristics of "unruly problems." They arise or behave unexpectedly in response to solutions (e.g., black swans, wild-card events, rude surprises, unintended consequences, boomerang effects, and paradoxical effects); are manifested in discontinuous ways (e.g., tipping points that mark the transition from one state to another); occur when the temporality of a problem is misaligned with the temporality of the problem response (e.g., crescive problems that grow so slowly that they are likely to be missed due to unstable attention cycles); are varied in intensity or are manifested differently over time (e.g., exponential growth, volatility, and escalations); have effects that may be delayed, cumulative, spillover, cascading, or contagious (e.g., discounting the future, small initial effects with large downstream effects, nonlinear interactive effects, and secondary effects that extend beyond the immediate effects); and generate vicious cycles (e.g., feedback effects that aggravate or deepen the original problem through deviation amplifying loops, lock-ins, and social traps that lock people into suboptimal situations).

As the properties of wicked problems broadened, so do the characteristics used to describe them: ill-structured,[41] intractable controversies;[42] unstructured or incorrigible;[43] unstructured and relentless; complex, uncertain, and divergent;[44] tangled,[45] with high degrees of scientific uncertainty and deep disagreements about values;[46] messy, confounding, and frustrating;[47] time sensitive;[48] undecidable—uncertain, unpredictable, under-specified, ill-defined, intangible, indeterminate, and subjective;[49] social messes; complex, constantly changing,[50] unpredictable, open-ended (never definitively solved), or intractable;[51] unruly;[52] messy or intractable or unstructured or contested;[53] highly complex and chronic;[54] "higher levels of problematicity in problem structuring;[55] messy, ambiguous, controversial, and unstructured;[56] and high complexity and uncertainty.[57]

Two questions arise from this brief overview of wicked problems and their properties and characteristics.[58] First, do problems have to exhibit all ten of Rittel and Webber's properties in table 1.1, and perhaps the additional properties of problems and solutions, to be wicked? If a wicked problem has only seven of ten Rittel and Webber's properties, or thirty of the fifty properties identified by all scholars (e.g., twenty-four problem properties and twenty-six solution generation and selection properties), what kinds of problems do we have? The term "super wicked problems" suggests a sliding

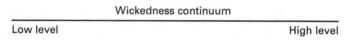

Figure 1.1
Continuum of wickedness

scale of wickedness, but to my knowledge no scale currently exists, although some researchers are attempting to assess the relative weight of various wickedness criteria.[59] Until we have more fine-tuned measures, one rule of thumb is to think of a problem-solving continuum of wickedness ranging from low to high, as illustrated in figure 1.1. Assume that we give each property in table 1.1 a score of 1 if it is present and zero if it isn't, and then total the scores for each problem and solution property. If the total score puts the properties on the low end of the wickedness continuum, we might question whether the problem is even wicked at all. Unfortunately, until and unless we have finer-tuned psychometrics, we will be unable to establish a cut point that distinguishes wicked problems from non–wicked problems.

Perhaps a more useful question at this juncture is to ask why differences among problem types are important to us. What advantage do we gain by differentiating wicked problems from other types of problems? My view is that the distinctions among problems are important because a strategy that is likely to be successful in addressing simple, technical problems, or even complicated problems, is very different from a strategy likely to be successful in addressing wicked ones. As most experts attest, our choice of problem-solving strategies depends on the type of problems that we are confronting.

There is a second reason why greater clarity among problem types is needed. The popularity of the term "wicked problem" has come at some cost. Critics have declared it to be "applied indiscriminately," "inflated and overused,"[60] and a "fad in contemporary policy analysis" that is conceptually "stretched" and "abused,"[61] and a concept that is not coherent philosophically or in terms of policy practice where it is used rhetorically.[62] Although I don't disagree with these criticisms, I do think the concept of "wicked problem" has some utility, but it needs to be reformulated. Reformulation should begin by acknowledging that the term "wicked problem" contains an inherent contradiction. By definition, wicked problems are not only highly contested, they are indeterminate without well-grounded theory, since each problem solver "must discover or invent a particular subject out of the problems and issues of specific circumstances,"[63] which makes it difficult for problem solvers to agree on what the problem is. So, then, why do we insist on naming specific problems as "wicked" (e.g., "poverty is a wicked problem," or "climate change is a wicked problem") when their very indeterminacy makes it difficult to get an agreement on the problem frame? Are we not privileging our preferred frames of reference over those of others and fanning the flames that contribute even more conflict to the problem-solving process? And might our label of a problem as "wicked" account for some of the indiscriminate use of this term in the literature and in practice? If the answer to these questions is "yes," and I believe it is, then perhaps we should stop naming and labeling problems as "wicked" and find another way to categorize issues on which we cannot agree.

In the hope of finding some way out of this conceptual tangle and to distinguish between wicked and other types of problems, we now turn to some of the more notable problem typologies in the literature. To evaluate these typologies, I followed the guidelines of D. Collier and colleagues, who describe typologies as "well established analytic tools in the social sciences" that can be useful in "forming concepts refining measures, exploring dimensionality, and organizing explanatory claims." They challenge critics who follow "the norms of quantitative measurement" and consider typologies as "old-fashioned and unsophisticated."[64] In their view, research on typologies can and should proceed, so long as it meets the high standards of rigor summarized in their guidelines. For example, there are important differences between conceptual categories, which describe types, and explanatory typologies, which explicate relationships among the types or their variables. The conceptual categories and explanatory typologies serve different purposes and should not be combined into one matrix. Unfortunately, these guidelines are not always followed. Moreover, problem types are sometimes confounded with change strategies to deal with them and/ with a problem's symptoms, causes, and consequences.

Problem Typologies

Rittel and Webber's Tame versus Wicked Problems

Table 1.2 contrasts tame and wicked problems as Rittel and Webber described them in their "General Theory of Planning."

A tame problem is clearly defined and accepted by all; has a common goal that problem solvers want to achieve; has information available to do a complete search for solutions to the problem; has an agreement on well-defined criteria to assess the solutions; has knowledge and understanding of the consequences for all solutions that are known in advance; generates an agreement on the optimal solution when the criteria are applied; provides clarity on whether the solution has succeeded or failed; and can derive the same results when the problem-solving process is repeated.

A wicked problem is difficult to bound and define; has no agreed-upon root cause; is unique, with no routine or standard procedures to deal with it; involves limited searches for solutions because people run out of time, resources, and political will during the search process; has no single set of criteria to assess solutions; is unable to reach an agreement on a solution or the "best" solution; has solutions that are reviewed and selected based on judgment—which are "better than" or "worse than" others; has no end point; generates solutions with unintended consequences that can make the problem worse; and derives solutions that are one-shot operations.

In juxtaposing tame and wicked problems, Rittel and Webber offered greater clarity between the two problem types, but they did so by describing a tame problem in terms of the properties it had, while they tended to describe a wicked problem in terms of the properties it lacked in comparison to a tame problem. This cataphatic description

Table 1.2
Rittel and Webber's comparison between tame and wicked problems

Problem Elements	Tame Problems	Wicked Problems
Problem Solving	Problems can be bounded and well specified.	Problems are difficult to bound. Every problem can be considered to be a symptom of another problem—a system of interconnected problems.
	Root causes of problems can be identified.	There are no identifiable root causes.
	Problems can be addressed in a linear, standardized way.	Every problem is unique. There are no agreed-upon routine or standard procedures to deal with them.
Problem Definition	The problem can be clearly defined.	The problem is difficult to define. People perceive the problem differently.
	There is agreement on the problem statement.	There are many problem statements.
Problem Solutions	Solutions can be identified.	The search for solutions stops when people run out of time, resources, and political will.
	Criteria used to select a solution are well defined.	No single set of criteria exists to select a solution. Criteria selected depend on problem solvers' preferences.
	Criteria are accepted by all.	Criteria are not accepted by all.
	Criteria are applied and solutions eliminated until the "best" solution is found.	Solutions are reviewed and selected based on selective judgments—which are "better than" or "worse than" others.
	There is agreement on the "best" solution.	There is no agreement on a solution, or the "best" one.
Consequences	The consequences are well specified and understood; the problem solver knows when she has succeeded or failed.	Problems do not have an end point. In the worst case, there are unintended consequences that make the problem worse.

of wicked problems requires the practitioner and researcher to identify these problems based on what is lacking in the problem-solving process. So when practitioners and researcher are working in the field to identify a wicked problem, they have to be more attuned to what *isn't* happening rather than what is occurring. That shift in perspective is not easy. Even Sherlock Holmes had difficulty. It took him some time in one of his cases before he realized that to solve it, he would have to pay attention to the dog that *didn't* bark. So if our problem-solving skills are not as finely tuned as Sherlock's, and there is variation in our ability to see and describe what doesn't occur, then it may explain why the concept of a "wicked problem" is sometimes conceptually stretched and abused. The challenge is to find a way to define and characterize wicked problems in terms of what they are rather than what they aren't.

One additional issue needs to be addressed. Rittel and Webber use the word "tame" in two ways. Tame is a problem type, as illustrated in table 1.2. There is also a suggestion in their article that "tame" describes a tactic or strategy that is used to domesticate wicked problems and make them more benign and manageable, such as when we "tame a problem prematurely" or refuse to recognize the inherent wickedness of social problems or when we set up and constrain the problem and the solution space.[65] Thus, a tame problem is different from a taming strategy. The goal of a tame problem is to find a solution; the goal of the taming strategy is to bound and limit the wickedness of problems and solutions to make them more manageable and solvable. Thus, we need to exercise care in setting up a typology so that problem types are distinguished from strategies employed to deal with them. In the table 1.2 comparison between tame and wicked problems, there is no issue. But this issue will arise in chapter 2, when we explore which strategies might be employed to deal with wicked problems. What follows are some of the typologies that have been developed to distinguish among problem types.

Heifetz Typology of Problem Situations in Organizations

Ronald Heifetz's work on leadership in organizations expands Rittel and Webber's two-fold comparison between tame and wicked problems.[66] As illustrated in table 1.3, type 1 work situations are comparable to tame problems. Experts are engaged in technical work so that problem definitions and solutions are clear. Type 3 work situations are comparable to wicked problems. Extensive, adaptive learning is required by all participants since both the problem definitions and the solutions are unclear and lack agreement. Type 2, positioned between types 1 and 3, describes a work situation where the problem definition is clear and agreed to, but the solutions aren't. Participants' adaptive learning also is required in type 2 work situations due to the difficulties involved in sorting out the relevant cause-and-effect relationships among problems and solutions.

Heifetz's threefold typology broadens the range of problem situations to type 1 technical work, type 2 technical and adaptive work, and type 3 adaptive work. He also includes a strategy/tactic that he calls "learning," which he views as central to understanding not only leadership, but problem solving which he believes is essential for generating both type 2 solutions and type 3 problem definitions and solutions.

There are several questions about this typology. The first is the implicit assumption that no learning is necessary in technical work. Once a technical system, however

Table 1.3
Heifetz typology of problem situations*

Situation	Type I	Type 2	Type 3
Problem definition	Technical	Technical and adaptive	Adaptive
Problem definition	Clear	Clear	Requires learning
Solutions and implementation	Clear	Requires learning	Requires learning

* Adapted from Heifetz (1994, 76).

defined, is set up, it apparently runs on autopilot, governed by standard operating procedures (SOPs). It begs the question: who sets up the technical system in the first place and who deals with the system failures and problems when they surface during the implementation of a technical system, since no technical system is failproof? Wouldn't learning be part of both of these efforts? The typology also confounds the problem type with the strategy/tactic advocated to address the problem situation. Rather than assume there is only one strategy to deal with type 2 and 3 problems, it is advisable to keep questions of strategy open and independent of problem classifications, especially if the problem classification may include complex, or even wicked problems.

Hoppe and Hisschemöller Typology of Policy Problems and Policy Strategy

Rob Hoppe and Matthijs Hisschemöller use two dimensions—certainty about a problem's relevant knowledge and consensus about relevant norms and values—to generate and compare four types of policy problems: structured, moderately structured (ends), moderately structured (means), and unstructured, as seen in table 1.4.[67] A *structured problem* has a high degree of consensus about the problem situation and the ways to convert it to a more desirable situation, and the relevant values. A *moderately structured problem (ends)* has a high degree of consensus on relevant values, but there is uncertainty or dissent on what the problem situation is and what the relevant knowledge is to convert it to a more desirable situation. A *moderately structured problem (means)* has a consensus on the knowledge of the problem situation and the ways to convert it to a more desirable situation, but there is ongoing dissent about the relevant values at stake. Finally, an *unstructured problem* has no consensus on relevant values, the problem situation, or ways to convert problems to a more desirable situation despite widespread discomfort with the status quo. This typology also identifies a particular strategy with each problem type: a *learning strategy* for unstructured problems, a *negotiation strategy* for moderately structured problems (ends), an accommodation strategy for moderately structured problems (means), and a *rule-based strategy* for structured problems.

The typology expands the problem types, which is useful, but we are left with two substantive issues. The vertical dimension appears to confound the relevant knowledge about a problem situation with the knowledge of how to convert the problem

Table 1.4
Hisschemöller and Hoppe typology of policy problems and policy strategy*

Certainty about Relevant Knowledge		Consensus on Relevant Norms and Values	
		No	Yes
	No	Unstructured Problem (policy as learning)	Moderately Structured Problem (Ends) (policy as negotiation)
	Yes	Moderately Structured (Means) (policy as accommodation)	Structured Problem (policy as rule)

* Adapted from Hisschemöller and Hoppe (1996, 56).

situation to a more desirable one. As an example, knowledge of a problem (e.g., global warming) is different from the knowledge needed to convert the problem situation to a more desirable one (e.g., ways to address global warming). Rather than combining both concepts into one dimension, the typology needs to have three dimensions: knowledge about a problem, knowledge about how to convert the problem situation to a more desirable one, and the level of consensus on norms and values. Together, the three dimensions would expand the 2×2 matrix to a 2×3 matrix. The second issue is the direct link between a particular strategy and each problem type. Assigning a particular strategy to a particular policy type assumes that there is one best strategy, independent of context, and leaves policy makers and problem solvers with a requirement, not a choice.

Alford and Head Typology of Problems and Contingency Framework

John Alford and Brian Head offer a typology of complex problems that vary in their degree of wickedness.[68] The typology has merit, in that it recognizes the increasing complexity and intractability of problems and solutions on the vertical dimension, as well as the evolving relationship between stakeholders from indifferent to cooperative to multiple parties with conflicting values and interests on the horizontal dimension. And, as the authors state, the purpose of the typology "is not to 'solve' the problem but to formulate a working hypothesis as to where in the matrix the particular situation sits."[69] Furthermore, once located, the problem solvers have a better understanding of a problem's "underlying causes and mechanisms," so they are in a better position to develop solutions and interventions that make progress in improving and managing the problem.

Attempting to gain a greater understanding of the problem-solution situation certainly has value, and the causal categories and factors listed in table 1.2 are an excellent start to help researchers define and operationalize the dimensions of complexity and stakeholder relations. But what is missing from Alford and Head's article is an explanation of the typology and the nine problem types that they derive from the two dimensions. The authors provide an explanation of only the tame problem and the wicked problem types, while bypassing the others. Although the title of the article signals the importance of a typology, the lack of attention to the other seven problem types suggests that the real purpose of the article is to generate criteria to operationalize the measurement of wickedness. This, I believe, is the article's value-added contribution to the discourse on wicked problems.

Roberts Problem-Solving Territories

As illustrated thus far, researchers have employed a range of concepts to explore wicked problems in terms of problem types, problem situations, consensus on norms and values, certainty about relevant knowledge, problem complexity, and stakeholder and institutional difficulties. These concepts certainly offer different ways to deconstruct wickedness. However, my preference is to return to Rittel and Webber and the stark picture they painted of the conflict-ridden context in the United States summarized at the beginning of this chapter. People in the 1970s were becoming increasingly pluralistic, with intergroup differences that often manifested as zero-sum conflicts over their values and beliefs. As division grew, people were left with no overriding theory or social ethic to ascertain which group is right and which should have its ends served, "what satisfies one may be abhorrent to another," and "what comprises problem solution for one is problem generation for another."[70] From Rittel and Webber's perspective, the heart of wicked problems were the deepening value conflicts that unfortunately have dramatically increased over time, as evidenced by the angry debates during the 2020 presidential election and the attack on Congress and the US Capitol on January 6, 2021.[71] At minimum, compared to other types of problems, wicked problems embroil us in higher levels of conflict, defined as a disagreement or argument, typically a protracted one, between people or parties with opposing views.[72]

So rather than constructing a typology of problems, I shift the unit of analysis from "the problem" to people's interactions and relationships as they attempt to socially construct some kind of agreement on problems and solutions.[73] The typology of *problem-solving territories*, as seen in figure 1.2, thus differentiates among four "problem

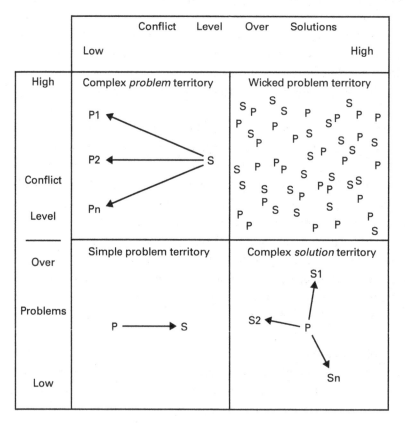

Figure 1.2
Roberts problem-solution territories

spaces"[74] that produce varying levels of conflict when people interact concerning problems and solutions within each quadrant. In *simple problem territory,* we find general agreement about a problem and a solution.[75] In *complex solution territory,* we find general agreement about a problem and conflict about the solutions. In *complex problem territory,* we find general agreement about a solution, but conflict about the problems. And in *wicked problem territory,* we find higher levels of conflict about both problems and solutions. Noordegraaf and colleagues, taking a "street-level" perspective, describe this problem-solving space as "situated wickedness."[76] The placement and distribution of problems (*P*s) and solutions (*S*s) *within* wicked problem territory indicate the variations among problem-solution conflicts that are possible, since not all problems and solutions have the same levels of conflict intensity in wicked problem territory. Some are "super wicked problems," likely located at the tip of the wicked problem quadrant, as Lazarus[77] and Levin and colleagues[78] have suggested based on the conflicts generated through people's interactions.

Simple problem territory. In simple problem territory, in the lower-left quadrant, there is a low level of conflict about a problem and its solution. In this configuration, we find a direct connection (shown by a solid line) between a problem (*P*) and a solution (*S*). Simple problems are technically well defined and structured and can be solved by people using standard techniques and procedures. My bicycle chain breaks. I take it to the bicycle repair shop, and the technician activates a routine to fix it; in this case, he replaces the chain. An engineer has a math problem. She solves the equation correctly. A short-order cook has twenty people to feed. He decides on a menu and follows a standard procedure of buying and preparing the food.

Complex problem territory. The term "complex" refers to something that is "composed of two or more separable or analyzable items parts, or constituents."[79] There is general agreement that complex problem solving has a number of dimensions, but two of these are most relevant for our purposes: complexity arises when people propose multiple definitions of the problem, and complexity arises when people pursue different goals embedded in solutions that they advocate.[80] Thus, complex problem territory lands us into two quadrants.

In complex solution territory, in the lower-right quadrant, people agree on the problem (*P*), but they disagree on the solutions (*S*). Hence, the configuration between the problem (*P*) and the solutions (*S*) are not well connected and are shown by dotted lines. One example is the San Clemente dam project in Carmel Valley, California. The community had a general agreement about the problem: the dam on the Carmel Valley River was failing, and something needed to be done about it. Conflict ensued over the solutions: shore up the dam, bypass the dam, or build another dam. (The ultimate decision was to forge a new channel in the river and bypass the dam, eventually eliminating it.) While the problem-solving process involved years of in-depth study and problem analysis, stakeholder deliberations and conflicts centered on the solutions, not on experts' well-specified technical problems with the dam.

We find another example in President John F. Kennedy's address to Congress about urgent national needs on May 25, 1961.[81] He challenged Americans to commit to the goal of landing a man on the Moon within the decade and returning him safely to Earth. The Soviet Union had launched Sputnik almost four years earlier and successfully sent a cosmonaut, Yuri Gagarin, into space in April 1961. The problem, as Kennedy framed it on September 12, 1962, to a crowd of 35,000 people at Rice University, was that the United States was losing and the Soviet Union was winning the space race. Space superiority translated into military superiority, and hence the urgent need. "Whether it will become a force for good or ill depends on man, and only if the United States occupies a position of preeminence can we help decide whether this new ocean will be a sea of peace or a new terrifying theater of war." Thus, said Kennedy, "we choose to go to the Moon in this decade . . . not because [it is] easy, but because [it is] hard; because that goal will serve to organize and measure the best of our energies and skills, because that challenge is one that we are willing to accept, one we are unwilling to postpone, and one we intend to win."[82]

A consensus on the problem quickly emerged—the lack of space superiority in the United States compared to the Soviet Union. The debate then shifted to the scientific and technical solutions needed to close the gap and get us safely to the Moon and back:

- *direct ascent* called for the construction of a huge booster to launch the spacecraft and send it on a direct course to the Moon, land a large vehicle, and send parts of it back to Earth;

- *Earth-orbit rendezvous* called for the launch of various modules required for the Moon trip into an orbit above the Earth, where they would rendezvous, be assembled on a space station into a single system, refueled, and sent to the Moon;

- *lunar-orbit rendezvous* called for sending the entire lunar spacecraft up in one launch, head to the Moon, enter its orbit, and dispatch a small vehicle to land on the lunar surface; and

- *lunar surface rendezvous* called for the launch of two spacecraft in succession. The first to land would be an automated vehicle carrying propellant for the return to Earth. The human-occupied vehicle would land some time later. Propellant then would be transferred from the automated vehicle to the other vehicle.

The debates on these four options were contentious, but in an all-day meeting on June 7, 1962, at the Marshall Space Flight Center, the advocates of the lunar-orbit rendezvous won out. Settling on a technical solution was just the beginning, however. There were layers of complexity in the project run by the National Aeronautics and Space Administration (NASA). Debates continued over its funding and the distribution of resources; the integration of disparate government organizations (e.g., research centers, laboratories, flight centers, and vehicle assembly and test facilities) and private-sector organizations (e.g., universities, research institutions, and businesses and contractors in the emerging aerospace industry) into a single unified path; the management of programs and their three interrelated constraints (cost, schedule, and reliability); different values and perspectives between engineers who usually worked in teams to build hardware and scientists who engaged in pure research and who were more concerned with designing experiments that would expand scientific knowledge about the Moon.[83]

The United States achieved its goal, landing Neil Armstrong and Edwin "Buzz" Aldrin on the moon on July 20, 1969 and returned them, along with the command module piloted by Michael Collins, safely back to Earth on July 24, 1969. Other achievements were noted in *Science*:

> [I]n terms of numbers of dollars or of men, NASA has not been our largest national undertaking, but in terms of complexity, rate of growth, and technological sophistication it has been unique. . . . It may turn out that [the space program's] most valuable spin-off of all will be human rather than technological: better knowledge of how to plan, coordinate, and monitor the multitudinous and varied activities of the organizations required to accomplish great social undertakings.[84]

James E. Webb, the NASA administrator from 1961–1968, concurred with this assessment. He contended that the project to send men to the Moon was much more a management challenge to ensure that technological skills were properly employed, political battles to acquire and manage resources were won, and good program management was followed to integrate complex organizations and their tasks to achieve the goal.[85]

In contrast, in the complex problem territory in the upper-left quadrant, we find people who disagree about the problem (*P*), but they agree on its solution (*S*). The configuration is shown with dotted lines moving "backward" from the agreed-upon solution to multiple problem formulations (*P*). This type of problem-solving space is more difficult to understand. How is it possible to agree on a solution but disagree on what the problem is? At first glance, the quadrant appears to be illogical. And indeed it doesn't make sense if one assumes a linear process of problem solving, in which to be "rational," one is advised to first identify a problem and then search for solutions, selecting one that is optimal based on well-chosen criteria. However, when I ask people to describe the decision-making process in the US Congress, they grudgingly admit that this solution-in-search of a problem does exist. Congressional representatives may differ on the problems facing the nation, but most will agree that spending money in their home districts is the solution. As Rittel and Webber reminded us, problems "can't be defined until the solution has been found."[86]

Coalitions also are formed on this basis. Countries agree on how to deal with an aggressor, but they don't necessarily agree on the problem that the aggressor presents. Madeleine Albright, the US secretary of state under President Bill Clinton, provided an example when she challenged Chairman of the Joint Chiefs Colin Powell during a 1993 meeting:[87] "What's the point of having this superb military that you're always talking about if we can't use it?" As General Powell later recalled, her problem-solving approach was so alien that he "thought [he] would have an aneurysm."[88] Rather than a solution in search of a problem, he advocated the rational-analytic approach as expressed in the Powell Doctrine: the United States should use military force only after a clear political goal has been set. Only if we have identified a problem, then and only can we set explicit military goals (solutions) to solve it.

In these cases and others, problem solvers start with their preferred solution and reverse-engineer the problem-solving process by attaching their preferred solution to whatever problems are handy or make the most sense to them. Rather than the "rational," linear logic of the traditional problem-solving process, there is a different logic, which some have dubbed "the garbage can model of decision making."[89]

Wicked problem territory. The space in the upper-right quadrant is populated with high levels of conflict surrounding problems (*P*) and solutions (*S*). The configuration is represented with many different *P*s and *S*s, without any clear connections. And as illustrated with the continuum of wickedness characteristics, there are likely to be different degrees of wickedness within the quadrant, depending on how well the problem and its solutions match Rittel and Webber's and others' criteria. Thus, a good rule of thumb to distinguish wicked problems from simple or complex ones is the level of discord on the topic. If many people are angrily debating problems and solutions, then it is a good guess that you have ventured into some space within wicked problem territory.

Take the example of climate change. Many define the changes in the Earth's climate to be human-induced global warming, and they advocate cutting carbon emissions as the solution. Others view the problem to be warming temperatures due to the Earth's natural or solar cycles, and thus they conclude that no solutions are needed since it is a natural phenomenon. Humans have survived past climate changes and will do so again. Still others deny the existence of global warming, challenge the science behind the problem statements, and therefore reject any proposed solutions to what they consider to be a nonproblem.

Implications for Those Venturing into Wicked Problem Territory

Dealing with High Levels of Conflict

High levels of conflict alert us to wicked problem territory, especially when people are more intensely focused on their areas of disagreement than on searching for areas of agreement. Sometimes the issues are so threatening and heated that people can't even be in the same room. Diplomats and mediators have developed a technique to deal with these extreme situations, which they refer to as "shuttle diplomacy." In this approach, a third party serves as an intermediary who goes back and forth between or among principals in a dispute, with no direct principal-to-principal contact. The term was first applied to Secretary of State Henry Kissinger's efforts to facilitate the cessation of the hostilities that followed the Arab-Israeli War in 1973.

My personal test of wicked problem territory is what it can feel like when you are caught in it—uncertain, anxious, fearful, stressed and angry. Arthur C. Evans, the chief executive officer (CEO) of the American Psychological Association, reports on one example—2020, which has been "a year unlike any other in living memory":

> Not only are we in the midst of a global pandemic that has killed more than 200,000 Americans, but we are also facing increasing division and hostility in the presidential election. Add to that racial turmoil in our cities, the unsteady economy and climate change that has fueled widespread wildfires and other natural disasters. The result is an accumulation of stressors that are taking a physical and emotional toll on Americans."[90]

I observed the toll that it was taking on those working on a UN mission team charged with developing a strategic framework for the reconstruction of Afghanistan in the late 1990s as the Afghanistan war was winding down and the Taliban was expected to take control of the country. I really had no idea what "the" problems or "the" solutions for Afghanistan would be, but the initial list of expected attendees—the major stakeholders in Afghanistan, including the Taliban—certainly had their own views on problems and solutions. The workshop that I was to design and facilitate risked being caught in an incessant "do-loop" of conflict, with no exit unless I found a way to help the stakeholders at least talk to one another. My goal was not to attempt to solve problems, but rather to help the stakeholders develop some shared appreciation of the situation so they could at least understand each other's positions well enough to have a dialogue about their differences and how they might want to address them.

So when venturing into wicked problem territory, be prepared to find it full of multiple stakeholders who hold competing values and views and vigorously defend their versions of the "truth" by making different claims about the problems and their causes, solutions, and potential consequences. Most important, be mindful of how to deal the significant stress that these conflicts will likely engender in all who are involved with them.

Social Construction of Problems and Solutions

Problems and their solutions are socially constructed.[91] They only exist phenomenologically when we agree by social definition that they do. Our values, beliefs, assumptions, interests, and preferences inform what we label as a problem, a cause, a solution, and a consequence. What we decide to call "wicked" one day can be reframed as "complex," "simple," or even "nonexistent" the next day to minimize the time and resources that wicked problems require and the aggravation and "dis-ease" they engender. As Wildavsky reminded us, "problems are not so much solved as alleviated, superseded, transformed, and otherwise dropped from view."[92] So for example, the Soviet Union was a US partner against Nazi Germany in World War II, but a US enemy in the Cold War. And when the Soviet Union officially ceased to exist on December 1, 1991, Russia and the United States became bilateral collaborators on a host of economic, commercial, regional, and security issues. After Russia's support for separatists fighting Ukraine, its occupation and annexation of Crimea, its backing of Bashar al-Assad of Syria, its alleged interferences in the US 2016 presidential election, and its ongoing invasion of Ukraine, Russia and the United States are now (fill in the blank with your own descriptor).

Language in wicked problem territory matters. Identifying problems first requires our interpretation, structuring, and labeling of people, things, and events. There are no givens when it comes to defining problems. In the case of "global warming," discussions seem to be refocusing on the "climatic disturbances" that are visible and evident—rising waters in coastal regions, hurricanes, and raging fires. As recent polls suggest, people seem to be more responsive to the term "climate change" than "global warming" and thus they are more willing to acknowledge the existence of the phenomenon.[93]

Lack of Conflict Doesn't Mean That We Agree on the "Facts"

Lack of conflict about a problem should not be confounded with an understanding of the "facts." Suppose that we all agree that the Earth is the center of our world system, as indeed most of us did at one point in history. There were few problems with that position, at least until Nicolaus Copernicus published *De Revolutonibus* in 1543, which expressed a heliocentric model of the universe (i.e., the Sun was at the center, not the Earth). Although Copernicus managed to escape the wrath of the Catholic Church, Galileo Galilei, who followed him, did not.[94] Describing observations made with his new telescope, Galileo began promoting Copernicus' theory. When he published his *Sidereus Nuncius* (Starry Messenger) in 1610, describing his observations and discoveries that the Sun was the center of the solar system and the Earth circled it, he prompted strong opposition from the Catholic Church. His first rebuke in 1616 resulted in a ban of his book and an order to abandon the heliocentric idea and to abstain from teaching, defending, or discussing his ideas, either orally or in writing. When he wrote his *Dialogue Concerning the Two Chief World Systems*, which continued to explore his ideas, he was ordered to stand trial in 1633. Galileo was interrogated, threatened with physical torture, tried, found guilty of heresy, and sentenced to indefinite imprisonment. His sentence was commuted to house arrest, which he served until his death in 1642. His offending book was banned and publication of his past and future work forbidden.

There are many ironies in this short narrative, the least of which is that neither the Earth nor the Sun is the center of our world, and now we are not even sure how many worlds and universes exist.[95] Although many think that science moves us beyond wicked problem territory in rational discussions of our physical world, others remind us that conflict over the Earth still generates a great deal of heat. Many of our problems are due to our own ignorance. We simply do not know what the "facts" are, and the worst part is that many of us do not know that we do not know—the unknown unknowns.

Time Is a Factor in Problem-Solution Territories

Problems and their solutions are not permanently affixed in any of the four quadrants. Take the example of tobacco. Neither a problem nor a solution, but simply part of a ceremonial tradition or a means to help a person relax, tobacco was not originally in the problem matrix. Then alarms sounded about the dangers of tobacco use. Conflicts erupted over tobacco research, a problem formulation, and potential solutions driving the issue of tobacco from a nonproblem into wicked problem territory. Eventually, mounting evidence convinced people that tobacco was indeed a health problem, and the use of tobacco gradually became a complex issue—which solution should we pursue to deal with this health problem? Ban it? Control its promotion, sale, and use? Tax it? Launch an information campaign and put warnings on packages?

Smallpox,[96] the scourge of humanity, is another example how issues move through the problem territory matrix. Evidence of its existence was found on the mummified body of Pharaoh Ramses V of Egypt (1150 BC), and historical records over millennia have documented its lethal worldwide transmission. Even when the problem was well defined and the solution (a vaccine) was well researched and accepted in the 1950s, over fifty million cases were estimated to be occurring each year throughout the world. As late as 1967, despite the successful vaccination campaigns that had been underway throughout the nineteenth and twentieth centuries, the World Health Organization (WHO) estimated that fifteen million people had contracted the disease and two million had died of it. But by December 1979, the WHO certified the eradication of smallpox, the only human infectious disease to have been completely eradicated. It had taken centuries and millions of people had died by then, but the pathogen and its causes had been identified and solutions had been discovered, tested, implemented, and proved successful.[97]

Thus, problems are not permanently relegated to one quadrant. It is possible to move them out of wicked problem territory and into other problem territories to the extent that people can agree on problems and/or their solutions, although movement likely necessitates a long time frame.

Separating Complex Problems from Complicated Ones

In the complex territories discussed in this chapter, there are conflicts over problems, their solutions, or both. But even though we may reach a consensus about a problem or its solution, complications do occur, as the smallpox case illustrates. The eradication of smallpox was complicated; it was difficult, involved many people, organizations, and countries, and required the application of well-established SOPs to deal with the disease. In 1972, a major European outbreak occurred in Kosovo, Yugoslavia. A pilgrim returning from Mecca via Iraq spread the virus to 175 friends, relatives, and hospital personnel, killing 35 people. When the virus reached Belgrade, Tito's communist government declared martial law, enforced quarantine, enlisted the help of WHO, and launched a vaccination campaign to prevent the epidemic's spread outside Kosovo. All public events were forbidden, including weddings. No one was permitted in or out of the area unless vaccinated. The work was exhausting, with no time off (not even holidays or Sundays). As Flight reports, "In the end almost the entire Yugoslavian population of 18 million people was vaccinated."[98] Although the causes and solutions to combat smallpox were known and understood, it still was complicated to quarantine a large number of people in a large geographic area in a short period of time in order to avert a pandemic. Routines and protocols continued to improve over the years with D. A. Henderson's more targeted strategy of containment and surveillance.[99] When an outbreak would occur, a WHO team arrived, vaccinated and isolated those were ill, and then traced and vaccinated all their contacts. The idea was to "fence in" the virus and prevent it from moving to others outside the fence. The team also traveled with a "recognition card" that would show what the disease looked like and offered rewards to encourage people to report any cases. The entire eradication process became less complicated and more medically efficient than vaccinating a whole country.

Be Wary of Those Offering Quick Fixes to Wicked Problems

Wicked problems are au courant. It may be that the growing references in the academic and popular press reflect their actual increase, in which case searching for their causes and solutions should be a priority. It also may be that "wicked problem" is simply an attention-grabbing label used without discretion, in which case greater clarity about problem types is needed. From my perspective, if people are telling me that they can tame, manage, or solve wicked problems, I question whether they are really dealing with them. Problems in wicked problem territory, some examples of which are listed in the introduction, defy quick fixes. Barring miracles or some yet-to-be-invented technology, they will not be tamed, managed, or solved, certainly not in the short term.

But I don't mean to say that we should stop trying to address them. Indeed, my point in this book is that there are problem-solving strategies that may serve us better than others when we find ourselves trapped in wicked problem territory. What it does mean is that we need to be realistic in what we are up against and be aware of our discomfort and frustrations in dealing with problems that we can't seem to define and solutions that defy our best efforts at resolution.

In Summary

In our journey into wicked problem territory thus far, we find wicked problems that we can't define, causes that we can't identify, solutions on which we can't agree, and results and consequences that we can't anticipate or control. If we accept a common definition of a problem as a perceived gap between an existing state and a desired state and a solution is whatever closes the gap,[100] then wicked problem territory can be understood as a social space where problem solvers are unable to conceptualize a gap or to close the gap due to high levels of conflicts over the existing state (an issue or presenting problem), its causes, and the desired state (a solution and its consequences). So instead of naming a problem as wicked and insisting that our frame is the "right" one, we need to find ways to categorize things on which we do not agree. I believe that replacing problems and solutions with different characterizations of problem spaces or territories provides problem solvers with that possibility. Most importantly, it enables us to pose a critical question, a topic that we take up in chapter 2. Which problem-solving strategies offer us greater leverage when we land in wicked problem territory?

2 Traditional Strategies in Wicked Problem Territory

> While strategy is undoubtedly a good thing to have, it is also a hard thing to get right.
> —Lawrence Freedman, 2013

Following Freedman's lead, attempting to get strategy "right"[1] entails attending to its key aspects: the *what* of a strategy, or its intent/purpose (e.g., particular goals being pursued); the *how* of a strategy, or its general approach (e.g., competitive strategy, which seeks to defeat opponents in business, trade, and warfare); and the *means* of a strategy, or its methods, techniques, tools, and other implements to execute the general approach. For example, in the collaborative strategy, people join forces and work together to define problems and agree on solutions, but they may use very different techniques to support the collaboration depending on the situation (e.g., citizen panels,[2] deliberative polling,[3] future searches and search conferences,[4] national issues forum,[5] soft system methodology,[6] and twenty-first-century meetings).[7] Due to space limitations, this book will not fully elaborate all three aspects of strategy, although it is important to remember that all three are interrelated. Instead, I focus on the "how" of strategy and probe five strategies in detail: competitive, authority/authoritative, rational-analytic, taming, and collaborative. I address the same question for all five of these strategies: What advantages and disadvantages do they have in wicked problem territory?

In "Dilemmas in a General Theory of Planning," Rittel and Webber eliminated the competitive strategy from consideration since the "zero-sum games" of winners and losers would likely exacerbate the intergroup differences and rivalries that were growing among increasingly pluralistic and contentious American subpublics.[8] However, many consider that the competitive strategy has its advantages, especially in wicked problem territory, so I include it here for our consideration.

Competitive Strategy

The competitive strategy has a long history and those who pursue it play a zero-sum game. Zero-sum can be best explained by thinking of a pie that I want to divide into six pieces. If I want to increase the size of my own serving, then I have to reduce the size of someone else's. To get more pie, I have to take it from someone else's share. So in terms of wicked problem territory, if my problem-solving strategy is competitive and my opponent wins the right to frame the problem and choose his preferred solution, then I lose. If I seize the opportunity to frame the problem and establish my preferred solution, then I win. Following the competitive strategy, the goal is to establish and sustain one's preferred problem statement and its solution over all those who challenge or disagree with it.

The competitive strategy has many adherents. Those who subscribe to this view find common cause with Thomas Hobbes, the seventeenth-century British philosopher who believed that human nature drives competition. According to Hobbes, man's natural instinct is to fight and war against his fellow man. Under such conditions, people constantly live in a war of all against all, which makes "the life of man solitary, poor, nasty, brutish, and short."[9] The win-lose mind-set and the tactics derived from it establish the rules of the game for all interactions, no matter what the topic, whom they involve, or where they occur. Thus, we find the competitive strategy manifested in warfare, markets, and public policy, as summarized below.

Warfare   Throughout world history, we have battled one another. The historians Will and Ariel Durant, in their 1968 book *The Lessons of History*, find that "war is one of the constants of history, and has not diminished with civilization or democracy." According to their calculations, "in the last 3,421 years of recorded history only, 268 have seen no war." They acknowledge that at present, war is "the ultimate form of competition and natural selection in the human species." Quoting the Greek philosopher Heraclitus, they view war and competition as "the father of all things, the potent source of ideas, inventions, institutions, and states."[10]

Twentieth-century warfare has seen particularly vicious forms of zero-sum competition among nation-states. Over 100 countries from Africa, the Americas, Asia, Australasia, and Europe fought in World War I between 1914 and 1918. Estimates for total military and civilian deaths vary between 15 million and 22 million.[11] With the exceptions of a few states that remained neutral, nearly every country in the world was involved to some degree in World War II, from 1939 to 1945. World War II estimates for total military and civilian deaths range from 70–85 million—about 3 percent of the world's population.[12]

Contests over problem definitions and solutions between the United States and Japan are only one example of the competing claims that landed the world in wicked problem territory. In the 1930s, Japan's need for oil and its expansion into the Pacific were considered to be a direct threat to US interests in the Pacific. American attempts to limit Japanese expansion were viewed as a direct threat to Japan's national security. Each country's competing claims on the problem and its solution and their inability to resolve their differences resulted in the Japanese bombing of Pearl Harbor, Hawaii, on December 7, 1941. After the attack, President Franklin Delano Roosevelt delivered his "Day of Infamy Speech," and on December 8, 1941, the United States entered World War II.

In Europe, Germany defined one of its wicked problems to be the Treaty of Versailles, which blamed Germany for World War I, required it to pay reparations for the war damages suffered by the international community, barred it from the League of Nations, demilitarized the Rhineland, and repossessed German territory. The Allies won the war and Germany lost it, and as a consequence, it had to forfeit all its colonies and lost 13 percent of its territory on the continent (more than 27,000 square miles) and one-tenth of its population (between 6.5 and 7 million people). France reclaimed Alsace-Lorraine. Belgium received Eupen and Malmedy. The League of Nations placed the industrial Saar region under its administration, and the largely German city of Danzig became a free city under its protection. Denmark received Northern Schleswig. Poland received parts of West Prussia and Silesia. Czechoslovakia received the Hultschin district. Lithuania received Memel, a small strip of territory in East Prussia along the Baltic Sea.

German attempts to repay the loans led to hyperinflation, which ultimately made the German mark worthless. Adolf Hitler gained popularity and in 1933 was appointed German chancellor, in part by promising to return the fatherland to its former glory, reversing the terms of the Versailles Treaty, regaining what was rightfully Germany's, and securing Germany's inalienable right of Lebensraum (living space). And so in the 1930s began Anschluss, the annexation of Austria, the annexation of Czechoslovakia's Sudetenland, the occupation of Czechoslovakia, and ultimately the invasion of Poland, the tipping point that pushed France and England to declare war on Germany.

A more recent example of zero-sum competition in wicked problem territory is Iraq's invasion of Kuwait on August 2, 1990, which triggered the 1990–1991 Persian Gulf War. The Iraq-Kuwait dispute centered on the huge Rumaila oil reservoir beneath the Iraq-Kuwait border. When oil formations run beneath political boundaries, participants who share the field typically use a formula that sets percentages of ownership to determine shared production costs and revenues. However, Iraq refused to negotiate with Kuwait, so Kuwait began extracting oil from Rumaila without any agreement. Kuwait's intention was to force Iraqi president Saddam Hussein to the bargaining table to extract a border truce that included a nonaggression pact and drilling rights.[13] But in an emergency meeting of the Arab League, Saddam spoke of the economic damage that Kuwait's oil policy had inflicted on Iraq, charging that it had stolen billions of dollars' worth of Iraqi oil from slant drilling. In addition, Saddam viewed Kuwait's refusal to decrease its oil production as an act of aggression against Iraq, stating: "We cannot tolerate this type of economic warfare. . . . We have reached a state of affairs where we cannot take the pressure."[14] So on August 2, Iraq invaded Kuwait, declared it to be its nineteenth province, drove its ruling family into exile, and installed its own leadership.

The zero-sum competition over the Rumaila oil reservoir, when each country claimed the oil and defended its national security interests to extract it, set off a chain of events. On August 3, 1990, the Security Council in the United Nations (UN) passed Resolution 660, which condemned the Iraqi invasion of Kuwait. Subsequent resolutions placed sanctions on Iraq and required Iraqi forces to withdraw by January 15,

1991, or face military action. In the aftermath of the Iraqi attack on Kuwait, US president George H. W. Bush directed American forces to Saudi Arabia to aid in the defense of its ally and prevent further aggression. This mission, dubbed "Operation Desert Shield," called for the rapid buildup of US and coalition forces in the Saudi desert and Persian Gulf. Ultimately, thirty-four nations contributed troops and resources to launch an aerial campaign against Iraqi targets, followed by a brief land campaign that ultimately liberated Kuwait from Iraqi control.

Terrorism landed the United States in wicked problem territory, and the War on Terror became its solution after four coordinated terrorist attacks on the United States on the morning of September 11, 2001. Al-Qaeda, led by Osama Bin Laden, was widely believed to be behind attacks. Having taken control of Afghanistan, the Taliban gave protection to Al-Qaeda under the laws of *Pashtunwali*, a nonwritten ethical code and a system of law and governance that the Pashtun people follow. In response to the attack, President George W. Bush said that countries faced a choice: "Every nation, in every region, now has a decision to make. Either you are with us, or you are with the terrorists."[15] With the zero-sum line drawn and the Taliban's refusal to hand over Al-Queda's leadership, Bush's solution to the wicked problem of terrorism was to invade Afghanistan. He eventually expanded his rationale for the war to include the search of weapons of mass destruction. Although an accurate count is difficult to make, speculation is that the US War on Terror has expanded to countries throughout the Middle East, South Asia, East and Central Asia, the Sahara/Sahel region of Africa, the Greater Horn of Africa, West and Central Africa, Central and South America, and Europe.

Market competition   In economics, competition is rivalry among sellers to offer more favorable terms to buyers for the goods and services they purchase, thus increasing the sellers' sales, profits, and market share. The underlying assumption of market competition is based on scarcity. Since there are never enough goods and services to satisfy human wants, when facing scarcity, market competition is believed to be an efficient way to determine who gets what.[16]

To achieve a competitive advantage, sellers develop competitive strategies—the ability to outperform present or potential competitors in the same industry or market. According to Michael Porter, businesses have their choice among three generic strategies: cost leadership, differentiation, and focus. When pursuing a cost leadership strategy, firms seek to be the lowest-cost producer in its industry. When pursuing a differentiation strategy, firms seek to establish a unique benefit among industry buyers that will command a premium price. When pursuing a focus or segmentation strategy, firms will narrow their scope and concentrate on a segment or group of segments in the industry, with either a cost focus or a differential focus, and serve consumers in those segments to the exclusion of others.[17] Recent criticism of the Porter model has dimmed its attractiveness to firms in the social media era, which value being fast, fluid, and flexible, although competition is still the name of the game. The competitive advantage is now developing a deeper understanding of consumers to identify their unarticulated needs and uncover opportunities before competitors do. Armed with such customer knowledge and customer signaling, companies attempt to gain the advantage by trying new things, directing production, and learning what works and what doesn't ahead of their competitors.[18]

Beyond the competition at the firm level, countries also engage in competition over trade. When foreign goods and services threaten to undercut the price of goods and services of country A, the government of country A decides to impose tariffs or quota restrictions on imports. And when other countries perceive the trading practices to be unfair, they retaliate and impose their own tariffs or quota restrictions on country A's exported goods and services, thus launching a trade war. For instance, the US-China trade war first centered on steel exports. China's steel output increased eightfold between 2000 and 2015. Its production was 823 million tons in 2014, which accounted for half of the world's total. Since China's demand for steel dropped 3.5 percent in 2015 and was expected to fall lower in 2016, and its domestic steel production continued to rise, China increased its steel exports 25 percent, to 112 million tons, to deal with its overproduction. Since China subsidizes steel production costs and can produce steel even at a loss, it was flooding the global market with steel that cost 25 percent to 50 percent less than its competitors. Foreign steel companies such as the Tata Iron and Steel Company in the British Commonwealth, the ArcelorMittal company mills in South Africa, and companies in the United States and Spain were forced to shut down or close their mills.

Western countries are vulnerable to cheaper steel imports since they have higher labor and environmental costs. To protect their local steel production, which is vital for industrial and economic growth, they began to impose heavy tariffs for what they saw as China's unfair "dumping" of cheap steel.[19] The US Commerce Department levied import taxes of up to 522 percent—a 266 percent antidumping duty and a 256 percent antisubsidy duty—on imports of Chinese cold-rolled flat steel.[20] In addition, antidumping and antisubsidy tariffs between 1 and 92 percent were applied to imports from various producers in South Korea, Italy, India, and Taiwan.[21] The duties went into effect the first week of March 2016. The American Iron and Steel Institute chair, John Ferriola, explained global overcapacity for steel in terms of the declining global demand from countries like China, which was exacerbated by Chinese subsidies of its own companies through grants, low-interest loans, free land, low-priced energy, and other raw material inputs. "Simply stated," said Ferriola, "the Chinese government is a company disguised as a country and they are waging economic war on the United States."[22] China began retaliation against its trading partners in April, announcing antidumping duties on steel from the European Union (EU), Japan, and South Korea.[23] The trade war between the United States and China continues, although there is less enthusiasm for it since the duties paid by US businesses ultimately result in higher prices for US consumers, and the trade deficits continue despite the tariffs on Chinese goods.[24] Lifting tariffs are currently under consideration.

Currency wars, or competitive devaluations, are another manifestation of international economic competition. They begin when a country attempts to gain a competitive advantage over other countries by weakening its currency and allowing its exchange rate to fall in relation to other countries' currencies. Countries have several options to weaken their currency.[25] They can cut interest rates, making it less attractive for its residents to save. They can print money, also known as "quantitative easing," which increases the supply of money (e.g., increased sales of government bonds) and leads to a fall in the value of the country's money. Alternatively, they can engage in intervention buying by purchasing the assets of other countries, which increases the value of other countries' currencies. The purpose of all three options is to boost economic growth and jobs by making a country's exports cheaper relative to goods priced in other countries, as well as increasing corporate profits for companies that do business in foreign markets.

Supply chains are other venues for international competition. A supply chain connects vendors who supply the raw materials with producers who convert the raw materials into products, warehouses that store the products, and distribution centers that deliver the products to retailers that offer the product to the ultimate user. According to Parag Khanna, "the nature of geopolitical competition in the 21st century is evolving from war over territory to war over connectivity" among supply chains.[26] Supply chain tugs-of-war are being fought over the flows of money, goods, resources, technology, knowledge, and talent. They are wars without end, with new opponents emerging constantly from all directions. The primary protagonists are cities, companies, and communities that are engaged in an all-encompassing struggle. Khanna describes "*competitive connectivity* (as) the arms race of the twenty-first century."[27]

Competitive public policy   Governments also pursue competitive strategies when landing in wicked problem territory by pursuing zero-sum foreign and domestic policies. Three policies are noteworthy: containment, a US policy to counteract expansion of the Soviet Union and other communist countries during the Cold War; the War on Drugs, a campaign in the United States to prohibit the illegal drug trade and the production and consumption of illegal drugs; and Brexit, the UK referendum on the country's membership in the European Union (EU).

Containment was a Cold War policy that the United States devised to check the spread of communism throughout the world from the end of World War II until 1989. It began as a response to the Soviet Union's movement into Eastern Europe and then gained momentum as proxy wars throughout Asia and Latin America. The diplomat George F. Kennan, credited as the originator of the US policy, believed that it was possible to contain the Soviet Union within its borders at the end of World War II without resorting to the two extremes: either complete rollback (war) or complete détente (appeasement). Keenan later turned against the containment policy and noted the deficiencies in its interpretation. Rather than a containment of a political threat by political means, it evolved to become the containment of a military threat by military means when the official US government policy interpreted it as a clash between totalitarian regimes and free peoples.

President Richard Nixon delivered a special message to Congress on Drug Abuse Prevention and Control in June 1971 and declared a "war on drugs."[28] Although more federal resources were devoted to rehabilitating addicts and preventing new ones, attention immediately focused on drug eradication and interdiction, as well as incarceration of users.[29] Nixon increased the size and presence of federal drug control agencies and pushed through mandatory sentencing and no-knock warrants. Ronald Reagan's presidency expanded the War on Drugs and saw a steep rise in incarceration. Nonviolent drug offenses increased from 50,000 in 1980 to over 400,000 by 1997 due to the zero tolerance policies in the mid-to-late 1980s. George W. Bush saw the militarization of domestic drug law enforcement, with about 40,000 paramilitary-style raids on Americans every year for primarily nonviolent, often misdemeanor drug offenses. As of July 2016, over 700,000 people had been arrested for marijuana offenses each year, and almost 500,000 were behind bars for drug-law violations.[30] The War on Drugs continues to this day, although a handful of states have regalized marijuana for adult use for either medical purposes or for general consumption.

The citizens of Great Britain played a zero-sum game when they voted on whether to leave the European Union, an economic and political partnership with twenty-seven other European countries that they had joined in the early 1970s. Dubbed "Brexit," the choice was either "Leave," for Britain's exit from the European Union, or "Remain," for staying in it. Those in favor of leaving argued that Britain would be liberated from the Brussel elite's top-down designs and political interference. It would be free from the unelected European Commission's monopoly in proposing all EU legislation, which it does in secret, with the power to issue regulations that are automatically binding in all EU member-states. The claim was that decentralized decision making would be a more successful strategy in an increasingly networked and interdependent world. And the intent was to enable and encourage more organic and self-organizing policy and program experimentation from the bottom up to meet Great Britain's unique needs and context. Britain also would be better positioned to regulate immigration, and its businesses would be better situated to trade with the rest of the world. In addition, it would eliminate the direct membership costs, which are more than the annual net contributions it received in return.[31]

On the other hand, those opposed to Brexit countered that since the end of World War II, the European Union has helped secure peace among previously warring Western European nations. Democracies in Spain, Portugal, Greece, and former Soviet bloc countries have been consolidated into the European Union, peace in the Balkans has been secured since the Balkans War, and the European Union, with the United Nations, has taken a leading role in conflict prevention, peacekeeping, and democracy building. Represented in many international organizations and EU delegations, Britain has played a major role in climate, world trade, and development issues. The EU arrest warrant replaced long extradition procedures, enabling the United Kingdom to extradite criminals wanted in other EU countries and the return of UK criminals who were hiding in other EU countries. In addition, UK authorities have worked with other EU countries to tackle international organized crime, such as drug smuggling, human trafficking, and money laundering. The United Kingdom also has been the second-largest beneficiary of EU research funds, a vital source of income for its universities and companies. Thus, Britain has enjoyed benefits and had more influence in the European Union than it would have on its own. In terms of the common market, the European Union has the world's biggest market and by having common rules for it actually cuts the red tape by eliminating twenty-eight sets of national regulations. The United Kingdom sells over 50 percent of its exports (54 percent of goods, 40 percent of services) to the European Union, and over 300,000 British companies and 74 percent of British exporters operate in other EU markets, while American and Asian firms build factories in Britain because it is well positioned in the single market. One in ten British jobs is directly linked to British membership in the common market. The European Union also negotiates trade agreements for the rest of the world, but if Britain were outside the European Union, all trade deals would have to be renegotiated and the United Kingdom would have less power on its own to negotiate these deals with other countries. Thus the market is stronger when all twenty-eight countries in Europe work together.[32]

On June 23, 2016, the vote took place. For the United Kingdom as a whole, the "Leave" proponents won by 51.1 percent to 48.9 percent; Scotland and Northern Ireland voted to stay in the European Union and England and Wales voted to leave it.

Advantages of competition   There are numerous advantages to a competitive strategy. Warfare can produce identifiable winners. The Allies stopped Hitler's aggression in Europe and Africa and Japanese aggression in the Pacific, defeated the Axis powers in World War II, set the terms of the peace and reconstruction of Europe and Asia, and contained Soviet expansion into Eastern Europe. The decisive victory against Saddam Hussein in the first Persian Gulf War repelled Iraqi forces from Kuwait, compelled Iraq to recognize Kuwait's sovereignty, and committed Iraq to getting rid of its weapons of mass destruction—nuclear, biological, and chemical.

Market competition also prompts commercial firms to develop new products, services, and technologies that offer consumers greater selection, better products, and lower prices compared to prices with no competition. Since a market economy engenders competitive pressures, resources tend to move to where they are needed and can be used more efficiently for the economy as a whole. The energy sector provides recent examples. Companies have developed renewable energy sources, such as solar power and wind power, which are touted to be cleaner and ultimately cheaper replacements for nonrenewable energy sources. What has appeared to be an intractable issue—environmental degradation that results from the use of oil and gas—may have found some resolution through the invention of these new technologies. Without competition among energy providers, it is unlikely that these innovative technologies would have been developed and brought to market.

The XPRIZE offers another high-profile example. It encourages public competitions among companies to develop innovative ideas and technologies that will bring about radical breakthroughs to solve grand challenges facing humanity. The XPRIZE has been awarded for innovations in suborbital space flight, superefficient vehicles, oil cleanup, precise and efficient small rocket systems, sensors and sensing technology to tackle health-care problems, and ocean health. Active scenarios include successfully launching, landing, and operating a rover on the Moon; creating a mobile device that can diagnose patients better than or equal to a panel of board-certified physicians; building a free Android app to teach reading, writing, and arithmetic skills, and prove their effectiveness over an eighteen-month period in African pilot communities; developing better technologies for mapping the sea floor; generating technologies that convert carbon dioxide (CO_2) into products with the highest net value in order to reduce CO_2 emissions of coal and natural gas power plants; finding improvements in literacy proficiency of adults in reading within a twelve-month period; and the latest challenge— making COVID-19 tests available to all.[33]

We also find advantages in the political economy, with clear decisions and outcomes deriving from the competitive strategy. The Soviet Union ceased to exist in 1989, and Britain has voted to exit the European Union. In announcing the War on Drugs, the US government provides focus and direction in public policy and clear indications of priorities and how its resources will be allocated. Competitive strategies also have the advantage, in that they challenge and check the institutionalization of power. The point of political parties is to keep power circulating—one day, one party wins, and the next election cycle, another party can win, so neither side is able to institutionalize its power. Power is not corrupting—it is the institutionalization of power that can be a problem.[34] Even when competition among stakeholders is great and no clear consensus emerges in a democratic system, the assumption built into the US Constitution and its "shared power" system of government is that it is preferable to wait until consensus evolves before making decisions on how to identify and solve problems.

Disadvantages of competition   Warfare is destructive even for the winners. The staggering losses of life and property in World War II and one of the outcomes of the war— the threat of nuclear war—are grim reminders that winning comes at high costs, with serious and unpredictable downstream consequences. The supposedly "limited" first Persian Gulf War, initially recognized as a decisive victory for the coalition, inflicted enormous damage, but it left Saddam Hussein in power and resulted in the brutal suppression of the Kurds in the north and the Shiites in the south. Saddam's refusal to comply with the peace terms and his defiance of UN weapon inspections ultimately led to the second Gulf War and the US occupation of Iraq. These events in turn led to a Sunni insurgency and the formation of the Islamic State (IS), which sought to establish an Islamic caliphate in the region. Thus, the world continues to face wars without end in the Middle East[35] in Afghanistan and Syria where winning battles is easier than winning hearts and minds and keeping the peace. The scars from these wars and conflicts in Israel and Palestine, Nigeria, Somalia, Yemen, Sudan, and Kashmir, just to name a few around the world, run very deep and continue to rend the social fabric.

For every winner of a war, there is at least one loser, as exemplified in Vietnam, where both the French and the United States were soundly defeated. Not only does defeat cost thousands their lives and damage a country's prestige and moral authority, but it risks even more devastating consequences, as in the case of the US-sponsored Bay of Pigs invasion of Cuba that provoked the Cuban Missile Crisis with the Soviet Union, when the world came as close as it has ever come to nuclear war. Losers in war also seek revenge, as we saw in the aftermath of World War I, when Germany rebuilt its military and launched its quest to regain its former territory and "living space," or when Al Qaeda launched its terror attacks against the United States in part due to its military presence in Saudi Arabia during and after the first Gulf War. And even when Israel has won all its wars since its independence, it has not succeeded in reaching peace with the Palestinians, and it now lives under a constant state of threat from some of its Middle Eastern neighbors.

The War on Terror, in the words of John Arquilla, has turned into "terror's war on the world."[36] According to terror specialists Peter Bergen and Paul Cruickshank in their 2007 study, the Iraq war "generated a stunning sevenfold increase in the yearly rate of fatal jihadist attacks, amounting to literally hundreds of additional terrorist attacks and thousands of civilian lives lost; even when terrorism in Iraq and Afghanistan is excluded, fatal attacks in the rest of the world have increased by more than one-third."[37] Between 2006 and 2016, there have been approximately 90,000 terrorist attacks worldwide, with around 130,000 fatalities.[38] In 2017 alone, there were 10,900 terrorist attacks that killed more than 26,400 people worldwide. The highest concentration was in Iraq (23 percent), Afghanistan (13 percent), India (9 percent), and Pakistan (7 percent), with more than half of all the deaths occurring in Iraq (24 percent), Afghanistan (23 percent), and Syria (8 percent).[39]

Market competition also can have disadvantages. Price fixing, predatory practices, mergers, and acquisitions can lead to the formation of oligopolies and monopolies that result in reduced competition, higher costs, and poorer service to customers. According to Robert Reich, "we are now in a new gilded age similar to the first Gilded Age, when the nation's antitrust laws were enacted. As then, those with great and resources are making the 'free market' function on their behalf. Big Tech—along with the drug, insurance, agriculture and financial giants—dominates both our economy and our politics."[40] The Nobel laureate Joseph Stiglitz and his colleagues concur; they recommend rewriting the rules of the American economy so that they work for everyone, not just for the wealthy.[41] Market competition also creates negative externalities or indirect costs that are not borne by the producer, nor are they passed to the end user. Instead, as in the example of pollution, those harmed by pollution bear the burden of higher health-care costs, decreased quality of life, and loss of opportunities in tourism, fishing, and other business interests.

The zero-sum game of currency wars may help some countries in the short term, but it can have negative effects for others. Since exchange rates are relative, as one currency declines, another has to go up. But when multiple countries try to maintain the competitiveness of their exports by devaluing currencies, there can be longer-term costs to the global economy as a whole. During the Great Depression in the 1930s, countries went into a vicious spiral of currency devaluations that resulted in unemployment among trading partners overseas. The "beggar thy neighbor" policy prompted other countries to retaliate with their own devaluations. The overall effect of this chain reaction was an increase in worldwide unemployment and a loss of global trade and investment.

Currently, there are some signs that currency devaluation strategies may be at play. Pursuant to Section 701 of the Trade Facilitation and Trade Enforcement Act of 2015, the US Treasury Department established a currency watch list. Analyzing fifteen years of data across dozens of economies, it found that no economy meets all three criteria set up to flag currency devaluations; however, five major trading partners of the United States met two of the three criteria. It therefore put China, Japan, Germany, South Korea, and Taiwan on the monitoring list, saying that their foreign-exchange practices merit close scrutiny to ascertain if they have an unfair trade advantage over the United States.[42] As the European Central Bank (ECB) president Mario Draghi warned at an ECB conference in Sintra, Portugal, currency devaluations with the intent to boost national competitiveness "are a 'lose-lose' for the global economy."[43]

Trade barriers and protectionism also limit the benefits of free trade, making economic activity less efficient, potentially reducing global economic growth, and disrupting supply chains. For example, US president Donald Trump's trade war with China did not achieve its objective. It did not revive American manufacturing, nor did it reverse the offshoring of factory production. Although it led to higher employment in certain industries, it also brought about a net loss of US jobs, estimated to be up to 245,000 according to a study commissioned by the US-China Business Council.[44] According to the US Department of Agriculture's Economic Research Service, "the Trump administration's tariffs also cost the American ag [agricultural] section 27 billion from mid-2018 through 2019."[45] In tracking the economic impact of US tariffs and retaliatory actions, the Tax Foundation's overall analysis revealed that the Trump administration "imposed nearly $80 billion worth of new taxes on Americans by leving tariffs on thousands of products," which they calculated was "equivalent to one of the largest tax increases in decades."[46] At the same time, the gross domestic product (GDP) grew just 2.3 percent between the fourth quarter of 2018 and the fourth quarter of 2019.[47]

Competitive public policies also have their downsides. George Keenan's policy of containment shifted away from his "third way" strategy of nonprovocative resistance and morphed into treating containment as a "line in the sand," a zero-sum demarcation that, if crossed, would and did lead to war, as in the case of the Korean War (1950–1953), the Vietnam War (1955–1975), and the failed US-sponsored invasion of Cuba in 1961. What was originally a foreign policy to limit war became a foreign policy to justify it.

The War on Drugs framed policy in the language of warfare, which many now believe was counterproductive. According to Gil Kerlikowske, the head of the White

House Office of National Drug Control Policy, the bellicose analogy to war was a barrier in dealing with the nation's drug issues. "Regardless of how you try to explain to people it's a 'war on drugs' or a 'war on a product,' people see war as a war on them. . . . We're not at war with people in this country."[48] Rather than treating drug use and addiction as a health problem that could be successfully prevented and treated, the war on drugs criminalized users who filled the criminal justice system. The United States annually spends more than 47 billion on the War on Drugs. Over 1.6 million people were arrested for violation of drug laws in 2018, and over 1.4 (86 percent) were for possession only. Although Blacks make up 13.4 percent of the US population and are not more likely to use or sell illegal drugs than white people, 27 percent of arrests for drug law violations are of Black people.[49] On the supply side, interdiction of drugs coming from Mexico results in rerouting and reorganization of the international drug trade, which ultimately benefits other drug cartels, especially those in Colombia. So long as there is a demand for drugs, the cartels have found land, air, and sea routes to get drugs into the United States.

While the referendum result on Britain's exit from the European Union was clear, the political consequences have produced uncertainty and discord:

- the campaign to leave resulted in Prime Minister David Cameron's resignation;
- a bitter Conservative Party leadership battle ensued over who would replace him;
- a coup was staged against Jeremy Corbyn, the leader of the opposition Labour Party for his half-hearted support for the European Union;
- talks occurred in Scotland and Northern Ireland about seccession from Great Britain;
- Spain pressed for the cosovereignty of Gibraltar;
- Theresa May was selected as prime minister, and she invoked Article 50 of the Lisbon Treaty on March 29, 2017, which began a two-year period of negotiations over the terms of the withdrawal;
- the potential for a reestablished border between Northern Ireland and the Republic of Ireland in the south, which would jeopardize the hard-won peace accord, and without a border, the potential for the Republic of Ireland to be used as a "back door" for immigration from the European Union and beyond;
- the potential loss of access of some sectors to some European markets, including the all-important financial sector in the City of London;
- opinion polls showing that a majority of people in the United Kingdom would vote to stop Brexit if asked to vote again;
- May resigned as prime minister effective June 7, 2019, when she was unable to gain acceptance from Parliament for her Brexit deal with the European Union;
- Boris Johnson became prime minister on July 24, 2019, with the likelihood of Britain crashing out of the European Union with a "no deal" exit on October 31, 2019;
- and the United Kingdom, after missing several deadlines, officially left the European Union on January 31, 2020, entering an eleven-month transition phase through

December 31, 2020, during which time most of the pre-Brexit arrangements remained while the details of the future EU-UK relationship were being worked out.

The economic impact of Brexit outcomes are uncertain and dependent on the UK negotiations with the European Union. Researchers have run various scenarios. All the economic analysis shows that the United Kingdom will be economically worse off outside the European Union under the most plausible scenarios. The key question for the United Kingdom is not whether it will be worse off post-Brexit, but by how much.[50]

Regardless of the outcome of this convoluted and tortuous problem-solving process, one thing is certain. Asking people to vote either "yes" or "no" on a very complex issue forces people to narrow their focus, drives them into their respective corners, and exaggerates their differences. What results is a dialogue of the deaf that makes deliberation, negotiation, and compromise very difficult. Zero-sum debates like Brexit tend to activate more heat than light and leave little room for exploring the complexity of an issue, especially its potential downstream second- and third-order effects. And, as is the case of all complex adaptive systems (CASs), we never know until it is too late if shocks such as Brexit can so destabilize a system that it collapses.

Authority/Authoritative Strategy

Rittel and Webber, writing in "Dilemmas in a Theory of Planning," also rejected the authority/authoritative strategy when dealing with wicked problems. They considered the expert/leader as a "player in a political game, seeking to promote his private vision of goodness over others." Since there was "no escaping that truism,"[51] they did not believe that the authority/authoritative strategy was a viable option when dealing with wicked problems. The authority/authoritative strategy relies on people in positions of power and those with expertise to frame problems and generate solutions. By virtue of their leadership or office, we entrust them to be our surrogates in the problem-solving process. Given the conflicts, uncertainties, and complexities involved in problem solving, the preference is to have leaders carry the burden of problem solving while the rest of us rely on their decisions. Ultimately, problems and solutions exist because our leaders say they do, and our compliance signals agreement with their assessments and solutions.

Examples of the authority/authoritative strategy abound. President Abraham Lincoln, rated highly among presidential historians, called up the militia, increased the size of the army and navy, allocated funds to purchase weapons, instituted a blockade, suspended the writ of habeas corpus, and issued the Emancipation Proclamation on January 1, 1863, all without congressional approval, in order to suppress the rebellion in the South. The American public accepted President Roosevelt's leadership through its domestic crisis of the Great Depression. His unparalleled four-term presidency launched the experimental economic and social programs of the New Deal that began the nation's recovery. President Harry S. Truman's range of political, diplomatic, military, and economic initiatives to contain Soviet communism and power became the accepted American approach to US-Soviet relations from the end of World War II until the end of the Cold War in the early 1990s. The US Constitution places the Supreme Court as the ultimate authority when overseeing actions by the legislative and executive branches. The United States relies on the authority of the Federal Reserve Bank (Fed) to supervise and regulate banking institutions, manage the nation's money supply, and, through its monetary policies, ensure maximum employment, prevent inflation or deflation, and moderate long-term interest rates. Christine Lagarde, as managing director of the International Monetary Fund (IMF), juggled the concerns of 188 member-countries while supporting IMF bailouts of Greece, Ireland, Portugal, and other financially struggling countries. We trust the military to defend us and prosecute our wars. George Washington led American forces in the war of independence against Great Britain. Dwight Eisenhower successfully oversaw the invasion of North Africa in 1942, was the Supreme Allied Commander for the D-Day invasion of occupied Europe during World War II, and was the first Supreme Commander of the North Atlantic Treaty Organization (NATO). Business leaders like Anne Mulcahy of Xerox and Alan Mulally of Ford turned their companies around during periods of crisis. And people around the world look to the moral authority of leaders: Mahatma Gandhi fought without violence to win freedom for the Indian people and for the "untouchables"; Martin Luther King, Jr., advocated for civil rights using nonviolent civil disobedience; Pope Francis leads 1.2 billion Catholics worldwide; and the Dalai Lama, the spiritual leader of the Tibetan people, campaigns for peace, nonviolence, democracy, and reconciliation among world religions.

Advantages   There are advantages to pursuing an authority/authoritative strategy, especially in wicked problem territory. Issues are complex and very difficult to sort through. Most of us don't have the time or the resources to explore problems, search for their causes, identify solutions, and track their anticipated effects. It would be better to turn problem solving over to leaders and experts who have dedicated their professional lives to building the knowledge, skills, and competences to solve problems and make decisions in the face of great challenges and crises. Similar to the assumption built into the US Constitution that calls on representative rather than direct democracy, it is best to trust leaders and experts to make the key decisions that affect our political and social lives. There is danger in putting full trust in a less-informed public who can suffer from faulty reasoning, emotional, knee-jerk reactions, and the inability to separate fact from fiction, especially when dealing with very complex issues. The Brexit vote appears to be a primary example of one of the dangers of direct democracy. According to *The Economist*, "the Brexit campaign [was] plagued by little white lies, half-truths and disinformation."[52] Indeed, it claimed that Britain has had a long and well-observed tradition of making false statements about Europe. The European Commission even set up a website to expose the deceptions.[53] These charges are supported by research during the campaign revealing that many Britons were misinformed about the European Union, especially on immigration and economic issues—the main focus in the referendum debate. It is telling that the second most frequent search in Britain as the results for the vote rolled in was "What is the EU?"[54]

Although leaders and authorities also have biases and make mistakes, the assumption is that their inbred skepticism is likely to make them less susceptible to fabrications and misinformation than the general public. The authority/authoritative strategy also has the advantage of reducing the number of people engaged in problem solving. The complexity of problem framing and solution generation in wicked problem territory increases dramatically as the number of problem solvers grows. It is easier to focus attention, sort out issues, and make decisions and guide the rest of us when fewer and more knowledgeable people are involved.

Disadvantages   Leaders and experts can be wrong—wrong when identifying the problems and wrong when formulating the solutions. Declassified documents reveal "failed intelligence, policy ad hockery, and propaganda-driven decision-making" in the lead-up to the second Iraq War in 2003. Iraq had no weapons of mass destruction and no ties to al-Qaeda, two major reasons that President George W. Bush used to justify the invasion of Iraq in 2003.[55] And the solution—the invasion of Iraq, the toppling of Saddam Hussein, and the disbanding the Iraqi army—undermined Iraq's civil and military infrastructure, weakened its economy, intensified internal ethnic and religious rivalries, and paved the way for the self-professed Islamic State of Iraq and eventually the Islamic State of Iraq and Syria (ISIS), which fueled Sunni-Shia religious conflicts and terrorism throughout the Middle East.

David Halberstam's book *The Best and the Brightest*[56] details how poor problem solving in the John F. Kennedy and Lyndon B. Johnson administrations led to flawed decisions about the Vietnam War, which most scholars conclude was a tragic event whose costs far exceeded any benefits. In 1995, Robert McNamara, the secretary of defense under the Kennedy and Johnson administrations, published a memoir, *In Retrospect: The Tragedy and Lessons of Vietnam*,[57] in which he described the mistaken assumptions of foreign policy and military misjudgments that combined to create the failure of Vietnam. Two important questions were never addressed by anyone in the White House: If South Vietnam fell to the communists, was it likely that all of Southeast Asia would fall? If the United States committed troops to fight alongside the South Vietnamese army, could this combined force win the war? General Maxwell Taylor, one of the architects of the war, summed up the military's failures in the following way:

> First, we didn't know ourselves. We thought we were going into another Korean war, but this was a different country. Secondly, we didn't know our South Vietnamese allies. We never understood them, and that was another surprise. And we knew even less about North Vietnam. Who was Ho Chi Minh? Nobody really knew. So, until we know the enemy and know our allies and know ourselves, we'd better keep out of this kind of dirty business. It's very dangerous.[58]

In a secret memorandum on May 12, 1975, to President Gerald Ford, Henry Kissinger, the president's assistant for national security affairs, summarized the lessons of

Vietnam from a number of perspectives, including the military's strategy and tactics: "We cannot help [but] draw the conclusion that our armed forces are not suited to this kind of war. Even the Special Forces who had been designed for it could not prevail. This was partly because of the nature of the conflict."[59] Ho Chi Minh and the Viet Minh forces, fighting a revolutionary war of independence first against the Japanese, then the French, and ultimately the United States, were much more adept at guerilla warfare, a war with no front. Guerrilla fighters blended in with the local population and disappeared within minutes of an attack into a geography that they knew well— jungles, river deltas, and hidden underground tunnels. The intent was to wage a war of attrition, a long, bloody, and expensive conflict that would turn the American public against US involvement. As Ho Chi Minh is reported to have warned French colonialists in 1946: "You can kill ten of our men for every one we kill of yours. But even at those odds, you will lose and we will win."[60]

The power that derives from leadership and expertise also can corrupt. President Richard Nixon's Watergate scandal in the 1970s included an array of illegal activities and dirty tricks—including burglarizing and bugging the offices of the Democratic Party, the cover-up of that break-in, and the use of the Federal Bureau of Investigation (FBI), the Central Intelligence Agency (CIA), and the Internal Revenue Service (IRS) to harass activists and political figures. The multiple abuses of power by the Nixon administration led the House Judiciary Committee to approve three articles of impeachment against the president, to the resignation of Nixon on August 9, 1974, to the indictment of sixty-nine people, many of whom were top administration officials, and to the convictions of twenty-five of them who served prison sentences. In a televised interview with David Frost a few years later, Nixon justified his actions by saying, "When the president does it, that means that it is not illegal."[61] And then there is the case of Donald J. Trump, who, after four tumultuous years, two impeachments (but no convictions), and his refusal to accept his loss in the 2020 presidential election, is now facing various criminal and legal actions.[62] After calling his supporters to Washington, telling them to "stop the steal" of the election and to "fight for Trump," several thousand of them stormed Capitol Hill; attacked the Capitol Police; disrupted a joint session of the US Congress that was intended to certify the electoral vote; threatened Vice President Mike Pence, congressional representatives, senators, and staff; damaged the building; and sacked offices. In the melee, five people died and many more were injured. Nearly two years after the deadly insurrection, the US House Select Committee on the January 6 Attack released its final report and recommended that former President Donald Trump be prosecuted on four charges: obstruction of an official proceeding; conspiring to defraud the United States; conspiracy to make a false statement; and conspiracy to defraud the United States by assisting, aiiding, or comforting those participating in an insurrection.[63] Indeed, the authority/authoritative strategy can have serious consequences.

There are also cases of corporate malfeasance, such as at Enron in 2001, when CEOs Kenneth Lay and Jeffrey Skilling borrowed money and hid their bad debt using creative accounting practices to inflate the company's share price; and when CEO Bernie Ebbers at Worldcom in 2002 underreported line costs and inflated company revenue with fake accounting entries. Then there was Bernie Madoff, the founder and chair of the Wall Street firm Bernard L. Madoff Investment Securities LLC, who operated a Ponzi scheme considered to be the biggest financial fraud in US history when it was discovered in 2008.

The Financial Crisis Inquiry Commission investigating the US 2008 crisis found that "the captains of finance and the public stewards of our financial system ignored warnings and failed to question, understand, and manage evolving risks within a system essential to the well-being of the American public. Theirs was a big miss, not a stumble."[64] Richard Kovacevich, the former chairman and CEO of Wells Fargo, had an even stronger opinion. In his view, the "shadow banks"—the investment banks and thrifts—caused most of the damage:

> If you don't remember anything else I say today, please remember this: Only about 20 financial institutions perpetrated this crisis. About half were investment banks, and the other half were savings and loans. Only one, Citicorp, was a commercial bank, but [it] was operating more like an investment bank. These 20 failed in every respect, from business practices to ethics. Greed and malfeasance were their modus operandi. There was no excuse for their behavior, and they should be punished thoroughly, perhaps even criminally.[65]

The Financial Crisis Inquiry Commission also placed responsibility with the public leaders who ran the regulatory agencies, saying, "The sentries were not at their posts, in no small part due to the widely accepted faith in the self-correcting nature of the markets and the ability of financial institutions to police themselves."[66] Two Fed chairs were singled out as well. Alan Greenspan's leadership was described as a prime example of negligence for his advocacy of deregulation and his "pivotal failure to stem the flow of toxic mortgages."[67] Ben Bernanke, his successor, was criticized for not foreseeing the crisis. Even when the problems of the subprime market first attracted national attention in March 2007, he testified before Congress that the problems "likely would be contained."[68] The Office of the Comptroller of the Currency, which regulates some banks, and the Office of Thrift Supervision, which oversees savings and loans, were "caught in turf wars"[69] and blocked states from curbing abuses concerning risky mortgage loans. The Securities and Exchange Commission (SEC) failed to require big banks to hold the capital needed to cushion potential losses and stop risky practices such as the use of poorly understood financial instruments. The Fed, the one agency empowered to stem the flow of toxic mortgages, failed to set prudent mortgage-lending standards. Deregulation, supported by successive administrations and Congresses, stripped away safeguards and opened oversight gaps, such as shadow banking and over-the-counter derivatives markets, and it even allowed financial firms to pick their preferred regulators. The Federal Reserve Bank of New York chose not to clamp down on Citigroup's excesses prior to the crisis, policy makers and regulators didn't stop mortgage securitization, and regulators continued to rate institutions they oversaw as safe despite their mounting troubles. As The Financial Crisis Inquiry Commission reported: "Where regulators lacked authority, they could have sought it. Too often, they lacked the political will . . . as well as the fortitude to critically challenge the institutions and the entire system they were entrusted to oversee."[70]

Serious blows to the moral authority of religious leaders occurred when Catholic priests throughout the world were charged and convicted of the sexual abuse of children. As of 2015, the *National Catholic Reporter*, an independent news source, estimates the payments to the survivors for the abuse and the Church's cover-ups of the abuses to be almost four billion dollars.[71] Other religious leaders have been convicted of violent and nonviolent crimes.[72] We have passed through what the journalist Chris Hayes calls "the Decade of Failure" (2000–2010), when the leaders of the nation's major institutions have let us down. The result has been a "crisis of authority," which he attributes to the malfeasance and corruption of elites. "We can't be sure . . . just who our elites are working for. But we suspect it is not us."[73]

This cascade of elite failures has done more than discredit leaders; it also has contaminated the very institutions that they lead. Americans' confidence remains below the historical average for most major US institutions in 2020. Based on those expressing "a great deal" or "quite a lot" of confidence in the institution, only the military (72 percent) and small businesses (70 percent) are currently rated higher than their historical norms. According to Gallup, the American public has lost confidence in the press, including newspapers (24 percent), television news (18 percent), and news on the Internet (16 percent); big business (19 percent); and church and organized religion (42 percent). Congress is rated lowest, at 13 percent.[74]

The ultimate blow to the authority/authoritative strategy in a democracy comes when people feel manipulated and deceived by their leaders. If instead of straight talk, leaders spoon-feed their constituents "spin" and outright lies, treat them as children who can't handle the truth, or make them think that their views don't matter, then people might do more than "throw them out of office." They can lose faith in democratic governance in general, disengage from their civic duties, and decide not to vote because it really doesn't matter. The irony is that their refusal to express themselves at the ballot box opens the door to more authoritarian leaders, who then are well positioned to deny people's right to participate in their own governance.

The Rational-Analytic Strategy

Rittel and Webber also critiqued and eliminated the rational-analytic strategy for consideration in "Dilemmas in a Theory of Planning." Although the rational-analytic strategy of problem solving had adherents in wide-ranging disciplines and professions such as economics, psychology, political science, sociology, business administration, education, information science, military science, and public administration, they also saw its limitations when dealing with wicked problems, especially in the assumptions made about the rational-analytic process used to solve problems and recommend actions. The generic rational-analytic model follows eight basic steps. The problem solver begins by doing the following:

- stating the problem;

- identifying the goal or result to be achieved;

- specifying the criteria to assess the expected results;

- identifying the total set of results and solutions to address the problem;

- estimating the consequences for each solution;

- deciding which solution is optimal by applying established criteria to the expected consequences;

- implementing the solution;

- and gathering data to judge the effectiveness of the solution's implementation.

Advantages   The rational-analytic strategy is now widely used and accepted by many as good practice. The careful collection and analysis of data, from the framing of a problem to the evaluation of results, infuse discipline, logic, and consistency in problem solving and decision making. Solutions and decisions that emerge from these processes are deemed to be objective and less susceptible to subjective judgments, distortions, guesswork, and errors.

Disadvantages   In wicked problem territory, defining the problem *is* the problem. In our battles and discord over what "the problem" is, we end up with different problem statements in the pursuit of different solutions and the application of different criteria to assess them. We are the proverbial blind men (or people in the dark) who touch an elephant to learn what it is like and find that we are in complete disagreement because we are touching different parts of the animal. Given the complexity and dynamism in wicked problem territory, we end up identifying and defending different problem statements, our pieces of the "elephant," making it difficult for us to recognize a problem in its entirety.

Information processing is central to the rational-analytic model. A rational choice model expects the problem solver to have complete information about the problem and its alternative solutions. Unfortunately, researchers find that people are not perfect information processors, as the rational model requires. People are limited in the amount of information they can process at any one point in time. According to George Miller, short-term memory can hold only five to nine chunks of information (seven plus or minus two), where a chunk is any meaningful unit.[75] Furthermore, all information may not be available for people to process. Access to information may be denied or the search for information may take too much time and require too many resources— time is money. Intractable, poorly defined problems, incomplete information about the full range of solutions, time restrictions, and cognitive limitations led Herbert Simon to describe humans as "boundedly rational agents." We have difficulties in processing (receiving, storing, retrieving, and transmitting) information and formulating and solving complex problems.[76] *Bounded rationality* is our response to a complex and dynamic world that pushes us to simplify the problem-solving process. Rather than search for an optimal solution, we satisfice by choosing the first solution that is satisfactory rather than continue a search for an optimal one. The rational-analytic model also fails to take into account our inability to predict or to forecast the future, despite the sophisticated tools and formal statistical methods we use to analyze time series, cross-sectional, or longitudinal data. Not only does the rational-analytic model expect us to identify the total set of solutions for our problem, but we are required to anticipate the consequences of each solution. Then when comparing and contrasting the anticipated consequences of the alternative solutions, we are expected to select one that is optimal.

Unfortunately, we lack information about the consequences of our solutions, and therefore we have no basis on which to identify one solution over all others to make the claim that it is optimal. And even if we did know the first-order consequences of CASs, which we don't, we have no idea what the second- and third-order effects might be. Instead, we are left with best-guess solutions that can produce "unintended consequences"—those that are not foreseen and intended by our choices.[77] Prohibition, originally enabled to reduce the consumption of alcohol and its trade, drove many small-time suppliers out of business and enabled large-scale organized crime to illegally control the alcohol industry. Rather than suppressing the illegal drug trade, the War on Drugs increased the power and profitability of the drug cartel. The policy to set aside national parks and to protect them from forest fires led to fewer fires, but now when fires do occur, they are larger and much more destructive. (I write this as evacuations from the Soberanes fire are underway in my community, smoke obscures the Sun, being outdoors is hazardous to one's health, and fine ash covers everything.) Rabbits, originally introduced to Australia and New Zealand as a source of food, became a major pest because no natural predators existed to check their explosive growth. During China's Great Leap Forward, Mao Zedong introduced a new hygiene initiative that targeted four pests: rats, flies, mosquitoes, and sparrows. Since sparrows fed on grain that the farmers sowed in their fields, Mao ordered sparrows to be reduced. Unfortunately, when the locusts came, there were no sparrows to eat them. Locust devastated entire crops, which resulted in mass starvation. Responses to drinking water and irrigation crises have resulted in drilling bore-holes deeper and deeper. Draining groundwater reserves that cannot be recharged ended up increasing saltwater intrusion in coastal areas, which contaminates the fresh water that remains. Ethanol subsidies in the United States intended to encourage ethanol production and use to lower greenhouse gases in the atmosphere ended up raising the prices for corn-based products used in food production and creating shortages and higher prices for food staples worldwide. Peace Corps workers helped install new stoves to alleviate smoke inside the huts, but that has had many serious health effects. The lack of smoke allowed mosquitoes in and around the huts, which increased the incidence of malaria.

The United States, under the Carter and Reagan administrations, funded the mujahedeen in Afghanistan to fight the Soviet Union. Some of those mujahedeen evolved into the Taliban, who supported and harbored Al Qaeda, who in turn attacked the United States on September 11, 2001. In launching a war to defeat the Taliban and Al Qaeda, the United States was fighting to defeat a group that it helped create. European

Christians began killing cats in the years leading up to the Black Death because religious zealots told them that cats were the devil's servants. When the Asian merchant ships brought rats bearing rat fleas, there were no cats to check the rats that spread the plague of the Black Death, which killed up to 60 percent of the population between 1348 and 1350. In nuclear reactors, the redundancy of multiple systems to ensure greater levels of safety can sometimes make things worse. As with most reactors around the world, zirconium cladding surrounds and protects the fuel. But in Fukushima, when the cooling system stopped working, the zirconium cladding overheated and interacted with water or steam to produce hydrogen gas. When hydrogen gas came into contact with air in the containment building, the explosion damaged the suppression pool beneath the reactor. In other words, the redundant safety systems had unexpected and negative consequences for safety.

As individuals, we suffer from serious limitations in our ability to follow the rational-analytic model of problem solving. The cracks in the rational-analytic facade first appeared when behavioral economists, psychologists, and social psychologists began researching what people actually did when they solved problems. They found that we suffer from multiple cognitive biases—systemic deviations, limitations, and deficiencies in our thinking that lead to illogical and subjective flaws in judgment, perceptual distortions, and illogical interpretations.[78] Daniel Kahneman, winner of a Nobel Prize in economics, summarizes this research in his book *Thinking Fast and Slow*.[79] His work builds on modern dual process theory, which posits two separate processes in the human brain: system 1 is a fast, intuitive, emotional, automatic, frequent, and subconscious process; and system 2 is a slow, logical, deliberative, calculating, controlled, infrequent and conscious process. System I operates most of the time. For the most part, it models familiar situations well and makes accurate short-term predictions and swift, generally appropriate responses to challenges. However, system I also produces cognitive biases that affect and inhibit our ability to be good problem solvers and decision makers.

Psychologists have identified over 100 cognitive biases or deviations from the norms of rationality. In combination, they underscore that we are not the rational, objective, and analytic thinkers that we believe we are, nor does the rational-analytic model provide a good description of our behavior.[80] Box 2.1 lists some of the cognitive biases to which we fall prey as individuals and in groups when System I is activated.

As group members, our cognitive biases also can lead us to "groupthink," where the desire for harmony and conformity in groups is so great that members try to minimize conflict, reach consensus without critical evaluation of alternative views, suppress dissent, and isolate themselves from outsiders.[82] The in-group dynamics end up producing an "illusion of invulnerability": an unquestioned belief in the group's morality and power; inflated certainty that the group knows best; overestimation of the group's abilities and underestimation of the outgroup's abilities; encouragement of risk taking; and refusal to consider the consequences of one's actions. The in-group dynamics also lead to "close-mindedness": rationalizing away challenges to the group's assumptions and information and dehumanizing those who don't belong to the in-group by

Box 2.1
Major cognitive biases[81]

When system I is activated, our tendency as individuals is to do the following:

- Make decisions on the basis of limited information (*what we see is what there is,* or *jumping to conclusions*)
- Unconsciously substitute things that are easier and more familiar to understand for those that are complex and difficult when confronted with a challenging problem, question, or decision (*attribute substitution*)
- Search for, interpret, and reference information that confirms our preconceptions and beliefs, while we ignore or dismisses counterexamples that don't fit our worldview (*confirmation bias*)
- Avoid options for which missing information makes the probability seem unknown (*ambiguity effect*)
- See what we expect to see (*selective perception*)
- Form our beliefs and make decisions based on what is pleasing to imagine rather than appealing to evidence or rationality (*wishful thinking*)
- Rely too heavily or fixate on one trait or piece of information or a past reference that limits our ability to compare and contrast only a limited set of items when making decisions (*anchoring*)
- Overestimate the likelihood of events with greater "availability" in our memory that are influenced by how recent or emotionally charged our memories may be (*availability heuristic*)
- React to disconfirming evidence by strengthening our previous beliefs (*backfire effect* or *continued influence effect*)
- Ignore generic information and focus on specific information that pertains to a certain case (*base rate neglect*)
- Place too much importance on one aspect of an issue or event (*focusing effect*)
- Draw different conclusions from the same information, depending on how that information is presented or framed (*framing effect*)
- To defend and bolster existing social, economic, and political arrangements, disparage alternatives even at the expense of individual and collective self-interest (*system justification, status quo bias*)
- To identify as true statements those we have previously heard, regardless of their actual validity, or to believe a familiar statement more readily than an unfamiliar one (*illusion of truth effect*)
- Devalue proposals when they originate with an adversary (reactive devaluation)
- Ignore obvious, negative situations (*ostrich effect*)
- Reject new evidence that contradicts our paradigm (*Semmelweis reflex*)
- Believe that something is true if our belief demands it to be true (*subjective validation*)
- Spend more time and energy discussing information that others are already familiar with, and less time and energy discussing information that only some members are aware of (*shared information bias*)

Box 2.1 (continued)

- Believe that we view reality objectively without bias, that facts are plain for all to see, and that rational people agree with us and those who don't are irrational, biased, or uninformed (*naive realism*)
- Have a stronger preference for immediate payoffs relative to later payoffs (*hyperbolic discounting*)
- Completely disregard probability when making decisions under uncertainty (*neglect of probability*)
- Believe that we can control or at least influence outcomes that that we cannot (*illusion of control*)

When system I is activated, our tendency in groups is to do the following:

- Overestimate the abilities and values of our immediate group and underestimate the abilities and values of people whom we do not know (*in-group bias or favoritism*)
- Do or believe things because many other people do or believe those things (*bandwagon effect* or *herd mentality*)
- Give collective beliefs increasing plausibility when they are increasingly repeated in public discourse (*availability cascade* or *repeat something long enough and it becomes true*)
- Examine things based on the conventions of one's profession, excluding broader points of view (*Déformation professionnelle*)

stereotyping and name calling. Ultimately, the dynamics lead to "pressure toward uniformity": the group self-censors any ideas that deviate from its consensus; views silence as agreement; directs pressure on those who question the group and calls those who do disloyal; and allows self-appointed "mind guards" to shield the group from dissenting information.

These cognitive biases reveal the limitations that people generally have in being rational-analytic problem solvers. But what about experts, people who have acquired knowledge and judgment to avoid the cognitive biases to which the rest of us fall victim? Surely they provide a justification for the rational-analytic model. Unfortunately, the sense-making machinery of system I subjects experts to illusions that exaggerate the role of knowledge and skill and underestimate the part that luck plays in outcomes.[83] Their flawed stories of the past (*narrative fallacy*) and experts' belief that they understand the past (*illusion of understanding*) feed the illusion that they can predict and control the future[84] (*illusion of control*). The confidence that they have in their judgments and skills (*illusion of skill*) can overrule statistical facts (*illusion of validity*). Their reliance on insider views (*insider bias*), their optimism (*optimistic bias*), and collective blindness can jeopardize planning for the future (*planning fallacy*). Their limitations are especially notable when making forecasts.

Philip Tetlock, who has asked experts (e.g., clinicians, stock pickers, and political scientists) to make thousands of predictions about the economy, stocks, elections, and wars, found that the accuracy of "the average expert was roughly as accurate as a dart-throwing chimpanzee."[85] (For those who don't know the capability of a dart-throwing chimpanzee, it is equivalent to random guessing.) Gary Klein also has studied the judgments and intuitive skills of experts like fire-ground commanders, firefighters, and clinical nurses, but he describes their process as naturalistic decision making.[86] In Kahneman and Klein's collaboration, they found that expertise can emerge under two conditions: "when an environment is *sufficiently regular to be predictable*," and experts have "an opportunity *to learn these regularities through prolonged practice*."[87] Unfortunately, neither condition informs expert problem solving and decision making in wicked problem territory. Kahneman thus concludes that when a problem is complex and people are asked to make summary judgments of complex information in a domain with significant degrees of uncertainty and unpredictability, their system I biases are activated. Unable to appreciate the limits of their expertise, their projections end up being no better than random guessing. So under these conditions, he recommends leaving final decisions to formulas, especially in low-validity environments (with high degrees of uncertainty and unpredictability) to maximize predictive accuracy.[88] His basic advice: "[D]o not trust anyone—including yourself—to tell you how much you should trust their judgment."[89]

It is wrong to blame anyone for failing to forecast accurately in an unpredictable world. However, it seems fair to question professionals for believing that they can succeed in an impossible task. Claims that intuitions in an unpredictable situation are correct are self-delusional at best, and sometimes worse. In the absence of valid clues, intuitive hits are due either to luck or to lies. If you find this conclusion surprising, you still have the lingering belief that intuition is magic. Remember this rule: intuition cannot be trusted in the absence of stable regularities in the environment.[90]

For all these reasons, the use of the rational-analytic model of problem solving faces severe restrictions in wicked problem territory. Limitations of the rational model should lead us to "an unbiased appreciation of uncertainty"[91] and a search for alternative methods of problem solving that might be a better fit in complex and uncertain environments. But rather than give up on the rational-analytic process in wicked problem territory and admit that our problem definitions are guesses and our "pretended knowledge is often the preferred solution,"[92] some prefer to modify their assumptions about wicked problem territory and suspend some of the restrictions that the rational-analytic model imposes on us. If we can't be perfectly rational, then the alternative is to change the rules of what rationality means in wicked problem territory, which leads us to the taming strategy.

Taming Strategy

Warning against taming "a wicked problem prematurely"[93] and proceeding "after the problem ha[d] already been tamed,"[94] Rittel and Webber had in mind a distinction between the *type of problem*—a tame problem that is described in "Dilemmas in a General Theory of Planning"—and the taming strategy, which was only implied in the article's text. Taming involves bounding a problem to make it more manageable so the problem solver can use the rational-analytic problem-solving process to address it. As C. West Churchman explained it, "sometimes, as in OR [Operational Research], it consists of 'carving off' a piece of the problem and finding a rational and feasible solution to this piece." It then "is up to someone else (presumably a manager) to handle the untamed part." "A better way of describing the OR solution might be to say that it tames the growl of the wicked problem: the wicked problem no longer shows its teeth before it bites."[95]

Central to the taming strategy, then, is the attempt to bound the problem space and/or the solution space. If being in wicked problem territory is too much for us to deal with, for whatever reason, then we circumscribe the problem space and/or its solutions. Recall from Rittel and Webber's analysis that a tame problem is a problem that can be clearly defined and agreed to; problem solvers agree on a goal they want to achieve; information is available to do a complete search for solutions and there is agreement on well-defined criteria to assess the solutions; the consequences of each solution are well specified and understood; when the criteria are applied, there is agreement about the optimal solution; problem solvers know whether they have succeeded in solving the problem; and the problem-solving process can be repeated and will produce the same results.

According to Rittel and Webber, science and the rational-analytic process fail when the problems of open, contentious societal systems are wicked. Building on their analysis, if the rational-analytic model is a poor fit, given the complexity and uncertainty of wicked problem territory, then to maintain some semblance of rationality, the problem solver attempts to simplify or tame some of the stringent requirements of the rational-analytic model to make it a better fit for the context. Thus problem solvers have four options: bound the problem space to reduce the uncertainty and conflict in problem identification; restrict the solution space by reducing the solution options and controlling the criteria by which a preferred solution is selected; domestic the problem-solving process to make it more manageable; and employ less stringent models of problem solving and decision making.

Bounding the problem space   As we saw in chapter 1, wicked problems tend to be a bundle of interconnected problems. One technique is to find a tame problem nested within the network of problems that can be solved and address it, or as Wexler described it, "hiving off" a simple component of a wicked problem.[96] So, for example, if climate change is putting residential communities and critical infrastructure in vulnerable waterfront areas at risk, then we can make changes in the zoning and building codes to minimize the damage done by flooding. Another technique is to define a problem so that it can be resolved. In *Taming the Waters: Strategies to Domesticate the Wicked Problems of Water Resource Management*, Denise Lash and colleagues found that one mode of handling water problems was to decompose them into functional areas of expertise, each having a narrowly defined purpose. So, for example, water problems were categorized into flood management; provision of safe drinking water; provision of irrigation water; and delivery of hydroelectric energy supplies. The overall challenge of water resource management was tamed into these discrete institutional and organizational areas and defined as "not having water in the right places at the right times, in the right amount, and/or of sufficient quality." Any issues that arose were turned over to experts in each problem domain rather than having all members address the governance and management of the water system as a whole.[97]

Jeff Conklin documents other options that he has observed in his work on software system design.[98] There is the problem of lock-down when the software designer develops a description of the problem, declares it to be "the problem," and resists all efforts to change it. "Freezing the requirements," thus prevents changes in project goals that delay projects and escalate costs, although the end product may not be what the client wanted. Another tactic is to cast the problem just as you have for another problem that you have already solved. First, refer to a previously resolved problem and claim that it is just like that problem you are now confronting. Then ignore or filter out any disconfirming evidence that complicates the comparison. This problem-bounding tactic is all too familiar among military officers who lament that "we always are fighting the last war" rather than dealing with the challenges of the current one. Alternatively, we can assign the problem to someone else—climate change is not our problem; it belongs to the countries responsible for the pollution. Alternatively, we can deny that there is a problem—what global warming?

Restricting the solution space   Similar to locking the problem down, we can lock down the solutions under consideration. Rather than do an exhaustive search for solutions to cut the budget, we can take 10 percent cuts across the board. We can proclaim the solution is just to do the same thing we did before. Or if we find out that our lake is polluted and we can't locate the source of the pollution, we can post signs telling people not to eat the fish. When the unemployment rate drops below 5 percent, we can assert that the problem is solved rather than consider those who are still unemployed or underemployed. We can say that our policing policy has driven out gangs and reduced the crime rate in our community, while ignoring the rising crime rates in surrounding communities where the gangs relocate. One particularly tried and true technique is to declare that there are only two issues to solve, and we know what they are: "Should we attack Iraq or let the terrorists take over the world?" And for the cynics among us, we can "give up on trying to get a good solution to the problem. Just follow orders, do [our jobs], and try not to get in trouble."[99]

Domesticating the problem-solving process   The search for decision-making aids to organize and manage the tremendous flow of information in wicked problem territory has been ongoing. Efforts include an Issue-Based Information System (IBIS) to support coordination and planning of political decision processes;[100] Dialogue Mapping to capture and connect participants' comments in a diagram or map as their interactions unfold;[101] Issue Mapping to reveal the deep structure of an issue by producing a graphical network that integrates many problems, solutions, and points of view;[102] Mess Mapping, combining interactive group processes with Visual Analytics to create graphical representations of wicked problems; Resolution Mapping, a knowledge-based, interactive group process, to analyze events and outcomes and enable problem solvers to select their most desirable outcome and the events that lead to that outcome;[103] and General Morphological Analysis (GMA), a group-facilitated, computer-aided, nonquantified problem-structuring method that leads problem solvers through a number of steps and cycles of analysis and synthesis to create a morphological field that represents the problem space and as many of the potential solutions as possible.[104] And some of the latest attempts to tame wicked problems use artificial intelligence (AI)—the integration of human and computer intelligence to produce intelligent behaviors.[105]

These contributions can and do make problem solving more manageable, but their success largely derives from tackling well-bounded simple and complex problems such as the "creation of algorithms that intelligently randomize schedules of park rangers to combat poaching in Africa and Asia"; the attempts to improve "security at Los Angeles International Airport, to better protect the Port of New York and to optimally deploy Federal Air Marshals to prevent airplane terror";[106] and agent-based models to address tobacco use.[107] While experts may proclaim their intent to solve some of the world's wicked problems, to date I am unaware of any information management, decision-making tools and techniques, and computer algorithms that have enabled them to do so. Algorithms, central to the way that software and computers process data, detail specific instructions to be performed in a specific order to do a specific task. But if we find ourselves in wicked problem territory, then algorithms have limited application since by definition, wicked problems are difficult to formulate, let alone solve.

Counterterrorism efforts illustrate this point. Algorithms are used for data mining to search for patterns in structured and relational databases to detect terrorist activities. These algorithms are not foolproof; results can and do produce false positives (i.e., identifying people and their activities as terror related when they are not) and false negatives (i.e., failure to identify people and their activities as terror related when they are).[108] Data-mining algorithms are as good as the assumptions that humans make when they construct and apply them. Figure 2.1, a relational map of worldwide terrorist organizations, offers an illustration of this principle.[109]

To apply the algorithms and generate this map, the analyst had to make a number of assumptions, as summarized in box 2.2.

These assumptions and others can introduce a great deal of variability into data cleaning, coding, structuring, and analysis. There is no such thing as a data set or data analysis free of human assumptions and preferences on how to collect data, analyze terror networks, and derive interventions to deal with them. To date, humans are very much in the "loop" in counter-terrorism efforts, no matter how sophisticated the analyst, the software and the analytical tools.

A taming strategy also includes tactics to manage group sessions among problem-solving teams for the purpose of bounding problem and solution spaces. We can

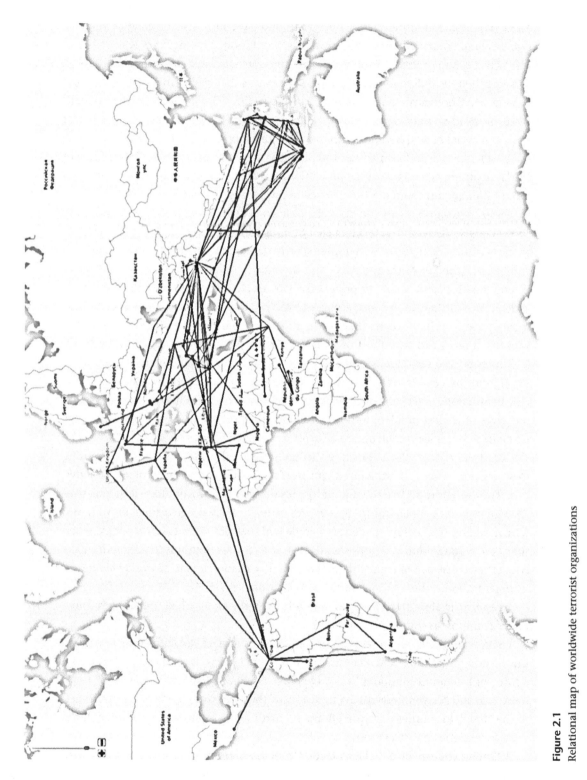

Figure 2.1
Relational map of worldwide terrorist organizations

Box 2.2

Assumptions made to apply algorithms to analyze terror data

- **"Good" data on terrorists and terrorist organizations are available and can be accessed.** Unfortunately, data are limited and often unavailable. Terrorist organizations and terrorists operate in secret. They keep information about their memberships and relationships on "close hold," making it difficult for outsiders to access, especially in open-source documents. Recent efforts by Twitter to suspend terror-related accounts online have led it to conclude that "there's no single 'magic algorithm' for identifying terrorist content online."[110] And on the classified side, government agencies are reluctant to share their data on terrorists and their networks with other agencies, let alone with researchers and analysts outside of government. The data generated by separate organizations often end up in silos, the property of one department, organization, or country, which makes it difficult to get a complete view of the terror data, especially if terrorist groups and organizations operate internationally.

- **Data collectors are consistent in how they collect and measure terror data.** Unfortunately, what data they do collect and measure depends on what questions they ask in fieldwork and data-mining exercises. Different methods of data collection and measurement can result in competing claims about what the data reveal. For example, researchers from the University of Chicago Project on Security and Terrorism (CPOST) challenged a US Department of Homeland Security Center of Excellence (START), at the University of Maryland, about the accuracy of its Global Terrorism Database (GTD). In particular, they criticized the Global Terrorism Database for inaccurately representing trends of suicide terrorism. What START sees as a dramatic rise of suicide attacks, CPOST claims is a function of a methodological change in how GTD collects data and is not an accurate portrayal of reality. The CPOST database, which researchers say has maintained a consistent collection methodology over time, is deemed more accurate in its statistics of 521 suicide attacks in 2007 and 423 in 2013.[111]

- **Analysts are consistent in how they code and structure the raw data collected from different sources.** Unfortunately, terror data do not arrive "clean" on the analysts' desks. Analysts have to make decisions on what people, groups, and organizations should be in the data set and how to eliminate duplications and remove any that don't belong, as well as reconciling different spellings of names and other discrepancies. As an example, the analyst who created figure 2.1 determined that an international "terrorist organization," the topic of interest, was defined as "an organization primarily involved in terrorist activities that is not registered as a political, business, or government organization."[112] However, acknowledging that the definition was vague and some organizations did not fit the definition perfectly, the analyst had to make some judgment calls. He combined suborganizations, such as the 44th and 39th Fronts of the Revolutionary Armed Forces of Colombia (*Fuerzas Armadas Revolucionarias de Colombia,* or FARC), into larger umbrella organizations, like "FARC." He included Hezbollah on the list of 100 organizations spread across the globe because the United States thinks that it is a terrorist group, even though it is also a political organization. And based on his best guess, he located the terror organizations' primary locations on the international map using geospatial coordinates.

Box 2.2 (continued)

- **Members of terror networks can be identified and their network boundaries can be established.** Unfortunately, algorithms can't determine if all terror members have been identified, nor can algorithms ascertain how people, groups, and organizations in the network are connected. To describe the relationships among the terrorist organizations in figure 2.1, the analyst aggregated all the active and former ties among the organizations found in a particular database, although he did not do an independent check on the status of those relationships in other open-source or classified databases. Moreover, a more complete analysis would have required him to collect data on over twenty-five types of relationships[113] (i.e., family ties, communication ties, school ties, and money ties) from numerous data sources that could possibly reveal how people, groups, and organizations might be connected, a difficult task given the paucity of fine-grained details about relationships and the amount of time and expense that it takes to collect data.

- **Social network analysis can be used to visualize terror networks.** Unfortunately, social network analysis algorithms that produce the visualizations are highly sensitive to missing data. The analyst who created figure 2.1 only visualized the main component of each network and eliminated minor components (i.e., subcomponents of the network with fewer interconnected nodes) and isolates (i.e., those people, groups, and organizations that surface in a database but who have no known connections to others) to reduce the clutter and complexity of the map. Visualizations also can vary greatly, depending on which algorithms generate them. Analysts have a wide range of centrality measurements, each producing a different relational map that identifies what is central to the network and what is less central. Moreover, the bias toward centrality in social network analysis algorithms obscures other aspects of the network that might be equally or more important, as a colleague and I discovered when we reanalyzed social network data from Syria. Initial analyses had missed a newly forming group, later called ISIS, because it did not rank highly on the centrality algorithms. Instead, analysts focused their attention on other groups that they deemed more central, so they missed the opportunity to track and possibly intervene in the ISIS network when it was in its early stages of development.[114]

- **The application of social network analyses and the algorithms behind them enable analysts to craft strategies to target and disrupt terror networks.** Unfortunately, the strategies identified and recommended to policy makers often depend on the analyst's interpretations and worldview. In social network analysis courses that I have taught to Special Operations Forces (SOFs), officers tend to recommend different strategies depending on their backgrounds and experiences. When viewing a terror network, field operators tend to opt for kinetic strategies that use force to target individuals and groups and their relationships. When viewing the same terror network, civil affairs officers gravitate toward community-building strategies with the goal of addressing the causes of terrorism and preventing terror networks from forming in the first place. Unless primed before viewing the same network, neither considers a reconciliation strategy that other countries have used to educate and reform terrorists so they can return to society.

exclude people with divergent views and invite only participants whose views and perspectives agree with ours so we can reduce disagreements and conflicts. I am reminded of a postconflict reconstruction expert at the Pentagon who called to ask educators at my university for help in getting into Pentagon meetings about the Iraq war. Discussions were underway on how to conduct the war, but not on how to stabilize Iraq after the fighting ended. Since the United States said it was not interested in "nation building," postconflict expertise was deemed unnecessary. The decision to exclude postconflict experts from meetings was a catastrophe for Iraq and the United States. With no postwar plans, Iraq was left with no governance and no army (the Baathists were removed from their positions) and there was no one to stop the massive looting and ethnic rivalries when they erupted.

This example also illustrates what happens when the number of people participating in meetings is limited—the smaller the group, the easier it is to arrive at a consensus, especially if the few are trusted advocates of one's position rather than outsiders. And when setting the agenda, we can tame the problem-solving process by listing only those issues that we want the group to address and omitting those that are likely to engender debates and decisions contrary to the predominant view. And if pressed to include a contentious topic, rather than place it at the top of the agenda, we can put it at the end, when time is limited and people are less engaged as they are preparing to rush out the door. And if none of these tactics are successful, limiting the criteria to assess our preferred solutions can narrow options and simplify selection. For example, we can shrink the solution space by establishing our preferred metrics to measure success. The claim that the United States was winning the war in Vietnam was based on the number of North Vietnamese and Viet Cong soldiers killed, which turned out to be a poor metric for a multitude of reasons, as the United States finally came to understand after it lost the war and thousands of lives in the process.

Substitute other models of problem solving and decision making. We can employ other problem-solving and decision-making models that are less ambitious and a better fit with the uncertainty and ambiguity of wicked problem territory. Herbert Simon's concepts of *bounded rationality* and *satisficing* were introduced earlier in this chapter as our fallback techniques when our rational-analytic strategy fails, but they deserve an extended treatment here. Simon was one of the first to identify the rational-analytic model as poorly suited for ill-structured problems.[115] As he described them, ill-structured problems dealt with incomplete information; ambiguous specification of the problem; no stopping rules or criteria to evaluate whether a solution is reached; no sources of knowledge that could be determined in advance; knowledge that needed to be integrated rather than treated independently; no predetermined solution path to reach a goal; and cognitive limitations of the problem solver. Thus, he recommended substituting bounded rationality for the rational model of problem solving when these conditions obtain. Using this simplified model, problem solvers first bound the problem until it becomes sufficiently well defined to be resolved, and then they evaluate solutions sequentially until a satisfactory alternative surfaces based on a minimal rather than an optimal set of solution criteria. Thus, the problem solver satisfices rather than optimizes. In addition, since only a few alternatives are seriously considered, the solutions chosen tend to be those that involve only small, incremental changes in existing policies and procedures. The result is change at the margin, or what is referred to as "incremental decision making." An oft-cited example is the budget. Rather than starting from scratch to construct a budget, start with this year's budget and add or subtract an incremental amount to establish the next year's budget. Thus, as the saying goes, the best predictor of next year's budget is this year's budget. Incrementalism also enables problem solvers and decision makers to take short cuts (heuristics) to save mental activity. When an implemented solution is found to be acceptable, the problem solver develops and invokes standard operating procedures [SOPs] and routines to avoid spending time and energy on solving similar problems from scratch. Charles Lindblom offered a variation on the same theme of incrementalism, which he called "muddling through" when describing policy change and decision making.[116] Rather than push for a major policy shift or radical change, he advocated a process of continuous improvements and gradual change.

Michael D. Cohen, James G. March, and Johan P. Olsen developed a different model called "the garbage-can model of organizational problem solving and decision making" as a counter to the rational-analytic model. The model describes choices under conditions of uncertainty and ambiguity, or what they referred to as "organized anarchy," when goals are contested and problematic, the process of decision making is unclear, and people's participation in problem solving is fluid—all characteristics of decision making in wicked problem territory. The assumption is that organizations are a "collection of choices looking for problems, issues and feelings looking for decision situations in which they might be aired, solutions looking for issues to which they might be an answer, and decision makers looking for work."[117] Meetings or any decision forum offer choice opportunities to discuss all sorts of disconnected problems, goals, interests, concerns, and solutions. However, decisions aren't reached through some orderly process of problem identification and solution generation and selection. Rather, organizations are like garbage cans into which unrelated streams of participants, problems, and solutions are dumped. A meeting to discuss faculty parking, for example, can easily morph into disorganized and conflict-ridden discussions of old grievances and wrestle with other issues not on the agenda, like research funding, student plagiarism, janitorial services, and hiring policy. Everyone has a say, no one sticks to the point, and major issues often don't get resolved. The flow of problems, solutions, and participants is continual, but every now and then, some of these elements cluster together to produce a decision. This clustering depends on the chance arrivals of participants, problems, solutions, and the time and energy that participants are willing to commit to a choice opportunity. Participants also can influence decisions in garbage-can situations by carefully timing issues, attending to shifting interests and involvement, tracking status and power in choice situations, and treating planning as largely symbolic opportunities for interaction. Two decision styles characterize participants' actions: *Oversight* involves making a quick choice when it can be made without distraction from existing problems and with a minimum expenditure of time and energy. *Flight* involves abandoning a choice when it gets hopelessly entangled with other problems or delaying a decision until a more attractive solution to the problem comes along. Consequently, in a garbage can process, there tend to be a large number of unresolved issues or problems.

Advantages   The taming strategy has a number of advantages. Our inability to be perfectly rational problem solvers and decision makers under conditions of uncertainty and ambiguity is acknowledged. Instead of overburdening us with expectations we can't possibly realize, our intentions become more realistic and goals more attainable when problems are tamed. The odds of getting things done in wicked problem territory are not in our favor, but at least a taming strategy enables us to be active and do something rather than stay frozen in uncertainty and confusion. Simon's model of bounded rationality has the added advantage of letting us hang on to the vestiges of the rational-analytic model and appear somewhat rationale in our problem solving. We are not perfectly rational, but being boundedly rational in wicked problem territory may be the best we can do. By bounding problems and solutions and domesticating the problem-solving process, we can make problem solving and decision making more manageable. Problem-solving tools also can help us manage the information flow and provide some coherence to our interactions and decision making. In addition, taming enables us to decompose problems into separate components and hand them off to specialists for resolution. Our search for solutions also can be limited to something that satisfices to save us time and money. And if necessary, we can bring in outside experts to provide legitimacy to our process and give us an aura of rationality. We also can use heuristics and rules of thumb to make educated guesses rather than searching for perfect solutions that we are unable to predict with any degree of accuracy. In the words of Charles Lindblom, we can "muddle through" and make decisions incrementally rather than addressing wicked problems in some comprehensive way.

The garbage can model also has advantages. By serving on committees, spending time on problems, and exploring issues and solutions, we become a major information source that offers value to others. We also can build our credibility and gain influence by freeing others from the endless committee meetings that they dread sitting through. In turn, we learn that persistence in a garbage can world is what really counts, since few issues are resolved once and for all. Our project that is rejected today may be accepted tomorrow if we remain vigilant when a new choice opportunity arises. We understand that we might get a "yes" response next time because in organized anarchies, decisions can be made, unmade, or modified in subsequent meetings when different people meet in different settings to address different problems and choices. We also learn that overloading a garbage can process with lots of proposals and solutions is to our advantage. While we might lose one of our proposals, we can't be stopped on all of them. We also understand that it is preferable to avoid direct confrontations since they tend to activate the garbage can process. Instead, we manage unobtrusively by redirecting efforts and making minor changes that have major effects, careful to keep others unaware of the consequences of our choices. Since most issues in wicked problem territory are complex and ambiguous and data are scarce, we can fill in the gaps by interpreting events and telling our version of the story of how problems, solutions, and consequences are connected. Our story, if accepted, can become *the* story to which others subscribe, laying the groundwork for collective action. We also might get lucky during the garbage can process. A serendipitous, chance connection among people, problems, and solutions may produce new ideas that offer a way out of wicked problem territory. And for those of a political mindset, working in organized anarchies and taking advantage of the uncertainty that the garbage cans generate, we can find rich opportunities to build our base of power. Whether our political preferences lie in gaining power *over* others or *with* others, a growing base of power activated by our political tactics can improve our chances of getting something done in wicked problem territory.

Disadvantages   Subdividing the problem space into components that are more manageable and measureable so that specialists can tame them does not address the underlying problems and risks of "solving the wrong problem precisely."[118] For example, changing the building codes to reduce the risk of flooding to homes and businesses won't stop rising seas in coastal areas. In one storm that battered Louisiana, over 40,000 people had to be rescued from major flooding. Arial photos reveal farmland under water, inundated shopping centers, flooded homes, and impassable streets. Decomposing problems so that functional experts can deal with them has not solved the water resource management problems in three large US river basins: the Columbia River, southern California, and the Potomac River Basin/Chesapeake Bay in the Washington, D.C., metropolitan area.[119] As noted previously, specialists initially treated water as a resource that they could manage by dividing water problems into functional areas: specialists to manage the flooding, specialists to ensure the delivery of safe drinking water, specialists to provide irrigation water, and specialists to manage the supply of hydroelectric energy. The challenge for functional specialists was the construction of the necessary infrastructure to clean, store, release, and channel water to places and times when and where it is needed. However, this strategy focused on delivering water to those in their service area, regardless of the impacts on those outside their organizational and geographical jurisdictions or the risks to the environment. One consequence has been ongoing legal battles over property rights and court cases that attempt to establish and manage the rights of all users and stakeholders, whose needs for an increasingly scarce resource with multiple and often conflicting uses continue to grow.

As in the case of water, environmental issues are multicriteria and multiobjective. To address them, we need to take into consideration many factors—impacts on human health, economic costs, and community well-being. Decomposing problems into separate functional categories masks the trade-offs that we need to make among the many objectives that we want to attain—clean water *and* plentiful jobs *and* robust communities. What water quality standards do we want to maintain, and at what environmental, economic, and social cost? Answers to these questions are matters of value that special-ists, including legal authorities, are unable to determine. Similar dilemmas arise in our attempt to deal with "fragile states" (i.e., countries that risk state collapse). A common approach has been to tame problems by segmenting then into subproblems that are less complex and to which well-known standard templates and operating procedures of state building and peace building among civilian and military specialists can be applied. Evidence mounts that decomposing state fragility into its component parts leads to oversimplified problems, unclear and conflicting goals among agencies' inter-vention policies and strategies, interagency turf battles, fragmented efforts, and limited results that sometimes lead to perverse outcomes.[120]

Working in wicked problem territory also carries a set of moral responsibilities that are different from working on tame problems. Given the uncertainties and challenges of wicked problem territory, problem solvers are responsible for providing to those with whom they work an accurate expectation of the outcomes of any problem-solving effort. People are only too eager to have someone solve their wicked problems, and people are only too eager to get paid for those services. But giving people false hopes that problems can be solved, at least in the short term, raises ethical issues, given what we know about the challenges of solving wicked problems. Wicked problems defy solution, and taming strategies risk making problems even worse. So consultants who champion new tools and techniques need to take care that they don't cross an ethical line when they assert that their taming efforts can deliver better results.[121] Granted, it is hard to sell products and consulting services if one can't solve an organization's prob-lems, but consultants and their tools and technologies by themselves aren't capable of resolving value conflicts that are central to wicked problem discussions. Giving people help in dealing with their anxieties surrounding wicked problems is one thing, but exacerbating their feelings of helplessness when taming strategies fail to deliver on their promises is quite another.

Collaborative Strategy

The fifth basic strategy in wicked problem territory is collaboration. This theory draws its name from the French verb *collaborer* (*col* means "together," and *laborare* means "work in combination with . . . especially at literary or artistic (or scientific) produc-tion").[122] Working together has two general interpretations. From a classic liberalism perspective, we work to achieve our own self-interests and goals by bargaining and negotiating with others, who in turn bargain and negotiate with us to achieve their self-interests. If successful, the "collaboration becomes an aggregation of private prefer-ences into collective choices."[123] In other words, through bargaining and negotiation, we find the points of overlap among our self-interests on which we all can agree, which some have described as the search for the lowest common denominator.

Rittel and Webber's recommended strategy of dealing with wicked problems is another approach to collaboration, which they called "argumentation." In the course of the argumentation process, "an image of the problem and the solution emerges gradually among the participants, as a product of incessant judgment, subjected to critical argument."[124] Through this process, one finds that "the modes of reasoning used in the argument are much richer than those permissible"[125] in rational discourse. Although not explained or developed in "Dilemmas in a General Theory of Planning," Rittel and Webber had been searching for and developing information tools to make arguments more transparent to facilitate understanding and agreements among those engaged in argumentation. Rittel called one of his information tools IBIS, which captured three elements central to problem solvers' reasoning: *issues* were the questions of concern; *positions* were the varied answers to the questions; and *arguments* offered reasons for the positions. Any of these elements could lead to a new issue or question of concern, which cycles through the three-step argumentation process.[126] Ideally, people can come to some agreement about an issue. In the worst case, they at least can agree on why they disagree.

In contrast, civic republicanism views collaboration as integrative;[127] it is the pursuit of something larger than our individual self-interests. At its core, it is the constructive exploration of differences that goes beyond each person's "limited vision of what is possible."[128] In the pursuit of integrative rather than self-interested collaboration, we join forces and work together to achieve what each of us is unable to do on our own, creating a synergy as the whole becomes greater than the sum of its parts. When successful, power is pursued *with* others for mutual gain rather than attempting to establish power *over* others in the pursuit of individual self-interests.

We also need to distinguish collaboration from two related concepts—coordination and cooperation. I draw from organization theory to define *coordination* as the management of interdependencies to ensure that work gets done by decomposing overarching goals, assigning tasks, allocating resources, and sequencing and synchronizing activities.[129] *Cooperation* is similar to collaboration, in that people work together to achieve a particular end, but its root term *operate* (meaning to "bring about" and "to accomplish"),[130] lacks the creative and transmutational properties of collaboration. Cooperation is more time bound and less complex, as exemplified in the single round of joint (reciprocal) purposeful interaction in the manner of Robert Axelrod's tit-for-tat theory of cooperation.[131] It relies on more informal relationships and information sharing on an as-needed basis and poses less challenge and risk to participants since a common mission/vision and shared authority, resources, and rewards aren't necessary. In comparison, *collaboration* requires more complex human interactions that are sustained over an extended period of time. It relies on formal relationships and structure for the purpose of: facilitating information sharing, resources, and rewards; integrating stakeholders; vesting authority in the collaborative, not just in the participating organizations; and generating a common vision and mission derived from joint planning and decision making.

Of particular interest to us is how to use collaborative problem solving in wicked problem territory. The seminal work of Barbara Gray gives us direction; she defines collaboration as "a process through which parties who see different aspects of a problem can constructively explore their differences and search for solutions that go beyond their own limited vision of what is possible" and, when successful, implement their solutions.[132] She further elaborates and defines collaboration as "a process that engages a group of autonomous stakeholders interested in a problem or an issue in an interactive deliberation using shared rules, norms, and structures, to share information and/or take coordinated actions"[133] Building on Gray's problem-centric focus, I thus define the collaborative strategy in wicked problem territory (where there is no agreement on problems or their solutions) as a collective effort to frame a problem and/or generate solutions and select one (or more) solutions for implementation. With the proviso that problems and solutions are socially constructed and always subject to reexamination and revision, it is possible to move from wicked problem territory into complex or possibly simple problem territories to the extent that people, through the collaborative-solving process, are able to come to some agreement on problems, and/or their solutions.

Advantages of Collaboration

Many have identified the benefits of collaborative problem solving when dealing with wicked problems.[134] We find examples in wide-ranging disciplines from health care,[135] education,[136] local governance and community development,[137] governance,[138] public management,[139] public policy,[140] resource and environmental planning and management,[141] economics,[142] and security.[143] Table 2.1 also summarizes the collaborative strategy's advantages in wide-ranging venues and activities.

Opening the "black box of collaboration," we also find advantages in understanding the dynamics of collaboration.[144] Rather than ask *what* the purpose or subject matter of the collaboration is, we ask questions about *governance*, or how to make decisions and agreements; *administration*, or how to set up coordination, roles, and responsibilities; *autonomy*, or how to reconcile individual and collective interests; *mutuality*, or how to forge equally beneficial relationships, and how to build social capital norms of trust and reciprocity.[145] Milward and Provan also offer guidance in network collaboration—how to manage accountability, legitimacy, conflict, and commitment.[146] Others provide very practical advice on how to design and plan collaborations,[147] manage stakeholders,[148] lead collaborations,[149] create and sustain dialogue,[150] encourage learning and generate knowledge,[151] build a consensus to reach agreement,[152] and use technology to enable and strengthen collaborative processes.[153]

Disadvantages of Collaboration

Collaboration also has its disadvantages in wicked problem territory. It is risky, with high failure rates; time consuming; costly; and difficult to manage—results that have been well documented in a series of comprehensive and comparative studies that explore collaboration in different contexts.[154]

Table 2.1
Collaborative strategy's applications and advantages in activities and venues

Collaborative governance*	Making meetings work[†]
Collaborative governance regimes[‡]	Negotiating and making decisions**
Collaborative networks[††]	Developing effective groups and teams[‡‡]
Collaborative public policy***	Crafting and implementing public policy[†††]
Collaborative management[‡‡‡]	Deepening participation in democracy****
Interorganizational and cross-sector collaboration[††††]	Improving governance[‡‡‡‡]
Emergency management*****	Solving multiparty problems[†††††]
	Creating cross-boundary relations to gain access to resources, share risks, and get things done[‡‡‡‡‡]

* Chris Ansell and Alison Gash, "Collaborative Governance in Theory and Practice," *Journal of Public Administration Research and Theory* 18, no. 4 (October 2008): 543–71, https://doi.org /10.1093/jopart/mum032; Kirk Emerson, Tina Nabatchi, and Stephen Balogh, "An Integrative Framework for Collaborative Governance," *Journal of Public Administration Research and Theory* 22, no. 1 (January 2012): 1–29, https://doi.org/10.2307/41342607.

[†] David Straus, *How to Make Collaboration Work* (San Francisco: Berrett-Koehler, 2002).

‡ Kirk Emerson and Tina Nabatchi, *Collaborative Governance Regimes* (Washington, DC: Georgetown University Press, 2015).

** Howard Raiffa, John Richardson, and David Metcalfe, *Negotiation Analysis: The Science and Art of Collaborative Decision Making* (Cambridge, MA: Harvard University Press, 2002).

[††] Vanessa R. Levesque, Aram L. Calhoun, Kathleen P. Bell, and Teresa R. Johnson, "Turning Contention into Collaboration: Engaging Power, Trust, and Learning in Collaborative Networks," *Society and Natural Resources* 30, no. 2 (February 2017): 245–60, https://doi.org/10 .1080/08941920.2016.1180726; Robert Agranoff, "Inside Collaborative Networks: Ten Lessons for Public Managers," *Public Administration Review* 66, s1(December 2006): 56–65, https:// onlinelibrary.wiley.com/toc/15406210/2006/66/s1.

[‡‡] J. Richard Hackman, *Collaborative Intelligence* (San Francisco: Berrett-Koehler, 2011).

*** Paul Williams, *Collaboration in Public Policy and Practice: Perspectives on Boundary Spanners* (Bristol, UK: Bristol University Press, 2012).

[†††] Judith E. Innes and David E. Booher, "Collaborative Policymaking: Governance through Dialogue," in *Deliberative Policy Analysis: Understanding Governance in the Network Society*, ed. Maarten Hajer and Hendrik Wagenaar (Cambridge: Cambridge University Press, 2003), 33-59. https://doi.org/10.1017/CBO9780511490934.003.

[‡‡‡] William D. Leach, "Collaborative Public Management and Democracy: Evidence from Western Watershed Partnerships," *Public Administration Review* 66, s1 (December 2006):100–10. https://onlinelibrary.wiley.com/toc/15406210/66/s1; Michael McGuire, "Collaborative Public Management: Assessing What We Know and How We Know It," *Public Management Review* 66, s1 (December 2006): 33–43, https://onlinelibrary.wiley.com/toc/15406210/66/s1.

**** Xavier de Souza Briggs, *Democracy as Problem Solving: Civic Capacity in Communities across the Globe* (Cambridge, MA: MIT Press, 2008); Tina Nabatchi and Matt Leighninger, *Public Participation for 21st-Century Democracy* (Hoboken, NJ: Wiley, 2015).

[††††] John M. Bryson, Barbara C. Crosby, and Melissa M. Stone, "The Design and Implementation of Cross-Sector Collaborations," *Public Administration Review* 66, s1 (December, 2006): 44–55, https://onlinelibrary.wiley.com/toc/15406210/66/s1.

Table 2.1
continued

Eran Vigota, "From Responsiveness to Collaboration: Governance, Citizens, and the New Generation of Public Administration," *Public Administration Review* 62, no. 5 (September/October, 2002): 527–60, https://doi.org/10.1111/1540-6210.00235. Mark T. Imperial, "Using Collaboration as a Governance Strategy: Lessons from Six Watershed Management Programs," *Administration & Society* 37, no. 3 (July 2005): 281–320, https://doi.org/10.1177/0095399705276111.

***** Louise K. Comfort, William L. Waugh, Jr., Beverly A. Cigler, and Christine G. Springer, "Emergency Management Research and Practice in Public Administration," *Public Administration Review* 72, no. 4 (July/August 2012): 539–49, https://www.jstor.org/stable/i40073944.

†††† Barbara Gray and Jill Purdy, *Collaborating for Our Future: Multi-stakeholder Partnerships for Solving Complex Problems* (Oxford: Oxford University Press, 2018); Judith E. Innes and David E. Booher, *Planning with Complexity: An Introduction to Collaborative Rationality for Public Policy* (Oxfordshire, UK: Routledge, 2010).

John M. Bryson, Barbara C. Crosby, and Laura Bloomberg, eds, *Discerning and Assessing Public Value: Major Issues and New Direction* (Washington, DC: Georgetown University Press, 2015).

Collaboration is risky and can fail to achieve its goal. Judith Innes and David Booher's criteria for successful dialogue/collaboration set a high bar: they are "deep and durable agreements" and "actions taken with strong support." They produce outcomes that address the "original problematic situation," result in "system adaptations," create "social and intellectual capital and build institutional capacity," "are adaptive to changing circumstances and evolve along with knowledge and conditions," and "produce spinoff and second- and third-order consequences such as institutional change."[155]

Although the range of collaborative applications is broad, it should come as no surprise that these researchers find only a small percentage of them are well managed and meet all of these criteria.[156] Introducing collaboration normally requires a change in the status quo that is threatening to the players—"something that would make matters worse or raise new risks."[157] Indeed, some conflicts may not be resolved. Robert Agranoff reached similar conclusions in his longitudinal studies of collaborative networks, noting that "collaborative successes are equaled or exceeded by stalemates or failures to launch."[158] Chris Huxham and Siv Vangen's concerns were so great that they warned practitioners of the dangers of "collaborative inertia"—when "the output from a collaborative arrangement is negligible, the rate of output is extremely slow, or stories of pain and hard grind are integral to successes achieved."[159] In the fifteen years that they have researched collaboration, they "have seen no evidence to shift [their]" view that collaboration should not be undertaken "unless the stakes are really worth pursuing."[160]

Many barriers to collaboration have been identified, such as vulnerability to changing political dynamics, lack of collaborative leadership, turf projection, power domination and unequal power among the participants, acrimony, the lack of trust, and policy restrictions and jurisdictional divides.[161] Three barriers warrant particular mention here. Collaboration is time consuming and requires incentives to sustain it; it is costly in terms of resources required; and it is messy, challenging, and difficult to manage.

Collaboration's time and resource requirements.   Collaboration is a dynamic process that evolves over a period of time. It is "best understood as a path rather than a destination."[162] Participants who land in wicked problem territory will likely be engaged over a number of years, and some say that it takes around two years just to establish a degree of trust,[163] with some successful collaborations requiring a ten-year time frame.[164] The advice to "budget a great deal more time for collaborative activities than you would normally expect to need" applies to the leadership as well as the participants.[165] Sustaining commitment on the part of organizational sponsors who resource the collaborations, leaders who guide and facilitate them, and participants who engage in them demands much of people's time and patience. It is one of the reasons that there are frequent reports of turnover—people and organizations dropping out because they have lost the will and interest to continue. For their substitutes, if there are any, building trust and sustaining relationships start the process anew. The shared collective memory that charted their history, informal agreements, and personal ties loses some of its depth and nuance, making it difficult for new members to assimilate into the collaborative.

Collaboration is costly.   Although not comparable to most collaborations in size or scope, a one-day citizen engagement for 4,500 people at the Javits Center in New York and a two-week online dialogue in the spring and summer of 2002 provided input to decision makers on the rebuilding of the World Trade Center site after the September 11 attack. The costs were estimated to be at least a million dollars and included expenses for the event planners, designers, and facilitators to staff a very large-scale project over a three-month period, contract support for outreach, communications, event management, and registration, and facility costs and technology to record and capture the meeting decisions.[166] As Carolyn Lukensmeyer and Steve Brigham report, events such as these are "resource intensive": Budgets rise by the size of the project. For meetings of 1,000 or more, the budget is likely to be at least several hundred thousand dollars; meetings of 3,000 or more can approach or even exceed a million dollars. Sponsors must not only devote significant organizational resources to the task, but also have access to significant funding sources or be savvy fundraisers.[167]

Innes and Booher, who study comparable longer-term collaborations, also report that additional expenses are need to support dedicated staff since "there is much to do behind the scenes as well as in meetings to make a process successful. All of our most successful cases had significant, trusted staff support, in contrast with the less successful ones."[168] There are agendas to be written, meeting summaries to prepare and distribute, experts to invite, information to gather, phone calls to be made, and meetings to attend or facilitate, as well as data to gather and analyze. A major staff job is to keep participants informed, make sure that they feel heard, and help them work through concerns that they may not feel comfortable discussing in the meetings.[169] And besides the direct costs of collaboration, there are the opportunity costs that people incur when they lose work time in their home organization—work that has to be made up when they return or passed on to others. The direct and opportunity costs involved in collaborations have led Huxham and Vangen to warn that "the overwhelming conclusion from our research is that seeking collaborative advantage is a seriously resource-consuming activity so it is only to be considered when the stakes are really worth pursuing. Our message to practitioners and policy makers alike is *don't do it unless you have to.*[170]

Collaboration is messy, challenging, and difficult to manage.   Collaboration is an "imperfect art."[171] "There are no easy routes to success,"[172] no recipes for success,[173] and no "prescriptions for best practice."[174] "Every project is different, and every day is different."[175] "A collaboration process cannot simply stay on a course, but has to be constantly in motion rethinking its tasks, membership and its incentive structure. There is no resting on laurels. There is no resting."[176] Huxham and Vangen, who have conducted long-term, in-depth field studies of collaborations, report some of the tensions, conflicts, contradictions, and dilemmas that are a natural part of the collaborative experience: "We must have common aims but we cannot agree on them";[177] "Sharing power is important but people behave as if it's all in the purchase strings";[178] "Trust is necessary for successful collaboration but we are suspicious of each other";[179] "We are partnership-fatigued and tired of being pulled in all directions";[180] "Everything keeps changing";[181] "Leadership is not always in the hands of members";[182] "Leadership activities continually meet with dilemmas and difficulties."[183]

There also are issues that make collaboration difficult, especially in the public sector, which operates in "the shadow of bureaucracy."[184] The traditional structures and systems of the public sector are not set up to deal collaboratively with wicked problems. The models and mindsets of bureaucracy can clash with "collaborative rationality," which assumes interdependent network clusters, distributed control, divided authority, various and changing goals, nonlinear planning, and the need for social learning and problem solving.[185] Summarizing public management's shortcomings in dealings with wicked problems, Brian Head and John Alford conclude that wicked problems are "challenging not only because of their inherent complexity but also because the mechanisms of public-sector management tend to complicate and hamstring efforts to resolve such issues."[186] Moreover, collaboration "is not always the primary or the best option among possible responses to wickedness.[187] It offers one way in dealing with the wickedness of a problem, but "it can be difficult to establish and sustain robust collaboration in a public-sector context subject to turbulence and accountability rules."[188]

Others are more critical of collaboration. Although collaboration has been viewed as an imperative for twenty-first-century public administration and management,[189] and even a moral imperative to deal with the challenges facing society,[190] its most ardent supporters warn that collaboration is not a "panacea."[191] Indeed, Innes and Booher call attention to what they refer to as "pseudo collaboration" and "inauthentic collaboration" that "co-opts, manipulates, or simply does not reflect a genuine agreement, much less a societally beneficial conclusion."[192] These so-called collaborations "may produce little or nothing and simply be a waste of time and money; [they] may be window dressing for decisions already made; or [they] may be a lowest common denominator agreement."[193] One of its most strident critics, Janine O'Flynn, calls collaboration an "obsession," a "cult," "the Holy Grail," the "one best way of operating,"[194] and "the King in a turbulent world where governments don't have all the answers to complex challenges, and where there is some impetus to move beyond both bureaucracy and markets."[195] I agree with O'Flynn that "what we are seeing is a phenomenon where everyone is talking about collaboration, but significant questions remain about whether they are actually doing collaboration."[196] I also am very concerned when its advocates highlight collaboration's potential and make claims that collaboration can solve wicked problems while they ignore the realities of wicked problem territory.

I accept that collaboration is an "inherently fragile system"[197] and an inexact art involving a great deal of judgment.[198] I agree that collaboration is difficult to design and facilitate. And I concur that its exacting praxis can limit its success.[199] Based on my experiences with the collaborative strategy, I see its merits when the problem territory is complex or when there is at least some consensus about problems or their solutions so that participants have some foundation on which to build. But when deep in wicked problem territory, when issues profoundly divide, and when little or no agreement exists about problems or solutions, the collaborative strategy has its limits in creating the conditions for effective problem solving.

In Summary

The competitive, authority/authoritative, rational-analytic, taming, and collaborative strategies have been widely touted as problem-solving approaches. This chapter's extensive literature review attests to their important contributions and advantages. However, as I also have demonstrated, these strategies have limitations, especially in wicked problem territory.

So what are our options now? Have we exhausted all the available problem-solving strategies? Is this the reason that problem solving in wicked problem territory is so difficult, challenging, and, dare I say, "wicked"? Perhaps, but I think there is a more hopeful possibility. I submit that there is another problem-solving strategy—the design strategy—that has the features, perspectives, and capabilities to make it particularly attractive in wicked problem territory. In part II, I describe the general parameters of the design strategy, trace its history and evolution, and describe its process, basic principles, mindsets, skill sets, and toolkits. Part III then follows, with cases in arenas where wicked problems tend to lurk—the strategic design of organizations, the systemic design of social systems, and the regenerative design of social and ecological systems—all of which demonstrate the design strategy's problem-solving potential in wicked problem territory.

II Design Strategy

3 Introduction to Design Strategy

Design is
    —an aspiration to create
    —our passion to help humankind
    —a strategy to effect change
    —the desire to impact the world
Warren Berger, 2009

The limitations of traditional problem-solving strategies summarized in chapter 2 prompted a search for alternatives in wicked problem territory. Richard Buchanan was one of the first to connect design's problem-solving potential and designers' creativity to deal with wicked, indeterminate problems and solutions.[1] Others followed, as Warren Berger captures in the epigraph that begins this chapter. Not only was design an "aspiration to create," a "passion to help humanind," and a "desire to impact the world," but some came to recognize it as "a strategy to effect change."

The concept of strategy is well known among those who work in private- and public-sector organizations, including military organizations. Countries have a "grand strategy," militaries have a "national security strategy," businesses have their "competitive strategies," and public-sector organizations and nonprofits have missions and purposes that they pursue and specific approaches they use to achieve them. As Lawrence Freedman describes it, strategy is the mobilization of resources and action to bring about some desired outcome.[2] And as noted in chapter 2, central to any strategy is its three parts—a goal or outcome, an identifiable approach to mobilize resources, and actions to bring about the outcome.[3] As previously noted, the three parts are generally described as the *what* of a strategy, or its intent/purpose; the *how* of a strategy, or its general approach; and the *means* of a strategy, or the methods, techniques, tools, and other elements used to support the approach and deliver results.

Design also has a three-part story. The *what* of design is the goal that designers want to achieve—the creation of a world that could be. The *how* of design describes the process that designers use to achieve their goal—variously described as "reflection-in-action," "the designerly way of knowing, thinking and acting," and "design thinking." The *means* of design are its skill sets, toolkits, methods, and techniques central to design practice. So when we combine the details of the *what*, the *how*, and the *means* of design, Design comes into bold relief as strategy that inspires creativity, effects change, transforms organizations, and "impacts the world."[4]

Accordingly, part II begins by offering a general overview of design as a strategy. Chapter 3 describes the *what* of design—its long history, discourse, landscape, and the growing fields and subfields of design disciplines. The convergence between design and innovation is noted, as well as design's distinguishing features compared to art and science. The *what* of design also includes design's eight basic principles that distinguish it from other types of strategies. Design is future oriented; human centric, context specific, exploration anchored, creativity dependent, prototype anchored, testing reliant, and implementation attentive. The chapter then ends with an overview of the *how* of design—the different ways that designers characterize the design process.

Chapter 4 continues to explore the *how* of design by probing designers' mindsets—the underlying assumptions that shape their perceptions, inform their values, attitudes, and understandings, and ultimately aid them in making manifest the external, material world. Seven mindsets illustrate this internal process: the growth mindset, benefit mindset, hyperattuned mindset, imaginative mindset, analytical mindset, maker mindset, and change-agent mindset. The chapter also draws from developmental theory to explore how a designer's consciousness is directly related to the generation of physical and material forms. Consciousness, we learn, can evolve from a system driven by a mindset of "me," which only cares for one's own well-being, to a system driven by the concern for the well-being of the whole, including oneself. The chapter then returns to the *what* of design and introduces the concept of metadesign—designers' intentional interventions that attempt to alter people's cultural values, beliefs, and consciousness.

Chapter 5 reviews designers' *means,* or the skill sets, toolkits, methods, and techniques that support their design process. They are organized into two general categories: change agent skill sets and toolkits, and designer skill sets and toolkits. All of these enhance designers' ability to explore context, frame problems, generate creative ideas, fashion and iterate prototypes, and test and adapt prototypes for field implementation.

Design's History, Discourse, and Landscape

Design has a long history. According to Friedman and Stolterman, "The urge to design—to consider a situation, imagine a better situation, and act to create that improved situation—goes back to our prehuman ancestors. Making tools helped us to become what we are; design helped to make us human."[5] *Homo habilis* fashioned the first tools over 2.5 million years ago. *Homo erectus*, living between 1.89 million and 143,000 years ago, created the earliest hand axes, the first major innovation in stone tool technology, and left evidence suggesting that they cared for the sick and the weak. From 400,000 to 40,000 years ago, *Homo neanderthalensis* made and used a diverse set of sophisticated tools, controlled fire, lived in shelters, made and wore clothing, skillfully hunted large animals, ate plants, and occasionally made symbolic or ornamental objects. Further evidence suggests that Neanderthals were the first to practice sophisticated symbolic behavior in deliberately burying their dead and occasionally marking graves with offerings such as flowers.[6]

Homo sapiens, the species to which humans belong, evolved in Africa about 200,000 years ago. We originally were noted for our ability to make and use stone tools, and then to make our tools smaller, more complex, refined, and specialized (tools making other tools), initially producing composite stone tools, fishhooks, harpoons, bows and arrows, spear throwers, and sewing needles. We controlled fire, lived in shelters, and collected and cooked shellfish 164,000 years ago. Within the last 12,000 years, we transitioned to producing food and changing our surroundings: we controlled the growth and breeding of certain plants and animals and farmed and herded animals. As food production grew, we settled down first in villages, then in towns, and eventually also in cities. We built broad social networks, exchanged resources over wide areas, created art, music, personal adornments, rituals, and a complex symbolic world, as illustrated in the graphic design and typography that emerged with the development of cuneiform in Sumeria 5,000 years ago. As our food availability increased, so did our population and eventually the size of our cities, city-states, empires, and ultimately nations.[7] Thus, as human evolution demonstrates, "stripped to its essence, design can be defined as the human capacity to shape and make our environment in ways without precedent in nature, to serve our needs and give meaning to our lives."[8] It affects the quality of human life and "every detail of every aspect of what [people] do throughout each day." Design is one of the defining "characteristics of what it means to be human."[9]

John Heskett describes design's historical diversity as a "process of layering, in which new developments are added to what design has already created. The layering, not "just a process of accumulation or aggregation, is a "dynamic interaction in which each new innovative stage changes the role, significance, and function of what survives."[10] Sticks and clamshells were extensions of the hand for digging, but digging became easier when a shell was tied with hide or fiber at a right angle to the end of a stick to fashion a hoe. The hoe was made more durable and less fragile when made of metal. Eventually, through language, writing, and visual representations and the ability to use "mind tools" to represent and articulate concepts of "what might be," humans were able to conceive how the physical power of animals could fortify the tools used to cultivate land and improve their yields.[11] Ultimately, "neither the hand alone, nor the hand allied to the other human senses, can be viewed as the source of design capability. Instead, it is the hand, allied to the senses and the mind, that forms the coordinated trinity of powers by which human beings have asserted ever-greater control over the world."[12]

Despite its long history, design as a profession is relatively new and still evolving. But ask the general public what design is and how designers go about their work, and the typical responses describe design as aesthetics or making things visually attractive and pleasing to the senses. To many, this is what design is all about. When the same question is asked of the design community, many will say that design is a fragmented discipline.[13] Indeed, Johansson-Sköldberg and colleagues[14] identified five discourses about design and designing:

- *Design is the creation of artifacts.*[15] For Herbert Simon, design is about the "artificial world"—the human-made world of artifacts. It is about shaping or producing objects (e.g., tools, weapons, and ornaments) intentionally made for a certain purpose.

- *Design is reflective practice.*[16] Donald Schön describes design as a practice-based relationship between the designer's creation and his or her reflection upon that creation. Reflective practice enables the designer to make constant improvements in whatever is being designed, and in so doing improve his or her competence in designing. Thus, reflection is not something separate from designing but rather is very much a part of design practice.

- *Design is problem solving.*[17] Building on Rittel and Webber's formulation of wicked problems, Richard Buchanan views designers as being challenged by a class of social system problems that have indeterminate problem definitions and solutions that require creativity in both defining problems and generating solutions. In contrast to Rittel and Webber's two phases of problem definition followed by solution generation, Buchanan introduces the process of contextualization, in which problem formulation and solutions go hand in hand, which he contends, is especially important in an increasingly complex technological culture.

- *Design is a way of reasoning or making sense of things.*[18] Design is making sense of and generalizing from observations to find patterns grounded in practical experience, which then can be described using practical examples. This form of reasoning relies on *abductive reasoning*, a form of logical inference that begins with an observation and then attempts to find the simplest and most likely explanation for the observation. Thus, we find Bryan Lawson distilling a model that describes the complex process of designing into a number of steps and Nigel Cross describing the recursive design process used by creative designers.

- *Design is the creation of meaning.* Instead of the creation of artifacts, Klaus Krippendorff[19] defines design and designers' work as meaning creation. Meaning and its semantic roots become the core of the design process, while the artifact becomes the medium through which the designer communicates that meaning. Verganti[20] extends this theme to the innovation process, maintaining that the innovation of meaning is as important as technological innovations. Thus, it is important for designers to research and explore the meaning that people attach to an artifact before its creation.

Despite this varied discourse, or perhaps because of it, the act of designing has produced incredible diversity. Box 5.1[21] captures some of design's expansive and every-growing fields and subfields.

This diversity begs the question of whether there is some underlying framework that systematizes the field of design. Answering this question has been challenging, as G. K. Van Patter points out:

Table 3.1
A subset of design's growing fields and subfields

Applied Arts	Fashion Design	Lighting Design	Software Design
Architecture	Floral Design	Modular Design	Sound Design
Automotive Design	Game Design	Organization Design	Spatial Design
Biological Design	Graphic Design	Process Design	Strategic Design
Cartographic Design	Information Design	Product Design	Systems Architecture
Configuration Design	Industrial Design	Production Design	Systems Design
Costume Design	Instructional Design	Property Design	Systems Modeling
Design Management	Interaction Design	Scenic Design	Urban Design
Engineering Design	Interior Design	Service Design	User Interface Design
Experience Design	Landscape Design	Social Design	Web Design

As a field of knowledge, design is an amorphous time warp that exists across several time zones, or paradigms, simultaneously. Some are old, rather static paradigms, while others are transforming and/or just emerging. Unlike in traditional science, the various paradigms within design do not necessarily replace [one another] as they emerge. As activity zones, the various paradigms within design . . . exist in parallel. . . . [and] simultaneously.[22]

Despite the parallel universe of design paradigms, there has been some attempt at systemization. Buchanan has explained design's expansive history and practice in terms of orders.[23] The Danish Design Center has considered design in terms of steps on a ladder.[24] Rabah Bousbaci[25] and Peter Jones[26] have interpreted design in terms of generations. John Heskett[27] and Kees Dorst[28] have viewed design in terms of layers. And Van Patter has conceptualized design in terms of levels.[29] All five perspectives add value and help us appreciate design's evolution. Table 3.2 integrates them into an overarching framework that not only captures design's range and diversity, but is flexible enough to add newer levels/layers as design continues to evolve. As Charles Owen reminded us, "as society evolves so does our ability to design,"[30] and as Elizabeth Sanders and Pieter Jan Stappers predict, design's landscape "will be infinite in space and time and continually changing."[31]

Beginning in column one, design produces different types of things, such as hand-crafted designs, architectural designs, graphic designs, product designs, and service designs. Column two aggregates these design types into nine design stages: *early design practice,* such as the fashioning of clothes and jewelry; *traditional design,* such as the construction of houses and bridges; *visual design,* or the communication of information in words and images; *value-added design,* or the production of products at a large scale; *experience design,* or the improvement of customer/user service, satisfaction, and involvement; *organizational design,* or the changes of an organizational strategy and its implementation; *cross-boundary design,* or the creation of dynamic networks to manage interdependencies in social systems; *ecological design,* or the redesign of natural and social ecosystems; and *sociocultural design,* or the change of frameworks, values, and paradigms.

Table 3.2
Design's landscape: Types, stages, and domains

Design	Generates Design Types	Aggregates into Design Stages	Characterized as Design Domains
	Handmade Design	Design 1.0: Early Design Practice (e.g., clothing, pottery, jewelry)	Craft Design
	Architecture Design Engineering Design	Design 2.0: Traditional Design (e.g., houses, bridges, roads, cities)	Infrastructure Design
	Graphic Design Media Design	Design 3.0: Visual Designs (e.g., communicating Information in words and images)*	Communication Design
	Product Design	Design 4.0: Value-Added Designs (e.g., producing products at a larger scale)**	Industrial Design
	Service Design Process Design	Design 5.0: Experience Designs (e.g., improving customer/user satisfaction and involvement)*	Interaction Design
	Work Design Job Design Organization Design	Design 6.0: Organizational Design (e.g., changing organizational strategy and its implementation)**	Strategic Design
	Policy Design Education Design Urban Design	Design 7.0: (e.g., creating networks to manage interdependencies in social systems).	Systemic Design
	Restoration Design Reconciliation Design	Design 8.0: Ecological Designs (e.g., redesign of social and natural ecosystems)	Regenerative Design
	Transition Design Disruptive Design	Design 9.0: Social-Cultural Designs (e.g., changing frameworks and shifting values and paradigms)	Metadesign

* Buchanan (2011).
** Van Patter (2009).

In column three, design levels are characterized as *design domains,* which are generalized arenas separating design into specified spheres of knowledge and thought: *craft design; infrastructure design; communication design; industrial design; interaction design; strategic design; systemic design; regenerative design;* and *metadesign.*

When scanning tables 3.1 and 3.2, it becomes clear that design is increasing in complexity[32] as it evolves and touches almost every facet of life, ranging from tangible objects to intangible systems. The boundaries of a design project, which Tim Brown refers to as "design's playing field,"[33] extend from those that have one designer who hand-crafts a product to those who codesign with large numbers of people who work in complex ecosystems and have competing worldviews. What they all have in common, whether dedicated to giving form to physical objects or to changing our social systems, is design's purpose—to improve and shape our "man-made environment," distinct from the "natural environment" that evolves without human intervention. In making this traditional distinction between a human-made environment that we design and the natural environment that nature designs, it is important to acknowledge that the boundary between the built and the natural environment has become very blurred of late. *Homo faber*[34] (meaning "man the maker") is now attempting to design and control the natural environment through the applications of tools. For example, scientists are using computer code to engineer deoxyribonucleic acid (DNA) circuitry and change how living cells behave—methods that are expected to revolutionize synthetic biology.[35] Clustered Regularly Interspaced Short Palindromic Repeats (CRISPR) technology is being employed for human genomic engineering,[36] and various techniques are being considered to geoengineer the planet's climate.[37] Through our interventions, as Juan Enriquez and Steve Gullans demonstrate,[38] we are evolving ourselves and changing life on Earth. And as we do so, designers are breaching the divide between the built and the natural environment and opening up complex ethical questions that need to be addressed—a subject to which we return in chapter 10.

Design Principles

A principle is a "comprehensive and fundamental law, doctrine, or assumption"[39] or "a fundamental truth or proposition that serves as the foundation for a system of belief or behavior or for a chain of reasoning."[40] Foundational principles of design exist, but there is little agreement among designers on what these principles are. Nor is there agreement on how to differentiate principles from mindsets, attitudes, skills, and tools,[41] or how to evaluate designers' personal attributes such as their "comfort with ambiguity," "ability to learn from failure," "openness to different perspectives," "curiosity," or "creative confidence."[42] The goal of this discussion, therefore, is to identify some basic design principles that are central to design's identity and purpose to which most designers tend to subscribe, and to offer a lexicon that differentiates design principles from other design elements.

I submit that there are eight major principles of design. Design is future-oriented, human centric, context specific, exploration driven, creativity dependent, prototype anchored, testing reliant, and implementation attentive. No doubt, this list is open for debate. Although these principles are recognized in their own right and can be found scattered throughout the design literature, they are rarely considered as a whole. But what makes design unique compared to other human endeavors is the way that these eight principles are woven together as a whole to create a sum that is greater than its parts. No doubt, additional clarifications and modification will be necessary as design evolves, but at least there is a foundation on which to build.

Design Is Future Oriented

Design is an intentional act, a conscious effort to seek something new. Rather than studying what is or what was, designers make a normative statement on what could be and what should be. As Harold Nelson and Erik Stolterman define it, "design is the ability to imagine that-which-does-not-exist, to make it appear in concrete form as a new purposeful addition to the real world."[43] Its future orientation establishes it as "the *first tradition* among the many traditions of inquiry,"[44] such as art and science.

Science generates knowledge that deals with what is "true" and the conditions under which something is "true." And what is "true" depends on the accumulated knowledge at a particular point in time. In the eighteenth century, Isaac Newton's theory of gravitation described a force acting at a distance between masses that results in their acceleration toward each other. The strength of that force depended on the size of the masses and the distance between them. By 1916, in what is referred to as the general theory of relativity, Albert Einstein proposed that gravity wasn't a force. Gravity stretched or shrank distances and warped spacetime. In essence, "mass tells space how to bend, and space tells mass how to move. . . . Space really is curved, and as a result objects are deflected from a straight path in a way that looks like a force."[45] Although the facts about gravity evolved as knowledge accumulated, what remained constant was the scientific method that scientists used to establish "truth." The scientific method is a process of problem solving that begins with an observation about some aspect of the world that scientists want to understand. A scientist then develops a tentative description—a hypothesis/prediction—that is consistent with the observation. Scientists then test the hypothesis/prediction using experiments and conducting carefully drawn and precise research studies. If the hypothesis/prediction is sustained, there is support for the original observation. If it is not sustained, scientists modify the hypothesis/prediction in light of the results or make new hypotheses/predictions and repeat the process. Thus, while "truth" evolves as knowledge evolves, the scientific process/method used to arrive at "the truth" remains constant and the most enduring aspect of science. Art, on the other hand, is not dependent on a particular process. As evident in the art of Michelangelo, Vincent Van Gogh, and Pablo Picasso, each artist has his or her own unique process that combines various subject matter, media, and styles to help others see and appreciate what they see. What matters is the artist's *personal expression* and their *unique interpretation* of their experienced reality in the art that they are producing, whether for themselves or for others. Eric Gibbons describes the artistic process as "often born of inner struggle. Artists are plagued by impulses they must express. Contentment does not seek action but struggle always seeks release, and for the creative it can take the form of art."[46] Thus, we value art for the artist's insight, originality, freshness, and stimulation, not for any formal rules that determine how he or she finds "truth."

Design is distinct from art and science. Art is the personal expression and unique interpretation of the artist's experienced reality, not constrained by any particular process. Science requires scientists to follow the scientific method to find explanations for natural phenomena to describe what is "true." In contrast, design is future oriented; it seeks to create and shape a world that currently does not exist but could eventually, as a consequence of the designer's intervention in the built environment. Thus,

Table 3.3

Comparison of design, art, and science

	Goal	Process	Output
Design	Generate new ideas	Designerly way	Artifacts for the built environment
Art	Artistic expression	Personal process	Unique insights and awareness
Science	Explore what is	Scientific method	Discovery of what is "true"

while artists express and scientists discover, designers invent and construct with an eye toward the future. They generate new ideas and concepts with unique goals, processes, and outputs.[47] Their goal is the generation of new ideas using the "designerly way of thinking" for the purpose of constructing the built environment. The goal of art is the interpretation of the artist's experienced reality using his or her distinctive process for the purpose of rendering the artist's original insights and awareness of the world. The goal of science is to explore the natural and social environment using the exacting process of the scientific method for the purpose of discovering, explaining, and sometimes predicting what is "true."

Despite this clarification, there remains some confusion concerning the relationship between design and science. I find references to "scientific design," "design science," "a science of design," "research for design," "research on design," and "research through design." One way to clarify this terminology is to use the phrase "research about design."[48] Research about design investigates designers and their frameworks, tools, processes, systems, and design practices.[49] The aim of this research is to use the scientific method to understand design and the conditions under which it is effective. So while designers create and construct designs, design researchers apply the scientific method to study designers' processes and results. Although design and science are separate and distinct traditions, one can use scientific methods to investigate the claims that designers make about how they are able to transform ideas into reality, as well as the efficiency and effectiveness of their processes and designs. So, for example, we find research about the core phases of the design process,[50] the designerly way of thinking and working,[51] how visualization unleashes the imagination,[52] how the design practices and design dispositions of novices and expert designers differ,[53] how empathy is important in design,[54] and how design thinking enhances the creative capacity of adults.[55]

Nigel Cross articulated the advantage of distinguishing between science and design. Design, he proposed, should be a separate discipline on its own terms in the pursuit of what could be. Fundamental to it are forms of knowledge unique to designers that are independent of their specific "domains of design practice. . . . What all designers know about is the 'artificial world'—the human-made world of artifacts" and the techniques to add, change, and even maintain the artificial world. Just as other intellectual cultures in the sciences and the arts concentrate on forms of knowledge that are unique to the scientist or artist, design concentrates "on the 'designerly' ways of knowing, thinking and acting."[56]

Design Is Human Centric

Human-centeredness hails from a long intellectual tradition.[57] Its earliest manifestation was expressed as *user-centered design*, a concept that originated in Donald Norman's research laboratory at University of California San Diego in the 1980s. In his book *The Psychology of Everyday Things*, Norman challenged designers to develop a deep knowledge of the people for whom they were designing.[58] To what extent do artifacts actually fit the human body and mind as determined by ergonomic, psychological, sociological, and anthropological studies? To address this question, the designer had to "know the user" on a fundamental level to ensure that users could employ designs as they were intended to be used, with minimum effort in learning how to use them. From his expanded view in the *Design of Everyday Things*, Norman warned that ignoring users' physical and psychological attributes and needs risked producing bad designs and producing human errors, of which there were far too many examples.[59]

The shift from user-centered design to human-centered design (HCD) occurred when designers wanted to understand people on their own terms rather than just testing and documenting their needs and problems when they use particular technologies and tools. Klaus Krippendorff's work was central to this evolution.[60] He maintained that artifacts were inseparable from how users conceived of them. People responded to the meaning of things as they engaged with them, not just to their physical qualities. It was therefore imperative that designers understand how people made sense of an artifact's meaning. From this point on, design moved from being technology-driven to being human-centered.[61]

Joseph Giacomin, drawing on the work of the anthropologist Lucy Suchman, treated design as an emergent property that resulted from the moment-by-moment interactions among designers and those for whom they were designing. Since the process of communication and learning in the design process could not "be fully defined or anticipated within the original physical, perceptual and cognitive objectives of the design,"[62] designers began to use techniques that enabled them to communicate, interact, and empathize with people to gain an understanding of their needs and experiences. Eventually, designers invited people for whom they were designing into the process, making designs visible as they unfolded. This more participatory process enabled designers to ask people's opinions and explore issues and potential problems before designs were finalized.

Proponents of the HCD approach now can be found at design centers throughout the world. The main tenet is that designers need empathy to understand the people for whom they are designing. Empathy is evident when designers put themselves "in others' shoes" to feel what they feel and understand what their experiences are. And to understand people's desires, aspirations, and experiences, designers must give priority to emotional resonance and the meaning of designs rather than design utility and product requirements. These empathy-driven insights then become the foundation on which the design process unfolds.[63]

The consequence of designing from an empathy-based understanding of people's needs and desires is that designers not only can come up with ideas that people can embrace, they also can arrive at unexpected solutions: the redesign of the hospital intake process from the patient's point of view,[64] redesigned cookstoves to improve the health of people living in poverty, and the generation of new ways to access clean drinking water.[65] As Harold Nelson and Erik Stolterman point out, design is a service relationship. As a service on behalf of others, designers work to meet human needs, which means more than making manifest what people already know and say they want, attempting to change their behavior for their "own good," or convincing them to buy something. Design is about exceeding their expectations and providing an "unexpected result that transcends original expectations." The result "is still recognizable as something that is in resonance with what is desired and anticipated yet adds something of significance."[66]

Richard Buchanan raised the stakes and significance of HCD in an important paper delivered at a national conference on "Reshaping South Africa by Design," held in Cape Town from June 22 to June 24, 2000. Entitled "Human Dignity and Human Rights: Thoughts on the Principles of Human-Centered Design," the paper described HCD as a fundamental "affirmation of human dignity," "an ongoing search for what can be done to support and strengthen the dignity of human beings as they act out their lives in varied social, economic, political, and cultural circumstances."[67] Buchanan's concept of HCD raises important questions about design ethics, a topic addressed in chapters 5 and 10, but his thoughts about Robben Island, where Nelson Mandela and other political prisoners were imprisoned, merit attention here. They are an important illustration of how far HCD has come in the twenty-first century and how far it has yet to go:

> The quality of design is distinguished not merely by technical skill of execution or by aesthetic vision but by the moral and intellectual purpose toward which technical and artistic skill is directed. Robben Island, site of the prison in which Nelson Mandela and other political prisoners were isolated so long from direct participation in the national life of South Africa, is another symbol of twentieth-century design gone mad when it is not grounded on an adequate first principle. It is a symbol of the wrongful use of design to shape a country in a system that denied the essential dignity of all human beings. Robben Island belongs with other disturbing symbols of design in the twentieth century, such as the one that my colleague, Dennis Doordan, chillingly cites. He reminds us that the Holocaust was one of the most thoroughly designed experiences of the twentieth century, with careful attention to every obscene detail.[68]

Design Is Context Specific

Ken Friedman and Erik Stolterman, editors of the MIT Press series on "Design Thinking and Design Theory," summarize their view of design as a "general human process" used "to understand and shape our world." But from their perspective, the process can't be used in "its general abstract form." Rather, designers meet design "in specific challenges, addressing problems and ideas in a situated context" that are as diverse as the problems clients bring to them:

> We are involved in design for economic anchors, economic continuity, and economic growth. We design for urban needs and rural needs, for social development and creative communities. We are involved with environmental sustainability and economic policy, agricultural competitive crafts for export, competitive products and brands for microenterprises, developing new products for bottom-of-pyramid markets and redeveloping old products for mature or wealthy markets. Within the framework of design, we are also challenged to design for extreme situations; for biotech, nanotech, and new materials; for social business; for conceptual challenges for worlds that do not yet exist (such as the world beyond the Kurzweil singularity); and for new visions of the world that does exist.[69]

The designer Eve Blossom certainly agrees, saying, "Design is contextual. It's about doing something appropriate for a particular place and time, for particular individuals, for a particular climate"[70]—what Nelson and Stolterman refer to as the "ultimate particular."[71] And even if designed products are widely distributed, such as the iPhone, they remain unique to their context. An iPhone is not the only way that phones can be designed, nor is it the only way to serve the multiple purposes that this product serves.

Early efforts to situate design in context can be found in Donald Schön's book *The Reflective Practitioner*, in which he described design as a "reflective conversation with the situation."[72] In accordance with a designer's initial appreciation and shaping of a design situation, the designer had to listen to how situations 'talk back,' and then respond "to the situation's back-talk."[73] As designers engage with distinctive medium, they need to listen to the "language" of their materials to guide their choices and decisions in a particular context. Kees Dorst makes a similar point in his discussion of design as "situated activity."[74] Design is conducted through the eyes of designers who face "local" design problems, not "overall," "abstract" problem statements. They derive basic issues and problems from the design brief, which makes their interpretations subjective. Thus, design problems do not objectively exist; rather, they are socially constructed in a particular context. Jesper Simonsen and his colleagues pick up this theme. Designing involves tinkering, negotiating, and making things tangible and intangible in a particular setting. The process also involves interdependencies among designers, their methods and designs, and interactions with other actors and the particulars in the broader context.[75]

Discursive design[76] also taps into context, but in a decidedly different way. Mostly found in exhibitions, print, film, and the research process, its purpose is to create utilitarian objects, services, and interactions as instruments that provoke reflections about substantive and debatable issues in context. When ideas from these instruments get internalized, they may result not only in the viewer's changes in behavior, but in ripple effects throughout society, as did Julia Lohmann's 2004 full-sized cow-benches upholstered with a single cowhide, which received a great deal of press and raised concerns about the use of animals as raw material.[77]

Design Is Exploration Driven

Design challenges, given to a designer from a client or an authorizing agent, are often abstract and not well defined or bounded, especially in wicked problem territory where problems and solutions are contested. People have a general sense that something is not quite right or there is something they want to achieve, but they don't know how to be more specific about it. This is why they have asked for a designer's help in the first place. It then is incumbent on designers to take a "deep dive" to explore the context. In the case of the Norwegian Special Operations Command (NORSOCOM), which is explored in detail in chapter 6, the commander of Norway Special Operations asked how the Norwegian Special Operations Force (NORSOF) should be designed for 2025 to address the potential challenges that it would likely face in the future. A very broad and general question like this one is typical of the design challenges in wicked problem territory, and they require deep exploration of the context before the design team can identify a more specific design purpose or problem. In this case, the design team began its exploration using three data-gathering approaches to explore the design space: *archival searches*, *interviews*, and *observations*.

Archival searches probe the literature for policies, documents, studies, and reports that might be relevant to the design challenge. In the NORSOCOM case, the design team began by attempting to understand the political, economic, environmental, social, and cultural trends anticipated within the next fifteen years. The team then focused more particularly on Norway's unique features that might counter or reinforce these trends or even add new twists to worldwide ones, such as Norway's involvement with Russia, the United States, Canada, and Greenland in the Arctic Circle. And finally, the team explored internal and external issues related to Norwegian Special Operations Forces that it was expected to confront in the next fifteen years, taking into account such things as its specializations in Artic maneuvers, its recent terrorist attacks, and its border and relationship with Russia, given its close proximity to Russia's heavily militarized Kola Peninsula, home to its Northern Fleet and Artic main combat forces.

Interviews involve informal questions and interactions with people whose knowledge, expertise, and experience might shed some light on the design challenge and their involvement in it. In the Norwegian example, people came from Norwegian and US government agencies and departments, and industries, and the Norwegian and international military personnel ranged in positions from the technical to the strategic levels of organizations.

Observations require designers to be present in actual work situations to see what people are doing as they go about their various activities. A great example comes from IDEO, an international consulting firm that the US navy hired to do some redesign work for the submarine community. Designers "rode submarines" to get a feel for life on a sub and shadowed submariners at their duty stations as they maneuvered subs through their training missions. Together with the crews, they identified problems and generated solutions to address them. Design teams that I have supervised also have participated in meetings, observed departmental workflows, and joined work teams to get a feel for the environment and how people engaged with one another and completed their tasks.

Some refer to these data-gathering exercises as "research." As a social scientist, as well as a designer, I reserve the term "research" to describe the scientific process that I use to build theory or to test theory about phenomena such as trying to understand people and their behavior. When I engage in design, I collect archival records, conduct discussions and interviews, and make on-site observations for the purpose of trying to understand the context of design challenge and to empathize with the people who live in it. I also can switch hats and become a social scientist conducting research about the design process and its outputs and outcomes as noted previously. Thus, designers can play two "roles," but serving in both at the same time is difficult since each serves a different purpose. Researchers test and build theory using the scientific process; designers create something new using the "designerly way of knowing."

I believe that much of the confusion between design and design research is the result of designers using some of the techniques that anthropologists, sociologists, and other qualitative researchers typically employ, such as interviews and participant observations. The use of these techniques does not automatically make designers researchers in the scientific sense of the word. Design data collection tends to be informal, time bound, and less attentive to documentation and sampling procedures required of scientific research. Borrowing from the title of Evelyn Fox Keller's book about Barbara McClintock, I liken the designer's data-collection effort as getting a "feeling for the organism."[78] Or, as Sanders and Stappers describe it, data collection is part of "the fuzzy front end" of design.[79] Formally called "predesign," the front end describes the many activities that take place that inform the exploration of open-ended design challenges such as, "How should NORSOF be designed for 2025 to address the challenges it will be facing?" This initial phase is messy and full of ambiguity and uncertainty as designers attempt to clarify what the challenge "really" means, what the sponsor "really wants," what the problem "really" is, and what the deliverable of the design process will "actually" be.

Design Is Creativity Dependent

Designers view creativity as infusing all aspects of design: being attentive to the nuances in the context, framing problems, and prototyping and testing solutions.[80] Beginning with imaginative "aha" moments that delight and surprise us with their novelty, creativity becomes the search engine for new ways of thinking and engaging in whatever activity designers do. Research on creativity is voluminous, with many theories and diverse perspectives that have engendered contemporary debate.[81] Psychologist Robert Sternberg, after years of studying creative people, concludes that they have one thing in common: "they decided to be creative." The decision to be creative "does not guarantee that creativity will emerge, but without the decision, it certainly will not."[82] Beyond deciding to be creative, experts identify what people can do to spark and cultivate their creativity. They can possess and develop particular attributes and intellectual habits and exploratory behaviors such as flexibility, openness, and inquisitiveness; employ particular thinking processes such as divergent thinking and visual thinking; write stories, draw pictures, generate ideas and create artifacts; and open themselves up to particular places and situations that reinforce curiosity rather than rote learning and conformity and offer access to resources.[83] Ultimately, people who make the decision to be creative and act on it are described as being creatively confident, playful, humorous, insightful, imaginative, intuitive, inspirational, courageous, and risk takers.

According to many who study creativity, we all have creative capacities but we don't all exercise or develop them. Indeed, many of us suffer from what James Adams calls "conceptual blocks"—perceptual, emotional, cultural, environmental, and thinking blocks—that impede our ability to be creative.[84] For those whose blocks have arrested their creative development, we need "creative confidence." According to Tom and David Kelley, "creative confidence is like a muscle—it can be strengthened and nurtured through effort and experience."[85] By changing people's intellectual habits, processes, and workplaces, the Kelly brothers "have been stunned at how quickly people's imagination, curiosity, and courage are renewed with just a small amount of practice and encouragement."[86]

A person can be the catalyst of creativity, but so can design teams. Indeed, Tom and David Kelly consider "creativity as a team sport"[87] since the best ideas often are the result of working with others, not from a lone genius. Many creatives acknowledged for their innovations had extensive design teams who joined and supported them in their work. Thomas Edison had a large lab that was central to his many designs. Steve Jobs had legions of people who worked with him and shared his vision for new designs and products. These examples and many others illustrate that to move ideas beyond a flash of insight requires long, hard work from a group of people who hone, shape, and improve the ideas to ensure that they actually work in practice. Even during implementation, things rarely go as anticipated, so constant updates and changes to the prototypes are needed. Thus, creativity is core to a designer's identity and aspirations as an individual and a team member. Whether described in terms of individual attributes, the design process, design results, or places where designers work, creativity is foundational.

Design Is Prototype Anchored
Developing new ideas and explaining them to others can be challenging. Even if designers find the right words and concepts, people can interpret what they hear very differently. Communication is quicker and easier when we show rather than tell others what we mean. Designers have found a shorthand way to communicate their new ideas. They "think with their hands" and generate protypes—small-scale designs or props that can take the form of drawings on napkins, images, storyboards, customer journey maps, mock-ups, skits, role-plays, scenarios, or whatever designers think best captures the essence of the new idea. Required materials are whatever is handy—paper, cardboard, foam, wood, and others—to fashion a physical approximation of the new

idea. Designers follow two simple rules of prototyping: "make it tangible" and "make it a good story."[88]

Thus, in creating prototypes, designers connect their imagined idea to something tangible and real so that others can see, experience, and probe it. Early prototypes are rudimentary—"fast, rough, and cheap"—so that designers can learn what works and what doesn't and quickly zero in on the best ideas and refine them without wasting money and time on ideas with less merit, commanding "only as much time, effort, and investment as is necessary to generate useful feedback and drive an idea forward."[89] Although there are many approaches to prototyping, "they share a single, paradoxical feature: They slow us down to speed us up."[90] By taking the time to prototype ideas, designers avoid costly mistakes, such as being too complex too early and sticking with a weak idea too long. Prototypes are not expected to work flawlessly, nor are they expected to be something of beauty. A successful prototype is "one that teaches us something—about our objectives, our process, and ourselves."[91] When feedback suggests that the prototype has value and merits continuation, then prototypes can move to higher fidelity or resolution.

Prototyping has other benefits. When designers learn by doing, the prototype becomes the springboard to their imaginations; they use it to unlock additional insights, think of new ideas, learn about the prototype's strengths and weaknesses, and identify what improvements and changes need to be made. As Brian Collins, a designer who teaches at New York's School of Visual Arts, observes, "a designer has one foot in imagination and one in craft. Envisioning "what might be" and by building representations of that idea, "the designer can put a version of the future in your hands and ask, 'Is this what we all want?'"[92]

Design Is Testing Reliant

Answering the question "Is this what we all want?" is a request for feedback on design prototypes. Designers make that request very seriously and often learn in the responses "that we didn't know as much as we thought we did about this idea."[93] The point is to reveal whatever flaws and limitations exist in the prototypes, and to do so quickly before designs become finished products and services that cost too much, don't appeal to the users, don't do the job they are supposed to do, are so error-prone they are unusable, or have unintended consequences that are worse than the problem they set out to solve. Their advice is to fail early and fail often, in order to succeed sooner.

I am reminded of the USS *Independence*, a navy littoral combat ship that was designed to be fast, highly maneuverable, and operational on the high seas and shallow coastlines—the littorals. Apparently "dissimilar metals" (i.e., when the aluminum hull interacted with salt water and other metals) produced extensive corrosion. The problem became so severe that the *Independence* had to be sent into dry dock for corrosion repairs and major design changes.[94] A navy ship that can't operate in salt water without corroding is hard to fathom, but it is an unfortunate demonstration of what happens when soliciting feedback is not taken as seriously as it needs to be.

Feedback is about figuring out what went wrong and what you need to do differently next time so you don't repeat your errors. And making the needed changes sooner rather than later saves money and time. Depending on the design project, feedback can be informal, such as undergoing rounds and rounds of feedback from team members during prototyping. Feedback also can be more formal, such as bringing in potential users to offer their opinions or most important, scheduling feedback sessions with sponsors to solicit their views on what is working or not, what offers possibilities for further development, or other pathways and ideas that hold greater promise.

No matter how one solicits and gives feedback, it needs to be as specific as possible. What do you like in the prototype; what works in its design? If something isn't working, what exactly is the problem—its size, shape, color, sustainability, human-centeredness, or something else? Also, if reviewers have suggestions, designers should welcome them, although they have the option of ignoring them (since it is their design, after all). But ignoring feedback comes with risks, especially when the prototypes are tested during implementation and the ship begins to sink.

Design Is Implementation Attentive

Designers put a high premium on their designs, and in the past they have shown less concern with how their designs actually work in practice. The wealthy industrialist Hibbard Johnson telephoned Frank Lloyd Wright, the eminent home designer, to complain that his roof was leaking and rain was dripping on his head. Wright is said to have retorted: "Why don't you move your chair?"[95] The priority of designs over their execution has been so widespread that Norman estimates that 75–95 percent of industrial accidents attributed to human error are mostly design errors. Instead of blaming humans, he proposes that we design and redesign our systems so they don't produce the errors in the first place.[96] Thus, design is no longer given free rein to trump reality; it now has to embrace it. The criteria for "good design" have expanded well beyond human desirability. Designers are expected to take into account and balance the often-competing constraints of feasibility, viability, desirability, and sustainability, and to face the consequences when things don't turn out as anticipated.

With the widening scope of design into more and more complex problems, designers in wicked problem territory are out of their studios and into the field to help people clean up the environment, improve cities and their infrastructures, deal with aging populations, transform education, and redesign health care. Designers who tackle challenges of this magnitude no longer see barriers between designing something and doing something. And the meaning of "doing something" has expanded beyond creating, prototyping, and testing ideas; it now includes actually implementing and evaluating prototypes in the field.[97] At the vanguard of this massive shift, we find designers like Bruce Mau helping Guatemala to design its future, Coca-Cola to design greater sustainability into its products and processes, and Arizona State University to reinvent education. All these design efforts require designers to work closely with people who are responsible and accountable for implementing the new ideas and practices.

This shift in design, sometimes referred to as "transformational design," or in Bruce Mau's term, "massive change," calls upon designers to move beyond creating things and instead orchestrating experiences in practice.[98] And with this expanded view, the definition of design has evolved from "the conscious and intuitive effort to impose meaningful order,"[99] to "the capacity to plan and produce desired outcomes,"[100] to "the power . . . to shape the world around us."[101]

Design and Innovation

One additional issue in this overview of the *what* of design is the relationship between design and innovation. Is design a phase in the innovation process? Or is design interspersed throughout the innovation process? Figure 3.1 illustrates how design is conceptualized as a phase in the policy innovation process.[102] My colleague Paula King and I found this pattern when conducting a longitudinal study of policy entrepreneurs in Minnesota. The policy entrepreneurs had developed a new idea—school choice—and they designed and fleshed out its details in position papers and reports (their prototypes), which they then circulated to others for feedback and revisions. When lawmakers introduced the reframed prototype (public school choice) as a bill in the legislature, and it went through revisions and ultimately became law and was successfully implemented in public schools, it was deemed to be an innovation. Eventually, the innovation was accepted as standard practice and institutionalized throughout the state of Minnesota.

Although engineers use different words, they describe the engineering process in similar terminology, at least for the first three phases.[103] *Initiation* begins the process with an early statement of the design brief, a statement of the problem, and the conceptualization and documentation of design solutions. During the second phase, *design*, often described as the production stage, engineers develop and continue to improve a solution and then test it in situ. The third phase, *implementation*, is the postproduction phase, when the designed solution is introduced to the environment. The redesign phase repeats any or all stages with corrections made before, during, or after production. Sir George Cox, the former chair of the Design Council in London, is a proponent of this view of design as a stage in the innovation process. He considers creativity as the

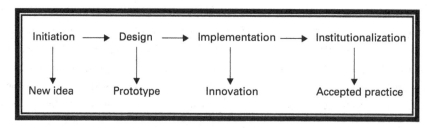

Figure 3.1
Design as a phase in policy innovation and engineering processes

generation of new ideas, innovation as the successful exploitation of new ideas, and design as "what links creativity and innovation."[104]

Describing design as "what links creativity and innovation" suggests that design is being narrowly construed as prototyping or production, as exemplified in policy design and engineering design. In contrast, design writ large offers a more holistic concept that captures an entire spectrum of activities, including the generation of new ideas and their prototyping and implementation in the field. I suspect that these two conceptualizations of design are a result of the residual tensions between the rational model and the reflection-in-action model of designing. It is more likely that the rational model sees design as a phase of the innovation process, while the reflection-in-action model portrays design as a dynamic flow of activities and interactions throughout the innovation process. Clearly, this linkage between the design and innovation merits further attention.

We know that both design and innovation produce output (things, products, or services). Both highlight the importance of creativity and the newness of ideas. Both are attentive to process: design is the generation of new ideas, the transformation and testing of the new ideas as prototypes, and the implementation prototypes into practice. Innovation involves the invention, development, and implementation of ideas.[105] And any idea is an innovation to the extent that the "idea, practice, or material artifact [is] perceived to be new by the relevant unit of adoption."[106] Both design and innovation develop ideas that produce different types of changes from first-order change (e.g., "change that occurs within a given system which itself remains unchanged")[107] to second-order change (e.g., "change that changes the body of rules governing a system's structure or internal order").[108] Both make distinctions between evolutionary and revolutionary change and between incremental and radical change, although there appears to be little consistency in either source on how these terms are defined and utilized.[109]

The similarities between design and innovation suggest that these two fields of endeavor are mutually compatible, although some observe that the concept of design thinking "seem[s] to be somewhat stuck in between the fields of innovation and design."[110] The difference appears to be that design thinking is more attentive to how the innovation process unfolds and builds innovative capacities.[111] As Tim Brown, the former chief executive officer (CEO) and president of IDEO, pointed out, "where you innovate, how you innovate, and what you innovate are design problems."[112] Moreover, the design process is "a system of spaces" of related activities "rather than a predefined series of orderly steps," which "together form the continuum of innovation."[113] This growing convergence between design and innovation has led at least one design researcher to conclude that "innovation and design thinking have become inseparable."[114] From this vantage point, it is not a stretch to consider design and innovation converging to the point that their differences do not add up to much of a distinction, so long as design thinking extends to and includes prototype implementation in the field. Implementation and evaluation are central to design thinking. Without them, designers may never know whether their designs have succeeded or failed, or which aspects of their designs need to be adapted, a point not always made clear in design process models that stop at in situ prototyping and testing. And finally, as Hernandez and colleagues[115] demonstrated, when this connection between design and innovation is forged,

> design language—communication based on visual tools, design development techniques, and research methods . . . effectively [becomes] the language of innovation. Design practices, design visualizations, and design methods—not to mention the push toward integrating design thinking—often form the common ground upon which conversations can be built in the complex context of innovation process. Design language, indeed, *is* the language of innovation.[116]

Design as Process

Lucy Kimbell identifies two streams of thought about design. The first views design as giving form to material objects. Christopher Alexander hails from this perspective when he describes design as giving "form, organization, and order to physical things."[117] Thus, material things are evident in the many subfields of design: architects design our homes; product designers design computers and iPhones; and aeronautical engineers design modules and ships that take us to the Moon and return us safely to Earth.

A second stream of thought, originating in the 1960s, focuses on how designers go about designing. Originating as an emphasis on design methods, interest gradually shifted toward how "[successful] designers went about design activity."[118] The emphasis came to be on designers' thoughts and actions as they designed, characterized by researchers as "design thinking,"[119] "designerly ways of knowing, thinking and action,"[120] and "reflection-in action."[121]

Kees Dorst and Judith Dijkhus further distinguished two models of designing: the "rational model" and "reflection-in-action."[122] Herbert Simon, in the *Sciences of the Artificial*,[123] is best-known for his view of design as a rational set of procedures. Evolving over time, the model typically involves a six-step process: define the problem, identify the decision criteria, generate alternative solutions to the problem, calculate the expected consequences of the alternative solutions, apply the decision criteria, and select the optimal solution.

In contrast to the rational model, the reflection-in-action model, as initially described by Donald Schön, views the design process as intuitive, dynamic, and iterative, especially suited to situations of uncertainty and conflict. Neither a predictable nor a linear process, design solutions derive from designers' imagination, creativity, insights, and skills in problem solving. Project goals are often unknown or contested when projects are launched, and as a result, project requirements and constraints continually evolve and change over time. Moreover, as the goals, requirements, and constraints evolve, so do design problems and their solutions. Thus, designers make no claims of optimality for their solutions.

In an attempt to clarify how designers actually design, researchers have conducted numerous empirical studies using different methodologies, including the following:

- Interviewed designers to gain their insights and reflections on what designers did for specific projects or in general terms
- Observed designers as they worked
- Conducted retrospective case studies to capture the designer's major activities and steps in the design process
- Artificially constructed and reconstructed design projects to view the unfolding process
- Conducted experimental studies where they ask the designer to think aloud as she or he does a specific task and then sort the statements and associated actions into protocols for analysis to distinguish differences between design experts and novices
- Used artificial intelligence (AI) techniques to simulate and understand human thinking
- Reflected and theorized about the nature of design ability[124]

The findings are fairly consistent. When asking designers what they do, deconstructing what designers do, and thinking about what designers do,[125] a general consensus has emerged. Designers do not design as the rational model says they should. Instead, their process is more in keeping with the reflection-in-action model. However, despite designers' proclivities for creativity and experimental thinking, they gravitate toward some kind of preferred design process. As Bruce Mau explains it, the design process becomes a "safety net" that enables experimentation: "People feel more comfortable experimenting with new ideas and venturing into unfamiliar turf when they carry with them an established method of working and solving problems. It means that even if they don't quite know what they're doing, they always know what to do."[126] Or as Kai Joffres explains it, "design processes don't give us good design—they're merely a scaffolding to help us get there."[127] Jeanne Liedtka has found similar results in her research, especially among novices. Using a structured process "appeared to free their creativity rather than stifle it: a highly structured approach to [design thinking] created engagement and produced psychological safety within teams that supported trying new behaviors—sometimes in the face of hostile external environments that viewed [design thinking] with suspicion."[128] Or, as one of her interviewees from Intuit explained:

> Anytime you're trying to change people's behavior, you need to start them off with a lot of structure so they don't have to think. A lot of what we do is habit, and it's hard to change those habits. So by having very clear guard rails, we help people to change their habits. And then once they've done it 20 or 30 times, *then* they can start to play jazz as opposed to learning how to play scales.[129]

Hugh Dubberly, in *How Do You Design? A Compendium of Models*, has compiled an extensive list of the models used in the design process—over 100 design and development processes from architecture, industrial design, mechanical engineering, quality management, and software development.[130] Although designers' goals, results, actions, and project scales differ, he is clear that what makes them similar "is that they are designing."

In what follows, I describe some of the better-known "handrails" that designers use to map their way as thinkers and doers in the design process. With variations, they all combine some form of problem framing, ideation, and implementation in the design thinking process.[131]

Tim Brown's Model of Design Thinking's Core Spaces and Activities

Tim Brown, the former CEO of the international consulting company IDEO, introduced three core spaces and activities of design thinking: inspiration, ideation, and implementation.[132] As shown in figure 3.2,[133] during *inspiration*, designers find a problem or an opportunity that motivates the search for solutions. They then go out into the world to interact with experts, put themselves in unfamiliar situations, connect with people to gain empathy for their needs and desires, conduct interviews, and observe people's behavior in their natural environment. The purpose of all these activities is to understand the major factors central to the design challenge and to trigger insights and ideas to launch their innovative efforts. *Ideation* is the generation, development, and testing of creative ideas. During this core activity, the designer explores many options to address the design challenge. Central to these efforts is building low-resolution prototypes to assist in the shaping, refining, testing, and selecting ideas with the most promise. *Implementation*, the final set of activities, is the pathway from the design shop to the market. It involves doing what it takes to communicate, demonstrate, and often adapt prototypes to local conditions to gain people's acceptance. The arrows in the graphic underscore the point that the activities are interconnected and iterative. Design doesn't progress in an orderly, linear, or step-by-step process. The designer can and does cycle back and forth through all activities during the life of the project.

Tom and David Kelley, respectively the general manager and cofounder of IDEO, build on Brown's model by adding an additional phase called *synthesis*.[135] They refer to this as "sense making," when designers identify themes, recognize patterns, and find meaning in what they have discovered during the inspiration phase. Designers typically use various data reduction techniques such as empathy maps and matrices to help them organize the data during synthesis. Refining the data and making sense of it often lead to a redefinition of the initial design problem and a refocusing of the design

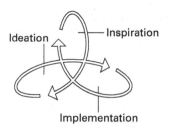

Figure 3.2
IDEO's three core activities of design thinking. *Source*: OpenIDEO, "Design Thinking Defined"[134]

project. With the addition of this phase, we have a four-phase model of design thinking: inspiration, synthesis, ideation/experimentation, and implementation.[136]

Jeanne Liedtka has a variant on the four-phase model, but she uses different terms to describe the phases: *What is? What if? What wows? What works?*[137] During the *What is?* phase, designers gather data, identify insights, and establish design criteria to bound the design problem (e.g., resources needed, time required, and constraints imposed). During the *What if?* phase, designers brainstorm ideas and develop concepts. During the *What wows?* phase, designers surface key assumptions, generate ideas, and make rapid prototypes. During the *What works?* phase, designers solicit feedback from stakeholders to shape the prototype into something that can be executed, conduct quick and inexpensive experiments in the marketplace (e.g., run learning launches), and enroll customers by designing on-ramps to how to use the prototype and enlist others in its use.

Don Norman's cycle of HCD also has four phases: *observation*; *idea generation*; *prototyping*; and *testing,* as shown in figure 3.4.[138] In his model, we see the variations that designers introduce to describe roughly the same phases: observation (inspiration or What is?); idea generation (ideation or What if?); prototyping (experimentation or What wows?), and testing (implementation or What works?). Norman also has a notation in his original diagram that underscores the iterative nature of the design process. He notes that the designer repeats the four phases until he or she is satisfied with the design.

Stanford's Hasso Plattner Institute of Design offers a five-phase model of design thinking: *empathy, define, ideate, prototype,* and *test,* as shown in figure 3.5.[139] It adds *define*, a problem-definition phase that is similar to the Kelleys' synthesis phase. It also substitutes the term "empathy" instead of "observation" or "What is?" to emphasize the strong connection that designers need to establish between the context and the people for whom they are designing. The placement of the hexagons in figure 3.5 also distinguishes the two phases of problem solving. *Empathize* and *define* are basic phases in problem identification, while *ideate, prototype,* and *test* are phases of the solution-generation and selection phases. The Stanford model also picks up the theme

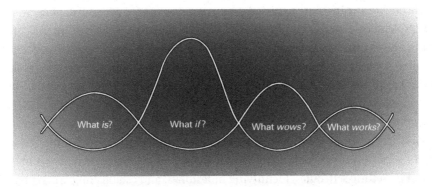

Figure 3.3
Liedtka's four-phase model of design thinking

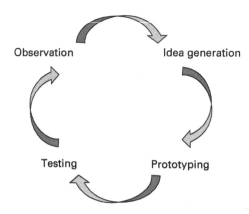

Figure 3.4
Norman's iterative cycle of HCD

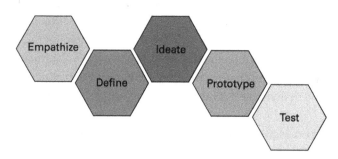

Figure 3.5
The Hasso Plattner Institute's five-phase model of design thinking

of convergence and divergence in positioning the hexagons. The downward flow from *empathize* to *define*, from *ideate* to *prototype*, and then to *test* are all meant to convey convergence. The upward flow from *define* to *ideate* illustrates divergence and the generation of new ideas when transitioning from problem finding to solution generation.

Based on my work in wicked problem territory, I decided to make some additions to the Hasso Plattner Institute model. As shown in figure 3.6, I added two phases—initiate and implement. *Initiation* begins with a design challenge, usually a general question that activates interests and gives direction to a design project. It involves identifying potential sponsors and gaining their commitment; making plans how the project will be resourced, funded, and launched; and building a team. Preparations can be long and complex during this phase, so the initiate phase expands designers' typical tasks beyond those in a traditional design brief. Design briefs are a contract between a client and the designer that identifies the general problem or opportunity, establishes the constraints under which the designers work, and gives a sense of direction for the project by setting schedules, identifying milestones, and establishing criteria by which the design outputs and outcomes will be measured. When first launching a design project in wicked problem territory, it is usually premature to expect this level of detail.

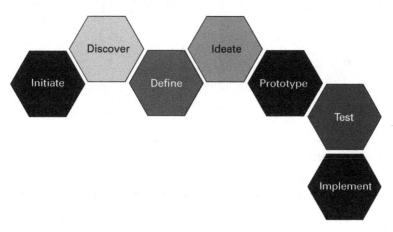

Figure 3.6
Roberts seven-phase model of design thinking in wicked problem territory

Defining a problem is "the problem" in wicked problem territory, so considerable time and effort go into problem framing before any milestones and criteria or design outputs and outcomes can be identified, let alone measured.

Implementation, anchoring the other end of the design thinking model, is a much more complex effort in wicked problem territory. Moving complex prototypes into the field, as we will see in chapters 6, 7, and 8, requires more than testing in design studios, labs, or market launches. Solutions proposed in wicked problem territory tend to be disruptive and often require changes in people's beliefs and values and transformation of systems in which they live and work. Thus, I highlight implementation as a separate phase in the design process due to the high level of fieldwork required, especially in communities whose physical, social, political, and economic situations are being designed or redesigned. And given the complexity of these design projects, it is not unusual for field-based implementations of new designs to recycle back into earlier phases of the design process, as we will see in part III of this book.

I also retitled the second phase of the design thinking to *discover* (with empathy), as seen in figure 3.6. This shift in emphasis is not to deny the importance of empathy but to signal that designers can and do use a range of data collection techniques beyond interviews and participant observations when empathy is demonstrably required. Designers also dig through archival records to review research pertinent to the design challenge. They glean insights from previous studies and surveys. And they read biographies and case studies of people and their communities, and other information.

Regardless of which design process model one uses, the assumption is that design is an iterative process not a linear one. Feedback loops can flow from define back to discovery when designers need a finer-grained understanding of the context. Ideation may lead back to problem definition, and even a return to the field for more data collection. Prototyping surfaces issues that may require restarts in problem definition and new ideas. And testing can prompt a renewal of the whole design effort.

Figure 3.7
Damien Newman's design squiggle

Damien Newman illustrates the messiness of the process using the design squiggle shown in figure 3.7.[140] He wanted to demonstrate to his clients how the creative process looks and feels like when going through it—unpredictable, uncertain, with many feedback loops throughout the process. The line begins to settle somewhat as some consensus emerges around key insights, concepts, and ideas, although iterations are still part of the process. Prototyping and lab-based testing provide more direction, but so-called failures and lessons learned can prompt a return to any phase of the design process. What is not included in Newman's model is the field-based testing that is characteristic of more complex designs in wicked problem territory. As we review in part III, prototyping and testing can take years before a design is accepted into practice.

In Summary

This chapter began with a brief summary of design's history, discourses, and major fields and subfields; growing landscape (design's types, levels, and domains); basic principles; and a clarification of the differences between design and innovation. It ended with an overview of the variations and descriptions of the design process. But there is more to the design story. In chapter 4, we begin to probe designers' interior world—their mindsets and consciousness that inform their values, attitudes, understandings, and actions. This probing opens the topic of metadesign—designers' intentional interventions to alter people's cultural values, beliefs, and consciousness to change their downstream design choices.

4 Design Strategist's Mindsets and Metadesigns

> The ultimate object of design is not artifacts, buildings, or landscapes,
> but human minds.
> —David Orr, 2001

While chapter 3 explored the exterior world of design, this chapter takes an inward turn. Its purpose is to explore designers' mindsets, which inform their values, shape their underlying assumptions, and guide their practice. Efforts to define the concept of a mindset[1] and operationalize it[2] are ongoing. Nonetheless, I have identified seven mindsets for designers that can serve as examples: growth mindset, benefit mindset, hyperattuned mindset, imaginative mindset, analytical mindset, maker-mindset, and change agent mindset.

The review of designers' mindsets opens up the related topic of metadesign—intentional interventions to alter people's values, beliefs, and consciousness to inform their downstream design choices.[3] The assumption is that many wicked problems surface because our worldviews and consciousnesses play a large part in creating them. So if designers are to deal with the life conditions of wicked problems and move out of wicked problem territory, they need to not only evolve their own consciousness but the consciousness of people they serve. Some designers see this as the major design challenge for the twenty-first century and concur with David Orr that "the ultimate object of design is not artifacts, buildings, or landscapes, but human minds."[4] Fortunately we have a vanguard of designers (four of whom are introduced in this chapter), who can guide us in this exploration of metadesign. They are helping us change our narrative to "give up what we know and who we are for what we could become,"[5] and to "bring forth a world not just through what we are doing, but through the quality of our being."[6]

Mindsets

Growth Mindset

Carol Dweck identified two general mindsets or self-perceptions that people hold about themselves.[7] People with a fixed mindset believe that their basic qualities, such as intelligence and talent, are stable and unchanging rather than developed. Instead of expanding their capabilities, they limit themselves to the abilities that they assume they have inherited. People with a growth mindset believe that their basic abilities and talents can be developed with dedication and hard work. Thus, a growth mindset affirms that a person's true potential is unknowable; it is not possible to foresee what anyone can accomplish or how much they can grow if they put their minds to it.

Designers align with a growth mindset. Regardless of their initial talent, aptitude, or IQ, they believe that it is possible for them to expand their capabilities with dedication, passion, training, and experience. As Tom and David Kelley define it, a growth mindset is a belief that your skills are not set in stone. You "believe that learning and growth are possible," "a belief that becomes your passport to new adventures."[8] To develop a growth mindset, Bruce Mau offers this advice: "Allow events to change you. You have to be willing to grow. Growth is different from something that happens to you. You produce it. You live it." [9] Roger Martin, author and former dean of the Rotman School of Management at the University of Toronto, adds: "designers live in an expansive world where they believe the only thing limiting [them] is the stuff [they] haven't figured out yet. And they're excited about it. You'll hear them say things like, 'I'm working on this really cool problem that has no answer!' That's what they live for."[10] What all this advice amounts to is designers deliberately puting themselves in situations that allow them to push the edge of the envelope, test their limits, and try new, even radical ideas.

Benefit Mindset

The benefit mindset entails questioning why we do what we do and searching for ways to make a meaningful difference in the world. It promotes individual and collective well-being and seeks to bring out the best in one another and the world, "not only being the best *in* the world, but also being the best *for* the world."[11] The benefit mindset derives from the "being well" perspective in positive psychology[12] and a "doing good" perspective in socially and environmentally engaged communities and organizations.[13] It is also informed by human development theory, such as Jane Loevinger's ego development theory[14] and Bill Torbert's action inquiry of leadership,[15] which describe how people can mature in terms of their meaning making and action logics to deal with the complexities of life.

An example of this emphasis on well-being and design is Annemarie Mink's work on *Design for Well-Being: An Approach for Understanding Users' Lives in Design for Development*. According to her findings, design's current toolkits and manuals are unsuited for users, particularly those in marginalized and disadvantaged communities. Based on poorly defined needs and preferences, standard toolkits and manuals do not clarify which information or insights should be collected to derive a full understanding of "users' valued beings and doings."[16] Drawing on insights from human-centered design (HCD) and from Nobel laureate Amartya Sen's capability approach,[17] Mink developed a social needs inventory to guide designers in conducting rapid and comprehensive user research, specifically in development projects. When using the inventory that explores users' potential and well-being, she finds that designers are better prepared and positioned to make informed decisions that improve the acceptance and adoption of their designs.

Hyperattuned Mindset

The hyperattuned mindset is wide open and all the designer's senses are on high alert, especially at the outset of a project. Bruce Mau describes it as a period of "not knowing" and a feeling of being "lost in the woods." As a consequence, "everything about your surroundings takes on added significance." "Suddenly you have to navigate and negotiate every detail of the environment, processing all of it while trying to regain your bearings."[18] Mau makes the analogy to the military's "fog of war," when "soldiers often make quick, instinctual decisions based on limited and degraded information." Similarly, designers have to "see through the haze, recognize the important pieces of information that are available . . . and ultimately trust their instincts."[19]

The challenge of developing this hyperattuned mindset is being open-minded, observant, and curious. According to Mau, it requires designers to do the following:

- "Listen carefully. Every collaborator who enters our orbit brings with him or her a world more strange and complex than any we could ever hope to imagine. By listening to the details and the subtlety of their needs, desires, or ambitions, we fold their world onto our own. Neither party will ever be the same."

- "Think like a traveler. Like a visitor to a foreign land, try turning fresh eyes on your surroundings, no matter how mundane or familiar. . . . Expose yourself to new ideas and experiences."

- "Ask questions, starting with 'why?' . . . to get to the heart of the matter."

- Assume "relaxed attention," which lies between meditation, when the mind is completely cleared, and a "laserlike focus" when the mind is tackling a tough problem. Relaxed attention provides space to the brain to make cognitive leaps.

- "Go deep. The deeper you go the more likely you will discover something of value."

- "Drift. Allow yourself to wander aimlessly. Explore adjacencies. Lack judgment. Postpone criticism."

- "Slow down. Desynchronize from standard time frames and surprising opportunities may present themselves."

- "Stay up late. Strange things happen when you've gone too far, been up too long, worked too hard, and you're separated from the rest of the world."[20]

Imaginative Mindset

Imagination is a basic human capability. When imagining, we bring forth images or concepts that are not real or present to our senses, but appear in our mind's eye. The psychologist Lev Vygotsky views imagination as the basis of all creativity and "an important component of absolutely all aspects of cultural life, enabling artistic, scientific, and technical creation alike."[21] Others certainly agree; as Albert Einstein reportedly said, the true sign of intelligence is imagination, not knowledge, and Sir Ken Robinson's body of work proclaims, "imagination is the source of all human achievement." Designers also see the close connection between imagination and creativity. Harold Nelson and Erik Stolterman maintain that "in order to create something, one must have the ability to imagine what the something is and how it can be made real. Imagination is required within all fields and all phases of design."[22] It led Mads Folkmann, in *The Aesthetics of Imagination in Design*, to view imagination to be "vital in design, as it is in all human thinking and creation. When we imagine, we obtain a visually oriented abstraction that can take us in new directions and lead us to examine new possibilities."[23] Robinson's story of a little girl makes the point quite well:

> An elementary school teacher was giving a drawing class to a group of six-year-old children. At the back of the classroom sat a little girl who normally didn't pay much attention in school. In the drawing class she did. For more than twenty minutes, the girl sat with her arms curled around her paper, totally absorbed in what she was doing. The teacher found this fascinating. Eventually, she asked the girl what she was drawing. Without looking up, the girl said, "I'm drawing a picture of God." Surprised, the teacher said, "But nobody knows what God looks like." The girl said, "They will in a minute."[24]

To be clear, imagination and creativity are not the same. "Imagination is the image-making power of the mind."[25] It enables us to form concepts, images, and even sensations in our mind. To imagine is to see the impossible or unreal, or what Einstein supposedly described as "a preview of life's coming attractions." In contrast, to create is to give form and shape to what the imagination evokes by transforming it into something concrete and tangible that can be shared with others. As Ann Pendleton-Julian and John Seely Brown explain it in their book *Pragmatic Imagination*,[26] imagination is without pragmatic intent; it enables us to find connections that are not obvious, play with boundaries and jump fences, and see unlikely relationships. In contrast, the intent of creativity is to generate things that have real-world purpose.

Analytic Mindset

The analytic mindset involves reflecting, reasoning, and examining something in a systematic way. It is particularly important in wicked problem territory, given the complexity of the design process. Vast amounts of data can be collected during discovery, especially in the strategic design of organizations (chapter 6), the systemic design of social systems (chapter 7), and the regenerative design of social and natural systems (chapter 8). Designers likely will be engaged in archival research that requires them to collect and sift through piles of documents on a wide-ranging set of topics. They will conduct one-on-one interviews, even group interviews, taking and condensing notes using an agreed-upon format. They will make observations in the field, immersing themselves in the life experiences of the people for whom they are designing, careful to capture what they have seen, heard, and experienced in a systematic way. As they engage in these data collection activities, they will have to decide which data are relevant, how to organize the data into topics and themes so they can review and analyze them with other team members, and eventually come to agreement as a team on how to interpret them. As Jeanne Liedtka and colleagues warn, "a sea of data is only as good as what you can learn from it, so a good design thinker takes time to look for patterns and insights in the mountain of notes."[27]

Beyond these initial qualitative data collection and analytic exercises, the design team may elect to employ quantitative techniques such as social network analysis and geospatial analysis, illustrated in chapter 5, which can be utilized to probe for underlying patterns in people's interactions and relationships that are difficult to see directly during field observations or elicit from interviews. Equally important, designers, throughout the data collection, data analysis, and data interpretation processes, will be looking for ways to understand how the many data pieces might fit together as an integrative whole. How might the data be reconfigured as a system, especially one that might produce undesirable and unintended consequences? Can the system and its interconnecting parts be described and diagrammed? And once the system's underlying dynamics are more fully explored and understood, can the designer identify what factors are driving the poor results? If located, the problem sources then become the focal point of design interventions to generate new ideas as solutions as illustrated in chapter 6. The analytical work continues, as prototyping often requires specialized knowledge and competencies, especially if advanced equipment and machinery are needed to fashion the prototype. And, as we will learn in chapter 9, given the complexity of some design interventions, more advanced evaluation approaches are needed to ascertain the extent to which designs have been successful.

Maker Mindset

Designers are makers. "They sketch and build, giving form to ideas as solutions. They take that faint glimmer of possibility and make it visible and real to others."[28] But they do more than that. Put designers together in a maker space, give them special tools for the project at hand, encourage them to play, experiment, work with others, share what they know, learn from and support one another, and they create communities of practice. Keep building these communities of practice and crowdfund their new ideas and products, and eventually a worldwide maker movement emerges with a manifesto closely linked to design: "Making is fundamental to what it means to be human. We must make, create, and express ourselves to be feel whole. There is something unique about making physical things. Things we make are like little pieces of us and seem to embody portions of our soul."[29] Add the global reach of the Internet and its new platforms that connect buyers and sellers and this new movement will begin to drive a new age of American manufacturing based on open-source design and do-it-yourself (DIY) manufacturing. Chris Anderson, the editor-in-chief of *Wired* and cofounder of 3D Robotics, a manufacturer of aerial robots and DIY drones, describes it as "the new industrial revolution."[30]

According to Anderson, this maker movement has many advantages.[31] Good ideas can come from anywhere, and this frees people from big companies with monopoly control. One example is Open Source Ecology, an online community that is creating a Global Village Construction Set with open-source designs for fifty machines ranging from a small sawmill to a microcombine for harvesting. Manufacture of things can be on demand, which drives down the costs of manufacturing, shipping, storage, inventory, and selling. Web-based entrepreneurship drops barriers to entry and advantages the nimblest players with the best innovation model. Thanks to automation, labor costs are falling and becoming a smaller percentage of production costs. Moreover, making things is more sustainable because design files are digital and products are custom made locally and have little or no transportation costs. Hatch says, "What we will see is simply *more*. More innovation, in more places, from more people, focused on more narrow niches. Collectively, all these new producers will invent the industrial economy, often with a few thousand units at a time" with the exactly right products, targeted niches and discriminating customers" that together will "reshape the world of making."[32]

Change Agent Mindset

Intentional change at all levels of human and social organization is defined as an action that alters, modifies, shifts, revamps, revises, reworks, or transforms something. And those who intentionally catalyze and guide a change process are recognized as change agents. The concept of "change agent" is not new to the design literature.[33] After all, it was Herbert Simon who reminded designers that "our task is not to *predict* the future; our task is to *design* a future for a sustainable and acceptable world, and then devote our efforts to bringing that future about. We are not observers of the future; we are actors who, whether we wish to or not, by our actions and our very existence, will determine the future's shape."[34] At the same time, as designers move deeper into wicked problem territory, they need to be more knowledgeable and skilled in change agentry. Attempting to alter, revise, and transform what is into what could be can generate support, but it also can activate resistance and pushback in an already conflict-ridden arena.

As agents of change, designers have a steep learning curve. The change literature is voluminous. It theories and practices are subdivided into separate topics based on *what change is*,[35] *what needs to be changed* (e.g., people, technology, systems, organizations, policies, laws, large-scale systems, and other elements), *how change occurs*, and how *people respond to changes*. I postpone a more in-depth treatment of change agentry and design until chapter 5, when the scaffolding of the design strategy's skill sets and toolkits take center stage. In the meantime, pay heed to these words of wisdom from Eve Blossom: "There's something going on in design—something powerful. People have realized a simple truth: Design is a legitimate way to change the world."[36]

Metadesigns

Think of design as a flowing river. The river of design begins with the immaterial—our mindsets, "conscious awareness, value systems, worldviews, and aspirations that define the intentionality behind materialized design." It also includes our biopsycho-logical systems and "the concepts and onto-epistemological assumptions we employ to define ourselves, and to make sense of our involvement in complex ecological, cultural, and social processes."[37] Eventually, the immaterial upstream of the river of design surfaces downstream material designs that are manifested as our cultural artifacts—the goods and services that we generate and the institutions of social, eco-nomic, and governance systems that we create. So if we want to change our material world and its downstream effects, then then we need to change "the up-stream end of the *river of design*":[38]

> The most up-stream transformation that has to take place before we set out to 'redesign the human presence on Earth' is to deeply question our way of thinking, our worldview and our value system. Up-stream changes in our mental models, basic beliefs and assumptions about the nature of reality will affect *how*, *what*, and *why* we design, the needs we perceive, the ques-tions we ask, and hence the solutions or answers we propose.[39]

Changing the Upstream End of the River of Design

Various interventions have been proposed to alter people's cultural values and beliefs. Donella Meadows, for example, viewed this transformation of values and basic beliefs as "changing our paradigms."[40] Another comparable term is "framework change"—change that "affects individual mindsets at a large scale" and ultimately seeks to "change behaviors across society as a whole."[41] Sociologists refer to these large-scale efforts of framework change as social movements—collective action by a group of people with shared beliefs, opinions, and collective identity who seek to change the social order.[42] Examples include the social movements that fought for abolition, public education, agrarian reform, labor rights, civil rights, women's rights, environmental protection, fair trade, and criminal justice reform.

Otto Scharmer, a senior lecturer at the Massachusetts Institute of Technology (MIT) and cofounder of the Presencing Institute and the MITx ULab,[43] probes even deeper to understand what informs our value, paradigm, and framework choices. His analysis begins with a review of the current state of the world and the three divides that afflict us:

- The ecological divide—unprecedented environmental destruction that is resulting in the loss of nature: "The ecological divide can be summed up by a single number: 1.5. Currently our economy consumes the resources of 1.5 planets. We use 1.5 times the regeneration capacity of planet earth. And that is just the average. In the United States, for example, the current consumption rate has surpassed five planets."

- The social divide—obscene levels of inequity and fragmentation that is resulting in the loss of society, the social whole: "The social divide can be summed up by another number: 8. Eight billionaires own as much as half of mankind combined. . . . A small group of people that you can fit into a minivan owns more than the 'bottom half' of the world's population of 3.8 billion people."

- And the spiritual divide—the increasing levels of burnout and depression that are resulting in the loss of meaning and the loss of Self (not the self of the current ego, but the self of the highest future potential): "The spiritual divide can be summed up by the number 800,000. More than 800K people per year commit suicide—a number that is greater than the sum of people who are killed by war, murder, and natural disasters. Every forty seconds there is one suicide."[44]

Scharmer, however, does not see the three divides as separate problems. For him, they are three faces of a root issue—"the inner place—the source—from which we operate."[45] Interpreted broadly, it is our consciousness that shapes what we do and how we create the external, material world around us. So he maintains that it is up to designers to realize and appreciate that "the quality of results in any social system is a function of the *consciousness* from which people in that system operate and create social reality. Boiled down to three words, the idea can be expressed as "*form follows consciousness.*"[46] So when designing, it is the designer's challenge to explore and probe his or her consciousness and a level of awareness and knowing that requires an open *mind*—"the capacity to suspend old habits of judgments" and "to see things with fresh eyes"; an open *heart*—"the capacity to look at a situation through the eyes of somebody else"; and an open *will*—"the capacity to 'let go' of the old and 'let come' the new."[47]

But there is more depth to this inward turn. The American philosopher Ken Wilber's Human Consciousness Project offers an excellent overview of its expansive possibilities, which he describes as a "cross-mapping of all of the states, structures, memes, types, levels, stages, and waves of human consciousness." His project is comparable to "the psychological correlate of the Human Genome Project, which involves the mapping of all of the genes in the human DNA."[48] His mapping begins with developmental psychology—the study and growth and development of the mind and conscious evolution. After assembling the conclusions of over 100 researchers and various developmental theories such as Erik Erickson's psychosocial theory of personality development, Clare Graves' theory of biopsychosocial systems, Jane Loevinger's theory of ego development and Bill Torbert's adaptation of it and its application to leadership development, and Laurence Kohlberg's theory of moral development, Wilber reported key similarities: "They all tell a generally similar tale of growth and development of the mind *as a series of unfolding stages or waves*" and the stage sequences that "can be aligned across a common developmental space."[49]

Three spaces tend to be shared by most developmental theories: "pre-conventional or egocentric" (e.g., impulsive and egocentric levels that focus on "me"); conventional or ethnocentric/sociocentric (e.g., conformist and conscientious levels that focus on "us"); and postconventional or worldcentric (e.g., individualistic, sensitive levels that focus on pluralistic relativism, communitarianism, and concerns for universal care, justice, and fairness that focus on "all of us").[50] Common to all developmental theories and maps is a successive decrease in egocentrism and narcissism and an "increasing consciousness, or the ability to take other people, places, and things into account and thus increasingly extend care to each."[51] It doesn't mean that we stop caring for ourselves as we evolve—only that we demonstrate an increasing concern and compassion for others. Wilber adds that when people create a society of individuals, they form a developmental *"center of gravity* . . . around which the culture's ethics, norms, rules and basic institutions are organized and this center of gravity provides the basic cultural cohesion and social integration for that society."[52] For example, developmental theorists and researchers have estimated that the bulk of the world's population is at the conventional/ethnocentric stage or lower.[53]

Developmental theory also acknowledges that not all people evolve to later stages; some remain at the preconventional or conventional stage. Although there are healthy aspects to all stages of development,[54] an important question is how people can evolve and do so without activating the unhealthy aspects of each stage. Wilber's answer begins with a four-quadrant integral map of human possibilities that can serve as our guide.[55] The first quadrant focuses on the individual's *interior or subjective experience*, represented by all levels of development. The second examines people's culture and worldview as *they understand and express their own intersubjective experience when they come together*. The other two quadrants offer an *external*, outsider's assessment of people from a rational-analytic, scientific perspective. The third quadrant is an objective exploration of the physical brain and the human body as an organism, and the fourth examines the interobjective social system that people create and the environment in which they live.[56] To fully appreciate and explore the full range of human possibilities, Ken Wilber recommends taking a "holonic" approach, which he refers to as "integral theory," which weaves together all four quadrants of his integrated map and does not just focus on one quadrant in order to understand, explore, and ultimately change human behavior.

However, Wilber cautions that we need more than an integrated map of human potential: "Even if we possessed the perfect integral map of the Kosmos, a map that is completely all-inclusive and unerringly holistic, that map itself would not transform people. We don't need a map; we need ways to change the mapmaker."[57] So a key question is: how do we change the mapmaker and transform his or her consciousness? Wilber recommends *integral transformative practice* regardless of whatever domain one is considering, whether it be physical exercise, emotional exercise, community service, dialogue, involvement in nature, or meditation (noting that meditation has shifted people's developmental levels). He also recommends books on how to get started on one's own integral transformative practice.

Transformative Practice to Change the Mapmaker

Following Wilber's recommendation on how to start an integral transformative practice, I turned to Clare Graves's developmental theory, which begins with the proposition "that the psychology of a mature human being is an unfolding, emergent, oscillating spiraling process marked by progressive subordination of older, lower-order behavior systems to newer, higher-order systems as an individual's existential problems change." When people are in one state of existence, they have a psychology particular to that state—feelings, motivations, ethics and values, biochemistry, belief system, conceptions of and preferences for education, economics, political theory and practice, and others.[58]

Graves's Spiral Dynamics identified what are variously referred to as eight "levels," "codes," "memes/value systems," or "colors"[59] of human development. Each level is a discrete structure of thinking that "reflects a world view, a valuing system, a level of psychological existence, a belief structure, an organizing principle, a way of thinking or a mode of adjustment." Representing a core intelligence that directs behavior and forms systems, each level *impacts upon all life choices* as a decision-making framework," which "can manifest in both *healthy and unhealthy* forms." And each level *can brighten and dim* as the **Life Conditions** (consisting of historic *Times*, geographic *Place*, existential *Problems*, and societal *Circumstances*) change."[60]

As seen in box 4.1, levels or ᵛMEMEs are divided into two tiers. The first six build the first tier of human development and represent a "culmination of our primate nature," with the acknowledgment that every new ᵛMEME is "a momentous leap" in human development.[61] But the transition from the sixth to the seventh ᵛMEME is the most critical leap. It requires a new type of thinking to deal with the level of societal complexity beyond the best first-tier thinking and its many unaddressed problems—the ecological, political, social, health care, race/ethnicity, and economic crises—of the first tier. The challenge of the seventh and eighth tiers is to address these crises and focus on all entities as integrated system "using collective human intelligence to work on large-scale problems without sacrificing individuality."[62]

Spiral Dynamics is not just a theory based on people's biological and psychological development. It is also a theory of sociocultural development. As humans evolve, so do their societies. Here are some of the fundamentals of the change process:

- "When *life conditions* change, humans, who are complex adaptive intelligences, adapt to new *life conditions*."[87] "Human nature is not static or finite."[88]
- Thus, "new systems are formed," while "old systems stay with us."[89] "Society is not static."[90]
- "As a new system is activated, our psychology and adaptation to new conditions emerge."[91] The brain can and does rewire itself,[92] which enables people to change their own psychology.[93]
- At the same time, "social systems (individual, groups, societies) can respond positively only to the principles, appeals, formulas, and legal and ethical codes that are congruent with (their) current level of human existence."[94]
- What results is an "open system of values with an infinite number of models of living available to us, and there is no final stage to which we all must aspire."[95]

In this brief exploration into mindsets and metadesigns of human and societal development and evolution, I came away with the following observations and conclusions: The design strategy's focus on the external world and its different types of designs is an important step in the evolution of twentieth- and twenty-first-century design, as well as its careful attention to the design's processes and principles that are necessary for all aspects of designing of whatever type. But if the warnings about the state of the world

Box 4.1
Clare Graves's eight levels or ^vMemes of development

First Tier:

- The **Instinctive** ^vMEME[63] centers on survival to satisfy basic physiological needs—food, water, temperature control, sex, and safety, among others. Behavior derives from instincts and reflexes rather than logical choices. People form protective and supportive bands to simply survive.

- The **Clannish** ^vMEME[64] moves beyond people's survival needs to broaden their focus on social needs. People seek safety and security for "our kind" through allegiance to blood relations, elders, and customs. Also curious about the world "out there," especially its potential for threats to their safety, people begin to link events with cause-effect sequences. So to protect themselves against unknown forces, they create sacred places, objects, and rituals, obey the desires of mystical spirits, and seek harmony with nature.

- The **Egocentric** ^vMEME[65] celebrates the impulsive "I," seeking to "avoid shame, defend reputation, be respected, gratify . . . senses immediately, fight remorseless and without guilt to break constraints, (and not) worry about the consequences that may not come."[66] As the egocentric ^vMeme gains in intensity, strong individuals take unilateral control. They use "intimidation, charisma, and physical force to impose" their will, "without guilt or compunction."[67] "Guilt is absent, and problems are always someone's fault."[68] The powerless revere the powerful individual's strength, willingness to break bonds, be free and courageous, and take control. Thus, a society dominated by the egocentric ^vMEME consists of a few dominant haves and many have-nots, in which "there is no altruism, but there is manipulation of indebtedness and exchange of favors. 'You scratch my back, I'll scratch yours'."[69] At its peak, when this ^vMeme predominates, "calm rational discourse is unlikely."[70]

- The **Purposeful** ^vMEME[71] states that "a single guiding force controls the world and determines our destiny." Life has meaning when people follow the appointed pathway and stand for what is "right, proper, and good, always subjecting [themselves] to the directives of higher authority."[72] People in this mode want to bring order and stability into their lives; control impulsivity; oppose evil and evildoers in an "ongoing battle for dominion," often leaving little room for compromise; restore traditions that made them great; reinforce family values and personal character; respond judgmentally; find fault and lay blame on "guilty" parties; prefer order and regimentation, "tight structure, certain schedules, and clear consequences"[73] where everything is in its proper place; and sustain an abiding belief that "there is meaning and purpose in living."[74]

- The **Strategic** ^vMEME[75] finds people who strive for autonomy and independence and have "an unquenchable thirst to explore, venture out, experience the novel, and to be the first to discover, invent, or conquer the many 'hidden' worlds of knowledge."[76] Letting go of myths, traditions, and beliefs, they are pragmatic and learn through experience. Their authority lies with their experiences and their 'right-thinking mind.' With a capacity for detailed, disciplined, and focused problem solving, they employ science and technology and the scientific method to search for the best solutions. For such people, who believe in human perfectibility through intelligent hard work and the testing of ideas, life becomes a series of challenges, tests, and unlimited possibilities to

(continued)

Box 4.1 (continued)

do better. Also believing in competition and achieving the good life and material abundance, they favor free-market, free-enterprise, and laissez-faire models. Ultimately, they believe in the inevitability of change and view nature as evolving through change, not permanence.

- The **Relativist** ᵛMEME,[77] at its peak, is "communtarian, consensual, egalitarian, and consensual."[78] Everyone is considered equal, although it is recognized that there is still not parity among people. The workplace is team oriented, with sharing of ideas and feelings. Authority lies with the group, not any external source, so everyone feels "in it together." Competition in the decision-making process yields to decisions based on understanding, appreciation, and acceptance. "Individuals benefit through elevation of the group as a whole; society is bettered through collaboration of groups. Social safety nets, investments in people-oriented programs, and 'socialized' health care are often run hand-in-hand with . . . communitarianism."[79] For individuals, it is better to be liked and accepted than to be a winner with material gain. Spiritualy tends to be nondenominational and nonsectarian.

Second Tier:

- The **Systemic** ᵛMEME[80] acknowledges that the first six systems of human living have created a disordered world that puts everything in jeopardy and at the same time opens up unprecedented opportunities. New social priorities and new decision-making modes are therefore required—new times require new thinking. The new thinking tolerates, or even enjoys paradoxes and uncertainties; honors value differences (while not necessarily agreeing with them) and facilitates people's movement up and down the human Spiral; and delights with the new and novel, lifelong learning, experimentation, and accessing knowledge from different domains and sources. People at this level of development are inner directed, have strong ethical anchors but are not trapped by rigid rules based on mandates from authority or external dogma. Taking an integrative and open systems perspective, they are skilled and imaginative problem solvers who link system parts and functions that form the whole in order to search for the root causes of problems, engage in complex problem-solving and decision-making initiatives, and "ride the explosive Spiral in search of major gaps, misfits, trigger points, natural flows and potential awakenings or regressions." They understand that "profound change only occurs around serious problems of existence. Like a heat seeking missile, they are drawn to hotspots where the evolving crisis demands new insights. They realize that many breakthrough ideas are forged within such crucibles."[81]

- The **Holistic** ᵛMEME[82] builds on the concept of "holon"—a Greek word that describes something that is simultaneously a whole and part of a larger whole. It "views a world of interlinked causes and effects, interacting fields of energy, and levels of bonding and communicating most of us have yet to uncover."[83] It is at this level "a Gaia view emerges, one that centers on life itself—all forms of life (not just humans)." "The planet itself is seen as a single ecosystem"[84] with multiple, interconnecting macro and micro levels. The Holistic ᵛMEME differs from the Systemic ᵛMEME in its shift toward a communal, collective point of view. The complex, expansive problems and the amount of information and disciplinary knowledge generated

Box 4.1 (continued)

to deal with challenges identified in the Systemic ʸMEME phase cannot be addressed or resolved by isolated individuals. They require focused, carefully directed collaborative efforts. "Joint activity across groups, factions, communities, and natures is necessary to gather enough human energy to find solutions" to the complexities of new life conditions. These purpose-driven collaborations integrate the full range of human feelings, intuitions, and knowledge, tapping into participants' conscious and unconscious minds and drawing on their brain/mind tools and competencies. And whole Spiral interventions are viewed as routine. "Business has a soul again, and the gaps between science and metaphysics close," suggesting "a unifying force and a set of guiding principles that sets the course of the universe and gives the appearance of consciousnes."[85] The self becomes "part of a larger, conscious, spiritual whole that also serves the self."[86]

are accurate, and I believe most are, for us to make the transition from our past to our future, we must assist designers and the people for whom they are designing to evolve their consciousness and behavior so that they fit better in the world in which we live and the world in which we hope to live. "Because our *life conditions* are so strewn with unsolvable problems, we literally [have to] change our minds, awakening neurologically pathways that propel us to new and higher-order thinking abilities."[96]

Facing problems that we are unable to solve "at our present level of being," our challenge is to make "a leap to a newer, higher-order system biologically, psychologically, socially, and spiritually.[97] Einstein, well ahead of his time on so many levels, offered this important advice to make the transition:

A human being is part of the whole—called by us "Universe," a part limited in time and space. He experiences himself, his thoughts and feelings as something separated from the rest—a kind of optical delusion of his consciousness. This delusion is a kind of prison for us, restricting us to our personal desires and to affection for a few persons nearest to us. Our task must be to free ourselves from this prison by widening our circle of compassion to embrace all living creatures and the whole of nature in its beauty. Nobody is able to achieve this completely, but the striving for such achievement is in itself a part of the liberation and a foundation for inner security.[98]

The Ultimate Design Challenge: Evolution of Human Consciousness

Some designers are already assisting people in opening their minds and hearts so that they can let go of the old, be receptive to the new, and transition from an egocentric to an ecosystem-centric awareness or consciousness. I have identified four as examples: Dr. Leyla Acaroglu, Carol Sanford, Dr. Otto Scharmer, and Dr. Daniel Christian Wahl.

Leyla Acaroglu, a sociologist and award-winning designer, offers an example of how to meet and work with people where they are developmentally. As a founder of Disrupt Design and creator of the Disruptive Design Method, she uses systems and design principles to actively intervene in complex problems to move people from where they are to where they could be. Although she doesn't frame her approach in this way, it would appear that she is helping people transition their consciousness and behavior from ᵛMEME 5, characterized by individualism, rationality, achievement, and materialism, to ᵛMEME 6, characterized by the exploration (along with others) of the caring dimensions of community, the use of reconciliation and consensus in decision making, an emphasis on feelings, sensitivity, and caring that supersede cold rationality, and a more equal distribution of the Earth's resources.[99] As part of her approach, Acaroglu has developed tools that activate and support a global community of change agents, "citizen designers," who are called to catalyze social change through their creative agency and practice. One example is the Post Disposable Initiative—a design challenge to rapidly redesign systems that sustain wastefulness and contribute to resource depletion and pollution, and in their stead substitute closed-loop circular solutions at all level of society. As she has said, "Everything is designed, even disposability—and therefore, everything can be redesigned to . . . move beyond disposability."[100]

Acaroglu also has created the Post Disposable Activation Kit which can provide inspiration for those who might want to join, and suggestions on how people can participate and what very specific actions they can take. The point is to help people overcome their frustrations and fear by flipping their narrative toward a positive future, taking action—first redesigning their own lifestyles, then influencing others in their communities, and ultimately shifting the status quo among companies and governments to create system change and take an active part in the new circular and green economy.[101] She also has developed a free Activation Toolkit and a series of three design challenges on e-waste, fashion, and plastic waste "to encourage creatives, visionaries and everyday people to take action and to re-design the production, consumption and waste systems to be circular, sustainable and regenerative." These free tools are devoted to helping people activate their leadership, make lifestyle changes, and tackle big issues that shift us to a postdisposable future.[102]

Carol Sanford, an author and executive in residence and senior fellow in social innovation at Babson College, also follows a developmental model to guide individuals "to create real change in the world." In her 2020 book *The Regenerative Life*, she moves beyond the "heroic and do-good" theories of change and offers a theory that develops "the capacity of ordinary people to see things differently."[103]

While social movements are driven by the power of compelling ideas, regenerative change "is built on the power of taking conscious charge of our thinking processes and helping others to do the same." Sanford advocates for the nonheroic path that "seeks a way to create profound and enduring change, not through large-scale movements or fighting the good fight, but by enabling people to transform themselves. When people learn how to evolve their own thinking—their beliefs, perspectives, aspirations, and thought patterns—they become change catalysts in all parts of their lives and with everyone they touch."[104] Box 4.2 summarizes the characteristics of her theory of change.

Box 4.2
Carol Sanford's theory of change

Change is:

- **Developmental.** This is built on "systems-thinking skills and personal mastery."[105] Its purpose is "to help individuals develop greater consciousness and agency in regards to their own thinking, in order to allow far more beneficial actions to flow from it."[106] Further, "[d]evelopment is intentional, not accidental. You have to design for it."[107]

- **Essence sourced.** This is "based on what makes every person or living thing specific and singular."[108] Essence is the "irreducible core of what allows us to experience ourselves as integrated beings with coherent selves that endure even as we grow and change throughout our lifetimes. Learning to engage in essence thinking . . . is foundational to understanding wholes and their potential"[109] in ourselves, others, and systems.

- **Regenerative.** This is committed to realizing "the evolutionary potential of life."[110] The focus of the Regenerative Life Paradigm is "on how to build capacity in people and other living systems to be self-determining in the world."[111] Seven principles guide this regeneration: focus on *wholes* rather than fragments; seek and understand the *potential*— the enduring, inherent qualities of a whole and how they could be expressed within a context that is constantly changing; understand the *essence*; pursue the *development* of consciousness and agency; understand *nestedness*—how things are connected and ordered into different levels of a system, such as individual humans nested within families, which are nested in communities, and which in turn are nested within ecosystems; explore *nodes*—the elements that have the potential to transform the system as a whole; and understand *fields*, the energy fields or patterns of energy that influence and respond to the activity within a system. "Fields are universal—all of us work and live within them. This means that the most powerful way to help people change their behaviors and the purposes they pursue is not to work on them individually, . . . but to reshape the fields that bring them into energetic connection." Field shifting "is a powerful way to create the conditions for change."[112]

- **Grounded.** This is "based on the idea that we can transform our world by transforming the roles we play in our lives."[113] "We make a better world by teaching ordinary people practices for shifting their thinking processes and enabling themselves to show up"[114] in completely new ways in the roles as *initiators*, who create the conditions for growth and development (e.g., parent, designer, and earth tender);[115] as *manifestors*, who bring new ideas into concrete existence that produce new value to the world (e.g., citizen, entrepreneur, and economic shaper); and *destabilizers*, who welcome and invite us to learn about how to manage uncertainty and to create conditions for transformation (e.g., educator, media content creator, blogger, journalist, or filmmaker), and *spirit resource* (e.g., spiritual teacher, mentor, minister, and sometimes psychologist).[116] Her intention in mapping the roles is to signal the "integrated approach" to transform and sustain whole healthy societies to help people who may have lost hope about how to revive meaning in their lives and efforts.[117]

Based on the complexity and comprehensiveness of Sanford's Regenerative Life Paradigm and its major themes, my assessment is that she is assisting people to move beyond the first tier of human development to the second tier of human development as it has been described in Graves's theory of Spiral Dynamics, although Sanford does not make this connection in her work. She refers to this transition as "stepping over." It appears to involve some combination of the Systemic 'MEME 7 (as discussed further in chapter 15 of *Spiral Dynamics*), which focuses on functionality, competence, flexibility, and spontaneity, discovery of personal freedom without harm to others or excesses of self-interest, and demand for integrative and open systems, with the Holistic 'MEME 8 (as discussed in chapter 16 of *Spiral Dynamics*), which focuses on blending and harmonizing a strong collective of individuals, the good of all living entities as integrated systems, and the self as a part of a larger, conscious, and spiritual whole.[118]

Otto Scharmer,[119] in his observations that "form follows consciousness" as already discussed, is also concerned with "stepping over," but he calls it "bridging the divide" between the past and the future, although again, there are no references to Graves's theory of development. According to Scharmer, we bridge the divide by developing principles and personal practices to shift from a system driven by a mindset of "me," which cares only for the well-being of oneself, to a system driven by the concern for the well-being of the whole, including oneself. The maximum-me mindset has created a world of "maximum material consumption, bigger is better, and special-interest-group decision making leading to a state of organized irresponsibility, *collectively creating results that nobody wants*."[120] It has produced an age of disruption—a state marked by crises, resource scarcity, climate chaos, mass poverty, mass migration, terrorism, fundamentalism, financial oligarchies, and other disruptive elements.

In part I of his book, Scharmer describes four social systems or social fields to bridge this divide. Each represent a separate level of consciousness, and each differs in terms of the "quality of relationships that give rise to patterns of thinking, conversing, and organizing, which in turn produce practical results."[121] *Field 1, the habitual social field*, describes an individual's actions that are triggered by external events and past habits. At this level of consciousness, there is a complete separation of mind and matter. *Field 2, the ego-system social field*, occurs when individuals or groups begin to suspend past assumptions, see things as they are, differentiate between an observer and the observed, and ultimately notice something new. *Field 3, the emotional-empathic-relational social field*, arises when social-system actors begin to sense reality from others' views and see things from a new perspective. And *field 4*, the generative-ecosystem, occurs when actors let go of old identities, open up a new space of creative awareness, and "co-create from a future potential that wants to emerge."[122] And each field is manifested and differentiated in terms of its organizing principles at the micro, meso, macro, and mundo levels of society.

In part II of his book, Scharmer describes a process for consciousness-based systems change that shifts the interior place or source from which we operate. The process, called Theory U, has five movements, each with its own principles and practices, as illustrated in figure 4.1:

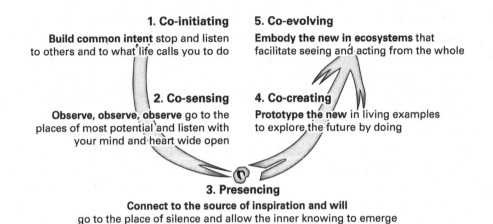

Figure 4.1
Otto Scharmer's Theory U

- *Co-initiating,* which builds common intent with others by listening to what life calls us to do
- *Co-sensing,* which tells us to go to the places with the greatest potential and observe and listen with an open heart and mind
- *Presencing,* which connects us to the sources of silence, inspiration, and will that allows inner knowledge about the future to emerge
- *Co-creating,* which explores the future by prototyping living examples of the new
- *Co-shaping,* which focuses on scaling the new while growing and evolving innovation for collective impact

Traveling down the U on the left side differentiates among the levels of perception that help people download past patterns and mental models, while moving to the right side passes through levels of action to engage in new practices from the perspective of the larger ecosystem.[123]

Scharmer concludes his book by focusing on a larger narrative. He asks how we can upgrade society's "operating systems"—our economic, democratic, health, educational, food, finance, and governance systems. He then charts a path from 1.0 operating systems, which are input and authority-centric; 2.0 operating systems, which are output and efficiency-centric; 3.0 operating systems, which are stakeholder and customer centric; to finally operating systems that are ecosystem-centric. In his final chapter, he invites participation in a worldwide movement that aims to bridge our ecological, social, and spiritual divides by developing our ability to listen, learn, sense and actualize the future as it emerges. At its core, Theory U is developmental: "the quality of the results that a system creates is a function of the awareness from which people in the system operate."[124] So if we want to change a system, we begin by creating holding spaces (action-research laboratories, programs, projects, and a global online platform) in which action-research communities explore our blind spot[125]—the interior condition from which we operate both individually and collectively. In these holding spaces, we also build a new narrative that helps us change as individuals and also guide others in the redesign of society to update our mental and institutional operating systems in all sectors of society.

Building on Clare Graves's dynamic map of the developmental stages in human consciousness, value systems, worldviews, and biopsychological systems, Daniel Christian Wahl asserts that the designer's next challenge is to design regenerative cultures that are "capable of continuous learning and transformation in response to, and anticipation of, inevitable change."[126] His argument is also developmental: "Humanity is coming of age" and "collectively undergoing a maturation process which requires us to redefine how we understand our relationship to the rest of life on Earth."[127] We are "stepping from our juvenile—and at times reckless and self-absorbed—phase as a young species into a mature membership of community life on Earth." We are now being "called to become productive members of this community and to contribute to its health and wellbeing."[128] As part of this reinvention process, "we need a new way of thinking, a new consciousness, a new cultural story" that questions deeply held current ways of being.[129]

In his book *Designing Regenerative Cultures*, Wahl offers some basic guidelines to help us develop our consciousness and build this cultural story. More than solutions, he begins with questions that he believes are the pathway to collective wisdom: "Questions can spark culturally creative conversations that transform how we see ourselves and our relationship to the world."[130] They help us examine our basic assumptions, worldviews, and value systems, and as such, they become our "cultural guidance system."[131] *Why questions*, for example, help to understand "purpose, a cause, a belief." *How questions* express "the values that guide our actions and how we aim to manifest the higher purpose in action. And *what questions* identify the "results of those actions."[132] Thus, "questions—and the conversations they spark—can unleash collective intelligence and help us value multiple perspectives. Living the questions, deep listening, and learning from diverse ways of knowing—these are all ways to transform consciousness and thereby create cultural and behavioral change."[133]

Daniel Wahl and Seaton Baxter also elaborate on the particular type of conversations and the deep listening and learning needed for this transformation. They recommend drawing on David Bohm's view of dialogue to "explore the wisdom of many minds and multiple perspectives."[134] As Bohm described it, "dialogue is really aimed at going into the thought process and changing the way the thought process occurs collectively. We haven't really paid much attention to thought as a process. We have *engaged* in thoughts, but we have only paid attention to the content, not to the process."[135] What is needed, according to Bohm, is to move into dialogue, well beyond current discussions, and explore how thought is generated and sustained at a collective level. The goal is to help us collectively question our deeply held assumptions about culture and identity.

Box 4.3

Daniel Wahl's call to change the narrative

A regenerative culture needs to facilitate the heathy development of human beings, which means paying attention to how our culture and educational systems shape our values and worldview. Not only do we need to encourage ongoing dialogue and lifelong learning, we need to collectively cocreate a new narrative for those dialogues and learnings. Wahl offers this guidance for our redesign and regenerative efforts:

- From a narrative of separateness and alienation from nature and one another to a new narrative of relationships, connectedness, interdependence, and interbeing[138]

- From a narrative of a "mechanistic, reductionist methodology of science,"[139] along with the specialization of human knowledge that "creates a tendency to lose ourselves in the details" of separate subjects or disciplines, to a narrative of fundamental interconnections and interrelatedness of all fields enabling us to see the "hidden connections" that maintain the long-term viability of life as a whole[140]

- From a narrative of exploitative and degenerative cultures, based on scarcity, zero-sum struggles for control and power, and competitive advantage, to a new narrative based on compassion, empathy, win-win collaborative advantages, and shared abundance[141]

- From a narrative that promotes the illusion of certainty, prediction, and control to a new narrative that accepts circular causality, ambiguity, unpredictability, and uncertainty[142]

- From a narrative that extols self-interest and self-absorption to a new narrative that encourages "enlightened self-interest" driven by care for humans, our communities, other species, and the Earth and life as a whole[143]

- From a narrative that describes "our current egocentric societies (materialistic, anthropocentric, competition-based, class stratified, violence prone and unsustainable)" to "a narrative of how we might grow whole, one life stage at a time, by embracing nature and soul as our "wisest and most trustworthy guides" and "a strategy for cultural transformation"[144] that facilitates healthy personal development "from ego-centric, to socio-centric, to species-centric, to bio-centric, and cosmos-centric perspectives of self"[145]

- From a narrative of ever-increasing consumption, resource depletion, and quantitative growth that have overshot a number of planetary boundaries that enable life on Earth to a new narrative of "regenerative use of renewable resources,"[146] qualitative growth found in natural systems, and a regenerative culture that is "healthy, resilient, and adaptable" at different scales from local, to regional, and global[147]

- From a narrative that advances technology for its promise without attention to its far-reaching social and environmental consequences to a narrative that raises ethical questions and applies "the precautionary principle" to make careful choices in the technologies we employ[148]

- From a narrative that values design in terms of its utility to a narrative guided by a Hippocratic oath of "do no harm" that challenges designers and others to evaluate their proposed actions in terms of their "life-sustaining, restorative, and regenerative potential"[149]

Wahl and Baxter also reinforce Richard Buchanan's call for design thinking to become the "new liberal art of technological culture" to help us integrate the knowledge of the natural, social, and humanistic sciences.[136] Rather than rely on a specific discipline or a limited perspective of a specific discipline, they propose "transdisciplinary design dialogue to ensure that our choices are conscious and well-informed by a holistic/integral perspective."[137] The designer's role in this process becomes the transdisciplinary integrator who facilitates this shift in development and consciousness. But, as they caution, transdisciplinary design dialogues need to meet and work with people where they are developmentally not where we want them to be.

Ultimately, as illustrated in box 4.3, the questions that we ask and the dialogues that they engender become the starting point for the creation of a new narrative that tells the story about our world and our place in it, highlighting what serves humanity and what doesn't.

In Summary

This chapter has taken an inward turn to explore seven types of designers' mindsets—growth, benefit, hyperattuned, imaginative, analytical, maker, and change-agent—that inform their values, shape their underlying assumptions, and guide their practice. Returning to an outward focus, the chapter then probed the concept of metadesign—the effort to alter people's cultural values, beliefs, and consciousness that inform their downstream design choices. Here, we learned that wicked problem territory exists because our worldviews and consciousness both play a part in creating it. If designers are to deal with the life conditions of wicked problems and move out of wicked problem territory, they need to focus on evolving their consciousness and the consciousness of the people they serve—the ultimate design challenge for the twenty-first century. Fortunately, there is a vanguard of designers, four of whom are introduced in this chapter, who are helping us change our narrative, "give up what we know and who we are for what we could become,"[150] and to "bring forth a world not just through what we are doing, but through the quality of our being."[151]

As essential as changing consciousness is, we also need to acknowledge that the design strategy requires not only being better, but doing better. If we can't connect the "being" of design with the "doing" of design, we will be severely handicapped in bringing about a world that could be. And doing better requires a mastery of the design strategy's skill sets and toolkits, the subject of chapter 5.

5 Design Strategy's Scaffolding: Skill Sets and Toolkits

As we will see in part III of this book, designers' work is taking them deeper into wicked problem territory in the strategic design of organizations, the systemic design of social systems, and the regenerative design of social and ecological systems. To match this growing complexity, design's skill sets and toolkits also must also evolve and expand. For purposes of this overview, I divide them into two general categories: change agent skill sets and toolkits and designer skill sets and toolkits.

Change Agent Skill Sets and Toolkits

Personal Development

Being self-aware Before we begin to design and redesign our world, we need to look inward to examine our assumptions and preferences to understand the kind of thinkers and problem solvers we are. We all have habits of the mind. Our thinking habits or "schema" have developed from repetitive activities and common knowledge that we have successfully applied in the past. Unfortunately, these same schemas can prevent us from developing new way of seeing, understanding, and problem solving. Becoming aware of our schemas and the perceptual, emotional, cultural, group, organizational, and environmental blocks that they can impose on us is an important step toward greater self-awareness and self-knowledge. The best work I know to develop these skill sets and toolkits is Jim Adams's book *Conceptual Blockbusting*.[1] Not only do the book's exercises help us gain greater awareness of our limitations, more important, they also move us beyond them to become better conceptualizers and creative problem solvers.

Developing emotional intelligence Change agents and designers need to regulate their emotions—a critical survival skill when working in wicked problem territory. Drawing from Aristotle's philosophical inquiry into virtue and the good life in *The Nicomachean Ethics*, Daniel Goleman lays out how we can "manage our emotional life with intelligence. . . . Our passions, when well exercised, have wisdom; they guide our thinking, our values, our survival." But as Aristotle understood, they can too easily lead us astray. Emotionality is not the problem, but "the *appropriateness* of emotions and their expression. The question is, how we can bring intelligence to our emotions—and civility to our streets and caring to our communal life?"[2]

As for *Homo sapiens*, the thinking species, we have ignored, until recently, the central role of emotion in our lives. Drawing from scientific studies that now reveal how important emotions are to shaping our decisions and actions, we have come to understand that "feeling counts every bit as much—and often more—than thought. . . . For better or worse, intelligence can come to nothing when the emotions hold sway."[3]

Goleman calls emotional intelligence "a master aptitude, a capacity that profoundly shapes all other abilities, either facilitating or interfering with them." If our emotions hinder our ability to think and plan, seek goals, and solve problems, they limit our use of our mental abilities and govern how we fare in life. But if motivated by enthusiasm and pleasure, our feelings can "propel us to accomplishment."[4] Thus, to work in wicked problem territory, designers need to establish an intelligent balance between head and heart, and they can do so by cultivating the five domains of emotional intelligence: "*knowing one's emotions*," or self-awareness that enables us to recognize a feeling as it happens so we can be "better pilots" of our lives; "*managing emotions*," or handling emotions appropriately so that we can "soothe" ourselves and "shake off rampant anxiety, gloom or irritability," and "distress" so that we can "bounce back far more quickly from life's setback's and upsets"; "*motivating oneself*," which requires us to stifle impulsiveness, marshal our self-control, and delay gratification to accomplish our goals and be productive; "*recognizing emotions in others*," which enables us to have empathy for and attunement to the feelings and needs of others; and "*handling relationships*," or the ability to manage others' emotions when required.[5]

Believing emotional literacy goes "hand in hand with education for character, moral development, and for citizenship,"[6] Goleman maintains that it can be taught and demonstrates how it is being taught and the important differences that it is making with students, teachers, and counselors in selective educational systems throughout the world, as he illustrates in chapter 16, "The Schooling of Emotions." As Goleman concludes, we have a "moral imperative" to help people fare better in life.

> These are times when the fabric of society seems to unravel at ever-greater speed, when selfishness, violence, and a meanness of spirit seem to be rotting the goodness of our communal lives. Here the argument for the importance of emotional intelligence hinges on the link between sentiment, character, and moral instincts. There is growing evidence that fundamental ethical stances in life stem from underlying emotional capacities. . . . Those who are at the mercy of impulse—who lack self-control—suffer a moral deficiency: The ability to control impulse is the base of will and character. By the same token, the root of altruism lies in empathy, the ability to read the emotions of others; lacking a sense of another's need or despair, there is no caring. And if there are any two moral stances that our times call for, they are precisely these, self-restraint and compassion.[7]

Developing a sense of well-being for self and others   Change agents and designers also need to cultivate a sense of well-being, given the challenges that they face in wicked problem territory. The most advanced skill set for well-being has been advanced by Martin Seligman.[8] As part of the movement in positive psychology, he has evolved and tested through rigorous research a theory about what makes life worth living and how people can build the enabling conditions to flourish regardless of their circumstances. Well-being has five elements: *positive emotions* ("what we feel: pleasure, rapture, ecstasy, warmth, and comfort, and the like");[9] *engagement* ("loss of self-consciousness during an absorbing activity");[10] *meaning* ("belonging to and serving something . . . bigger than the self");[11] *accomplishment* (achievement and mastery for its own sake);[12] and *positive relationships* (seeking good relations with others").[13]

Seligman also notes that it is important to distinguish between values and ethics. "What you care about—your values—is more basic than ethics" and "most of what we care about is learned."[14] For example, he contrasts the values of two groups with whom he has worked: Wharton master's of business administration (MBA) graduates, who care about making money, and West Point cadets, who care about serving the nation. According to Seligman, how we learn to value and care about something is currently "speculative and incomplete," but he believes that they include the cultivation of meaning, engagement, positive emotion, positive accomplishment, and positive relations.[15]

Seligman and his associates offer interactive exercises, coaching techniques, and online courses and curricula, all of which he summarizes in his book and on his website.[16] Professionals from diverse backgrounds in psychology, medicine, education (from grade school to the university), and the military have benefited from his techniques not only to develop their own well-being, but also to assist others in developing their own. Seligman also includes a short version of the Signature Strengths Test in the appendix, to help people identify their strengths and weaknesses in six major areas: wisdom and knowledge, courage, humanity and love, justice, temperance, and transcendence. The full version can be found on Seligman's Happiness website, along with other toolkits and references. Seligman's book *Learned Optimism: How to Change Your Mind and Your Life*[17] also will be of interest. It offers many simple techniques to develop one's potential and encourage optimistic behavior for every phase of life. It is especially useful for designers who need to learn how to retain their optimism despite the many challenges and setbacks they face in wicked problem territory.

Cultivating intuition   Intuition is the ability to understand something or make conclusions without conscious reasoning, proof, or evidence of support. As Malcolm Gladwell described it in *Blink*, intuition is "thinking without thinking."[18] It is a way of knowing without knowing how we know what we know. Sometimes referred to as "gut feeling," "sixth sense," or "insight," intuition is generally recognized as a source of creativity.[19]

In contrast to those in the social sciences, change agents and designers openly acknowledge the importance of intuition in design and view it as foundational in driving the design process.[20] Boris Müller, for example, credits intuition for enabling us to act, make decisions, deal with unforeseen events, and handle ill-defined problems despite limited information. "Most design projects are—by definition—open, vague, unclear and sometimes chaotic, where intuition plays a prominent role." He therefore concludes that "intuition does not necessarily lead to good design—but good design is always based on intuition."[21]

Beyond intuition, researchers are learning that there is much more that unfolds from our unconscious mind. Our perceptions, behaviors, memories, and social judgments likely are driven by our subliminal, precognitive processes rather than our conscious ones.[22] For example, Rosalind Picard and her team at MIT's Media Laboratory have been exploring the autonomic nervous system as bedrock of human emotion which enables the brain to deal with external environmental demands and internal emotional states. Their findings challenge what we think we know about human decision making and raise important questions about how the neuroscience of the unconscious might one day inform human decision making, and ultimately design.[23] The neuroanatomist Jill Bolte Taylor, drawing from her personal experiences in her book *My Stroke of Insight*, acknowledges that "we live in a world where we are taught from the start that we are thinking creatures that feel. The truth is, we are feeling creatures that think."[24] Designers from frog, a design company based in San Francisco, add that "even when we believe we're thinking our way towards a logical solution, we are often simply feeling our way towards a decision we've pre-made via intuition."[25]

For those who want to strengthen their intuitive powers, I would start with Frances Vaugh's book *Awakening Intuition*.[26] Beginning with an examination of the role of intuition, her book guides readers through the discovery and development of intuition as a vital resource for creativity and problem solving. For those whose interests lie more in the metaphysical aspects of intuition than the psychological and biological, Judith Orloff's book *Second Sight* might be of interest.[27] Supported by scientific rationale, real-life anecdotes, and her personal reflections, part 1 of her book describes how she integrated unconscious intuition in her work as a psychiatrist. Part 2 of her book offers teachings—how others might pursue their own journeys through exercises such as dream interpretation, meditation, and seeking a spiritual path.

Perspectives on Change

Three horizons of change framework   Change agents engage in different time horizons, particularly in large systems, and so do designers. Bill Sharpe's book *Three Horizons: The Patterning of Hope*[28] provides an excellent illustration of this framework (see figure 5.1). The vertical axis indicates the relative dominance or prevalent pattern among the interplay of Horizons 1, 2, and 3, which represent three waves of change at different points in time.[29] The first line, labeled Horizon 1, describes business as usual—doing things to keep daily life functioning. It represents the perspective of those who are responsible for current system activities, such as keeping the lights on. This type of change consists of making incremental modifications and adjustments to the stable patterns of everyday life that are necessary to maintain current values, approaches and technologies. However, the downward decline of Horizon 1 suggests that the pattern is losing its appeal and is not a good fit, given the emerging conditions in the environment. In contrast, Horizon 3 represents the visionary's aspirations of a yet unknown or undeveloped future pattern that ultimately is shown to be the long-term successor to Horizon 1. It begins with seemingly minor changes, but then it takes

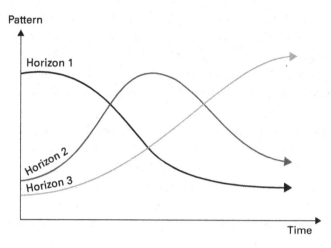

Figure 5.1
The three horizons of change framework

an upward transformational turn that over time becomes dominant pattern since it is a more viable fit with the changing environmental conditions. Horizon 2 represents the middle horizon, a transitional zone when the shortcomings of Horizon 1 are becoming apparent and the seeds of Horizon 3 begin to emerge. As a "zone of innovation,"[30] we find creatives at odds with conservative pressures to conform and the sunk costs of the current way of doing things. This transitional zone can erupt in conflict, as well as transactional interactions and compromises where innovators are attempting to shift the landscape between Horizons 1 and 3.

This three-dimensional view of time has several advantages. As the case studies in part III of this book reveal, this framework can facilitate people stepping out of their mindsets, listening and learning from one another, and bringing about workable structures for complex, transformative change under conditions of uncertainty. The diverse applications in rural community development, education, the National Health Services in the UK, the Scottish Broadcasting Commission, the Southcentral Foundation healthcare system in Alaska, and the Glasgow Community Action on Climate Change attest to the framework's ability to help people create a shared vision of the future.

Awareness of the three horizons also "legitimizes each of the different perspectives and highlights the value of each" and "can result in a shift from holding a horizon as a mindset to using it as a flexible perspective on the situation."[31] "We won't always agree, but we can significantly improve the processes by which we disagree, and sometimes even find fresh ways to get along together to support the transformations that we all need—if no one keeps the H1 lights on we won't be able to see where we are going."[32]

The three horizons of change framework also enables people to shift from a one-dimensional view of time, which stretches from the present to the future, toward a three-dimensional view of time, in which each horizon represents a different relationship between the present and the future. For example, what is today's Horizon 1 "was once the future, the third horizon of a previous era"[33] that no longer fits the emerging environmental conditions. We also find "examples of the third horizon in the present (pockets of future in the present), and consider how this new pattern can emerge through the transitional second horizon."[34] Thus, the three horizons can help people "situate the present moment in relation to the future" since each horizon is regarded "as a quality of the future in the present."[35]

The three horizons of change framework also maps reasonably well with the innovation literature, so long as the concepts are treated metaphorically rather than literally. Horizon 1 is similar to what Clayton Christensen referred to as sustaining innovations in businesses—changes to the status quo and adjustments to the current ways of doing things in order to improve efficiency and sustain existing systems [36] Horizon 2 is akin to what Christensen called disruptive innovations, such as the creation of new markets that eventually disrupt and displace established markets. [37] As represented in the three horizons of change framework, disruptive innovations shake things up and subvert the current system and can take many forms—new technologies like the smartphone, a new election like Brexit, or a social movement like Black Lives Matter. Ultimately Horizon 3 is the vision of the future that people want to attain—"new ways of living and working that will be a better fit with emerging need and opportunity."[38] "The outlook is visionary and aspirational"[39] and relies on radically new transformative innovations, the seeds of which are present today, which "will pave the way for their Horizon 3 vision."[40] Taken together, the three horizons represent a "framework for transformative change"[41] that calls for "a deep transformation in the way we *think together* to inform our actions"[42] and ultimately how we will repattern our collective lives.

Graham Leicester develops the concept further in his book *Transformative Innovation*,[43] a practical guide about the practice of transformative innovation and the development of capacities. It includes discussions of being comfortable with complexity rather than being overwhelmed by it (chapter 2); imaging the transformative innovation that needs to be initiated (chapter 3); bringing people together to make a stand for something radically different, organizing, leading, and managing their efforts, and expanding members over time to prevent burnout (chapter 4); being effective in action by introducing the new in the midst of the old and dealing with challenges along the way (chapter 5); ensuring enabling policy, strategy, and financing in support of transformative innovation (chapter 6), and supporting investments in intentionally designed systems and structures that support a culture of renewal in public, civic, and social systems (chapter 7).

Social movements Cass Sunstein's book *How Change Happens* is directed toward those engaged in social movements, like the civil rights and the #MeToo movements, and how they can succeed.[44] They begin with small influences or "nudges," like the refusal of a Black woman to sit at the back of the bus, that represent seemingly small perturbations in the status quo. These acts of defiance or protest then unleash suppressed feelings and beliefs in others—what Sunstein refers to as "preference falsification," or hidden preferences that might have existed all along but were discouraged from being public because of the existence of social norms.[45] When others cross their personal thresholds for change and say "Me Too," and then are drawn in and activated in greater numbers in a cascade of social interactions, a tipping point is eventually reached, where social norms collapse and are replaced with new ones.

Changing laws   John Thibault's book *How to Change a Law* offers a blueprint on how to change public policies and laws to assist elected leaders in generating solutions that affect the public—student debt, violence, immigration, cybersecurity, privacy, energy independence, health care, taxes, and other areas of concern. It also offers guidance on how people can come together around issues, build coalitions, get funding, and empower themselves with actionable tools and strategies to make changes in law and policy.[46]

Organizational change   By far, the change literature has focused the most attention on organizational change, with numerous theories how organizations change and innovate.[47] Paul Gibbons's *The Science of Successful Organizational Change: How Leaders Set Strategy, Change Behavior, and Create an Agile Culture*, and his second book, *Impact: 21st-Century Change Management, Behavioral Science, Digital Transformation, and the Future of Work*, are two excellent resources.[48] They are founded on science, and yet they are full of practical wisdom and evidence-based insights into how to make changes so that businesses can become more agile and "antifragile," and therefore more successful. In *The Science of Successful Organizational Change*, chapters 7 and 8 are particularly noteworthy about developing a change agent's mindset and responding to people's so-called resistance to change.

   Warner Burke's *Organization Change: Theory and Practice* offers a more traditional overview of the theoretical foundations, types, levels, and processes of change, but he too addresses the challenge of resistance to change. In his view, "people do not *always* resist change." What they "resist is the imposition of change," which takes away their freedom of choice.[49] Moreover, not all forms of resistance are the same. Some people may resist for ideological and political reasons, while others may resist because of system constraints that impede their ability to change. Remove the impediments, and these people will accept change. Still others may resist due to ambivalence. Give them time to make sense of and understand the implications of the new ideas, and they eventually will accept them. Moreover, resistance can be treated as a "form of engagement"—a concept in keeping with the design strategy. Rather than attempting to impose submission or end-run change with power and politics, one can treat resistance as a form of energy that "can be redeployed as a resource" in service to change instead of a barrier to it.[50]

   And for those attempting to change large-scale organizations, John Kotter and Dan Cohen's book *The Heart of Change* offers some important insights. Although the authors acknowledge that an organization's strategy, structure, culture, and systems are part of change, they find that central to its success is speaking to people's feelings rather than their thoughts and analysis: "The heart of change is in the emotions."[51]

And if you still need more books to make the point, I recommend reading *Switch: How to Change Things When Change Is Hard* by Chip and Dan Heath. Drawing from research in psychology, sociology, and other fields, the authors identify key elements to *any* successful change effort. Their humor, insights, and stories of amazing changes give a light touch to a very serious book. According to the authors, for things to change, "somebody somewhere has to start acting differently."[52] Unfortunately, people's minds are ruled by two systems—their rational mind and their emotional mind—each competing for control. The rational mind (the rider) attempts to analyze, plan for, and control change, and the emotional mind (the elephant) attempts to drive, motivate, and energize change through powerful emotions. When the two minds disagree about which way to move, change is doomed. Change can be successful in any situation if you connect the two minds by following a three-part framework:

- *Direct the rider*: Follow the bright spots (what is working) and expand on them; script the critical moves in terms of specific behaviors; and point to where you are going and why the destination is worth it.
- *Motivate the elephant*: Find the feeling; don't just rely on knowledge; shrink the change by breaking it down into manageable parts so it no longer spooks the elephant; and grow your people to cultivate a growth mindset and a sense of identity.
- *Shape the path*: Tweak the environment; change the situation that induces the behavior; build habits and set action triggers so that the rider is not overtaxed in the change process; and rally the herd by making behavior contagious and encouraging it to spread.

The Heath brothers then end their book with twelve common problems that people encounter in fighting for change and some advice on how to counter and overcome them.

Fundamentals of Change Agentry

Dialogue In his book *Dialogue and the Art of Thinking Together*, William Isaacs defines dialogue as "shared inquiry, a way of thinking and reflecting together."[53] It is based on the belief that "if we cannot talk together, we cannot work together."[54] In part II of his book, Isaacs offers guidance and practices on the four essential behaviors of dialogue: *listening*, not just as a singular activity, but listening together as part of a larger whole; *respecting*, which means honoring others and their boundaries and viewing them and their views as legitimate; *suspending*, which entails a deferment of judgment and the certainty that lies behind it, with the willingness to stop, step back, see things with new eyes, and change direction; *speaking* or *voicing*, which is courageous speech revealing what is true for oneself, regardless of other influences. Part III probes how people can improve their "predictive intuition" by separating advocacy from inquiry, exploring people's underlying motives and intentions and overcoming structural traps—"the set of frameworks, habits, and conditions that compel people to act as they do."[55] Isaacs further explores how "conversational fields" and "ecologies of thought" form and emerge, how they are governed, and the methods and practices (including leadership) that generate dialogue. He widens the circle in Part V with cases and examples that illustrate the importance of dialogue for the new economy, organizational and system change, and the future of democracy. He maintains that the goal is to address "problems farther 'upstream' than conventional approaches" and "bring about change at the source of our thoughts and feelings, rather than at the level of results our ways of thinking produce."[56] So ultimately, the intent of dialogue is not only to raise the level of shared thinking, but also to improve "how people act, and, in particular, how they act all together.[57]

Two other books offer more "downstream" approaches but are very helpful in preparing design teams to work together. Deborah Flick's book *From Debate to Dialogue*[58] is an excellent introduction to how to transform conversations. She begins by comparing two processes: the conventional discussion process and the understanding process in terms of their premises, goals, attitudes, focuses, behaviors, roles, and outcomes.[59] Then, in chapters 5–9, she takes the reader through various experiential exercises and applications in how to transform destructive conflicts, bridge the diversity divide, transform groups into teams, and enhance the civility of our public conversations. Jeff Conklin's book *Dialogue Mapping: Building Shared Understanding of Wicked Problems*[60] uses software to demonstrate how dialogue can be used as a facilitation technique to enable team members to see how their comments contribute to the coherence and order of the team's thinking and how they can improve group communications.

Prosocial groups   Using the same principles that underlie biological evolution, referred to as *multilevel section (MLS) theory*, the authors Paul Atkins, David Sloan, and Steven Hays posit that people can be cooperative, collective, and altruistic (prosocial), depending on the social ecologies in which they live and work,[61] despite the pernicious view that humanity's nature is basically selfish. Drawing on Nobel laureate Elinor Ostom's eight core design principles for the commons, the authors broaden their scope to all kinds of groups and how to improve them. Chapter 3 offers a brief overview of eight *core design principles* and how they can work flexibly as a whole to shift behaviors (see table 3.1, which compares Ostrom's principles and the prosocial version and their functions). Chapter 4 then lays out the multilevel psychological and learning skills that people need to adopt and apply these principles.

In part II, the authors demonstrate with tools, exercises, and cases how to help groups function more effectively. Chapter 5 introduces the "psychological flexibility model," featuring a tool called the *acceptance and commitment training (ACT) matrix*, which maps individual and collective interests to articulate both their personal interests and their internal concerns and barriers that often go undiscussed and interfere with group behavior. Chapter 6 describes six interlocking modules that make up the prosocial process, which can be used separately or in combination, with two pathways to combine the modules. In chapters 7–14, the authors explore the eight core design principles, show how, through their integration, they can enhance conversations and ultimately end in agreements that instantiate the principles. Chapter 15 illustrates how to convert a group conversation to real action by setting group goals. The book concludes with the wider implications of prosocial—scaling nested networks of groups to cooperate and address regional, national, and even global challenges.

Building community   Peter Block's book *Community: The Structure of Belonging*[62] is written for those who want to come together to support the well-being of their community and the common good. According to Block, the essential challenge is to shift attention from the problems of community to its possibilities. He maintains the key to community restoration is connectedness or social capital that begins with our language and conversations—"all the ways we listen, speak, and communicate meaning to each other"[63] and the context in which these meanings take place. "We cannot problem-solve our way into fundamental change, or transformation, or community. . . . This is not an argument against problem solving; it is an assertion that the primary work is to shift the context and language and thinking about possibility within which the problem solving takes place.[64]

Part II of Block's book offers a methodology, what he calls the "alchemy of belonging"[65] to help fragmented communities be restorative and transforming. It includes convening leadership; the small group that becomes the unit of transformation; questions of possibility that open the door to the future and invite engagement; six types of conversations[66] that materialize belonging; hospitality that welcomes the stranger; and the design of physical and social space that supports belonging.

Large-group collaborations   From chapter 2 of this book, we understand that collaboration means to *colabor*—people pooling their talents and capabilities and producing something of value together that they could not accomplish on their own, making all of us "smarter than any of us."[67] Most design teams are relatively small, but there are occasions when designers may need to work with groups of more than thirty, even those extending into the hundreds or even thousands of people, such as those sponsored by AmericaSpeaks.[68] Known in the literature as "large group interventions," "interactive events," and "large-scale changes," these collaborations typically last between one and five days, with a common set of features: an intense period of planning prior to meeting, basic agreements on process, a focus on the future, broad participation, and implementation that may require an extended period of time. They began in the 1960s with the Search Conference and Future Search, and thereafter gained momentum as other methodologies emerged, such as Real Time Strategy Change, the ICA Strategic Planning Process, The Conference Model, Fast Cycle Full Participation Work Design, Real Time Work Design, Participative Design, Simu-Real, Work-Out, and Open Space Technology.[69] Other engaging whole systems followed, including Appreciative Inquiry, Collaborative Loops, Whole Scale Change, and The World Café. Too numerous to probe in any depth here, readers will find additional details in *The Change Handbook*.[70] More examples of citizen engagement in their democracy and its governance can be found in *The Deliberative Democracy Handbook* and *How People Harness Their Collective Wisdom and Power to Construct the Future in Co-laboratories of Democracy.*[71]

Leading and facilitating a large-group collaboration, or any meeting for that matter, constitute an art. In *How to Make Collaboration Work*,[72] David Straus provides very practical guidance on how to deal with the challenges of collaboration in order to increase its effectiveness. He recommends putting a common focus on content, establishing an agreed-upon collaborative process, and setting an agenda with clearly defined and assigned roles and resonsibilities—facilitator, recorder, group member, and leader. Strauss also recommends designing collaborations in phases—keeping the whole group focused and together in the same phase of the problem-solving process using the same method. Collaborations also need to have a *process map*—a clear, flexible plan detailing how the team will approach its challenge and the sequence of steps that it will take to get there. The "pathways to action" model in chapter 4 demonstrates how to create a process map, which is useful for designers who are guiding stakeholders through contentious, long-term design projects. The maps are one-page diagrams that identify the people involved (e.g., senior management, steering committees, task forces, and outreach, among others); the phases of the collaboration (e.g., the steps that occur over time in terms of the process design and its planning); and the results that are expected at each step (e.g., the creation of ground rules, identification of strategic issues, problem statements, interim reports, feedback, and a final report and implementation plan). I highly recommend the Strauss model when designing and facilitating large-group collorations, especially in wicked problem territory.

Power and politics of design   "Power" refers to the ability to get something done, and "politics" describes the relations that people form and the various activities in which they engage to get things done. So one can find power and politics in all facets of life—any time people assume a future orientation; attempt to change attitudes, norms, and ideals; influence individuals and communities in taking new courses of action; and shape society in preferred ways. Designers also recognize that design involves a political process, referring to it as the "politics of design."[73] As Ramia Mazé points out, when we accept Herbert Simon's formulation of design as devising "courses of action aimed at changing existing situations into preferred ones"[74] and we seek change, progress, transition, and transformation from what is to what could be, design becomes "a profoundly political act, whether we are reflexive or intentional about this or not."[75] Richard Buchanan makes a similar case when he views design as "political rhetoric" . . . an art of shaping society, changing the course of individuals and communities, and setting patterns for new action."[76]

This political orientation is apparent, although often not explicit, in *concept design*, which induces desires and cultural imaginaries for the future, such as those featured in trade shows and world expositions that prototype "the ideal home," "the future city," or "the world of tomorrow"; *critical design*, which produces artifacts that provoke debates about current norms and generates critiques about models of production and consumption; and *persuasive design*, directed to changing norms and behavior, such as in the area of sustainability.[77] None of these are value-neutral activities. Since there are many ways to image the "ideal" home, car, or city, as well as socioeconomic and tech-nomaterial possibilities, design "choices are normative—they are made from and for particular ideological positions, in relation to specific conditions, contexts, and world-views." Thus, the elaboration of possibilities becomes "an exercise of power . . . , even if position or preference is not articulated or neutrality is claimed."[78]

Based on this short overview, what are the skill sets of power and politics for design-ers? The first is to understand what power is. Rather than assume the traditional view of power, getting what you want against resistance,[79] we can adopt the view that power is "the ability to get things done."[80] Thus, power does not necessarily represent a dilemma for designers when they support people in improving and changing things, especially when people participate in the process. But what is at issue is the *politics* of getting things done—its manipulative, coercive, and destructive aspects—such as making false claims that products have been sustainably produced, creating user interfaces specifi-cally designed to trick users into doing actions that they might not otherwise do, or convincing the public that public policies have produced positive outcomes when they have not. Designers need to move toward the "lighter side" of politics—being collec-tive, collaborative, and generative. The challenge is to resist moves to its "darker" side that have the potential to make design into an instrument of manipulation, control, and repression. The point is to be more reflexive and discerning about the projects in which we engage in terms of their politics, as well as their ethics.[81]

In that regard, two books are of value. Allison M. Vaillancourt's *The Organizational Politics Playbook*[82] offers important insights and strategies for designers who need to understand that surviving in highly political environments does not mean sacrificing moral principles in order to be both ethically and politically savvy. As she reminds us, the word "politics" emerged from Aristotle's writings and describes how to govern communities in the best interests of citizens, which includes finding productive ways to resolve competing interests. One book, although not written as a toolkit for power and politics, is Jeffrey Pfeffer's *Managing with Power*,[83] which describes how to recognize when power is utilized and to identify the sources of power that people have. Several chapters are devoted to the strategies and tactics that people employ for the effec-tive use of power—how they frame problems, their skills of interpersonal influencing, their politics in the use of information and analysis, the symbolic action of language, ceremonies, and settings, how power is lost, and how to manage political dynamics productively.

Managing, resolving, and transforming conflict   Before launching design projects in wicked problem territory, a reading or rereading of Peter Marris's *Loss and Change* is advised. We need to be reminded that when people's familiar patterns of life are dis-rupted by change, the "conservative impulse" is to try to sustain the continuity and stability of their life purposes and relationships. But to change what is and transition to what could be, individuals need to go through a form of bereavement. Not only must they come to terms with their losses, but they must learn how to reconstruct meaning in their lives based on the changes. Marris offers three principles to navigate individuals through this change process: first, we "must always expect and even encourage conflict" to give people an opportunity to react, express their ambivalence, and make sense of the change; second, we must respect people's responses and experiences without forcing "alien" ideas upon them; and third, change requires time and patience "because conflicts involve not only the accommodation of diverse interest, but the realisation of an essential structure of meaning. . . . People have to find their own meaning in . . . changes before they can live with them."[84]

Conflict is a natural part of the design process. People will disagree on a whole host of things—what is being designed, how it is being designed, for whom it is being designed, and whether it merits being designed in the first place. Add to the mix stakeholders' different bases of power and their competing views about a design's usefulness, costs, and contributions to society, and disagreements of all kinds can surface in a design challenge. But the issue is whether conflicts are constructive and increase people's understanding, learning, and contributions to the design effort or whether they are destructive and undermine people's ability to be creative problem solvers. Unless conflict is addressed and managed so that people can come away energized by the experience, it can wreak havoc on the design process.

A comprehensive and multidisciplinary source for understanding how to make conflict constructive is Lisa Amsler, Janet Martinez, and Stephanie Smith's book *Dispute System Design*.[85] They raise an important question: how can one design systems to manage conflict in a way that is fair, provides meaningful justice, has control over the final design, is most effective in resolving conflict, and gives people access to voice and justice? To answer this question, the book is divided into two general areas. The foundation of Dispute System Design (DSD) includes six chapters on its definition, analytic framework, building blocks, practice, accountability, and ethics. The second general area is case applications that explore DSD across a range on contexts. Cases are subdivided into four parts: part I focuses on conflicts that touch people's lives in their neighborhoods; part II examines the management of conflict in private, public organizations, and systems. part III moves the design to the national and international levels. And part IV sets its sights on issues of networks, collaborative public management, and collaborative governance.

Systems thinking   Systems thinking can be viewed as a paradigm, a language, and a methodology.[86] As a *paradigm*, it requires dynamic thinking—acknowledgment that change is constant and the world is not static. Since organizations are complex adaptive systems (CASs), we must accept that the relationship between a cause and its effect is not necessarily linear, thanks to feedback loops when effects often influence their causes. As a *visual and diagrammatic language*, systems thinking has a precise set of rules that translate perceptions and concepts into pictures that illuminate interdependencies and relationships. And as a *methodology*, systems thinking employs a set of modelling and learning technologies that can be used to understand the structure of a system, the interconnections among its components, and how change in any part or component of the system can affect the whole system.

A *system* is defined as a collection of parts or components that interact to form a unified whole. For example, the human body is a system made of subsystems like the circulatory, digestive, and circulatory subsystems, which all work together to maintain life. An organization is a system that has many differentiated parts: units that set the organization's direction; people with specific skill sets and competencies required to do the work; technologies needed to support the workflow; the organization's structure that differentiates among specialized organizational units; and organizational processes such as planning and decision making, communications and information management, budgeting and accounting to ensure that the organization can deliver its intended results. For example, the Roberts Organizational System Framework (ROSF), which will be discussed in chapter 6, demonstrates how to collect data on an organization's major elements, not only to assess how well the elements are aligned or fit together to produce results, but also to identify any unintended outcomes or consequences, such as harm to people and the environment, that need to be rectified in the organization's strategic redesign.

Depending on the system and the level of detail required, *system diagrams* can be very complex, as seen in figure 5.2, which was an attempt to understand the effectiveness of civilian-military activities to counter the Afghan insurgency. The aim was to identify the insurgency's root causes and then develop strategies and tactics that focused on them rather than their symptoms.[87]

Some system maps, also referred to as *causal loop diagrams (CLDs)*, can use *archetypes* to reduce the complexity of the system and yet retain a system's problem architecture. Figure 5.3 illustrates one example, the archetype known as the "Tragedy of the Commons."[88] Here, we see two actors (A and B) pursuing actions that are individually beneficial. But if the amount of their joint activity grows too large for the system to support, the common resource or "the Commons" becomes overloaded, and both parties experience diminishing benefits or net gains. If this behavior continues over time, the Commons faces collapse. Although the Commons typically involves many parties, the interactions of just two parties in a CLD can demonstrate the same underlying problem architecture.

What is revealing about a system's map is that we often find that there is no single concept or variable that represents "the problem." What system maps and CLDs do is help the designer, as a systems thinker, to understand how "the problem" is embedded in the dynamic interconnections among the system elements as a whole. Choosing one variable or concept to be "the problem" misses the pattern of relationships and interactions that produce, in this case, the Tragedy of the Commons. Thus, designers face a dilemma: Where and how do they intervene in a system if they can't pinpoint where a particular problem is? And how they develop solutions if they are unable to find a

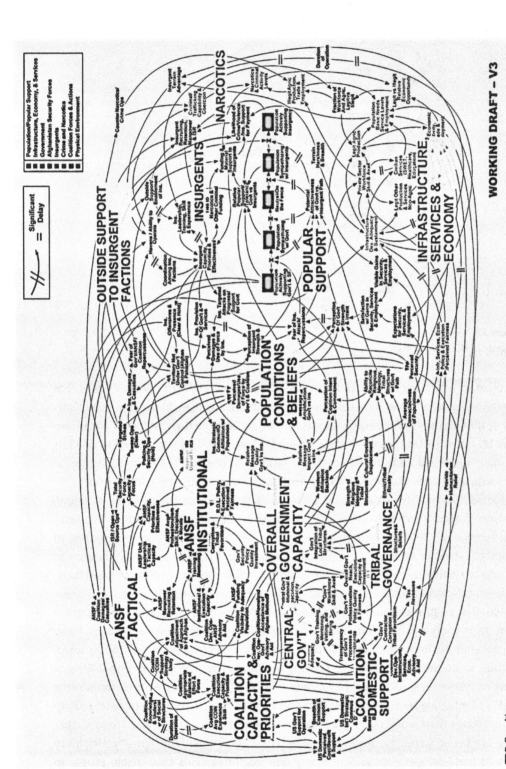

WORKING DRAFT – V3

Figure 5.2

Afghanistan stability / COIN dynamics

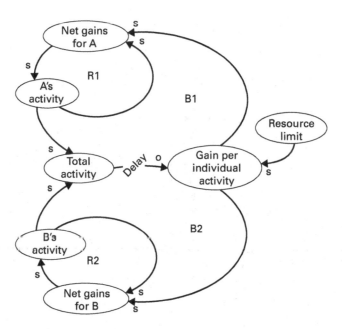

Figure 5.3
Tragedy of the Commons

problem to which they can attach it? The answer from a system's perspective is that effective solutions "never lie at the level of individuals." Instead, in the case of the Tragedy of the Commons, the designer needs to ask questions such as: "What are the incentives for individuals to persist in their actions?" How "can the long-term collective loss be made more real and immediate to the individual actors?" What are the ways "to reconcile short-term individual rewards with long-term cumulative consequences"?[89]

For additional ways to map and understand systems, see *Design Journeys through Complex Systems: Practice Tools for Systemic Design* by Peter Jones and Kristel Van Ael.[90] The handbook's focus is on complex systemic design practices—those described in chapter 7—that cross sector, disciplinary, cultural, and organizational boundaries to address challenges such as regional development, urban design, health care, and large-scale educational systems redesign. The toolkit runs through the life cycle of systemic design change projects guided by eleven principles over seven stages, accompanied with thirty tools and over forty modeling canvasses to guide workshop designs. I also recommend Anthony Hodgson's *Systems Thinking for a Turbulent World*[91] as an introduction to the next generation of systems thinking—what he calls second-order systems or cybernetics—that deal recursively with multiple scales and time frames. His goal is to integrate second-order systems theory with futures thinking in order to help people adapt their worldviews, practical knowledge, consciousness and ethics so that they are better suited for turbulent times. His foundational concept—"anticipatory present moment"—is central to learning new cognitive skills that enable people to view the world as a "mutually interdependent living system"[92] with consciousness. The practice of 'participative patterning,'[93] aided by methods of visual and artful facilitation, also offers a new way that people can collaborate to deconstruct and reconstruct their thinking and behavioral patterns, and thus deepen their efforts to make a paradigmatic shift. This short summary doesn't do justice to this important book. Full of wisdom and insight, it is highly recommended for designers who want to go beyond first-generation systems thinking.

Designers' Skill Sets and Toolkits

Data Collection

The design challenge launches the discovery process and data collection. It begins with searches of *secondary or archival data sources*—books, reports, journals, and newpapers anything that informs issues surrounding the challenge and the questions that it generates. Based on this background information, the design team then moves to interviews and observations of people in their own settings. For example, the design challenge for the Special Operations Command in the Pacific required the team to collect general information about the command, the forces and trends in its environment, its stakeholders, and the challenges and opportunities that it faced. Once the design team gathered this information, it was ready to interview people who were positioned to answer questions generated during the archival search. The interviews not only gave the team additional insights about people's views and opinions, but they also opened up opportunities for the team to observe people as they worked. The observations then provided a deeper understanding of how the command operated, often beyond the awareness of the people themselves. Thus, data collection, especially in wicked problem territory, is a multilayered process.

But the most difficult aspect of archival data collection is knowing how much of it is enough to get started. Too much data, and the danger is getting trapped in analysis paralysis; too little, and the danger is not having a broad enough perspective to capture different points of view. So how far should data collection extend from the micro to the macro level, and what and whom should it include? Each project is unique. In the case of the regeneration of rain forest in Samboja Lestari (discussed in chapter 9), the designer had to delve into the large-scale political, economic, social, and environmental forces that were destroying Indonesian rain forests and all living things on the land, examine the unique factors that were at play near Samboja Lestari and the city of Balikpapan in East Kalimantan, Borneo, and delve into the science of creating a rain forest on land where nothing lived—which no one said could be done. Thus, the discovery phase in wicked problem territory can require an extended period of time before the designer is able to frame the problems that will anchor the subsequent phases of the design process.

Conducting interviews Interviews form the second round of data collection. Ideally, designers are in the field to ask questions of the people for whom they are designing in order to hear, in their own words, about their experiences, hopes, and concerns. People, who are selected based on their expertise, stakeholder group, or perspective on the design challenge, can be interviewed individually or in groups. Since this topic has been well covered by others who note the importance of empathy and open-ended explorations in the interviews, I refer readers to two resources: The Stanford d-School *Design Project Guide*[94] and IDEO's *Field Guide*.[95] Both resources, which are free, guide the design team through interview preparation and the basic steps of the interview process.

Observations and immersion in the field   Direct observation requires designers to "have all their receptors on—and frequently turned up to eleven."[96] When engaging with a "beginner's mind," they put aside their assumptions to look and see things with fresh eyes, staying alert to contradictions between what they see and what they expect that signals a need to dig deeper. Direct observation of group meetings, the physical layout of work settings, and interactions in formal and informal settings all speak volumes about people's underlying beliefs, values, and views, of which they may not be consciously aware.

When immersed in settings in which people work,[97] the designer's goal is to observe what people are doing, record exactly what they see and hear, and then add their impressions and interpretations. One immersion technique is to shadow people for a day (with their permission), watching them as they work, socialize, and relax, and even asking them questions about how they make decisions and lead their lives. It was through immersion that the embrace design team came to understand that the design challenge in Nepal was not the neonatal incubators that had broken down. The problem was the distance that parents had to travel to the hospital, which accounted for many of the neonatal deaths since premature infants lack body fat and cannot survive the cold for long distances.

Training design teams to see when they are in the field is an essential skill. Tina Seelig's *inGenius* has an excellent chapter on paying attention.[98] Exercises in Stanford's Bootcamp Bootleg[99] are also useful. They range from how to assume a beginner's mind-set, training people to view and interpret situations using the What, How, Why tool, conducting camera studies, engaging with extreme users whose behavior is not the norm, and searching for analogous spaces or examples that are tangential to the design, but share enough attributes to offer crossover insights—like the hospital emergency room design team that went to NASCAR events to observe how winning pit crews worked together under intense pressure and achieved excellent results.

Qualitative Data Analytics

Mathew Miles and colleagues[100] describe three concurrent activities of qualitative data analysis: data condensation, data display, and conclusion drawing/verification. *Data condensation*, sometimes referred to as *data reduction*, involves writing summaries and memos of field notes, interviews, and observations. *Data display*, sometimes referred to as *data visualization*, compresses, structures, and presents the collected information into a more easily understood, accessible, and compact format. And *conclusion drawing and verification* involve writing up tentative conclusions and then verifying them with others.

Data display In terms of data display, Rudolf Arnheim's seminal work on visual thinking equates it with the most important kind of thought, for which language is only a translation. The goal is to convert information, stories, and concepts into images to make ideas more tangible and concrete.[101] The transformation of insights and what is in the mind's eye can be an image, a graphic, a representation, or a picture, as illustrated in *empathy maps*, *point-of-view statements*, *personas*, and *journey mapping*. Journey mapping, for example, presents a flowchart in a graphic format that documents people's experiences as they go about their work or daily lives. It is a way for the designer to "walk in their shoes" and to identify problems and frustrations that people may encounter as they go through their day. It was particularly useful, for example, when one of my design teams wanted to understand how new personnel entered their organization. Using journey mapping, the team identified various pain points and issues that made entry for newly rotated personnel very frustrating and difficult. Problems then became opportunities to change new personnel orientation programs to facilitate how personnel could enter the organization and assume their duties.[102]

The ubiquitous sticky notes, sketches, pictures, and photographs that cover the walls in design studios have made visualization "the mother of all design tools."[103] For an excellent overview of visual thinking graphics, see David Sibbet's book *Visual Meetings: How Graphics, Sticky Notes, and Idea Mapping Can Transform Group Productivity*.[104] Liedtka and Ogilvie also present an excellent overview of visualization in chapter 3 of *Designing for Growth*[105] and demonstrate the use of tools such as posters, flowcharts, storyboards, and journey maps in the *Designing for Growth Field Book*.[106] Other excellent sources are David Straker's *Rapid Problem Solving with Post-it Notes*[107] and Dan Roam's *The Back of the Napkin: Solving Problems and Selling Ideas with Pictures*.[108] For a delightful beginner's guide to sketching people, emotions, actions, and relations, see *Creative Confidence* by Kelley and Kelley.[109] Colin Ware's book *Visual Thinking for Design*[110] is also of value to probe human perception and explore how humans think visually and design.

Conclusion drawing and verification Conclusion drawing and verification involve writing up tentative conclusions and then verifying them with others. Jon Kolko describes the effort as forging a synthesis and making "connections between seemingly unrelated issues through a process of selective pruning and visual organization" in order to extract themes and patterns.[111] Two skill sets are valuable in this effort: *sensemaking* and *abductive reasoning*.

Kolko describes sensemaking as "an "action-oriented process that people automatically go through in order to integrate experiences into their understanding of the world around them." It involves "manipulating, organizing, pruning, and filtering data in the context of a design problem" using methods of "reframing, concept mapping, and forging connections."[112] Robert Thayer's description of leaders as "sense makers" and how they construct meaning in situations that are puzzling and uncertain also may be of interest to designers working in organizations.[113]

Abductive reasoning differs from inductive reasoning, which moves from specifics to a general conclusion, and deductive reasoning, which moves from a general principle to a specific conclusion.[114] In contrast, designers begin with incomplete data collected during discovery. They synthesize the data and attempt to make some sense of it[115] by coming up with an explanation based on what they have read, observed, experienced, and learned. Like Sherlock Holmes, who examined the evidence at a crime scene, designers call on their intuition and inspired guesswork to make an inferential leap from the data they see to some plausible explanation that seems to fit the available "facts." As a very practical way of reasoning, abduction enables designers to move forward provisionally and take action despite the lack of complete evidence and certainty, a situation that plagues all designers in wicked problem territory.

Designers also use multiple ways of thinking related to sensemaking. *Divergent thinking* expands options, and *convergent thinking* zeroes in on a selective few. The most comprehensive toolkit that I have found for divergence and convergence thinking is Robert Curedale's section on the ideation phase in his book *Design Thinking Process and Methods*. Although the section does not distinguish activities in terms of divergence and convergence, the techniques of brainstorming are excellent examples of divergent thinking. The section includes an overview of the many types of brainstorming and how to prepare for and conduct brainstorming sessions. Illustrations of convergent thinking (e.g., how to vote, review, arrange, focus and evaluate ideas) also are summarized.[116]

Lateral thinking is a way to generate more creativity and insight in the problem-solving process. Edward de Bono's book *Lateral Thinking: Creativity Step by Step* offers a range of techniques and exercises such as fractionation, analogies, random stimulation, and the rearrangement, restructuring, and juxtaposition of information that can lead to different ways of doing things, different ways of looking at things, and different ways to break out of the "concept prison of old ideas."[117]

Integrative thinking is well described in *Creating Great Choices: A Leader's Guide to Integrative Thinking* by Jennifer Riel and Roger Martin.[118] Rather than choosing one solution or making trade-offs to placate opposing positions, leaders can walk through four phases and steps within each phase to resolve the tensions between opposing ideas or models. Although the book is written for business leaders, it can be useful for anyone dealing with high-conflict design projects in wicked problem territory.

Quantitative Data Analytics
Quantitative data analysis is the collection of numerical data or the transformation of collected or observed data into numerical data.

Value chain analysis *Value chain analysis* describes and tracks end-to-end interactions that an organization has with its partners—those that supply the materials it needs and assist in the production of its products and/or services, as well as the marketing, distribution, and support of its offerings. The goal of value chain analysis is to identify where along the chain that costs can be minimized and values increased. Designers then recommend where and how to make changes to improve organizational performance and to differentiate the organization from those that offer similar products and services.

Geospatial and temporal analyses   *Geospatial and temporal analyses* collect, store, manage, visualize, analyze, and present geographic and temporal data. For geospatial analyses, designers can use software programs (e.g., ARCGIS) to input raw data, which the software then transforms and displays in the requested format. Alternatively, before launching into more complex geospatial software packages, designers can use programs such as Google Earth or Ed Ferrari and Alasdair Rae's book *GIS for Planning and the Built Environment: An Introduction to Spatial Analysis*.[119] To collect and display temporal data, designers should refer to the seven types of time series data on the Humans of Data website.[120]

One example of geospatial analysis can be found in figure 5.4. The dark spaces on the land masses locate where the designers geospatially mapped the presence and operations of the Army Civil Affairs Regiment and its units from 2006–2014.[121] Until then, the units' locations were neither widely understood nor appreciated until the data were visually displayed.

Social network analysis   Designers also can conduct *social network analysis* using a software program (e.g., ORA), to convert raw data about people, organizations, and other entities into nodes and their connections (e.g., family ties, friendship ties, work ties, or organizational ties) into lines. The lines or connections among the nodes depict a *social network*. In figure 5.5, using a software program called ORA, Civil Affairs designers also generated a social network to graphically display how the nodes (different Civil Affairs organizations) were interconnected. The analysts then circled the four *subnetworks* that had the greatest centrality measures—meaning that they identified organizations that were more tightly interconnected than others in the command's network. The visualizations then informed discussions about how the command's network of organizations was interconnected and the extent to which this network structure supported the command's mission and purpose.

The size of social networks grows substantially as people and organizations cross organizational, sectoral, and disciplinary boundaries to contribute their time, resources, and expertise to work together. Social networks grow even larger when people use the web to share ideas and information to achieve a common goal.[122] Some are collaborative innovation networks (COINs), but others can extend to even larger groups of people—collaborative networks (CNs) and collaborative interest networks (CINs). Taken together, these networks have delivered some impressive innovations—the World Wide Web, the Linux operating system, and Wikipedia. All have a similar pattern of working together. They self-organize online, they work and learn from one another, and they evolve an ethical code based on trust, honesty, and transparency.[123]

Figure 5.4
US Army Civil Affairs Regiment's worldwide presence (95th, 85th, USACAPOC), 2006–2014

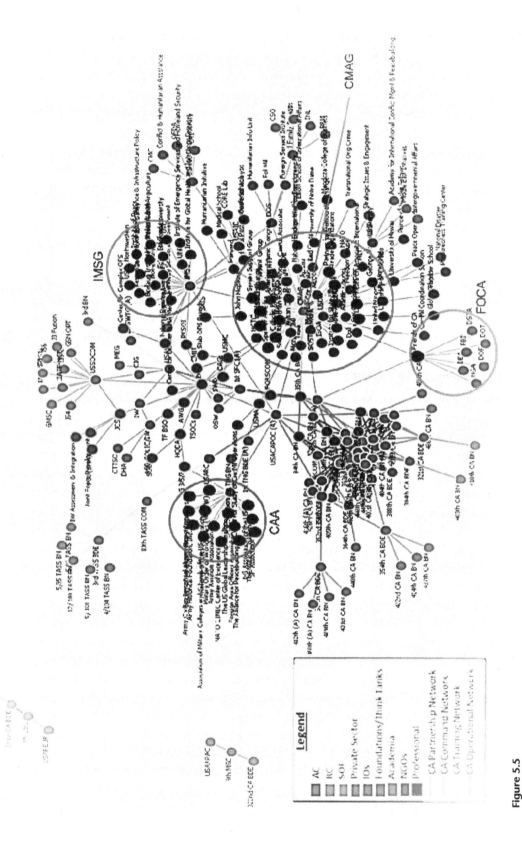

Figure 5.5
US Army Civil Affairs organizational network, 2006–2014

Perspective Taking, Problem Finding/Framing, and Solution Generation

Ultimately, the quality of designs depends on the quality of designers' ability to synthesize data, make sense of it, take a perspective, frame or reframe a problem, and come up with a tentative solution.[124] To get a sense of perspective taking, I recommend the *Powers of Ten* film and animation made by the Office of Charles and Ray Eames for IBM.[125] It begins with a view of a lakeside picnic in Chicago and then transports us to the outer edges of the universe. It then returns us to the sleeping picnicker and moves us inward into his hand to the point where we ultimately view a proton of a carbon atom within a deoxyribonucleic acid (DNA) molecule in a white blood cell. It is a wonderful film to help designers consider which perspective will inform the next steps in the design process.

For finding and framing problems and generating solutions, two books are particularly noteworthy. Kees Dorst's very important book *Frame Innovation*[126] provides examples of how designers generate new ideas and solutions where others see none, and find opportunities where others only see problems. Bryan Lawson's book *How Designers Think* describes design "as much a matter of finding problems as it is of solving them."[127] Drawing from his guidance, Box 5.1 summarizes the challenges of problem finding, framing, and solution generation using homelessness as an example.

Prototyping, Getting Feedback, Storytelling, and Advocating

Prototyping Kathryn McElroy's book *Prototyping for Designers*[136] offers examples of prototypes, differentiates among various types of prototypes (low fidelity, mid-fidelity, and high-fidelity), identifies five dimensions of fidelity, and then walks the reader through processes of prototyping. She devotes a chapter to prototyping digital products, a chapter on physical products, and a chapter to illustrate how to test prototypes with users. Her final chapter offers a case that pulls together all aspects of prototyping.

Chapter 6 of Luis Perez-Breva's book *Innovating: A Doer's Manifesto for Starting from a Hunch, Prototyping Problems, Scaling up, and Learning to be Productively Wrong* presents a "kit to drive innovation, anywhere."[137] After a short overview of the two paths to prototyping, the kit details the second path. It begins with "a hunch . . . phrased as a problem," which usually surfaces a "'family' of problems to be discovered and potentially addressed." "Thus, a problem—or, more accurately, a hunch with the structure of a problem—is the first component of the kit."[138] The second component of the kit is "parts"—whatever is needed to materialize the problem and to quickly arrive at its tangible demonstration. The third component is "people"—those brought together in the team and a list of those who might be tapped as subject matter experts. The fourth component is a "primer," conceived to "help a team overcome the fear of being wrong" and to focus on demonstrating their own version of the problem at scale. [139] The focus then turns to ideas that could lead to solutions, what must be accomplished to solve the problem, and how to verify how a problem could be solved.

Make Space, a book by Scott Doorley and Scott Witthoft,[140] is highly recommended for those who want to set up design space, including the space and tools for prototyping. It describes how to convert and configure available space, build furniture and

Box 5.1
Challenges in Problem Finding, Framing, and Solution Generation

- The challenge that launches a design project can be broad, sometimes with constraints that bound the challenge. In either case, the design challenge offers a general direction, but the problem statement requires a more specific focus. Let's say that the design challenge is to address homelessness in a particular city. Detailed inquiry during discovery is needed before the designer can zero in on a problem definition about a city's homelessness. The designer doesn't know what the problem is until he or she makes sense and knows much more about the city and its context.

- Design problems also can be symptoms or consequences of higher-level problems or causes of lower-level problems. For example, the issue of homelessness depends on how one views its causes. Could it be due to the psychological and mental health issues of the homeless, a lack of jobs for unskilled laborers, the loss of affordable housing due to demolition and deterioration of aging properties, the expiration of federal contracts, or the weak economic conditions and the foreclosure crisis that turned millions of homeowners into renters? Since "problems tend to be organized hierarchically" from the policy level down to the individual level, "there is no objective or logical way of determining the right level on which to tackle such problems."[128]

- In addition, "design problems and solutions are inexorably interdependent. It is obviously meaningless to study solutions without reference to problems, and the reverse is equally fruitless."[129] We often don't fully understand a problem unless we have an acceptable solution to illuminate and explore it. Thus, we should view design as an emergent process in which a problem and a solution develop in tandem and each is viewed as a reflection of the other.

- Design problems and their framing "require subjective interpretation."[130] Homelessness is perceived differently by city planners who create housing policy, architects who design housing, medical personnel who treat illnesses, social workers who find people places to live and work, and the police who try to keep people safe. Therefore, we "should not expect objective formulations of design problems"[131] based on their sense-making routines.

- Thus, "problems cannot be comprehensively stated." The designer never can be sure that all aspects of a problem have surfaced, and many of its components "cannot be expected to emerge until some attempt has been made at generating solutions." Indeed, many features of design problems may never be fully uncovered and made explicit. Design problems are often full of uncertainty, both about the objectives and their relative priorities. In fact, both objectives and priorities are quite likely to change during the design process as the solution implications begin to emerge.[132]

- The number of design solutions is "inexhaustible." Since wicked design problem can't be definitively and comprehensively stated, "it follows that there can never be an exhaustive list of all the possible solutions to such problems."[133] There are no optimal solutions to design problems. Multiple requirements are embedded in a design, so "rarely can the designer simply optimize on one requirement without suffering some loses elsewhere" such as when motorists demand acceleration *and* good gas mileage.[134] Design involves trade-offs and compromises, so instead of an optimal solution there are a range of acceptable solutions, each of which "is likely to prove more or less satisfactory in different ways to different clients or uses." And ultimately, since there are no established methods to decide whether the design offers a good or bad solution, the "best test of most designs is to wait and see how well it works in practice."[135]

tools, construct see-through walls with an overhead grid with spring-leaded studs and jacks, and create and design completely new spaces. It also describes prototyping toolkits, stocking a prototyping cart, and a design template of spatial characteristics with suggestions for lighting.

For those who want to explore the power of digital tools and the desktop fabrication revolution, Chris Anderson's book *Makers: The New Industrial Revolution*[141] provides an excellent introduction, especially chapter 7, "Open Hardware," and chapter 8, "Financing the Maker Movement." His appendix, "The 21st Century Workshop: How to Become a Digital Maker," recommends tools on getting started, including CAD, a desktop program to work with designs onscreen with two- and three-dimensional drawing programs; three-dimensional printing; laser cutting; computer numerical control (CNC) machines; and electronics gear to make physical objects programmable and connected to the web—a particularly important feature in the emerging Internet of Things.

Getting feedback Feedback is ongoing throughout the design process. The point is to ascertain whether designs are desirable, feasible, and viable. Does a design solution meet the needs and expectations of the sponsor, clients, and stakeholders? Is the solution technically doable, or does it require adaptation to current or emerging technology and expertise? Is the solution financially viable as well as environmentally safe, or does it exceed the costs that people are willing to pay and open up questions sustainability amid growing concerns about the environment and climate change?

Many factors influence design feedback that is needed to assess a design's desirability, feasibility, and viability: the fidelity needed to present an idea (high, medium, or low fidelity); the types of solutions to be developed (e.g., products, processes); the particular stage in the design process (e.g., testing a proof of concept; testing a tangible or functional manifestation of an idea—often referred to as a prototype; conducting a pilot or service rollout; only testing the essential core of a concept rather than the full solution, otherwise known as "minimal viable product";)[142] or testing the prototype as it is implemented in the field with its users and stakeholders.

Thus prototyping requires multiple rounds of feedback, beginning with team members and then extending to a range of stakeholders specific to the design project. Getting feedback can take the form of a simple 2×2 matrix that asks what works, what needs to be improved, what the evaluator doesn't like, and what recommendations for change are proposed. But evaluations can get more complex. IDEO's Design Kit[143] provides answers to a number of detailed questions: "How do I choose a solution to take forward? "How do I get feedback?" "How do I integrate the feedback and iterate?" "How do I assess if my solution is working?" "How do I prepare for scale?" See chapter 17 of Curedale, which discusses validation and describes even more sophisticated testing tools.[144]

Storytelling and advocating Jeanne Liedtka and her colleagues warn that "in a world with too much information, much of it badly communicated, we are drowning in data. Design's ability to cut through the clutter, to distill the essence of what is important, and to communicate that vividly and with a human face—what could be more valuable than that?"[145] Thus, they call stories "an innovator's best friend," which bring people toward a design project "the way nectar brings bees to a flower."[146] Stories are not only time efficient, but they offer people a compelling invitation to explore the problem space and search for solutions. Although storytelling is important as part of the prototyping process, stories also are an effective skill set of advocacy to help people understand why the design challenge is important and how they might become involved in it.

An outline and techniques for developing a good story can be found in the *Designing for Growth Field Book*.[147] Chapter 8 of Perez-Breva offers more extensive details on practicing advocacy, beginning with a "story arc that makes sense," which reaches a conclusion with a demonstrable impact. He describes advocacy meetings as a "ballet in three movements": movement 1 gets someone's attention; movement 2 outlines the value proposition in joining the designer, which hinges on the problem solved, what has been demonstrated, and the magnitude of the impact foreseen; and movement 3 lays out the specifics for a deal.[148]

Project Management for Designers

Project management is an important subject in the management literature, and it is no less important in design, especially in wicked problem territory. Regenerative design projects, for example, can extend over years, span large geographic areas, include thousands of people, and require massive funding and resources. To undertake projects of this magnitude, designers need to be directly involved in project management. In-depth consideration of this important topic is not possible in this short overview. Instead, the subsections here highlight key issues that designers need to think about before pursuing the organizational, systemic, and regenerative designs described in part III.

Funding a design project   Foundations and organizations are sponsoring design competitions that award those who are seeking creative solutions to major social, economic, environmental, and cultural issues concerning education, poverty, water, the environment, housing, and other elements.[149] However, funding and awards are distributed based on the designer's creative ideas and the potential to solve problems that are already known. But if the problem is known, by definition we are in complex, not wicked problem territory. A key question is how designers get funding for problem finding, not just solution generation.

One answer comes from Jock Brandis, who describes the "Rambo school of design."[150] The designer literally stumbles on a problem—bleeding fingers from shelling sun-dried peanuts in Mali, Africa. He then works with no budget, no materials other than what he can scrape together, and no support to share and develop his ideas. He eventually creates the universal nut sheller, a low-cost tool that has caused productivity to jump in Mali and generates biofuel and a good fertilizer when used to press oil from the Jatropha plant in India. Other examples of problem finding on very low budgets can be found in David Bornstein's book on how social entrepreneurs who, as designers with little to no funding, have generated new ideas that indeed have changed the world.[151] His case studies provide details of how social entrepreneurs scrape together funds and resources for the design or redesign of rural electrification, nursing, assisted living for the disabled, health care (including caring for AIDS patients), college access, disability rights, and child protection.

To generate funding, the following resources are useful in getting designers started: Alex Daly's *Crowdsourceress: Get Smart, Get Funded, and Kickstart Your Next Big Ideas*; Vilius Stanislovaitis's *Your First Kickstarter Campaign*; and William Eggers and Paul Macmillan's *The Solution Revolution*, especially chapter 5, "Public Value Exchanges."[152]

Framing design challenges and writing design briefs   Designers are in a double bind in wicked problem territory. It is difficult to get funding unless designers provide information about the nature of a design project—what is the purpose, who will be involved, what resources will be required, and what time frame bounds the project. But providing this level of detail is difficult before designers have been involved in the discovery phase in some depth. In wicked problem territory, we don't know what we don't know, and it is difficult to predict what will surface as we explore unfamiliar terrain and discover potential problems and solutions. Any agreement with an authorizing person or organization has to balance the designer's need for exploration and flexibility with a sponsor's constraints and requirements in terms of time, money, and resources. Rather than a premature closure, I take a two-step process with the sponsor: first, getting agreement on a design challenge; and second, finalizing the design brief.

A design challenge in wicked problem territory lays out the design project's general direction and gives just enough guidance to attract interest and support, but avoids prematurely specifying problems or solutions. For example, when I worked with the Civil Affairs Regiment in the Special Operation Forces, we opened with the question on what could the Civil Affairs Regiment be in 2025, rather than identifying the many problems that it was experiencing that needed fixing. Although offering design solutions was our ultimate aim, we had no idea which problems and issues should be the focus of our efforts until we finished gathering data through the discovery phase.

Once the design team has gone through at least one iteration of discovery, it can be more specific in the design brief, usually two or three pages in length, which more formally defines the project and its goals, identifies the resources needed, provides a timeline, establishes reporting relationships, and specifies the design criteria based on the scope of the design solutions. For this task, I recommend the *Designing for Growth Field Book*'s instructions for drafting a design brief.[153]

Leading and managing design projects   In wicked problem territory, increasing numbers of people are affiliated with long-term design projects measured not in months but in years, especially those that require extensive field-based testing and implementation. Designers not only attend to the design team and the dynamics of the design process, they also need to build a culture that encourages dialogue, transforms conflict, and maintains motivation. In addition, they need to interface with the sponsors, secure funding, network with stakeholders, plan and organize the project, schedule activities, and evaluate the results of their interventions.[154] I have found it prudent for design teams of long duration and a larger number of team members to have at least two people in the leadership role, and possibly a team of people depending on the project. For example, one person can be the lead designer, who works with the design team and facilitates its process, and one person can serve as the project manager. As illustrated in chapter 6, the design team for the Norwegian project had two people—a designer and a project manager who spoke Norwegian, interfaced and negotiated with the Norwegian sponsor, managed the resources, coordinated the team's travel and activities, and assisted in evaluating the results of the yearlong, ten-person design project that spanned two continents.

Aidan Hornby's article "How Design Teams Can Avoid Bad Project Management" is a good place to prepare for project management, especially his advice on how to balance structure and freedom and differentiate the differences between good design project management and poor project management.[155] Although Katherine Best's *Design Management* is for organization-centric designs, part 1 has guidance on how to manage client relations, guide design decisions, and develop good working relationships; part 2 offers suggestions on how to initiate design projects and manage creative teams; and part 3 offers an overview of the project management process, design's social and environmental responsibilities, design's policy, procedures and guidelines, and how to measure the success of designs, as well as how to differentiate design leadership and management.[156] Steven Wu on the *Creative Bloq* offers a good overview of the best project management software for designers.[157] He features Trello, Basecamp, Teamwork projects, Resource Guru, ActiveCollab, Zoho Projects, Jira, Asana, Podio, Freedcamp, and Wrike, with prices that range from free to nominal monthly fees.

Building a design team   Some design teams have a history of working together and are well versed in the design process. So when one project finishes and the team wants to continue working together, it searches for design challenges to which it wants to commit. Alternatively, in many design consultancies, those responsible for negotiating with a sponsor set up the general terms of the design challenge and the particulars of the design brief, and then they assign people to the projects based on the content expertise required. Catapult Design,[158] a nonprofit design firm in San Francisco, uses another strategy in building a design team. A lead designer goes in-country and searches for content experts interested in joining the team and working on a design challenge. The lead designer then instructs the team in the design process as they tackle the design challenge and project. In other words, the new team learns design by doing design. When the lead designer returns home, the rest of the design team remains there, ready to apply the newly acquired design competencies to future design challenges.

As designers tackle more abstract and complex challenges in wicked problem territory, they typically invite others based on their perspectives, expertise, and skills. This broadening has changed design's landscape.[159] Design has gone from treating users as subjects to inviting them to be partners in the design process. Even beyond that, design's landscape is now extending to include "participative projects." *Taking [A]part: The Politics and Aesthetics of Participation in Experienced-Centered Design* considers a series of research projects in human-computer interaction (HCI), in which the design of digital technology is central to the participative experience. These "projects explore and harness the capacity of people to create participatory experiences" that enable "them to take part in new ways of defining themselves and their relationships with others."[160] Going well "beyond the desire simply to provide solutions to problems already given," these boundary-pushing projects in HCI "redefine social arrangements, challenge institutional norms, and make new social relations possible."[161] So when HCI designers are working to bring diverse communities together, engaging them in dialogue and relationship building, empowering them to challenge conventional perceptions, and assisting them to devise alternative ideas, frameworks, practices, and systems of knowledge, there is "the potential for a new participatory democracy . . . emerging in our everyday lives. This emergence represents a massive shift in our collective experience, and its potential to scaffold a citizen-led participatory culture represents an opportunity for those who research and design human-centered digital technology to shape a more egalitarian future."[162] Thus, *Taking [A]part* has a dual meaning. It means not only participating in design, but also disrupting "ideologies that position inequality as natural."[163]

This more inclusive participation in design opens up a number of questions that need to be considered. Who should be on a design team, and what competencies do they need? How many people should be added if fuller participation is warranted, and what will be their roles? Will the team have a design lead and a project manager? Is advanced training needed in terms of cross-cultural understanding, interpersonal skills, and team building? How will the team communicate, make decisions, and maintain trust, especially if they are not colocated? For long-term design projects, how does the team sustain the motivation of all its members or, if necessary, replace them with others who join the team? Answers to these questions will be specific for each design team and its particular design challenges. For a general overview of designers' toolkits and resources for developing a team and facilitating its evolution through the design process, two resources are free and available online: *The Field Guide to Human-Centered Design*, published by IDEO;[164] and the Stanford d-School's *Design Project Guide*, from the Hasso Plattner Institute of Design.[165] More expansive descriptions of the design process and its toolkits and resources can be found in *Designing for Growth: A Design Thinking Tool Kit for Managers* by Jeanne Liedtka and Tim Ogilvie;[166] and *Designing for Growth Field Book: A Step-by Step-Project Guide.*[167]

Evaluating design projects   Evaluation is a central skill set in design project management. But rather than take up the subject here, the reader is referred to two sections in chapter 9 of this book. "Evaluating the Evaluations" describes the limitations of formative and summative evaluation and "Developmental Evaluations" recommends Michael Patton's research into and work on projects in wicked problem territory.[168]

In Summary

This wavetop summary of designer skill sets and toolkits is by no means complete. I offer it as a foundation on which designers can build. The most important message to take from this overview is that designers are also agents of change. Not only do they have to learn the craft of design, but they have to learn how to navigate the "whitewater rapids" of the change process, especially in wicked problem territory. Changes ignite emotions and passions, competing worldviews, and different action logics. Without understanding the deep currents that run beneath all design projects, they risk getting swamped. Think of designing as comparable to running actual rivers. Before a whitewater river trip even starts, you learn what kind of river you want to run and decide whether your knowledge and skills match the challenge that you want to undertake. Just as there are different categories of rapids, there are different categories of problems. Beginners don't run category 5 rapids, and people should not jump into wicked problem territory without some previous training and experience. Design is a discipline that is learned over time, through apprenticeship and experience. If you are not ready for whitewater, select a challenge lower on the ladder of design and carefully choose the guides who will help you hone your craft and basic skill sets. For those who are ready to test themselves in whitewater territory, part III offers three options—the strategic design of organizations, the systemic design of social systems, and the regenerative design of social and ecological systems.

III   Designing in Wicked Problem Territory

6 Strategic Design

Strategic design builds on the fundamentals of strategic management—the formulation of an organization's direction and its implementation and evaluation for the purpose of improving the organization's performance. Direction setting begins with an assessment of the organization's external and internal environments. Based on those assessments, top management, in collaboration with others, identifies a long-term vision and a course of action or strategy to carry out that vision. Implementation addresses questions of how organizational resources (e.g., the people, tasks, technology of work, organizational structure, and organizational subsystems and processes) should be configured and mobilized to support the organization's vision and strategy. Evaluation then ascertains the extent to which the vision and strategy have been successful. Having identified areas of success and failure, executives then repeat the process, making the necessary changes, be they incremental or transformational, to realign the organization vis-à-vis its environment to improve its performance. Strategic design, however, parts ways with formal strategic management in its use of design thinking to formulate, implement, and evaluate an organization's strategy. Creativity, imagination, learning, and innovation are more predominant features of design-led strategy making compared to the more analytical, linear, planned, and transactional processes of strategic management.[1] As James Carlopio underscores in his book *Strategy by Design*, strategy creation is a process of strategy innovation, especially in a dynamic global environment.[2] He recommends design as the means to generate the innovative changes that enable organizations to adapt and thrive. Although he acknowledges the existence of a few organizations (e.g., Cirque du Soleil and Apple) that constantly generate creative strategies, what is not clear is how they do it. "How do we create strategy innovations and find these uncontested, radical, nonlinear, innovative breakthrough strategies, business models, industries, and solutions?"[3] To answer his question, his work explores how design can be the engine of strategy innovation in launching the "radical redesign of industries for the design of solutions to some of our most pressing large-scale social and global problems."[4]

Giuila Calabretta and her colleagues extend Carlopio's argument to highlight the spread of design throughout the entire organization, which makes the designer's role strategic. Involvement with an innovation strategy is important, but involvement in strategic decisions like the company's overarching vision, its corporate strategy, and its organizational culture has even more impact since they drive decisions and practices within the organization.[5] Thus design supports the strategic design of an organization by doing the following:

- Positioning design at the organization's board level with the commitment of top management
- Demonstrating how design can be the source of competitive advantage
- Highlighting the interplay between design and business strategy
- Using design as a catalyst for change that contributes to the organization's overall goal and direction
- Illustrating how design meets challenges in different markets and captures emerging ideas and trends
- Providing the tools to visualize and communicate business strategy and corporate objectives to external and internal audiences
- Using design tools to interpret and address client or end-user needs, which opens up new insights to strategic options; and defusing design throughout the organization and making it part of the organizational culture[6]

Examples of where design has expanded its reach can be found in *Fortune* 500 companies that started hiring chief design officers, investing in design and innovation centers, using design thinking to forge and guide business strategy, and making design and design thinking a part of their organizational DNA. In 2013, the Design Management Institute, in collaboration with Motiv Strategies and funded by Microsoft, created a market index to compare how these design-focused companies performed in the aggregate relative to the S&P 500. Companies were selected based on six criteria:

- Design operates at scale across the enterprise.
- Design holds a prominent space on the company organization chart and designers either sit on the leadership team or directly report to a leadership team member.
- Experienced executives manage the design function.
- Design sees a growing level of investment to support its growing influence.
- Design enjoys senior leadership support from the top tier of the organization.
- The company has been publicly traded on a US exchange for the last ten years and thereby adheres to GAAP accounting.[7]

Sixteen companies met the criteria as "design-centric." The Design Value Index in figure 6.1 reveals a 211 percent return of these companies over the S&P 500, supporting the growing body of research that design is related to shareholder value.[8] Design is not a "fad," the study concludes, but "a highly *integrated* and *influential* force that *enables* organizations to achieve outsized results." Indeed, "the widespread use of design as a strategic capability is unlikely to go away anytime soon."[9]

Since the ten-year the study was completed, other companies such as SAP have joined the list, and Honeywell, 3M, PepsiCo, Capital One, and General Electric are

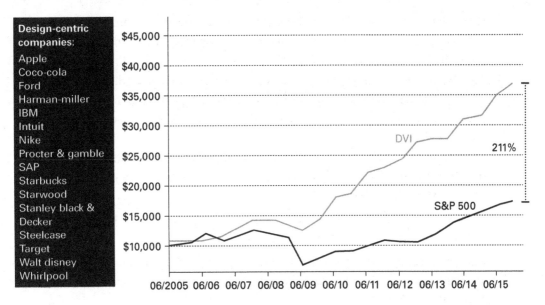

Figure 6.1
Design Value Index 2005–2015

currently building enterprisewide design functions and have strong commitments to design and design thinking. Fortune's 2018 Business by Design List now includes Dyson, Google, Samsung, Amazon, Huawei, Microsoft, IBM, Airbnb, Musical.ly, Snap, Meitu, Instagram, Tesla, Ford, Audi, Hyundai, Starbucks, IKEA, PepsiCo, Capital One, Uniglo, Nike, Zalando, and Philips, companies in which design has become a central feature in their ability to innovate.[10] The growing interest in the application of design to business led the editors of the *Academy of Management Journal* to release a special issue entitled "Managing by Design," which concluded that design's current contributions to the workplace has the potential to "become for the experience economy what the assembly line was to industrialization."[11] An update by McKinsey released in October 2018[12] captures the results of this growing interest in design. It documents "how the best design performers increase their revenues at nearly twice the rate of the industry counterparts." The research entailed tracking the design practices of 300 publicly listed companies in multiple countries and industries over a five-year period; collecting their financial data; recording design actions[13] (more than 100,000 of them); conducting regression analysis that uncovered twelve design actions with the highest correlations with financial performance; clustering design actions into four broad themes; and using the themes as the basis for the McKinsey Design Index (MDI), which rates companies by linking their financial performance with their strength in design.

Sheppard and colleagues, the authors of the McKinsey research, revealed several significant results:

• We found a strong correlation between high MDI scores and superior business performance. Top-quartile MDI scorers increased their revenues and total returns to shareholders (TRS) substantially faster than their industry counterparts did over a five-year period—32 percentage points higher revenue growth and 56 percentage points higher TRS growth for the period as a whole.

- The results held true in all three of the industries we looked at: medical technology, consumer goods, and retail banking. This suggests that good design matters whether your company focuses on physical goods, digital products, services, or some combination of these.

- TRS and revenue differences between the fourth, third, and second quartiles were marginal. In other words, the market disproportionately rewarded companies that truly stood out from the crowd.[14]

These design actions with the highest correlations with improved financial performance were companies in which the following was the case:

- Leadership combines design and business in crafting a bold vision and developing an analytic framework to measure and drive design performance with the same rigor as revenues and costs.

- Cross-functional talent breaks down silos and internal walls between physical, digital, and service design to make user-centric design everyone's responsibility.

- Continuous iteration de-risks development by continually listening, testing, and iterating with end users.

- User experience integrates physical, digital, and service designs.[15]

Procter and Gamble

Procter and Gamble (P&G) is one company that has been very open about its strategic redesign efforts to shift its businesses away from their traditional ways of operating and toward more creative and innovative approaches. In 2001, chief executive officer (CEO) A. G. Lafley declared that P&G "will not win on technology alone. We need to build design into the DNA of P&G."[16] To guide this organizational transformation, he turned to Claudia Kotchka, eventually naming her vice president of design innovation and strategy and charging her to build a design mindset and culture throughout P&G. In a company that viewed the function of its small design unit as putting labels on products and making them look pretty, this task was quite a challenge. So, according to Katchka, P&G's efforts proceeded in phases. Phase 1 began with projects to shift corporate identity from a focus on research and development (R&D) and technology to the consumer. Office spaces and buildings were plastered with pictures of real people in their everyday lives and natural surroundings to remind P&G of the people that the company was serving. Phase 1 advanced when Kotchka hired external designers to help transform product lines like Pampers and Olay, where the company was "getting their butts kicked" by the competition. The successes of these efforts produced some important lessons learned. Designers were different and thought differently. Rather than rely on quantitative research to describe customers by the numbers, "designers listened with their eyes" to look at people and empathize with them as human beings. Their wider aperture enabled them to fuse meaning, pleasure, and function when redesigning products. P&G also discovered that designers worked differently. They couldn't work in standard-issue cubicles, so they received approval from corporate to redesign their spaces. (It turned out that these open spaces actually reduced building costs, which then changed how building and rooms were designed throughout the company.) Designers also needed Mac computers to do their work, so they got them.

Phase 1 design "wins" opened up greater opportunities in phase 2. Designers were challenged to demonstrate how they could improve the functionality of products or user experiences. For example, designers were adding more success stories to champion design throughout the organization: how to change measuring cups; how to improve how Swiffer mops functioned; and how to redesign the display space of Olay in China, which became the number one Olay counter worldwide. The important lesson in phase 2, according to Kotchka, was improving people's experiences and creating things that people loved. Central to these efforts was the change in the P&G process of problem solving and decision making to incorporate a human-centered approach in designing and redesigning products. The new process of problem solving reached executive levels when the external design board met three times a year to respond to managers' questions and decide how to solve problems. The company also started projects with IDEO, where P&G managers were sent to work on some of their wicked problems. Lafley's leadership team met twice a year to spend a full day with IDEO to go through the whole process of design thinking on particular challenges that required them to collect data, define the problem, ideate, prototype, and test their new designs. Kotchka also started a mentoring program, where designers paired with executives and took them shopping and told them what the designers were seeing.

P&G entered phase 3 when it moved design thinking into direction setting, coming up with breakthrough ideas and demonstrating what brands could emerge in the future. These strategic design efforts started off with ten P&G people who were sent to work as a team for ten weeks using the design thinking process. The team culminated its efforts by briefing leadership on their new ideas and prototypes. Kotchka also built design into P&G's sustainability efforts by introducing the ideas expressed by Bill McDonough in his book *Cradle to Cradle* in order to inform how the company designed its manufacturing plants and how compaction could reduce material, save water in the making of their products, and reduce shipping costs. In addition, Roger Martin, former dean of the Rotman School of Management, Patrick Whitney, dean of the Institute of Design at the Illinois Institute of Technology, and David Kelley, founder of the Stanford D. School and IDEO, were brought in to design two-day experiential workshops to teach design thinking to P&G business leaders. As part of the overall effort, facilitators were taught how to run workshops and websites were created to highlight the lessons learned. Ultimately, designers and design "make a difference," said Kotchka as design talent was embedded in product lines throughout the world. And for Lafley, who "wanted P&G to become the number-one consumer design company in the world," design had become "part of P&G's strategy" and "its innovation process."[17]

P&G's successes, along with the achievements of other businesses, have captured the attention of public and nonprofit organizations,[18] which also are introducing design thinking to spur innovation, transform work, and make changes that enhance people's lives. Design interventions in these organizations follow a trajectory similar to P&G and other businesses. They tend to start with a limited scope in order to demonstrate the potential and power of design—the design/redesign of an organization's products, services, and processes. Eventually, designers move into executive suites to tackle more complex strategic design projects and introduce the concept of strategic design. They ask: How do we employ design to imagine and steer our organization toward a new future, and how do we make the necessary organizational adaptations to get us there? How do we "backcast" from our desired future to spur the needed organizational changes that will enable us to become what we want to be? Thus, designers plan a key role in the strategic design process by doing the following:

- Helping organizational members decide who they are, what they want to achieve, and how they want to chart a course to realize their desired future despite their inability to predict with certainty the future states of the world or forecast the consequences of their actions
- Encouraging organizational members to view themselves as an organic whole, with the expectation that all people and organizational elements need to fit together and be mutually supportive, notwithstanding their divergent values and perspectives
- Activating and supporting creative thinking and problem solving among organizational members
- Putting a high premium on generating innovative solutions and adaptations to the organization's volatile, uncertain, complex, and ambiguous environment

In probing more deeply into the discipline of strategic design, Anna Meroni also identifies eight processes that she believes are foundational to strategic design practice. Designers must be aware of and actively engaged in the following:

- A dialogical process that guides organizational members toward a shared interpretation of the future and how to transform the organization to achieve it
- A codesign process that shifts from user-centered design to community-centered design
- A problem-setting process and a problem-solving process
- A scenario-building process to transform visions into structure
- A capacity-building process to create the knowledge and tools to implement visions
- An integrated product-service design process oriented to producing solutions
- A social innovation process that drives a product-service design toward a distinctive identity
- An evolutionary process of exploration and change[19]

Strategic Design in Public and Nonprofit Organizations

Although not always identified as strategic designs, cases are surfacing in public and non-profit organizations,[20] where design thinking is being used to strategically design and renew organizations. The Monash Medical Center in Melbourne, Australia, is one example.[21] It faced numerous organizational and health-care challenges, such as extended patient stays, hand hygiene, and mental health services. Its strategic efforts and organizational transformation eventually led to the redesign of general medicine and mental health clinics, along with a cultural change that made design thinking central to the organization's problem solving. This case also illustrates greater potential. It ends with a vision of an international hub for design education and applied research and practice, where designers would draw together a network of stakeholders—including hospitals, design agencies, and university design teachers, hospital partners, patients and their communities, health services providers, and government insurers—to educate and train medical personnel. Should this transboundary international hub of relationships and connections materialize, it would be an example of systemic design, a topic addressed in chapter 7.

A second case is the NORSOCOM Design Challenge. From September 2014 through June 2015, the commander of Norwegian Special Operations Command (NORSOCOM) sponsored a group of ten Naval Postgraduate School (NPS) officer-students from Norway, Canada, Netherlands, Sweden, Switzerland, and the United States to envision the future of NORSOCOM. The design team, led by myself, a professor of defense analysis, and Espen Berg-Knutsen, a visiting research scientist from the Norwegian Defense Establishment (FFI), set out to answer the initial question: How should the Norwegian Special Operations Force (NORSOF) be designed for 2025? We turn to the specifics of the case to illustrate how design can be employed to envision a public organization's future. It also is a good example how some military organizations are experimenting with design thinking to invite more creative and innovating problem solving at all organizational levels.[22]

NORSOCOM Design Challenge

Background Similar to the counterterrorism (CT) efforts of many nations in the aftermath of the 9/11 terrorist attacks, the NORSOF began a buildup that doubled its size in less than ten years.[23] Its growth prompted the establishment of an independent joint Norwegian Special Forces Command with official requirements, guidelines, and budgets to oversee all NORSOF activities. In preparation for this shift, the command teamed up with FFI (the Norwegian Defense Research Establishment) to conduct scenario-based analysis, capability analysis, and gap analysis as a prelude to long-term planning. This analytical, linear approach to planning ensured the traceability and identification of gaps between the anticipated scenarios and NORSOF capabilities. The analysis captured well the current threats, missions, tasks, courses of action (COAs), and capability requirements, but it was limited in its ability to generate and capture new ideas that might anticipate future challenges. Determined not to make the mistakes of great companies that have failed due to their inability to move beyond current successes, FFI initiated several activities to capture the technological, doctrinal, and organizational ideas that were out there. One of these places was the Defense Analysis Department at the Naval Postgraduate School, widely recognized as the world's premier institution for Special Operations graduate thinking and education.

The ten-person NPS Design team of officer-students who volunteered for the project brought a unique and broad background, including extensive field experience and knowledge of NORSOF. But instead of employing FFI's more traditional approach to strategic planning, the team agreed to an alternative methodology—the design strategy. The hope was that design would enable them to take a longer-term focus, generate creative ideas to inform NORSOF's future, and formulate a set of recommendations in answer to some fundamental questions that launched the study: What is the future of Special Operations? What can SOF expect in 2025? How should NORSOF be designed to address the challenges that it may face in 2025?

Sponsor guidelines An active and engaged sponsor is central to launching a design challenge. The team was fortunate to have the commander of NORSOCOM, Rear Admiral Nil J. Holte, personally overseeing its process. Admiral Holte outlined four guidelines for the design project:

- Design the future of NORSOF, regardless of historical structures and restrictions, giving the team the latitude to start from scratch and design a completely new NORSOF.
- Follow three mission priorities: homeland defense, alliance commitments, and military support to homeland security (listed by order of importance).
- Keep within a reasonable budget, which the team and the commander agreed meant a modest increase by 2025.
- Generate creative ideas that could be turned into innovative solutions for NORSOF's future.

Initial team preparations In the best-case scenario, design teams would have a great deal of design experience before tackling complicated strategic design projects. Unfortunately, few of us live in Dr. Pangloss's world, especially those of us wandering through wicked problem territory. The best that could be done, given the project's time constraints, was to offer a workshop to introduce the team to design and design thinking. After the workshop, the team agreed that design thinking would be a good process to respond to the commander's design challenge since it enabled them to combine both creative and analytical efforts and foster cross-disciplinary collaboration. After additional preparation in organization design, as discussed next, the team launched a five-phase design thinking process of discovery, define, ideate, prototype, and test.

Organizational configuration The starting point for strategic designs and redesigns is knowledge about an organization and how it is configured.[24] Since team members had different exposure to concepts of organizational design, the team paused for a short review. I introduced them to a configurational organizational framework,[25] which views an organization as a whole system. The major system components include the organization's external environment, strategy (or what I call its "direction"), design elements (e.g., people, tasks, structure, technology, and processes), and results. An important aspect of assessing an organization's performance is the extent to which there is a *fit* or *congruence* among the major components. So, for example, do people have the knowledge, skills, and competencies to do their jobs, does the organization's structure support the technology of the work to be performed, and are all the organization's components mutually supportive? Achieving fit or congruence is difficult enough in a placid environment, but most modern organizations operating in dynamic environments are challenged to adjust and adapt continually to ensure that all the organizational components have some compatibility.

I chose a variant on the configurational framework called the Roberts Organizational System Framework (ROSF), shown in figure 6.2.[26] The framework consists of four major components: inputs, organizational direction, organizational design elements, and results. *Inputs* are the political, economic, social, ecological, and technological trends and forces that shape the organization's general and domain-specific environments. It also includes an assessment of the competitive threats, customer preferences, government regulations, and new technologies, as well as the evolving physical environment.

Scanning the external environment is a complicated and time-consuming process, especially finding the key factors that are central to an organization's success. For example, airlines have to be attuned to any disruptions that can impede the flow of oil, which would affect the company's cost structure and profitability. Construction and insurance companies continually monitor and adapt to changes in building

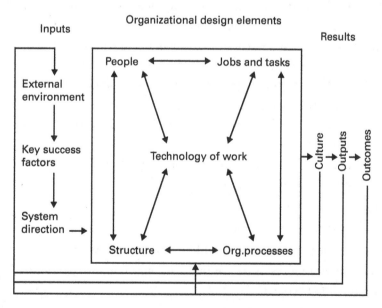

Figure 6.2
Roberts organizational system framework (ROSF)

codes, especially in highly forested areas and coastal regions threatened by fires, rising seas, and flooding. Businesses heavily invested in international trade are particularly sensitive to changing laws regarding tariffs and embargoes. And depending on voter preferences and the changing issue agenda—whether we are fighting the war on terror, the war on drugs, or climate change—government bureaus may have their budgets cut or increased. Although all public, private, and nonprofit organizations face similar general trends and forces, their domain-specific environments—airlines, building construction and insurance, international trade, and public service in these examples— usually present specific challenges and unique success factors.

Drawing on information from environmental scans and key success factors, an organization then sets its *direction*. Organizations can and do use different words to describe their direction, such as "mandate," "mission," "vision," "values and beliefs," "strategy," "goals," and "objectives."[27] The words are less important than their intent. The intent of the direction-setting process is to establish an organization's unique identity, espouse its particular values and beliefs, outline the future that it hopes to achieve, and present a strategy for how it expects to actualize that future. The bottom line is that an organization's direction explains how it plans to deliver value to its stakeholders.

The third major component of the system's framework contains the *organizational design elements* needed to implement the organization's direction. Figure 6.2 identifies five major building blocks of organizational design that are modified or redesigned to match any changes in the organization's environment and direction:

- *People*—What is the level of their knowledge, skills, and competencies?
- People's *jobs and tasks*—What are the basic tasks and jobs, how formalized, specified, and differentiated are they in doing the organization's work, and how well do the tasks and jobs match people's competencies?
- *Technology of work*—What services or goods does the organization produce, how are they produced, and what technology supports their production; and to what extent does the technology of work support the organization's direction and purpose?
- *Structure*—What is the organization's division of labor, how centralized or decentralized is its structure, and how does the structure integrate the differentiated parts to form a whole system?
- *Organizational* processes—How are the organizational processes designed to support the work effort, including the following:
  - Communication and information processes?
  - Planning and decision processes?
  - Financial management, measurement, and control processes?
  - Human resource processes (recruiting, selecting, training, promoting, termination, and retiring people)?
  - Acquisition and contracting processes?
  - R&D processes?

The fourth component of the systems framework is the *results*. Tracking results enables the organization to monitor the extent to which it has succeeded in achieving and implementing its direction. Managers assess results in terms of the organization's culture, outputs, and outcomes:

- *Culture* describes how people in the organization treat one another and their stakeholders. Values and beliefs are espoused during direction setting, but an assessment of the actual culture reveals how people manifest those values and beliefs in practice. Organizational culture does not assume that what people espouse and believe is necessarily congruent with how they act. Culture is treated as an emergent property of the organization's direction and design elements and is an important way to evaluate whether an organization practices what it preaches.

- *Outputs* are the actual goods or services that the organization provides to its customers and clients. They are measured in terms of performance metrics that are linked directly back to the organization's direction, specified in the mission, vision, strategy, goals, and objectives.

- *Outcomes* are the consequences of the outputs for the organization's various stakeholders. They are measured in terms of performance metrics that directly link to outputs and, most important, to organizational direction.

Thus, the use of the organizational system framework from a design perspective is based on the following set of premises:

- An organization is a complex adaptive system (CAS) with very permeable or open boundaries. As an open system, the goal is to keep the organization in dynamic equilibrium with its environment. As the environment changes, the organization's direction and design elements need to adapt for organizational survival. For example, if competitors are adopting new technology (i.e., automation), if personnel need new skills, or if customers have complaints about products or services, the organization needs to take corrective action and make changes in its direction, its design elements, or both. Organizations also influence their environments to the degree that their strategies and the goods and services that they produce are successful. If customers through their purchasing power signal their approval of an organization's new products and services, competitors take note and attempt to introduce new products and services to stay competitive. Thus, the constant interaction and mutual adaptation among organizations, their component parts, and the environment are central features of CASs.

- Organizational results provide feedback to judge organizational performance and to signal changes when needed. If the organization's stakeholders view the culture, outputs, and outcomes in a positive light, then the organization usually continues on its trajectory with few modifications in its design. However, if stakeholders view the culture, outputs, or outcomes as negative or less than stellar, then managers and organizational members are required to design interventions to change the organization's direction, design elements, and results. When changes aren't forthcoming or successful and the thinning cash flows leave it with little money to reinvest in improvements, the company becomes irrelevant, as the bankruptcies of Toys "R" Us and Sears Holdings have recently demonstrated.

- Corrective interventions can involve the whole organization (strategic designs or redesigns) or involve only certain system elements or components. Total system change or system redesign is often referred to as *transformational change*, in contrast to *targeted change*, which makes adjustments and adaptations in some system elements. Related concepts are *episodic change*, which is an infrequent, explicitly defined, and distinct period of change, and *continuous change*, in which an organization is constantly changing various aspects of its design.[28]

- Whether organizational interventions are intended to change the whole system (strategic design/redesign) or only specific elements, change interventions create ripple effects throughout the organization. As the connecting arrows illustrate in figure 6.2, the organization is a system composed of interdependent parts. A change in one system element will eventually have an impact throughout the entire system, and even its environment. These constant changes and adaptations, especially heightened in a VUCA[29] environment, put the organization in a state of constant flux.

- A major challenge is how to lead, design, and manage an organization that is in a state of flux. All the organizational system elements need to be a good fit with one another, but a good fit is difficult to achieve when, for example, resources have been drastically reduced, certain elements like technology are racing far ahead of changes in human resource management, or when organizational members are told to be creative and innovative, but the organization's culture penalizes risk-taking and deviations from standard operating procedures (SOPs). If they are not paying attention to organizational congruence or fit, organizations suffer from misaligned parts that are not in sync with one another and result in reduced efficiency and effectiveness. At the same time, organizations need agile and flexible organizational architectures that enable them to change quickly as conditions warrant, especially in a VUCA world. It is not easy to thread the needle that requires both organizational adaptation *and* coherence, but that is the fundamental challenge of strategic leadership and design.

Launching Design Thinking

Initial design team preparations were time consuming but absolutely necessary to provide the team with a common frame of reference. The Roberts Organizational System Framework (ROSF) provided the team with a conceptual model to understand NORSO-COM, both in terms of how it was currently designed and how it could be redesigned in the future. The design thinking workshops then enabled the design team to generate and test creative prototypes that would inform the redesign. In what follows, the team's activities are organized around each phase of the design process. Although the process appears to be linear, it was not. As new data, ideas, and feedback surfaced, the design team had to return to earlier phases of the process to reexamine and update its environmental assessment, key success factors, direction setting, and key organizational components.

The Discovery Phase

Discovery (with empathy) initiated the exploration of the design challenge and its context. Designers can use many techniques to gather information about the context and the people in it. In this case, the team examined archival records, including documents, books, and readings about the environment and Special Operations Forces (SOFs), and conducted more than twenty-five face-to-face interviews with subject matter experts for their personal views of future trends and challenges and how NORSOF might deal with them. These experts were experienced professionals from various Norwegian governmental offices, Norwegian and international senior ranking military officers, and prominent representatives from academia and the private sector. As the team gathered information, they used the ROSF to organize the data about the organization and its environment.

Archival records   The archival records revealed a number of sources on future trends. Most were assessments from the allied intelligence community and academic institutions. The design team organized the information into four categories: relative certainties for future environments; critical game changers; Norway and Geo-politics 2025; and Russian and Norwegian defense planning. All these factors were expected to influence Norwegian security in 2025.

Relative certainties included the following:[30]

- *Worldwide individual empowerment*, especially strengthened religious and ethnic identities.
- *Diffusion of power*, specifically the rise of rogue nations and terrorist and criminal networks.
- *Changing demographic patterns*, in particular aging populations due to rapid extensions of life expectancy, are likely to lead to declines in economic growth in some countries. At the same time, countries in sub-Saharan Africa and South Asia are expected to continue to have youthful and growing populations because deaths from communicable diseases are projected to drop by more than 40 percent. Increased migration also is expected to spread to emerging powers and urbanization is projected to grow by almost 60 percent.
- *Increasing demands for resources* are expected due to a global population increase from 7.1 billion to 8 billion by 2030. Demand for food is expected to rise by 35 percent, and energy is expected to increase by 50 percent over the next fifteen to twenty years. Nearly half of the world's population is likely to live in areas of severe water

stress. Increasing food, water, and energy requirements have a high potential to provoke conflicts over scarce resources.

Critical game changers include the following:[31]

- *Governance deficits* are likely to drive rapid political and social change.
- *Countries moving from autocracy to democracy* have a proven record of high instability, and about fifty states are falling into this category.
- *There will be a more complicated political landscape*: megacities and regional groupings are likely to assume increasing powers; and networks, some between rogue states and terrorist movements, are expected to be harder to address directly.
- *Information and communication technology* will make possible multiple and simultaneous action, near-instantaneous responses, and mass organization across geographical boundaries, which increases the potential for more frequent change in the international system and governments' ability to monitor their citizens.
- *Intrastate conflicts are likely to increase* due to resource constraints and a rising young male population, particularly in sub-Saharan Africa, South Asia, and parts of the Middle East. And these types of conflict are likely to take the form of irregular warfare, with the spread of precision weaponry expected to change the dynamics of these conflicts.
- *Interstate conflicts are likely to arise* due to a more fragmented international system, spillover from regional conflicts, and resource competition. The Middle East is expected to remain the most volatile region, and future wars in Asia and the Middle East possibly could include a nuclear element. And many of these conflicts, once begun, will not be easily containable and will have global impacts.

Norway and Geo-Politics 2025 features the following points:

- *The Asia Pacific will emerge as an important economic and political center of gravity* for Norway's biggest ally, the United States, which may affect US willingness to maintain a clear and credible commitment in northern Europe.
- *There is no credible opposition to Russian president Vladimir Putin's goal of restoring Russia as a world power.* Russia is aggressively countering Western expansion into its sphere of interest, as illustrated by the war in Georgia, annexation of the Crimea, and most recently, the full spectrum/hybrid war in Ukraine. A Norwegian contribution to the collective North Atlantic Treaty Organization (NATO) defense of former Warsaw pact members is one of the highest-probability scenarios.
- *Southwest Asia and North Africa will continue to be characterized by poverty, deep cultural differences, and the expansion of militant Islam.* Norway has been struck by terror at home and overseas, and this is likely to continue.
- *Current threats will continue,* including the proliferation of weapons of mass destruction, terrorism, the weaponization of information, and cyberwarfare. Geographic distance will have less significance, as Norway is attacked in cyberspace every day,

particularly by Russia and China. All these factors will continue to affect Norwegian security in 2025.

Norwegian and Russian defense planning includes the following:

- *Russia will be the dominating factor in Norwegian defense planning in the foreseeable future, given the geographic situation.* Norway borders on Russia's Kola Peninsula, which contains 70–80 percent of Russian strategic nuclear capabilities. As such, the peninsula can be described as militarized, with Russian forces increasing their training level, responsiveness, mobility, and range over the past few years. Although Norway and Russia recently settled a forty-year-long dispute about the common border at sea, issues concerning the continental shelf are unresolved. In addition, the strategic geographic position of Spitsbergen, a demilitarized Norwegian archipelago with a minority population of Russians, will be important in any war effort to dominate the North Atlantic.

- *Structurally, Norway is part of the Western security alliance and world order, while Russia is not.* Russia views NATO as a threat to its borders, and its ambition is to challenge the Western-made international system or even bring about its dismantling.

- *Norway maintains well-developed diplomacy and military channels to Russia, and they remain open based on common interests and the desire to avoid misunderstandings.* It is Norway's intent to continue the balancing act between deterrence and reassurance in the future.

- *In a conflict between Russia and other NATO powers, Russia may want to secure parts of Norwegian territory (land and sea) for its defensive purposes.* This is the classic article 5 scenario of the NATO Washington Treaty—an attack on one is an attack on all.

- *In the case of a purely bilateral crisis, Norway's current and future ambition will be to establish a threshold designed to trigger article 5.* On the other hand, it is anticipated that Russia will likely use the full spectrum of its powers to pressure the small state of Norway to comply, but stop just short of triggering NATO's involvement.

Interviews and key success factors   Three factors were projected to be critical to Norway's success in the 2025 environment: flexibility, integration, and innovation. During discovery, especially during discussions with subject matter experts, *flexibility* was a recurring theme. As described in the environmental overview, the future was expected to be complex and turbulent, with dramatic shifts and rapid changes in the social, economic, and political landscape. In such a context, NORSOF would have to be prepared for vastly different scenarios that might occur in rapid succession, with little time for planning and organizational learning. For example, a high level of adaptation would be needed to balance its homeland defense, faraway alliance commitments, and homeland security, especially if they all occurred at the same time. In addition, designing NORSOF for full-spectrum operations with a homeland defense emphasis on Arctic and maritime arenas would require adjustments in the command's current structure, resource allocations, and capabilities. Thus, the team agreed that flexibility of mind and agility in the organization's design and culture would be NORSOF's best defense against future challenges.

Also central to NORSOF in the 2025 time frame would be the ability to work with others in an interdependent world. The aforementioned global diffusion of power and the challenges that it presents would be beyond Norway's ability to deal with on its own, and thus the effort would require multiple agencies, organizations, and nations working together. Moreover, few anticipated threats and challenges would fit within the purview of traditional bureaucracies rigidly defined by military, civil, and political boundaries. Where borders of all types were porous and no longer as sacrosanct as they once were, cross-boundary coordination and integration would be critical success factors. Thus, the design team envisioned a governmental and coalitional approach that involved multiple agencies, organizations, and nations in ideation and problem solving. Although effective integration might take place between senior national and international personnel, the design team noted a need for increased cooperation and interoperability at all levels. This integrated governmental and coalitional approach was expected to have significant implications for NORSOF's organizational and warfare designs.

A third theme among the subject matter experts was the importance of innovation for NORSOF 2025. *Innovation*, defined as the introduction of new ideas and prototypes and their implementation in organizational practice, included setting new organizational directions and generating new ideas for the design of warfare (doctrines, technology, structures of fighting units, and information technology) and for NORSOF's organizational structure and systems. Most important, NORSOF's leaders needed to be champions of the change process to ensure that new ideas and prototypes were successfully executed. Simply put, if NORSOF wanted something that it didn't have, it needed to do something that it had not done before—launch an all-out effort to innovate its way into the future.

Problem Definition Phase

The problem definition phase reframed the design challenge. Often, these challenges are general and represent only the presenting questions, not the underlying problems or issues facing the organization. In this instance, the design team decided to reframe the problem statement informed by data gathering during discovery. With input from the sponsor, the NORSOF design team framed the problem as a question: how might we strategically design Special Operation Forces to best serve Norway's security interests in 2025?

Ideation, prototyping, and testing phases of organizational direction The design team quickly realized that their "how might we" question required a two-part process. First, it needed to brainstorm, prototype, and then test new ideas that set NORSOF's direction. Only when the direction setting was sufficiently complete would the team be able to address another question: how might we design an organization to execute this direction? The goal of the brainstorming sessions was to widen the solution spaces by building on others' ideas, generating a wide spectrum of ideas, especially creative and original ones, while at the same time deferring judgment on anyone's suggestions.

Ideation on direction setting provided a range of new ideas   The new ideas centered on issues of identity: Who are we? What do we do? Why do we do it? And how do we do it? NORSOF's new direction then became the answers to these four questions:

- *Who are we?* Highly selected professional soldiers, warrior-diplomats, strategic thinkers, and problem solvers
- *What do we do?* Perform full-spectrum NORSOF operations in all environments, deliver strategic effect, fulfill tasks that no one else is capable of accomplishing, and provide unmatched return on investment
- *Why do we do it?* To address and help solve Norway complex strategic problems and provide the country with a highly trained and equipped force to ensure high readiness and flexibility with a track record of proven success
- *How do we do it?* With purpose, speed, security, and surprise, and by nurturing a culture of innovation through interservice, interdepartmental, and international partnering, enabled by a lifelong career perspective

When first prototyping the identity statement, it appeared to be a description of any SOF command in the Global SOF Network. But further analysis during testing revealed eye-opening shortfalls between reality and future ideals. For example, the "who are we" discussion centered on what the terms "strategic thinking" and "warrior diplomat" actually mean. While common in the military lexicon, members of the design team questioned whether NORSOF currently developed strategic thinkers and warrior diplomats and selected highly selected, professional soldiers with the appropriate attributes. For the "how do we do it" question, there was a general agreement that NORSOF was not designed to produce innovation and the acceptance of change, nor was it effective in developing a career perspective among NORSOF and encouraging partnering both within and beyond Norwegian borders. In terms of "why do we do it," the design team questioned whether NORSOF was as flexible as it thought it was or needed to be, and whether operators were properly trained in the right capabilities. Finally, the team also expressed concerns about the "what do we do" question in terms of NORSOF's preparation for all environments, particularly maritime and Arctic, in support of national defense. It challenged the view that NORSOF was actually focusing on missions that no one else was capable of accomplishing. And it questioned whether NORSOF was focusing on the right mission sets and was leveraging other services and departments effectively. It also probed the extent to which NORSOF provided a better return on investment by focusing more or less on niche capabilities.

The prototyped identity statement, when tested and revised with the sponsor and other stakeholder inputs, proved to be robust enough to guide NORSOF's direction setting for 2025. Most important, the gaps identified between the current situation and the future direction anticipated for 2025 became the impetus of a second round of ideation, prototyping, and testing driven by the question: how might NORSOF design the organization to execute this new direction?

Ideation, prototyping, and testing of NORSOF's organizational design The "how might we" question opened up a range of new ideas on how to redesign NORSOF to be a better fit with its new identify and direction. The design team used the ROSF to categorize and group the new ideas into five general areas: NORSOF tasks; NORSOF people and their knowledge, skills, and competencies; the NORSOF human resource management subsystem; NORSOF warfare design (a term used instead of "technology of work" when military organizations operate under warfare conditions); and the NORSOF structure for the whole organization. Given time constraints, rather than have the entire design team prototype all new ideas in the five areas, the team decided to break into five subgroups, with members serving on multiple groups depending on their interest and expertise. For brevity's sake, I have selected only two subgroups—NORSOF Tasks and NORSOF Design of Warfare—to illustrate some of the basic ideas and deliberations that informed all the subgroups' prototypes.

NORSOF Tasks subgroup The NORSOF Tasks subgroup began by reviewing the trends and forces in the global and national environments. It then explored NORSOF's general role and unique tasks vis-à-vis other services, comparing them to how NATO SOF and US Special Operations Command (USSOCOM) were positioning themselves for the future.

In contrast to the US Special Operations Forces (USSOF) community, which had increased its core tasks and made them more specialized, NORSOF followed traditional SOF tasks that were in line with NATO requirements for a Special Operations Task Force (SOTF): Special Reconnaissance (SR),[32] Direct Action (DA),[33] and Military Assistance (MA).[34] In addition, NORSOF had national requirements to conduct hostage rescue operations worldwide, as well as domestic CT operations, both maritime and on land, in support of police in the federal Justice Department. On a more irregular basis, NORSOF supported other government agencies, and when tasked, conducted close protection for the Norwegian chief of defense.

Thus, NORSOF's traditional mission sets and tasks prioritized broad preparation rather than specialization. And its preparation was closely linked to the unique Norwegian environment and its specific requirements: operating on Arctic, winter, littoral, and mountainous terrain, as well as defending, when called upon, Norway's large merchant fleet and its extensive gas and oil platforms. Broad preparation, rather than task specialization combined with relative sparse resources, forced NORSOF to be a jack of all trades. This strategic positioning produced a number of trade-offs and dilemmas for Norway's relatively small SOF community. One dilemma was to be constantly ready to conduct the high-end strategic tasks of CT, hostage rescue operations, and national defense. These were "no failure missions" with high public and political visibility and global and domestic impact, although they had a low probability of occurrence. At the same time, NORSOF was expected to be prepared on a daily basis to conduct support missions abroad that were more frequent and had a lower strategic significance due to their smaller footprint and long-term focus, with less visibility and public attention.

Based on its assessments, the design team thus recommended a shift of NORSOF toward more military assistance (MA) rather than direct action (DA) tasks, such as those involved in the large-footprint deployments in Afghanistan and Iraq. Conducting small, cost-efficient, and proactive MA missions and tasks, especially those that were part of an integrated interagency effort, would avoid large-scale operations, and be viewed as more politically acceptable in an economically and politically constrained environment. At the same time, the task subgroup recognized that NORSOF should retain its DA capability, including the ability to strike a high-tech opponent's key installation in high-intensity scenarios.[35] With regard to special reconnaissance (SR) tasks, the demand was expected to be stable in the future. Thus, the task subgroup believed that NORSOF should keep SR, DA, and MA as its core tasks, broadly defined and in line with NATO's and Norway's requirements. These well-known tasks within the international SOF community would enable NORSOF to continue to be a flexible and responsive strategic tool in future national defense and national and international crisis response scenarios.

The task subgroup also highlighted three tasks that they believed would become even more important in the future: research and development (R&D), counter-UW (unconventional warfare/hybrid warfare), and interagency coordination. To survive on the battlefield and be as cost efficient as possible, and to stay in front of or at least keep up with innovations in both technology and doctrine, the subgroup recommended that NORSOF put greater emphasis on R&D. Indeed, it viewed NORSOF as the innovative laboratory for the Norwegian armed forces in the development of its future warfare designs (a subject explored in greater depth in the next section).

Second, as a consequence of Russia's strategic and political show of force in Eastern Europe, the task subgroup saw the need to develop ways to counter Russian unconventional/hybrid warfare, a type of warfare that operates in an environment between peacetime police scenarios and full-blown article 5 scenarios. To explore the wide range of instruments and actions that might go into a hybrid/unconventional attack, the entire design team organized a war game with the assistance of twenty international subject matter experts from diverse backgrounds in academe and the defense sector. The point of the war game was to identify an aggressor's possible order of battle and probable courses of action. Insights gained were then used to identify key capabilities needed to counter an aggressor's operations in such a complex environment.[36]

Third, the task subgroup stressed the need to integrate all aspects of Norway's power—its diplomacy, information, military, and economic capabilities. Not only was an integrated approach to hybrid/unconventional warfare a key success factor in the war game, but it underscored how central NORSOF's ability to build and participate in cross-boundary networks and work in combined/joint teams was to that effort. Thus, the task subgroup saw NORSOF as an important bridge in the interagency, interdepartmental, and international arena, central to coordinating a Norwegian whole-government approach to the nation's defense.

Antiterrorism was an area of SOF community underutilization and could offer new domestic solutions and capabilities. However, SOF involvement in antiterrorism activities for homeland defense would require some changes to current Norwegian laws and political acceptance, and as such, this was a topic that the subgroup did not explore in its prototypes.

Design of Warfare subgroup   Warfare design, the technology of work for warfighting, relies on four essential components: innovative technology, doctrine, information systems, and the organization of fighting units.[37]

Innovative technology   History has demonstrated that whoever is first to recognize, understand, and successfully field an innovation can gain a decisive advantage over an opponent. Past examples of technology-driven innovation in military affairs were the machine gun, the submarine, and aircraft. However, the subgroup was quick to point out that technology alone was not a "silver bullet" in designing warfare. Neither was choosing between high-tech solutions over low-tech ones. The subgroup cautioned that NORSOF always should be able to choose the right technology to fight degraded or low-tech opponents as well as high-tech ones.[38] But it did identify two areas of technological innovation that it believed were central to the future revolution in military affairs: unmanned systems and nonlethal technology.

Unmanned systems are expected to replace humans or manned systems at the battle front lines. Soldiers and operators will have remote control of unmanned systems. Linked with robotics and artificial intelligence (AI), unmanned systems will become smaller and be equipped with more advanced weapon systems, which will improve their range and lethality. Operators also should anticipate that a wide range of unmanned systems will become available to even low-tech opponents, whether state or nonstate actors. And national decision makers, with a greater range of technologies at their disposal, are expected to have greater say on when, how, and under what conditions they will deploy SOF.

Nonlethal technology is another area of technological innovation. For example, laser weapons, frequency interference, and gas and drugs can temporarily immobilize rather than do permanent physical damage to an enemy. As the field of biometrics evolves, incentives and opportunities for cooperation among departments of defense, justice, and the interior are expected to open up and increase. Thus, the subgroup expects nonlethal technologies will spark a whole new discussion on the *jus in bellow* criteria on when, how, and why deadly force can be used if other alternatives to war are available, in order to limit the suffering.[39]

Innovation in information systems.   The subgroup found many technologies and systems that have the potential to radically change future warfare designs. On a very broad scale, think of a world of ubiquitous satellite, drone, and Internet coverage that collects data, combines it with data from signal surveillance, and processes and fuses the data using AI to locate an adversary and know what the adversary is doing. As the individual soldier level, think of haptic technology, a feedback technology that uses computer applications to take advantage of the user's sense of touch by applying force vibrations and/or motions to the user, a technology currently used in smartphones, game controllers, and joysticks that is spreading rapidly. Also, think of brain wave sensing, which enables the control of technology functions by the brain. A possible future use of this technology could be to monitor the mental state of the SOF operator through helmet sensors in order to perceive the level of fatigue that the individual is experiencing. In addition, think of laser-based eyewear technology, which displays images directly onto retinas while not blocking vision. It can be used in eyeglasses and has applications ranging from e-gaming to military defense. So in the next ten to twenty years, experts predict that Internet glasses will replace smartphones, and this would enable NORSOF operators to see building schematics and the locations of enemy forces in the corner of their eyeglasses.

Doctrinal innovation Doctrine is a guide and framework of reference for military forces on how they will accomplish their tasks and conduct operations. For example, forces can be conventional—weapons and battlefield tactics that rely on well-defined massed forces and firepower, used in open confrontations between two or more states that primarily target the opponent's military. In contrast, forces like NORSOF are irregular—weapons and battlefield tactics that are maneuverable, indirect and asymmetric, such as counterinsurgency, CT, foreign internal defense, and stability operations, all of which require them to quickly adapt to the environment. In the view of the Design of Warfare subgroup, NORSOF was operating at the maneuver end of the spectrum, but it recommended moving as far within the maneuver spectrum as possible. It viewed doctrinal innovations such as swarming and distributed operations as essential to NORSOF's future success. *Swarming* describes numbers of relatively small, synchronized operators and weapons that act faster than their opponents to gain the advantage. Executed by small teams, or even individual operators,[40] and armed with new information systems and technology, NORSOF would be able to offset the risks of committing limited manpower to swarming operations. *Distributed operations*, also a form of maneuver warfare, occur when small, highly capable units disburse to find targets, gather intelligence, and secure lightly defended infrastructures. Although separated and spread over a large area of operations, they continue to coordinate their independent tactical actions with robust communications and tactical mobility assets. At the same time, all the units are capable of coalescing and concentrating all their capability on high-value targets, sometimes in combination with air and sea bombardment. The Design of Warfare subgroup thus recommended that NORSOF adjust and develop a new doctrine for swarming and distributed operations to respond more effectively to unconventional/hybrid threats, as demonstrated in the aforementioned war game.[41]

Doctrine in hybrid warfare to defeat an opponent on civilian-led terrain also needed development. It required a flexible, adaptable, and resilient military response to blend conventional warfare with the subversive efforts of irregular warfare, cyberwar, and diplomacy. In these instances, NORSOF likely would be working more closely with other government agencies, as well as civilian partners and enablers. As such, a stronger link between NORSOF and the Norwegian Home Guard units needed to be forged.

Given the massive number of unmanned systems available, NORSOF also required a new doctrine to guide the integration of manned and unmanned systems. The challenge of integrating multiple systems will only accelerate, but no NORSOF doctrine existed. Unmanned and remote-controlled systems have the advantage of enabling NORSOF to increase its physical distance from their adversaries, while keeping or even increasing their accuracy. Current tactics, techniques, and procedures needed to be adjusted to benefit from these developments. Unmanned and remote-controlled systems also are expected to force NORSOF to rethink SR tasks and missions. They beg the question: will the SR deception and discrete and clandestine operations become obsolete, or are humans still essential for its critical success? This question, as well as issues concerning the increasing vulnerability of large base camps like forward operating bases and the adversaries' increased use of advanced technology, were left unanswered by the subgroup.

Organizing warfare units   The subgroup on innovative warfare design recommended that NORSOF units operate more as self-organizing networks that would allow greater flexibility and adaptability in a complex, dynamic environment. A reliance on a hierarchical chain of command when NORSOF is moving toward maneuver warfare and adversaries are becoming more sophisticated and adept in building and employing "dark networks" would be a "misalignment" and put them at a distinct disadvantage. Quoting one of their professors, Dr. John Arquilla, the subgroup noted that "it takes a network to fight a network." Assessing NORSOF to be at the beginning stage of network evolution, the subgroup therefore advocated a greater emphasis on how these self-organizing units could be configured into smaller combat teams given the increased connectivity, range, and effectiveness of weapon systems. For example, the subgroup envisioned small teams dedicated to international and national UW (unconventional warfare/hybrid warfare) and MA tasks. Such shifts opened up questions whether the six-man team would continue to be the nucleus of the warfighting units or if technology and connectivity would enable teams to become even smaller.

Viewing current warfare as "technology driven," the subgroup supported the view that military leaders "will have to be masters of both the art of war and technology,"[42] a point reinforced by Arquilla, who believes that officers need to know what is technologically possible to be effective innovators. The subgroup therefore recommended the establishment of a new, well-resourced, and well-connected R&D entity charged with the mission of finding, developing, and implementing new technology, including information systems, doctrine, and the structure of fighting units to ensure that new warfare designs can be implemented within the larger NORSOF system. The R&D unit also would need to be closely coordinated and networked with other interservice, interagency, and international organizations to encourage the free flow of ideas and underscore the mindset that "everybody is an innovator" in NORSOF.

Beyond the separate challenges of configuring technology, information systems, doctrine, and fighting units lay the overarching challenge of integrating all four elements of warfare design into a mutually supportive coherent whole. A range of strategies were possible. NORSOF could hedge its bets through greater specialization, as USSOCOM had done, and prepare to execute a broad range of future warfare designs. Alternatively, it could put all efforts on one particular big bet that combined all four elements of warfare design in a unique and particular way. One example of such a big bet was the integration of manned and unmanned/remote-controlled systems to equip NORSOF operators with the latest technology that was linked to integrated systems.

A quick reality check suggested that neither greater specialization nor the big bet strategy were likely options for NORSOF. Greater specialization would be costly for Norway's relatively small NORSOF community. And policy makers who employed NORSOF as a "multitool problem solver" would be less inclined to approve specialization, such as technical integration into high-tech systems, at least in the near term. Instead, the Design of Warfare subgroup agreed that NORSOF should continue to be a jack of all trades in the foreseeable future, but it did see value in institutionalizing innovation within NORSOF to encourage, develop, and field new ideas, whether they be technological, informational, doctrinal, or organizational. Although creativity and tactical and operational innovation are hallmarks of SOF, high-level NORSOF leadership and a supportive culture would be needed to make innovation a core competency throughout the entire NORSOF system.

Subgroup process   All five subgroups managed their process with support from the lead designer on an as-needed basis. Periodic "all-hands" meetings pulled together the entire design team to keep all subgroups updated on their progress. These meetings were extremely valuable for several reasons. Subgroups reported on their evolving prototypes so everyone could see the progress being made. Other design team members then became the first testers of the prototypes by providing feedback to the presenting subgroup on what aspects of their prototypes worked, what didn't, what needed to be changed, and what new ideas might be added. Most important, the subgroups came to appreciate that their new ideas and their prototypes were not just stand-alone efforts in redesign. All the subgroups' efforts needed to fit together as a whole.

It did no good to fix one element of NORSOF's design and find that it was incompatible with other subgroups' prototypes. NORSOF's structure was a case in point. As originally prototyped by a subgroup, the structure was more hierarchical than the other members of the design team thought appropriate, given the key success factors. In contrast, other subgroups' initial prototypes had been based on the assumption of a decentralized structure to foster greater flexibility and encouraged creativity and innovation. The all-hands meetings then became the occasions for the design team as a whole to iron out the differences among their prototypes and key success factors informed all prototyping efforts. The process, which was challenging and sometimes contentious, ultimately enabled the subgroups to work through their differences and create a NORSOF organizational design in which all subgroup contributions fit together to form a configurational whole.

Additional rounds of prototype testing continued with a wider set of stakeholders. NPS staff and students were asked for their input using the same procedures as subgroup feedback sessions. They listened to presentations, asked questions, and pointed out what they thought worked and what didn't, and offered additional suggestions and ideas for the next rounds of prototyping. The final feedback session occurred during a special workshop for leaders (both officers and civilians) of NORSOCOM. Admiral Holte sent members of his staff to NPS to learn about the design team's thinking process, as well as its recommended prototypes. The design team incorporated and summarized its feedback in the last round of prototyping and the final report to NORSOF.[43]

Evaluation of NORSOF 2025 The NORSOF 2025 design prototypes recommended that NORSOF be: transformed into a truly strategic instrument; oriented to defend against hybrid and unconventional warfare, with a greater emphasis on MA; configured to fight as a flexible, adaptable, highly maneuverable, and well-connected network supported by a flat organizational structure; organized to enable interservice, interdepartmental, and international cooperation and to integrate R&D with fighting units to sustain organizational innovation; and renewed with a lifelong perspective on career development, with multiple career tracks to recruit, select, train, educate, and retain the appropriate personnel.

It may be argued that few, if any, of these recommendations are individually unique, as many have been put forward elsewhere by others in one form or another. However, if one examines the recommendations as a whole, probes deeper into the underlying assumptions and analyses that guide them, it becomes clear that this set of recommended prototypes have not been proposed in the Norwegian context before. Were they to be implemented, NORSOF in 2025 would have a very different strategic design compared to its current configuration. Thus, it is reasonable to conclude that the design effort succeeded in adding new ideas and prototypes to inform NORSOF's long-term planning process, a conclusion supported by both the sponsor, the commander's staff, and the officer-student design team after the workshop presentations in May 2015.

Additional evaluations conducted post workshop in Norway reinforced this view. Sponsoring a summative evaluation, a goal-based assessment,[44] NORSOCOM assessed whether the NORSOF 2025 design project achieved its intended goals—the generation and design of creative ideas and their prototypes. The study compared the results of the design approach at NPS against the results of FFI's Traditional Strategic Planning Approach, which ran independently and currently in Norway. The Norwegian sponsor and Norwegian stakeholders who assessed both projects scored the design thinking approach higher than the traditional approach on all indicators and rated its results "more innovative than the Traditional Approach." The evaluators observed that "design thinking appears to encourage creativity and innovation more than the Traditional Planning approach does."[45] They noted that the differences between the two models were particularly visible in the later stages of the two processes. Whereas traditional approach to problem solving included an initial creative session, it had, over time, a tendency to become more a programming exercise for the decided course of action. Design thinking allowed, and even encouraged, creativity until the final product was delivered. Although eventually leading to more creative results, the flip side of that creativity was students' impression of a more chaotic, unpredictable, and at times frustrating process compared to their previous experiences in more traditional planning. These results reinforce Tim Brown's assessment that "convergent thinking is a practical way of deciding among existing alternatives. What convergent thinking is not so good at, however, is probing the future and creating new possibilities."[46] And this apparently is where strategic design and design thinking excelled in the NORSOF case.

In Summary

Strategic design is organization-centric design—an organization employing the principles of design and design thinking to chart its future and specifiy how it intends to achieve its future and hoped-for results. In addition, as a CAS, an organization is constantly updating its decisions and practices to remain aligned with the general and task environments in which it is embedded. To reflect this alignment, or to identify any misalignments, it is important for designers and change agents to be able to map the organization as a system. This chapter introduced the ROSF, which maps the key aspects of an organization: its direction setting; organization design (tasks, people and their skills, technology of work, organizational structure and organizational processes); emergent culture; and results. Applying the ROSF, designers and change agents are then able to pinpoint where misalignments occur and where to intervene in the system to make changes.

These organizations can be private enterprises like P&G or public organizations like NORSOF, both of which are featured in this chapter. In the ideal, regardless of their type, all organizations have a clear purpose and identity and, in the case of public organization, a specific mandate. They also have boundaries that distinguish the organization from other organizations, and each one has its own unique purpose and identity. Organizations also have well-identified members who have official positions and roles, either full time or part time, including contractors who may be on short- or long-term assignments with the organization.

Organizational boundaries also become more fluid as members engage in cross-boundary relationships to tackle issues and challenges that no single organization can handle on its own. We call these cross-boundary efforts *systemic design*—the topic of chapter 7.

7 Systemic Design

Systemic design, an evolving domain of design, calls for a better means of change through the design of systems.[1] Diverging from the engineering and hard science epistemologies of system design and systems engineering, systemic design links human-centered design (HCD) with systems thinking to prepare designers to deal with the greater complexities of twenty-first-century design challenges.[2] It typically includes the design or redesign of multiple, interconnected, and overlapping subsystems—social, economic, technical, and political—that together make up a whole social system.[3] These *multistakeholder service systems*,[4] such as those that exist in education, health care, and megacity planning and management,[5] are noted for their social complexity, integration, and scale.

The socially complex map of stakeholders that need to be considered in the pursuit of better educational outcomes offers an example. Comprehensive systemic educational design to improve student learning takes into account: students in the classrooms; parents who support their children's educational endeavors; teachers who guide and evaluate students' learning; school leaders and staff who support the teacher and students engaged in the learning process; communities that sustain schools with their volunteer time and tax dollars; authors and companies that create the learning materials, technologies, and books for classroom use; the state educational system that oversees and funds schools and certifies their results; universities that educate the teachers and educational leaders; in-service training organizations that update teacher and staff skills and competencies; states' elected leaders (e.g., superintendents, governors, and legislators), who formulate and change educational policy in terms of what is taught, why it is taught, how it is taught, when it is taught, and to whom it is taught; federal laws and organizations that govern education policy at the national level; and businesses and organizations that rely on educated students to be contributing members of their organizations and communities.

Systemic design also relies on systems thinking that takes a holistic approach to problem solving. It begins with efforts to establish a system's boundary, identify its constituent parts, and ascertain how the parts are interdependent such that they form an interconnected whole. Once the system and its interdependent parts have been mapped, the next step is to ascertain how the system is functioning. Does the system produce its intended results? Are the children learning what the educational system and stakeholders intend them to learn? Or does the system produce unintended consequences, such as children dropping out of school? If some of the system outcomes produce unintended consequences or harmful effects to the system and its stakeholders, systemic designers then need to decide where and how to intervene in the system. Change interventions typically focus on one part of a system to prompt concurrent shifts in the system's other parts. Ideally, taken together, the shifts are intended to realign the system and its constituent parts to form a new integrated whole, with improved results and outcomes.[6]

A key question for designers is where to launch systemic designs and who should drive them. In the case of education, should systemic design begin in school districts with local stakeholders? If the new ideas are successful, they then can be adopted and scaled to the state, or even the federal level. Or should systemic design opt for a top-down strategy that brings together a coalition of support to generate innovative policy designs at the state or federal level, which are then implemented in local school districts? Alternatively, as Ray Ison and Edward Straw argue in *The Hidden Power of Systems Thinking: Governance in a Climate Emergency*, rather than zeroing in on specific policy initiatives, the better option is to redesign outmoded and dysfunctional governance systems that sustain the status quo and makes it difficult to tackle wicked problems like climate change. Instead, they advocate for new systems of governance, practices, institutions, and even constitutions that are better suited to deal with the complexities and challenges of the twenty-first century.[7] Whether designers use a top-down or a bottom-up approach to policy initiatives, some hybrid process that is a combination of the two,[8] or even top-down governance redesign, they need to address the necessary building blocks of systemic design: the social networks needed to develop and support new ideas and the social ecosystems that nurture and support them.

Systemic Design and Social Networks

Early efforts in social system design began when businesses and public and nonprofit organizations came to recognize the potential benefits of coordinating, cooperating, and even collaborating with stakeholders to accomplish organizational missions. The literature recognizes these initiatives as the pursuit of "cross-sector partnerships," "interorganizational relations," "intergovernmental relations," "intergovernmental collaborations," "multigovernmental collaborations," and "collaborative governance." Later literature referenced "social networks," "governance networks," "policy networks," and "collaborative networks," and even the "metagovernance of hierarchies, networks, and markets."[9] Regardless of the label, all had similar features that distinguish them from earlier types of designs:

- Recognizing the difficulties that individuals and organizations have in independently addressing transboundary issues, what Russell Ackoff referred to as "messes,"[10] organizations and stakeholders acknowledge their interdependencies and begin to work together on complex initiatives such as those involved in education and health care.

- Initial stakeholder connections and relationships form unbounded, fuzzy, porous, and fluid network boundaries as stakeholders come and go, have different levels of commitment to resolving transboundary concerns, and lack an overarching authority to guide problem solving unless network participants agree to create some mechanism to coordinate and govern their interactions.[11] Clear boundaries characteristic of strategic designs that are established by organizational mandates, missions, and membership are typically missing from systemic designs, resulting in a more emergent and self-organizing design process.

- The wide-ranging diversity of stakeholders' interests and capabilities, their discipline-based expertise (e.g., from economics to anthropology), the reach of their operations (e.g., from local to regional levels), and the various sectors in which they work (e.g., public, nonprofit, and business) can drive network members apart and make problem-solving contentious. Employing design thinking when working on any systemic design/redesign project plays an important role in helping network members view their diversity as a strength rather than a source of conflict.

- Systemic design, as all design levels, depend on the generation of new ideas and their prototyping and testing. But generating new ideas among the network depends on the nature of transboundary relationships. We know, for example, that "a high degree of trust provides relative certainty that other actors will not abuse initiatives to interact in order to realize their own objective at the cost of other participants."[12] Indeed, trust has been shown to enhance network performance and the innovation of the network's solutions.[13] Design thinking's values, principles, and processes play an important role in building trust among the stakeholders and sustaining it over time.

- Place-based systemic design comes in a range of sizes, depending on the design challenge: small-scale networks with a few stakeholders at the local level, midscale networks with greater numbers of stakeholders at the state and regional levels, and large-scale networks that can span national and international levels. All are examples of how people and organizations come together to address complex, transboundary issues and problems that are well beyond the expertise and capacity of any one stakeholder to tackle on its own. In contrast to large-scale change initiatives, which typically involve an array of stakeholders that come from multiple domains and disciplines, all with divergent views on problems and their solutions,[14] systemic design differs in that it incorporates design into its change and transformation process.

An early example of systemic design is CHILDLINE 1098, a twenty-four-hour, toll-free emergency telephone service that offers India's street children's quick access to police assistance, health care, and follow-up support. The idea of CHILDLINE took root in 1993, when Jeroo Billimoria,[15] then a professor at the Tata Institute of Social Sciences, launched an experimental, action-based project to deal with the growing numbers of street children, estimated at that time to be 130,000 in Bombay (Mombai), with

48 million throughout India. Her on-the-ground experience in problem solving took different pathways. Billimoria originally opened negotiations with the police department to use the Mumbai police control room for an emergency telephone service for the city's street children. When that idea didn't pan out, she approached the Mahanagar Telephone Nigam Limited, the government's telecom agency, and requested a toll-free number. The number—1098—was approved and became the official toll-free CHILDLINE number available to all. CHILDLINE differed from standard rehabilitation efforts that were organization-based, entirely adult-led, heavy on cost and infrastructure with limited reach, and resistant to cross-organizational coordination. Instead, it was led and manned by a network of trained volunteer street children themselves. They took the calls and routed them to networked partner service organizations in the zone closest to the caller. The partner organizations that received 1098 calls offered night shelter, managed the volunteer staff of street children, and maintained a referral network of support agencies who undertook long-term follow-up and rehabilitation. The ongoing support of the Tata Institute included the design of an information management system, training documentation, advocacy, and liaising with the police, the health system and other collateral agencies. The computer database logged every recorded call and provided the quality control to track and monitor the service's effectiveness. This network of support for the street children eventually grew into the nationwide, government-funded program committed to providing CHILDLINE 1098 service to children in every Indian city with a population of 10 million by 2002. The program is now overseen by the CHILDLINE India Foundation, which is responsible for establishing the CHILDLINE 1098 services and monitoring its operations in cities and districts throughout India.[16] In the meantime, Billimoria, the founder of CHILDLINE India, moved on to a new role in Child Helpline International, a new initiative that practices the model of CHILDLINE India in other nations, such as Vietnam, Mongolia, and Egypt.

Later examples of systemic design come from Dodge County, a rural agricultural region in southeastern Minnesota. The stakeholders included the Optimized Care Team in the Kasson Clinic in Dodge County, the Dodge Refreshed Partnership among the Dodge County community, the Kasson Clinic, and the Center for Innovation.[17] The optimized care model that they developed moved from "conveyor belt care" to "team-based care," which relied on a network of providers (a doctor of medicine and nurse practitioner/physician assistant mix), a registered nurse, three licensed practical nurses or medical assistants, and one scheduler.[18] Patients and team members rated the new care model as performing well on every metric. Prototype testing demonstrated that the Optimized Care Team was more efficient, reduced costs, increased patient and provider satisfaction, and improved overall system performance. The Dodge Refreshed Partnership also moved from a reliance on disconnected groups that acted independently to a network of providers who delivered wellness-based health care. It too began to measure health in terms of the total cost of care rather than the number of clinic visits and fees for service. The Mayo Clinic's Office of Population Health Management is now disseminating the Optimized Care Team to over eighty clinics across three states. It also is integrating Dodge Refreshed with other initiatives (e.g., partner management, community engagement, finance management, and operational management) into the Mayo Model of Community Care to assist clinics across the US Midwest in improving community health care and making the transition from fee for service to total cost of care.

Related to systemic design are cases that take a "systems approach" combining "system-based practices" and "design thinking."[19] Despite the narrow characterization of design thinking in a report from the Organisation for Economic Co-operation and Development (OECD),[20] the four design projects described in chapter 3 capture the essence of systemic design. The most prominent case comes from the Prime Minister's Office of Finland, which combined systems and design thinking approaches to establish a policy design program. Its purpose was to encourage "strategic experiments" such as the basic income experiment and a grassroots experiment to build an "experimental culture" in Finland's public sector.[21] In addition to the government's original six strategic experiments, hundreds of experiments and policy pilots emerged both at the central government and municipal levels throughout the country. And in 2017, the government launched a digital platform—the Place to Experiment—to support its key goal of finding innovate ways to develop public services.

Systemic Design and Social Ecosystems

Systemic design, initially reliant on complex social networks as its defining feature, eventually broadened its language and scope to focus on social ecosystems—the network of interdependent people, collectives, and institutions that need to be taken into account in supplying resources and creating a culture of innovation and change. The Children's Medical Center of Dallas provides an example. It originally launched a strategic design effort to assist the organization in rethinking the fundamentals of its business model to increase its value to stakeholders. When attempts to strategically redesign the organization failed, the center then launched a redesign effort at a broader ecosystem level. Changing its name to the Children's Health System of Texas, it signaled the creation of "a new ecosystem" of heath care that was "wellness (versus sickness) centered, citizen (versus physician) driven, prevention (versus intervention) focused, partnership based and community supported."[22] Working with a wide-ranging set of system stakeholders, it developed a new business model based on family health and well-being. It also created the Health and Wellness Alliance for Children, a community-based network of more than seventy-five organizations and agencies serving children, to assist the Children's Health System of Texas in testing new programs and developing new funding sources and opportunities to support the new business model.

BRAC,[23] the largest global development nongovernmental organization (NGO) in the world, also demonstrates the power and potential of systemically designed social ecosystems. Established in Bangladesh in the 1980s, it created a low-cost system of health care by training and developing community women, who, as self-employed health promoters, went door to door in villages and slums with a basket of goods—vitamins, antimalaria pills, sterile bandages, and other supplies—that they sold at affordable prices. The *shasthya shebikas*, as they are called in Bengali, also inquired about their neighbors' health needs or problems, which they then relayed to other health-care professionals for follow-up. From this humble beginning, BRAC evolved into a global leader in assisting marginalized people in poor, conflict-prone, and postdisaster settings. Using the same development principles, it expanded its programs beyond health care to education, women's and girls' empowerment, human and legal rights, agriculture, microfinance, and production.[24]

BRAC's programs in Uganda, a country recovering from a twenty-year old conflict that displaced an estimated 1.5 million people, serves as an excellent example how social ecosystems are the focal point in its developmental model. BRAC's "entrepreneurial ecosystem" began when it partnered with the government to create "'second chance' learning centers" for children who had been denied an opportunity to get an education due to poverty, violence, or both.[25] The curriculum in these "feeder" schools offered informal primary education based on the building blocks of entrepreneurship—treating children "not just as job seekers but as potential job creators."[26] As part of its holistic approach to reducing poverty and building entrepreneurship, BRAC also set up a chain of girls' clubs—safe spaces under the name "Empowerment and Livelihood for Adolescents" to address the problems of teen pregnancy to help girls stay in school and develop their financial literacy and ability to spot business opportunities when they arise. As girls matured, they also received training on how to take out microloans and start a microfranchise. All these efforts were designed to deal with the barriers to being a "self-employed and self-empowered economic actor."[27] BRAC viewed poverty as "capability deprivation" and treated children as "potential entrepreneurs with untapped talents and latent capabilities that are only waiting to break through the many barriers that keep them from achieving their potential."[28] Thus, building an ecosystem of entrepreneurship at the base of the economic pyramid became the way to attack the market distortions that work against the poor.

Beyond its educational programs, BRAC also partnered with the MasterCard Foundation to build out its system in Uganda. The strategy was to combine microfinance with livelihood development and youth empowerment to generate a "job-creation machine" reliant not only on wage employment for its 1,960 employees, but also on developing and supporting entrepreneurs.[29] Central to this strategy was lowering the barriers to entrepreneurship at multiple touch points in the respective value chains of the agriculture, poultry and livestock, and health-care sectors. As an example, the process in agriculture began when people received livelihood training and microloans to start a business. In return, rather than paying a fee, BRAC only asked that they offer their neighbors free advice on more efficient farming techniques. Sarah Mukama, a farmer who supports a family of seven on a small plot of land by rearing livestock and growing beans and vegetables, illustrates how the process works. She gets a regular supply of seeds for herself and supplements her income by distributing high-yield seed varieties of maize, beans, and vegetables to other farmers in her village and surrounding areas.

Due to the assistance that she received from BRAC, her farm yield increased threefold, and farmers in her village began coming to her to buy seeds and for training. BRAC has reported that farmers are doubling and sometimes tripling their yields as a result of the inputs and advice that they receive from entrepreneurs like Mukama. Beyond the agricultural yields, the farmers' increased income now is rippling out to benefit other families and vendors in the community.

Mukama thus became part of an "ecosystem, a network of likeminded people from poor communities who are reinforced to help both their neighbors and themselves."[30] Currently, about 5,000 BRAC-trained micro-entrepreneurs like her work in Uganda. Each operates as an independent enterprise without wages or salaries from BRAC, but each makes money by reselling goods at a small markup to rural farmers who have not been served by the existing distribution systems. Besides the seed network, other networks provide cattle insemination and chicken vaccines, and their results have been equally impressive. The scaled-up network of microfranchised chicken inoculators, for example, successfully delivered thirteen million doses of vaccine and helped to reduce the chicken mortality rate from 35 percent to 10 percent, which enabled the poultry microborrowers to repay their BRAC loans and for BRAC to redeploy capital to others even more quickly.

For the BRAC ecosystem of development to work, the producers of the distributed products have to break even. So, for example, to keep the unit cost of high-yield seeds low, it engages a network of contract growers in the seed production and processing enterprises that BRAC established. Taken together, the network of growers, the low-cost distribution network, and the microfinance network produces BRAC's "end-to-end value chain." It seamlessly integrates these networks to deliver economics of scale that "makes prices fair for everybody in the value chain, from producer to end-user—something that the market mechanisms driven purely by profit have failed to do." Moreover, the cost benefits of operating at scale "passes savings onto other actors in the value chain, who are mainly poor and disadvantaged women." To expand its operations and compete on price, BRAC continuously streamlines and routinizes its processes by removing unnecessary steps, minimizing waste and inefficiency, and taking a "zero-tolerance stance on corruption in its ranks."[31]

BRAC's interlinked efforts all work "in the service of the bottom line that is not financial return but social good."[32] It views its "microfinance, microfranchising, pro-poor value-chain interventions, health care education, social enterprises, and girls' empowerment through a single lens: one of bringing down barriers to entrepreneurship"[33] at the base of the economic pyramid to overcome the market distortions that work against the poor and marginalized people.[34]

Systemic Design and Social Innovation

HCD, systems thinking, collaborative social networks, and social ecosystems are important features that inform the systemic design of social systems. When successful, these collective efforts result in social innovation and social change.[35] Although writings on social innovation and social change have yet to form a consensus on definitions,[36] Goff Mulgan finds some agreement that social innovators are "social both in their ends and their means." They produce new services, organizational forms, rules and regulations, changes in social relations, and other innovations that are "better ways to meet human needs." Through their collective and collaborative engagements, they simultaneously strengthen "bonds of commitment and solidarity."[37] Thus, social innovation has become "a loose movement founded on ideas: above all the idea that in the right circumstances people can make, shape and design their world, and more specifically, that they can invent and grow new forms of social organization . . . [that enables them] to take control of their lives and their world."[38]

We find evidence of social innovation in the cases of CHILDLINE's social networks, which provided support and protection to India's street children, and BRAC's social ecosystems in Uganda, which empowered people through microfinance, microfranchising, social enterprises, pro-poor value-chain interventions, and improved health care and education. Not only did these interventions find new ways to meet people's needs and protect their rights better than their current alternatives, but the results that they produced engendered greater community trust and social capital, which increased people's willingness to take collective action for the common good, opening up the potential for future innovations.

Thus, Mulgan and his colleagues see social innovation "as an urgent task—one of the most urgent there is" due to "a wide, and probably growing, gap between the scale of the problems we face and the scale of solutions on offer." They contend that problems haven't been solved and cannot be solved by conventional practices and institutions because of people's "pressing unmet needs." [39] Alex Nicholls and his colleagues agree, adding that these needs have not been met due to "problems of social welfare efficiency or distribution and imbalances and inequalities in social structures and relations"[40] and "the failure . . . of established systems (technology, markets, policy, governance, etc.) to deliver well-being and economic prosperity."[41] To address these failures, Roberto Unger highlights the key role of connectors in the systemic design and innovation process—the broker, the entrepreneur, and the institutions that link people, ideas, money, and power in the search for solutions to intractable social problems. He describes this connector as a "social innovator," a "social entrepreneur," and a "civic activist—"the self-created agent of the social innovation movement . . . a practical visionary [who] offers tangible down payments on another future."[42] This "agent of social innovation"[43] operates in arenas where "conceptions of a market economy or of a political democracy are always wedded to flawed, relatively accidental institutional arrangements." Thus, the activist is challenged to "redesign these arrangements for the sake of interests and ideals that [these institutional arrangements] fail to satisfy,"[44] especially those "that have not been solved by either the state or the market."[45] In other words, agents of social innovation intervene in systems "to do what needs to be done to address the unresolved problems of society";[46] they are "the lifeblood of the social innovation movement."[47] Some examples of these agents of social innovation can be found on the "Design for the Other 90%" website.[48] Rather than designing to serve only 10 percent of the population, participants are dedicated to designing for those who lack money and power to deal with their economic, political, and cultural life challenges. The Milan-based DESIS Network (whose name stands for "Designers for Social Innovation and Sustainability") also promotes social innovation in higher education to advance meaningful social change through network collaboration.[49]

In what follows, two systemic design approaches to social innovation are detailed—those driven by social entrepreneurs working at the grassroots level, and those launched by grassroots policy entrepreneurs who ultimately were successful in crafting state policy from the top down. We can better understand how these agents of innovation function in this capacity by comparing them to a business entrepreneur like Mukama in the BRAC example given previously. She started her enterprise, a commercial undertaking, with a new idea or concept—selling seeds to her neighbors to make a profit. Although BRAC absorbed the initial risks in giving Mukama the seeds, she took the risk of using her land (which provided a livelihood for her family) to demonstrate to herself, and eventually to her neighbors, that the seeds could produce greater commercial value than those they were using. Thus, business entrepreneurship is the capacity and willingness to risk a new idea, and all that is entailed to develop it, to launch an enterprise for the purpose of making a profit.

Developing business entrepreneurs was part of BRAC's mission. But Fazle Hasan Abed, who founded BRAC, and Jeroo Billimoria, who established CHILDLINE, are entrepreneurs of a different type. Some call them *changemakers* or *disrupters*, while others, as noted previously, call them *social entrepreneurs*[50]—people who focus on social problems, go after their root causes, and seek innovative social solutions that enhance not only people's well-being and change the status quo, but also ideas and practices that can be replicated and scaled.[51]

Social Entrepreneurs as Agents of Social Innovation

Many people and institutions have contributed to the evolution of the field of social entrepreneurship: Charles Leadbeater[52] coined the term "social entrepreneurship"; Michael Young founded the School for Social Entrepreneurs in 1997; Charles Schwab established the Foundation for Social Entrepreneurship in 1998 in partnership with the World Economic Forum; J. Gregory Dees taught a course on social entrepreneurship at the Yale School of Management, and then at the Center for Social Entrepreneurship at Duke Business School; Jeff Skoll, the founder of the Skoll Foundation and the Skoll World Forum, established the Saïd School of Business at Oxford University and launched the Skoll Award for Social Entrepreneurship in 2005; and Bill Drayton, considered by many to be "the father of modern social entrepreneurship," established the field of social entrepreneurship and inspired others to expand it.[53]

In 1980, Drayton launched Asoka, which today is the largest global social entrepreneurship organization, with 3,500 entrepreneurs operating in ninety-two countries.

Ashoka's comprehensive survey of its successful social entrepreneurs worldwide under-scores the importance of developing a "changemaking ecosystem," in which everyone takes a part in being a changemaker.[54] These results underscore Bloom and Dees's[55] recommendations that social entrepreneurs cultivate their ecosystem by developing "an ecosystem strategy" for long-lasting and significant change.[56] Not only do social entrepreneurs need to understand the broad environment in which they work, but it is incumbent upon them to learn how to shape the environment, which begins by mapping the social ecosystems and identifying all the social actors who need to be included in the change process—the resource providers, competitors, complementary organizations, bystanders, beneficiaries, opponents, competitors—whether friendly or not, and complementary organizations.[57]

In *Getting beyond Better*, Roger Martin and Sally Osberg describe in greater detail how social entrepreneurship actually works. The four-phase model that they employ has parallels with design thinking. Comparable to the discovery phase, it begins with "understanding the world" before one attempts to change it. The second phase, "envi-sioning the future," sets a direction and develops new ideas for "specific, targeted con-stituents," akin to problem definition and idea generation in design thinking. The "build" phase creates a model of change that "reduces costs or increases value in a sys-temic and permanent way that can be quantified and captured," similar to prototyping and testing in design thinking. And finally, implementation means "scaling the solu-tion." [58] This phase means designing "explicitly for scale economies" so that the costs of scaling up are not prohibitive; "leveraging other actors in an ecosystem rather than attempting to work as a solo actor"; and encouraging "others to build on their models" and be "open source in their approach."[59] They also underscore the point that all the phases rely on social entrepreneurs' critical skills of empathy, working in empowered teams, and building trust.

To illustrate the finer points of social entrepreneurship and demonstrate how social entrepreneurs are designers at their core, I now turn to the case of Bunker Roy, a social entrepreneur from India. Roy received international recognition when he received the Skoll Award for Social Entrepreneurship in 2005[60] and when *Time* magazine selected him as one of the most influential people in the world in 2010.[61] Influenced by Mahatma Gandhi's spirit of service, he went to Bihar, an Indian state that was suffering a terrible famine in 1965, and it changed his life. Upon returning home, he told his mother that he wanted to live and work in a village. So in 1967, hav-ing completed his elite education, even becoming the Indian national squash cham-pion for three years,[62] Roy went to live and work in Tilonia as an unskilled laborer digging and blasting wells from 1967–1971. As part of his five-year discovery process, he learned that youths left their villages to look for jobs "because the predominant value system denigrated rural life, skills, and traditions and offered little hope of improved incomes or quality of life." Instead the youth gained "certificates" from "uninspiring mediocre technical institutes and colleges located in small towns" that produced thousands of "graduates" who hoped to get good-paying jobs in the cities.

Unfortunately, their "paper degrees had no value," and the youths ended up as educated unemployables in India's slums, unable to return home because of the shame that would bring upon their families.[63] Equally tragic, when the youths left their families, no one was left in the villages to pass on the traditional professions of weavers, blacksmiths, potters, builders, carpenters, and farmers that had been developed and adapted to local conditions over generations.

Roy eventually came to understand the fundamental problem as a "gross underestimation of people's infinite capacity to identify and solve their own problems with their own creativity and skills, and to depend on each other in tackling problems."[64] Conventional approaches to development at that time that were top-down, expensive, and ignorant of local knowledge and left the poor and the marginalized even more disempowered, dependent, and ill prepared to improve their lives. From his perspective, the challenge was to unlearn "the predominant value system [that] denigrated rural life, skills, and traditions"[65] and to create a new one. So he and his friend Merghaj, a farmer from the small village of Tilonia, leased an abandoned tuberculosis sanatorium from the government for one rupee a month and founded the Social Work and Research Centre, which eventually came to be known as the "Barefoot College." Located in Tilonia, 350 kilometers southwest of Delhi in Rajasthan state, its mission was to work in poor rural communities to do the following:

- Raise the standard of living
- Improve the quality of life
- Upgrade people's existing traditional skills and knowledge through training
- Guide the community in taking responsibility for providing some of these basic services
- Struggle and campaign for justice and the rule of law
- Be transparent and publically accountable to the community in whose name they receive funds.[66]

Founding the Barefoot College was the new idea, and it met with initial success—a 1974 survey covering over 500 square miles assessing 110 villages' groundwater situation informed the government's decision to extend the electrical grid to 100 villages. Unfortunately, a series of crises followed due to differences in the college's ideology and approaches, decision making, and management between its rural members and its urban-trained professionals who vastly outnumbered them. By 1977–1978, many professionals left the organization, which forced the college to look inward to build on its own strengths.

Other difficulties also arose. The college had antagonized the rural rich in the surrounding villages when it bypassed its hierarchy to work directly with the rural poor, creating tension between the poor and the local politicians. In its attempts to tackle corruption, the college also opened itself up to questions and scrutiny from the state assembly. In January 1979, the government told it to vacate the unused center that it had leased. The visit of Robert McNamara (then president of the World Bank) and McGeorge Bundy (then president of the Ford Foundation) eased the tensions with the politicians, and when Indira Gandhi returned to power in January 1979, the order to vacate was cancelled. So, in dealing with these crises, Bunker believed that the college became stronger:

> In the eyes of the rural poor we established a certain degree of credibility in taking on the local dominant political leadership and surviving. As local people started to be a part of the collective decision-making process, the thinking within the Barefoot College changed fundamentally. The college recognized that its dependence on urban expertise and paper credentials did damage to the mindset of the rural poor, in effect preventing them from coming out of poverty on their own.
>
> We also decided to take on the local political structure by persuading the local staff to run in the panchayat (village) elections as "independents." Our presence in the political process shook the political environment when several of our candidates won.[67]

The Barefoot College was—"a radical departure from the traditional concept of a 'college'." It was "built by the poor, for the poor," and over the forty-five years or so of its operations, it has been "managed, controlled, and owned by the poor." Its name is both "symbolic and literal"—"those who work, teach and learn in the college go barefoot and remain so when they return to their villages." The college's fundamental "belief [is] in the knowledge, creativity, practical wisdom, and survival skills of the rural poor." Instead of requiring written tests, it emphasizes "a hands-on-learning-by doing-process to gain practical skills." The goal is not to give attendees "paper degrees" that contribute to urban migration, but to help them gain the basic skills needed to provide vital services to their communities.[68] Four elements are central to the college's philosophy:[69]

- It offers an alternative education that values practical skills and knowledge needed to solve day-to-day problems essential to develop rural India.
- It prioritizes the ideas, thoughts, and wishes of the rural poor and values their traditional knowledge, skills and practical wisdom, including their oral traditions.
- It builds the poor's self-confidence and self-reliance by giving them access to learning that enables them to serve their own communities. Only illiterate or barely literate village youths, both males and females with no hope of getting the lowest government job, are selected. They then are trained to be "'barefoot' educators, doctors, teachers, engineers, architects, designers, communicators, hand pump mechanics, and accountants."[70]
- It disseminates its approach all over India and the world. The Barefoot College international currently operates in ninety-three countries.[71] The ripple effect of its direct training and services affects about two million people.

A good way to illustrate how this innovative college operates is to describe how illiterate and semiliterate rural poor physically built the new Barefoot College campus between 1986 and 1989. Even before the building began, the college had been encouraging and promoting male and female barefoot architects. So 12 of them, directed by an illiterate farmer in Tilonia,[72] assisted by 50 village masons and over 100 day laborers, and with input from those who lived and worked in the college, designed and built the main campus. An architect had attempted to draft blueprints, but they turned out to be useless since so many changes had to be made to accommodate the needs of the community. Instead, the design team refined and redrew the plan with rough sketches on the ground, measured the depth of wells and floor spaces using their hands, arms, and a hath, a traditional measure of about eighteen inches, or the length or a human arm from the elbow to the end of the middle finger. The construction process, reliant on traditional knowledge, local materials, and villagers' skills, ultimately created a campus that contained 2,800 square meters of buildings on 35,000 square meters of land at the cost of $20,000, or $1.50 per square foot. The buildings, which surrounded decorative courtyards, faced the wind to take advantage of air circulation to keep the courtyards cool. Local materials included stone, lime mortar for load-bearing walls, and stone slabs for the roofs, which the women waterproofed using a process that they insisted be carried out in secret. (In a 2011 TED talk, Bunker Roy claims that the roofs have never leaked.)[73] The Barefoot architects also connected all the building roofs so that they could collect rainwater in an underground 400,000-liter tank. On top of the tank, they constructed a community venue for performances that could accommodate 2,000 people for puppet shows and musical evenings. In addition, the Barefoot architects and village blacksmiths built seventy geodesic domes from discarded agricultural equipment, bullock carts, and pump sections, covering them with thatch to avoid using scarce wood. The domes serve as meeting halls, a dispensary, a milk booth, a pathology lab and an Internet cafe. And by 1989, the Barefoot solar engineers had installed "40 kilowatts of solar panels and 5 battery banks, each containing 136 deep-cycle batteries" using "solar components (inverters, charge controllers, battery boxes, stands)" all of which were fabricated by the college.[74]

The principles of "learning by doing," "learning from failure," "taking risks, trying new ideas, failing and trying again"[75] has been part of a respected process at the Barefoot College that has produced social innovations in five major areas:[76]

- **Education.**[77] *Digital Night Schools* teach children 6–14 who are unable to attend the formal education day schools due to their family responsibilities. They are taught literacy, mathematics, scientific skills, and digital literacy, as well as the values of democracy and environmental sustainability. Students also actively participate in school management through the innovative Children's Parliament program. *Residential Bridge Schools* enable children not previously enrolled in the formal education system to catch up with their peers in a special ten-month program to fill in the gaps in their knowledge in order to reintegrate them into the formal school system. The *Shikshaniketan Day School*, an experimental primary school in Tilonia, is a research and development center that develops tools and techniques for the rural context, with an emphasis on the local environment, sustainability, science, and digital literacy. Taken together, these schools have trained 14,000 grassroots educators and educated 75,000 children since the college's inception. A total of 65 percent of the students are girls, 40 percent have been reintegrated into mainstream education, and 85 percent have settled in their own villages.

- **Solar energy.**[78] The Barefoot College in Tilonia trains semiliterate and illiterate rural women "to build, install, maintain, and repair solar electrification systems in off-grid villages." It also has developed and installed India's first solar-powered reverse osmosis plant that produces 3,600 liters of clean water daily to supply drinking water for over 1,000 villages, and it has been teaching rural youths how to build and install water heaters for people who live in remote villages in eight states of India. In addition, solar cooker engineers have learned how to fabricate, install, and maintain parabolic solar cookers for homes.

  The college also has a global mission.[79] It brings in women from countries in Africa, South and Central America, Asia, and the Pacific Islands, who speak no English and have no educational qualifications, to learn how to build solar electrification systems, such as light-emitting diode (LED) lamps, charge controllers, home lighting systems, and solar lanterns. As Barefoot solar engineers (or "Solar Mamas," as they are often called), the women also learn how to establish village rural electronic workshops where the equipment and components needed for solar unit repair and maintenance are stored. When their course is completed, the college ships their equipment back to their villages for installation. To date, over 750 solar engineers have provided 550,000 people with light in 1,300 villages worldwide. In terms of overall impact, 4,020 grams of carbon emissions from burning firewood and kerosene have been avoided with the use of solar energy as a source for light, heating, and cooking in ninety-seven countries, thanks to over 2,200 trained solar engineers who have installed solar systems in 18,047n households.

- **Water.**[80] The Barefoot College teaches people how to harness fresh rainwater from rooftops and store it in simple, low-cost underground tanks, which represents 90 million liters of rainwater collected in eighteen states for two million people. It also has supported the construction of four dams, bringing drinking water to 48,000 people from twenty villages. A total of 1,766 people have been trained as mechanics to install and maintain 1,735 hand pumps that provide water to over 60,000 people in 530 villages spread across four states in India. The Barefoot College's six solar-powered desalination plants, constructed from booster pumps and sand and carbon filters, provide drinking water from the nearby Sambhar Lake, which is stored in 5,000-liter tanks that supply water to nearby villages. The college also has designed a village-based, interactive water-mapping website (Neer Jaal) controlled and managed by rural committees to catalog village water tables and water sources. It is designed to scale nationally for gathering and monitoring water consumption data. The Barefoot College also provides three annual trainings and mobile water test kits to interested community members who disseminate knowledge about water resources throughout their villages. In terms of total impact, 1,600 schools and communities now have access to drinking water, 50 billion liters of drinking water is available through rainwater harvesting, and 1,042 rural water engineers are now employed.

- **Health.**[81] The Barefoot health reach, facilitated by a team of doctors, health workers, and midwives, extends to over fifty villages in rural Rajasthan. The college has
  "fostered health awareness among rural men, women, and children on issues such
  as hygiene, food and nutrition, family planning and reproductive health, immu-
  nizations, midwifery and HIV prevention." The college also works with the Medic
  Mobile Network to use mobile technology to collect data on services, track and regis-
  ter diseases, keep stock of essential medicines, and communicate about emergencies.
  In terms of general impact, 6,674 patients in 80 villages have been treated, more
  than 2,000 women and girls have benefited from the Women's Wellness Program
  in 50 villages, and over 200 camps have been conducted on family planning and
  gynecology, dental health, and emotional well-being in over 500 villages.

- **Women's Empowerment.**[82] Enriche offers "education, enterprise and empowerment, by and for rural women." The goals are to give them the confidence, knowledge, and skills to enhance their awareness and aspirations; enable sustainable
  livelihoods relevant to local resources and market opportunities; engage communities and local partners to transform community aspirations into practical solutions
  and actions; and provide participants with access to financial services, local mentoring opportunities, and market contacts to help them become self-reliant entrepreneurs and agents of change. The curriculum is designed in collaboration with
  partner organizations and uses audio, visual, and digital content in local languages
  that are adapted for a rural, nonliterate audience.

Central to all these activities are five key values that inform all of the Barefoot College's operations:[83]

- *Equality*—"[A]ll people in the college are equal regardless of gender, caste, ethnicity,
  age, and schooling."[84]

- *Collective decision making*—The collective, not individuals, makes decisions. So, for
  example, each person's salary is based on criteria and a point system and decided by
  everyone in the organization.[85]

- *Decentralization*—The college's structure is decentralized, with a full-time director
  assisted by a team in charge of different sections, to encourage the free flow of information and to give voice to all.[86] The director meets monthly with people in charge
  of the sections, as well as the directors of field centers, to review the work completed
  in the previous month, make plans for the next month, and discuss any issues of
  coordination that might have arisen. *Field centers*[87] are run by a team consisting of
  a coordinator and field workers who plan and implement village-level initiatives.
  Village-level committees, with equal numbers of men and women who come from
  among the poorest in the villages, review the initiatives and endorse their implementation. The four most common village-level communities are water committees,
  village education committees, children's parliaments, and women's groups.

- *Self-reliance*—The college gives those in charge their own budgets and bank accounts.
  For example, the village committees are empowered to purchase materials, select

those who will work on special projects as wage laborers, disburse wages, oversee the systems that they install, and even collect monthly fees.[88] Minutes that record decisions are circulated to all concerned. Hearings that share confidential information (e.g., funding sources, amounts received, expenditures, and staff bank accounts and audits) are open to anyone in the community.[89]

- *Austerity*—"[E]veryone in the college receives a living wage, not a market wage."[90] The monthly wage ranges from 75 to 150 dollars. Living conditions provide basic needs and minimize waste.

The Barefoot College is also comprised of three distinct entities, each with its own unique registration and operating mechanisms designed to support the college's vision and mission:[91]

- *The SWRC*, known as the *Barefoot College*, was the original organization founded by Roy. It manages the local Barefoot College campus, engages in activities with local Rajasthan communities, and partners with the Silicon Andhdra Music, Performing Arts, and Dance Academy (SAMPADA) network[92] of twenty-seven organizations in sixteen states of India to develop and innovate in the programmatic areas of water sanitation, alternative energy, education, women's health and wellness, traditional communications, and women's and girls' rights advocacy.
- The *Barefoot College International*, established in 2015, brings the Barefoot College empowerment programs to a global scale in the areas of enterprise, technology (renewable energy, digital education, and research and development (R&D)), and education.
- *Hatheli Sansthan* develops and trains artisans who produce products for sale within India and abroad, and works to develop a viable cottage industry that honors regional crafts.[93]

Policy Entrepreneurs as Agents of Social Innovation

In contrast to social entrepreneurs, who typically begin delivering social innovations from the bottom up, policy entrepreneurs can be found working at the policy level, generating new ideas, formulating policies, and even facilitating their enactment into law and overseeing their implementation in practice.[94] In their pursuit of policy change,[95] policy entrepreneurs have driven innovative policies in education,[96] climate change,[97] health-care reform,[98] urban poverty,[99] water policy,[100] and science research.[101] And when new policy initiatives (e.g., regulations, programs, and services, and even tools and processes) result in improved public outcomes and experiences, policy entrepreneurs become catalysts of social innovation.[102]

Having defined design "as the ability to imagine 'that-which-does-not exist' to make it appear in concrete form as a new purposeful addition to the real world,"[103] it is natural to extend it to the intentional creation of public policy in the pursuit of systemic change. Indeed, policy design, an area of study that links the design and the policy fields, is dedicated to this effort.[104] From Peters and Rava, we learn that "new lenses" of design are needed in the design of policy in order to expand the policy problem-solving space; rely on foresight rather than forecasting; iterate to an approximate the ideal and to muddle through rather than attempting to solve a problem using a linear, analytic process; consider the path dependencies and the political economy in policy design (e.g., its "throwness") rather than viewing policy making as a tablula rasa; change policy design practices to include a "'design attitude'" rather than a "'decision' attitude"; and interactively move upstream, downstream, and sideways across silos in the process of designing.[105] And we can find these new lenses surfacing in the applications of design and design thinking to policymaking processes worldwide[106] and in worldwide design, innovation, and change labs.[107]

Six policy entrepreneurs outside formal positions in government are examples of how to intentionally pursue systemic change and advocate innovative social policy initially from the bottom up, and eventually from the top down.[108] Together with a complex social network of people and organizations, they created a social ecosystem of educational reform that successfully passed and implemented the nation's first mandatory K–12 public school choice program in the United States. To understand how they achieved this educational social innovation, we must go beyond some traditional descriptions of the policy phases identified in the left column of table 7.1: *policy initiation*[109]/*agenda setting*,[110] *policy design/formulation/analysis*,[111] *policy legitimation*,[112] *policy implementation*,[113] and *policy evaluation*.[114] Although these general phases of the policy process can be discerned in the case, the right column represents the finer-grained details of the policy entrepreneurs' design strategy that occurred within the traditional parameters of the policy process.

This comparison between the two lenses underscores three points. First, the two lenses of the policy process capture different levels of detail, not different frameworks. The left column of table 7.1 captures the general phases of the policy process as described in the policy literature, and the right column captures a more detailed map of policy entrepreneurs' activities through the same process. Second, a deeper dive into

Table 7.1

The policy process through two lenses

Traditional Policy Lens	Design/Design Thinking Lens
Policy initiation/agenda setting	Discovery
	Problem framing
	Ideation
Policy design/formulation/analysis	Prototyping
	Policy entrepreneurs' ideas/prototypes
	Governor's ideas/prototypes
	Administrators' ideas/prototypes
Policy legitimation	Prototypes that become law
Policy implementation	Laws implemented in practice
Policy evaluation	Laws (if tested and approved) accepted as standard practice

the activities in each phase of the policy process in the right column shows the lens of design to be compatible with the lens of the traditional policy process, but with one important difference. In the left column, the word "design" describes one phase in the policy process when concepts are put into a more concrete form—a positon paper or a model that formulates a policy so it can be reviewed, approved, and legitimated by those in governmental authority. In contrast, the word "design" in the right column refers to the entire policy process and its outcomes. and the term "prototyping" is substituted for the word "design" in the left column. Prototyping is then defined as a subset of the design activities that hone and shape new policy ideas generated during ideation so that they take a more substantive form for testing and evaluation. And finally, whether one seeks incremental or transformative changes in policy, both lenses offer a pathway to forge something new in a particular context—the standard definition of innovation.[115]

In what follows, I explore the policy process through the design lens and offer a secondary analysis of policy entrepreneurs' activities organized into the design phases (discovery, problem formulation, ideation, prototyping, and testing). Looking through this lens does not change any details of the case. It simply reframes the policy entrepreneurs' and their network activities as a policy design—a social innovation that changed the educational system in the state of Minnesota.

Minnesota Public Policy Innovation Viewed through the Design Lens

Discovery

Every new idea springs to life molded and shaped by its context. To fully appreciate the appearance of a new policy idea, we must have some understanding of the forces that give it life. In the case of policy entrepreneurs, it is difficult to pinpoint with certainty when the discovery phase began, but as early as 1978, two of them began meeting informally with other educators and change agents to discuss the declining quality of Minnesota and US education. Evidence of performance declines began to appear in the early 1970s and increased over the next decade to reach a peak in April 1983 with the publication of *A Nation at Risk*, a report issued by the National Commission on Excellence in Education. The commission, appointed by the Secretary of Education, warned that the US education was threatened by a "rising tide of mediocrity." Statistics from the report, such as the following, sent shock waves across the country:

- By the simplest test of everyday reading, writing, and comprehension, some twenty-three million adult citizens were functionally illiterate.
- Scores on the College Board's Scholastic Aptitude Tests declined from 1963 to 1980, with average verbal scores falling over fifty points and average mathematics cores dropping nearly forty points.

- Average achievement of high school students was lower on most standardized tests than it had been when Sputnik was launched, twenty-six years earlier.
- Many seventeen-year-olds did not possess the higher-order intellectual skills expected of them. Nearly 40 percent could not draw inferences from written materials; 80 percent were unable to write a persuasive essay; and 66 percent could not solve a mathematics problem requiring several steps.
- Between 1972 and 1980, remedial mathematics courses in public, four-year colleges increased by 72 percent. They constituted one-quarter of all mathematic courses taught in those institutions.
- Business and military leaders spent millions of dollars on costly remedial education and training programs in basic skills such as reading, writing, spelling, and computation.

The report tapped a nagging fear that the United States was slipping behind other industrial nations and losing its ability to compete in another area—education. With stark language, the report issued a call to arms: "If an unfriendly foreign power had attempted to impose on America the mediocre educational performance that exists today, we might well have viewed it as an act of war: As it stands, we have allowed it to happen to ourselves. . . . We have, in effect, been committing an act of unthinkable, unilateral educational disarmament."[116]

Performance declines at the national level were evident even in Minnesota, which had enjoyed a reputation for excellent schools.[117] Scores on national tests, such as the PSAT and the ACT, were declining faster than the national average. Minnesota colleges had to provide substantial remediation in mathematics. The proportion of respondents rating public school performance as good or excellent dropped from 63 percent in 1974 to 36 percent in 1979.[118] And both employers' complaints about the skills of their new employees and students' complaints about the emptiness of their high school experience added to the chorus of concern.[119] In the months and years that followed, reports on the status of education blanketed the country. By 1985, over 350 separate reports were issued.[120] Scholars added their voices in highly publicized books. The flurry of activity came to be known as "The Great School Debate" on the status of US education.[121] Why had these declines occurred, and what was the nation going to do about them? The public wanted answers.

Policy entrepreneurs eventually identified three major forces that they believed were responsible for these declines. The first was the changing social fabric. Minnesota children and families had undergone a dramatic transformation. By 1980, 58 percent of married women with children worked outside the home, resulting in more preschoolers being cared for outside the home and more children spending time alone and unsupervised before and after school. While it was difficult to tie poor student performance directly to the increases in the divorce rate and the number of single-parent families, out-of-wedlock births, and female-headed households, the argument was a compelling one that many offered as an explanation for educational declines. Children from five to eighteen years old were spending 11 percent of their lives in school and 89 percent outside of school; if they were not learning, it was important to look beyond the school to find the major causes. There were other issues as well: the widespread use of alcohol and drugs, increased sexual activity at an early age, greater reliance on television and decreased time spent reading books and doing homework, and a greater number of students who worked during the school year.[122] All these issues worked to reduce the schools' efficacy and increased teachers' challenges in dealing with the new mores and youth culture.

The worsening economy was a second factor that needed to be taken into account. The United States was slowly recovering from the backbreaking recession and double-digit inflation that occurred in the early 1980s. The US economy had lost 23 percent of its share of world markets, representing 125 billion dollars in lost production and the loss of at least two million industrial jobs.[123] The national psyche took a beating as people began to question whether major industrial sectors could compete with other countries and debated causes and cures for the loss of competitive strength. From 1980 through 1984, Minnesota lagged the recovery from the recession by the nation as a whole. Unemployment rates in the Iron Range, in the northern part of the state, reached record highs when taconite mines closed and firms were forced to downsize due to intense competition from low-cost, foreign steel manufacturers and US minimills. The farm economy experienced the most serious depression since the 1930s, with bankers and farmers locked into a deadly dance to see who would survive. During this same period, interstate competition for new jobs was becoming fierce, and there were a growing number of complaints about Minnesota's business climate. The state's largest employer, Minnesota Mining and Manufacturing (3M), transferred 1,600 jobs to Austin, Texas, citing Minnesota's high unemployment compensation and income and property tax burdens as some of the reasons for the move.

These economic challenges had a dramatic impact on education. Budget cuts caused an abrupt halt to reform efforts in special education, school financing, technology in the classroom, early childhood services, and community education. From the summer of 1980 to the end of 1982, the state suffered severe revenue shortfalls. As of 1981–1982, the state's share of school revenues was 71 percent; by 1982–1983, it had reached a low of 45 percent.[124] To add to this budgetary distress, federal aid to education was consolidated into block grants and a number of programs were cut back, hitting programs for the disadvantaged, child nutrition, and vocational education the hardest.

Declining enrollments of school-age children also drained critical resources. Between 1972–1973 and 1982–1983, enrollment dropped 21 percent, as opposed to the average national decline of 14 percent. This contraction rippled throughout the entire state system: schools closed, districts consolidated, and teachers and staff were laid off. Minnesota lost over one-tenth of its classroom teachers during the decade. Rapidly rising school costs also contributed to the bleak picture. Inflation rose by almost 120 percent during the 1973–1974 to 1982–1983 period in Minneapolis/St. Paul, just when demand for new programs increased. Schools were required, and funding was needed, to foster racial integration, eliminate sex discrimination, improve access for the handicapped, minimize fiscal disparities among districts, and broaden the age groups that they served. These expectations came at a time when demands for new technology also increased. Teachers needed computers, software, and staff development to retool for the information age. These were costly add-ons in a period of retrenchment, and it became increasingly difficult to achieve economies of scale. Declining enrollment, underutilization of buildings and classrooms, rising inflation, and new services, programs, and technology drove up per-pupil costs.[125] One legislator summed up the situation as follows:

> The state economy almost collapsed in 1980 and '81. The Iron Range is dead. The Feds have cut the rug out from under us in a dozen different ways and the South and the Southwest are draining our potential reorganization capital by the costs of energy while they kidnap our industry. Sure we care about schools. It's the biggest chunk of our state budget if nothing else. But there were and are a hell of a lot of things we talk about first in Minnesota, and I don't just mean in the legislature.[126]

Moreover, with the declining rates of economic growth and the increasing international competition, it became more and more difficult to draw money from the private sector to fund the public sector. By the end of the 1970s, an array of tax limitation measures had passed in states across the nation. These trends, along with interstate competition for economic development, kept state fiscal systems under pressure. All levels of government were finding it harder and harder to support programs that had flowered in the period of sustained growth after World War II. Education suffered, along with housing, health care, social insurance, welfare, civil rights, conservation and environment improvement, and rural and urban development. Under siege from all sides, governments seemed unable to sustain their commitment to services, including education. For a growing number of people, the only alternative appeared to be smaller government and lower spending.

Thus, the policy entrepreneurs identified a third factor—the role of government. The American public, concerned about the effectiveness, responsiveness, and cost of government and less interested in an activist, progressive government bent on social reform, elected Ronald Reagan as president in 1980. Hoping to stimulate the growth of the economy and shake the country out of its lethargy, the president envisioned a new role for government. Under the banner of "New Federalism," the goal was to free the government from the social service burdens that it had adopted from Franklin D. Roosevelt's New Deal to Lyndon Johnson's Great Society. Obligations best handled at the national level, such as defense, would be retained, but other programs better left to the states, such as education, would be dismantled or reduced. State and local governments, closer to the needs of their communities, were expected to assume more responsibility for the funding and delivery of services. Key economic sectors, such as transportation, financial services, telecommunications, and health care, were to be deregulated. Market forces would replace government controls in these areas, providing fiscal accountability lacking in most government-regulated programs. Thus, the themes of decentralization, deregulation, and fiscal accountability were the defining element of the New Federalism.

The search for a new role for government was evident even in Minnesota, a state with a reputation for supporting populist causes and Democratic candidates. However, it took a different turn from the national version of New Federalism. Against New Federal proposals to do less and progressive proposals to do more, what surfaced in Minnesota communities, nonprofit organizations, and policy research institutes were proposals to do things differently. During the search for new ways to conduct the public's business, new terms surfaced: "alternative service delivery," "load shedding," "contracting," "vouchers," and "coproduction." The Citizens League was a leader in this exploration. In 1980, this nonprofit policy analysis organization issued a statement that set forth a new perspective on public services and called for consumer solutions to public problems. While not denigrating traditional public administration and design, it argued giving resident-users of public services the power to do more than simply elect public officials. They offered citizens and other residents an expanded role, an option to withdraw if the services did not fulfill their expectations, and a voice to articulate how services should be run more effectively and efficiently. Thus, the league envisioned a market-driven public service system governed by consumer sovereignty and regulated by market pricing.

Problem Framing

Having undertaken an extensive period of discovery, the policy entrepreneurs' problem reframing initially took the form of an analogy. Borrowing liberally from trends and events in the private sector, they declared that education was like the steel and textile industries or any other declining industries. Said one entrepreneur, "If they are ailing they ask for protection . . . they want import quotas, they want tariffs, they want anything to reduce the amount of competition in the marketplace."[127] Referencing educational and social theorists,[128] they drew analogies between mature bureaucracies, regulated monopolies, and education. Education, they believed, suffered from the same ills: inertia; protectionism; lack of either accountability or competition; excessive rules and regulations; inconsistent goals; attempts to stake out, defend, and expand policy territory; and inadequate concern for performance and the customer. The educational system—designed for an earlier, industrial age—had been pushed to its limits and could no longer adapt to the challenges of the information age. It lacked the capacity to be flexible, innovative, efficient, and supportive of diversity, with so many entrenched interests protecting the status quo and keeping the system from adapting. Innovation and change would not be possible without breaking the monopolistic hold that school districts had on students. It was time for a major overhaul.

Ideation

Improvement approach Ideas on how to address the problem of Minnesota public education revolved two contrasting views on how to deal with student performance declines. Those who subscribed to the "improvement approach" believed that performance problems were (or could be) temporary. The economic dislocation, fiscal exigencies, declining enrollments, explosive costs, changing social fabric, and new youth culture were all responsible for the deterioration of student performance. They insisted that the trends could be reversed and student learning could be improved with the infusion of funds and public support. Based on a series of studies, the state had a quality public school system and continued to earn a national reputation for excellence:[129]

- In 1982, Minnesota spent 122 percent of the US average for education—$572.77 per capita, compared to $468.34 in the country as a whole.

- The state had one of the highest high school completion rates in the nation, second only to North Dakota.

- A total of 91 percent of students graduated from high school, a figure that exceeded President Reagan's goal of 90 percent by 1990.

- The state's historically high SAT scores compared favorably with other states.

- Although occasional news stories offered negative anecdotes about a district, school, or teacher, for the most part the general consensus was quite positive, with 79 percent of people in one poll in 1984 ranking the schools as good or excellent.[130]

To make up for ground lost to harsh economic realities and counter the trends, they urged the state to restore historic levels of funding so that the state could respond to the tremendous social changes and maintain its competitive edge in education. In addition, they recommended setting higher standards for its students and teachers and pumping more resources into the educational system—more money for better-trained teachers, updated technology and curricula, new services, and modern facilities. Implicit in their argument was the belief that the ultimate responsibility for teaching and learning rested with the state government. The state constitution was the source and legal embodiment of the obligation to provide education for state residents. Minnesota possessed the authority to define what education was and determine how it should be delivered to the citizenry: it established the number of days in a school year, the minimum qualifications for teachers and educators, the core subjects to be taught, and the list of textbooks from which schools were to make their selections. And its authority had increased with school consolidations, pressures to subsidize local districts' expenditures, and school finance reform that required states to equalize educational funding among districts.

New ideas for systemic redesign   Policy entrepreneurs, convinced that educational performance declines were indicative of far more serious global and national problems, wanted fundamental, structural changes, not "tinkering around the edges," as they described the improvement approach. Although they acknowledged the impact of external forces, they called for a total revamping and redesign of the educational system. For them, education could not be substantially better without being substantially different. Advocates of improvement offered policy makers only two choices—either pay more for services rendered or reduce the quality and quantity of services delivered.

Neither alternative was attractive to the policy entrepreneurs. They believed that new ideas could be found to change the system without adding a greater burden to the taxpayers and business community. Policy makers were growing resistant to spending tax dollars without clear proof that the funds would yield a commensurate return, especially since results from educational research were finding "no relationship between expenditures and the achievements of students.[131] Moreover, financial conservatism was expected to continue into the 1980s, with states preparing for huge deficits due to the economic recession, faltering federal assistance, and increasing welfare costs. As a Citizens League report[132] warned, there was national and state reluctance to spend more on public services. It cited a Gallup poll finding that 60 percent of Minnesota respondents would vote against a tax increase if local public schools said that they needed more money. Calling strategies to improve education "well-meaning but misguided and costly," policy entrepreneurs insisted that more had to be delivered for less.

As writers, authors, analysts, researchers, and educators, these policy entrepreneurs were in the idea business. They firmly believed in the power of ideas to shape the direction of history and their search for ideas started without constraints. In group meetings with other change agents and educators, they challenged education's underlying assumptions and took nothing as given. School district boundaries, teacher education requirements, tenure practices, certification procedures, district governance structures, stare core curriculum, length of the school day and year, differentiated staffing practices, and accountability systems were all called into question in the search for a school system that was better suited for a postindustrial society.

New ideas in group meetings came from different sources. Some were adapted from other policy domains, some were original with the policy entrepreneurs, educators, and change agents, and others were derived from their collaborations with the Citizens League and the Minnesota Business Partnership, both of which issued reports recommending educational reforms consistent with, or in some cases identical to, ideas espoused by the policy entrepreneurs. Eventually, discussions centered on nine ideas that the policy entrepreneurs thought were worth pursuing: parent-student school choice; school-site management, which assigned decisions about curriculum, budget, and personnel to the schools rather than school districts; teacher partnerships (teachers in private practice); shared facilities; a model schools program that explores and demonstrates new educational ideas, methods, and approaches for their efficacy in other schools; technology for tomorrow's schools; alternative pathways to a teaching career; and new career advancement patterns for teachers.[133]

The policy entrepreneurs also wrote books, position papers, and journal and newspaper articles to publicize and get feedback on their new ideas. On occasion, they drafted speeches or parts of speeches for politicians, served as guests on local and national radio television shows, and one even hosted a local public television public affairs program. They also gave speeches on educational issues to a wide range of audiences and taught courses in leadership development and graduate programs in public affairs to vet their ideas. They were in constant contact with a large network of people who cited their phone calls and personal contacts, as well as the articles and documents that they sent to keep everyone updated on the ongoing educational policy debate. These policy entrepreneurs even created forums to discuss their redesign proposals, bringing together national education experts with state and local political and educational leaders. As an amazed observer at one of these events commented about an entrepreneur: "He is phenomenal—the most effective organizer I've ever run into. . . . He just makes a couple of phone calls and says, 'Gee, I'm having a little gathering at my office. Would you like to come?' The governor shows up, the commissioner shows up, everybody shows up."[134]

Policy Entrepreneurs' Prototyping and Testing

Excited about their new proposals, but lacking funding and official support, the informal group of policy entrepreneurs, educators, and change agents decided to form a 501(c)(3) nonprofit corporation called Public School Incentives (PSI) in 1981. The purpose of PSI was "to translate ideas into demonstration projects to test their efficacy and potential for success in Minnesota schools."[135] If results from the prototyping revealed problems, corrections could be made before widespread dissemination occurred. And since the policy entrepreneurs needed resources to translate their ideas into testable programs, PSI also served as a fiscal agent for foundations willing to support innovative projects in education. A total of 1.2 million dollars eventually was funneled through the organization, some of it supporting proposals for school-site management and parent-student choice. PSI also advocated for a limited voucher system for low-income families and the expansion of choice in Minnesota.

What Came Next

Table 7.2 summarizes what followed from 1984 to 1988. The debates on what should be done about Minnesota schools drew in the governor, the legislature, the Minnesota Department of Education, educators, parents, and the general public.[136] The policy entrepreneurs' ideas and prototypes, initially strongly opposed and dismissed, were eventually, after adaptations from the governor and legislators, accepted into law. On May 6, 1988, Governor Rudy Perpich signed the Omnibus Education Bill, which established the nation's first mandatory K–12 public school open enrollment program. He called the law "a historic reform, and a model for the nation." The national and international press hailed it as an innovation, and U.S. secretary of education William Bennett, announcing that the idea had won, predicted that other states would likely follow. Over four legislative sessions, ideas almost identical to those that the policy entrepreneurs first proposed in 1985 were discussed, and public school choice across district lines became a reality in Minnesota by the end of the legislative session in 1988.

Table 7.2
Design history of Minnesota public school choice

Policy Entrepreneurs (1978–1984)
Discovery
Problem finding and framing
Ideation: systemic educational redesign
Prototyping: PSI and demonstration projects
Field testing (1983–1984) 1.2 million to test efficacy and potential in schools

Legislature (1983–1984)
Ideation: Voucher option debate for students from low- and moderate-income families

Governor (1985)
Ideation: *Access to Excellence* (PE ideas + open enrollment only within public schools)

Legislature (1985)
Ideation—postsecondary enrollment option; state school for the arts; testing program
Prototype—Postsecondary Enrollment Options Act (PSEOA)
Implementation—PSEOA 1985
Implementation—PSEOA 1986
Final testing and evaluation of PSEOA 1986–1987

Governor (1985–1986)
Ideation and prototype: governor's discussion group and signing of the Visionary Plan

Legislature (1987)
Ideation and prototype: Voluntary K–12 Enrollment Options Act; High School Graduation
Incentives Act; Area Learning Centers and Alternatives Programs Act

Governor (1987)
Signed three acts into law; public school choice became mainstream in the state

Legislature (1988):
Ideation and prototype: the "Silent Bill"—K–12 Mandatory Enrollment Options Act passed

Governor (1988)
Signed into law the first mandatory K–12 public school enrollment across district lines in the
country

In Summary

Systemic design, including the design and redesign of social systems, is a complex and
wide-ranging endeavor, as reflected in the myriad of cases in this chapter. It extends
well beyond strategic design that is anchored and circumscribed by organizational
boundaries. Instead the following features are descriptive of systemic designs:

- *Participants* are drawn together into social networks whose reach can extend from
  local to state, national, even international levels as illustrated in the case of Jeroo
  Billimoria's CHILDLINE.

- *Sustained cross-boundary networks* create social ecosystems—people, collectives, and institutions that together build a culture of innovation and change, as demonstrated by the BRAC case in Uganda.
- *Subsystems*—social, technical, and organizational—when interwoven and integrated, result in the redesign of complex systems in education, solar energy, health care, and water resources, as exemplified by the Barefoot College in India.
- *Designers* answer to the name of *change agent, activist,* and *entrepreneur,* as in the cases of Bunker Roy in India, who initiated design from the bottom up, and the policy entrepreneurs in Minnesota, who used a combined bottom-up and top-down process of policy redesign.
- The *time frame* typically involves a longer period, given the number of stakeholders and intertwined networks involved in generating ideas, as well as prototyping, testing, and implementing them as part of the ecosystem's social innovation process.
- *Design efforts* typically begin small to address a local social problem. When successful, the local innovative changes then ripple throughout a system and establish new patterns of behavior. Scaling mechanisms from local to systemwide vary.[137] Some employ an organizational model to mobilize people and resources to serve a common purpose (e.g., BRAC), others develop a program that integrates a set of specialized activities (e.g., the solar energy program of Barefoot College), and still others follow a set of principles that establish guidelines and values about how to serve a particular purpose (e.g., the optimized care model in Dodge County, Minnesota).[138]
- And its design efforts can be purposeful as ideas are generated, shaped into prototypes and implemented in practice as social innovations. But design efforts also can be political when designers take on the role of agents of change to protect their ideas and prototypes against critiques, as they did in Minnesota to enact public school choice, or when staff from Barefoot College in India took on the local political structure and ran and won as independents in village elections. This blend of design and politics is an important issue that we already have addressed in chapter 5 and will revisit in chapter 10.

Thus, systemic designs are complicated and complex. But when we expand the designer's purview to the regenerative design of *social and ecological* systems, the complexity increases dramatically, as we shall see in chapter 8.

8 Regenerative Design

Recognizing the limitations of studying species separate from their social and natural environment, biologists originated the concept of *ecology*. The term has come to mean the study of living things (i.e., plants, animals, and other organisms) in a given area that interact with each other and with elements of their nonliving environments—weather, earth, sun, soil, climate, and atmosphere. They also expanded the concept of *environment* to include species' *surroundings*—natural forces and other living things that provide conditions for development and growth, as well as danger and damage. Thus, an *ecosystem* is defined as a unit formed by the interaction of a community of organisms that function together in a particular place (e.g., a forest, grassland, desert, or coral reef).[1] From an evolutionary perspective, the minimum unit of survival becomes the species plus its environment—never a single organism, nor even a species. Moreover, survival depends on a process of trial and error, learning, adaptation, and innovation that results in the selection of what is most fitting for the species in a particular environmental niche. Ultimately, ecology has come to be understood as the study of ecosystems and their healthy function and adaptation to the biosphere.

Building on our understanding of ecology and ecosystems, regenerative design is understood as the renewal and realignment of social systems with the natural world so that humans and the built environment can coexist and coevolve in a way that maintains the integrity of both society and nature. As we have seen in previous chapters covering the strategic design of organizations and the systemic design of social systems, regenerative design is informed by a systems approach. Yet in this case, humanity is embedded in more complex interrelationships—"natural systems, human social systems, and the conscious forces behind their actions."[2] These relationships occur within a "multilayered network of living systems within a geographic region that results from the complex interactions, through time, of the natural ecology (climate, mineral and other deposits, soil, vegetation, water and wildlife, etc.) and culture (distinctive customs, expressions of values, economic activities, forms of association, ideas for education, traditions, etc.)."[3] Thus, regenerative design broadens the design challenge to encompass the design of both natural **and** social systems for the purpose of creating a place-based natural and social ecology.

One way to have a fuller appreciation of regenerative design is to compare it to related practices. *Conventional practice* seeks efficiencies to reduce "the damage caused by excessive resource use."[4] *Greening* seeks "relative improvements" "toward a generalized ideal of doing no harm," without focusing on the interrelated wholeness of society and nature.[5] *Sustainability* seeks "effectiveness," doing no more damage and moving toward "effectiveness thinking" without addressing a fundamental question: "effective for what, or to what end," which becomes the search for the neutral point of being "less bad" and not doing any more damage.[6] *Restoration* seeks to assist and repair natural systems and their return to a natural state as a self-organizing ecosystem.[7] *Reconciliation* seeks the understanding "that humans are an integral part of nature and that human and natural systems are one."[8] And eventually we arrive at *regeneration*, which seeks the coevolution of human systems with nature to ensure ecosystem integrity, maintain diversity, cultivate systemic health, and fortify the planetary life support system on which we all depend.[9]

Social Acupuncture Points

Chapter 4 of this book focused on metadesigns—the shifts in values and consciousness that have changed our frameworks and worldviews. This chapter illustrates the impact that this shift has been having in small-scale prototypes and well-targeted interventions in large, complex systems throughout the world. Daniel Wahl describes these creative design interventions as "social acupuncture points"[10] that are catalyzing transformative change and creating "regenerative systems and cultures that share a unifying narrative of collaboration."[11] Examples abound in wide-ranging fields such as agriculture, architecture, business, economics, education, energy sources, food systems, development, governance, and water management, as illustrated in table 8.1.

Three Concepts That Inform Regenerative Design

Despite these wide-ranging practices in regenerative design, three concepts inform design interventions: biomimicry; cradle-to-cradle production; and nested systems and change.

Biomimicry

In her book *Biomimicry: Innovations Inspired by Nature*, Jane Benyus describes biomimicry as an imitation of life and nature.[12] Rather than extracting from nature, biomimicry focuses on what can be learned from nature to inform the search for innovative solutions to complex problems, particularly those at the juncture of ecology, material science, agriculture, medicine, product design, computing, commerce, architecture, community design, industry, and urban and regional planning. Biomimicry follows nature's nine principles of life, as summarized in box 8.1, which offer a new way to value and view nature.[13]

Nature can be a model—communities modeled on nature do not bankrupt their ecological capital. Nature also can be a measure. Based on the nine principles summarized in box 8.1, nature can provide guidance for standards that judge the "rightness" of decisions and actions: "Are they life promoting? Does the resultant action fit

Table 8.1
Regenerative design's social acupuncture points

Regenerative agriculture	Farming and grazing practices are redesigned to rebuild soil and organic matter and restore degraded soil biodiversity that has the additional benefit of drawing down carbon, improving the water cycle and reversing climate change.*
Regenerative architecture	Buildings are designed and operated to reverse damage and have a net-positive impact on the environment,[†] and at the macro scale, they can serve as carbon sequestration sites.
Regenerative business	Businesses cultivate human potential, talent, and agency to redesign work and achieve extraordinary outcomes that benefit individuals, business, society, and nature.[‡]
Regenerative economics	Ecological economics, bioeconomics, or ecoeconomics redesign the interdependence of human economies and natural ecosystems. Standard economic theory doesn't recognize or value original capital assets such as the Earth and the environment. It frames the economy as an isolated and circular model of goods and services exchanged between companies and households without physical contact with the natural environment. The result, says Herman Daly, a leading ecological economist, has been unsustainable economic conditions and growth. He advocates steady-state economics where the human economy "is an economy of stable or mildly fluctuating size." "To be sustainable, a steady state economy may not exceed ecological limits." It "entails stabilized population and per capita consumption" and minimizes waste.**
Regenerative education	Education is redesigned from teaching people *what* to think to teaching them *how* to think. It is a process of "disruption and liberation that enables students or learners to develop the critical thinking necessary to form thoughts and judgments independently. . . . It is our primary resource for maturation and the development of agency" for the purpose of transforming society and natural systems.[††]
Regenerative energy sources	Energy is redesigned from nonrenewable to renewable energy sources. Conventional nonrenewable fossil fuels like oil and coal are mined or extracted from the Earth and produce energy when they are burned. They have two major disadvantages. Their supply is limited because they don't naturally replenish themselves on a time scale short enough for human use. They also release carbon dioxide (CO_2) into the atmosphere that contributes to global warming and climate change. Alternative or renewable energy sources, such as solar energy, wind energy, hydroenergy, tidal energy, geothermal energy, and biomass energy, are constantly replenished through natural processes and do less damage to the environment. None of the renewable sources can meet all the world's current energy needs, but if taken together, they provide reliable energy throughout the day and year without increasing the cost of electricity.[‡‡]
Regenerative food systems	Food production, whether on land or at sea, is redesigned to restore habitat, protect biodiversity, and preserve the livelihoods of those who provide our food, now and in the long run.***
Regenerative development	Towns and urban and regional areas are redesigned to create a balance where buildings, their occupants, and the surrounding systems, both natural and manmade, enhance well-being and happiness and work together to create resources rather than deplete them. Central factors and aspirations in regenerative development include livability, equity, ecology, nutrition, access, a closed-loop waste system, water, resiliency, energy, and heritage.[†††]

(continued)

Table 8.1
(continued)

Regenerative governance	Governance is redesigned to connect regenerative development with the concept of collaborative governance, defined as "processes and structures of public policy decision-making and management that engage people constructively across the boundaries of public agencies, levels of government, and the public, private, and civic spheres"[‡‡‡] for the purpose of generating solutions and policies to improve practice in city-regions.[****]
Regenerative water management	The disruptions and anomalies in our weather patterns, often attributed to atmospheric CO_2, are recognized as manifestations of distorted water cycles. For example, increasing urbanization, draining marshes, and loss of forest cover have diminished water cycling in the Western Mediterranean basin. It has resulted in accumulated moisture piling up in layers over the sea or moving inland, causing torrential rains and mudslides on the continent. Regenerative water management thus acknowledges that human activities are affecting the water cycle. If we want to have an impact on climate change, then we also need to revise our water policies and practices.[††††]

* Regenerative International, *Why Regenerative Agriculture?* accessed October 31, 2020, https://regenerationinternational.org/why-regenerative-agriculture/. See also Nicole Masters, *For the Love of Soil: Strategies to Regenerate Our Food Production System* (Waitakere, New Zealand: Printable Reality, 2019); Mark Shepard, *Restoration Agriculture: Real World Permaculture for Farmers* (Austin, TX: Acres USA, 2013); Gabe Brown, *Dirt to Soil: One Family's Journey into Regenerative Agriculture* (White River Junction, VT: Chelsea Green Publishing, 2018).

† HMC Architects, "Regenerative Architecture Principles: A Departure from Modern Sustainable Design," accessed October 31, 2020, https://hmcarchitects.com/news/regenerative-architecture-principles-a-departure-from-modern-sustainable-design-2019-04-12/.

‡ Carol Sanford, *The Regenerative Business* (New York: Nicholas Brealey, 2017).

** Center for the Advancement of the Steady State Economy, "What Is a Steady State Economy?" accessed February 17, 2023, https://www.keepandshare.com/doc19/36906/what-is-a-sse-briefing-paper-pdf-262k?da=yhttps://steadystate.org/discover/definition/.

†† Carol Sanford, "The Regenerative Education System and Practice—Part 1," accessed October 31, 2020, https://medium.com/@carolsanford/the-regenerative-education-system-and-practice-part-1-23ffcc86326e; Carol Sanford, "The Regenerative Education System and Practice—Part 2," accessed October 31, 2020, https://medium.com/@carolsanford/the-regenerative-education-system-and-practice-part-2-d6c07a7beac5; Carol Sanford "The Regenerative Education System and Practice—Part 3," accessed October 31, 2020, https://medium.com/@carolsanford/the-regenerative-education-system-and-practice-part-3-c4e7d04cde11; Seed Communities, "The Regenerative Educator Community," accessed October 31, 2020, https://seed-communities.com/regeneducatorfounders/.

‡‡ EDF, "Energywise," accessed October 31, 2020, https://www.edfenergy.com/for-home/energywise/renewable-energy-sources.

*** Nature Conservancy, "Beyond Sustainable: A Food System to Restore the Planet," accessed October 31, 2020, https://www.nature.org/en-us/what-we-do/our-insights/perspectives/regenerative-agriculture-food-system-restore-planet/. See also Jessica Duncan et al., eds. *Routledge Handbook of Sustainable and Regenerative Food Systems* (New York: Routledge: 2021).

††† Maibritt P. Zari, *Regenerative Urban Design and Ecosystem Biomimicry* (London: Routledge, 2018); Filippo Boselli, *Regenerative Cities in China: Roadmap for a Better Urban Future* (Hamburg, Germany, World Future Council, 2016), accessed November 2, 2020, https://www.worldfuturecouncil.org/wp-content/uploads/2016/03/WFC_2016_Regenerative_Cities_in_China_En.pdf; Toby Hemenway, *The Permaculture City: Regenerative Design for Urban, Suburban, and Town Resilience* (White River Junction, VT: Chelsea Green Publishing, 2015).

Table 8.1

(continued)

---

‡‡‡ Lorena F. Axinte et al., "Regenerative City-Regions: A New Conceptual Framework," *Regional Studies, Regional Science* 6, no 1 (March 2019):117–129, 123, https://doi.org/10.1080/21681376.2 019.1584542.

**** Pamela Mang and Ben Haggard, *Regenerative Development and Design* (Hoboken, NJ: John Wiley, 2016).

†††† Judith D. Schwartz, *Water in Plain Sight: Hope for a Thirsty World* (White River Junction, VT: Chelsea Green Publishing, 2019). For updates on many of these regenerative initiatives, see Daniel C. Wahl, "Planetary Health and Regeneration Resource Compilation," September 11, 2018, http://newstoryhub.com/2018/09/planetary-health-and-regeneration-resource -compilation-daniel-wahl/; Daniel C. Wahl, "Regenerative (R)evolution: Reclaiming Humanity's Oneness with Nature," *Medium*, May 2, 2017, https://medium.com/insurge-intelligence /regenerative-r-evolution-f1058a975e96; Daniel C. Wahl, "'Regeneration Hits the Mainstream," *Medium*, Nov. 1, 2018, https://medium.com/age-of-awareness/regeneration-hits-the-mainstream- but-what-about-the-deeper-practice-746c4aa7ea1b; and Daniel C. Wahl, "Human and Planetary Health," *Resilience*, December 5, 2018, https://www.resilience.org/stories/2018-12-05 /human-and-planetary-health-ecosystem-restoration-at-the-dawn-of-the-century-of-regeneration/.

with nature? Will the results or the impact last in a positive way?" Nature also can be a mentor. From master to teacher to mentor—nature can be a source of ideas, inspiration, innovation, and knowledge. As McGregor cautions, "Nature has had 4.3 billions of years to evolve and gain experience of living systems in evolving complex, efficient, resilient and adaptive systems. Humans would do well to watch and learn rather than exploit and destroy."[14]

Biomimicry's design process—the design spiral—also can be used to address key questions and assist designers in becoming better problem solvers and decision makers.[15] For example, rather than ask what the designer wants to design, ask what the designer wants the designs to do (their function), and then ask why the designer wants the designs to do that. Then ask how the designer could improve the design or how the solutions could be changed to best emulate nature and apply life's principles? As questions are posed and addressed, the design spiral unfolds as an iterative process "in such a way that life's principle are respected and emulated."[16]

The "Cradle-to-Cradle" Approach to Industrial Production

The architect William McDonough and the chemist Michael Braungart launched a new approach to industrial production in the 1990s. Instead of cradle-to-grave, which relies on "downcycling" (reduce, reuse, and recycle), which casts off as much as 90 percent of the materials used as waste (much of it toxic), they call for cradle-to-cradle, which remakes the way that we make things. When products reach the end of their useful life, they are designed to be either "biological nutrients," for something new that can safely reenter the environment, or "technical nutrients," which can remain within closed-loop industrial cycles. The advantage of cradle-to-cradle production is that it eliminates the

Box 8.1
Biomimicry's nine principles of life

Principle 1: Nature "rewards cooperation and integration" and makes working together as "rewarding and necessary." "Natural ecosystems operate in a symbiotic, complex network of mutually beneficial relationships." Nature "even allows predation and competition *through* cooperation."

Principle 2: Nature "optimizes rather than maximizes," "fits form to function," and builds "within the confines of available resources." It shapes designs that are based on what they are intended to do, are "organic and only as big as they need to be to fit their function," and "co-evolve" by "adapting to the changes of others."

Principle 3: Nature "depends on and develops diversity of possibilities to find the best solution(s) (rather than a one-size-fits-all, homogeneous approach." Nature also "depends on randomness . . . because randomness creates anomalies that open opportunities for diversity." To remain viable, "a system must be as diverse as its environment" and "respect [the] regional, cultural and material uniqueness of a place."

Principle 4: Nature "recycles and finds uses for everything. Everything becomes recyclable; everything has a use." "In closed systems, each co-existing element consumes the waste of another as its lifeline!"

Principle 5: Nature "requires a rich bio-diversity to adapt to change and to grow," and "local ecosystems require a rich range of interlocking resources and the involvement of many local species to create a vibrant natural community." "Natural ecosystems are tied to the local land; hence, sustainability requires reliance on local expertise and Indigenous knowledge."

Principle 6: Nature "avoids internal excesses and 'overbuilding' by curbing excesses within. . . . It remains in balance with the biosphere . . . that is capable of supporting life."

Principle 7: Nature "taps into the power of limits and manages not to exceed them." Species live "within the boundaries that surround them, . . . do not seek elsewhere for resources," and "use existing materials sparingly." Nature relies on "constant feedback mechanisms . . . to maintain balance." It uses limits as a "focusing mechanism" to stay "within the carrying capacity of the boundaries" and maintain "an energy balance that does not borrow against the future."

Principle 8: Nature "runs on natural sunlight" as a source of energy. "All energy is sunlight." Plants use the Sun to turn light into sugar, their natural food, and then humans eat the plants as food. Photosynthesis also uses water and releases oxygen, which many organisms need to stay alive.

Principle 9: Nature "uses only the energy and resources that it needs. . . . It does not drawdown resources" or "[consume] them unnecessarily." Each organism makes "optimal and maximum use" of its limited habitat by finding "a niche" and "using only what it needs to survive and evolve."

concept of "waste." Everything produced become a resource for something else, or to put it another way, "waste" in one system becomes input or "food" for another. Thus, cradle-to-cradle design is advocated as a positive, regenerative force that can improve manufacturing and production quality, decrease waste, increase value, and spur innovation.

Nature's Nested Systems, Scale, and Regenerative Change

Nature is structured as nested systems within systems (or processes within processes). Each individual system is an integrated whole. It has its own adaptive cycle, which consists of four distinct phases: "r" stands for growth or exploitation, "K" stands for conservation of established patterns and resource distribution, "Ω" stands for collapse or release, and "α" stands for reorganization, as illustrated in figure 8.1.[17]

At the same time, each system is simultaneously composed of smaller subsystems, as well as being integrated into larger systems. A nested hierarchy of systems is known as a "panarchy"[18] or "holarchy,"[19] the interconnected wholes within wholes. For example, a federal government as a system divides power among three subsystems at different scales. At the largest scale, there is a national government subsystem that makes decisions affecting the country as a whole on issues such as national security and cross-country transportantion. Its adaptive cycle is large scale, with long/slow cycling. There is also government at the province or state level that deals with regional issues and citizen concerns. As a subsystem, its adaptive cycle is shorter and faster than that of the federal subsystem. At the smallest scale, local governments such as villages, towns, cities, and counties address issues of the immediate area. As a subsystem, its adaptive cycles are the shortest and fastest.

Nature too is fundamentally scale-linking. Nested hierarchies can interlink all levels from the molecular to the planetary, from the local to the bioregional, national, and global levels, and range from small scale to large scale and from short, fast cycles to long, slow cycles, as illustrated in figure 8.2.[20] Critical to panarchy theory is that these nested adaptive cycles can influence each other. In the case of a federal government, the fast and small governments at the local scale can influence the regional and

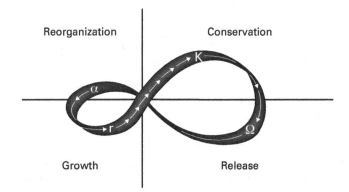

Figure 8.1
The adaptive cycle

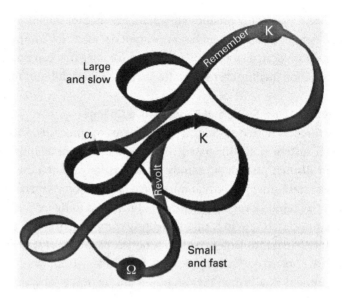

Figure 8.2
Adaptive cycles at various spatial and temporal scales in a panarchy

national levels should citizens demand it, while policies at the national level can influence policies at the regional and local levels. These government subsystems also can go through the release or collapse phase should they experience perturbations, including protests and civil unrest. And depending on the scale at which these perturbations occur, small forms of unrest at the local level may have a ripple effect and have the potential to destabilize the national government.

Panarchies are continually changing at different rates and at different scales as they move through their adaptive cycles. Panarchy transitions include:

- *Pathway 1: Revolt*[21] occurs when fast, small events accumulate and overwhelm large and slow ones, which may produce new processes and structures at higher levels. One example would be a series of insurrections at the local level that could change an election and governance at the national level.

- *Pathway 2: Remember*[22] occurs when a particular local scale enters the omega phase and collapses. But instead of a revolt, the scale enters a renewal phase and reorganizes to fit the pattern of the larger and slower scale above it. In this instance, the higher scale retains its memory of its institutional structures and processes, while the lower scale uses that memory to reconstitute itself in a similar way as the patterns that existed in the past.

The adaptive cycles at different spatial and temporal scales in a panarchy have important implications for regenerative design. As Wahl comments, "The larger and longer the adaptive cycles, the less predictable and controllable they are"[23] and the more difficult it is to change them. But there is an advantage to them as well. Larger ecosystems and large-scale systems can provide a stability that makes innovation (and experimentation) at the smaller scale possible. Thus, we might expect to find more transformative and revolutionary innovations in systems of smaller scale that can respond to opportunity and change. Moreover, if viable alternatives are successfully tested at the local and regional scales, then these innovations have greater potential not only to adapt to local and regional conditions, but to eventually spread globally.[24] We return to this topic in chapter 10, when we examine design's advantages in going to scale by integrating multiple levels of design.

Exemplars of Regenerative Design

To more fully explore regenerative design and appreciate its breadth and depth, we turn to four examples in economics, development, agriculture, and landscapes.

Regenerative Economics and the Monetary System

A fundamental question informs the calls for a regeneration of economics and the monetary system: "Does our current economic system work for 100 percent of humanity without ecological offence and disadvantage to anyone?"[25] The answer from a growing number of thought leaders suggests not:

- "Money as debt created out of nowhere" drives extreme inequality and sets "competition" as the rule.
- Compound interest on loans and deposits creates an economic time bomb that drives the perverse necessity for exponential growth and unbridled consumption, structurally establishing a win-lose rather than a win-win "playing field."
- Inappropriate and misguided measures of economic success like gross domestic product (GDP) divert our attention from creating systemic health and well-being (caring about qualities) to economic throughput (caring about quantities).
- Anachronistic subsidies and international trade policies established under the economic stranglehold of big lobbies favor the wrong kind of industries and energy sources.
- Current trade rules favor financial gains for the shareholders of multinational corporations and yet sabotage local and regional production and consumption (to the detriment of most of humanity's 5 billion poor and of ecosystem functions).
- Tax systems that are set up to tax work rather than resource-use structurally increase inequality and drive environmental and social degradation.
- Value creation is based on an exploitative system of extraction, production, and consumption that externalizes the social and ecological costs of (and damage caused by) degrading our resource base and causing dangerous climate change.
- The flow of investments and subsidies is not supporting salutogenic and regenerative activities and technologies, as would be the case if value creation was based on healthy ecosystems functions and regeneration.[26]

Moreover, as Robin Murray and his coauthors explain in the *Open Book of Social Innovations,*[27] the existing structures and policies of not only the market, but also of government and civil society, have proved to be inadequate to tackle many large-scale challenges:

> The market, by itself, lacks the incentives and appropriate models to solve many of these issues. Where there are market failures (due to non-competitive markets, externalities or public goods), these tasks have fallen either to the state or civil society. However, current policies and structures of government have tended to reinforce old rather than new models. The silos of government departments are poorly suited to tackling complex problems which cut across sectors and nation states. Civil society lacks the capital, skills and resources to take promising ideas to scale.[28]

Rather than pursue the linear economy, which uses a "take, make, dispose" model of production, a growing number of thought leaders are searching for alternative ways "to design, make, and use things within planetary boundaries." For example, Paul Hawken, Amory Lovins, and L. Hunter Lovins's book *Natural Capitalism* critiques traditional "Industrial Capitalism" and its accounting principles that liquidate capital and call it income and neglect to assign any value to natural resources and living systems that are the basis of human capital. For these authors, the "next economy" or "next industrial revolution" relies on four central strategies: resource conservation through the redesign of manufacturing processes, the reuse of materials found in natural systems, a shift in values from quantity to quality, and the restoration and sustainability of natural resources.[29]

Others advocate *circular economics*, sometimes described as circularity or a closed-loop system that decouples growth from the consumption of finite resources. Instead, growth is measured in terms of increased productivity and positive societywide benefits that come from building economic, natural, and social capital; the minimization of resource inputs by keeping products, equipment, and infrastructure in longer use; the elimination of waste and pollution through reusing, sharing, repairing, refurbishing, and remanufacturing; and keeping resources, products, and materials in continual use to regenerate national systems.[30] Everyone is invited to participate in new economics redesign efforts—businesses, governments, individuals, cities, manufacturing, and others.

The concept of circular economics has many progenitors, such as those introduced earlier in this chapter—Janine Benyus's concept of biomimicry and William McDonough and Michael Braungart's concept of cradle-to-cradle manufacturing and production. The Ellen MacArthur Foundation also has been instrumental in concept development. MacArthur commissioned a McKinsey & Company report entitled *Towards the Circular Economy: Economic and Business Rationale for an Accelerated Transition.* It was the first to consider the economic and business opportunities to transition from a linear economy (based on extraction, production, consumption, and disposal/waste) to a circular economy (based on refurbishment, reuse, remanufacturing, and recycling to extract maximum value).[31]

The contributions of new-economy designers continue to expand. Box 8.2 provides a partial list of some of their major initiatives.

Box 8.2

Regenerative designers for a new economy

- *Kate Raworth* is an economist who explores the economic mindset needed to meet the challenges of the twenty-first century. Her book *Doughnut Economics: Seven Ways to Think Like a 21st-Century Economist*[32] is a counterproposal and reconsideration of mainstream economic thinking and its focus on economic growth. She offers the doughnut model of social and planetary boundaries, which, if followed, would enable us to formulate conditions for a sustainable economy, ensuring that everyone on Earth has basic needs (e.g., adequate food and education) while protecting the ecosystem for future generations.

- *Gar Alperovitz and James Gustave Speth* are cofounders of the Democracy Collaborative,[33] a research institution pursuing practical policy-focused options to catalyze the transformation of the economy based on democratic ownership and stewardship over capital, democracy in the workplace, and the flourishing of democratic and community life. Alperovitz and Speth are also cochairs of the collaborative's Next System Project.[34] It works with researchers, theorists, and activists involved in launching a national debate on the nature of the "next system," which will offer alternative political-economic models capable of delivering superior economic and ecological outcomes compared to the failed systems of the past.[35]

- *John Fullerton*, a former J. P. Morgan managing director and member of the Club of Rome, founded the nonpartisan think tank Capital Institute, dedicated to developing and promoting regenerative economy models and exploring what a regenerative economy might entail at the local, regional, and global scales. A white paper from the institute, "Regenerative Capitalism: How Universal Principles and Patterns Will Shape the New Economy,"[36] explores how an economy, functioning like an ecosystem, could regenerate wealth and resources in ways that serve people and the planet. The institute's *Field Guide to a Regenerative Economy* also offers a framework and national and international examples of regenerative economies.

- *Hazel Henderson*, with the socially responsible investment firm Calvert, led the development of the Ethical Markets Quality of Life indicators, which measure economic performance based on twelve indicators: education, employment, energy, environment, health, human rights, income, infrastructure, national security, public safety, recreation (self-renewal and development), and shelter.[37]

- *David Korten* is the author of *Change the Story, Change the Future: A Living Economy for a Living Earth*; *Agenda for a New Economy: From Phantom Wealth to Real Wealth*; *The Great Turning: From Empire to Earth Community*; *The Post-Corporate World: Life after Capitalism*; and *When Corporations Rule the World*. In his books, Korten describes the connection between the social and environmental devastation that he was witnessing abroad and the economic policies practiced and advanced by the United States through its foreign policy, use of military power, and corporate reach.[38]

- *Bernard Lietaer, Christian Arnsperger, Sally Goerner, and Stefan Brunnhuber* explore how complementary regional currencies can be designed to address our current monetary system in *Money and Sustainability: The Missing Link*.[39]

(continued)

Box 8.2 (continued)

- *Ethan Roland and Gordon Landua*, rather than defining wealth in terms of financial capital, proposed eight forms of capital in *Regenerative Enterprise: Optimizing for Multiple-
  Capital Abundance*. They are *social capital*—connections, relationships, and social
  networks that link people, businesses, and communities; *material capital*—raw and processed resources, infrastructures, and technologies; *financial capital*—money, securities,
  and financial instruments as tools for exchanging goods and services; *living capital*—plants,
  water, soil, organisms, animals, and healthy ecosystems; *intellectual capital*—knowledge;
  experiential capital—experiential learning, embodied learning, which is built from experience; *spiritual capital*—internal connection to and awareness of a greater whole; and
  cultural capital—the shared ideas, experiences, and creations of a community, city, or
  nation.[40]
- *Carol Sanford*, the author of *Regenerative Business: Redesign Work, Cultivate Human Potential, Achieve Extraordinary Outcomes*, and *The Responsible Business: Reimaging Sustainability
  and Success*, is a regenerative business educator who works to transform businesses and
  regenerate the productivity of companies, communities, and ecosystems. Rather than
  pursue a competitive advantage that produces winners and losers, regenerative businesses operate in collaborative business ecologies and learn from healthy ecosystem
  dynamics to achieve collaborative advantage for all.[41]
- *James Speth and Kathleen Courrier* (2021), in The *New Systems Reader*, offer an excellent overview of some of the major alternatives proposed for a new economy, such as "community-
  based wealth building," "stakeholder economics," "participatory economics" a "civic
  economy," "subsidiarity" (economic devolution and decentralization), "solidarity economy for people and the planet," and an "economy for the common good."[42]

Many of these new-economy initiatives are grassroots efforts dedicated to building
communities from the bottom up, not only to meet people's material needs but to
establish the social and psychological conditions in which people can thrive. The *solidarity economy*, for example, builds cultures and communities of cooperation that foster
relationships of mutual support and solidarity and rely on shared responsibility and
democratic decision making. Rather than prioritizing profit over all else, they encourage
a commitment to shared humanity, expressed as social, economic, and environmental
justice.[43] The solidarity economy also includes "the practice of 'commoning'—holding
a natural or cultural resource as a 'commons' that is not owned "but cared for and
regenerated so it can be passed on to the next generation in as good or better condition
than the current generation received it."[44]

Other approaches to the solidarity economy, such as the Democracy Collaborative,
combine both top-down and bottom-up initiatives. For example, its policy-focused
interventions, such as the Community Wealth Building Program, are derived from the
Cleveland Model.[45] The model works with "anchor institutions" (e.g., hospitals and
universities) and draws on their purchasing power—some 3 billion dollars of goods
and services a year—to build local community businesses in economically devastated

neighborhoods near the universities and hospitals. Then, from the bottom up, a non-profit cooperative like the Community Wealth Evergreen Cooperatives of Cleveland,[46] links a revolving loan fund with the common goal of rebuilding economically devastated communities.

Researchers of the Democracy Collaborative also track the cutting edge of the "solidarity economy," or what Robin Murray and colleagues describe as the "social economy,"[47] and Gar describes as "the pluralist commonwealth." All of them share a similar interest and objective—the exploration of alternative ways to democratize how wealth is owned and managed among the diverse forms of democratized ownership, such as worker cooperatives, municipally owned institutions, public banks, utilities and transportation, and land trusts.[48] Examples include 11,000 companies owned entirely or partially by some 13.6 million employees; social enterprises that use profits for environmental, social, and community-serving goals; companies that are owned entirely or in a part by employees with stock ownership plans, some of which involve participatory management; 1.6 million nonprofit corporations that often cross over into economic activity; B corporations, which allow companies to subordinate their profits to social and environmental goals; and cooperatives in which 130 million members in the US participate[49] and a billion people in total membership worldwide. These latter include the following:

- Credit unions—member-owned financial cooperatives
- Agricultural cooperatives (e.g., Sunkist, Ocean Spray, Land o' Lakes, Organic Valley)
- Purchasing cooperatives (e.g., Ace, Coast to Coast, and True Value)
- Consumer cooperatives (e.g., REI and a host of independent grocery stores)
- Housing cooperatives, which address the needs of seniors, students, mobile home park residents, and low-income communities[50]

Four examples further demonstrate the scope of the new-economy redesign efforts: Mondragon, a group of cooperatives based in the Basque region of Spain; Lulan Artisans, a social enterprise headquartered in Charleston, South Carolina, that develops cottage industries in Southeast Asia; the Grameen Bank, a microfinance and community development bank founded in Bangladesh by Muhammad Yunus to provide banking services to the poor; and the Self-Help Credit Union, a nonprofit loan fund, founded in North Carolina by Martin Eakes and Bonnie Wright.

Mondragon.[51] Founded in the town of Mondragon in 1956 by Father José María Arizmendiarrieta and graduates of a local technical college, Mondragon is the world's largest and most advanced cooperative system, with 11,936 billion euros in total revenue. It integrates 266 businesses and autonomous and independent federated cooperatives employing 80,818 members who are worker-owners and 15,000–20,000 employees in the industrial and distribution segments of the economy that compete successfully in global markets. In addition, it has its own schools, bank, university, research laboratories, business incubators, and a supermarket chain. Its social welfare program includes health care, pensions, and unemployment benefits. Retirees receive 80 percent of their former salary as a pension—60 percent from the government and 40 percent from the Mondragon system. Mondragon's governance system combines democratic decision making with a General Assembly of worker-owners who elect the Governing Council. The Governing Council selects the managing director of the enterprise, and it also decides the basic questions governing it—where to produce, how to produce, what technology to use, how to coordinate the cooperatives, how to expand the cooperative, and the range of pay and benefits. The highest-paid person is not allowed to get more than 4½ times what the lowest-paid person does, although there are some exceptions where the gap is allowed to be 6½ times. A Social Council has an advisory role and represents the concerns of the worker-owners to the Governing Council and managing director. Should an agenda issue be contentious and a decision opposed by the Social Council, it can be brought to the General Assembly for a one-member, one-vote binding decision. In decision making, Mondragon's purpose is to benefit members, not shareholders.

Lulan Artisans. Lulan Artisans is a for-profit social venture or social enterprise business that uses its revenue to make a social and environmental impact and contribute to the well-being of the community and society.[52] Founded in 2002 by Eve Blossom and headquartered in Charleston, South Carolina, it designs, produces, and markets luxurious, handwoven, hand-dyed, and sustainable textiles in partnership with more than 600 artisans and developing local cottage industries in South East Asia. Blossom began her work with the question: "Could I create a sustainable business that opened up economic options for artisan communities threatened by human trafficking? And could my business model provide the weavers with steady jobs and enough money not just to survive but also to thrive and help fuel their local economies?"[53] To create her social enterprise, Blossom relied on the major principles of design thinking and systems thinking: listening to artisans and understanding their needs; developing strong collaborations with all stakeholders and embracing the community as a partner; prototyping and testing different designs, dyes, textiles, and production arrangements; making meaningful and sustainable products that added value to artisans, their families, and their communities; and building and structuring the social enterprise around the local culture and its needs.[54] She also redesigned and attended to the entire product-creation cycle to ensure that the overall impact of production reflected her values and those of her customers,[55] measured in terms of the triple bottom line, expressed as "planet, people, and profit."[56] Her business network is expanding worldwide to support artisans and combat human trafficking in Cambodia, Laos, Thailand, Vietnam, India, and Bangladesh. She also is working with artisans in Africa, South America, Central America, the United States, and Europe to expand jobs in the maker movement. Her ultimate aim is to create a social enterprise that is sustainable on six levels: social, economic, communal, personal, cultural, and ecological. In response to the question of why Lulan got involved in so many aspects of a system, she said. "This is how you create, a holistic, sustainable business. Everything is interconnected and impacts everything else in the ecosystem—the people, products, and ecology—in many different ways. This is how business should work."[57]

Grameen Bank. Grameen is a microfinance and community development bank founded in Bangladesh by the social entrepreneur Muhammad Yunus to provide banking services to the poor.[58] It has disbursed, based on trust, over 24 billion dollars in collateral-free loans to over 9 million borrowers/members, 97 percent of whom are women. Majority owned and governed by its borrowers, it has 2,568 branches and offers services (e.g., loans, saving accounts, pension plans, and loan insurance) in 81,677 villages, which include more than 93 percent of the total villages in Bangladesh. The overall goal of the Grameen Bank is to use credit as a weapon to fight poverty by helping people who have been kept out of commercial banking on the grounds that they are poor and not bankable. Given microcredit on terms and conditions that were reasonable, the poor have become generators of social and economic development from below. Given its positive impact on poor and formerly poor borrowers, 65 percent of whom have lifted themselves out of extreme poverty, the Grameen Bank and Yunus were awarded the Nobel Peace Prize in 2006.

Self-Help Credit Union. Cofounded by Martin Eakes and Bonnie Wright, Self-Help is a family of two credit unions, a nonprofit loan fund, a policy advocacy group, and a designated community development financial institution, all of which work to expand ownership and economic opportunities for its 188,800 members who have accounts online and in branches in eight states in the US. They provide financial services to low- and moderate-income consumers and underserved communities; promote homeownership to help families, especially in neighborhoods hit by foreclosures; lend to small businesses and nonprofits, including affordable housing developments and commercial real estate to invigorate downtown areas and neighborhoods; and promote fair financial practices that benefit communities of all kinds, including people of color, women, rural residents, and low-wealth families and communities. For over forty years, as one of the fastest-growing community development financial institutions in the country, the National Center for Community Self-Help and its affiliates have provided more than $10.5 billion in financing to help more than 150,000 borrowers buy homes, start and grow businesses, and strengthen community resources. [59]

Regenerative Development

Regenerative development is based on three fundamental concepts: *living systems thinking*, which focuses on relationships and the interconnectedness of social, economic, and ecological systems in a particular context; *permaculture*, which consists of ecosystem integrity, biodiversity, resilience, and sustainable resource use and waste regeneration; and *developmental change processes*, which build on equity, empowerment, social cohesion, and the development of human capital.[60]

The work of the Regenesis Group, cofounded by Pamela Mang and Ben Haggard, illustrates how regenerative development works in practice. The group's mission is to transform the development industry so that it contributes to rather than undermines the health of the planet by assisting cities, towns, and other human communities to align themselves with the unique ecological systems of which they are part.[61] Ultimately, the group posits that all development should coevolve with natural living systems regenerating both environments and cultures. Rather than applying a checklist or template, or generic one-size-fits-all thinking, a place's unique ecosystem becomes the foundation for the development, health, and prosperity of a community. Projects begin by engaging members of the local community to understand their aspirations, challenges, and potential. These interactions, combined with what is known about the owners' goals, build a common language, understanding, and commitment to a shared story of *place*, which becomes the touchstone for every aspect of design, construction, operations, and marketing. From this research-based story and awareness of a place and its essence—how it functions, what it contributes to the world, and its geology, hydrology, and flora and fauna—the regenerative design process then moves each project from research to concept to integrative practice to deliver tangible results: "schools, farms, resorts, and parks; housing, commercial and mixed-use projects; neighborhoods and planned communities; and community and regional economic development and sustainability plans."[62]

Playa Viva. One example of regenerative development and design is Playa Viva,[63] a 200-acre regenerative ecoresort adjacent to the village of Juluchuca and 3 kilometers from Rancho Nuevo, in the Costa Grande region of Guerrrero on the western coast of Mexico. Developed by coowners David Leventhal and Sandra Kahn and assisted by the Regenesis Group between 2006 and 2007, Playa Viva boasts a hotel, pristine beaches, a private nature preserve, a turtle sanctuary, ancient ruins, and a natural estuary home to more than 200 bird species. When the project began, the village of Juluchuca was dying. From the 1920s on, the majority of its coastline suffered from government-subsidized deforestation for monoculture plantations of coconut, mango, and tamarind, as well as cattle ranching. The new dependency on agrochemistry, unbalanced crop nutrition, uncontrolled coastal development, and the tourist industry collectively led to soil degradation, declining water quality, water shortages due to loss of key vegetation and rapid discharge, and declining yields. In more recent years, palm plantations had collapsed, businesses had closed, and young people were leaving in search of opportunities in the big cities. Playa Viva's regenerative concept emerged in response to this degeneration. By taking a systems approach, the founders believed that the place could return to the biodiverse ecosystem that it once had been by focusing on both environmental and social impacts, including estuary regeneration, regenerative agriculture, community development (health, education, and economic development), and transformational guest experiences (i.e., tourism) that would be a point of leverage for regeneration.[64]

Regenerative initiatives were extensive throughout the community, as illustrated in table 8.2.

Table 8.2
Sequence of regenerative design initiatives at Playa Viva

Routing traffic through the village, which required building a bridge in order to link the community to the eco-resort

Establishing a training program in biodynamics to help local farmers launch a partnership that provides high-quality local produce for the hotel kitchen

Sponsoring a local cooperative to brand and sell its distinctive, organically produced artisanal salt, Sal Viva, and working with top chefs in the United States to increase the price obtained for the members of the salt coop

Offering local farmers organic agriculture courses to help them clean up the watershed, improve human health, and expand the supply of organic food

Expanding the organic food market and helping the farmers set up Canasta Viva, a community-supported agriculture cooperative to deliver baskets of organic produce to local homes, bed-and-breakfasts, and hotels in the region

Constructing buildings with the best available green technology and having local artisans build hotel furniture from native and locally harvested woods

Orienting rooms for natural cooling, and designing them to feel like an extension of the natural surroundings

Moving toward the creation of more energy than used with 100 percent off-grid solar energy

Relying on construction crews with 50 percent local workers, who were provided training and workshops in sustainable and permaculture techniques

Designing landscaping to balance native, drought-tolerant, and aesthetic/food-bearing species that attract birds and beneficial insects

Establishing a recycling program to raise money, keep trash out of the river and in the surrounding area, and reduce burning

Encouraging small businesses to support development, such as a nursery that provides plants and trees for the restoration and regeneration of the preserve

Supporting an on-site turtle sanctuary set up by local volunteer staff working to preserve Mexico's endangered green sea turtle population

Establishing the Playa Viva Reserve, which is working to restore 80 percent of the resort's 200 acres to coastal forests and wetlands with mangroves, hardwood trees, and a variety of indigenous flora and fauna

Working to ensure cleaner water, estuary and lagoon regeneration, healthier soil, and increased biodiversity

Managing water, which includes both gray water on gardens and black water on mini-living systems

Removing pollutants to protect the local wetlands, and reusing water for landscaping and extraction of nutrients to enrich the soils, and using biodegradable cleaning and hygiene products to improve the well-being of both the natural systems and community

Increasing business profitability and viability through economic assistance such as business training and broader access to resources and markets

---

The initial outside assessment of Playa Viva's development was very positive. It noted the: returning vitality and abundance to the landscape, shift in worldviews based on collaborative and reciprocal relationships, ability to add value across scales, regenerative capacity in the whole system and the evolution of its living economies, and return of its young people to the area.[65] The *Social Impact 2018 Report* by Melissa Luna, using an alternative methodology based on interviews of Playa Viva staff and people from the nearby villages of Juluchuca and Rancho Nuevo, and the village of Coyuquilla Sur as a control, was less positive. David Leventhal and Sandra Kahn, Playa Viva owners who commissioned the report, offered their insights on their regeneration efforts from the interviews:

- *Communication is key*: Playa Viva was doing a "pretty good job" of communicating the commitment for social and environmental impact to the "outside world," but it was not communicating these same goals, activities, and achievements with equal effectiveness with the team/staff and the local community.

- *Give back to the most vulnerable*: The local turtle volunteers who gave the most were those who were in most need in the community. Efforts needed to be redoubled to integrate them into the Playa Viva community and improve their morale and ability to gain financially from their role in conservation.

- *Develop a strong sense of community*: Social cohesion, the feeling of being part of a community, is key to creating positive impacts in the local community. It starts with getting volunteers to spend more time in Juluchuca and Rancho Nuevo, as well as engaging resort guests in the community.

- *Listen more and engage people at a deeper level*: A key learning was to host more town halls and listen to the needs of the community. Regenerative engagements had tended to be tactical and responsive rather than strategic, with a focus on social impact. Volunteer efforts need to be better aligned with strategic goals.

- *Train and support employees as the ambassadors in the local community*: More time was needed for training and supporting employees. They are the best and most effective advocates and promoters of environmental and social consciousness, so it is essential that they know and understand the purpose of Playa Viva and what it does.

- *Leverage collective impact*: To be a catalyst for change, it is important to engage a larger network of nongovernmental organizations (NGOs), educational institutions, government, and for-profit entities in the Playa Viva ecosystem to address the larger and more systemic issues.

- *Be patient and keep at it*: Impact takes time. [66]

French Gulch Concept Plan. Other examples of regenerative development can be found in Allan Berger's work, which combines political, economic, geospatial, ecological, and social factors in a redesign practice, although he frames his work as systemic design.[67] Incorporating landscape architecture, urban studies, and community design, he begins with research around "integrative reclamation" and the redesign of "wasted landscapes," defined as "overlooked and undervalued" areas that are left after humans have scoured the landscape of its raw materials and left behind destroyed habitat and wastelands of pollution. Berger's French Gulch Concept Plan, requested by the Environmental Protection Agency (EPA), is illustrative. He developed a solution for a retired mine near Breckenridge, Colorado, which, due to neglect, had been gradually flooded over eighty years and contaminated with high levels of sulfuric acid. Berger's vision for the project began by asking what the immediate community needed and wanted for the site. He then based the plan on three steps: correcting the abandoned mine's environmental problems, providing affordable housing and open-space planning, and presenting it as a demonstration project for thousands of similar mines in the United States. Other more recent projects have included French president Nicolas Sarkozy's Grand Paris Competition, designed to rethink Paris's metropolitan region with regard to a more sustainable future, and the regeneration of Pontine Marshes in central Italy, focused on cleaning the polluted water more effectively and efficiently using naturally occurring ecosystems.

Regenerative Agriculture

A third example of regenerative design is *regenerative agriculture*, a term introduced by the Rodale Institute in the early 1980s. The concept describes a holistic land management practice that seeks the restoration of highly degraded soil and improvements in the health and biodiversity of soil, which in turn "symbiotically enhances the quality of the water, vegetation and land-productivity."[68] As shown in table 8.3, there is a range of regenerative agriculture practices.[69]

Table 8.3
Examples of regenerative agricultural practices

Aquaculture	The cultivation of aquatic plants and aquatic animals for food
Agroecology	The study of ecological processes applied to agricultural production systems
Agroforestry	The planting and growth of trees and shrubs around or among crops of pastureland to increase biodiversity and reduce erosion
Biochar	The use of biomass charcoal to increase the ability of soils to sequester carbon and improve soil health
Compost	The composting of organic matter, which produces soil rich in nutrients
Holistic planned grazing	Animal health and welfare and the integration of livestock with crops, wildlife, and land regeneration
No-till	The growth of crops or pasture without disturbing the soil through tillage in order to increase water, the soil's retention of organic matter, and the cycling of nutrients
Pasture cropping	The direct drilling of cereal crops into living summer growing perennial pastures, which then become dormant and allow year-round growth, eliminating fallow and bare ground
Silvopasture	The integration of trees and forage plants to provide food and shelter for livestock

Agricultural regeneration has some important advantages. In addition to the production of food and resources for regional bioeconomies, it offers a way of sequestering carbon in the soil (known as *carbon drawdown*).[70] From its current adoption of 11.84 million hectares, future regenerated croppings are expected to increase to 221–322 million hectares by 2050, thanks to organic agriculture and the projected conversion from conservation agriculture to regenerative annual cropping. These changes could result in a total reduction of "14.5–22.3 gigatons of carbon dioxide, from both sequestration and reduced emissions. Regenerative annual cropping could provide a $2.3–3.5 trillion lifetime operational cost savings and lifetime net profit gain of $135–206 billion on an investment of $79–116 billion," according to Project Drawdown.[71]

Walker's Sand Quarry and Walker's Reserve. A number of organizations promote regenerative agriculture around the world,[72] an excellent example of which is Walker's Sand Quarry in Barbados.[73] For five decades, it had been an open-pit mine providing sand for Barbados's construction industry. When Ian McNeel, a social entrepreneur and impact investor, inherited his family's business and property in 2006, he began to explore whether it was possible to regenerate degraded quarry land and make it viable for food production in Barbados, an island that imports an estimated 80 percent of foodstuffs. When his first efforts at planting cashew seedlings failed, he started to learn about permaculture and how to put it into practice in the quarry. When he found permaculture, a concept developed by Australian researchers David Holmgren and Bill Mollison in 1978 that utilizes patterns and features seen in natural ecosystems to create holistic agricultural systems, "it was evident to me that the way I was looking at things before was not a whole systems approach."[74] His search for people who could help him regenerate the degraded quarry to ecological health led him to Gregory Landau, the chief executive of Terra Genesis International,[75] a firm that specializes in permaculture and agricultural systems; Ethan Soloviev Roland, a regenerative agriculture designer; and Erle Rahaman-Noronha, an implementation consultant who applied permaculture principles to degraded land. McNeel then brought in Terra Genesis International to offer some initial training, including a certified permaculture design course, to help develop a cohesive vision and provide an initial set of strategies and techniques, which the Barbados participants could then adapt to their unique environment.

The combined expertise in regenerative agriculture, along with a cooperative group of experienced farmers, pickers, and community members, transformed the quarry into a 300-acre food forest called Walker's Reserve. It is a mixed-use agroforestry site for short- and long-term yields. In over five years of engagement, they added thousands of tons of green waste to generate compost with sheep, chicken, and horse manure, created twelve planting patterns and fifty-two planting plots, and put in 18,000 trees and nitrogen-fixing plants, as well as bananas, cassava, and moringa to provide shade. They also established test zones for products such as aloe, bananas, figs, plantains, lemongrass, watermelons, and turmeric, as well as pineapples and arrowroot, which are traditionally grown in northern Barbados. In the future, the food forest might also contain pomegranates and Bajan cherries, as well as guava, soursop, jamun, and goose-berries. By stabilizing the soil and replacing windswept dunes with sheltered wetlands, new growth is now protected from strong easterly winds and salt spray. The reserve also has restored a native forest that forms a sanctuary for migratory birds, endemic amphibians, and reptiles under pressure from habitat loss.

Walker's Reserve currently offers workshops for employees and the public, led by international and local professionals who teach a mix of sustainable and regenerative techniques—composting, beekeeping, and earth building are just some of the topics covered. Future plans being discussed include a food hub with a cold storage room and an on-site farmers' market that features produce from other local growers, distilling essential oils, growing and weaving natural fibers, and ecotourism. Knitting together the agroecological diversity of the surrounding landscape and the community's social system and the transition from sand quarry operations to mixed agricultural and eco-logical land provides an excellent case of postextraction regeneration.

Regenerative Landscapes

A fourth example of regenerative design closely related to regenerative agriculture is *regenerative landscapes*—the process of restoring a landscape's ecosystem services and the benefits that people obtain from nature to ensure human well-being.[76] These efforts, referred to as *natural capital*, include:

- *Provisioning*—products drawn from ecosystems such as food, fresh water, wood, fiber, genetic resources and medicines
- *Regulating*—benefits derived from the regulation of ecosystem processes such as water purification, waste treatment, pollination, pest control, climate regulation, flood control, and natural hazard regulation
- *Supporting*—services necessary for providing all other services, such as soil forma-tion, nutrient cycling, and oxygen production, primary production
- *Cultural*—nonmaterial benefits that people derive such as spiritual enrichment, intellectual development, recreation, and other aesthetic values[77]

The Assessment Report on Land Degradation and Restoration by the Intergovernmental Science-Policy Platform on Biodiversity on Ecosystem Services provides an update of the state of knowledge on natural capital and the drivers, status, and trends of ecosystem degradation occurring in all parts of the world.[78] The recent data presented in table 8.4 are alarming.

The *Assessment Report* concludes that land degradation tends to be the result of mul-tiple interacting economic, demographic, technological, institutional, and cultural drivers.[79] Although there does not appear to be a "one size fits all approach to sustain-able land management,"[80] it notes the importance of collective action by communities and the management of common pool environmental resources and multistakeholder approaches in building long-term socioecological resilience.[81] There also is general agree-ment on the rationale for restoring degraded landscapes to healthy ecosystems—"they

Table 8.4
Degradation of the Earth's land surface through human activities

Land surface degradation	"Currently, degradation of the Earth's land surface through human activities is negatively impacting the well-being of at least 3.2 billion people, pushing the planet towards a sixth mass species extinction, and costing more than 10 per cent of the annual global gross product in loss of biodiversity and ecosystem services."[*]
Global direct driver of land degradation	"Rapid expansion and unsustainable management of croplands and grazing lands is the most extensive global direct driver of land degradation."[†]
Impact of land degradation	"Transformation and degradation of various types and intensity are causing predominantly negative impacts on biodiversity and ecosystem functions" on three-quarters of the Earth's land surface. "Wetlands are particularly degraded, with 87 per cent since 1900."
	"Land degradation, especially in coastal and riparian areas, increases the risk of storm damage, flooding and landslides."[**]
	"Although land degradation exists in both developed and developing parts of the world, it tends to have the strongest negative impacts on the well-being of people in vulnerable situations and of those living in economically poor areas."[††]
Predictions for 2050	"By 2050, land degradation and climate change together are predicted to reduce crop yields by an average of 10 percent globally and up to 50 per cent in certain regions. Decreasing land productivity, among other factors, makes societies, particularly on drylands, vulnerable to socioeconomic instability. In dryland areas, years with extreme low rainfall have been associated with an increase of up to 45 per cent in violent conflict. Every 5 per cent loss of [gross domestic product (GDP)], itself partly caused by degradation, is associated with a 12 per cent increase in the likelihood of violent conflict. Land degradation and climate change are likely to force 50 to 700 million people to migrate by 2050."
Benefits of regenerative landscapes	"On average, the benefits of restoration are 10 times higher than the costs, estimated across nine different biomes. While challenging, the benefits of restoration include, but are not limited to, increased employment, increased business spending, improved gender equity, increased local investment in education and improved livelihoods. Investing in avoiding land degradation and the restoration of degraded land makes sound economic sense; the benefits generally by far exceed the cost."[‡‡]

[*] Luca Montanarella, Robert Scholes, and Anastasia Brainich, eds., The *Assessment Report on Land Degradation and Restoration* (Bonn, Germany: Secretariat of the Intergovernmental Science-Policy Platform on Biodiversity and Ecosystem Services (IPBES), March 24, 2018), https://zenodo.org/record/3237393#.YDQoh-hKiMo, 22. Ecosystem services are free of charge—the current economy, which is based on manufacturing, does not include them. So ecological economists have developed techniques to capture their direct and indirect benefits and worth by assigning monetary valuations to services that humans receive from naturally functioning ecosystems.

[†] Montanarella et al., *Assessment Report*, 14.

[‡] Montanarella et al., *Assessment Report*, 18.

[**] Montanarella et al., *Assessment Report*, 24.

[††] Montanarella et al., *Assessment Report*, 25.

[‡‡] Montanarella et al., *Assessment Report*, 10.

form the basis of all wealth creation,"[82] since restoration provides people with food, water, clean air, climate stability, and economic wealth, and even their happiness and well-being. The ultimate challenge, as the report concludes, is "how to make the restoration of ecosystem functions and biodiversity a flourishing part of our economy and move from the current degradation economy to a restoration economy."[83]

Rwanda's Rugezi wetland ecosystem.   A variety of multifaceted approaches have demonstrated to be effective in avoiding, reducing, and reversing land degradation in both urban and rural settings.[84] One initiative is the restoration of Rwanda's Rugezi twenty-kilometer-long-wetland ecosystem that supplies water to the Ruhondo and Bulera lakes.[85] By 2004, the deforestation of the mountains surrounding the lakes, the draining of the wetlands for cultivation and grazing that affected their buffering function, together with below average rainfall and poor plant maintenance, led to a 50 percent drop in the two lakes' water level. This sharp drop in the Lake Bulera water reservoir, where the Ntaruka and Mukungwa hydropower stations were located, set off an energy crisis and then a countrywide economic crisis. In response, the Rwandan government decided to halt the ongoing degradation and drainage of the area and reclaim the Rugezi wetland's ecological and economic function. It sponsored extensive erosion control with reforestation and agrointensification measures such as the building of terraces. It also introduced new plant species to help farmers secure their livelihoods. By 2008, both hydropower stations had returned to full operation capacity.

Regeneration of the Loess Plateau.   Another example of land restoration is China's Regeneration of the Loess Plateau (1994–2005),[86] a project jointly financed by the World Bank and the Chinese government.[87] Home to 50 million people, the plateau and its people suffered from land overuse, overgrazing, widespread poverty, and one of the highest erosion rates in the world. The project's primary objectives were to restore the heavily degraded 35,000 square kilometers of land in nine tributary watersheds of the Yellow River in the Loess Plateau, an area roughly the size of Belgium, return the area of sustainable agricultural production, and increase people's income. At the end of the project implementation in 2008, the World Bank reported its findings, shown in table 8.5.

In Summary

Daniel Wahl warns us that "humanity is challenged to fundamentally redesign the human presence on Earth within the lifetime of generations alive today."[88] Regeneration design—the coevolution of human systems with nature to ensure ecosystem integrity, maintain diversity, cultivate systemic health, and fortify the planetary life support system on which we all depend—is central to this effort. Regenerative designs are underway in agriculture, architecture, business, economics, education, energy sources, food systems, development, governance, and water management. Three concepts inform regenerative design practice: biomimicry, a cradle-to-cradle approach to

Table 8.5
Results of the Regeneration of the Loess Plateau project

People out of poverty	More than 2.5 million people in four of China's poorest provinces—Shanxi, Shaanxi, Gansu, and the Inner Mongolia Autonomous Region—were lifted out of poverty.
Impact on income	Incomes doubled: People in project households saw their incomes grow from about $70 per year per person to about $200 through agricultural productivity enhancement and diversification.
Natural resource protection and regeneration	The degraded environment was revitalized and natural resources were protected: Uncontrolled grazing, subsistence farming, fuel wood gathering and cultivation of crops on slopes had left huge areas of the plateau devastated. The project encouraged natural regeneration of grasslands, tree and shrub cover on previously cultivated slope lands. Replanting and bans on grazing allowed the perennial vegetation cover to increase from 17 to 34 percent.
Waterway sedimentation reduced	Sedimentation of waterways was dramatically reduced: The flow of sediment from the plateau into the Yellow River has been reduced by more than 100 million tons each year. Better sediment control has reduced the risks of flooding with a network of small dams helping store water for towns and for agriculture when rainfall is low.
Employment rate increased and diversified	Employment rates increased: more efficient crop production on terraces and the diversification of agriculture and livestock production have brought about new on- and off-farm employment. During the second project period, the employment rate increased from 70 percent to 87 percent. Opportunities for women to work have increased significantly.
Secured food supplies and high-value products	Before the project, frequent droughts caused crops cultivated on slopes to fail, sometimes requiring the government to provide emergency food aid. Terracing not only increased average yields, but also significantly lowered their variability. Agricultural production has changed from generating a narrow range of food and low-value grain commodities to high-value products. During the second project period, per capita grain output increased from 365 kilograms to 591 kilograms per year.
Restructured agricultural sector	The project significantly contributed to the restructuring of the agricultural sector: introduced sustainable farming practices; adjusted to a market-oriented economic environment; and created conditions for sustainable soil and water conservation.
Restored ecological balance	Even during the lifetime of the project, the ecological balance was restored in a vast area considered by many to be beyond help.
Second-order effects	Terracing required the development of roads that facilitated the access of vehicles and farm equipment and labor to these areas. Sediment control and capture transformed previously unproductive land into valuable cropping areas, helped increase water storage for communities and agricultural use and reduced flood risk. Terraces reduced labor inputs and allowed farmers to pursue new income-earning activities.

Source: World Bank, "Restoring China's Loess Plateau," March 15, 2007, http://www.worldbank .org/en/news/feature/2007/03/15/restoring-chinas-loess-plateau.

industrial production, and nature's nested systems for adaption and change. And the examples of regenerative design presented in this chapter demonstrate its breadth and depth: *regenerative economics and the monetary system* (e.g., Mondragon; Lulan Artisans; the Grameen Bank; and the Self-Help Credit Union); *regenerative development* (e.g., Playa Viva; French Gulch Concept Plan); *regenerative agriculture* (e.g., Walker's Sand Quarry and Walker's Reserve); and *regenerative landscape* (e.g Rwanda's Rugezi wetland ecosystem and China's Loess Plateau).

These success stories of regenerative design certainly offer hope and optimism for the future. But there is a larger question to be addressed: is the design strategy always successful as demonstrated in these cases, or are there limitations in its applications? And even more to the point, to what extent is the design strategy more advantageous compared to other problem-solving strategies, especially in wicked problem territory? Part IV, which follows, addresses these two important questions.

IV Assessing the Design Strategy

9 Critiques of Design/Design Thinking

Is the design strategy always successful, or are there limitations in its application? And to what extent is the design strategy more advantageous than other problem-solving strategies, especially in wicked problem territory? This chapter addresses the first question and begins by summarizing some design practitioners' and academics' criticisms of design and design thinking that have appeared in the literature. As with other evolving disciplines, there tends to be differing views about what constitutes design as a discipline. Physicists typically don't dispute what physics is, but as illustrated with counterpoints to these criticisms in conferences and online chatter, designers do disagree about design and its process. And I should note that these criticisms were published in practitioner journals where findings from design research did not appear to be factored into the commentary, although research published prior to these criticisms could have informed the views expressed. The chapter ends with several explanations of why this level of dissension occurs within the design community and what is being done to address it.

Practitioners' Criticisms of Design and Design Thinking

Criticisms about design and design thinking cover a range of topics organized into two general categories—those that specifically focus on design thinking and those that focus on design as a profession and a practice.

Design Thinking

- is "ill-defined." "Its adaptability has led to varied definitions and interpretations. This confuses those who want to try it but don't know which path to take."[1]
- is not how real designers work. Design thinking "is too general a framework and too ideation-based: it's more focused on generating new ideas than on understanding how they might actually work."[2] We need to focus on design doing, not just on design thinking.[3]
- "dilutes design into a structured, linear, and clean process." "*Real* design is messy, complex, and nonlinear."[4] It can't be simplified or watered down into oversimplified steps.[5]

- "is too process-oriented" and results in a rigid system that seeks efficiency rather than producing innovative ideas. "There is nothing efficient about creativity or design." The focus on process rather than results seriously compromises the quality of the output.[6]

- "promises more than it can deliver." There is "a false promise that design thinking guarantees innovation."[7] "The value and effectiveness of creativity offered in design thinking is diluted, and results become an incremental innovation at best." "Innovation requires more than launched prototypes of concepts as the end result. It requires . . . a more holistic approach to innovation . . . in order to implement and create real impact in the organization."[8] "The unfantastic truth is that building a powerful innovation growth-engine does require changing your organization and finding ways to transcend the constraints of your business, industry and market. And that's really hard. Harder than merely finding new ways to meet the needs of your customers. Design thinking is great for winning hearts and minds, but the big prize innovation remains out of reach."[9]

- "The one thing I feel is missing (in design thinking) is a kind of skepticism from designers." "Not all user feedback is good."[10]

- is limited to the extent it doesn't bring "people from a range of disciplines—business strategists, technologists, product managers, human insights, and interaction designers—together into a unified, weaponized team that brings cross-disciplinary thinking to bear on a problem all at once."[11] Cross-pollination between domains is better than democratized design.[12]

Design as a Profession and Practice:

- "Design thinking is full of jargon, and most of it is confusing and doesn't mean much at all." "Design is much more nuanced, but because of a lack of vocabulary, we begin to see simplistic words used over and over again." We have too much jargon."[13]

- Design thinking knowledge needs to focus not just on process, but also on design abilities.[14] Design tools "can't work effectively without a skillful facilitator and experienced team to identify accurately the different aspects of the problem addressed. Otherwise, you will end up with a nonsense meeting that wastes time and effort."[15] Design teams also lack knowledge of team dynamics and change management and understanding of the obstacles (e.g., groupthink) that can prevent teams from reaching solutions and solving complex problems.[16]

- Designers also need to maintain design's professional ethical standards.[17] Design lacks "skepticism and reflection." "Designers need to question more. 'Are we doing the right thing? Or are we doing good design right now'?"[18] "Good design never happens if designers aren't in a position to answer the important questions."[19] "One specific aspect that is missing is the design critique. Critiques are a common practice in design studios and in some learning experience design departments. They are a valuable part of the feedback loop."[20]

- Human-centered design (HCD) is "superficial" and "not good design." "Good design goes back and forth between user needs and strategic needs, and planetary needs, and societal needs . . . to frame challenges that incorporate multiple considerations." "An essential design ability is the ability to create elegant solutions at the intersection of a variety of different—and sometimes seemingly contradictory—considerations." "So design thinking is nice for users, but it doesn't pay enough attention to strategy, or the planet." "Instead we need: life-centered design" that considers how "all life on the planet is connected—not design for people." "Designers need to take a more expansive view of what they design."[21] Therefore, design needs to be more "holistic."[22]

Academics' and Scholars' Criticisms of Design Thinking

What follows is a summary of views based on papers, articles, and blogs written by their publication date.

- In *Design Thinking: A Useful Myth*, design thinking is described as "a public relations term for good, old-fashioned creative thinking" characteristic of great artists, engineers, scientists, and designers. The 'new' approach "is nonsense, but like all myths, it has a certain ring of plausibility although lacking any evidence." Its broad acceptance, especially in industry, is due to its "fashionable format" and the "'hero'-function ascribed to the designer. However, the emerging breadth of the construct has led to a dilution of the concept."[23]

- In *Design Thinking: A Paradigm on Its Way from Dilution to Meaninglessness*, the emergence of a design research community and culture has produced broad-ranging results on various aspects of design thinking. However, "the whole picture is still not convincing—because there is no such thing as a *whole* integrated picture. The knowledge gained appears to be fragmented, without obvious approaches to arrive at a moment of consolidation." Moreover, current research topics are "mainly following and repeating topics and methods of the last decades," and as a consequence, they are losing their "innovative force." Instead, three research questions should be addressed and readdressed: (1) Designing is comprised of thinking processes, but what roles do motivation, emotion, preferences, and attitudes play during design thinking? (2) The focus on design teams has increased, but if the design team is interdisciplinary and geographically and culturally diverse, "where is the individual designer?" (3) "Most research in the field of design thinking seems to be explorative, with a lack of scientific rigor in terms of data assessment, analysis and interpretation," so "is there more than case studies and protocol analysis?"[24]

- *The Craze for Design Thinking: Roots, a Critique, and Toward an Alternative* views design thinking "as a force broadly hostile to technological innovation." It makes consumer needs seem preferable to technical progress as an innovation driver. The "frenzy" and "craze" of design thinking stands in "marked contrast to the gradual but gathering stagnation of Western R & D [research and development] over the past 50 years." "Sometimes explicitly, DT [design thinking] counterposes itself to technological innovation, intimating that faith in technology is just a bit out of date." It offers a "'modernising' but low-risk, technology-lite" solution that "may be both a product and reinforcer of the West's diminishing interest in and passion for investment in technological innovation." In addition, design thinking helps Western elites "maintain their political legitimacy" because design thinking "advocates the participation of the users of design, and particularly the participation of users of services," and thus "it can appear to some as a useful means of legitimation—democratic, bottom up, a world apart from the stuffy laboratory of old. Here DT can once again, and perhaps inadvertently, encourage a casual attitude to the practice of science and technology." Moreover, the role of technologists has become "less distinct," obscuring the basic role of basic scientific research and technological development, "while DT came out smelling of roses." By the 1990s, as technology's prestige was falling and Western business and government expenditures on R&D were stagnating, there was a "growing confidence in and scope for design and DT," resulting in a growing "triumphalist feeling" among designers. The British government, "in a quest to be popular and legitimate," expanded the role of design, and civil servants narrowed technology's scope to focus on sustainable, low-carbon energy-saving technologies in response to climate change warnings. Books on green design multiplied. Design ideas proliferated: design should be ethical; workplaces should be designed for employee "health," "wellness," "interactivity," and "creativity" rather than viewing workplace technology "as key to productivity and the creation of wealth." Tim Brown's *Change by Design* illustrates all these themes: "ridicule for technology," the "triumphalism about design," the neglect of technological innovation, the lack of attention to costs and economics, and more interest in "sustainability" and "energy conservation than in the generation of new energy."

For the future, design should: deal critically with *"all* the data" that is relevant to *"forecasts of the future"*; "eschew triumphalism"; "make sure that designers have a bit of humility in their dealings with scientific and technological innovation"; and realize "that DT pursued with zeal can only detract from the more vigorous pursuit of R&D; do not "take DT's claims that it facilitates stakeholder participation at face value." "The de-legitimation of those stakeholders known as scientists and technologist seem to be the main results of DT." "The fact is that major scientific and technological innovations have benefited mankind much more than innovations in design." [25]

- *Design Thinking Is a Failed Experiment. So What's Next?* announces a shift away from design thinking and toward a conceptual framework described as "creative intelligence." True design thinking had made major contributions to society and the field of design, but it had given the design profession and society all the benefits that it could. It was beginning to "ossify and actually do harm." Chief executive officers (CEOs) were implementing the design thinking process as an "efficiency-based" process, and design consultancies were promoting design thinking as "a process trick" to produce "significant cultural and organizational change." But the "real deliverable" of design thinking was "creativity." Unfortunately, design thinking "was denuded of the mess, the conflict, failure, emotions, and looping circularity that is part and parcel of the creativity process." Although a few CEOs and managers accepted the mess and real innovation occurred, most did not. "The success rate for the process was low, very low." The new focus should be on "creative intelligence," defined as "the ability to frame problems in new ways and to make original solutions," a process that "can be learned." [26]

- *Toward Sustainable Design Thinking*[27] begins with Victor Papanek's opening lines in *Design for the Real World*: "There are professions more harmful than industrial design, but only a few of them," given their designs that contribute to landfills, pollution, climate change, and a host of sociocultural problems.[28] This critique of design, which is called the Human-Business-Technology (HBT) model of design thinking, is its "glaring omission": its tendency toward "unsustainability and ethical neutrality." In terms of unsustainability, design has the power "to create both desirable and undesirable futures." "Good design thinking processes aim to uncover unmet needs as opposed to simply catering to 'easy wins'." But unfortunately, with HBT, "the importance and skill of articulating unmet needs is often sacrificed." Its reliance on surface-level wants has produced designs that can be "overly simplistic" and "unsustainable." Thus, sustainability (not human desirability) should be the most important constraint of HCD. And defining sustainability should focus on unsustainability—the "practices of modern, industrialized humans that work to foreclose on The Future," or what Tony Fry refers to as "defuturing"[29] actions such as the release of carbon emissions and planned obsolescence that decrease resilience. Unsustainability is driven by consumerism—"the belief that any design solution is worth creating as long as it satisfies human, business, and technological needs." Unless people distance themselves from this belief, "we will never break from defuturing forces."

In terms of ethical neutrality, "the HBT model is missing an ethical component." Besides asking themselves whether a design meets a human need, or whether money can be made from it, or whether it is feasible to build, designers also should be asking: "Does this contribute to a future that promotes a positive existence for humans and their environment?" "If not, it should not be designed." Injecting an "ethical attitude into an already ethically neutral practice" will not be easy. It will entail more than asking "why should we" questions instead of "how might we" questions, or introducing new methods such as scenario planning and critical systems thinking. "Instead, ethical design practice calls for a radical shift"; how humans can relate to our artificial world; "how commercial design mediates relationships between designers and clients/bosses"; and how design needs to be redefined to "include its various paradoxes, ambiguities, and effects on experience." "It means an acknowledgement that some design solutions should not exist, despite their potential for profit, and the satisfaction of a human need is not the most important criteria for deciding what to design, unless the definition of 'need' includes sustainability." [30]

- "Design Thinking Is a Boondoggle," and it is indicative what is happening in American universities.[31] "Innovation-centric reformers" have "manufactured (a) general perception of crisis" that universities need to change. As a consequence, "universities have cast themselves as engines of innovation." Professors become entrepreneurs. Students become customers who receive science, technology, engineering, and mathematics (STEM) education that prepare them for corporate positions. "University presidents and provosts create new initiatives, generate funding streams, and develop incentives that "encourage, or even force" faculty to define themselves and their work as innovative. The universitywide perception of crisis then provides opportunities for faculty to initiate new programs, centers, and institutes that will make the university more innovative, and transform "students into little innovators and entrepreneurs." With STEM as the dominant model of education and innovation, other disciplines are then forced into contortions to fit that profile.[32]

Against this backdrop, criticisms of design thinking zero in on its "roots in consulting."[33] Business consultants are using design thinking as a marketing and consulting tool, a "model for retooling all of education," including higher education, with claims that it should be part of the liberal arts, "a central part of what students learn, a lens through which graduates come to approach social reality." "In other words, we should view all of society as if we are in the design consulting business."[34] Design thinking is also "design lite." Without students developing "any specific expertise," it gives "students power without knowledge, 'creative confidence' without actual capabilities." "There is nothing new about design thinking. It is common sense tarted up in mumbo jumbo."[35] It is an example of "innovation speak,"[36] but it fails to deliver innovation. An "even deeper problem" is that "design thinking isn't focused on generating . . . fundamental technological transformations; it's centered on repackaging existing technologies behind slick interfaces."[37] "The picture gets even worse when you compare design thinking's 'social innovation' with movements that lead to deep and abiding social change," such as the civil rights movement. "In the end, design thinking's not about design. It's not about the liberal arts. It's not about innovation in any meaningful sense. It's certainly not about 'social innovation' if that means significant social change. It's about *commercialization*. It's about making education a superficial form of business training."[38] "In time, design thinking will fade away like so many other management fads. "To the degree that higher ed Design Thinkers are successful, they will make our universities more like corporations and our curricula more like shoddy, shallow forms of business schooling."[39]

- *The Divisiveness of Design Thinking*[40] summarizes critiques against design thinking and the "emergent backlash" against the methodology of designers and design organizations, describing them "just" for four reasons: "it takes a thoughtful, complex, iterative, and often messy process and dramatically oversimplifies it in order to make it easily understandable"; "it trivializes the role of craft and making things, which is fundamental to the process of design"; "it promotes 'empathy lite'—as if an empathetic and meaningful connection with people could be forged in hours or even days"; and "it's become a tool of consultancies to sell work, not to drive real impact."

  When viewing design's historic roots, there are two emerging paths of design. Designing demands more than design thinking. It actually requires doing design—learning design fundamentals and the craft of giving form to things ranging from material objects to organization strategy. "Today's design thinkers lack craft, lack intellectual foundations, and can't make things." As a consequence, design thinking "has warped into something superficial." "The act of making things takes time to learn. It's something that, again, everyone should be able to do; but it is not something everyone can do without years of practice." In a follow-on interview, one more sentence was added to this statement: "Big, nasty design problems should probably be approached by people with more experience than small, tame problems."[41]

- In *Design Thinking Is Fundamentally Conservative and Preserves the Status Quo*,[42] The claim is that "most critics have missed the main problem with design thinking. It is, at its core, a strategy to preserve and defend the status-quo—and an old strategy at that. . . . Both design thinking and the rational-experimental approach implicitly establish problem solving as the remit of the powerful, especially when it comes [to] design for social ends. They turn the everyday ability to solve a problem into a rarified practice, limited only to those who self-consciously follow a specialized methodology. In fact, problem solving is always messy and most solutions are shaped by political agendas and resource constraints. The solutions that win out are not necessarily the best—they are generally those that are favored by the powerful or at least by the majority. Both rational experimentation and design thinking provide cover for this political calculus."

  "There has [long been] a push to make problem-solving design more open and democratic. . . . However, even in these more open processes, the designer or policy maker ultimately decides which ideas and preferences are included in the solution" which "reaffirms the privileged role of designer, positioning her as the vessel through which all the implicit understanding that make it into the final design must first pass. She is the instrument that transforms messy ambiguity into the clean lines of an elegant solution. Because the input she brings into the design process can't be articulated, she is to some extent liberated from the requirement to explain and defend the rationale for her design choices."

"Moreover, because the designer herself generates the tacit understandings she uses by connecting empathetically . . . whatever needs . . . she perceives are refracted through her personal experience and priorities. . . . This subjectivity is inevitable." It "signals that the designer, as creative visionary, is somehow suspended above the fray of bias, blind spots, and political pressure." Thus, "privileging the role of the designer, or even a small circle of designers . . . radically narrows the potential for innovation."

"The political dimensions of design thinking are problematic enough on their own, but the method is particularly ill-suited to problems in rapidly changing areas or with lots of uncertainty." The design competition to rehabilitate the New York region devastated after Hurricane Sandy is one example of this. Two design submissions were awarded funding: the Big U/Dryline design and the Living Breakwaters design. The first won the lion's share of the one billion dollars for its proposed "ten-mile segmented wall, made of landscaped bridging berms and moveable gates, to protect the low half of Manhattan and the very valuable real estate locate[d] there." The second, which is characterized as a "radically open alternative," was based on the premise that the way to address climate change is not to barricade against it, but instead to embrace the change that it represents and to reimage catastrophe as an opportunity to create a new ecological future." It received "only modest seed funding" for its proposal of a "necklace" of small islands along the south shore of Staten Island, one of the areas that suffered the worst erosion effects. These islands, constructed of concrete boxes, would be "floating schools" that would offer lodging for "oysters, seals, fish, algae, and other marine species" and platforms for "educational and economic engagement with the ecosystem."

The Big U/Dryline design selection has many problems: the costs (one billion to three billion dollars); protection only from storms the size of Sandy, but not much larger; projections that the wall will last against surges only through 2050, at which point the wall will hold floodwater inside the city; real estate will continue to build behind the wall and face increasing risks when the barrier is breached; construction will displace "one of the last pockets of affordable housing on the island; and those displaced—"many of whom participated in good faith in the repeated community consultations"—will suffer from "a wave not of water but of gentrification." Thus, "in selecting the Big U/Dryline proposal, *Rebuild by Design* affirmed the political, economic, and physical status-quo."

In contrast, the Living Breakwaters design process and solution were radically open on two counts. Residents in the area participated as "lay designers," who were not limited to the role of "providers of feedback." The concept of the designer was "dethroned," and participants were invited to engage in a "messy" and "generative" process of meaning making, which is described as "interpretive engagement." Participants also shaped "the physical elements of the solution and the social and economic projects" to allow "a complete re-imagination of what counts as a solution." For example, the project entertained "the possibility that the breakwaters will have to be invented as the seas around them rise." Each "water hub" was left undetermined in its design, "inviting residents to define both their form and their function"—some could be "a business incubator, a lighthouse, a lab for the study of wildlife, a kayak depot, and a place for contemplation." Interpretive engagement also has its tensions. Politics shaped and forcefully challenged design choices, while at the same time it helped surface highly creative solutions, welcomed people affected by the solution into the process, and supported "transformative solutions."[43]

Empirical Assessment of Design and Design Thinking

Evaluations of Strategic Designs

Seeking a research base on which to make judgments about design and design thinking especially in wicked problem territory, I turned to the strategic design literature. Unsurprisingly, I found its success rate depends on the research methodologies used and the extent to which the research focus is on the design process, its results, or its outcomes. For example, as mentioned in chapter 6, the latest of two large-scale empirical studies by McKinsey[44] collected both financial and design data on 300 publicly listed companies in multiple countries and industries over a five-year period. Using regression and cluster analysis, the researchers created an index that linked financial performance with strength in design to demonstrate that design performers increased their revenues at nearly twice the rate of their industry counterparts.

Smaller-scale case studies based on interviews[45] and dissertations reliant on mixed methods[46] also exist. I also found one large-scale empirical study[47] that conducted a survey with worldwide organizations of all sizes that had experiences with design thinking. The researchers also interviewed organizational members who had significant experiences with design thinking. The study found that although design thinking is applied in all industry sectors, for-profit organizations report the greatest usage. Probing how design thinking is practiced in organizations, the study also revealed what they believed accounts for its successes and failures. Building on Junginger's model,[48] Schmiedgen and colleagues found that design thinking is localized in organizations:[49]

- On an organization's periphery, reliant on external consultants to facilitate design thinking and booked on demand with no continuous presence in the organization (21.4 percent)

- In organizational units or departments, such as marketing and R&D, where design initiatives tend to originate and are offered as an internal or external service (72.3 percent).

- In the organization's core, a central and official position with access to leadership and linked to the organization's overall strategy, which gives it access to the executive suite and the opportunity to transform it (17.5 percent).

• As an established and intrinsic mindset and practice that is integral to all aspects of the organization and its culture. Design thinking serves "to discover and invent solutions for all kinds of organizational problems. . . . Managing and designing are no longer treated as activities that apply to different organizational realms" (27.2 percent).[50]

The researchers also identified three major reasons that account for the discontinuation of design thinking in organizations.[51] The first is that design thinking was introduced as a "one-off affair," without efforts to embed it within an organization.[52] Design projects, offered by commercial service providers and educational institutions, were not designed to foster knowledge transfer or build a long-term organizational commitment. Second, management support was lacking. Design thinking was often practiced by "single actors in parts of the organization—usually without an official mandate."[53] Thus design thinking was not accepted as good management practice in which everyone needed to be proficient. As a result, it often lacked financial support and investment in training and education, as well as time allocated for participation in creative projects. When design teams were localized into separate units and isolated from the rest of the organization, they had, as one interviewee commented, "'a lot of problems convincing people that [they are] doing useful work'." Their contributions were often measured against "indiscriminate criteria, which often were execution-oriented . . . with no understanding of . . . creative detours" needed in problem solving.[54] As designers, they complained that

> we were never really acknowledged. Our insights were handed over to some guy in the engineering department and when the time came to redesign the [device] he would just say: "Oh, I had this wonderful idea." There wasn't a meeting where the director said: 'Look what great work the CDT [Center for Design Thinking] did!'[55]

Moreover, as one interviewee commented, throwing creative ideas "over the wall" to others in the organization did not give them

> much of a chance of being implemented. The rest of the organization [lacked] the appreciation, awareness, and strategic context to understand the contributions design thinking [was] making. The will to develop commitment [was] also lacking. In the worst instance, this [may even have led] to internal animosity.[56]

Consequently, when organizational leaders were not willing to advocate for and experiment with design thinking themselves, their organizations lacked direction, vision, and mandates to signal its importance. As the authors of the report acknowledged, these missed opportunities "may [have led] to failed diffusion and implementation although the method was introduced with the best of intentions."[57] Citing the design experts interviewed, the report concluded that "design thinking is more likely to fail if applied in an isolated manner without the rest of the organization practicing, appreciating or even being familiar with the concepts."[58]

Third, some of the failures can be related directly to design thinking and its practices. The difficulties begin with the concept of design thinking.[59] Although design is well established in many fields, references to design thinking has increased dramatically only within the last twenty years. As the research study concludes, "there are vastly disparate understandings" of design thinking. "No standards exist" in the various training programs for beginners,[60] so unsurprisingly, as reflected in practitioners' discourse, different interpretations result in no shared definition of design thinking.[61] As the title of the study underscores, the current state of design thinking *practice* is "parts without a whole":

> There exist different understandings of and emphases on what design thinking is. Understandings develop along a range of perceptions viewing it as a tool box, process, method(ology) or mindset. . . . Experts emphasize that the whole is more than the sum of the parts, as it forms a system. They point to organizational shortcomings when merely applying isolated elements without an awareness for the interdependencies of mindset, principles, practices and tools that constitute the concept for them.[62]

Design thinking, according to the survey results, is also difficult to measure. Of the study respondents (n=235), when asked if they measured the success of design thinking in their organizations, 127 said "no" and 101 provided reasons for not measuring design thinking in their organizations. The top ten themes that were mentioned at least three times for not measuring the "success" were:

- Respondents have no idea how to do it.
- Design thinking has just been introduced and is not yet established. It is too early to make claims about its impact, as there is not enough experience with it yet.
- No resources are available for measuring, especially in terms of people who have the knowledge of how to do this.
- No design thinking key performance indicators (KPIs) exist that are known or available to the organization.
- Insufficient time leads to perception of measurement as an additional labor-intense task.
- Measurement is seen as another cost-incurring task and therefore is avoided.
- Design thinking is not formally or officially introduced in the organization. As it operates under the radar, it is not supported by the management and hence not measured: "What has never been introduced formally won't be measured."
- Respondents believe that it is impossible to measure mindset or culture.
- It is not clear against what standard one should measure: Competing method(ologies), other project management techniques or . . . ?
- Evaluating design thinking via measures or KPIs makes no sense. Reflection (in action) is seen as more important than measuring.[63]

As one respondent commented, "Design thinking is part of the culture and the approach to work with customers. And it is adapted to our needs, approaches and mixed with methods processes. So what should we measure? A mindset? A part of a method?"[64]

Of the forty who replied "yes" as their organizations measured the success of design thinking, only twenty-three provided details on what got measured and how it was measured. The researchers reported that "the only strong similarity between them was their measuring of *customer feedback and satisfaction*, e.g., via NPS (net promoter score) or brand perception surveys."[65] Other reported measures were specific to the responding organization: "success stories and case studies; extent of employee engagement and team collaboration; # of projects with second-round funding and conversion rate from projects to strategic plans for implementation; # of projects or innovation opportunities created; # of trainings; # of people exposed to design thinking; # of coaches/innovation facilitators; special evaluation procedure . . . for recognizing high levels of organizational performance; and wins and losses of placed innovation bets."[66] Other reported metrics were "use-related, such as those affecting user experience such as "conversion rates, # of live customers, task level satisfaction."[67]

The interviewees responded in a similar way:

- "Basically everyone wants to measures something but realizes that is it 'hard to trace back design thinking's dedicated impact on financial performance (as) there are too many confounding variables'."[68]

- "Once design thinking is part of the company's DNA, it's even much harder to separate it out and say (what) caused (what). It was easier when there was just a session (author's note a workshop)."[69]

- "In our company it takes years until a product is launched on the market and a patent is granted. Keeping track of all the projects and measuring the overall impact—especially the business impact—of design thinking after a short period of time is extremely difficult for us."[70]

Respondents from Intuit, an organization well known for its success with design thinking,[71] offered additional insights:

- "The way we look at success is not so much about metrics. There are so many things that can confound a metric. . . . It is better to use stories! Stories that had a significant financial impact."[72]

- "We look at all the usual metrics the company cares about: revenue, cost, profit, employee engagement and customer engagement. Basically these stories are all about that."[73]

- The innovation catalysts then "decide what makes sense for them when compiling a story."[74]

Based on these results, the researchers concluded that what they found in their study "was vaguely coherent. There [were] hardly any ideas about how to operationalize adequate metrics,"[75] despite the fact that a majority of respondents had rated design thinking as "producing, concrete outcomes."[76] As one respondent concluded:

> How would you measure it? Measuring implies that metrics can be derived and tested against competing methodologies. . . . If design thinking is embedded in your organization, it cannot be measured in a single concept. . . . We measure our general performance with several KPIs, but we cannot determine specifically to which level design thinking contributed to this.[77]

Evaluating the Evaluations

If evaluating design thinking in organizations has been challenging with results that are "vaguely coherent," as reported in this study, I would expect assessing systemic and regenerative design to pose even greater difficulties. The purpose of systemic design is to generate social innovations, but the "dizzying variety of definitions" of social innovation and their dynamic and exploratory character "raise dilemmas for evaluators tasked with their evaluations."[78] Comprehensive evaluations of systemic design require an assessment of how designers (often described as innovators and social and policy entrepreneurs) solve problems (e.g., the strategies, tactics, and processes that they employ), build social networks (e.g., make connections among hundreds of people, groups, and organizations across disciplines and sectors), form social ecosystems (e.g., involve stakeholders that include resource providers, value chain members, and others that extend from local to international levels in specific capacities), and pursue and deliver social innovation (e.g., "new programs, products, laws, institutions, relationships, or patterns of interaction, and it is often a mix of many of these"[79] that change people's social relationships to better meet their social needs). Moreover, evaluations of systemic designs need to include all these factors and do so in such a way that could capture the changing nature of problems and solutions, "support adaptation and leave space for the unexpected, . . . give innovators the information and data they need to discover new patterns and pathways, to rapidly test solutions and abandon the ones that fail, and to detect what's emerging in response to their efforts." The findings continue:[80]

> While the long-term goals of a social innovation might be well defined, the path to achieving them is less clear—little is known about what will work, where, and under what conditions, how, and with whom. Instead decision makers need to explore what activities will trigger change; and activities that successfully trigger a desired change may never work again. Further, once one change occurs, decision makers often need to take stock of the context before they decide which activities to try next. Formative and summative evaluation designs are typically not structured in a way that gives decision makers timely information or data that supports new developments where next steps are unknown."[81]

For example, traditional formative evaluations describe assessments aimed at improving the intervention or model. They focus on the details of how a program takes out bugs and problems and improves, refines, and standardizes the model so the fixed model can be judged. If found worthy, it then can be funded, disseminated, and taken to scale.[82] Traditional summative evaluations address the question—did the program intervention work as intended? The assumption is that we know what the program is and can state that the program is "identifiable, specifiable, stable, implementable, standardized, and replicable."[83] Only then can we know what is being evaluated and whether the program should be continued, expanded, or terminated. But unfortunately, neither formative or summative evaluations address the question: how is the model developed in the first place so that downstream formative and summative evaluations can be conducted and adaptions can be tracked?

Regenerative design poses even greater challenges than systemic design. Both are wickedly complex undertakings that need to be understood as a journey guided by a general vision and principles for the purpose of realigning people's beliefs, values, and worldviews in the redesign of major social and natural systems, but without specific, long-term answers about where the journey will lead. Moreover, regenerative design, composed of complex social, economic, political, technological, and ecological subsystems, require dedicated resources and the commitment of large numbers of people over a long period of time. Often driven from the bottom up, these large-scale design interventions tend to rely on self-organization for coordination and a large network of supporters to fund activities. As a result, these designs are not evaluated in months or years, but often in decades. And given the time frame and the costs of undertaking assessments of this scale, evaluations tend to focus on outcomes rather than probing underlying dynamics of the change process. The subtle aspects of the design process—the learnings, experimentations, adaptations, and course corrections often are not well documented. Bottom-line results rather than the messy details of design thinking become the focal point. In other words, as design strategy interventions get more complex, so do the challenges of evaluating them.

More and more evaluation experts are concluding that formative and summative evaluations are poorly suited for new design interventions that explore different problem frames, search for creative ideas and solutions, engage in interactive trial-and-error learning and experimentation, and make adaptations in a particular context.[84] Moreover, new design interventions are not well matched when rapid, dynamic changes occur; the past does not necessarily predict the future; conventional wisdom is challenged by conflicting theories of social change; no clear pathways exist between problems and solutions; problems and solutions have many multiple interdependent variables interacting together in iterative and nonlinear feedback loops; and small changes create large and often unintended effects, making it difficult to predict outcomes.[85]

Despite the fact that many evaluators have concluded that traditional evaluation's insistence for "up-front, preordinate specificity doesn't work under conditions of high innovation, exploration, uncertainty, turbulence, rapid change, and emergence," some continue to demand it because that is what "they understand to be good evaluation." But in fact, "premature specificity can do harm by constraining exploration, limiting adaptation, reducing experimental options, and forcing premature adoption of a rigid model."[86] A good analogy is a ship captain who confronts rough seas and unpredictable weather and yet continues to follow a preplanned route that sends his ship straight into a storm rather than charting a new course into calmer waters.

Thus, when strategic, systemic, or regenerative interventions are attempted, the key question is whether we have an evaluation approach that matches their design's growing levels of complexity and the increasing volatility, uncertainty, and ambiguity in their environments. Perhaps the "vaguely coherent" results that we have accumulated thus far are due more to *how* we are evaluating rather than *what* we are evaluating. If traditional formative and summative evaluations are not up to the task of capturing the dynamics, learnings, and adaptations that are central features of strategic, systemic, and regenerative design, the question is what evaluation approach is.

Developmental Evaluation

Michael Quinn Patton offers developmental evaluation (DE) as an answer to this question. Rather than trying to impose order on a disorderly and uncertain world, the purpose of DE is to provide people with timely and ongoing evaluative information and feedback to inform their projects and programs and facilitate their adaptive, emergent, and creative development in complex dynamic environments.[87] Its purpose is development, and its intended users are those who are working to bring about major change.

As preformative evaluation, DE nurtures emergent, learn-by-doing, innovative, and transformative activities in contrast to traditional evaluations that seek to control, predict, and bring order out of chaos. It "adapts to the realities of complex adaptive systems rather than to impose order and certainty on a disorderly and uncertain world,"[88] and "is especially useful for tracking strategic changes."[89]

> Developmental evaluation . . . centers on situational sensitivity, responsiveness, and adaptation, and is an approach to evaluation especially appropriate for situations of high uncertainty where what may and does emerge is relatively unpredictable and uncontrollable. Developmental evaluation tracks and attempts to make sense of what emerges under conditions of complexity, documenting and interpreting the dynamics, interactions, and interdependencies that occur as innovations unfold.[90]

At some point, DE can lead to the generation of a model for formative and summative testing, but its particular value-added contribution is its attention to dynamic situations that support "ongoing observation, assessment, and feedback about how things are unfolding, what's working and what's not, and what's emerging, toward what outcomes."[91] As Patton elaborates, DE does the following:

- It illuminates, informs, and supports something that's being developed, whether it be a program, policy, or some idea to shape the vision and process with the goal of producing an innovation.

- It adapts and applies principles of whatever is being developed, rather than attempting to replicate the knowledge and principles developed from elsewhere.

- It explores real-time adaptions, solutions, and innovative responses to crisis, intractable challenges, and wicked problems[92] by identifying the patterns of development and the implications and consequences of those patterns.

- It works toward new innovation models that may not exist and may need to be developed and explored as new possibilities when current systems show signs of dysfunction, or even collapse.

- It supports the disruption of an existing system and tipping it into a new desired direction, including taking new ideas as innovations to scale, which add levels of complexity, uncertainties, conflicts, and unexpected consequences to continued evaluations.[93]

Consequently, the evaluator's role in developmental evaluations is very different than the evaluator's role in formative and summative evaluations.[94] In both formative and summative evaluations, the evaluator is an external, independent, and objective observer who relies on predictive logic and follows a fixed plan, the focus of which is to test models that specify a hypothesized chain of cause and effect. In addition, both assume the evaluation's purpose is to refine the program or model, measure success against predetermined goals, and render a judgment of success or failure.[95] In contrast, each developmental evaluation is considered to be unique; there is "no one best way to conduct an evaluation."[96] The developmental evaluator becomes a *bricoleur*, a "jack-of-all trades do-it-yourself person who draws on eclectic traditions and integrates diverse approaches to get the job done usefully in a way that fits the situation at hand."[97] The *bricolage* includes a range of activities and skill sets: reflective practice, abductive reasoning, "critical thinking, creative thinking, design thinking, inferential thinking, strategic thinking, and practical thinking,"[98] along with collaborative learning, adaptation, and experimentation.[99] In this new role,[100] the evaluator

- Is a team member who acts as a coach and facilitator of data-based reflection and decision making in the developmental process, which requires everyone to support the innovator's [designer's][101] values and vision

- Centers accountability for the project on the innovator's [designer's] fundamental values and desire to make a difference, and works with funders to ensure what gets developed and learned becomes the focus of accountability, all the while being sensitive to unintended results and side effects

- Encourages and nurtures a leader's [designer's] and his team's reality-testing, results-focus, and learning, in order to try things out and quickly assess what happens, both intended and unintended, to inform the next steps of a project's development

- Conducts developmental evaluations that are rigorous, data-based, and empirically driven, although there are no set methods, tools, techniques, steps, recipes, formulas, or standardized procedures to follow. Assessments rely on rapid feedback, real-time evaluation, ongoing environmental scanning, outcome monitoring, and reflective practice.[102]

Thus, the developmental evaluator's role shifts from external bystander to active partner in the change process. Evaluations are deemed successful to the extent that they "are useful, practical, ethical and accurate," with the understanding that all evaluations emerge "from the special characteristics and conditions of a particular situation—a mixture of people, politics, history, context, resources, constraints, values, needs, interests, and chance."[103] As Mark Cabaj, an experienced developmental evaluator summarizes, DE is not for everyone or for all situations:

> *Developmental evaluation is situational, responsive, and emergent.* If you crave evaluation templates, formulas, and frameworks, you will be frustrated with developmental evaluation. Developmental evaluation work is unavoidably situational, focused on asking the right questions at the right time, developing practical evaluative methods that take into account who

needs what information, when, and for what purpose. Moreover, given the emergent nature of most developmental situations, with changing contexts, new players, and new learnings, the questions and evaluative processes are apt to evolve as well. I suspect that people who are comfortable with modern jazz are more likely to feel comfortable with this reality than those who prefer meticulously interpreted and orchestrated sounds of a symphony by Mozart.[104]

The Case of Samboja Lestari

To appreciate the evaluation challenges of regenerative design and how to address them, I turn to a case in Borneo. I have summarized this complicated case as much as possible, but the details are important. They offer insights and explanations why this design project, dismissed by some as "unsuccessful" and a "failure," actually offers important insights and learnings about which aspects of the design intervention worked, which were less successful, and why. The case also demonstrates what happens when developmental evaluators do not work with designers and innovators in the design process, not only to give ideas a fair hearing but also to capture the important lessons learned and adaptations needed for the next generation of design interventions.

The story begins with mechanical logging and slash-and-burn techniques that have denuded Borneo's forests, reducing them by 50 percent today, down from 75 percent in the mid-1980s.[105] These forests sit on top of peat bogs, waterlogged ecosystems often more than twenty meters deep, storing massive amounts of carbon. When the soil dries out, disturbing the water table below it, organic matter quickly disintegrates or burns, emitting greenhouse gases. When combined with oxygen, the gases explode into ecological disasters during the dry season.[106] They spew noxious gases, including carbon dioxide (CO_2), methane, and fine particulate matter, that not only warm the climate, but also close schools and businesses, cancel, divert, or delay air travel, and result in very serious negative health effects linked to respiratory disease, heart problems, and premature deaths.[107] An Air Quality Index reading above 100 is classified as unhealthy and anything above 300–500 is hazardous. The fires in September 2019 generated haze that sent the Air Quality Index to 2,000 in the capital of Kalimantan. The Pollutant Standards Index (measured in terms of the concetration of sulfur dioxide, particulate matter, fine particulate matter, nitrogen dioxide, carbon monoxide, and ozone) is unhealthy at 101–200. It reached a very unhealthy level of 208 in several Malaysian districts and 100 (moderate) in Singapore, where previous fires and haze in 2015 had sent the index to 341. The haze even spread to south of Thailand and the Philippines, causing significant deterioration of air quality in those areas as well.[108] And the fires of 2019 weren't as bad as the 2015 fires, which had caused an estimated sixteen billion dollars in economic losses, produced haze that sickened half a million people, and emitted emissions in just six weeks that catapulted Indonesia, a country with little industry, from the sixth-largest CO_2 emitter in the world to the fourth-largest.[109]

Dr. Willie Smits,[110] a Dutch-born forester and an Indonesian citizen, wanted to break the cycle of fires that were destroying the forests and the life within them. His vision entailed giving impoverished people from the surrounding communities an alternative to poaching from the forest, clearing their land with slash-and-burn techniques, cultivating destructive palm trees to supplement their income, or selling their land to companies that would raze the forests to create monoculture palm tree plantations to meet the international market's demand for products with palm oil as their main ingredient. So on February 6, 2009, in Long Beach, California, Smits presented a twenty-minute TED talk employing dramatic slides and vignettes, detailing how he had transformed barren land located about thirty-eight kilometers from Balikpapan in East Kalimantan on the island of Borneo, Indonesia. Securing the rights to the land and following good forestry practices, he and a team of 100 local workers turned approximately 5,000 acres of infertile land, savaged by clear cutting, drought, and life-choking alang-alang grass, into a second-growth biodiverse tropical rain forest that integrates agroforestry into a closed-canopy forest ecosystem. The regenerated land, Samboja Lestari, whose name, roughly translated, means "everlasting forest" in Indonesian,[111] also serves as a refuge for the critically endangered orangutans driven from their homes by deforestation and illegal smuggling. Not only is it now a safe place to nurse abused and sick orangutans back to health, it is a forest school that teaches orangutans raised in captivity how to be orangutans. If they can learn how to climb, build nests, and forage and feed themselves, graduates from the six stages of the school are then reintroduced into the remaining first-growth forests in Kalimantan.[112] To accomplish these seemingly impossible tasks, Smits added two other goals—he designed economic and social systems to support the people who would live and work in Samboja Lestari. The plan called for protecting people by offering them training, jobs, and homes so that they could protect the forest, which in turn would protect the orangutans.

The design of Samboja Lestari located the orangutans in the center of the forest, along with a gene bank reforestation area and an ecolodge where visitors could stay. A thicket of thorny palms was planned to separate the center from a 100-meter-wide belt of sugar palms growing around the perimeter of the forest, which would serve as a barrier protecting against fires. A total of 648 families, supplied with water and electricity from Samboja Lestari, would live on small plots of land within this exterior belt, close to access roads. Not only would they have a place to build homes using reforested, fast-growing acacia trees, they also could plant vegetables both for themselves and to sell to others. In addition, they would get training and jobs to regenerate the forest, fight fires, and care for the animals, and their children would be educated in a community-supported school. On their allocated land, workers would earn income by tapping the valuable sugar palm trees, the products of which have economic and ecological advantages over the destructive oil palm trees, which grow only in monocultures.[113] Thirty-three groups, each with twenty families, would have the responsibility of monitoring what was going on and taking appropriate action should anyone violate agreements, similar to the arrangements that Smits supported with the Tomohon democratic cooperative of 6,285 people with whom he worked in North Sulawesi.

The Tomohon cooperative is self-governing and distributes the profits that the collective derived from processing juice and wood products from sugar palms. The juice from the sugar palm trees, tapped twice a day, is harvested and processed in Smits-designed "village hub" factories situated on the outskirts of forests.[114] These mini-factories are smaller versions of the regional hub at the Tomohon factory that Smits designed and built in North Sulawesi in collaboration with the SPIE Engineering Group[115] and sponsored by the Masarang Foundation.[116] The factories, big and small, demonstrated the economic benefits of processing products from sugar palm trees that can grow in a biodiverse forest (e.g., premium organic sugar, low-grade ethanol, wood crafts, and other products) using a low-carbon method.

Taken together, Smits's vision for Samboja Lestari and his factory innovations in Tomohon and elsewhere offered powerful economic incentives to build trust and increase people's quality of life. Most strikingly, thanks to satellite monitoring, Smits demonstrated that the regenerated forest produced increasing cloud cover and changes in the microclimate that turned Samboja Lestari into a "rain machine." The increased rainfall not only benefited Samboja Lestari, but the water supply project offered a supply of fresh water to the city of Balikpapan, which has a serious problem of seawater intrusion.

After the talk posted online, congratulations and comments poured in from hundreds of viewers worldwide, but so did some challenges and criticisms. Some people who had been to Samboja Lestari, or had contacted the Borneo Orangutan Survival (BOS) Foundation that Smits founded, reported that there was no ring of sugar palms. The handful of sugar palms that did exist were not being tapped, so they were unable to deliver promised economic, social, and environmental benefits. Questions also arose about the number of animal species in Samboja Lestari and the forest's rainmaking capabilities. As a result, TED directors invited the critics to point them to a scientist who would provide them with a written critique. The letter from Dr. Erik Meijaard, a forest conservation scientist in Indonesia since 1992, and Smits's response to Meijaard's comments are posted online.[117]

The discrepancies between Smits and his critics' comments were a puzzle. Smits has a distinguished biography with extensive expertise in forestry, animal conservation and activism, and innovations in economic and community development, all of which have been acknowledged with national and international awards. In 1999, the Indonesian government awarded Smits its highest Indonesian conservation medal of merit, making him the first non-Indonesian to receive the Satya Lencana Pembangunan Award. In 2009, Smits was elected to the Ashoka Fellowship. And in 2010, he was awarded the equivalent of knighthood from the Netherlands for his conservation work. Something didn't make sense. I wanted to know more, so I decided to conduct my own post-hoc evaluation and headed off to Borneo in August 2012. Here is what I found:

- Samboja Lestari, a regenerated second-growth forest, did indeed exist. I stayed in the beautifully designed ecolodge, where guides escorted me through the forest, the arboretum, the sun bear enclave, and to a position where I could view the islands where older orangutans are kept and younger ones played, and clinics where ill and abused animals are treated and nursed back to life.

- The orangutans and the sun bears were well fed and cared for, although due to funding difficulties and licensing agreements, the orangutans that had graduated from the forest schools had long waits before they could be transported to the first-growth forests in Central Kalimantan.

- I counted five sugar palms in the forest, none of which were being tapped. I was told that some sugar palms were planted in the perimeter as an experiment, but they were limited in number and no family plots existed among the sugar palms.

- I visited the administration building and asked to see data about planting, timber, and water generation, but was told that the database was being updated and researchers were needed to help with assessments. The person who had been in charge of collecting climate data had recently left for Ramadan celebrations.

- I visited village businesses on the outskirts of Samboja Lestari that produced and sold food—including tempeh, soya, soya milk, tofu, and fruit—for the animals.

- I explored an abandoned mine next to Samboja Lestari and saw the environmental damage that it had created. All the topsoil was gone from the once-dense forest, none of the land had been reclaimed, areas of the mine were still smoldering, and water pooled in small, polluted lakes. My guide also took me to some of the homes that had flooded in the rainy season as a result of the mine's runoff.

As I reviewed my interview notes with Samboja Lestari's program manager and my guides and other staff, and checked my personal observations and online searches, I surfaced an alternative explanation for the discrepancies between Smits's TED talk and what I found at Samboja Lestari. Among his many responsibilities, Smits was also the director of the Gibbon Foundation. Its benefactor, who had funded the animal rescue and rehabilitation centers like Samboja Lestari, died in 2006. By 2008, the foundation's funding had dried up and the animal rescue and reintroduction centers could no longer be subsidized. The government of Indonesia then announced an early termination of cooperation with the Gibbon Foundation in the development and management of animal protection centers in Indonesia, and the animal rescue center network collapsed. During this financial crisis, Smits was out of the country doing presentations to attract funding for the BOS Foundation, generate investments for sugar palm factory development, and market his book *Thinkers of the Jungle: The Orangutan Report*, published in 2007.

In response to the crisis, the BOS Foundation decided to terminate the sugar palm venture when it became clear that it was not achieving its intended result and was costing funds that were needed to feed the orangutans. As Smits commented in his response to Meijaard and the TED community, there was a "takeover where all the operational management and many of the people were replaced, planting was virtually stopped by the new decision makers." But sugar palm planting also stopped for another reason, as I learned from the Samboja Lestari staff. Processing sugar palms juice was a very successful venture when Smits worked with the Christian community in Tomohon, North Sulawesi. That community had no problems with one of the sugar palm's by-products—alcohol. But in East Kalimantan, where Samboja Lestari is located, "Muslims didn't want to touch the sugar palms due to the alcohol that could be produced from them. More community development and lots more talking were needed to get them to accept the sugar palms. So what else could he do?" asked one interviewee.

What Smits did do was continue working as a member of the BOS foundation to obtain permits enabling him to manage large tracks of land in which to relocate orang-utans in East and Central Kalimantan. His long-term vision—to use sugar palms in preventing forest fires, preserving the biodiversity of the forest (sugar palms only grow in diverse forests), and supporting the local community by using the substantial financial proceeds from sugar palms to improve their well-being—was no longer part of Samboja Lestari's ambitious plan for the future. If developmental evaluators had been involved with Smits and Samboja Lestari, would they have made a difference in the outcome? It's impossible to say, but here are a few of the activities in which they might have been helpful:

- Utilizing their "people skills," they could have served as a coach early on, to facilitate community engagements to identify and appreciate the unique features of the social context, especially the beliefs of the Muslim population and how they might affect Samboja Lestari's developmental plans.

- Having identified community concerns, they could have worked with Smits and the community to find ways to adapt sugar palm processing technology to address community concerns about alcohol.

- If adaptations weren't technically feasible and reliance on sugar palms were not a viable economic strategy to sustain Samboja Lestari for the long term, they could have invited the community and stakeholders to search for other long-term alternatives to make Samboja Lestari economically sustainable, making it clear that without such alternatives, the project would not be able to fund future training, jobs, housing, and community development.

- Utilizing their evaluation skills, they could have assisted Smits in collecting and analyzing the tremendous amount of data generated about climate change, community development, and "recipes" used to prepare the soil and decide what could be planted where, depending on the microclimate and soil fertility.

- They could have assisted Smits, an extremely busy and successful entrepreneur and innovator, in posting online written reports and publishing scientific articles in peer-reviewed journals to substantiate Samboja Lestari's contributions and its approach to development.

- They could have written articles for general audiences describing Samboja Lestari's innovative design interventions, its results, lessons learned, and implications for design practice.

- They could have helped Smits prepare his presentations for international audiences, giving him credit for all that he accomplished, and at the same time linking his vision and plans for Samboja Lestari with the actual results as they were evolving on the ground.

The irony of Smits's TED talk is that he did follow the "people, profit, planet" principles that he described. But his design interventions did not occur in one place. They were located in two different Indonesian provinces, separated by about 1,317 kilometers and an approximate thirty-nine hours of transit by car and ferry over the

Makassar Strait. In Tomohon, North Sulawesi, his sugar palm village hubs and factory indeed generate economic benefits, raise the standard of living, promote democratic self-governance, equally distribute the cooperative's profits, and limit opportunities for corruption. And in Samboja Lestari, East Kalimantan, his designs were successful in regenerating a second-growth rain forest, protecting endangered species, and serving a rehabilitation center until orangutans could be transported for release into Central and East Kalimantan's first-growth rain forests. But his presentation gave people the impression that everything actually had occurred in Samboja Lestari when it had not. The integrated system that he envisioned did not exist in the Samboja Lestari community.[118] Instead of establishing Samboja Lestari as a self-sufficient, sustainable, and regenerated forest upholding the principle "people, profit, planet," it continues to be, according to a staff member, an "international beggar" reliant on funding from generous worldwide donors. And, at least in the short run, the challenges to his credibility distracted people's attention from the innovative and important contributions that Smits has made and continues to make as a designer and innovator in agroforestry, animal conservation, and economic and social development.

In Summary

There are explanations that I believe are a likely source of many design criticisms. Two are particularly noteworthy. First, I find that the diverse opinions and views about design and design thinking exist because there is "an inherent, continuous and critical question of what design is and could be"[119] which, as noted in this chapter, is characteristic of newly forming disciplines. Moreover, design educators admit that design education is not keeping up "with the new demands of the 21st century."[120] Much like the Flexner Report of 1910, which led to the restructuring of medical education, and the Ford and the Carnegie Foundation reports in 1959, which led to the restructuring of business education, design leaders are undertaking efforts to make design education more professional as an academic discipline, with a common core that all designers will share in addition to specializations and subdisciplines that differentiate them (e.g., graphic designers or industrial designers).[121] Their goal is to develop a framework to assist international educators in the redesign of design education at all levels,[122] a topic that I return to in the conclusion of this book.

Second, I find that the success rate—whether a type of design addresses the design challenge to the satisfaction of the designers, sponsors, and stakeholders—depends on the research methodologies used and the extent to which the research focus is on the design process, its results, or its outcomes. In my view, some of the so-called failures found in strategic design assessments are due to the limitations of summative and formative evaluations that are ill suited to capturing the complexities and dynamics of design interventions in wicked problem territory. Formative evaluations focus on ways to improve and enhance innovative ideas and programs, eventually getting them stabilized, standardized, and ready for summative evaluations. Summative evaluations then assess the overall effectiveness, merit, worth, and significance of a program for the purpose of informing decisions about the continuation or termination of experimental programs, projects, policies, and other actions.[123]

A fairer appraisal of the design strategy in wicked problem territory awaits evaluators who can capture its complexity and dynamism. Traditional formative and summative evaluations require up-front, preordinate specificity that is not a good match for conditions of high uncertainty, exploration, rapid change, and innovation. In fact, premature specificity constrains exploration, limits adaptation, reduces experimental options, and forces premature adoption of well-specified models. Design interventions in wicked problem territory also are complicated, with many moving parts, and complex, with multiple interdependent variables that often interact in iterative and nonlinear feedback loops, as illustrated in the Samboja Lestari case. Taken together, these factors can produce emergent and often unpredictable results and rapid changes, where the past does not necessarily predict the future and small changes can have large and unanticipated effects.

Under these conditions, it can be difficult to predict outcomes and untangle what causes what.[124] Designers in wicked problem territory simply do not have enough control over all the factors and people to deliver outcomes in the same way as evaluators of stable programs can. Neither do they have a proven path to achieve their vision. They may know where they want to end up, as Smits did, but they lack a predetermined path to get there or a timetable that specifies how long will take them to arrive. They live with uncertainty and the knowledge that plans will shift as circumstances change, constantly learning and adapting as the design process evolves.[125]

Accordingly, when design interventions are undertaken, the key question is whether we have an evaluation approach that matches design's growing levels of complexity and the increasing volatility, uncertainty, and ambiguity in the environment. I suggest that the vaguely coherent results accumulated thus far in evaluating strategic designs are due less to *what* we are evaluating than *how* we are evaluating. Finding the traditional formative and summative evaluations limiting, I therefore recommend Patton's developmental evaluation theory for the strategic design of organizations, the systemic design of social systems, and the regenerative design of social and ecological systems. Its virtues include not only being highly attuned to what is being designed, but how it is being designed, what learning is captured along the way, and what adaptions are necessary to improve the success rate of design interventions. The case of Samboja Lestari illustrates the unfortunate results that can happen when developmental evaluation is not part of the evaluation process. And for global change interventions that work toward a sustainable future across national boundaries, sectors, and issues, Patton's *Blue Marble Evaluation* offers the next generation of evaluation.[126]

But there is more to the issue of assessing design in wicked problem territory. The question is not just about the effectiveness of the design strategy, but also to what extent it offers more advantages than other problem-solving strategies. This issue guides our final assessment in chapter 10.

10 Design Strategy: Overall Assessment

There is hyperbole in the list of criticisms about design that are summarized in chapter 9. Design is not dying or dead, and neither is it a failure. Parts II and III of this book more than amply demonstrate its contributions and staying power, and so does the substantive research accumulated thus far. "Design is becoming a real force in the world,"[1] according to Dorst, and its field of operation is "radically expanding" and increasing its scope and range. Not only do design-trained people have access to a broad range of professions, they are wielding broader influence in senior positions in management, government, and academia, all of which are "a testament to the quality of design practices and the relevance of design education in contemporary society."[2] Highly successful people also have moved beyond traditional design disciplines to address societal problems. And de facto designers[3] and citizen-designers who haven't been trained as traditional designers are applying their design knowledge, skills, and competencies to wide-ranging sets of problems, as the cases in part III demonstrate. Yet according to Dorst, this expansion of design is not without its contradictions and tensions, as was evident in chapter 9. Designers' objectives and motivations "can range from the financial to the social"—"commercial success versus common good"; designers can be autonomous creators or serve a client—"creation versus problem solving"; designers' drive can be idealistic or down to earth—"utopianism versus pragmatics"; designers' results can be a "thing," a service, an experience, and even learning—"materiality versus immateriality of outcome"; and the design process can be based on intuition or knowledge and research—"art school versus academic design."[4]

But there are other issues, especially with strategic, systemic and regenerative design. Such designs can be expensive and time consuming, require leadership, a vision, a long time frame, and a great deal of patience, commitment, and resources in order to stay the course. They also necessitate expertise in developmental and blue sky evaluations, which, although expanding both nationally and internationally, are not as yet widely employed in field settings. And without investments of time, resources, and talent, designs can and do fail, or as Buckminster Fuller reportedly put it, "come up with unexpected results," to which I would add that results and learning that are not necessarily appreciated by sponsors and funders, which can be driven by efficiency and bottom-line concerns.

Strategic, systemic, and generative design also depend on expertise in change management, which many designers do not have. Questions arise in launching a design project—what is the designer's role, especially given the increasing number of people who participate in them? If goals and problems launch a design challenge, they likely will be changed and reframed. Whoever makes those changes invites questions of accountability—should changes be made by the sponsors, the designers, or the many stakeholders who participate or are affected by them? And how should designers incorporate the multiple perspectives into the design process? We also know that design interventions risk failure if they are localized in separate units and leaders fail to undertake them as part of a comprehensive change program linked to strategic management and cultural change.[5] And when leadership changes occur that prompt a shift in priorities, designers have to be ready to adapt and shift their design interventions accordingly, as Willie Smits demonstrated in Samboja Lestari and Tomohon in chapter 9.

We also need to acknowledge that the design strategy, in whatever venue it is practiced, is not value neutral. All change initiatives are value-driven.[6] The question is: whose values will inform the change process? Design depends on designers' ethical codes and moral reasoning, but they are not always acknowledged, understood, or even appreciated by the designers themselves. "Designers materialize morality,"[7] as Verbeek reminds us, whether they are technology-centered, business-centered, human-centered, earth-centered, or some combination thereof. Smits offers a case in point in his Samboja Lestari vision to support "people, profits, and planet." We know that values and political views inform choices that designers make and results they produce. They also inform what evaluators and stakeholders determine to be "good" and innovative designs. And we should not be surprised, given the land mines and level of conflicts about problems and their solutions in wicked problem territory, that the design strategy requires knowledge about power and politics, particularly[8] the differences between power with people and power over others. Recognizing when and how power and politics are activated and what responses are warranted is a major factor in delivering successful outcomes, but unfortunately this knowledge and sensitivity is not taught in design schools; instead, it is learned in the school of hard knocks as designers attempt to change reality from what is to what they hope it can be.[9]

Claims that design delivers innovation also can be challenged to the extent that design doesn't move beyond thinking and doing in design labs.[10] Innovation requires more than in situ prototyping and testing. Designers need to be engaged in field settings where additional prototyping and testing occurs, herein described as the implementation phase of the design process. While design generates creative ideas and tested prototypes, unless ideas survive field tests to become accepted practice, they will not achieve their intended result—innovation. And then there are the first-, second-, and third-order consequences of innovation that often cannot be anticipated. Who assumes responsibility for these, especially when downstream issues of social inequity and environmental destruction arise?

And last but certainly not least, attendance in design thinking crash courses and introductory boot camps does not a designer make. These are important entry points to begin learning about design and design thinking, especially for those who have been educated in other disciplines and practices. People have to start somewhere, and these opportunities may be the only vehicle that they have, since most are unlikely to pursue additional education in design programs. But in their enthusiasm for design, instructors can leave people with unrealistic expectations of what they can accomplish. Rarely are cautions raised about the investment of time, knowledge, and experience required to be a good designer, never mind an expert one. People certainly can celebrate their first design steps, which can and do make valuable contributions to learning and practice. But in all fairness to the rich design tradition, people also need to understand that there are many more rungs on the ladder of design expertise than what a few days or weeks of training can allow them to access. And as to whether the design strategy should inform educational practice, I answer with an unqualified "yes," although when, how, and in what manner this happens are ongoing questions over which educators will continue to deliberate. Personally, given what confronts us in the twenty-first century, I believe that educators are remiss if they do not provide students with design's age-appropriate problem-solving capabilities in order to assist them in forging a future for the world that they will inherit.

The good news is that there appears to be a growing consensus on the fundamentals of design thinking that one could teach in these educational programs. Despite the complaints, "fundamental attributes of design thinking have been consistently noted in the design research literature. This indicates that whilst interpretations of design thinking may vary, the design community is not as inconsistent as many believe."[11] Moreover, we find that "most definitions present design thinking as a mindset, method, process, attitude or a combination of all four."[12] And this consistency within the foundational attributes of design thinking "allows people to use, adapt, and apply design thinking to different disciplines, outside of traditional design practice."[13] Ultimately, "an examination of both theoretical work and actual management practice reveals a process that is both internally consistent and coherent and that constitutes a distinctive practice."[14]

Even those who criticize aspects of "designerly thinking" acknowledge its benefits. Pieter Vermaas and Udo Pesch, for example, believe that "designerly thinking is an effective and viable approach to addressing social problems."[15] However, they acknowledge that further developments in designerly thinking are warranted. They challenge the unconditional acceptance of designerly thinking as the way to resolve wicked societal problems, since designerly thinking is unable to determine goals that all social groups can endorse [although it is not clear why all social groups must endorse the goals]. They recommend the reassignment and oversight of design consequences to designers, the development of responsible practices within design teams, and the acknowledgment of potential negative consequences for products designed [although what the responsible practices would be and how designers would anticipate the first-, second-, or third-order effects of theses designs are not explored]. They seek designers' acceptance that they will not "always arrive at a fair distribution of a design's potential consequences," and therefore, they should be ready to listen and learn when challenged about issues of social equity [although it is not clear how this discussion would occur, who would be involved in it, and how conflicts would be resolved]. Finally, they endorse designers' involvement in the back end of design, where downstream consequences of design surface [although there is no indication what length of time would be reasonable, given the long-term requirements of many major social change efforts and who would absorb the expenses that long-term developmental evaluations would likely require].

In a different vein, Kipum Lee seeks to set design thinking models "free from entrapments of the making paradigm that keeps design on the fringes."[16] He continues, "Design thinking left to its own devices, can, paradoxically and unwittingly, 'go native' and become swallowed up by the mangerialist and materialist establishment it seeks to change," and therefore be "silent with regard to the inegalitarian landscape of the organizational terrain."[17] Beyond the world of making, production, and the technical artifact "lies the world of the social," where designers become, in the words of Dieter Rams, "critics of civilization, technology, and society" and, in Lee's words, "builders of enabling, life-giving institutions."[18]

Design Strategy's Comparative Advantage

By far, the most important comparison is not between designers who work in design labs, use specialized language, seek to retain expertise in insular communities, and designers who invite more participation and expansion of design's reach into organizations, communities, and complex systems. The real test of design strategy is how it stands up against the other well-known problem-solving strategies in wicked problem territory. I believe that it offers at least six major advantages: the exploration of and reliance on feedback and learning; the social technology embedded in design thinking which helps designers break free from biases and behavioral norms that block imagination, impede creativity, and hinder innovation; the reliance on paradoxical and dialectical thinking in response to tensions and conflicts; the acceptance of ethical codes that guide designers' moral reasoning and choices; the ability to go to scale by integrating multiple levels of design; and the integration of key elements from other problem-solving strategies into the design strategy.

Design Strategy's Reliance on Exploration and Learning

Nothing in the design strategy can be taken as a given—not the design challenge, the problem, the context, the solutions, or the results. For nondesigners, the open-endedness of design can be anxiety producing. But for designers and aspiring designers, they are energized by the freedom to be curious, original, imaginative, and resourceful problem solvers. As Kolb reminds us, design is a "process whereby knowledge is created through the transformation of experience,"[19] particularly in unfamiliar terrain that has no finite boundaries, answers, or solutions. Explorations[20] and learning[21] begin immediately in an attempt to make sense of the design challenge and to understand the unique context in which designers work. They are evident in the struggles to zoom in and out of the problem space to frame and reframe the issues. They surface in the interactive juxtaposition of problems and creative ideas as potential solutions. They appear in the tussles over which criteria will be used to select ideas for prototyping. They are present when giving form and shape to ideas and manifesting them as prototypes. And they are apparent as designers, learning from feedback what works and what doesn't, make successive adjustments and adaptations and decide whether prototypes can be field-tested, implemented, and ultimately established in practice as an innovation.

Thus, the design strategy, equipping designers with design principles, processes, mindsets, skill sets, and toolkits, does the following:

- Offers a practical approach to problem solving that employs simple, basic language that everyone can use
- Encourages people to be flexible, agile, and resilient problem solvers who engage emotionally, analytically, and physically as explorers and learners in the design process
- Invites active cross-functional, cross-organizational, cross-sectoral, and cross-disciplinary cocreation with a broad representation of users, customers, and stakeholders
- Taps people's desire to be catalysts for positive change in the world by offering a safe space to hold dialogues in which to explore and learn about future possibilities and envision what could be
- Provides people with the perspective, skill sets, and toolkits to manage conflicts and design integrated systems that form a new whole

Design Strategy's Social Technology

Embedded in the design strategy is the social technology of design thinking, a process geared to helping people overcome their cognitive biases and break free from behavioral norms that block imagination, creativity, and innovation. Jeanne Liedtka summarizes its major features as follows:[22]

- Working without specific guidance on how to change habits and behaviors to innovate, people can wonder off track and focus more on "preventing errors than seizing opportunities" and "opt for inaction rather than action when a choice risks failure."[23] Having a structured design thinking process can offer psychological safety and a sense of security as people move through the activities in discovery, problem framing, ideation, and prototyping and testing.

- Collecting massive amounts of data and makings sense of it can be overwhelming, but design thinking's collaborative data reduction techniques (data sharing, combining, and sorting) build a common database that facilitates interactions, the sharing of insights, and the generation of different data interpretations.

- Collecting and analyzing market research offer general, impersonal data from which analysts make inferences about user needs, but deep immersion into the context to understand people can uncover hidden, unexpressed needs that people have.

- Framing problems in conventional ways can lead to incremental improvements, but asking challenging questions offers people the opportunity to break out of traditional patterns of behavior and decision making, view problems from a different perspective, take advantage of agile and iterative processes to try out concepts and ideas, and generate more original ideas and creative solutions.

- Including diverse voices and opposing views in the problem-solving process can lead to incoherence and deteriorate into divisive arguments, but a well-managed design thinking process can integrate opposing views and lead to improved solutions.

- Pursuing efficiency drives out variation and focusing on constraints imposed by the status quo can limit options, but design teams are better positioned to uncover new pathways and options for the future, open up possibilities and variation in a dynamic world, and reach consensus and alignment on design criteria.

- Having a portfolio of options and ideas can dilute focus and resources, but having many ideas makes it easier to let go of bad ideas and reduces the risk of launching new ideas.[24]

- Making choices among the competing ideas generated can be difficult due to unchallenged "behavioral biases" (e.g., overoptimism, confirmation bias, and first-solution fixation), but design thinking frames the discussion "as an inquiry into what would have to be true for an idea to be feasible" and vets the idea in terms of the necessary conditions to achieve success.

- Negotiating compromises when differences arise can lead to the lowest common denominator, but using design criteria to brainstorm, share and build on others' ideas opens up a greater range of new ideas.

- Regarding prototyping as "fine-tuning a product or service that has already largely been developed" runs the risk of being too far into the process to make needed corrections, but prototyping early opens up the potential for radical changes, or even complete redesigns.[25]

- Building high-resolution, high-fidelity prototypes takes time and resources on products and services that can fail, but building incomplete, low-resolution prototypes invites people to "pre-experience" or vividly imagine something novel that is low-cost, captures the prototypes essential features, yet is flexible enough to be easily altered in line with feedback.

- Waiting to the end to test the viability of a new idea, product, or service risks increased commitment to a failing course of action, but design thinking offers "learning in action" in real-world experiments throughout the process not only to identify what changes are needed to make ideas workable, but also to reduce people's normal fear of change.

Leigh Thompson and David Schonthal[26] provide additional reasons for design's comparative advantage, assuming that designers are attentive to "the social psychology of design thinking," which can enhance rather than degrade the creative process. Building on four design thinking tenets as described by Sara Beckman and Michael Barry,[27] they zero in on the social psychology of design:

- How *people observe and notice* by abandoning their cognitive lenses or preexisting scripts, inductively learning via inferences, finding patterns, and dealing with inattentional blindness and the illusion of transparency

- How *people frame and reframe problems* by focusing on attaining attractive goal states (promotion frames) and avoiding unattractive, negative outcomes; putting weight on certain traits while ignoring others; avoiding cognitive set effects that use one method of problem solving for all problems and instead employ analogical reasoning to find parallels between situations and problems that on the surface seem to be very different

- How *people imagine and design* by ideation and being attentive to group size, brainstorming, brainwriting, and speedstorming

- How *people make and experiment* by narrowing ideas, playing, and rapidly iterating and learning with a growth mindset rather than a fixed mindset, and by asking "how might we" questions to get beyond constraints

Design Strategy's Response to Tension and Contradiction

By definition, tension and contradiction are defining features of wicked problem territory—the result of high levels of conflict over problems and solutions. In this arena, responses can be a search for agreements reliant on trade-offs—give up one thing to get another, and thus be content with compromise, reconciliation, or some middle ground.[28] Alternatively, the search for agreement can lead to framing tensions as a dilemma, thus forcing a choice between two equally beneficial options.[29] The Samboja Lestari case in the previous chapter offers an example of this scenario. The goal of the project was to make sugar palms the economic foundation on which Samboja Lestari would build to ensure its long-term viability. However, the goal was in direct conflict with the Muslim community's beliefs that sugar palms led to the production of alcohol, and the use of alcohol in any form was in direct conflict with their values. As the tensions became more pronounced and were heightened by concerns over resources, they were eventually dissolved by replacing Samboja Lestari's leadership team and the principle of "people, profit, planet" with a new goal—a single focus on the support for and survival of endangered orangutans. It resulted in what some view as a third option in dealing with tensions—separate the two opposing views spatially or temporally.[30] In this instance, that is exactly what happened. Smits continues to serve as a board member of the BOS Foundation and supports Samboja Lestari and other centers whose goal it is to conserve the endangered Bornean orangutan and its habitat.[31] But Smits also had founded the Masarang Foundation,[32] where he continues his innovative work in agoforestry and sugar palm projects in Tomohon, North Sulawesi, as well as the Tengkawang sugar factory and the Biochar plant in West Kalimantan.[33]

Designers have and prefer other options when dealing with tension and contradiction. The first is the *paradox perspective*—the acknowledgment that "contradictory yet interrelated elements [can] exist simultaneously and persist over time."[34] So, for example, organizations face competing demands—the need for certainty and flexibility, stability and change, exploitation and exploration, and efficiency and flexibility.[35] The major challenge in dealing with paradox is how to accept the coexistence of contradictions, acknowledge their functional interdependencies, and differentiate, coordinate, and manage the contradictions. People surmount these difficulties by creating *synergy*—a means to differentiate and coordinate the two poles of a contradiction. Synergy takes many forms, but as a means to an end, it creates a sum that is greater than its parts. It encourages comfort with tension, acceptance of contradiction, and a willingness to break free from either-or thinking to search for new perspectives. The result of synergy is the combined effect of mutually advantageous practices and arrangements.[36]

In the case of the design strategy, intuition, imagination, and affect combine to offer one way of knowing and processing information and while reasoning, experimentation, and analysis offer another. But instead of dismissing one or the other way of knowing and information processing, designers are ambidextrous. They acknowledge and accept both as interdependent and simultaneously valid. The point is to understand the tension and contradiction that arise, accept their copresence, and establish practices in the design process that build a synergy that is mutually advantageous for both ways of knowing and information processing. Thus, architects learn to deal with the paradoxical tensions of form and function, product designers deal with functional performance and emotional satisfaction, interior architects deal with cost-efficiency and aesthetics, and social entrepreneurs deal with social and commercial logics.[37]

Designers have long recognized design's paradoxical nature. For instance, consider the following:

- Alain Fideli considered the essence of design to be paradoxical; "an attempt to eliminate one pole to the benefit of the other inevitably distorts its fundamental nature." The goal is "to transform this antagonism into a constructive dynamic."[38]

- Fred Collopy, in his article "Think with My Hands," offers a description of balancing *both* the analytical and intuitive aspects of designing.[39]

- Kees Dorst, in "Design Problems and Design Paradoxes," views a design problem "as a paradox, made up out of the clash of conflicting discourses." To resolve the paradox, designers need to construct a meta-discourse that transcends or connects discourses. From their understanding of the various discourses and a meta-discourse, designers create "a framework in which a solution is possible for the paradoxical situation." Thus, the "paradoxical problem situation works as both a trigger to creative imagination and as a context for the evaluation of the design. For the solution to *be* a solution, it needs to be recognized as such in the contexts of all the relevant discourses," which means "it should be acceptable to all the relevant stakeholders)."[40]

- Kathrina Dankl, in "The Paradox of Design Methods: Towards Alternative Functions," explores the toolboxes of social innovation, design thinking, and cocreation and recommends attending to their "communicative and aesthetic potential," not just their methodologies "for transferring project goals to stakeholders and the wider public."[41]

- Medhanie Gaim and Niles Wålin, in "Search of a Creative Space," map how design thinking—rooted in pragmatic philosophy and reliant on an integrative perspective based on both-and, best-of-both logics, an open mindset, and the design thinking process characterized by abduction and reframing—can assist organizations and their members to frame and cope with tensions and paradoxes as they search for future possibilities.[42]

- Paul Rodgers, Giovanni Innella, and Craig Bremner acknowledge some of the many paradoxes of design thinking: as a discipline, design is really undisciplined; the easier it becomes to design, the harder it is; and the claim that good design equals good business has impoverished design. They present a six-point manifesto to address and manage these paradoxes, including *lightness* in design to remove its weight; *intellectuality* in design for a more critical stance in design culture to reveal its contradictions, rock the boat, and continually contest the legitimization of power; concern for the *public domain* to reflect the kind of society in which we want to live; concern for *otherness* rather than privilege interests of the dominant economies; *visuality* to reestablish thinking in images, not just thinking in terms of numbers and text; and an interest in *design theory* to inform professional practice since all practices occur within a theoretical framework.[43]

Designers have a second way to deal with tension and contradiction between two elements—the *dialectical perspective*. According to Hargrave and Van de Ven, "Like the paradox perspective, the dialectical perspective is rooted in the premise that human understanding of reality is composed of logically and socially constructed contradictions—opposed yet interdependent elements which each presuppose each other for their existence and meaning." However, in dialectics, "the relationship of contradictory elements plays out through a process in which actors espousing one element, the affirmation, engage in conflict with actors promoting the opposed element, the negation. This conflict releases the tension between the contradictory elements and produces a new set of arrangements and practices, the transformation."[44]

Throughout the design literature, we also find designers attuned to the dialectics of design and design thinking:

- Gabriela Goldschmidt describes the dialectics of sketching as the "oscillation of arguments which brings about gradual transformation of images, ending when the designer judges that sufficient coherence has been achieved."[45]

- Jeanne Liedtka, in "In Defense of Strategy as Design,"[46] views design as dialectical, agreeing with Buchanan and Margolis that it is a mediation between divergent forces situated at "the intersection of constraint, contingency, and possibility."[47] Successful design remains ever mindful of the constraints imposed by the materials and situation at hand, as well as the changing and contingent preferences of the audience it serves. Simultaneously, however, it holds open the promise of the creation of new possibilities, which is available by challenging the status quo, reframing the problem, connecting the pieces, synthesizing the learning, and improvising as opportunities emerge.[48] Liedtka offers Frederick Law Olmsted and Calvert Vaux's design of New York's Central Park in the 1850s as an example. Instead of envisioning the park as a two-dimensional space, the designers won the competition for the assignment by envisioning it as a three-dimensional space that would allow carriages to transverse the park using the construction of buried roadways that were out of sight of those enjoying the park. She concludes that the tension created by the often-diverging pulls of necessity, uncertainty, and possibility define design's terrain: "It is a landscape where a mindset that embraces traditional dichotomies—art versus science, intuition versus analysis, the abstract versus the particular, ambiguity versus precision—finds little comfort."[49]

- Roger Martin describes innovative leaders who have the predisposition and the capacity to hold two diametrically opposing ideas in their heads. And then, instead of panicking and settling for one alternative or the other, they can produce a synthesis that is superior to either idea. "Integrative thinking" is his term for this process—or, more precisely, the discipline of consideration and synthesis—which he believes is the hallmark of exceptional leaders and the businesses they run.[50] And later, Martin finds the battle between analytical and creative thinking to be misguided. Both are necessary. As he summarizes, "the most successful businesses in the years to come will balance analytical mastery and intuitive originality in a dynamic interplay that I call *design thinking*."[51]

- Anne Tomes and Peter Armstrong, in "Dialectics of Design: How Ideas of 'Good Design' Change," demonstrate with three successive design movements—arts and crafts, art nouveau, and modernism—how each rejected the virtues of what was the prevailing idea of "good design" and moved toward its opposite. Thus, they consider good design to be an illusion. What appear to be fundamental principles are instead positions between relatively stable but opposed conceptions of design virtues. The framework that they propose creates a "dialectic in which a particular idea of a 'good design' both crystalizes the priorities of school or era and creates the discontents which will eventually undermine it."[52]

- Ian Gonsher, in "On Creative Dialectics," explores the progression of history "as a creative process, a creative dialectic. A proposition is made, then negated, differentiated and unmade, from which a new synthetic unity emerges. And it repeats again, over and over again. With each iteration the boundary conditions are set as opposing terms that afford and constrain possibilities."[53]

- Stephen Beckett uses a Hegelian dialectical approach to probe the logic of the design problem. He clarifies the method of dialogical logic, identifies the logical paradox at the heart of the design problem, and applies this logic to the design problem to demonstrate how problems and solutions simultaneously emerge as a single concept.[54]

- Richard Buchanan, in "Creativity and Principles in the Flourishing Enterprise," describes fourth-order design as the movement into environments, organizations, and systems. He refers to fourth-order design as "dialectical design," which elevates discussions and conversations that designers facilitate in an effort to surface the core ideas and principles that animate the work that people do and the values that they hold.[55]

- Cameron Tonkinwise, in "Prototyping Risks when Design Is Disappearing," describes designing as the process of future making with at least two aspects: "One is disruptively innovative; its seeks to break with how things currently are, open to the new. The other is more instrumentally pragmatic; it seeks to work out how current things might be transformed, what it is practicable to make." As "equal part fantasists and realists," designers "can imagine the most far-fetched things; but then they can also focus on questions of practicability, how to make those imagined things real. Designing should be a dialectic between . . . these two different kinds of possibility." And designers' tools and skills help them manage this dialectic and gives "the expertise of designing its distinctiveness."[56]

In summary, the paradox perspective in design focuses on how to accept the coexistence of tension and contradiction, acknowledge their functional interdependencies, and differentiate, coordinate, and manage the contradictions by creating a synergy among ongoing mutually advantageous practices and arrangements. In the dialectic perspective, the focus is on how tension and contradiction, embedded in practices and arrangements as well as in society's institutional orders, are transformed through mobilization and conflict between proponents of the affirmation and of the negation that produce a new affirmation, which begins the dialectical process anew.[57] Whether attempting to manage paradoxes or to transform them, designers are prepared with the design strategy's principles, process, mindsets, skill sets, and toolkits to address and deal with the following contradictory forces shaping wicked problem territory:

- Collective good and individual self-interests[58]
- Constraints, contingencies, and possibilities of design projects[59]
- People- and planet-centered designs[60]

- Concern for the whole system, as well as its parts[61]
- Demands for exploration, flexibility, and change, as well as the need for exploitation, stability, and control[62]
- Pursuit of bottom-up and top-down change[63]
- Evolutionary, incremental small wins and radical, revolutionary change[64]
- Radical innovation and incremental innovation[65]

Designers' Responses to Ethical and Moral Dilemmas

C. West Churchman first alerted us to the "moral principle" of problem solving when he warned that problem solvers, working on wicked problems at the knowledge frontier, have a different set of moral responsibilities compared to problem solvers who work on routine or tame problems. He took particular aim at those who would hive off and tame a relatively simple component of a wicked problem, "but not the whole" problem, calling them "morally wrong."[66] Mark Wexler expanded on Churchman's views in "Exploring the Moral Dimension of Wicked Problems" and compared tame problems and wicked ones on four moral issues: the *responsibility nexus*—tame problem solvers' *negligence* and violation of the norms of competence versus problem solvers' *raised expectations*, capitalizing on claims to make improvements on the knowledge frontier; the *risk of false assurance*—*low risk* in tame problems, with clear solutions versus *high risk*, with those that stress the new and improved methods and drop the risks; the *politics of urgency or criticality*, a *weak signal* that is organized around established funding with tame problems versus a *strong signal* when problem solution are not organized around established funding and must capture attention; and *confusion over wicked problem solutions* when problem solvers *distance themselves from unsolvable problems* or *abandon the idea that problems are unsolvable.*[67]

Beyond the moral implications of how problem solvers address tame versus wicked problems, we find wicked problem territory rife with ethical and moral dilemmas.[68] When facing the complexities, conflicts, and uncertainties, what values do designers uphold? Whose values do they uphold? Michael Hardt asks, "What guidelines do designers follow for themselves, towards others, towards nature and the environment, towards future generations?"[69] These questions are particularly relevant when "the world is becoming more and more a human artifact, a designed space."[70] Most everything that we encounter on a daily basis is part of the built environment. As S. D. Noam Cook explores in his essay "Design and Responsibility: The Interdependence of Natural, Artefactual, and Human Systems," "design entails crafting artifactual systems by imposing aims and values from human systems onto the raw materials of natural ones."[71] Life as we now experience it requires us not only to distinguish among the three systems (natural, artifactual, and human), but to recognize that life as we now live it depends on the stability of their interdependencies and "our ability to make the value judgments" to determine whether "a design is worth making and how best to realize it."[72]

Sitting at the interface of the natural, artefactual, and human, design can be viewed as "an act of world creation" and the designer as "the co-creator of a new world" who "is consciously or unconsciously midwifing" the world "into existence through her or his designed contribution."[73] If a designer is to take this calling seriously, there are many ethical and moral issues at stake:

> Do I have the right to cause such significant change in the world? What is the right approach to take when making such changes? What kind of changes are good, or just, and for whom? As a designer, am I fully responsible and accountable for my designs, and to whom? Can I be relieved of responsibility in some way? If not, how can I prepare for this responsibility and assume the liability of being fully accountable for my design judgments and actions?[74]

Thus, ethics and morality are fundamental to design practice. Designers are trained to solve problems and improve people's lives, but improving lives is not a value-neutral activity. Where one designer meets demands for the latest technological gadgetry, another complains about the "brainless mass consumption with the effect of an overconsumption of valuable resources," which requires "talented designers to seduce people to buy things they don't need with money they don't have to impress people they don't like."[75] And the results of all these design efforts have a tremendous impact on how people behave and live their lives. Ethics is "not an appendage to design but an integral part of it."[76] It "is an inherently ethical activity,"[77] and designers at every phase of the design process confront questions of ethics. Should I take on design challenges for certain people, groups, and organizations whose values and beliefs are inconsonant with mine, in the hope that I can influence or change them? Should I work for those whose values are in conflict with mine, but say nothing and just collect a paycheck? Or should I only work with those whose values and beliefs I share? Once I have accepted a design challenge, how should I interface with the sponsor—delegate responsibility and accountability to that entity to make the key decisions, make our responsibility and accountability joint, or hold myself solely responsible and accountable as a designer? When I gather data during the discovery phase, how comprehensive should I be, since I understand that there is no such thing as perfect knowledge about the design challenge?

Time and costs are just two factors that limit data collection. Not everyone can provide input, nor can all information can be gathered, processed, and interpreted. Judgments and choices have to be made about who should be consulted, what data need to be gathered, and how data should be analyzed, and especially how to factor multiple perspectives and points of view into very complex design projects. Each decision point along the way raises important issues—are certain groups or people or points of view excluded from data gathering, is that justified, and who should make that call?

Problems also can be framed in a number of ways. There is the potential for ethical and moral breaches when the designer directs attention to certain problems and redirects attention away from others. What is a designer's or an organization's particular position on contested topics in wicked problem territory, such as policing, abortion, and climate change? Ideation surfaces many new ideas, but which ideas will be selected and what criteria will be chosen to make that determination? Are environmental impacts and people's health and safety considered when assessing new ideas, or are the criteria limited to issues of costs and efficiency? Prototypes require materials, but some of these materials may be unsustainable, of lower quality, or unnecessary add-ons that raise the cost of the products or processes, waste resources, and damage the environment. Testing requires assessments of the prototypes, but when the tests are manipulated to serve particular interests, they open ethical and moral questions. And when the real-world consequences of designs produce unintended consequences that have detrimental effects on people, the society, and the environment, questions inevitably will be raised about whether the consequences were natural, accidental, or willfully evil.[78]

Natural evil is the result of the consequences of a change process that brings something new into the world and displaces or destroys something old. Because change is disruptive, some people will be unhappy, which often generates resistance or hostility. *Accidental evil* is the result of chance occurrences that happen due to the designer's "ignorance, carelessness, or inattention." Both natural and accidental consequences can be rectified or mitigated when designers become more aware and more knowledgeable about the consequences of their actions. In contrast, *intentional evil* produces "willful evil." In these instances, design uses people as a means to an end, destroys life, and wields "power without charity and agency without community."[79]

Designers generate natural consequences as part of the change process, and even accidental consequences occur because designers are imperfect in an unpredictable world. But of greatest concern are those who willfully and intentionally produce evil. Examples of this include the entrepreneurs and engineers who built gas ovens to kill millions of people, as documented by Eric Katz in *Death by Design: Science, Technology, and Engineering in Nazi Germany*,[80] and the technicians who "had to apologize to the Nazis for their gas chambers not being good enough—i.e., not killing their 'clients' quickly enough."[81] Design depends on having the right information and knowledge, but good design also depends on "good" designers as much as on the best information or know-how. So how does one become a "good" designer?

Designers can begin by familiarizing themselves with professional guidelines and ethical codes. For example, the Institute of Architects has developed its 2020 Code of Ethics and Professional Conduct, arranged in three tiers of statements. Canons "are broad principles of conduct," such as obligations to the public. Ethical standards "are more specific goals toward which Members should aspire in professional performance and behavior." Rules of conduct are mandatory; a violation of a rule is grounds for disciplinary action by the institute. [82] Some design labs issue their own codes of ethics, such as Mule Design of San Francisco,[83] and so do individual designers like David Berman, whose book *Do Good Design: How Designers Can Change the World* invites other designers to take the "do good" pledge intended to establish ethical activism within the designer.[84] There is even specific guidance about the particular phases of the design process, such as IDEO's *Little Book on Design Research Ethics*,[85] as well as particular skill sets and tools[86] that designers need to develop moral sensitivity (recognize the moral dimensions of their designs), moral creativity (explore the creative solutions to moral problems) and moral advocacy (communicate their ethical standpoint to stakeholders).

These steps are important, but are they enough to guarantee that designers will make the "right" decisions for the "right" reasons to produce "good" products and services with "good" outcomes for clients and other stakeholders in society? Herald Nelson and Erik Stolterman say no:

> As designers, we cannot depend on a source of wisdom outside of ourselves for guidance that will relieve us of our ultimate responsibility. Design decisions are based on judgment and judgment is both personal and situational. In the end, design is always an act of faith in our abilities and ourselves.[87]

Accepting this level of responsibility is unnerving for some designers, and they resort to various ways to escape or avoid accountability.[88] But "if you want to be a good designer there are no justifiable ways to move, hide, or remove responsibility for your actions."[89] Nor can you rely on any "'guarantor-of-design' 'out there',", say Nelson and Stolterman:

> Design is about creating a new reality, and there are no givens in that process. There are no theories, methods, techniques, or tools that can calculate, predict, or envision the truly best future reality. The true future does not exist as a predetermined, objective fact. As human beings, we have the capacity to create a different future—restricted only by our present reality and our imagination.[90]

So if there are no guarantors on which designers can rely, what is the alternative? Character counts, say Nelson and Stolterman:[91] "To be good designers, we must base our design actions and judgments on our own to develop core character."[92] But how does one develop a core character, or know one's core character, or learn to trust it? Drawing on others' work, Nelson and Stolterman offer these suggestions:[93]

- "Live the examined life." Be guided by your own thoughts and not someone else's.[94]
- Constantly examine design practice and thoughts through "reflection-in-action" (first-order reflection that centers on a judgment or action in the process of designing something) and "reflection-on action" (second-order reflection that focuses on design behavior and process as a whole).[95]
- Live in accordance with your calling, which from a design perspective means developing a design character in line with one's calling.[96]

Ben Sweeting takes a slightly different tack when searching for way to help designers navigate the tricky ethical and moral currents that they face. He agrees that "ethical considerations . . . are implicit within core aspects of design activity,"[97] and he concurs with Horst Rittel and Melvin Webber, who say that designers in wicked problem territory have "no right to be wrong," given the significant impact they have on others.[98] He also points out that designers "have no way to be right as design questions have no right answers or ultimate tests" which "leaves designers in a bind from which they cannot escape."[99] "Designers cannot work passively or objectively with wicked problems, as there are no right answers to be deduced, no overall goals to be optimized and the criteria against which proposals are to be measured are known only in part at the onset."[100] Moreover, quoting from Rittel and Webber, Sweeting agrees that "it becomes morally objectionable for the planner to treat a wicked problem as though it were a tame one, or to tame a wicked problem prematurely, or to refuse to recognize the inherent wickedness of social problems."[101] In ethics as well as design, conflicting premises and criteria make actions contestable. Thus, Sweeting finds design processes and their outcomes interwoven with ethical concerns as designers assume responsibility, consider options, and take actions for reasons of both design and ethics.

However, Sweeting does not rest on "normative ethical theories"[102] to give designers moral and ethical guidance. While they may "contribute in particular circumstances, the sorts of reasoning on which they rely . . . are unworkable with wicked problems, and may even be counter-productive."[103] "Consequentialist ethical theories involve the optimisation of our actions against a predefined overall goal. Yet, given that a wicked problem has no definitive formulation, there is no clear goal against which to optimize."[104] Deontological approaches to ethics require us to "conform to predefined rules." However, "the situation of a wicked problem is not fully known and is, in any case, transformed into a new one through designers' action with the result that, even if one had rules to follow, it is not clear which rules to apply."[105] Sweeting does acknowledge that virtue ethics as well as pragmatic or care ethics are more compatible with wicked problems, but "there still remains the issue that different approaches imply different responses and there is no way to resolve between them."[106]

What Sweeting does recommend is that we look to design to inform ethical problem solving. He suggests Caroline Whitbeck's *Ethics in Engineering Practice and Research* as one avenue in practical ethical reasoning.[107] It serves "as an example of the sort of practical problem solving that has been neglected in ethical theory."[108] Whitbeck believes that "people confronted with ethical problems must do more than simply evaluate alternatives; they must also come up with those alternative responses; they must figure out what to do and *devise* a plan of action."[109] Thus, ethical problems become practical problems, leading Whitbeck to find "similarities between ethical problems and a specific class of practical problems, design problems."[110] She then illustrates with a number of cases how a design approach can inform ethical problem solving in engineering.[111] Sweeting also recommends Kees Dorst and Lambèr Royakkers's article "The Design Analogy: A Model for Moral Problem Solving,"[112] a designer's guide to explore the analogy between design and ethics and solve moral problems in a manner closely modeled on the design method of problem solving.

Design's Ability to Go to Scale by Integrating Multiple Levels of Design

Some construe the microlevel design projects as a disadvantage, especially in dealing with large, complex, transdisciplinary, and transgovernmental issues such as climate change. How can hundreds and thousands of decentralized, uncoordinated design challenges at the local level be successful in dealing with issues of climate change?

The growing body of research and practice in transition design offers some important insights in answer to this question.[113] Designers can amplify and accelerate their design efforts either by going to scale horizontally and connecting similar experimental design efforts across the same level or going to scale vertically by building out and linking design efforts from local initiatives to the state, regional, national, and international levels.[114] As Mintrom and Luetjens demonstrated, policy entrepreneurs/designers in the C40 Cities Climate Leadership Group and the Carbon Disclosure Project were able to scale up both horizontally and vertically to develop policies and programs in response to the challenge of climate change.[115]

A justification for this bottom-up design approach can be found in Elinor Ostrom's work, which frames global warming as a collective action problem.[116] Ostrom begins by challenging the conventional collective action theory, which assumes that "no one will change behavior and reduce their energy use unless an external authority imposes enforceable rules that change the incentives faced by those involved."[117] The assumption is that rules are necessary because there will be free riders who take advantage of others' restraint in using shared resources or their contributions to collective action. Thus, "without externally imposed regulations at the scale of potential externalities, the theory predicts that the benefits that might be achieved through collective action are impossible to obtain."[118] However, Ostrom was quick to point out the multiple issues arising in the pursuit of this conventional theory of collective action. First, there is a lack of empirical support for the conventional theory of collective action related to natural resource problems.[119] There also is the issue of "waiting for a single worldwide 'solution' to emerge from global negotiations."[120] The wait is problematic due to the debate over who or what was responsible for the levels of carbon dioxide (CO_2) in the atmosphere and should bear the burden of paying for its solutions, as well as whether proposed remedies would actually work.[121] Moreover, "it is important that we recognize that devising policies related to complex environmental processes is a grand challenge and that reliance on one scale to solve these problems is naïve."[122] "All policies adopted at any scale can generate errors, but that without trial and error, learning cannot occur."[123] We also need to recognize that

> while many of the effects of climate change are global, the causes of climate change are the actions undertaken by individuals, families, firms and actors at a much smaller scale. The familiar slogan "Think Globally but Act Locally" hits right at a major dilemma facing all inhabitants of our globe. To solve climate change in the long run, the day-to-day activities of individuals, families, firms, communities, and governments at multiple levels—particularly in those in the developed world—will need to change substantially. Many of those who need to change, however, have not yet accepted the reality of the threat and their need to act locally in a different manner.[124]

Thus, Elinor Ostrom draws on the polycentric approach to "coping with climate change" and concludes that "an important lesson is that simply recommending a single governmental unit to solve global collective action problems—because of global impacts—needs to be seriously rethought and the important role of smaller-scale efforts recognized."[125] Mutual benefits can derive from diverse action at multiple scales, even at the household and community levels, where people begin to build commitment and learn to trust that others also are taking responsibility: "The advantage of a polycentric approach is that it encourages experimental efforts at multiple levels, as well as the development of methods for assessing the benefits and costs of particular strategies adopted in one type of ecosystem and comparing these with results obtained in other ecosystems." Thus, she maintains, finding ways to reduce emissions "can be more effectively undertaken in *small-to medium-scale* governance units that are linked through *information networks and monitoring* at all levels.[126]

Design Strategy Embeds Elements from Other Problem-Solving Strategies

Design strategy is unique among the other problem-solving strategies in its reliance on imagination and creativity, discovery, and learning to make manifest a world that could be. At the same time, it is not completely divorced from the other strategies. Often, without acknowledgment, or even awareness, it incorporates and embeds certain elements of competition, authority, reason, taming, and collaborative problem-solving strategies into its basic framework. But rather than working counter to the basic values or undercutting the design strategy's viability, these elements paradoxically are integrated in such a way that they increase its potential and power.

Steven Ney and Marco Verweij offer an explanation to understand this apparent paradox.[127] Drawing on Mary Douglas's cultural theory,[128] they identify four ideal types of organizing and decision making: individualism, hierarchy, egalitarianism, and fatalism. The individual model is based on competition and self-interest. People, adhering to different views on how to define and resolve problems, compete with others to demonstrate that their ideas are of higher quality and superior to others' ideas. The hierarchical model is based on authority and expertise. The authority decides who participates in deliberation, what is to be discussed, when and where meetings take place, and which solutions should be accepted. The egalitarian model invites open deliberation among all those affected by the final outcomes. People who participate are expected to listen to others in public fora, frame their arguments in terms of the public good and not private interests, eliminate differences of rank and power, and make decisions based on consensus. The fatalistic model resorts to chance. The argument is that solutions can't be planned; rather, they are stumbled upon. Similar to Charles Lindblom's theory, the best one can do is "muddle through" by limiting analysis and making small, incremental steps to see what happens.[129]

Each way of organizing has its drawbacks, and so, according to Ney and Verweij, any attempts to impose a single way of organizing are bound to fail. And even though these four ways appear to be in opposition, each needs the others to be sustainable. Indeed, "more sustainable and effective forms of governance tend to nimbly mix all four ways of organizing and thinking."[130] They refer to this mixing as "clumsy solutions"—those that emerge from decision making based on messy pluralism that combines all four ways of organizing. Most significantly, not only do they maintain that we need just this type of decision making to tackle our wicked problems, they identify design thinking as one example of "clumsy solutions."

So how does the design strategy incorporate elements of the other problem-solving strategies? In terms of competition, design teams participate in criterion-based design challenges to ascertain whose problem frames and solutions offer a better response to the design challenge. The Stanford Center on Longevity offers an example. It invited university students from around the world to compete in The Design Challenge 2020: Reducing the Inequity Gap.[131] The center acknowledged that there have been many product and service advancements, but "far too often they only reach the wealthiest people in a society." Noting the rising levels of inequity worldwide, the center challenged students to assist people of all ages in achieving long and healthy life outcomes, while at the same time significantly reducing design costs. Designs could range from targeting the health and well-being of young people, to monitoring heath and managing chronic disease, to encouraging higher levels of community engagement.

To participate, students were to create and submit a design before December 6, 2019, for a product, service, or program that addressed the challenge. The judges prescored each design on a scale from 1–10 in the following areas:

- *alignment with the topic* (this rating was used to weight the final score resulting from the other three); the potential for impact—would successful implementation of the design change the world for the better? If so, how much? (40 percent);
- *affordability for the target market*—teams must identify their target population for the design, as affordability means different things in different places (40 percent); and *feasibility*—would the design work? Could it be produced at scale? (20 percent).

Eight teams made a presentation at the finals. Then, on April 7, the judges awarded the first prize to the Shishu, Sui aur Dhaaga team from the Srishti Institute of Art, Design and Technology in India, which beat 159 other entries from thirty-five countries.[132] Its design was a bracelet that converts a common local cultural practice into an immunization tracker for infants. The School in the Sky team from Brigham Young University in Utah won second prize for its cloud-computing-based education system for very poor areas that links US students and retirees as mentors and teachers. And the First Desk team from the Beijing Institute of Technology won third prize for an extremely low-cost education station for rural youth and their grandparents.

Authority of position and expertise also informs the design strategy. In well-defined and centralized systems found in most organizations, authority establishes and approves the design challenges, generates resources to support them, establishes criteria to assess designs, and hires and oversees designers who answer the design challenge. Design authority also can be decentralized and delegated to others, even within organizations. As illustrated in the NORSOCOM Design Challenge described in chapter 6, external designers took the initiative, received approval from organizational leaders, consulted with authorities on an as-needed basis, and led a design team whose results were welcomed and accepted by the organization. And even when authority tends to be weak in organizations, designers can proceed from the bottom up rather than the top down, although, as evidenced in chapter 6, unsupported design initiatives in organizations tend to fail without authority's sponsorship. Bottom-up systemic and metadesigns in underorganized social and ecological systems tend to fare much better, especially when they depend on a hybrid process that combines the interactions of people at the community level supported by top-down interventions of institutions, civic organizations, and companies.[133] However, even these design initiatives can be compromised if authorities do not make clear the criteria by which design decisions are made, a point Natasha Iskander implies in her article entitled "Design Thinking Is Fundamentally Conservative and Preserves the Status Quo" described in chapter 9.[134]

Designers also borrow and adapt certain features of the rational-analytic model. For example, they gather data, although the process tends to be more informal, time-constrained, and less attentive to the documentation and sampling procedures required of scientific research. Designers also are more reliant on qualitative data drawn from observations and interviews, although some have begun to incorporate quantitative data collection and analytics into the discovery phase, such as systems thinking, social network analysis, and temporal analysis, as in the Civil Affairs project described in chapter 5.[135] Designers also go through a series of "what if" speculations about problems and their solutions, but their problem solving is much more fluid, dynamic, and emergent. Liedtka likens designers' virtual world of "if-then" thinking to two types of "hypothesis testing." Primary is the design hypothesis, which "is conjectural and, as such, cannot be tested directly." However, there are a series of assumptions embedded in the primary hypothesis about cause-effect relationships that can be identified and tested directly with a series of "what if"'and "if-then" questions. As Liedtka points out, "As successive loops of 'what if' and 'if then' questions are explored, the hypotheses become more sophisticated and the design unfolds.[136]

Willie Smits, whose project is discussed in the previous chapter, serves as an example. His conjectural hypothesis was that it is not only possible to regenerate rain forests, which experts said was impossible, but it should be done as an important way to counteract climate change. His conjecture, being a value judgment, could not be tested directly. Instead, he sought to support his idea by identifying and testing a set of cause-and-effect relationships needed to transform denuded land into a rain forest that would offer a safe haven for orangutans. Over many cycles of "what if" and "if-then" questions and answers, he developed various "recipes" of what could grow, where, and under what conditions given the variations in light, type of soil, specific nutrients, availability of water, type of terrain (steep or gentle), and the mix of other trees and plants in the area. His iterative hypothesis generation and testing eventually resulted in the creation of Samboja Lestari, a second-growth rain forest. And the increased rainfall in the previously denuded area lends support to his claim that regenerated forests could reduce some of the detrimental effects of climate change. So in this case, the virtual and the physical worlds actually did merge, at least in terms of forest regeneration.

Designers, as evidenced in the Reducing the Inequity Gap challenge, also specify criteria for assessing design results. However, the criteria tend to be very broad and general in order to invite a range of creative solutions. And unlike the rational model, the creative solutions generated do not pretend to represent the total range of potential solutions to address a problem or a particular goal, nor do designers know the consequences of their recommended design solutions. Both conditions are required to establish the optimality of a chosen design and to establish it as the best solution. The design strategy also calls for the evaluation of field-based implementation, as does the rational-analytic model of problem solving. However, as was argued in the previous chapter, the design strategy requires more sophisticated developmental evaluation capabilities to capture the environmental complexity, dynamism, and conflicts that surface when designers engage in strategic, systemic, and regenerative designs.

The design strategy thus draws on the taming strategy. It recognizes the critiques of the rational analytic approach to problem solving, especially under conditions of high conflict, complexity, and uncertainty. Most importantly, it reduces the stringent requirements of the rational-analytic approach by searching for "good" solutions rather than "optimal" ones in order to take some of the "bite" out of wicked problems."[137] The design strategy also finds affinity with Lindblom's version of incrementalism which he describes as "muddling through."[138] Lindblom criticized the rational, comprehensive model's unrealistic expectations of people's ability to make rational decisions, given their cognitive limitations in dealing with complex problems and their widespread value conflicts. So instead of pushing for major shifts or radical changes and attempting to deal with problems in a comprehensive way, he advocated "continually building out from the current situations, step-by-step and by small degrees."[139] Later, in 1979, he argued that "a fast-moving sequence of small changes can more speedily accomplish a drastic alteration of the *status quo* than can an only infrequent major policy change." As he noted, "incremental steps can be made quickly because they are only incremental. They do not rock the boat, do not stir up the great antagonisms and paralyzing schisms as do proposals for more drastic change."[140]

Others have built on Lindblom's insights. Karl Weick elaborated on his ideas of continuous and incremental change in his concept of "small wins" and applied it to the field of complex societal problems. A small win is "concrete, complete, implemented outcome of moderate importance." Although a small win may appear unimportant, "a series of wins at small but significant tasks . . . reveals a pattern that may *attract allies*, *deter opponents*, and *lower resistance* to subsequent proposals. Small wins are controllable opportunities that produce visible results."[141] In addition, small wins "provide information that facilitates learning and adaptation . . . miniature experiments that test implicit theories about resistance and opportunity and uncover both resources and barriers that were invisible before the situation was stirred up."[142] Weick also found psychological advantages of small wins in making problems "manageable, understandable, and controllable"; producing compliance; reducing stress; and building order into unpredictable, disordered, and fragmented environments.[143] Political advantages also accrue when because small wins are dispersed and "harder to find and attack than is one big win that is noticed by everyone who wants to win big." In small wins, "stakes are reduced, which encourages the losers to bear their loss without disrupting the social system."[144] And in their studies of continuous adaptation, learning, and improvisation in organizations, Karl Weick and Robert Quinn have found that small steps have the potential to generate transformational organizational change when they occur simultaneously and cumulate across units, or when small units become "pockets of innovation that may prove appropriate in future environments."[145]

Designers also find advantages in small wins. Elizabeth Gerber views prototyping through the lens of small wins. When designers engage in low-fidelity prototyping, they break tasks into modest-sized pieces, take frequent actions, attribute positive effects to self-action, reduce their anxiety of failure, and increase their sense of control—all of which enables them to remain committed to the design process despite the uncertainty of the outcomes.[146]

Catrien Termeer, Art Dewulf, and Robert Biesbroek[147] also rely on the small wins framework to overcome what they describe as the evaluation paradox in wicked problem territory—the attempt to assess policy solutions that according to Rittel and Webber have "no solutions."[148] To deal with this evaluation paradox, they recommend using the small-wins framework because small wins, located at the micro level, are of moderate importance and therefore are easier to address, have concrete outcomes, produce in-depth change (including changes in routines, beliefs, and values), and can generate positive judgments about a shared ambition. Small wins also can scale up using six mechanisms—"energizing, learning by doing, logic of attraction, bandwagon effect, coupling, and robustness."[149] These mechanisms not only give a boost to initial small changes, but together, through feedback loops, small changes can become larger, stronger, and more intense, which ultimately can accelerate, amplify, and escalate their consequences.

The design strategy also draws on aspects of the collaborative strategy. It relies on team collaboration in the search for a common purpose and invites cross-disciplinary, cross-functional, and cross-boundary stakeholder interactions. Although, as Gray carefully noted in her book *Collaborating: Finding Common Ground for Multiparty Problems*, even successful collaboration does not necessarily result in innovation, nor is it expected to: "Collaboration is a process through which parties who see different aspects of a problem constructively explore their differences and search for solutions that go beyond their own limited vision of what is possible."[150] Although the potential to discover innovative solutions is enhanced in collaboration, it is not expected, nor is it required, as demonstrated in the case of the Afghanistan stakeholder collaboration that I designed and facilitated.[151] However, I quickly should add that the knowledge, skills, and competencies of the collaboration strategy—dialogue, organizing, planning, and facilitating team interactions, along with managing change, conflicts, power and political dynamics—all are important skills that designers need in wicked problem territory. But based on the extensive design literature and my own experiences in both the public and private sectors, these collaborative skill sets, while necessary, are not sufficient. They require the added-value contribution of the designer to deliver creative and innovative designs in wicked problem territory.

In Summary

I find that the design strategy draws elements from the alternative ways of organizing and thinking described herein as the competitive, authoritative, rational-analytic, taming, and collaborative strategies described in chapter 2. And building on Ney and Verweij's analysis, I believe that it is this mixing, this messy pluralism, that is responsible for the design strategy's potential and power in wicked problem territory. The fundamental issue in this overall assessment of the design strategy has not been whether it is a perfect problem-solving process. It isn't. The issue has been, and continues to be, whether the design strategy positions us to be better problem solvers compared to the other options that we currently have in wicked problem territory. I believe that the evidence to date demonstrates that it does.

Conclusion: Transitioning from Age of Disorder to Age of Design

The Earth is about 4.5 billion years old. The International Commission on Stratigraphy has developed a system called the geologic time scale that divides the Earth's history into various time periods. Currently, there is a debate about which epoch we are in—Holocene or Anthropocene. The Holocene began approximately 11,650 years ago with the glacial retreat and the beginning of human effects on the Earth with the agricultural revolution. In 2000, the Nobel laureate Paul Crutzen and Eugene Stoermer coined the term "Anthropocene" to describe a new epoch, signalling human's increasing impact on the Earth's geology and ecosystems and the alterations of atmospheric, geologic, hydrologic, biospheric, and other Earth system processes. There has been

- an order-of-magnitude increase in erosion and sediment associated with urbanization and agriculture
- marked and abrupt anthropogenic perturbations of the cycles of elements such as carbon, nitrogen, phosphorus and various metals together with new chemical compounds
- environmental changes generated by these perturbations, including global warming, sea-level rise, ocean acidification and spreading oceanic "dead zones"
- rapid changes in the biosphere both on land and in the sea, as a result of habitat loss, predation, explosion of domestic animal populations and species invasions
- and the proliferation and global dispersion of many new "minerals" and "rocks" including concrete, fly ash, and plastics, and the myriad "technofossils" produced from these and other materials.[1]

Various start dates have been proposed for the Anthropocene: the beginning of the Industrial Revolution in the 1800s, the first test of the atomic bomb in Alamogordo, New Mexico, at 5:29:45 a.m. on July 16, 1945, the "great acceleration" since the 1950s of carbon dioxide (CO_2) emissions, sea level rise, global mass extinction of species, plastic pollution, high levels of nitrogen and phosphate in soils, and the transformation of land by deforestation and development. Whatever date is chosen—a decision is expected soon—it is clear that humans have become a force of nature, and not necessarily in a good way. As Simon Lewis and Mark Maslin note in their book *The Human Planet: How We Created the Anthropocene*, "the only unambiguously good aspect recognizing that we live in the Anthropocene is to gain new perspectives, think in new ways, and see the society we live in more clearly, in order to develop practical ways of steering society towards a better future."[2]

Design certainly offers a new way of thinking and acting and steering society "towards a better future." Indeed, we have seen the evolution of design from making everyday things more attractive to using design to raise provocative questions, address social and political issues, and creatively transform our social and ecological systems. So, at the beginning of the Anthropocene age that marks the increasing human impact on the Earth's geology and ecosystems and the alteration of Earth's systems, we also are celebrating potentialities in the so-called Age of Design.[3] As Jeff Conklin describes it, the Age of Design shifts our activities and harnesses our creative energies to create what might be. "These are exciting times," he says. Not only are we "empowered to come up with a radically new solution, but we are, in fact, *expected* to, since all of the existing opinions are unacceptable."[4]

But are these celebrations premature? We know that humanity's designs and their consequences have unwittingly pushed us deep into wicked problem territory. For example, we have learned that

> in many ways, the environmental crisis is a design crisis. It is a consequence of how things are made, buildings are constructed, and landscapes are used. Design manifests culture, and culture rests firmly on the foundation of what we believe to be true about the world. Our present forms of agriculture, architecture, engineering, and industry are derived from design epistemologies incompatible with nature's own. It is clear that we have not given design a rich enough context. We have used design cleverly in the service of narrowly defined human interests but have neglected its relationship with our fellow creatures. Such myopic design cannot fail to degrade the living world, and, by extension, our own health.[5]

These words of warning, written in 1996, are prescient, especially as I thought about this conclusion in the midst of a worldwide pandemic, an economic recession that threatened to deepen, a rising inflation rate, a growing gap between rich and poor, and disruptive, divisive, and confrontational politics that undermine democracies worldwide. If we have designed our way into the many messes of the Anthropocene, many of which are enumerated in the introduction and chapter 1, then to what extent is it reasonable to assume that we can design our way to a new and better future? We know that humanity's ecological footprint continues to expand, pushing us into overshoot days well beyond the Earth's carrying capacity. And the "code red for humanity" from the former secretary-general of the United Nations (UN), António Guterres, should give all of us reason to pause: "Conflicts have deepened and new dangers have emerged. Global anxieties about nuclear weapons are the highest since the Cold War. And climate change is moving faster than we are. Inequalities are growing. And we see horrific violations of human rights. Nationalism and xenophobia are on the rise."[6]

But I think some progress has been made. We have greater understanding of the trends and forces shaping our world and how they are pushing us deeper into wicked problem territory. We have learned that traditional problem-solving strategies have their limitations, especially in arenas of high conflict over problems and solutions. We have come to appreciate the design strategy and its growing landscape in strategic design, systemic design, and regenerative design. And our assessments of the design strategy have made us more cognizant of how its advantages outweigh its disadvantages, especially when compared to other problem-solving strategies. But is this all we need to design our way to a new and better future?

I believe that the design strategy offers an important beginning. Its open-ended attention and celebration of imagination, creativity, learning, and innovation are important means to an end. More and more designers, many of whom who have been introduced in this book, are tackling some of the greatest challenges facing this world using design principles and ethics as their guide. And the good news is that there are a growing number of governmental agencies, foundations, organizations, and people that are funding design challenges in what I would describe as wicked problem territory. The following is just a sample:

- The Bill and Melinda Gates Foundation's Grand Challenges Programs such as "Disrupting Dehumanizing Narratives of Black Men in Poverty" and "'Good' Neighbors: Shifting Segregation Paradigms."[7]

- USAID, an agency of the US government, sponsors "Grand Challenges for Development," such as "All Children Reading," "Powering Agriculture," "Securing Water for Food," "Scaling Off-Grid Energy," "Ensuring Effective Heath Supply Chains," and "Water and Energy for Food."[8]

- XPRIZE competitions such as the Carbon Removal $100M XPRIZE, a four-year global competition to pull CO_2 directly from the atmosphere or oceans that scale to gigaton levels in order to lock away CO_2 permanently in an environmentally benign way;[9] the $10 million Rainforest XPRIZE, a five-year competition to enhance our understanding of the rain forest ecosystem;[10] the $5 million Rapid Reskilling XPRIZE, a contest to reimagine the entire work process from education to employment and quickly reskill underresourced communities facing systemic barriers to learning, mobility, and progress;[11] the $20 million NRG COSIA Carbon XPRIZE, designed to develop breakthrough technologies to convert CO2 emissions into usable products;[12] the $1.75 million Water Abundance XPRIZE for alleviating the global water crisis with energy-efficient technologies that harvest fresh water from thin air;[13] and the $2 million Healing Our Oceans, The Wendy Schmidt Ocean Health XPRIZE, designed to measure ocean chemistry from its shallowest waters to its deepest depths.[14]

The growing sponsorship of opportunities for designers in wicked problem territory offers some reason for optimism, but more designers need to answer these calls. And time is of the essence if we are to believe the Intergovernmental Panel on Climate Change (ICC) Special Report on Global Warming of 1.5°C.[15] But for me, the key question for designers is not "How much time do we have left?" but rather "Where and how should I start my redesign efforts?"

Like the Roman god Janus with two faces (figure 11.1), we have options. We can engage in different streams of time. We can learn by reflecting on the past to help us inform our future, or we can learn by sensing and actualizing emerging future possibilities to inform our present.[16] Thus, the real challenge, and why the Romans relied on Janus, the god of transitions,[17] is to figure out how to cross the abyss that divides the past from the future and how to move from here to there. Currently trapped in an Age of Disorder, which derives from a past that we collectively have created and the results of which few want—including climate change, resource depletion, financial instability, and a growing gap between rich and poor[18]—the key question is: how do we transition from the Age of Disorder to the Age of Design?

Transition Movement

The three horizons framework (introduced in chapter 5 and shown again in figure 11.2) represents the interplay of three horizons or waves of change—horizon 1, horizon 2,

Figure 11.1
Janus, the Roman god of transitions

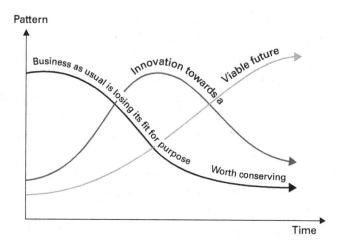

Figure 11.2
The three horizons framework, explained

and horizon 3. Horizon 2 represents transitional activity where the shortcomings of horizon 1 are becoming apparent and the seeds of horizon 3 are beginning to emerge.

Designers working in the horizon 2 zone are experimenting and innovating to shift the landscape between horizons 1 and 3. Although they come from different fields and disciplines in pursuit of top-down and grassroots initiatives, their aims are similar—the realignment of the social order with the natural world. So, what is the challenge? Find ways to transition from where we are now to what we aspire to be (hence the term "transition movement"). Some examples include the following:

- *Commons Transition* champions a civil society based on the Commons, which includes the collaborative stewardship of shared resources to bring about a more egalitarian, just, and environmentally stable society.[19]

- *Forum for the Future*[20] and its School of Systems Change[21] specialize in catalyzing change in three critical areas with high change potential: the 1.5°C challenge to transition to a carbon-positive economy; a challenge to change the way that food is produced and consumed; and a challenge to build transparent business models and transform value chains to distribute value more equally and to provide sustainable jobs and livelihoods to farmers, workers, and communities.

- *Just Transitions* pursues the principle that a healthy economy and a clean environment can coexist; upholds the fundamental rights of workers, community residents, and Indigenous peoples to clean air, water, land, and food; requires the development of fair economic trade, health, safety and environment policies; and upholds people's rights in challenging any government, military, corporation, or international bodies that commit economic or environmental injustices.[22]

- *Sociotechnical Transition* takes a multilevel perspective or "big-picture" view of sociotechnical transitions that span three analytical levels: (1) long-term secular developments; (2) development in incumbent systems—strategic games, political games, political struggles, and sociocultural debates; and (3) radical niche innovation, including local implementation projects.[23]

• The *Sustainability Transitions Research Network* is an independent, international, research-driven network of over 2,000 scholars whose mission it is to deepen the scientific understanding in established industries, sociotechnical systems, and societies, and to aid in their transition to more sustainable modes of production and consumption.[24]

• The *Great Transition Initiative* is an online idea forum and an international network of thinkers and activists to explore the concepts, strategies, and visions needed to contribute to a new praxis for global transformation, enrich the scenarios, sharpen the theory of change, and spread awareness. By 2014, the Tellus Institute had reimagined and relaunched the initiative to serve as a formal journal of great transition studies that also offers essays, viewpoints, reviews and interviews to advance a vision and praxis for a decent planetary civilization.[25]

• The *Transition Network* connects international communities who come together to reimagine and rebuild our world by starting locally, supporting one another, and crowdsourcing solutions to reclaim the economy, spark entrepreneurship, reimage work, and develop new skills.[26]

The transition movement and their social experiments have had several progenitors. Some attribute its inspiration to Rob Hopkins, the author, activist, and environmentalist.[27] Others credit the permaculture activists and designers in Devon, United Kingdom, in 2004[28] and Louise Rooney, who introduced the term "transitional design" in 2005 to describe a townlike initiative in Kinsale, Ireland. In what has now become a worldwide undertaking, people are coming together to address big challenges and catalyze activities at the local level to increase self-sufficiency and reduce the potential effects of oil, climate destruction, and economic instability. They begin by reimaging and rebuilding their communities to make them more resilient, ignite entrepreneurship, gain new skills, reclaim their economies, and weave worldwide networks of connections and support. The approach has now spread to transition towns, cities, villages, islands, peninsulas, and other entities (now referred to as "transition initiatives") in over 1,400 communities in fifty countries.[29] Basic principles guide these efforts: "we respect resource limits and create resilience"; "we promote inclusivity and social justice"; "we adopt subsidiarity (self-organization and decision making at the appropriate level"; "we pay attention to balance"; "we are part of an experimental, learning network"; "we freely share ideas and power"; "we collaborate and look for synergies"; and "we foster positive visioning and creativity."[30]

Ezio Manzini's book *Design When Everybody Designs*[31] provides a fuller description of some of these transition communities. He views them as caught in "a "double world where two realities live together in conflict: the old 'limitless' world that does not acknowledge the planet's limits, and another that recognizes these limits and experiments with ways of transforming them into opportunities."[32] The first represents the dominant worldview that shapes our economic and institutional infrastructures. The second surfaces in an "archipelago of new microworlds" illustrated throughout his book: Ainonghui, A Case of Community-Supported Agriculture;[33] Slow Food, Italy (and Worldwide);[34] the Park Slope Food Co-op, in Brooklyn, New York;[35] Community-Supported Agriculture;[36] the Green Map system, which plots local "green" projects worldwide;[37] the Neighborhood, A Living Lab, in Malmö, Sweden;[38] "Via Scarsellini": A Collaborative Living Project, Milan;[39] Feeding Milan: Energy for Change;[40] and the Xianqiao Sustainable Community Project, Chongming Island, Shanghai.[41]

Transitional Redesigns in Education

Educational institutions are joining the movement to redesign their curricula to assist designers in understanding and appreciating the dramatic changes occurring in the world, the impact that changes are having on the boundaries of design practice, and by necessity, the new roles that designers are challenged to take on as agents of change.[42] Here are some initiatives currently underway.

Parsons Masters of Fine Arts in Transdisciplinary Design

The Parsons School of Design at the New School announced its Masters of Fine Arts in transdisciplinary design in the fall of 2010.[43] The program is dedicated to the reintegration and recontexualization of diverse disciplinary knowledge in science, philosophy, psychology, social science, anthropology, and the humanities. In 2012, the *Journal of Design Strategies* celebrated its contributions and devoted the entire issue to the topic of "Transdisciplinary Design."[44] James Hunt, the guest editor, provided a rationale for the program:

> The inception of the MFA in Transdisciplinary Design at Parsons is a response to a confluence of forces—social, technological and environmental—that have knotted themselves together in a way that make this approach not just timely, but also urgent. From the vexing challenges of sustainable growth to the disintegration of the United States' nineteenth-century infrastructure; from the intractable complications of risky human settlement patterns to the perverse co-presence of obesity and hunger epidemics in developed and developing countries; and from problems in our own backyard to those of global span: the world is on fire and many of us believe that design can play a role in extinguishing some of the blazes. Or at least that it is time for practitioners of design to move on from projects that privilege stylistic novelty to ones that grapple with meaningful social change.[45]

Hunt then highlighted the role that designers are anticipated to play in transforming the landscape of wicked problems and sparking innovations, signaling that there will be "a gradual but very real recalibration of the designer's potential as an agent for change."[46] In this new role, designers will be expected to shift their attention from objects or artifacts to the complex systems that contextualize them. The change also will entail a transition from discipline-based design where outcomes that are typically knowable, "relatively discrete, bounded, and (for the most part) tangible"[47] to trans-disciplinary design that forces designers to reconsider the boundaries of their design practice. The changes will also require them to reconfigure expectations, reimagine what they are creating, engage in experimentation in new contexts, invent new languages and syntaxes, and generate outcomes that "do not necessarily take material form,"[48] all with the intent of catalyzing new social outcomes. A key characteristic of this shift will be the reliance on collaborative practice that is "distributed, open, and emergent,"[49] remaking the relationships among designers, producers, consumers, users, and other citizens. Transdisciplinary design, therefore, calls for designers to be "fluent in the mechanics of working together" to "deliver methods that maximize the effects of multiple perspectives rather than letting the process devolve into chaos, miscommunication, and dysfunction—as it often can."[50] Since designers will be shaping processes of innovation and change, it also follows that their theoretical underpinnings and "the rules of the game and terms of engagement must evolve as well."[51] Design practices that will be situated in new and different contexts will entail greater emphasis on critical reframing, systems diagramming, scalar thinking, experimental prototyping, assessment metrics, design-led research, and reflective practice.[52]

Stanford School of Education's ChangeLabs

ChangeLabs is located within the Stanford Graduate School of Education and is part of the Human Sciences and Technologies Advanced Research Institute (H-Star).[53] It offers a ten-week Stanford graduate class, taught at the Hasso Plattner Institute of Design (d.school), in which students throughout Stanford's seven schools—Business, Earth, Energy and Environmental Sciences, Education, Engineering, Humanities and Sciences, and Law—can apply for admission through a competitive selection process. The immersive and advanced project-based course, entitled "Collaborating with the Future: Innovating Large-Scale Sustainable Transformations," pairs student teams with a partner for a full quarter to work on a real-world challenge. Previous partners have included government agencies such as the UN Development Programme, the New Zealand Ministry of Primary Industries, USAID, and the City of Miami; nongovernmental organizations (NGO) such as the Nature Conservancy, Mayo Clinic, CreditDo, and Mastercard Foundation, and technology companies and start-ups such as Google and Facebook. The course, informed by design theory, processes, tools, and methods, prepares the students to create initiatives that their partners can implement in the real world. Previous projects have included planning a new town's waste and energy future and large-scale distributed electrification for rural India.

The System Transformation Masterclass Series is a program for strategists, leaders, managers, and decision makers who work in multistakeholder arenas marked by uncertainty, rapid changes, and global challenges, especially where innovation and scale are needed to develop system-based strategies and robust, resilient solutions. Three modules (each held as a two-day workshop) make up the series: (1) System Acupuncture:

Rethinking Leadership and Innovation, (2) Designing the Scale Advantage, and (3) Mastering Systems Leadership.

Carnegie Mellon School of Design

By far the most developed program in transition design is at the Carnegie Mellon School of Design.[54] Terry Irwin, head of the school from 2009–2019, and her colleagues Gideon Kossoff and Cameron Tonkinwise, led a two-and-a-half-year collaborative effort dedicated to expanding the role of design and designers in transitioning to a sustainable society. They, along with the Carnegie's design faculty, revitalized curricula at the undergraduate, master's, and doctoral levels. Approved by the university's college council, the new programs launched in the autumn of 2014.[55]

A continuum of design approaches are embedded in the new programs: Design for Service focuses on solutions within the business area and the existing dominant economic paradigm; Design for Social Innovation challenges existing paradigms and seeks positive social changes; and the centerpiece of the new programs, Transition Design, "challenges existing paradigms, envisions new ones, and leads to radical positive social and environmental change."[56]

At its core, transition design is dedicated to using the tools and processes of design to reconceive entire lifestyles, as well as society's infrastructure (i.e., policies, energy resources, transport, manufacturing, economy and food, health care, and educational systems).

When engaged in transition design, designers are taught to utilize a heuristic model that identifies "four interrelated and mutually reinforcing and coevolving areas of knowledge, action and self-reflection":[57]

- *Vision for transition*: "A vision for the transition to a more sustainable society is needed. It calls for the reconceptualization of entire lifestyles in which communities are in symbiotic relationship with the environment. Lifestyles are place-based yet global in their exchange of technology, information and culture."
- *Theories of change*: "Ideas, theories and methodologies from many varied fields and disciplines inform a deep understanding of the dynamics of change in the natural and the social worlds."
- *Mindset and posture*: "Living in and thru transitional times requires a mindset and posture of openness, mindfulness, a willingness to collaborate, and 'optimistic grumpiness'."
- *New ways of designing*: "The transition to a sustainable society will require new ways of designing that are informed by a vision, a deep understanding of the dynamics of change, a new mindset and posture"[58] and new knowledge and skill sets.

The Ojai Workshops in southern California illustrated how these coevolving areas of knowledge came to life and showcased designers' skills and competencies as they attacked the wicked problem of water shortage and helped the community move toward a sustainable future.[59]

In addition to the revised curricula, Carnegie Mellon University has launched the Transition Design Institute to support the practice of transition design and the educators, policymakers, and communities around the world who want to learn how to transition to better long-term futures.[60] Central to these pedagogical and practitioner efforts will be a growing body of research and theory that has grown out of science and technology studies since the 1990s. Under the umbrella term "design for sustainability transitions," the focus is on how to realign of our institutions, organizations, technologies, and sociocultural norms, values, and lifestyles so they are more compatible with and supportive of a sustainable worldview.[61]

The Future of Design Education

The most ambitious efforts undertaken thus far is fhe Future of Design Education Initiative, founded in late 2019 as a partnership between the Design Lab of the University of California, San Diego, and IBM's Global Design Group, with the World Design Organization as a cosponsor. It is led by a small executive team, a steering committee of leading designers from academia and industry, and more than 600 volunteers—undergraduate students, deans, department chairs, and industry executives representing every region of the world—who serve on working groups and provide overall assessment of and advice on concept development. Anticipated ten-year reviews, each taking roughly three years to complete, signal a dedication to the continual renewal of design education. The scope of the initiative includes two-year technical degrees, three- or four-year undergraduate education programs, graduate education, terminal professional master's degrees, and PhD programs. The initiative's priority is twofold: "provide an in-depth, evidence-driven academic foundation for design decisions" for the twenty-first century and enable designers "to become advocates for social and environmental responsibility." The initiative is structured around four issues: *principles* underpinning work in design that guides situational decision-making in practice; *categories of themes*—which as of December 2020 have identified fourteen core, specialized, and elective themes, along with six themes defined by the teaching context; and *characteristics of students*.[62]

The Evolution of Design

Mindful of Stuart Brand's *Whole Earth Catalog*'s statement of purpose ("we are as gods and might as well get used to it")[63] and Tony Fry's affirmation "that the history of the impossible is the history of humanity,"[64] I began this book with six goals in mind. The first, as elaborated in the introduction of this book, was to acknowledge VUCA—the volatility (V), uncertainty (U), complexity (C), and ambiguity (A) that characterize our current life experiences and to link them to the massive transformations underway in all aspects of life—our technologies, economics, environment, politics, and social relations. The second, presented in chapter 1, was to appreciate how these transformative shifts and changes and the dis-ease we feel in trying to cope with them are landing us in what I call "wicked problem territory"—a terrain so conflict-ridden that we find it difficult to agree on our problems, much less their solutions.

The third goal, presented in chapter 2, was to identify our current problem strategies on which we have long relied and to explain why they don't work particularly well as we attempt to deal with the conflicts that these transformations provoke. The short answer is that each of the problem-solving strategies—competitive, authoritative, rational-analytic, taming, and collaborative—has its limitations. And none are well equipped when values and worldviews collide and people are unable to agree on problems and solutions. The consequence has been people moving to their respective corners, insisting that they are right, and calling on the like-minded to join them in resistance to "the other."

The fourth goal was to propose the design strategy in part II as an alternative problem-solving approach in wicked problem territory, summarizing its history, discourse, landscape, principles, and process in chapter 3 and reviewing some of its basic skill sets and toolkits in chapter 5. In keeping with Rittel's view that design solutions depend on the "Weltanschauung [worldview] of the designer"[65] and Wahl and Baxter's assessments that "all design decisions are fundamentally worldview and value-system dependent,"[66] Chapter 4 shifted the focus from the exterior and material world of design to the interior world of the designer. This inward turn challenged us to examine the source of wicked problems that lies within our own ways of thinking, and yes, designing. The chapter then introduced some designers who are making this turn inward. Their explorations of developmental stages, value systems, mindsets, worldviews, and biopsychological systems of human consciousness are an important turning point in design's evolution. No longer needing Janus, the god of transition, to guide their path, the developmentally based interventions and transformative practices that they advocate to change people's consciousness—both designers and the people they serve—open up pathways to "step over" and bridge the divide between the past and the future as follows:

- Beyond a focus on the exterior world of design, designers have extended their gaze to their interior world in terms of their thinking styles, emotional intelligence, and worldviews that seek well-being for self and others.

- Beyond a focus on things, designers are becoming more attentive to transitions, the dynamics of the change process, and *how* things can be accomplished.

- Beyond the theories of design practice, the ethics of design is taking its rightful place in guiding complex and contentious design interventions.

- Beyond their traditional role, designers are adding new roles of social and political entrepreneurs, educators, and change agents.

- Beyond an attention to products and processes, designers are applying their knowledge, skills, and competencies to understand large-scale systems and their redesign.

- Beyond a practice that ends with prototyping in innovative design labs, designers are broadening their responsibilities to include place-based implementation, testing and adaptations.

The fifth goal was to explore the expanding domains of design in part III—the strategic design of organizations (chapter 6), the systemic design of social systems (chapter 7), and regenerative design (chapter 8), which renews and realigns social systems with the natural world so that humans and the built environment can coexist and coevolve in a way that maintains the integrity of both society and nature.

The sixth goal was to assess the design strategy's contributions as a problem-solving approach. The criticisms about design presented in chapter 9 identified areas for improvement, but they struck me as limited in scope, especially when one considers that as designs get more complex, and more sophisticated forms of developmental evaluation (DE) are needed to fully understand and appreciate design's contributions. Thus, I concluded in chapter 10 that the design strategy offers decided advantages in wicked problem territory, particularly in terms of its emphasis on the following:

- Design's reliance on imagination, creativity, exploration and learning
- The social technology of the design thinking process
- The options that designers employ to deal with tensions and contradictions to either manage paradox or transform it
- Designers' ability to respond to ethical and moral dilemmas
- Design's ability to integrate multilevel designs and go to scale
- Design's inclusion of central elements from other problem-solving strategies

Despite the design strategy's advantages, the transition from what we are to what we want to become will be neither quick nor easy. Change and transformation in a complex, interconnected, and interdependent world with local, regional, and global networks will take time, resilience, and grit. And if levels of individual development do exist—and we have a large body of literature and research that says that they do—then people will be operating at different levels in terms of their consciousness, cognition, morality, and ego development. Not everyone will be open, willing, and able to making the transition from egocentric to ecocentric system designs. We know from research that people neither understand nor appreciate developmental levels a half step to a full stage beyond where they are. So developmentally based interventions and transformative practices will need to be specifically designed to appeal to people at different developmental levels. We also understand that these interventions may not succeed. Watching the horrific images of the Russia invasion of Ukraine, I am reminded how some people can remain fixated, with no change or movement in their levels of consciousness—a serious impediment when attempting to shift from a world that *is* to a world that *could be*. So in this age of transition, finding a narrative that appeals to all of us, regardless of our worldview and level of consciousness, becomes a formidable challenge, but an absolutely necessary one to undertake if we are to take advantage of the design strategy's full potential.

With these intriguing possibilities and daunting prospects of how we might link the material and external world of design to the consciousness and interior world of designers and those for whom they design, I close this book. Like a kaleidoscope whose rotation results in ever-changing views, we have come to appreciate the design strategy's many facets. Turn it one way, and we see designers who are the catalysts of creative change. Turn it another way, we uncover the underlying dynamics of design thinking and the change process. Rotate it again, and we observe the results of the design strategy's many creative and innovative efforts. Rotate it once more, and we see our own reflections and realize that we are all are designers in this Age of Design. How we think, what we value, and everything we do has an impact on our planet and those who inhabit it. In completing this final rotation, we also come to understand that the world that we have designed ultimately designs *us*—it affects our values, worldviews, and choices in the things we create. So as we cross the divide from the past into the future, either as expert or citizen designer, we are left with new questions, perhaps the most important ones of all—who are we, and what do we want to become in this Age of Design?

Notes

Preface

1. Horst W. J. Rittel and Melvin M. Webber, "Dilemmas in a Theory of Planning," *Policy Sciences* 4 (1973): 155–69, https://doi.org/10.1007/BF01405730.

2. See Nancy C. Roberts, "Wicked Problems and Network Approaches to Resolution," *International Public Management Review* 1, no. 1 (2000): 1–19.

3. Rittel and Webber, "Dilemmas in a Theory of Planning," 168.

4. Rittel and Webber, "Dilemmas in a Theory of Planning," 169.

5. Rittel presented his ideas about wicked problems in C. West Churchman's seminars at the University of California, Berkeley. Based on these discussions, Churchman then wrote a guest editorial entitled "Wicked Problems," and attributed his comments about "wicked problems" to Rittel. See C. West Churchman, "Wicked Problems," *Management Science* 14, no. 4 (December 1967): B-141, https://www.jstor.org/stable/2628678.

6. Rittel and Webber, "Dilemmas in a Theory of Planning," 162.

7. Kees Dorst, *Frame Innovation: Create New Thinking by Design* (Cambridge, MA: MIT Press, 2015), 21.

8. Willie Smits, "How to Restore a Rainforest," filmed February 2009 at TED, video, 20:24, https://www.ted.com/talks/willie_smits_how_to_restore_a_rainforest?language=en.

9. Lawrence Freedman, *Strategy: A History* (Oxford: Oxford University Press, 2013), xi.

10. Warren Berger, *Glimmer: How Design Can Transform Your Life, and Maybe Even the World* (New York: Penguin Press, 2009), 29.

11. Marco Verweij, "Wicked Problems, Clumsy Solutions, and Messy Institutions in Transnational Governance," in *The Problem-Solving Capacity of the Modern State: Governance Challenges and Administrative Capacity*, ed. Martin Lodge and Kai Wegrich (Oxford: Oxford University Press, 2014), 183–97.

12. Bela H. Bernathy, *Designing Social Systems in a Changing World* (New York: Springer Science+Business Media, 1996), vii.

Introduction

1. Horst W. J. Rittel and Melvin M. Webber, "Dilemmas in a General Theory of Planning," *Policy Sciences* 4, no. 2 (June 1973): 155–69, https://doi.org/10.1007/BF01405730.

2. US Army Heritage and Education Center, "Origin of the Term VUCA," updated May 7, 2019, https://usawc.libanswers.com/faq/84869.

3. Sandra Bichl/Career Angels, HR Team, "Career Advice in a VUCA World," *Career Angels* (blog), August 21, 2017, https://blog.careerangels.eu/career-advice-in-a-vuca-world/. (My thanks to Sandra for giving permission to reproduce her image.)

4. Charles Eames and Ray Eames, "IBM Mathematics Peep Show: Legend of the Chessboard," 2011, YouTube video, 1:58, https://www.youtube.com/watch?v=t3d0Y-JpRRg.

5. Ray Kurzweil, *The Age of Spiritual Machines: When Computers Exceed Human Intelligence* (New York: Penguin, 1999).

6. Ray Kurzweil, "The Law of Accelerating Returns," accessed August 29, 2020, https://www.kurzweilai.net/the-law-of-accelerating-returns.

7. Sveta McShane and Jason Dorrier, "Ray Kurzweil Predicts Three Technologies Will Define Our Future," *Singularity Hub*, April 19, 2016, http://singularityhub.com/2016/04/19/ray-kurzweil-predicts-three-technologies-will-define-our-future/.

8. The term "$1,000 genome" refers to an era of predictive and personalized medicine during which the cost of fully sequencing an individual's genome (whole genome sequencing, or WGS) is roughly $1,000.

9. R. Buckminster Fuller and Kiyoshi Kuromiya, *Critical Path* (New York: St. Martin's Press, 1981).

10. David R. Schilling, "Knowledge Doubling Every 12 Months, Soon to Be Every 12 Hours," *Industry Tap*, April 19, 2013, http://www.industrytap.com/knowledge-doubling-every-12-months-soon-to-be-every-12-hours/3950.

11. Paul J. Crutzen, "The 'Anthropocene,'" *Journal de Physique* 12, no. 10 (November 2002): 1–5, https://doi.org/10.1051/jp4:20020447.

12. International Geosphere-Biosphere Programme, "Global Change," accessed August 28, 2020, http://www.igbp.net/globalchange/greatacceleration.4.1b8ae20512db692f2a680001630.html.

13. Will W. Steffen et al., "The Trajectory of the Anthropocene: The Great Acceleration," *Anthropocene Review* 2, no. 1 (2015): 81–98, https://doi.org/10.1177/2053019614564785.

14. Will W. Steffen et al., *Global Change and the Earth System: A Planet under Pressure* (Berlin: Springer, 2004), 131.

15. Steffen et al., "The Trajectory of the Anthropocene," 11.

16. *Collins Dictionary*, "Complexity," accessed August 28, 2020, https://www.collinsdictionary.com/dictionary/english/complexity.

17. US Census Bureau, "U.S. and World Population Clock," accessed August 29, 2020, http://www.census.gov/popclock/.

18. United Nations, Department of Economic and Social Affairs, "World Population Prospects: The 2015 Revision," https://www.un.org/en/development/desa/publications/world-population-prospects-2015-revision.html.

19. The Islamic State is also known as Islamic State of Iraq and Syria (ISIS), Islamic State of Iraq and the Levant (ISIL), and Daesh.

20. Stratfor Worldview, "How Many Countries Are There in the World in 2019?" April 15, 2019, https://worldview.stratfor.com/article/how-many-countries-are-there-world-2019.

21. David M. Eberhard, Gary F. Simons, and Charles D. Fennig, eds., *Ethnologue; Languages of the World*, 23rd ed. (Dallas: SIL International, 2020), https://www.ethnologue.com/.

22. David Barrett, George Thomas Kurian, and Todd M. Johnson, eds., *World Christian Encyclopedia: A Comparative Survey of Churches and Religions in the Modern World, Vol. 1: The World by Countries: Religionists, Churches, Ministries*, 2nd ed. (Oxford: Oxford University Press, 2001).

23. James Fearon, "Ethnic and Cultural Diversity by Country," *Journal of Economic Growth* 8, no. 2 (June 2003): 195–222, https://www.jstor.org/stable/40215943?origin=JSTOR-pdf&seq=1.

24. Leon P. Baradat and John A. Philips, *Political Ideologies: Their Origins and Impact*, 12th ed. (New York: Routledge, 2017).

25. James Burke, *Internet Archive*, "Connections, Seasons 1–3," 1978, updated November 7, 2018, 18:57, https://archive.org/details/ConnectionsByJamesBurke/.

26. James Burke, *Internet Archive*, "Connections: The Trigger Effect," 1978, video 49:24, February 15, 2015, http://www.dominoprinciple.com/2015/02/15/connections-trigger-effect-james-burke/.

27. Robin M. Helms, "Going International," *Higher Education Today* (blog), January 23, 2015, https://www.higheredtoday.org/2015/01/23/going-international/.

28. UN World Tourism Organization, "UNWTO World Tourism Barometer and Statistical Annex, January 2019," *eLibrary*, accessed August 28, 2020, https://www.e-unwto.org/doi/abs/10.18111/wtobarometereng.2019.17.1.1.

29. United Nations, Department of Economic and Social Affairs, Population Division, "Migration and Population Change—Drivers and Impacts," *Population Facts*, no. 2017/8 (December 2017), https://www.un.org/en/development/desa/population/migration/publications/populationfacts/docs/MigrationPopFacts20178.pdf. Note that "net migration" refers to the difference between the numbers of immigrants and emigrants, who arrive in or depart from a particular country or area in a given time period, regardless of country of birth or citizenship. Tourists, foreign aid workers, temporary workers employed abroad for less than a year, and overseas military personnel typically are not counted as migrants.

30. Çağlar Özden et al., "'Where on Earth Is Everybody?' The Evolution of Global Bilateral Migration: 1960–2000," *VOX*, last modified August 6, 2011, https://voxeu.org/article/where-earth-everybody-global-migration-1960-2000.

31. United Nations, Department of Economic and Social Affairs, *Population Facts* (New York: Population Division, 2019), https://www.un.org/en/development/desa/population/migration/publications/populationfacts/docs/MigrationStock2019_PopFacts_2019-04.pdf.

32. Steven A. Camarota and Karen Zeigler, "Foreign-Born Population Hits Record in January 2022," Center for Immigration Studies, February 23, 2022, https://cis.org/Camarota/Foreign Born-Population-Hits-Record-466-Million-January-2022.

33. Bureau of Transportation Statistics, US Department of Transportation, *Estimated January 2019 U.S. Airline Traffic Data* (Washington, DC: US Department of Transportation, February 14, 2019), https://www.bts.gov/newsroom/estimated-january-2019-us-airline-traffic-data.

34. International Civil Aviation Organization, "Economic Impacts of COVID-19 on Civil Aviation," Updated December, 2022. https://www.icao.int/sustainability/Pages/Economic-Impacts-of-COVID-19.aspx.

35. Leslie Josephs, "A Flood of Job Losses Looms as Airline Industry Struggles in Pandemic," CNBC, August 16, 2020, https://www.cnbc.com/2020/08/16/a-flood-of-job-losses-looms-as-airlines-industry-struggle-in-coronavirus-pandemic.html.

36. DevelopmentSeed, the University of Wisconsin–Madison Cartography Lab, and Dr. Parag Khanna, *Connectivity Atlas*, last updated August 28, 2020, https://atlas.developmentseed.org/all/.

37. Parag Khanna, *Connectography: Mapping the Future of Global Civilization* (New York: Random House, 2016).

38. Harvard University, *Exploring the World of Connectography*, accessed August 28, 2020, http://worldmap.harvard.edu/maps/connectography.

39. Center for Geographic Analysis, Harvard University, accessed August 28, 2020, https://gis.harvard.edu/.

40. Pablo Kaluza et al., "The Complex Network of Global Cargo Ship Movements," *Journal of the Royal Society Interface* no. 7 (January 2010): 1093–1103, https://royalsocietypublishing.org/doi/pdf/10.1098/rsif.2009.0495.

41. DevelopmentSeed, University of Wisconsin-Madison Cartography Lab, and Dr. Parag Khanna, *Connectivity Atlas*.

42. A zettabyte is a measure of digital storage capacity. It is read as 2^{70} bytes, which are equal to 1,000 exabytes, a billion terabytes, or a trillion gigabytes. In other words, it means one billion, one terabyte hard drives would be needed to store one zettabyte of data.

43. Sean M. Kerner, "Global Internet Traffic on Track to Hit 4.8 Zettabyes by 2022," *Enterprise Networking Planet*, December 7, 2018, http://www.enterprisenetworkingplanet.com/netsp/global-internet-traffic-on-track-to-hit-4.8-zettabytes-by-2022.html.

44. Internet World Stats, "Internet Growth Statistics," accessed August 30, 2020, https://www.internetworldstats.com/emarketing.htm.

45. GSM Association, *The Mobile Economy*, accessed August 30, 2020, https://www.gsma.com/mobileeconomy/#key_stats.

46. Paul James and Manfred B. Steger, "A Genealogy of 'Globalization': The Career of a Concept," *Globalizations* 11, no. 4 (September 2014): 417–34, https://doi.org/10.1080/14747731.2014.951186. See also David Held et al., *Global Transformations: Politics, Economics, and Culture* (Stanford, CA: Stanford University Press, 1999) for an expanded view of globalization beyond the big four markers that weaves together all the domains of social activity to include political-legal, cultural, financial, military, and environmental interdependencies.

47. *Cambridge Dictionary*, "Globalization," accessed August 30, 2020, https://dictionary.cambridge.org/us/dictionary/english/globalization.

48. James Manyika et. al, *Digital Globalization*, McKinsey Global Institute, February 23, 2016 Report, 12.

49. Steven Altman, Pankaj Ghemawat, and Phillip Bastian, *DHL Global Connectedness Index 2018: The State of Globalization in a Fragile World* (Bonn, Germany: Deutsche Post DHL Group,

January 2019), https://www.dhl.com/content/dam/dhl/global/core/documents/pdf/glo-core-gci -2018-full-study.pdf.

50. Altman et al., *DHL Global Connectedness Index*, 8.

51. Altman et al., *DHL Global Connectedness Index*, 12.

52. Altman et al., *DHL Global Connectedness Index*, 14.

53. Altman et al., *DHL Global Connectedness Index*, 15.

54. Altman et al., *DHL Global Connectedness Index*, 28.

55. John H. Holland, "Studying Complex Adaptive Systems," *Journal of Systems Science and Complexity* 19, no. 1 (2006): 1–8, https://doi.org/10.1007/s11424-006-0001-z. Also see the excellent videos that demonstrate CAS: Systems Innovation, "Complex Adaptive Systems Overview," 2014, YouTube video, 4:53, https://www.youtube.com/watch?v=rl0yFwcGx_o; Systems Innovation, "Complex Adaptive Systems," 2015, YouTube video, 10:22, https://www.youtube.com/watch?v =IWhkUne8T68.

56. Ilya Prigogine and Isabelle Stengers, *Order out of Chaos: Man's New Dialogue with Nature* (Portsmouth, NH: William Heinemann, 1984). Note: Far-from equilibrium systems are what Prigogine calls "dissipative structures"—structures that dissipate entropy.

57. Prigogine and Stengers, *Order Out of Chaos*.

58. Malcolm Gladwell, *The Tipping Point: How Little Things Can Make a Big Difference* (New York: Back Bay Books, 2000).

59. My thanks to Raymond Trevor Bradley for his suggestion on how to visualize a complex adaptive system as depicted in Figure Intro.4. Note the imagery is idealized—the actual fluctuations in a CAS are more irregular and varied.

60. Yoav Ben-Dov, "Hanoi Traffic," 2009, YouTube video, 2.34, https://www.youtube.com/watch ?v=LzjifmHavAQ.

61. Joseph Tainter, *The Collapse of Complex Societies* (New York: Cambridge University Press, 1990).

62. Tainter, *The Collapse of Complex Societies*, 4.

63. Tainter, *The Collapse of Complex Societies*, 202.

64. Tainter, *The Collapse of Complex Societies*, 193.

65. Jared Diamond, *Collapse: How Societies Choose to Fail or Succeed* (New York: Penguin, 2006).

66. William Ophuls, *Immoderate Greatness: Why Civilizations Fail* (North Charleston, SC: Create Space Independent Publishing Platform, 2012), i.

67. Ophuls, *Immoderate Greatness*, ii.

68. Systems Innovation, "Self-Organization Overview," 2014, YouTube video, 5:53, https://www .youtube.com/watch?v=BTR17I_Eb_o.

69. NOVA *Science Now*, "Emergence: Everyday Examples," accessed August 30, 2020, http://www .pbs.org/wgbh/nova/sciencenow/3410/03-ever-nf.html.

70. Charles Perrow, *Normal Accidents: Living with High-Risk Technologies* (New York: Basic Books, 1984).

71. Thomas Homer-Dixon, *The Upside of Down* (Washington, DC: Island Press, 2006).

72. Nassim N. Taleb, *Black Swans*, 2nd ed. (New York: Random House, 2010), 323.

73. University of Southampton, "Scientists Identify Climate 'Tipping Points'," *Science Daily*, October 15, 2015, https://www.sciencedaily.com/releases/2015/10/151015084348.htm.

74. Richard Harris, "Predicting the Crash: Tracking Tipping Points," NPR, September 16, 2009, http://www.npr.org/templates/story/story.php?storyId=112886911.

75. Johan Rockström et al., "A Safe Operating Space for Humanity," *Nature* 461, no. 24 (September 2009): 472–75, https://doi.org/10.1038/461472a.

76. Stockholm Resilience Centre, Stockholm University, "The Nine Planetary Boundaries," accessed January 7, 2021, https://www.stockholmresilience.org/research/planetary-boundaries/planetary-boundaries/about-the-research/the-nine-planetary-boundaries.html.

77. Rockström et al., "A Safe Operating Space," 474–75.

78. Steffen et. al, "The Trajectory of the Anthropocene,"

79. Kate Raworth, *Doughnut Economics: Seven Ways to Think Like a 21st-Century Economist* (White River Junction, VT: Chelsea Green, 2017), 38.

80. Kate Raworth, "A Doughnut for the Anthropocene: Humanity's Compass in the 21st Century," *The Lancet Planetary Health* 1, no. 2 (May 2017): e48–e49, https://doi.org/10.1016/S2542-5196(17)30028-1.

81. Raworth, *Doughnut Economics*, 43–44.

82. Raworth, *Doughnut Economics*, 44–45. Also see the interactive model of social and planetary boundaries on Kate Raworth's website (https://www.kateraworth.com/doughnut/).

83. UN Food and Agriculture Organization (FAO), *The Water-Energy-Food Nexus: A New Approach in Support of Food Security and Sustainable Agriculture* (Rome: FAO, 2014). https://www.fao.org/3/bl496e/bl496e.pdf.

84. FAO, *The Water-Energy-Food Nexus*, 2.

85. FAO, *The Water-Energy-Food Nexus*, 5.

86. Kate Raworth, "A Safe and Just Space for Humanity: Can We Live within the Doughnut?" Oxfam discussion paper (February 2012), 6, https://www-cdn.oxfam.org/s3fs-public/file_attachments/dp-a-safe-and-just-space-for-humanity-130212-en_5.pdf.

87. Joseph E. Stiglitz, Amartya Kumar Sen, and Jean-Paul Fitoussi, *Report by the Commission on the Measurement of Economic Performance and Social Progress* (Paris: Commission on the Measurement of Economic Performance and Social Progress, 2009), 9, https://www.cpc.unc.edu/projects/rlms-hse/publications/1921.

88. Global Footprint Network, "Overshoot Days 1970–2021," accessed January 11, 2022, https://www.overshootday.org/newsroom/past-earth-overshoot-days/.

89. Peter H. Diamandis and Steven Kotler, *Abundance* (New York: Free Press, 2012).

90. Diamandis and Kotler, *Abundance*, ix–x.

91. Peter H. Diamandis, "Abundance Is Our Future," filmed February 2012 at TED, video, 15:59, https://www.ted.com/talks/peter_diamandis_abundance_is_our_future?language=en.

92. Peter H. Diamandis, "Abundance—The Future Is Better Than You Think," *Singularity Hub*, June 28, 2012, https://singularityhub.com/2012/06/28/abundance-the-future-is-better-than-you-think/.

93. Hans Rosling, "The Best Stats You've Ever Seen," filmed February 2006 at TED, video, 19:38, https://www.ted.com/talks/hans_rosling_the_best_stats_you_ve_ever_seen.

94. Max Roser, "Research and Data to Make Progress against the World's Largest Problems," *Our World in Data*, accessed August 28, 2020, https://ourworldindata.org/.

95. World Bank, "World Bank Forecasts Global Poverty to Fall below 10% for First Time; Major Hurdles Remain in Goal to End Poverty by 2030," October 4, 2015, https://www.worldbank.org/en/news/press-release/2015/10/04/world-bank-forecasts-global-poverty-to-fall-below-10-for-first-time-major-hurdles-remain-in-goal-to-end-poverty-by-2030.

96. Bill H. Gates, "What Gives Me Hope about the World's Future," interview by Nancy Gibbs, *Time*, January 4, 2018, https://time.com/5086907/bill-gates-nancy-gibbs-interview/.

97. Steven Pinker, *The Better Angels of Our Nature: Why Violence Has Declined* (New York: Penguin Books, 2012).

98. Homer-Dixon, *The Upside of Down*.

99. Donella H. Meadows et al., *The Limits to Growth: A Report for the Club of Rome's Project on the Predicament of Mankind* (New York: Universe Books, 1972).

100. Donella H. Meadows, Dennis Meadows, and Jørgen Randers, "Beyond the Limits to Growth," Donella Meadows Archives, Summer 2002, http://donellameadows.org/archives/beyond-the-limits-to-growth/.

101. Donella H. Meadows, Jørgen Randers, and Dennis L. Meadows, *Limits to Growth: The 30-Year Update* (White River Junction, VT: Chelsea Green, 2004).

102. Michael Huesemann and Joyce Huesemann, *Techno-Fix: Why Technology Won't Save Us or the Environment* (Gabriola Island, BC, Canada: New Society Publishers, 2011).

103. Peter Turchin, *Ages of Discord: A Structural-Demographic Analysis of American History* (Chaplin, CT: Beresta Books, 2016).

104. George Packer, *The Unwinding: An Inner History of the New America* (New York: Farrar, Straus and Giroux: 2013).

105. Jeff Connaughton, *The Payoff: Why Washington Always Wins* (Westport, CT: Prospecta Press, 2012).

106. Dale Maharidge and Michael S. Williamson, *Someplace Like America: Tales from a New Great Depression* (Berkeley: University of California Press, 2011).

107. Evan Osnos, *Wildland: The Making of America's Fury* (New York: Farrar, Straus and Giroux, 2021).

108. Steven W. Webster, *American Rage: How Anger Shapes Our Politics* (Cambridge: Cambridge University Press, 2020).

109. Tom Ashbrook, "Time for a Guaranteed Basic Income?" *On Point*, January 19, 2016, https://basicincome.org/news/2016/01/audio-on-point-with-tom-ashbrook-time-for-a-guaranteed-basic-income/.

110. Justin Lahart, "The Fed Fought the World and the World Won," *Wall Street Journal*, January 22, 2016.

Chapter 1

1. Nassim Taleb, *The Black Swan: The Impact of the Highly Improbable* (New York: Random House Trade Publications, 2010), 323.

2. Andrejs Skaburskis, "The Origin of 'Wicked Problems,'" *Planning Theory and Practice* 9, no. 2 (June 2008): 277–80; Johanna Lönngren and Katrien van Poeck, "Wicked Problem: A Mapping Review of the Literature," *International Journal of Sustainable Development and World Ecology* 28, no. 6 (December 2020): 481–502, https://doi.org/10.1080/13504509.2020.1859415.

3. C. West Churchman, "Wicked Problems," *Management Science* 14, no. 4 (December 1967): B-141, https://www.jstor.org/stable/2628678.

4. Horst W. J. Rittel and Melvin M. Webber, "Dilemmas in a General Theory of Planning," *Policy Sciences* 4, no. 2 (June 1973): 155–69, https://doi.org/10.1007/BF01405730.

5. Rittel and Webber, "Dilemmas," 157.

6. Rittel and Webber, "Dilemmas," 168.

7. Rittel and Webber, "Dilemmas," 167.

8. Rittel and Webber, "Dilemmas," 167.

9. Rittel and Webber, "Dilemmas," 156.

10. Rittel and Webber, "Dilemmas," 157.

11. Rittel and Webber, "Dilemmas," 168.

12. Rittel and Webber, "Dilemmas," 168.

13. Rittel and Webber, "Dilemmas," 169.

14. The literature on wicked problems is voluminous. Rittel and Webber's article touched off a fifty-year quest to understand wicked problems—their properties, characteristics, causes, and ethics, comparison to other problem types, and their expansion into many other disciplines. Rather than to summarize this entire body of work, the intent here is to highlight certain aspects of the wicked problem literature that are central to our search for problem-solving strategies better equipped to deal with them. The design strategy will be one of those strategies.

15. Rittel and Webber, "Dilemmas," 161.

16. Rittel and Webber, "Dilemmas," 165.

17. Hasan Özbekhan, "The Predicament of Mankind: Quest for Structural Responses to Growing Worldwide Complexities and Uncertainties: A Proposal (to the Club of Rome)," 1970. https://www.futureworlds.eu/wiki/The_Predicament_of_Mankind. For an updated discussion, see Richard Slaughter and Chris Riedy, "Understanding and Resolving the Global Problematique: Assessing the Balance between Progressive and Socially Conservative Foresight," *Foresight* 11, no. 5 (August 2009): 21–39.

18. Eduardo Porter, "Finding Common Ground on Poverty," *New York Times*, February 3, 2016. http://www.nytimes.com/2016/02/03/business/finding-common-political-ground-on-poverty.html.

19. Rittel and Webber, "Dilemmas," 166.

20. Rittel and Webber, "Dilemmas, 164

21. Crime and Justice News, "Illinois Town of 26,000 Has Nation's Highest Murder Rate," *The Crime Report*, April 24, 2019, https://thecrimereport.org/2019/04/24/e-st-louis-il-has-the-nations -highest-murder-rate/.

22. Aron Wildavsky, *Speaking Truth to Power* (Boston: Little Brown, 1979), 386.

23. Finance Online: Reviews for Business, "Income Inequality: Views & Solutions from Experts," accessed September 2, 2020, http://financesonline.com/income-inequality-views-solutions-from -experts/.

24. David J. Kilcullen, *The Accidental Guerrilla: Fighting Small Wars in the Midst of the Big One* (Oxford: Oxford University Press, 2009).

25. Wikipedia, "The original cobra effect," last modified July 10, 2020, https://en.wikipedia.org /wiki/Cobra_effect.

26. Rittel and Webber, "Dilemmas," 163.

27. Rittel and Webber, "Dilemmas," 163.

28. Rittel and Webber, "Dilemmas," 162.

29. Rittel and Webber, "Dilemmas," 163.

30. Office of the High Comissioner for Human Rights, "UN Human Rights Office Estimates More than 306,000 Civilians Were Killled over 10 Years in Syria Conflict," June 28, 2022. https://www .ohchr.org/en/press-releases/2022/06/un-human-rights-office-estimates-more-306000-civilians -were-killed-over-10.

31. Rittel and Webber, "Dilemmas," 163.

32. Russell L. Ackoff, *Redesigning the Future: A Systems Approach to Societal Problems* (New York: John Wiley & Sons, 1974), 21.

33. Robert E. Horn and Robert P. Webber, "New Tools for Resolving Wicked Problems: Mess Mapping and Resolution Mapping Processes," v. 1.2, 2007, https://www.strategykinetics.com/new _tools_for_resolving_wicked_problems.pdf.

34. Australian Public Service Commission, *Tackling Wicked Problems: A Public Policy Perspective* (Canberra: Australian Public Service Commission, 2007).

35. Richard J. Lazarus, "Super Wicked Problems and Climate Change: Retraining the Present to Liberate the Future," *Cornell Law Review* 94 (2009), 1160. https://scholarship.law.cornell.edu/cgi /viewcontent.cgi?article=3143&context=clr.

36. Lazarus, "Supper Wicked Problems," 1174.

37. Lazarus, "Supper Wicked Problems," 1174.

38. Lazarus, "Super Wicked Problems," 1225–1231.

39. Kelly Levin et al., "Overcoming the Tragedy of Super Wicked Problems: Constraining Our Future Selves to Ameliorate Global Climate Change," *Policy Science* 45 (2012):123–52, https://doi .org/10.1007/s11077-012-9151-0.

40. Chris Ansell and Martin Bartenberger, "Tackling Unruly Public Problems," in *Governance in Turbulent Times*, ed. Christopher K. Ansell, Jarle Trondal and Morten Øgård (Oxford: Oxford University Press, 2016), 107.

41. Ian I. Mitroff and Richard O. Mason, "Structuring Ill-Structured Problems: Further Explorations in a Methodology for Messy Problems," *Strategic Management Journal* 1, no. 4 (1980): 331–42, https://doi.org/10.1002/smj.4250010404.

42. Donald A. Schön and Martin Rein. *Frame Reflection: Toward the Resolution of Intractable Policy Controversies* (New York: Basic Books, 1994).

43. Maatthijs Hisschemöller and Robert Hoppe, "Coping with Intractable Controversies: The Case for Problem Structuring in Policy Design and Analysis," *Knowledge and Policy: The International Journal of Knowledge Transfer and Utilization* 8, no. 4 (winter 1995–1996): 40–60.

44. Brian W. Head, "Wicked Problems in Public Policy," *Public Policy* 3, no. 2 (2008): 104.

45. Sharon S. Dawes, Anthony M. Cresswell, and Teresa A. Pardo, "From 'Need to Know' to 'Need to Share': Tangled Problems, Information Boundaries, and the Building of Public Sector Knowledge Networks," *Public Administration Review* 69, no. 3 (May/June 2009): 392–402, https://doi.org/10.1111/j.1540-6210.2009.01987_2.x.

46. Peter J. Balint et al., *Wicked Environmental Problems* (Washington, DC: Island Press, 2011), 2.

47. Balint et al., *Wicked Environmental Problems*, 209.

48. Lazarus, "Super Wicked Problems and Climate Change," 2009; Levin et al., "Overcoming the Tragedy of Super Wicked Problems," 2012.

49. Ranulph Glanville, "A (Cybernetic) Musing: Wicked Problems," *Cybernetics and Human Knowing* 19, nos. 1–2 (2012): 163–73, http://ranulphglanville.org.za/publications/; Ranulph Glanville, "Try Again. Fail Again. Fail Better: The Cybernetics in Design and the Design of Cybernetics," *Kybernetes* 36, no. 9 (October 2007): 1173–206, https://doi.org/10.1108/03684920710827238.

50. Tom Richey, "Wicked Problems: Modelling Social Messes with Morphological Analysis," *ACTA Morphologica Generalis* 2, no. 1 (2013): 1–8, https://vdocuments.net/amp/wicked-problems-modelling-social-messes-with-morphological-analysis.html; Robert E. Horn, "Social Messes," Nautilus Institute, https://nautilus.org/gps/solving/social-messes-robert-e-horn/.

51. Brian W. Head and John Alford, "Wicked Problems: Implications for Public Policy and Management." *Administration & Society* 47, no. 6 (August 2015): 712, https://doi.org/10.1177/0095399713481601.

52. Ansell and Bartenberger, "Tackling Unruly Public Problems."

53. Kate Crowley and Brian W. Head, "The Enduring Challenge of 'Wicked Problems,'" *Policy Science* 50 (2017): 542. https://doi.org/10.1007/s11077-017-9302-4.

54. Allan McConnell, "Rethinking Wicked Problems as Political Problems and Policy Problems," *Policy & Politics* 46, no. 1 (2018): 165, https://doi.org/10.1332/030557317X15072085902640.

55. Nick Turnbull and Robert Hoppe, "Problematizing 'Wickedness': A Critique of the Wicked Problems Concept, from Philosophy to Practice," *Policy and Society* 38, no. 2 (2018): 315, https://doi.org/10.1080/14494035.2018.1488796.

56. Brian W. Head, "Forty Years of Wicked Problems Literature: Forging Closer Links to Policy Studies," *Policy and Society* 38, no. 2 (2019): 189, https://doi.org/10.1080/14494035.2018.1488797.

57. Steven Ney and Christoph Meinel, eds., *Putting Design Thinking to Work: How Large Organizations Can Embrace Messy Institutions to Tackle Wicked Problems* (Cham, Switzerland: Springer Nature, 2019), 76.

58. Table 1.1 builds on Rittel and Webber's framework, but researchers make other distinctions between problems: routine versus nonroutine; programmed versus nonprogrammed; well-defined versus ill-defined; structured versus ill-structured; unstructured versus simple; and complex versus intractable. For those who wish to take a deeper dive into this literature, I recommend starting with Herbert Simon and Allen Newell, *Human Problem Solving* (Englewood, NJ: Prentice Hall, 1972); Donald Schön and Martin Rein, *Frame Reflection: Toward the Resolution of Intractable Policy Controversies* (New York: Basic Books, 1994); Ian I. Mitroff and Richard O. Mason, "Structuring Ill-Structured Problems: Further Explorations in a Methodology for Messy Problems," *Strategic Management Journal* 1, no. 4 (1980): 331–42, https://doi.org/10.1002/smj.4250010404.

59. John Turnpenny, Irene Lorenzoni and Mavis Jones, "Noisy and Definitely Not Normal: Responding to Wicked Issues in the Environment, Energy and Health," *Environmental Science & Policy* 12, no. 3 (2009): 347–58, https://doi.org/10.1016/j.envsci.2009.01.004.

60. John Alford and Brian W. Head, "Wicked and Less Wicked Problems: A Typology and a Contingency Framework," *Policy and Society* 36, no. 3 (2017): 398, https://doi.org/10.1080/14494035.2017.1361634.

61. B. Guy Peters, "What Is so Wicked about Wicked Problems? A Conceptual Analysis and a Research Program," *Policy and Society* 36, no. 3 (2017): 385, 392, 389, https://doi.org/10.1080/14494035.2017.1361633.

62. Nick Turnbull and Robert Hoppe, "Problematizing 'Wickedness': A Critique of the Wicked Problem Concept, from Philosophy to Practice," *Policy and Society* 38, no. 2 (2019): 315–37, https://doi.org/10.1080/14494035.2018.1488796.

63. Richard Buchanan, "Wicked Problems in Design Thinking," *Design Issues* 8, no. 2 (Spring 1992): 16, https://doi.org/10.2307/1511637.

64. David Collier, Jody LaPorte, and Jason Seawright, "Putting Typologies to Work: Concept Formation, Measurement, and Analytics Rigor," *Political Research Quarterly* 65, no. 1 (2012): 217–32, https://doi.org/10.1177/1065912912437162.

65. Rittel and Webber, "Dilemmas," 161.

66. Ronald A. Heifetz, *Leadership without Easy Answers* (Cambridge, MA: Harvard University Press, 1994).

67. Maatthijs Hisschemöller and Robert Hoppe, "Coping with Intractable Controversies: The Case for Problem Structuring in Policy Design and Analysis," *Knowledge and Policy: The International Journal of Knowledge Transfer and Utilization* 8, no. 4 (Winter 1995–1996): 56. See also Robert Hoppe, "Policy Analysis, Science and Politics: From 'Speaking Truth to Power' to 'Making Sense Together,'" *Science and Public Policy* 26, no. 3 (1999): 201–10, https://doi.org/10.3152/147154399781782482.

68. Alford and Head, "Wicked and Less Wicked."

69. Alford and Head, "Wicked and Less Wicked," 403.

70. Rittel and Webber, "Dilemmas" 169.

71. Barbara F. Walter, *How Civil Wars Start* (New York: Crown, 2022); Steven Levitsky and Daniel Ziblatt, *How Democracies Die* (New York: Broadway Books, 2019).

72. Merriam-Webster, "Conflict," accessed September 2, 2020, https://www.merriam-webster.com/dictionary/conflict.

73. Nancy C. Roberts, "Wicked Problem Territory and the Design Strategy," paper presented to the International Public Policy Workshop on Wicked Problems and Agenda Setting, June 26–28, 2018, 15–20, IPPA—IWPP, Pittsburgh 2019, Policy (ippapublicpolicy.org).

74. The concept of space or territory draws from Allen Newell and Herbert Simon's problem-space theory, presented in their 1972 book *Human Problem Solving*. They theorize that people solve problems by searching in a problem space that consists of the current state, the goal state, and all possible states in between and conducting an operation or a series of operations to transform the actual state of a system into the goal state. See also "What Is Problem Solving?" *Cognitive Psychology*, last edited April 14, 2009, http://cognitivepsychology.wikidot.com/cognition:problem-solving.

75. For illustrative purposes, only three options are shown: simple problem territory, complex solutions territory, and complex problems territory. There likely are many other options in all three territories.

76. Mirko Noordegraaf et al., *Policy and Society* 38, no. 2 (2019): 278, https://doi.org/10.1080/14494035.2019.1617970.

77. Lazarus, "Super Wicked Problems."

78. Levin et al., "Overcoming the Tragedy."

79. "Complexity," *Webster's Third New International Dictionary*, 16th ed. (1971), 465.

80. Andreas Fischer, Samuel Greiff, and Joachim Funke, "The Process of Solving Complex Problems," *Journal of Problem Solving* 4 (2012): 19–42, https://doi.org/10.7771/1932-6246.1118; Peter A. Frensch and Joakim Funke, "Definitions, Traditions, and a General Framework for Understanding Complex Problem Solving," in *Complex Problem Solving: The European Perspective*, ed. Peter A. Frensch and Joachim Funke (New York: Psychology Press, 2014), 3–25; Dörner Dietrich, *The Logic of Failure: Recognizing and Avoiding Error in Complex Situations*, trans. Rita and Robert Kimber (New York: Metropolitan Books, 1996).

81. John F. Kennedy, "Special Message to Congress on Urgent National Needs," John F. Kennedy Archives, May 25, 1961, https://www.jfklibrary.org/asset-viewer/archives/JFKWHA/1961/JFKWHA-032/JFKWHA-032.

82. John F. Kennedy, "Address at Rice University on the Nation's Space Effort," John F. Kennedy Archives, September 12, 1962, https://www.jfklibrary.org/archives/other-resources/john-f-kennedy-speeches/rice-university-19620912.

83. Courtney G. Brooks, James M. Grimwood, and Loyd S. Swensen, Jr., *Chariots for Apollo: A History of Manned Lunar Spacecraft*, NASA Special Publication-4205 in the NASA History Series, 1979, https://www.hq.nasa.gov/office/pao/History/SP-4205/contents.html; NASA, "Project Apollo: A Retrospective Analysis," updated April 21, 2014, https://history.nasa.gov/Apollomon/Apollo.html.

84. Dael Wolfle, "The Administration of NASA," *Science* 162, no. 3855 (November 15, 1968): 753.

85. Wolfle, "The Administration of NASA," 753.

86. Rittel and Webber, "Dilemmas," 161.

87. My thanks to Dr. John Arquilla for suggesting this example.

88. Walter Isaacson, "Madeline's War," *Time*, May 17, 1999, http://content.time.com/time/world/article/0,8599,2054293,00.html.

89. Michael D. Cohen, James G. March, and Johan P. Olsen, "A Garbage Can Model of Organizational Choice," *Administrative Science Quarterly* 17, no. 1 (March 1972): 1–25, https://doi.org/10.2307/2392088.

90. American Psychological Association, "2020 Presidential Election a Source of Significant Stress for More Americans than the 2016 Presidential Race," October 7, 2020, https://www.apa.org/news/press/releases/2020/10/election-stress.

91. Ludwig Wittgenstein, *Philosophical Investigations*, trans. G. E. M Anscombe, 4th ed. (Hoboken, NJ: Wiley-Blackwell, 1998); Peter L. Berger and Thomas Luckmann, *The Social Construction of Reality* (Garden City, NY: Doubleday, 1966); John R. Searle, *The Construction of Social Reality* (New York: Free Press, 1995).

92. Aaron Wildavsky, *Speaking Truth to Power: The Art and Craft of Policy Analysis* (New York: Routledge, 1987), 386.

93. Sheril Kirshenbaum, "'Climate Change' or 'Global Warming'? Two New Polls Suggest That Language Matters," *Scientific American*, December 15, 2014, https://blogs.scientificamerican.com/plugged-in/climate-change-or-global-warming-two-new-polls-suggest-language-matters/.

94. William R. Shea and Mariano Artigas, *The Rise and Fall of a Troublesome Genius* (Oxford: Oxford University Press, 2003).

95. Ethan Siegel, "Yes, The Multiverse Is Real, But It Won't Fix Physics," *Forbes*, January 25, 2018, https://www.forbes.com/sites/startswithabang/2018/01/25/yes-the-multiverse-is-real-but-it-wont-fix-physics/#132b47e33a67.

96. World Health Organization (WHO), *The Global Eradication of Smallpox: The Final Report of the Global Commission for the Certification of Smallpox Eradication* (Geneva, Switzerland: WHO, 1980), http://apps.who.int/iris/bitstream/10665/39253/1/a41438.pdf.

97. Larry Brilliant, an epidemiologist who helped eradicate smallpox, accepted the TED Prize in 2006. Larry Brilliant, "My Wish: Help Me Stop Pandemics," TED2006, 25:38, https://www.ted.com/talks/larry_brilliant_my_wish_help_me_stop_pandemics.

98. Colette Flight, "Smallpox: Eradicating the Scourge," BBC History, last updated February 17, 2011, http://www.bbc.co.uk/history/british/empire_seapower/smallpox_01.shtml.

99. Flight, "Smallpox."

100. "What Is Problem Solving?" *Cognitive Psychology*, last edited April 14, 2009, http://cognitivepsychology.wikidot.com/cognition:problem-solving. See also Allen Newell and Herbert A. Simon, *Human Problem Solving* (Englewood Cliffs, NJ: Prentice-Hall, 1972). Newell and Simon define problem solving as the successful search for an operation or a series of operations that will transform the actual state of a system into the goal state.

Chapter 2

1. Lawrence Freedman, *Strategy: A History* (Oxford: Oxford University Press, 2013), 608.

2. Ned Crosby, Janet M. Kelly, and Paul Schaefer, "Citizen Panels: A New Approach to Citizen Participation," *Public Administration Review* 46, no. 2 (March/April, 1986):170–78, https://doi.org/10.2307/976169.

3. James S. Fishkin, "Consulting the Public through Deliberative Polling," *Journal of Policy Analysis and Management* 22, no. 1 (Winter 2003): 128–33, https://doi.org/10.2307/3325851.

4. Merrelyn Emery and Ronald E. Purser, *The Search Conference* (San Francisco: Jossey-Bass, 1996); Marvin R. Weisbord and Sandra Janoff, *Future Search: Getting the Whole System in the Room for Vision, Commitment, and Action* (San Francisco: Berrett-Koehler, 2010).

5. Keith Melville, Taylor L. Willingham, and John R. Dedrick, "National Issues Forum: A Network of Communities Promoting Public Deliberation," in *The Deliberative Democracy Handbook: Strategies for Effective Civic Engagement in the Twenty-First Century*, ed. John Gastil and Peter Levine (San Francisco: Jossey-Bass, 2005), 37–58.

6. Peter Checkland and Jim Scholes, *Soft Systems Methodology in Action* (Chichester, UK: John Wiley, 1999).

7. Carolyn J. Lukensmeyer and Steven Brigham, "Taking Democracy to Scale: Creating a Town Hall Meeting for the Twenty First Century, *National Civic Review* 91, no. 4 (Winter 2002); 351–66, https://doi.org/10.1002/ncr.91406l; Carolyn J. Lukensmeyer and Steven Brigham, "Taking Democracy to Scale: Large-Scale Intervention—for Citizens," *Journal of Applied Behavioral Science* 41, no. 1 (March 2005): 47–60, https://doi.org/10.1177/0021886304272656.

8. Horst W. J. Rittel and Melvin M. Webber, "Dilemmas in a Theory of Planning," *Policy Sciences* 4 (1973): 168, https://doi.org/10.1007/BF01405730.

9. Thomas Hobbes, "Of Man, Being the First Part of Leviathan," *Harvard Classics, Vol. 34, Part 5* (New York: P. F. Collier & Son, 1909–1914), accessed September 5, 2020, www.bartleby.com/34/5/.

10. Will Durant and Ariel Durant, *The Lessons of History* (New York: Simon & Schuster, 1968), 81.

11. Wikipedia, "World War I Casualties," last modified September, 2, 2020, https://en.wikipedia.org/wiki/World_War_I_casualties.

12. Wikipedia, "World War II Casualties," last modified September, 4, 2020, https://en.wikipedia.org/wiki/World_War_II_casualties.

13. Thomas C. Hayes, "Confrontation in the Gulf; The Oilfields Lying below the Iraq-Kuwait Dispute," *New York Times*, September 3, 1990, http://www.nytimes.com/1990/09/03/world/confrontation-in-the-gulf-the-oilfield-lying-below-the-iraq-kuwait-dispute.html?pagewanted=all.

14. Abbas Alnasrawi, The Economy of Iraq: Oil, Wars, Destruction of Development and Prospects, 1950–2010 (Westport, CT: Greenwood Press, 1994), 116).

15. President George W. Bush's Address to Joint Session of Congress (transcript), CNN.com/US, September 30, 2001, http://edition.cnn.com/2001/US/09/20/gen.bush.transcript/.

16. Paul L. Heyne, Peter J. Boettke, and David L. Prychitko, *The Economic Way of Thinking*, 13th ed. (New York: Pearson, 2013), 102–6.

17. Michael E. Porter, *Competitive Advantage* (New York: Free Press, 1985), 11–15.

18. A. G. Lafley and Roger L. Martin, *Playing to Win* (Boston: Harvard Business Review Press, 2013); A. G. Lafley, Roger L. Martin, and Jennifer Riel, "A Playbook for Strategy: The Five Essential Questions at the Heart of Any Winning Strategy," *Rotman Magazine* (Winter 2013), 5–9, https://matthewemay.com/wp-content/uploads/2014/08/Play2Win-Roger1.pdf.

19. Peter Pham, "China's Steel Industry Is Dominating the Global Market—But Will It Last?" *Forbes*, April 27, 2016, http://www.forbes.com/sites/peterpham/2016/04/27/chinas-steel-industry-is-dominating-the-global-market-but-will-it-last/#ceeed04380b1.

20. Edward Flanagan, "China's 'Zombie' Steelmakers Hit with Huge U.S. Tariffs," NBC News, May 18, 2016, http://www.nbcnews.com/business/business-news/china-s-zombie-steelmakers-hit -huge-u-s-tariffs-n576006.

21. Holly Ellyatt, "US Hits China and Others with More Steep Steel Duties," CNBC, updated May 26, 2016, http://www.cnbc.com/2016/05/26/us-hits-china-and-others-with-more-steep-steel -duties.html.

22. Flanagan, "China's 'Zombie' Steelmakers."

23. Tyler Durden, "China Furious after US Launches Trade War 'Nuke' With 522% Duty," *Zero Hedge*, May 19, 2016, http://www.zerohedge.com/news/2016-05-19/china-furious-after-us -launches-trade-war-nuke-522-duty. For an updated guide to Trump's trade war, see Chad P. Brown and Melina Kolb, "Trump's Trade War Timeline: An Up-to-Date Guide," Peterson Institute for International Economics, December 18, 2020, https://www.piie.com/blogs/trade-investment -policy-watch/trump-trade-war-china-date-guide.

24. US Census, "Trade in Goods with China," https://www.census.gov/foreign-trade/balance /c5700.html.

25. Michelle Gibley, "Currency Wars: Is a Weaker Currency Good or Bad?" Charles Schwab, September 16, 2019, http://www.schwab.com/public/schwab/nn/articles/Currency-Wars-Is-a-Weaker -Currency-Good-or-Bad.

26. Parag Khanna, *Connectography: Mapping the Future of Global Civilization* (New York: Random House, 2016), xvii.

27. Khanna, *Connectography*, 6.

28. Drug Policy Alliance, "A Brief History of the Drug War," accessed September 5, 2020. http:// www.drugpolicy.org/new-solutions-drug-policy/brief-history-drug-war.

29. Drug Policy Alliance, "A Brief History of the Drug War."

30. Drug Policy Alliance, "A Brief History of the Drug War."

31. Campaign for an Independent Britain, "7 Reasons Why We Should Leave the EU," accessed September 5, 2020, http://campaignforanindependentbritain.org.uk/the-economy/.

32. European Movement United Kingdom, "Reasons to Remain in the European Union," May 20, 2019, http://www.proeuropa.org.uk/twelvereasons.

33. *XPRIZE*, "XPRIZE Rapid COVID Testing," accessed September 5, 2020, https://www.xprize .org/prizes/covidtesting.

34. Jeffry Pfeffer, *Power in Organizations* (New York: Harper Business, 1981), 344–45.

35. Andrew J. Bacevich, "Endless War in the Middle East," *CATO Institute* 14, no. 3 (Summer 2016): 1–7, https://www.cato.org/publications/catos-letter/endless-war-middle-east.

36. John Arquilla, personal communication, May 21, 2016.

37. Peter Bergen and Paul Cruickshank, "The Iraq Effect," *Mother Jones*, March 1, 2007, https:// www.motherjones.com/politics/2007/03/iraq-101-iraq-effect-war-iraq-and-its-impact-war -terrorism-pg-1/.

38. Statista Research Department, "Terrorism—Facts and Statistics," Statista, accessed September 5, 2020, http://www.statista.com/topics/2267/terrorism/.

39. National Consortium for the Study of Terrorism and Responses to Terrorism (START), Global Terrorism Database, accessed September 5, 2020, https://www.start.umd.edu/gtd/.

40. Robert B. Reich, "Big Tech Has Become Way Too Powerful," *New York Times*, September 18, 2015, http://www.nytimes.com/2015/09/20/opinion/is-big-tech-too-powerful-ask-google.html.

41. Joseph E. Stiglitz et al., *Rewriting the Rules of the American Economy: An Agenda for Growth and Shared Prosperity* (New York: Roosevelt Institute, 2015), https://rooseveltinstitute.org/wp-content /uploads/2015/05/RI-Rewriting-the-Rules-201505.pdf.

42. US Department of Treasury Office of International Affairs, *Foreign Exchange Policies of Major Trading Partners of the United States*, April 29, 2016, https://www.treasury.gov/resource-center /international/exchange-rate-policies/Documents/2016-4-29%20(FX%20Pol%20of%20Major%20 Trade%20Partner)_final.pdf.

43. Tom Fairless, "ECB Mario Draghi Urges Central Bank to Align Monetary Policy," *Wall Street Journal*, June 28, 2016, http://www.wsj.com/articles/ecbs-mario-draghi-urges-central-banks-to -coordinate-monetary-policy-1467104849.

44. Michael Pettis, "How Trump's Tariffs Really Affected the U.S. Job Market," Carnegie Endownment for International Peace, accessed January 23, 2023, https://carnegieendowment .org/chinafinancialmarkets/83746#:~:text=A%20January%202021%20study%20 commissioned,the%20United%20States%20245%2C000%20jobs.

45. Bill Tomso, "USDA: Trump Tariffs Cost $27 Billion in Lost Exports over Year and a Half," accessed January 23, 2023, https://www.agri-pulse.com/articles/17053-usda-trump-tariffs-cost -27b-in-lost-exports-over-year-and-a-half#:~:text=The%20retaliatory%20duties%20imposed%20 on,by%20USDA's%20Economic%20Research%20Service.

46. Erica York, "Tracking the Economic Impact of U.S. Tariffs and Retaliatory Actions," *Tax Foundation Tariff Tracker*, accessed January 23, 2023, https://taxfoundation.org/tariffs-trump -trade-war/.

47. Center on Budget and Policy Priorities, "Chart Book: Tracking the Post-Great Recession Economy," updated May 27, 2022, https://www.cbpp.org/research/economy/tracking-the-post -great-recession-economy.

48. Gary Fields, "White House Czar Calls for End to 'War on Drugs'," *Wall Street Journal*, updated May 14, 2009, https://www.wsj.com/articles/SB124225891527617397.

49. Drug Policy Alliance, "Drug War Statistics," accessed September 6, 2020, https://www .drugpolicy.org/issues/drug-war-statistics.

50. Charles P. Ries et al., *After Brexit: Alternative Forms of Brexit and Their Implications for the United Kingdom, the European Union, and the United States* (Santa Monica, CA: RAND Corporation, 2017). https://www.rand.org/randeurope/research/projects/brexit-economic-implications.html.

51. Rittel and Webber, "Dilemmas," 169.

52. "Debunking Years of Tabloid Claims about Europe," *The Economist*, June 22, 2016, https:// www.economist.com/graphic-detail/2016/06/22/debunking-years-of-tabloid-claims-about -europe.

53. Niall McCarthy, "How Many British Euromyths Has the EU Debunked?" Statista, November 22, 2018, https://www.statista.com/chart/16181/how-many-british-euromyths-has-the-eu-debunked/.

54. Lena Masri, "After Brexit, Many 'Leave' Voters Express Buyer's Remorse," ABC News, June 27, 2016, https://abcnews.go.com/International/brexit-vote-leave-voters-express-buyers-remorse/story?id=40158309.

55. Joyce Battle and Malcolm Byrne, ed., "The Iraq War Ten Years After," *National Security Briefing Book*, no. 418, March 19, 2013, *National Security Archive* (Washington, DC, George Washington University, 2013), https://nsarchive2.gwu.edu/NSAEBB/NSAEBB418/.

56. David Halberstam, *The Best and the Brightest* (New York: Ballantine Books, 1969).

57. Robert McNamara, *In Retrospect: The Tragedy and Lessons of Vietnam* (New York: Times Books, 1995).

58. Stanley Karnow, "A Verdict on Vietnam," *Washington Post*, October 28, 1984, https://www.washingtonpost.com/archive/entertainment/books/1984/10/28/a-verdict-on-vietnam/ca05dbd0-1838-4998-8be0-42c14b5ad1e5/.

59. Office of the Historian, Department of State, "280 Memorandum from the President's Assistant for National Security Affairs (Kissinger) to President Ford," May 12, 1975, *Foreign Relations of the United States, 1969–1976, Vol. X, Vietnam*, January 1973–July 1975, https://history.state.gov/historicaldocuments/frus1969-76v10/d280.

60. James M. Lindsay, "The Vietnam War in Forty Quotes" (blog post), From the Water's Edge, Council on Foreign Relations, April 30, 2015, https://www.cfr.org/blob/vietnam-war-forty-quotes.

61. "Nixon's Views on Presidential Power: Excerpts from a 1977 Interview with David Frost," May 19, 1977, https://ilearn.marist.edu/access/content/user/10043047@marist.edu/my%20documents/EDAC631/Lesson%20Presentation%20Final%20Project/Nixon%20interview.pdf.

62. Karl Milm, Jacob Apkon, and Sruthi Venkatachalam, *Just Security*, "Litigation Tracker: Pending Criminal and Civil Cases against Donald J. Trump," originally published February 28, 2021, continually updated. https://www.justsecurity.org/75032/litigation-tracker-pending-criminal-and-civil-cases-against-donald-trump/.

63. GovInfo, *Select Juanuary 6th Committee Rinal Repot and Supporting Materials Collection*, https://www.govinfo.gov/collection/january-6th-committee-final-report?path=/GPO/January%206th%20Committee%20Final%20Report%20and%20Supporting%20Materials%20Collection.

64. Financial Crisis Inquiry Commission, *The Financial Crisis Inquiry Report* (Washington, DC: US Government Printing Office, 2011), xvii, http://fcic-static.law.stanford.edu/cdn_media/fcic-reports/fcic_final_report_full.pdf.

65. John Maxfield, "25 Factors That Caused or Contributed to the Financial Crisis," *The Motley Fool*, updated October 2, 2018, http://www.fool.com/investing/general/2015/02/28/25-major-factors-that-caused-or-contributed-to-the.aspx.

66. Financial Crisis Inquiry Commission, *Financial Crisis Inquiry Report*, xviii.

67. Financial Crisis Inquiry Commission, *Financial Crisis Inquiry Report*, xvii.

68. Financial Crisis Inquiry Commission, *Financial Crisis Inquiry Report*, xxi.

69. Financial Crisis Inquiry Commission, *Financial Crisis Inquiry Report*, xxiii.

70. Financial Crisis Inquiry Commission, *Financial Crisis Inquiry Report*, xviii.

71. Jack Ruhl and Diane Ruhl, "NCR Research: Costs of Sex Abuse Crisis to US Church Under-estimated," *National Catholic Reporter*, November 2, 2015, https://www.ncronline.org/news/accountability/ncr-research-costs-sex-abuse-crisis-us-church-underestimated.

72. Wikipedia, "List of Religious Leaders Convicted of Crimes," last modified March 15, 2020, https://en.wikipedia.org/wiki/List_of_religious_leaders_convicted_of_crimes.

73. Chris Hayes, *Twilight of the Elites: America after Meritocracy* (New York: Crown Publishers, 2012), 175.

74. Gallup, "Confidence in Institutions," accessed September 6, 2020, https://news.gallup.com/poll/1597/confidence-institutions.aspx.

75. George A. Miller, "The Magical Number Seven, Plus or Minus Two: Some Limits on Our Capacity for Processing Information," *Psychological Review* 63 (1956): 81–97.

76. Herbert A. Simon, *Models of Man* (New York: Wiley, 1957).

77. Robert K. Merton, "The Unanticipated Consequences of Purposive Social Action," *American Sociological Review* 1, no. 6 (December 1936): 894–904, https://doi.org/10.2307/2084615.

78. Ori Brafman and Rom Brafman, *Sway: The Irresistible Pull of Irrational Behavior* (New York: Doubleday, 2008); Zachary Shore, *Blunder: Why Smart People Make Bad Decisions* (New York: Bloomsbury, 2008).

79. Daniel Kahneman, *Thinking Fast and Slow* (New York: Farrar, Straus and Giroux, 2011).

80. Kahneman, *Thinking Fast and Slow*, 411.

81. Kahneman, *Thinking Fast and Slow*, 411.

82. Irving L. Janis, *Groupthink*, 2nd ed. (Boston: Wadsworth, 1982).

83. See Kahneman. *Thinking Fast and Slow*, Part 3, "Overconfidence," 199–265, which describes these fallacies in greater detail.

84. Kahneman, *Thinking Fast and Slow*, 205.

85. Philip E. Tetlock and Dan Gardner, *Superforecasting: The Art and Science of Prediction* (New York: Crown Publishers, 2015), 4.

86. Gary Klein, *Sources of Power: How People Make Decisions* (Cambridge, MA: MIT Press, 1998).

87. Kahneman, *Thinking Fast and Slow*, 240 (emphasis added).

88. Kahneman, *Thinking Fast and Slow*, 225.

89. Kahneman, *Thinking Fast and Slow*, 240.

90. Kahneman, *Thinking Fast and Slow*, 241.

91. Kahneman, *Thinking Fast and Slow*, 263.

92. Kahneman, *Thinking Fast and Slow*, 263.

93. Rittel and Webber, "Dilemmas," 161.

94. Rittel and Webber, Dilemmas," 162.

95. C. West Churchman, "Guest Editorial: Wicked Problems," *Management Science*, 14, no. 4 (1967): B-141.

96. Mark N. Wexler, "Exploring the Moral Dimensions of Wicked Problems," *International Journal of Sociology and Social Policy* 29, no. 9–10 (2009): 535. https://doi.org/10.1108/01443330910986306.

97. Denise Lash, Steve Raynor, and Helen Ingram, "Taming the Waters: Strategies to Domesticate the Wicked Problems of Water Resource Management," *Water* 3, no. 1 (2005): 3.

98. Jeff Conklin, *Dialogue Mapping: Building Shared Understanding of Wicked Problems* (Chichester, UK: John Wiley and Sons, 2006), 21–22.

99. Conklin, *Dialogue Mapping*, 22.

100. Conklin, *Dialogue Mapping*, "IBIS: A Tool for All Reasons," 87–122.

101. Conklin, *Dialogue Mapping*, "The Dialogue Mapping Experience," 57–83.

102. Jeff Conklin, "Issue Mapping FAQs," CogNexus Institute, accessed September 7, 2020, http://www.cognexus.org/issue_mapping_faqs.htm.

103. Robert E. Horn and Robert P. Webber, "New Tools for Resolving Wicked Problems: Mess Mapping and Resolution Mapping Processes," v. 1.2, 2007, https://www.strategykinetics.com /new_tools_for_resolving_wicked_problems.pdf.

104. Tom Ritchey, *Wicked Problems—Social Messes* (Berlin: Springer, 2011).

105. *ScienceDaily,* "Human-Machine Superintelligence Can Solve the World's Most Dire Problems," January 4, 2016, https://www.sciencedaily.com/releases/2016/01/160104080041.htm; Anne-Marie Grisogono, "How Could Future AI Help Tackle Global Complex Problems?" *Frontiers in Robotics and AI,* April 21, 2020, https://www.frontiersin.org/articles/10.3389/frobt.2020.00050/full.

106. Marc Ballon, "Artificial Intelligence: Are We Facing a Future of Robots Running Wild?" *USC News,* August 31, 2016, http://news.usc.edu/106565/artificial-intelligence-for-a-better-tomorrow/.

107. Nancy A. Rigotti and Robert B. Wallace, "Using Agent-Based Models to Address 'Wicked Problems' Like Tobacco Use: A Report from the Institute of Medicine," *Annals of Internal Medicine* 163, no. 6 (September 2015): 469–71. https://doi.org/10.7326/M15-1567.

108. Spencer Ackerman, "How the US's Terrorism Watchlists Work—and How You Could End up on One," *The Guardian,* July 24, 2014, https://www.theguardian.com/world/2014/jul/24/us -terrorism-watchlist-work-no-fly-list.

109. Dan Cunningham, "Social Network Map," *CORE Lab,* Naval Postgraduate School, July 17, 2017. My thanks to Dan Cunningham for his depiction of this social network and the assumptions he had to make to generate it.

110. Terry Collins, "Twitter Suspends Another 235,000 Terrorism-Related Accounts," C/Net, August 18, 2016, https://www.cnet.com/news/twitter-suspends-another-235000-terrorism-related -accounts/.

111. Robert Pape et al., "How to Fix the Flaws in the Global Terrorism Database and Why It Matters," *Washington Post,* August 11, 2014, https://www.washingtonpost.com/news/monkey -cage/wp/2014/08/11/how-to-fix-the-flaws-in-the-global-terrorism-database-and-why-it-matters/.

112. Dan Cunningham, personal communication, CORE Lab Research Associate, Department of Defense Analysis at the Naval Postgraduate School, July 17, 2017.

113. Sean F. Everton, *Disrupting Dark Networks* (New York: Cambridge University Press, 2012).

114. Nancy C. Roberts and Sean F. Everton, "Monitoring and Disrupting Dark Networks: A Bias toward the Center and What It Costs Us," in *Eradicating Terrorism from the Middle East,* ed.

Alexander R. Dawoody (Berlin: Springer, 2016), 29–42, https://doi.org/10.1007/978-3-319-31018 -3_2.

115. Herbert A. Simon, "The Structure of Ill-Structured Problems," *Artificial Intelligence* 4, no. 3–4 (Winter 1973):181–201, https://doi.org/10.1016/0004-3702(73)90011-8.

116. Charles E. Lindblom, "The Science of Muddling Through," *Public Administration Review* 19, no. 2 (Spring 1959): 79–88; Charles E. Lindblom, "Still Muddling, Not Yet Through," *Public Administration Review* 39 (November–December 1979): 517–26.

117. Michael D. Cohen, James G. March, and Johan P. Olsen, "A Garbage Can Model of Organizational Choice," *Administrative Science Quarterly* 17, no. 1 (March 1972):1–25, 1, https://doi.org /10.2307/2392088.

118. Ian L. Mitroff and Abraham Silvers, *Dirty Rotten Strategies: How We Trick Ourselves and Others into Solving the Wrong Problems Precisely* (Stanford, CA: Stanford University Press, 2010).

119. Denise Lash, Steve Rayner, and Helen Ingram, "Taming the Waters: Strategies to Domesticate the Wicked Problems of Water Resource Management," *International Journal of Water* 3, no. 1 (2005): 1–17, https://doi.org/10.1504/IJW.2005.007156.

120. Derick W. Brinkerhoff, "State Fragility and Failure as Wicked Problems: Beyond Naming and Taming," *Third World Quarterly* 35, no. 2 (March 2014): 333–44, https://doi.org/10.1080 /01436597.2014.878495.

121. Wexler, "Exploring the Moral Dimensions of Wicked Problems."

122. "Collaboration," *The Concise Oxford Dictionary*, 5th ed., 1964, 234.

123. Ann M. Thomson and James L. Perry, "Collaboration Processes: Inside the Black Box," *Public Administration Review* 66 (December 2006): 20, https://doi.org/10.1111/j.1540-6210.2006.00663.x.

124. Rittel and Webber, "Dilemmas," 162.

125. Rittel and Webber, "Dilemmas," 166.

126. For further elaboration of Rittel's views on information systems, see two chapters in Protzen and Harris (2010). Chapter 3.1 is Rittel's article on the "Structure and Usefulness of Planning Information Systems" (171–180) and chapter 3.2 is Werner Kunz and Horst Rittel's article, "Issues as Elements of Information Systems" (181–186), a paper that was originally published as Working Paper No. 131, Berkeley, CA: Institute of Urban and Regional Development, July 1970, and reprinted in 1978.

127. Thomson and Perry, "Collaboration Processes," 20.

128. Barbara Gray, *Collaborating: Finding Common Ground for Multiparty Problems* (San Francisco: Jossey-Bass, 1989), 5.

129. Thomas W. Malone and Kevin Crowston, "The Interdisciplinary Study of Coordination, *ACM Computing Survey* 26, no. 1 (1994): 87–119; Gerardo A. Okhuysen and Beth A. Bechky, "Coordination in Organizations: An Integrative Perspective," *Academy of Management Annals* 3, no. 1 (2009): 463–502, https://doi.org/10.5465/19416520903047533.

130. "Cooperation," *The Concise Oxford Dictionary*, 5th ed. (1964), 848.

131. Robert Axelrod, *The Evolution of Cooperation* (New York: Basic Books, 1984).

132. Gray, *Collaborating*, 5.

133. Donna J. Wood and Barbara Gray, "Toward a Comprehensive Theory of Collaboration," *Journal of Applied Behavioral Science* 27, no. 2 (June 1991): 11, https://doi.org/10.1177/0021886391272001.

134. Judith E. Innes and David E. Booher, "Collaborative Rationality as a Strategy for Working with Wicked Problems," *Landscape and Urban Planning* 154 (October 2016): 8–10, https://doi.org/10.1016/j.landurbplan.2016.03.016; William D. Eggers and Paul MacMillan, *The Solution Revolution: How Business, Government, and Social Enterprise Are Teaming up to Solve Society's Toughest Problems* (Boston: Harvard Business Review Press, 2013).

135. Ewan Ferlie et al., *Making Wicked Problems Governable? The Case of Managed Networks in Health Care* (Oxford: Oxford University Press, 2013); Ben Hannigan and Michael Coffey, "Where the Wicked Problems Are: The Case of Mental Health," *Health Policy* 101, no. 3 (2011): 220–27, https://doi.org/10.1016/j.healthpol.2010.11.002; Marshall W. Kreuter et al., "Understanding Wicked Problems: A Key to Advancing Environmental Health Promotion," *Health Education & Behavior* 31, no. 4 (August 2004): 441–54, https://doi.org/10.1177/1090198104265597.

136. Kerri-Lee Krause, "Addressing the Wicked Problem of Quality in Higher Education: Theoretical Approaches and Implications," *Higher Education Research & Development* 31, no. 3 (2012): 285–97, https://doi.org/10.1080/07294360.2011.634381.

137. Anne Tietjen and Gertrud Jørgensen, "Translating a Wicked Problem: A Strategic Planning Approach to Rural Shrinkage in Denmark," *Landscape & Urban Planning*, 154 (October 2016): 29–43, https://doi.org/10.1016/j.landurbplan.2016.01.009.

138. Catrien Termeer, Art Dewulf, and Gerard Breeman, "Governance of Wicked Climate Adaptation Problems," in *Governance of Wicked Climate Adaptation Problems*, ed. J. Knieling and Filho W. Leal (Heidelberg, Germany: Springer, 2013), 27–39, https://doi.org/10.1007/978-3-642-29831-8_3.

139. Brian W. Head and John Alford, "Wicked Problems: Implications for Public Policy and Management," *Administration & Society* 47, no. 6 (August 2015): 711–39, https://doi.org/10.1177/0095399713481601; Edward P. Weber and Anne M. Khademian, "Wicked Problems, Knowledge Challenges, and Collaborative Capacity Builders in Network Settings," *Public Administration Review* 68, no. 2 (March/April 2008): 344–49, https://doi.org/10.1111/j.1540-6210.2007.00866.x.

140. Brian W. Head, "Forty Years of Wicked Problems Literature: Forging Closer Links to Policy Studies," *Policy and Society* 38, no. 2 (April 2019): 1–8, https://doi.org/10.1080/14494035.2018.1488797; Falk Daviter, "Coping, Taming, or Solving: Alternative Approaches to the Governance of Wicked Problems," *Policy Studies* 38, no. 6 (2017): 571–88, https://doi.org/10.1080/01442872.2017.1384543.

141. Brian W. Head, Helen Ross, and Jennifer Bellamy, "Managing Wicked Natural Resource Problems: The Collaborative Challenge at Regional Scales in Australia," *Landscape and Urban Planning* 154 (October 2016): 68–92, https://doi.org/10.1016/j.landurbplan.2016.03.019; Vanessa R. Levesque, Kathleen P. Bell, and Aram J. K. Calhoun, "Planning for Sustainability in Small Municipalities," *Journal of Planning Education and Research* 37, no. 3 (September 2017): 322–33, https://doi.org/10.1177/0739456X16655601.

142. Sandra S. Batie, "Wicked Problems and Applied Economics," *American Journal of Agricultural Economics* 90, no. 5 (December 2008): 1176–91, https://doi.org/10.1111/j.1467-8276.2008.01202.x.

143. Charles Hauss, *Security 2.0: Dealing with Global Wicked Problems* (Lanham, MD: Rowman & Littlefield, 2015).

144. Kirk Emerson and Tina Nabatchi, *Collaborative Governance Regimes*, ch. 3 (Washington, DC: Georgetown University Press, 2015).

145. Thomson and Perry, "Collaboration Processes," 24–25.

146. H. Brint Milward and Keith G. Provan, *A Manager's Guide to Choosing and Using Collaborative Networks* (Washington, DC: IBM Center for the Business of Government, 2006).

147. Richard D. Margerum, *Beyond Consensus: Improving Collaborative Planning and Management* (Cambridge, MA: MIT Press, 2011); Ralf Brand and Frank Gaffikin, "Collaborative Planning in an Uncollaborative World," *Planning Theory* 6, no. 3 (November 2007): 282–313, https://doi.org/10.1177/1473095207082036.

148. R. Edward Freeman, Jeffrey S. Harrison, and Stelios Zyglidopoulos, *Stakeholder Theory* (Cambridge: Cambridge University Press, 2018).

149. David D. Chrislip and Carl E. Larson, *Collaborative Leadership* (New York: Wiley, 1994); Barbara B. Crosby and John M. Bryson, *Leadership for the Common Good: Tackling Public Problems in a Shared-Power World*, 2nd ed. (San Francisco: Jossey-Bass, 2005).

150. Judith E. Innes and David E. Booher, "A Turning Point for Planning Theory? Overcoming Dividing Discourses," *Planning Theory* 14, no. 2 (2015): 195–213, https://doi.org/10.1177/1473095213519356; William W. Isaacs, *Dialogue and the Art of Thinking: A Pioneering Approach to Communication* (New York: Currency, 1999).

151. Deana D. Pennington, "Cross Disciplinary Collaboration and Learning," *Ecology and Society* 13, no. 2 (December 2008), http://www.jstor.org/stable/26267958; Peter M. Senge, *The Fifth Discipline: The Art and Practice of the Learning Organization*, 2nd ed. (New York: Currency, 2006).

152. Judith E. Innes, "Consensus Building: Clarifications for the Critics," *Planning Theory* 3, no. 1 (July 2004): 5–20, https://doi.org/10.1177/1473095204042315; Lawrence Susskind, Sarah McKearnan, and Jennifer Thomas-Larmer, eds., *The Consensus Building Handbook* (Thousand Oaks, CA.: SAGE, 1999).

153. Robert Goodspeed, "Smart Cities: Moving beyond Urban Cybernetics to Tackle Wicked Problems," *Cambridge Journal of Regions, Economy, and Society* 8, no. 1 (March 2015): 79–92, https://doi.org/10.1093/cjres/rsu013; Don Tapscott and Anthony D. Williams, "Innovating the 21st Century University: It's Time!" *Educause Review* 45, no. 1 (January/February 2010): 16–29, https://kofd.pw/uploads-innovating-the-21st-century-university-its-time.pdf.

154. Emerson and Nabatchi, *Collaborative Governance Regimes*; Chris Huxham and Siv Vangen, *Managing to Collaborate* (New York: Routledge, 2005).

155. Judith E. Innes and David E. Booher, *Planning with Complexity: An Introduction to Collaborative Rationality for Public Policy* (Oxfordshire, UK: Routledge, 2010), 89.

156. Innes and Booher, *Planning with Complexity*, 85.

157. Innes and Booher, *Planning with Complexity*, 91.

158. Robert Agranoff, *Collaborating to Manage: A Primer for the Public Sector* (Washington DC: Georgetown University Press, 2012), 18.

159. Huxham and Vangen, *Managing to Collaborate*, 60.

160. Huxham and Vangen, *Managing to Collaborate*, 42.

161. Agranoff, *Collaborating to Manage*, ch. 7.

162. Innes and Booher, *Planning with Complexity*, 95.

163. Huxham and Vangen, *Managing to Collaborate*, 152.

164. Innes and Booher, *Planning with Complexity*, 67–72.

165. Huxham and Vangen, *Managing to Collaborate*, 37.

166. Carolyn J. Lukensmeyer and Steven Brigham, "Taking Democracy to Scale: Creating a Town Hall Meeting for the Twenty-First Century," *National Civic Review* 91, no. 4 (Winter 2002): 351–66. https://doi.org/10.1002/ncr.91406l.

167. Carolyn J. Lukensmeyer and Steven Brigham, "Taking Democracy to Scale: Large Interventions—for Citizns," *Journal of Applied Behavioral Science* 41, no. 1 (March 2005): 47–60. https://doi.org/10.1177/0021886304272656.

168. Innes and Booher, *Planning with Complexity*, 94.

169. Innes and Booher, *Planning with Complexity*, 94–95.

170. Huxham and Vangen, *Managing to Collaborate*, 13 (emphasis in the original).

171. Huxham and Vangen, *Managing to Collaborate*, 41.

172. Huxham and Vangen, *Managing to Collaborate*, 12–13.

173. Huxham and Vangen, *Managing to Collaborate*, 116.

174. Huxham and Vangen, *Managing to Collaborate*, 34.

175. Huxham and Vangen, *Managing to Collaborate*, 87.

176. Innes and Booher, *Planning with Complexity*, 115.

177. Huxham and Vangen, *Managing to Collaborate*, 61. See also chs. 6 and 7.

178. Huxham and Vangen, *Managing to Collaborate*, 64. See also ch.10.

179. Huxham and Vangen, *Managing to Collaborate*, 66. See also ch. 9.

180. Huxham and Vangen, *Managing to Collaborate*, 69. See also ch. 8.

181. Huxham and Vangen, *Managing to Collaborate*, p. 72. See also ch. 8.

182. Huxham and Vangen, *Managing to Collaborate*, 75. See also ch. 12.

183. Huxham and Vangen, *Managing to Collaborate*, p. 78. See also ch. 13.

184. Michael McGuire and Robert Agranoff, "Networking in the Shadow of Bureaucracy," in *Oxford Handbook of American Bureaucracy*, ed. Robert F. Durant (Oxford: Oxford University Press, 2010), 372–420.

185. Innes and Booher, *Planning with Complexity*, ch. 8, esp. 197–205.

186. Brian W. Head and John Alford, "Wicked Problems: Implications for Public Policy and Management," *Administration & Society* 47, no. 6 (August 2015): 719. https://doi.org/10.1177/0095399713481601.

187. Head and Alford, "Wicked Problems," 722.

188. Head and Alford, "Wicked Problems," 728.

189. Donald K. Kettl, "Managing the Boundaries in American Administration: The Collaboration Imperative," *Public Administration Review* (SI December 2006): 10–19, https://doi.org/10.1111/j.1540-6210.2006.00662.x.

190. Huxham and Vangen, *Managing to Collaborate*, 7.

191. John M. Bryson, Barbara C. Crosby, and Melissa M. Stone, "The Design and Implementation of Cross-Sector Collaborations," *Public Administration Review* 66, no. s1 (December 2006), https://onlinelibrary.wiley.com/toc/15406210/66/s1: 44.

192. Innes and Booher, *Planning with Complexity*, 41.

193. Innes and Booher, *Planning with Complexity*, 41.

194. Janine O'Flynn, "The Cult of Collaboration in Public Policy," *Australian Journal of Public Administration* 68, no. 1 (2009): 112, https://doi.org/10.1111/j.1467-8500.2009.00616.x.

195. O'Flynn, "The Cult of Collaboration in Public Policy," 113.

196. O'Flynn, "The Cult of Collaboration in Public Policy," 115.

197. Thomson and Perry, "Collaborative Processes," 29.

198. Huxham and Vangen, *Managing to Collaborate*, 4.

199. Innes and Booher, *Planning with Complexity*, ch. 4.

Chapter 3

1. Richard Buchanan, "Wicked Problems in Design Thinking," *Design Issues* 8, no. 2 (Spring 1992): 5–21, https://doi.org/10.2307/1511637.

2. Lawrence Freedman, *Strategy: A History* (Oxford: Oxford University Press, 2013), xi.

3. Freedman, *Strategy: A History*, 608.

4. Warren Berger, *Glimmer: How Design Can Transform Your Life, and Maybe Even the World* (New York: Penguin Press, 2009), 29.

5. Ken Friedman and Erik Stolterman, eds., "Series Foreword," *Design Thinking, Design Theory Series,* in *Making Design Theory*, ed. John G. Redström (Cambridge, MA: MIT Press, 2017), ix.

6. Smithsonian Natural Museum of Natural History, "What Does It Mean to be Human?" Last updated January 6, 2001, http://humanorigins.si.edu/evidence/human-family-tree.

7. Smithsonian Natural Museum of Natural History, "What Does It Mean to be Human?"

8. John Heskett, *Design: A Very Short Introduction* (Oxford: Oxford University Press, 2005), 5.

9. Heskett, *Design*, 5.

10. Heskett, *Design*, 6.

11. Heskett, Design, 12.

12. Heskett, *Design*, 12-13.

13. Lucy Kimbell, "Rethinking Design Thinking: Part I," *Design and Culture* 3, no. 3 (2011): 285–306, https:// doi.org/10.2752/175470811X13071166525216.

14. Ulla Johansson-Sköldberg, Jill Woodilla, and Mehves Çetinkaya, "Design Thinking: Past, Present and Possible Futures," *Creativity and Innovation Management* 22, no. 2 (2013): 121–46, https://doi.org/10.1111/caim.12023.

15. Herbert A. Simon, *The Sciences of the Artificial* (Cambridge, MA: MIT Press, 1969).

16. Donald A. Schön, *The Reflective Practitioner* (New York: Basic Books, 1983).

17. Buchanan, "Wicked Problems in Design Thinking."

18. Bryan Lawson, *How Designers Think: The Design Process Demystified*, 4th ed. (London: Routledge, 2005); Nigel Cross, *Design Thinking: Understanding How Designers Think and Work* (Oxford, UK: Berg, 2011).

19. Klaus Krippendorff, *The Semantic Turn: A New Foundation for Design* (Boca Raton, FL: CRC, 2006).

20. Roberto Verganti, *Design-Driven Innovation* (Boston: Harvard Business School Press, 2009).

21. Wikipedia, "Design," accessed September 2, 2020, 06:06, https://en.wikipedia.org/wiki/Design.

22. G. K. Van Patter, "Design 1.0, 2.0. 3.0. 4.0," *NextD Journal: ReRe Thinking Design* (March 2009), 3, https://pdfslide.net/documents/design-10-20-3040-the-rise-of-visual-sensemaking.html.

23. Richard Buchanan, "Design Research and the New Learning," *Design Issues* 17, no. 4 (Autumn 2001): 3–23, https://doi.org/10.1162/07479360152681056.

24. Danish Design Center, "The Design Ladder: Four Steps of Design Use," May 6, 2015, https://danskdesigncenter.dk/en/design-ladder-four-steps-design-use.

25. Rabah Bousbaci, "'Models of Man' in Design Thinking: The 'Bounded Rationality' Episode," *Design Issues* 24, no. 4 (Autumn 2008): 38–52, https://doi.org/10.1162/desi.2008.24.4.38.

26. Peter H. Jones, "Design Research Methods in Systemic Design," paper presented at the Design Research Methods for Systemic Design: Perspectives from Design Education and Practice (58th Annual Meeting of the International Society for the Systems Sciences, Washington, DC, July 27—August 1, 2014), https://www.researchgate.net/publication/289551227_Design_research_methods_for_systemic_design_Perspectives_from_design_education_and_practice.

27. John Heskett, *Toothpicks and Logos: Design in Everyday Life* (New York: Oxford University Press, 2002), 6–7.

28. Kees Dorst, "Layers of Design Practice," paper presented at the International Association of Societies of Design Research (Seoul, South Korea, October 18–22, 2009), 157–66, https://opus.lib.uts.edu.au/bitstream/10453/11246/1/2009003488.pdf.

29. Van Patter, "Design 1.0, 2.0. 3.0. 4.0."

30. Charles Owen, "Considering Design Fundamentally," *Design Processes Newsletter* 5, no. 3 (1993), 2.

31. Elizabeth B.-N. Sanders and Pieter J. Stappers, "Co-creation and the New Landscapes of Design," *CoDesign* 4, no. 1 (March 2008): 5–18, https://doi.org/10.1080/15710880701875068.

32. Van Patter, "Design 1.0, 2.0. 3.0. 4.0."

33. Tim Brown, "Strategy by Design," *Fast Company*, June 1, 2005, https://www.fastcompany.com/52795/strategy-design.

34. Hannah Arendt, *The Human Condition*, 2nd ed. (Chicago: University of Chicago Press, 1998); Vilém Flusser, *The Shape of Things: A Philosophy of Design* (London: Reaktion, 1999).

35. George Church and Ed Regis, *Regenesis: How Synthetic Biology Will Reinvent Nature and Ourselves* (New York: Basic Books, 2012).

36. James Kozubek, *Modern Prometheus: Editing the Human Genome with Crisper-Cas9* (Cambridge: Cambridge University Press, 2016).

37. Oliver Morton, *The Planet Remade: How Geoengineering Could Change the World* (Princeton, NJ: Princeton University Press, 2016).

38. Juan Enriquez and Steve Gullans, *Evolving Ourselves: Redesigning the Future of Humanity—One Gene at a Time* (New York: Current, 2015).

39. Merriam-Webster, "Principle," accessed September 16, 2020, https://www.merriam-webster.com/dictionary/principle.

40. Google, "Principle," accessed September 16, 2020, https://www.google.com/search?q=principles+definition&rlz=1C1NHXL_enUS704US704&oq=principles+definition&aqs=chrome.0.69i59j0l5.9512j0j9&sourceid=chrome&ie=UTF-8#xxri=1.

41. See Clio Rosati, Francesca Rosati, and Matteo Vignoli, "Measuring Design Thinking Mindset," paper presented at *DS 92: Proceedings of the Design 2018*, 15th International Design Conference (Dubrovnik, Croatia, May 21-24, 2018): 1991–2002, https://doi.org/10.21278/idc.2018.0493; Walter Brenner, Falk Uebernickel, and Thomas Abrell, "Design Thinking as Mindset, Process, and Toolbox," in *Design Thinking for Innovation*, ed. Walter Brenner and Falk Uebernickel (Cham, Switzerland: Springer, 2016), 3–21. https://doi.org/10.1007/978-3-319-26100-3_1; Lisa Carlgren, Ingo Rauth, and Maria Elmquist, "Framing Design Thinking: The Concept in Idea and Enactment," *Creativity and Innovation Management* 25, no. 1 (March 2016): 38–57, https://doi.org/10.1111/caim.12153; Lotta Hassi and Miko Laakso, "Making Sense of Design Thinking," in *IDBM Papers, Vol. 1*, ed. T.-M. Karjalainen, M. Koria, and M. Salimäki (Helsinki: IDBM Program, Aalto University, 2011), 50–63, https://www.researchgate.net/publication/274066130_Making_sense_of_design_thinking.

42. Rosati et al., "Measuring Design Thinking Mindset."

43. Harold G. Nelson and Erik Stolterman, *The Design Way: Intentional Change in an Unpredictable World* (Cambridge, MA: MIT Press, 2012), 12.

44. Nelson and Stolterman, *The Design Way*, 12 (emphasis in the original).

45. Brian Koberlein, "Gravity," *Cradle to Grave* (blog), February 26, 2015, https://archive.briankoberlein.com/2015/02/26/cradle-to-grave/index.html#:~:text=In%20Einstein's%20model%2C%20gravity%20isn,tells%20mass%20how%20to%20move.&text=Space%20really%20is%20curved%2C%20and,that%20looks%20like%20a%20force.

46. Thom Reaves, "Eric Gibbons: Reflecting Our Humanity, Beauty, and Imperfections," *Thom Reaves' Studio Tour Magazine: The Artists behind the Art*, August 28, 2016, https://www.studiotourmagazine.com/single-post/2016/08/27/Eric-Gibbons-Reflecting-Our-Humanity-Beauty-Imperfections.

47. Others refer to design as a discipline distinct from the disciplines of science and art. See Bruce Archer, "Design as a Discipline," *Design Studies* 1, no. 1 (July 1979): 17–20; Nigel Cross, "Design as Discipline," in *Designerly Ways of Knowing* (London: Springer-Verlag, 2006), 95–103, https://doi.org/10.1007/1-84628-301-9.

48. Hasso Plattner, Christoph Meinel, and Larry Leifer, eds., *Design Thinking Research: Making Design Thinking Foundational* (Heidelberg, Germany: Springer, 2016).

49. See, for example, the dimensions of human-centered design (HCD) research in the design and development of products and services in Sanders and Stappers, "Co-creation and the New Landscapes of Design."

50. Cross, *Designerly Ways of Knowing*; Nigel Cross, "From a Design Science to a Design Discipline: Understanding Designerly Ways of Knowing and Thinking," in *Design Research Now*, ed. Ralf Michael (Basel, Switzerland: Birkhäuser, 2007), 41–54; Kees Dorst and Nigel Cross, "Creativity in the Design Process," *Design Studies* 22, no. 5 (2001): 425–37, https://doi.org/10.1016/S0142-694X(01)00009-6; Hasso Plattner, Christopher Meinel, and Larry Leifer, eds. *Design Thinking: Understand, Improve, Apply* (Berlin: Springer, 2011), https://doi.org/10.1007/978-3-642-13757-0.

51. Nigel Cross, Henri Christiaans, and Kees Dorst, eds. *Analysing Design Activity* (New York: Wiley, 1997); Cross, *Design Thinking: Understanding How Designers Think and Work*.

52. Colin Ware, *Visual Thinking for Design* (Amsterdam: Morgan Kaufmann, 2008).

53. J. H. L. Koh et al., "Developing and Evaluating Design Thinking," in *Design Thinking for Education: Conceptions and Applications in Teaching and Learning* (Singapore: Springer, 2015), 109–20.

54. Eva Köppen and Christoph Meinel, "Empathy via Design Thinking: The Creation of Sense and Knowledge," in *Design Thinking Research: Building Innovators*, ed. Hans Plattner, Christoph Meinel, and Larry Leifer (Cham: Springer, 2015), 15–28, https://link.springer.com/chapter/10.1007%2F978-3-319-06823-7_2.

55. Manish Saggar et al., "Developing Novel Methods to Assess Long-Term Sustainability of Creative Capacity Building and Applied Creativity," in *Design Thinking Research: Understanding Innovation*, ed. Hasso Plattner, Christoph Meinel, and Larry Leifer (Bergen: Springer, 2015), 29–39, https://doi.org/10.1007/978-3-319-06823-7_3.

56. Nigel Cross, "Designerly Ways of Knowing: Design Discipline Versus Design Science," *Design Issues* 17, no. 3 (Summer 2001): 49–55, https://doi.org/10.1162/074793601750357196.

57. Krippendorff, *The Semantic Turn*, ch. 2.

58. Donald A. Norman, *The Psychology of Everyday Things* (New York: Basic Books, 1988).

59. Norman, *The Psychology of Everyday Things*, ch. 5.

60. Klaus Krippendorff, "On the Essential Contexts of Artifacts or on the Proposition That 'Design Is Making Sense (of Things)'," *Design Issues* 5, no. 2 (1989): 9–39, https://doi.org/10.2307/1511512; Krippendorff, *The Semantic Turn*, 2006.

61. Joseph Giacomin, "What Is Human Centred Design?" *Design Journal* 17, no. 4 (2014): 606–23, https://doi.org/10.2752/175630614X14056185480186.

62. Giacomin, "What Is Human Centred Design?" 609.

63. Jon Kolko, *Well-Designed: How to Use Empathy to Create Products People Love* (Brighton, MA: Harvard Business Review Press, 2014).

64. "IDEO's Human-Centered Design Process: How to Make Things People Love," *IDEO* (blog), December 4, 2018, https://www.usertesting.com/blog/2015/07/09/how-ideo-uses-customer-insights-to-design-innovative-products-users-love/.

65. John Cary, "What Is Design If Not Human-Centered?" *Stanford Social Innovation Review*, June 25, 2013, https://ssir.org/articles/entry/what_is_design_if_not_human_centered.

66. Nelson and Stolterman, *The Design Way*, 42.

67. Richard Buchanan, "Human Dignity and Human Rights: Thoughts on the Principles of Human-Centered Design," *Design Issues* 17, no. 3 (Summer 2001): 37, https://www.jstor.org/stable/1511799.

68. Buchanan, "Human Dignity and Human Rights," 37–38.

69. Friedman and Stolterman, eds. "Series Foreword,"xiii.

70. Eve Blossom, *Material Change: Design Thinking and the Social Entrepreneurship Movement* (New York: Metropolis Books, 2011), 42.

71. Nelson and Stolterman, *The Design Way*, 27–40.

72. Schön, *The Reflective Practitioner*, ch. 3.

73. Schön, *The Reflective Practitioner*, 79.

74. Kees Dorst, "Design Problems and Design Paradoxes," *Design Issues* 22, no. 3 (Summer 2006): 11, https://doi.org/10.1162/desi.2006.22.3.4.

75. Jesper Simonsen et al., eds. *Situated Design Methods* (Cambridge, MA: MIT Press, 2014), 1.

76. Bruce M. Tharp and Stephanie M. Tharp, *Discursive Design: Critical, Speculative, and Alternative Things* (Cambridge, MA: MIT Press, 2018).

77. Julia Lohmann, "Waltraud" Cow-Bench, Museum of Modern Art, New York, 2004, https://www.moma.org/colection/works/110306.

78. Evelyn Fox Keller, *A Feeling for the Organism* (New York: W. H. Freeman, 1984).

79. Sanders and Stappers, "Co-creation and the New Landscape of Design," 7.

80. Tom Kelley and David Kelley, *Creative Confidence: Unleashing the Creative Potential within Us All* (New York: Crown Business, 2013); Tina Seelig, *inGenius: A Crash Course in Creativity* (New York: HarperOne, 2012).

81. James C. Kaufman and Robert J. Sternberg, eds. *Cambridge Handbook of Creativity* (Cambridge: Cambridge University Press, 2010).

82. Robert J. Sternberg, "Creativity as a Decision," Comment, *American Psychologist* 57, no. 5 (2002): 376, https://doi.org/10.1037/0003-066X.57.5.376a.

83. James Melvin Rhodes, "An Analysis of Creativity," *Phi Delta Kappan* 42, 1961: 305–10.

84. James L. Adams, *Conceptual Blockbusting: A Guide to Better Ideas*, 4th ed. (Cambridge, UK: Perseus, 2001).

85. Kelley and Kelley, *Creative Confidence*, 2–3.

86. Kelley and Kelley, *Creative Confidence*, 4–5.

87. Kelley and Kelley, *Creative Confidence*, 103.

88. Christoph Meinel and Larry Leifer, "Introduction—Design Thinking Is Mainly about Building Innovators," in *Design Thinking Research: Understanding Innovation*, ed. Hasso Plattner, Christophe Meinel, and Larry Leifer (Cham, Switzerland: Springer, 2015), 1–11, 4, https://doi.org/10.1007/978-3-319-06823-7_1.

89. Tim Brown, *Change by Design* (New York: HarperCollins, 2009), 91.

90. Brown, *Change by Design*, 105.

91. Brown, *Change by Design*, 105.

92. Berger, *Glimmer*, 73.

93. Berger, *Glimmer*, 75.

94. James F. Dunnigan, "Cracked, Leaking and Limping Along," *Strategy Page*, February 24, 2012, https://www.strategypage.com/dls/articles/Cracked,-Leaking-And-Limping-Along-2-24-2012.asp.

95. Brown, *Change by Design*, 125.

96. Norman, *The Psychology of Everyday Things*, ch. 5.

97. Danielly De Paula, Franziska Dobrigkeit, and Kathryn Cormican, "Doing It Right—Critical Success Factors for Design Thinking Implementation," in *International Conference on Engineering Design* 1, no. 1 (August 2019): 3851–860. https://doi.org/10.1017/dsi.2019.392.

98. Berger, *Glimmer*, 37.

99. Victor Papanek, *Design for the Real World: Human Ecology and Social Change*, 2nd ed. (London: Thames & Hudson, 1985), 4.

100. Bruce Mau, quoted in Berger, *Glimmer*, 3.

101. Brown, *Change by Design*, 1.

102. Figure 3.7 adapted from Nancy C. Roberts and Paula J. King, *Transforming Public Policy: Dynamics of Policy Entrepreneurship and Innovation* (San Francisco: Jossey-Bass, 1996), 9.

103. Gerhard Pahl et al., *Engineering Design: A Systematic Approach*, 3rd ed., trans. Ken Wallace and Luciënne T. M. Blessing (London: Springer-Verlag, 2007). The preproduction stage includes a design brief (an early statement of design goals), analysis of design goals, research that investigates design solutions, specified requirements of a design solution for a product or service, conceptualization and documentation of design solutions, and presentation of design solutions. The production stage includes development and continued improvement of a design solution and testing in situ of a design solution. The postproduction stage includes implementation (the introduction of the designed solution to the environment), the evaluation stage (a summary of the process, its results, and suggestions for future improvements), and the redesign stage that repeats any or all stages with corrections made before, during, or after production.

104. Design Council, "Introducing Design for Europe," accessed September 14, 2020, https://www.designcouncil.org.uk/news-opinion/introducing-design-europe.

105. Raghu Garud, Philipp Tuertscher, and Andrew H. Van de Ven, "Perspectives on Innovation Processes," *Academy of Management Annuals* 7, no. 1 (2013): 773–817, https://journals.aom.org/doi/10.5465/19416520.2013.791066.

106. Gerald Zaltman, Robert Duncan, and Jonny Holbek, *Innovations and Organizations* (New York: Wiley, 1973), 10.

107. Paul Watzlawick, John Weakland, and Richard Fisch, *Change: Principles of Problem Formulation and Problem Resolution* (New York: W. W. Norton, 1974), 10.

108. Watzlawick et al., *Change*, 11. For more on proposed third-order change, see Karl E. Weick and Robert E. Quinn, "Organizational Change and Development," *Annual Review of Psychology* 50 (1999): 351–86.

109. Michael L. Tushman and Charles A. O'Reilly III, "Ambidextrous Organizations: Managing Evolutionary and Revolutionary Change," *California Review* 38, no. 4 (Summer 1996), 8–30, http://web.mit.edu/curhan/www/docs/Articles/15341_Readings/Organizational_Learning_and_Change/Tushman_&_OReilly_1996_Ambidextrous_Organizations.pdf; Donald A. Norman and Roberto

Verganti, "Incremental and Radical Innovation: Design Research vs. Technology and Meaning Making," *Design Issues* 30, no. 1 (Winter 2014): 78–96, https://doi.org/10.1162/DESI_a_00250.

110. Lisa Carlgren, *Design Thinking as an Enabler of Innovation: Exploring the Concept and Its Relationship to Building Innovation Capabilities* (PhD diss., Chalmers University of Technology, Gothenburg, Sweden, 2013).

111. Sara L. Beckman and Michael Berry, "Innovation as a Learning Process: Embedding Design Thinking," *California Management Review* 50, no. 1 (Fall 2007): 25–56, https://doi .org/10.2307/41166415; Carlgren, "Design Thinking as an Enabler of Innovation"; Lisa Carlgren, Maria Elmquist, and Ingo Rauth, "Design Thinking: Exploring Values and Effects from an Innovation Capability Perspective," *Design Journal* 17, no. 3 (2014): 403–24, https://doi.org/10 .2752/175630614X13982745783000; Jeanne Liedtka, "Putting Technology in Its Place: Design Thinking's Social Technology at Work." *California Management Review* 62, no. 2 (March 2020): 53–83. https://doi.org/10.1177/0008125619897391.

112. Brown, "Strategy by Design."

113. Tim Brown, "Design Thinking," *Harvard Business Review* (June 2008): 88, https://readings. design/PDF/Tim%20Brown,%20Design%20Thinking.pdf.

114. Stefanie Di Russo, "Understanding the Behavior of Design Thinking in Complex Environments" (PhD diss., Swinburne University of Technology, Melbourne, Australia, 2016), 51, https:// researchbank.swinburne.edu.au/file/a312fc81-17d3-44b5-9cc7-7ceb48c7f277/1/Stefanie%20 Di%20Russo%20Thesis.pdf.

115. Ricardo J. Hernández et al., "Design, the Language of Innovation: A Review of the Design Studies Literature," *She Ji: The Journal of Design, Economics, and Innovation* 4, no. 3 (Autumn 2018): 249–74, https://doi.org/10.1016/j.sheji.2018.06.001.

116. Hernández et al., "Design, the Language of Innovation," 266 (emphasis in the original).

117. Kimbell, "Rethinking Design Thinking: Part I," 290.

118. Kimbell, "Rethinking Design Thinking: Part I," 289.

119. Peter G. Rowe, *Design Thinking* (Cambridge, MA: MIT Press, 1991); Cross, *Design Thinking: Understanding How Designers Think and Work.*

120. Nigel Cross, "Designerly Ways of Knowing," *Design Studies* 3, no. 4 (October 1982): 221–27, https://doi.org/10.1016/0142-694X(82)90040-0; Nigel Cross, "Designerly Ways of Knowing: Design Discipline Versus Design Science," *Design Issues* 17, no. 3 (Summer 2001): 49–55, https:// doi.org/10.1162/074793601750357196.

121. Schön, *The Reflective Practitioner.*

122. Kees Dorst and Judith Dijkhus, "Comparing Paradigms for Describing Design Activity," *Design Studies* 16, no. 2 (April 1995): 261–74, https://doi.org/10.1016/0142-694X(94)00012-3.

123. Herbert Simon, *The Sciences of the Artificial* (Cambridge, MA: MIT Press, 1969.

124. See, for example, Schön, *The Reflective Practitioner*, 1983; Rowe, *Design Thinking*, 1991; Cross, *Design Thinking: Understanding How Designers Think and Work.*

125. Cross, *Design Thinking: Understanding How Designers Think and Work*, 16–29.

126. Berger, *Glimmer*, 271.

127. Kai Joffres, "Design Thinking Isn't the Problem—Here's What It Takes to Do Good Design," UX Collective, December 29, 2019, https://uxdesign.cc/design-thinking-isnt-the-problem-but-here-s-what-it-takes-to-do-good-design-eb4cf4278c63.

128. Jeanne M. Liedtka, "Putting Technology in Its Place: Design Thinking's Social Technology at Work," *California Management Review* 62, no. 2 (March 2020): 53–83.

129. Jeanne Liedtka, "Exploring the Impact of Design Thinking in Action," Charlottesville: University of Virginia, Darden Working Paper Series, 2018, 27, https://designatdarden.org/app/uploads/2018/01/Working-paper-Liedtka-Evaluating-the-Impact-of-Design-Thinking.pdf.

130. Hugh Dubberly, *How Do You Design? A Compendium of Models* (San Francisco: Dubberly Design Office, 2005), last edited March 18, 2005, http://www.dubberly.com/articles/how-do-you-design.html.

131. There are other variations in the design process. As an example, see the references to Dr. Leyla Acaroglu's "Disrupt Design" process in the conclusion of this book.

132. Brown, *Change by Design*, 16.

133. OpenIDEO, "Design Thinking Defined," Facebook, May 4, 2020, https://www.facebook.com/openideo/photos/a.157018881007518/3839137512795618/?type=3.

134. OpenIDEO, "Design Thinking Defined."

135. Kelley and Kelley, *Creative Confidence* (New York: Crown Business, 2013).

136. Kelley and Kelley, *Creative Confidence*, 22–24.

137. Jeanne Liedtka, "Design Process: *What Is? What If? What Wows? What Works?*" Image adapted from Jeanne Liedtka and Tim Ogilvie, *Designing for Growth: A Design Thinking Toolkit for Managers* (New York: Columbia Business School, 2011), 21.

138. Donald A. Norman, *The Design of Everyday Things* (New York: Basic Books, 2013), adapted from figure 6.2, 222.

139. Stanford d School, "Design Thinking Bootleg," accessed September 14, 2020, https://dschool.stanford.edu/resources/design-thinking-bootleg. A seven-phase variant of this Stanford dSchool model can be found in Michael Lewrick, Patrick Link, and Larry Leifer, *The Design Thinking Toolbox* (New York: Wiley, 2020).

140. Damian Newman, "Design Squiggle," accessed September 14, 2020, thedesignsquiggle.com.

Chapter 4

1. Some refer to mindsets as "attitudes"—an established way of thinking or feeling about someone or something that is reflected in one's behavior. See Christian Bason, "Design Attitude as an Innovation Catalyst," in *Public Innovation through Collaboration and Design*, ed. Christopher Ansell and Jacob Torfing (London: Routledge, 2014), 209–28; Kamil Michlewski, "Uncovering Design Attitude: Inside the Culture of Designers," *Organization Studies* 29, no 3 (2008): 373–92. https://doi.org/10.1177/0170840607088019. My preferred term is "mindset," which I use throughout this chapter.

2. See Clio Dosi, Francesca Rosati, and Matteo Vignoli, "Measuring Design Thinking Mindset," in *Proceedings of the DESIGN 2018 15th International Design Conference*, ed. D. Marjanović, M. Štorga,

S. Škec, N. Bojčetić, and N. Pavković (Glasgow: Design Society, 2018), 1991–2002. https://doi .org/10.21278/idc.2018.0493; Walter Brenner, Falk Uebernickel, and Thomas Abrell, "Design Thinking as Mindset, Process, and Toolbox," in *Design Thinking for Innovation*, ed. Walter Brenner and Falk Uebernickel (Cham, Switzerland: Springer, 2016), 3–21. https://doi.org/10.1007/978-3 -319-26100-3_1; Jochen Schweitzer, Lars Groeger, and Leanne Sobel, "The Design Thinking Mindset: An Assessment of What We Know and What We See in Practice," *Journal of Design, Business & Society* 2, no. 1 (March 2016): 71–94. https://doi.org/10.1386/dbs.2.1.71_1.

3. Metadesign should not be confounded with the company Meta Design, which was founded in Berlin with affiliates in San Francisco and Zurich, nor with the concept of "meta-organizations"— large-scale organizational systems in the strategic management literature. The concept is also different from Gerhard Fischer and Elisa Giaccardi's concept of "Meta Design," which is more in line with systemic design as it is defined and explored in chapter 7 of this book. See Gerhard Fischer and Elisa Giaccardi, "Meta Design: A Framework for the Future of End-User Development," in *End User Development*, ed. Henry Lieberman, Fabio Pataernó, Markus Klann, and Volker Wulf (New York: Springer, 2006), 427–57.

4. David Orr, "Architecture, Ecological Design, and Human Ecology," 89th ACSA Annual Meeting, Baltimore, March 16–20, 2001, 23.

5. Daniel C. Wahl, *Designing Regenerative Cultures* (Axminster, UK: Triarchy Press, 2016), 43.

6. Wahl, *Designing Regenerative Cultures*, 47.

7. Carol S. Dweck, *Mindset: The New Psychology of Success* (New York: Ballantine, 2006).

8. Tom Kelley and David Kelley, *Creative Confidence* (New York: Crown Business, 2013), 31.

9. Bruce Mau, "Incomplete Manifesto for Growth," *Chicago Magazine*, May 17, 2010, https:// www.chicagomag.com/Chicago-Magazine/June-2010/Bruce-Mau-Manifesto-for-Growth/.

10. Warren Berger, *Glimmer: How Design Can Transform Your Life, and Maybe Even the World* (New York: Penguin Press, 2009), 47.

11. Ashley Buchanan and Margaret L. Kern, "The Benefit Mindset: The Psychology of Contribution and Everyday Leadership," *International Journal of Wellbeing* 7, no. 1 (June 2017): 2, https:// doi.org/10.5502/ijw.v7i1.538 (emphasis in the original).

12. Reuben Rusk and Lea Waters, "Tracing the Size, Reach, Impact, and Breadth of Positive Psychology," *Journal of Positive Psychology* 8, no. 3 (2013): 207–21, https://doi.org/10.1080/1743976 0.2013.777766.

13. Paul Hawken, *Blessed Unrest: How the Largest Movement in the World Is Restoring Grace, Justice, and Beauty to the World* (New York: Viking Penguin, 2007).

14. Jane Loevinger, *Ego Development* (San Francisco: Jossey-Bass, 1976).

15. Bill Torbert and Associates, *Action Inquiry: The Secret of Timely and Transforming Leadership* (San Francisco: Barrett Koehler, 2004).

16. Annemarie Mink, *Design for Well-Being: An Approach for Understanding Users' Lives in Design for Development* (Delft, Netherlands: Delft Academic Press, 2016).

17. Amartya Sen, *Development as Freedom* (Oxford: Oxford University Press, 1999).

18. Berger, *Glimmer*, 52–53.

19. Berger, *Glimmer*, 53.

20. Mau, "Incomplete Manifesto for Growth."

21. Lev S. Vygotsky, "Imagination and Creativity in Childhood," *Journal of Russian and East European Psychology* 42, no. 1 (January/February 2004): 9.

22. Harold G. Nelson and Erik Stolterman, *The Design Way: Intentional Change in an Unpredictable World* (Cambridge, MA: MIT Press, 2012), 128.

23. Mads Nygaard Folkmann, *The Aesthetics of Imagination in Design* (Cambridge, MA: MIT Press, 2013), 67.

24. Sir Ken Robinson, "Do Schools Kill Creativity?" filmed in February 2006 in Monterey, CA, TED video, 19:12, https://www.ted.com/talks/sir_ken_robinson_do_schools_kill_creativity.

25. WikiDiff, "What Is the Difference between Imagination and Image?" accessed September 18, 2020, https://wikidiff.com/imagination/image.

26. Ann Pendleton-Julian and John Seely Brown, *Pragmatic Imagination* (San Francisco: Blurb, 2016).

27. Jeanne Liedtka, Tim Ogilvie, and Rachel Brozenske, *The Designing for Growth Field Book* (New York: Columbia Business School, 2014), 17.

28. Berger, *Glimmer*, 3.

29. Mark Hatch, *The Maker Movement Manifesto* (New York: McGraw-Hill Education, 2014).

30. Chris Anderson, *Makers: The New Industrial Revolution* (New York: Crown Business, 2012).

31. Hatch, *Maker Movement Manifesto*, 225–29.

32. Hatch, *Maker Movement Manifesto*, 229.

33. Banny Banerjee, "Designer as Agent of Change: A Vision for Catalyzing Rapid Change," in *Changing the Change Conference Proceedings*, ed. Carla Cipolla and Pier Peruccio (Torino, Italy: Allemandi Conference Press, July 2008), https://uploads-ssl.webflow.com/5a9898f92fa8fa00017acfa3/5c63e109cbc13e075f6db2aa_Banny%20Banerjee-Designer%20as%20Agent%20of%20Change.pdf.

34. Herbert A. Simon, "Forecasting the Future or Shaping It?" Complex Information Processing, Working Paper no. 550, presented at the Carnegie Mellon University Earthware Symposium, sponsored by the Department of Computer Science, Carnegie Mellon University, Pittsburgh, October 19, 2000, 1.

35. Paul Watzlawick, John Weakland, and Richard Fisch, *Change: Principles of Problem Formation and Problem Resolution* (New York: W. W. Norton & Company, 1974).

36. Eve Blossom, *Material Change: Design Thinking and the Social Entrepreneurship Movement* (New York: Metropolis Books, 2011), 16.

37. Daniel C. Wahl and Seaton Baxter, "The Designer's Role in Facilitating Sustainable Solutions, *Design Issues*, 24, no. 2 (2008): 73.

38. Daniel C. Wahl, "Meta-Design for Whole Systems Health," *Age of Awareness*, April 8, 2017, https://medium.com/age-of-awareness/design-for-whole-systems-health-e700f1f030c6.

39. Wahl, *Designing Regenerative Cultures*, 20.

40. Donella H. Meadows, "Leverage Points: Places to Intervene in a System," Donella Meadows Archives, accessed October 4, 2020, http://donellameadows.org/archives/leverage-points-places -to-intervene-in-a-system/.

41. Marina Kim, "Rethinking the Impact Spectrum," Ashoka U, April 30, 2015, https://ashokau .org/blog/rethinking-the-impact-spectrum/.

42. I view social movement theory from the cultural perspective. Its central themes are identity, moral principles, emotions, and agency rather than political conflict. For further elaboration, see Alberto Melucci, *Challenging Codes* (Cambridge: Cambridge University Press, 2009); Jeff Goodwin and James M. Jasper, ed. *Rethinking Social Movements* (Lanham, MD: Rowman and Littlefield, 2004); James M. Jasper, *The Art of Moral Protest* (Chicago: University of Chicago Press, 1997); and James M. Jasper, *The Emotions of Protest* (Chicago: University of Chicago Press, 2018).

43. The MITx u.lab is a massive open online course for activating and leading a global ecosystem of societal change and personal renewal, accessed October 21, 2020, https://www.ottoscharmer. com/programs/ulab.

44. C. Otto Scharmer, *The Essentials of Theory U* (Oakland, CA: Berrett Koehler, 2018), 4–5.

45. Scharmer, *The Essentials of Theory U*, 6.

46. Scharmer, *The Essentials of Theory U*, 16 (emphasis in the original).

47. Scharmer, *The Essentials of Theory U*, 25 (emphasis in the original).

48. Ken Wilber, *A Theory of Everything: An Integral Vision for Business, Politics, Science, and Spirituality* (Boston: Shambala, 2001), 7.

49. Wilber, *A Theory of Everything*, 5 (emphasis in the original).

50. Wilber, *A Theory of Everything*, 19, figure 2–1, 21.

51. Wilber, *A Theory of Everything*, 18.

52. Ken Wilber, *A Brief History of Everything: 20th Anniversary Edition* (Boulder, CO: Shambhala, 2017), 126.

53. See Wilber, *A Theory of Everything*, 8–13; Keith E. Rice, "vMemes #4," *Integrated Socio-Psychological Blog*, accessed October 21, 2020. https://www.integratedsociopsychology.net /theory/vmemes/vmemes-3/.

54. Don E. Beck and Christophe C. Cowan, *Spiral Dynamics: Mastering Values, Leadership, and Change* (Malden, MA: Blackwell, 2006).

55. Wilber, *A Theory of Everything*, 2001, figures 4.4 and 4.5, 70–71.

56. For a short description of Ken Wilber's integral theory and its implications for design's evolving mental models and worldviews, see Wahl's overview in *Designing Regenerative Cultures*, 73–75.

57. Wilber, *A Theory of Everything*, 55.

58. Clare Graves, "Summary Statement: The Emergent, Cyclical, Double-Helix Model of Adult Human Biopsychosocial Systems," Boston, May 20, 1981, cited in Wilber, *A Theory of Everything*, 2001, 5–6. However, as best as I am able to ascertain, the Graves quote is a compellation of his statements, not a direct quote from his text. See https://www.clarewgraves.com/articles_content/1981 _handout/1981_summary.pdf.

59. Color-coding the levels or memes was a result of Beck and Cowan's work in South Africa. See Don E. Beck and Graham Linscott, *The Crucible: Forging South Africa's Future, in Search of a Template for the World* (Columbia, MD: Graphic Press, 1991).

Instead of keeping people trapped in mindset of Black versus white, they use the color scale to describe eight levels of development.

60. Beck and Cowan, *Spiral Dynamics*, 4–5.

61. Beck and Cowan, *Spiral Dynamics*, 274.

62. Beck and Cowan, *Spiral Dynamics*, 11.

63. Beck and Cowan, *Spiral Dynamics*, ch. 9.

64. Beck and Cowan, *Spiral Dynamics*, ch. 10.

65. Beck and Cowan, *Spiral Dynamics*, ch. 11.

66. Beck and Cowan, *Spiral Dynamics*, 215.

67. Beck and Cowan, *Spiral Dynamics*, 216.

68. Beck and Cowan, *Spiral Dynamics*, 222.

69. Beck and Cowan, *Spiral Dynamics*, 224.

70. Beck and Cowan, *Spiral Dynamics*, 225.

71. Beck and Cowan, *Spiral Dynamics*, ch.12.

72. Beck and Cowan, *Spiral Dynamics*, 229.

73. Beck and Cowan, *Spiral Dynamics*, 236.

74. Beck and Cowan, *Spiral Dynamics*, 237.

75. Beck and Cowan, *Spiral Dynamics*, ch. 13.

76. Beck and Cowan, *Spiral Dynamics*, 259.

77. Beck and Cowan, *Spiral Dynamics*, ch. 14.

78. Beck and Cowan, *Spiral Dynamics*, 264.

79. Beck and Cowan, *Spiral Dynamics*, 268.

80. Beck and Cowan, *Spiral Dynamics*, ch. 15.

81. Beck and Cowan, *Spiral Dynamics*, 283.

82. Beck and Cowan, *Spiral Dynamics*, ch. 16.

83. Beck and Cowan, *Spiral Dynamics*, 289.

84. Beck and Cowan, *Spiral Dynamics*, 290.

85. Beck and Cowan, *Spiral Dynamics*, 288.

86. Beck and Cowan, *Spiral Dynamics*, 287.

87. Don E. Beck, Teddy H. Larsen, Sergey Solonin, Rica Viljoen, and Thomas Q. Johns, *Spiral Dynamics in Action: Humanity's Master Code* (Hoboken, NJ: Wiley, 2018), 27.

88. Beck et al., *Spiral Dynamics in Action*, 12.

89. Beck et al., *Spiral Dynamics in Action*, 12.

90. Beck et al., *Spiral Dynamics in Action*, 108.

91. Beck et al., *Spiral Dynamics in Action*, 12.

92. Beck et al., *Spiral Dynamics in Action*, xix.

93. Beck et al., *Spiral Dynamics in Action*, 108.

94. Beck et al., *Spiral Dynamics in Action*, 13.

95. Beck et al., *Spiral Dynamics in Action*, 12.

96. Beck et al, *Spiral Dynamics in Action*, 27.

97. Beck et al, *Spiral Dynamics In Action*, xix.

98. Walter Sullivan, "The Enstein Papers: A Man of Many Parts," *New York Times*, March 29, 1972, 1.

99. Wilber, *A Theory of Everything*, 8–13.

100. Leyla Acaroglu, "Disrupt Design: Post Disposable," accessed October 21, 2020, https://www.disruptdesign.co/post-disposable.

101. Leyla Acaroglu, "Disrupt Design" Post Disposable Workshops," accessed October 21, 2020, https://www.disruptdesign.co/workshops.

102. Leyla Acaroglu, "Toolkit: Free Post Disposable Activation," accessed October 21, 2020, https://online.unschools.co/courses/post-disposable-activation-kit.

103. Carol Sanford, *The Regenerative Life: Transform Any Organization, Our Society, and Your Destiny* (Boston: Nicholas Brealey, 2020), xxvi.

104. Sanford, *The Regenerative Life*, 1.

105. Sanford, *The Regenerative Life*, xxiv.

106. Sanford, *The Regenerative Life*, xxvii.

107. Sanford, *The Regenerative Life*, 28.

108. Sanford, *The Regenerative Life*, xxiv.

109. Sanford, *The Regenerative Life*, 27.

110. Sanford, *The Regenerative Life*, xxiv.

111. Sanford, The Regenerative Life, p. 6.

112. Sanford, *The Regenerative Life*, 32.

113. Sanford, *The Regenerative Life*, xxiv.

114. Sanford, *The Regenerative Life*, xxviii.

115. Of particular note is Sanford's description of the regenerative designer role, which is activated by the desire to make something new. See chapter 5 in *The Regenerative Life* for a fuller exploration of this role, which involves the pursuit of functionality, relatability, and the promotion of agency in others.

116. Sanford, *The Regenerative Life*, 39–45.

117. Sanford, *The Regenerative Life*, 183–86 (emphasis in the original).

118. Beck and Cowan, *Spiral Dynamics,* and Beck et al., *Spiral Dynamics in Action.*

119. Scharmer, *Theory U*, 34–50.

120. C. Otto Scharmer and Katrin Kaufer, *Leading from the Emerging Future: From Ego-System-to Eco-System* (San Francisco: Barrett-Koehler, 2013), 1 (emphasis in the original).

121. Scharmer, *Theory U*, 14.

122. Scharmer, *Theory U*, p. 36.

123. Image from C. Otto Scharmer, "Leading from the Future: A New Social Technology for Our Times," *Systems Thinker*, accessed October 22, 2020, https://thesystemsthinker.com/leading-from -the-future-a-new-social-technology-for-our-times/, based on a Creative Commons ShareAlike 4.0 license.

124. Scharmer, *Theory U*, p. xiv.

125. Scharmer, *Theory U*, pp. 6-8.

126. Wahl, *Designing Regenerative Cultures*, 46.

127. Wahl, *Designing Regenerative Cultures*, 22–23.

128. Wahl, *Designing Regenerative Cultures*, 23.

129. Wahl, *Designing Regenerative Cultures*, 23.

130. Wahl, *Designing Regenerative Cultures*, 19.

131. Wahl, *Designing Regenerative Cultures*, 21.

132. Wahl, *Designing Regenerative Cultures*, 36.

133. Wahl, *Designing Regenerative Cultures*, 21.

134. Wahl and Baxter, "The Designer's Role in Facilitating Sustainable Solutions," 76.

135. David Bohm, *On Dialogue* (London: Routledge, 1996), 10.

136. Richard Buchanan, "Wicked Problems in Design Thinking," *Design Issues* 8, no. 2 (Spring 1992), https://doi.org/10.2307/1511637

137. Wahl and Baxter, "The Designer's Role," 75.

138. Wahl, *Designing Regenerative Cultures*, 24–26.

139. Wahl, *Designing Regenerative Cultures*, 79.

140. Wahl, *Designing Regenerative Cultures*, 83.

141. Wahl, *Designing Regenerative Cultures*, 26.

142. Wahl, *Designing Regenerative Cultures*, 28–30.

143. Wahl, *Designing Regenerative Cultures*, 31–33.

144. Wahl, *Designing Regenerative Cultures*, 39. Quote from Bill Plotkin, *Nature and the Human Soul: Cultivating Wholeness and Community in a Fragmented World* (Novato, CA: New World Library, 2007).

145. Wahl, *Designing Regenerative Cultures*, 35.

146. Wahl, *Designing Regenerative Cultures*, 42.

147. Wahl, *Designing Regenerative Cultures*, 43.

148. Wahl, *Designing Regenerative Cultures*, 42–44.

149. Wahl, *Designing Regenerative Cultures*, 44.

150. Wahl, *Designing Regenerative Cultures*, 43.

151. Wahl, *Designing Regenerative Cultures*, 47.

Chapter 5

1. James L. Adams, *Conceptual Blockbusting: A Guide to Better Ideas*, 4th ed. (Cambridge, UK: Perseus, 2001).

2. Daniel Goleman, *Emotional Intelligence: Why It Can Matter More Than IQ* (New York: Bantam, 1995), xiv (emphasis in the original).

3. Goleman, *Emotional Intelligence*, 4.

4. Goleman, *Emotional Intelligence*, 80.

5. Goleman, *Emotional Intelligence*, 43.

6. Goleman, *Emotional Intelligence*, 286.

7. Goleman, *Emotional Intelligence*, xii.

8. Martin Seligman, *Flourish* (New York: Free Press, 2011).

9. Seligman, *Flourish*, 11.

10. Seligman, *Flourish*, 11.

11. Seligman, *Flourish*, 12.

12. Seligman, *Flourish*, 18.

13. Seligman, *Flourish*, 20–24.

14. Seligman, *Flourish*, 229.

15. Seligman, *Flourish*, 230–31.

16. "Happiness Website," accessed September 19, 2020, www.authentichappiness.org.

17. Martin Seligman, *Learned Optimism: How to Change Your Mind and Your Life* (New York: Vintage Books, 2006).

18. Malcolm Gladwell, *Blink: The Power of Thinking without Thinking* (New York: Little Brown, 2005).

19. Frances Vaughan, *Awakening Intuition* (Garden City, NY: Anchor Books, 1979), 3.

20. Petra Badke-Schaub and Ozgur Eris, "A Theoretical Approach to Intuition in Design: Does Design Methodology Need to Account for Unconscious Processes?" in *An Anthology of Theories and Models of Design*, ed. Amaresh Chakrabarti and Lucienne T. M. Blessing (London: Springer, 2014), 353–70, https://doi.org/10.1007/978-1-4471-6338-1_17.

21. Boris Müller, "Intuition Is the Key to Good Design," *MODUS*, accessed September 20, 2020, https://medium.com/@borism/in-defence-of-intuition-f924ab82f76b.

22. frog, "Design and the (Ir)Rational Mind: The Rise of Affective Sensing," May 1 2014, accessed September 20, 2020, https://designmind.frogdesign.com/2014/05/design-irrational-mind-rise -affective-sensing-2/.

23. Rosalind W. Picard, *Affective Computing* (Cambridge: MIT Press, 2000).

24. Jill Bolte Taylor, *My Stroke of Insight* (New York: Viking, 2006).

25. frog, "Design and the (Ir)Rational Mind," 2014.

26. Vaughan, *Awakening Intuition*.

27. Judith Orloff, *Second Sight* (New York: Three Rivers Press, 2010).

28. Bill Sharpe, *Three Horizons: The Patterning of Hope* (Axminster, UK: Triarchy Press, 2013).

29. Bill Sharpe et al., "Three Horizons: A Pathways Practice for Transformation," *Ecology and Society* 21, no. 2 (June 2016): 47. https://doi.org/10.5751/ES-08388-210247.

30. Sharpe, *Three Horizons*, 23.

31. Sharpe et al., "*Three Horizons*," 46.

32. Sharpe, *Three Horizons*, 29.

33. Sharpe, *Three Horizons*, 19.

34. Sharpe et al., "Three Horizons," 47.

35. Sharpe et al., "Three Horizons," 47.

36. Clayton M. Christensen, *The Innovator's Dilemma: When New Technologies Cause Great Firms to Fail* (Boston: Harvard Business School Press, 1997).

37. Clayton M. Christensen, Michael E. Raynor, and Rory McDonald, "What Is Disruptive Innovation?" *Harvard Business Review Magazine*, Decmber 2015, https://hbr.org/2015/12/what -is-disruptive-innovation.

38. Sharpe, *Three Horizons*, 13.

39. Sharpe, *Three Horizons*, 14.

40. Sharpe, *Three Horizons*, 70.

41. Sharpe, *Three Horizons*, 41 (emphasis in the original).

42. Sharpe, *Three Horizons*, 98.

43. Graham Leicester, *Transformative Innovation: A Guide to Practice and Policy* (Axminster, UK: Triarchy Press, 2016).

44. Cass R. Sunstein, *How Change Happens* (Cambridge, MA: MIT Press, 2019).

45. Sunstein, *How Change Happns*, 4.

46. John Thibault, *How to Change a Law* (Menlo Park, CA: iLobby, 2016).

47. Marshall S. Poole and Andrew H. Van de Ven, *Oxford Handbook of Change and Innovation*, 2nd ed. (Oxford: Oxford University Press, 2021).

48. Paul Gibbons, *The Science of Successful Organizational Change: How Leaders Set Strategy, Change Behavior, and Create an Agile Culture* (Oslo: Phronesis Media, 2019); Paul Gibbons, *Impact: 21st-Century Change Management, Behavioral Science, Digital Transformation, and the Future of Work* (Oslo: Phronesis Media, 2019).

49. Warner Burke, *Organization Change: Theory and Practice*, 5th ed. (Thousand Oaks, CA: SAGE, 2018), 377.

50. Burke, *Organization Change*, 378.

51. John Kotter and Dan Cohen, *The Heart of Change* (Boston: Harvard Business Review, 2012), 2.

52. Chip Heath and Dan Heath, *Switch: How to Change Things When Change Is Hard* (New York: Broadway Books, 2010), 259.

53. William Isaacs, *Dialogue and the Art of Thinking Together* (New York: Currency, 1999), 9.

54. Isaacs, *Dialogue*, 329.

55. Isaacs, *Dialogue*, 204.

56. Isaacs, *Dialogue*, 20.

57. Isaacs, *Dialogue*, 22.

58. Deborah Flick, *From Debate to Dialogue: Using the Understanding Process to Transform Our Conversations* (Boulder, CO: Orchid Publications, 1998).

59. Flick, *From Debate to Dialogue*, 36–37.

60. Jeff Conklin, *Dialogue Mapping: Building Shared Understanding of Wicked Problems* (Chichester, UK: Wiley, 2006).

61. Paul W.B. Atkins, David S. Wilson and Steven C. Hays, *Prosocial: Using Evolutionary Science to Build Productive, Equitable, and Collaborative Groups* (Oakland, CA: Context Press/New Harbinger Publications, 2019).

62. Peter Block, *Community: The Structure of Belonging*, 2nd ed. (Oakland, CA: Barrett-Koehler, 2018).

63. Block, *Community*, 32.

64. Block, *Community*, 83.

65. Block, *Community*, 87.

66. Block, *Community*, 115–51.

67. Tim Brown, *Change by Design* (New York: Harper Business, 2009), 26.

68. For an example of large-scale intervention for thousands of citizens, see Carolyn Lukens-meyer and Steven Brigham, "Taking Democracy to Scale," *Journal of Applied Behavioral Science*, 41, no. 1 (2005): 47–60.

69. Barbara B. Bunker and Billie T. Alban, eds. *The Handbook of Large Group Methods: Creating Systemic Change in Organizations and Communities* (San Francisco: Jossey-Bass, 2006).

70. Peggy Holman, Tom Devane, Steven Cady, and Associates, *The Change Handbook* (San Francisco: Berrett Koehler, 2007).

71. John Gastil and Peter Levine, eds. *The Deliberative Democracy Handbook: Strategies for Effective Civic Engagement in the 21st Century* (New York: John Wiley and Sons, 2005); Alexander N. Christakis and Kenneth C. Bausch, *How People Harness Their Collective Wisdom and Power to Construct Their Future in Co-laboratories of Democracy* (Greenwich, CT: Information Age Publishers, 2006).

72. David Straus, *How to Make Collaboration Work* (San Francisco: Barrett Koehler, 2002).

73. Claire Bingham, "Inside the Growing Nexus of Politics and Design," *Architecture + Design*, November 8, 2018, https://www.architecturaldigest.com/story/political-design; Carl DiSalvo, *Adversarial Design* (Cambridge, MA: MIT Press, 2015); Tony Fry, *Design as Politics* (Oxford, UK: Berg Publishers, 2011); Mateo Kries, Amelie Klein, and Alison Clarke, (eds.), and Victor Papenek (artist), *Victor Papanek: the Politics of Design* (**Weil am Rhein**, Germany: Vitra Design Museum, 2018; Ruben Pater, *Politics of Design: A (Not So) Global Manual for Visual Communication* (London: Laurence King Publishing, 2016); Ruben Pater, *CAPS LOCK: How Capitalism Took Hold of Graphic Design and How to Escape from It* (Amsterdam: Valiz, 2021).

74. Herbert Simon, *The Sciences of the Artificial*, 3rd ed.(Cambridge, MA: MIT Press, 1996), 130.

75. Ramia Mazé, "Politics of Designing Visions of the Future," *Journal of Future Studies* 23, no. 3 (March 2019): 34.

76. Richard Buchanan, "Declaration by Design: Rhetoric, Argument, and Demonstration in Design Practice," *Design Issues* 2, no. 1 (Spring 1985): 6, https://www.jstor.org/stable/1511524.

77. Mazé, "Politics of Designing Visions of the Future," 27.

78. Mazé, "Politics of Designing Visions of the Future," 28.

79. Jeffrey Pfeffer, *Managing with Power* (Boston: Harvard Business Press, 1992), 30.

80. Rossabeth M. Kanter, *Men and Women of the Corporation* (New York: Basic Books, 1977), 166; Dennis Wrong, *Power: Its Forms, Bases, and Uses* (New York: Routledge, 2017).

81. I also believe that being ethical is a value and a critical skill set of design and change agentry. We revisit the topic of design ethics in chapter 10, so it is not included here.

82. Allison M. Vaillancourt, *The Organizational Politics Playbook: 50 Strategies to Navigate Power Dynamics at Work* (Tucson, AZ: Wheatmark, 2021).

83. Pfeffer, *Managing with Power*.

84. Peter Marris, *Loss and Change* (London: Routledge & Kegan Paul, 1974), 156.

85. Lisa B. Amsler, Janet K. Martinez, and Stephanie E. Smith, *Dispute System Design: Preventing, Managing, and Resolving Conflict* (Stanford, CA: Stanford University Press, 2020).

86. Kambiz E. Maani and Robert Y. Cabana, *Systems Thinking and Modelling* (Auckland, New Zealand: Pearson Education, 2000), 6–11.

87. Although PA Consulting created a thirty-one-page document to explain the causal diagram, the audience saw none of this material. Apparently, there was time for only one slide, without a narrative, without explanations of the causal loops and how they were constructed, and without any help in interpreting the diagram or understanding how it might inform their work. The slide was dismissed as a misuse of government resources and an example of Microsoft PowerPoint failure. Most notably General Stanley McChrystal is reported to have said: "When we understand that slide, we'll have won the war." Simon Rogers, "The McChrystal Afghanistan PowerPoint

Slide: Can You Do Any Better?" *The Guardian*, April 29, 2010, https://www.theguardian.com /news/datablog/2010/apr/29/mcchrystal-afghanistan-powerpoint-slide. My advice to those who create CLDs of their wicked problem territory is to strive to uncover the deep structure of a system. We go into cognitive overload when slides such as the one in figure 5.2 are presented to us, especially when we haven't had a hand in creating them.

88. Daniel H. Kim, "Using 'Tragedy of the Commons' to Link Local Action to Global Outcomes," *Systems Thinker*, accessed September 20, 2020, https://thesystemsthinker.com/using-tragedy-of-the -commons-to-link-local-action-to-global-outcomes/.

89. Daniel H. Kim and Virginia Anderson, *Systems Archetype Basics: From Story to Structure* (Waltham, MA: Pegasus Communications, 1998), 182.

90. Peter Jones and Kristel Van Ael, *Design Journeys through Complex Systems* (Amsterdam: BIS, 2022).

91. Anthony Hodgson, *Systems Thinking for a Turbulent World: A Search for New Perspectives* (London: Routledge, Taylor and Francis Group, 2020).

92. Hodgson, *Systems Thinking for a Turbulent World*, 1.

93. Hodgson, *Systems Thinking for a Turbulent World*, 107.

94. Hasso Plattner Institute of Design at Stanford, *A D.School Design Project Guide* (2016), 5–12, accessed September 19, 2020, https://static1.squarespace.com/static/57c6b79629687fde090a0fdd /t/589ba9321b10e3beb925e044/1486596453538/DESIGN-PROJECT-GUIDE-SEPT-2016-V3.pdf.

95. IDEO.org, *The Field Guide to Human-Centered Design: Design Kit* (2015), 39–43, accessed September 19, 2020, https://www.designkit.org/resources/1.

96. Tom Kelley and David Kelley, *Creative Confidence: Unleashing the Creative Potential within Us All* (New York: Crown Business, 2013), 78.

97. IDEO.org, *The Field Guide to Human-Centered Design*, 52–56.

98. Tina Seelig, *inGenius: A Crash Course in Creativity* (New York: HarperOne, 2012), chapter 4.

99. Stanford's Bootcamp Bootleg, *Method: Interview Preparation*, 9–16, accessed September 19, 2020, https://static1.squarespace.com/static/57c6b79629687fde090a0fdd/t/58890239db29d6cc6 c3338f7/1485374014340/METHODCARDS-v3-slim.pdf.

100. Mathew B. Miles, A. Michael Huberman, and Jonny Saldaña, *Qualitative Data Analysis*, 4th ed. (Thousand Oaks, CA: SAGE, 2020). I am using the Miles et al. reference here not to imply that data analysis for social scientist is the same as data analysis for designers. It could be, but typically designers' interactive process of data condensation, data display, and conclusion verification is less scientific and more inventive than what is required of social scientists. Although some designers refer to the process as "social research" or "design research," I prefer the term "discovery" to capture designers more open-ended, artistic, and imaginative field-based data collection and analysis efforts.

101. Rudolf Arnheim, *Visual Thinking*, 2nd ed. (Berkeley: University of California Press, 2004).

102. For more on on journey mapping and how it can be used in other phases of the design process, see Jeanne Liedtka, Tim Ogilvie, and Rachel Brozenske, *The Designing for Growth Field Book* (New York: Columbia Business School, 2014), 61–73; and Jeanne Liedtka and Tim Ogilvie, *Designing for Growth: A Design Thinking Toolkit for Managers* (New York: Columbia Business School, 2011), chapter 4.

103. Liedtka and Ogilvie, *Designing for Growth*, 49.

104. David Sibbet, *Visual Meetings: How Graphics, Sticky Notes, and Idea Mapping Can Transform Group Productivity* (Hoboken, NJ: Wiley, 2010).

105. Liedtka and Ogilvie, *Designing for Growth*, ch. 3.

106. Liedtka et al., *Designing for Growth Field Book*, 2014.

107. David Stracker, *Rapid Problem Solving with Post-it Notes* (Boston: Da Capo Press, 1997).

108. Dan Roam, *The Back of the Napkin: Solving Problems and Selling Ideas with Pictures* (New York: Portfolio/Penguin, 2013).

109. Kelley and Kelley, *Creative Confidence*, 59–63.

110. Colin Ware, *Visual Thinking for Design* (New York: Morgan Kaufmann, 2008).

111. Jon Kolko, "Abductive Thinking and Sensemaking: The Drivers of Design Synthesis," *Design Issues* 26, no. 1 (Winter 2010): 15–28, https://doi.org/10.1162/desi.2010.26.1.15.

112. Kolko, "Abductive Thinking and Sensemaking," 27.

113. Robert L. Thayer, "Leadership/Communication: A Critical Review and a Modest Proposal," in *Handbook of Organizational Communication*, ed. Gerald M. Goldhaber and George A. Barnett (Norwood, NJ: Ablex, 1988): 231–63.

114. Charles S. Peirce, *The Collected Works of Charles Sanders Peirce* (Cambridge, MA: Harvard University Press, 1958).

115. Karl E. Weick, *Sensemaking in Organizations* (Thousand Oaks, CA: SAGE, 1995); Karl E. Weick, Kathleen M. Sutcliffe, and David Obstfeld, "Organizing and the Process of Sensemaking," *Organization Science*, 16, no. 4 (July/August 2005): 409–21, https://doi.org/10.1287/orsc.1050.0133.

116. Robert Curedale, *Design Thinking Process & Methods*, 4th ed. (Los Angeles: DCC, 2018): 411–412; 414–420.

117. Edward de Bono, *Lateral Thinking: Creativity Step by Step* (New York: Harper & Row, 1970).

118. Jennifer Reil and Roger L. Martin, *Creating Great Choices: A Leader's Guide to Integrative Thinking* (Boston: Harvard Business School Press, 2017).

119. Ed Ferrari and Alasdair Rae, *GIS for Planning and the Built Environment: An Introduction to Spatial Analysis* (London: Red Globe Press, 2019).

120. Humans of Data, accessed September 20, 2020, https://humansofdata.atlan.com/2016/11/visualizing-time-series-data/.

121. Samuel L. Hayes and Ken Nguyen, "CA 2025: The Strategic Design of Civil Affairs," Calhoun Institutional Archive of the Naval Postgraduate School, Monterey, CA, http://hdl.handle.net/10945/45870. The map's creators are Hayes and Quinn.

122. Peter A. Gloor, *Swarm Creativity: Competitive Advantage through Collaborative Innovation Networks* (Oxford: Oxford University Press, 2006), 4.

123. Gloor, *Swarm Creativity*, 53.

124. Donald A. Schön, *The Reflective Practitioner* (New York: Basic Books, 1983); Donald A. Schön and Martin Rein, *Frame Reflection: Toward the Resolution of Intractable Policy Controversies* (New York: Basic Books, 1995).

125. Charles and Ray Eames, "Power of Ten (1977)," YouTube, accessed September 21, 2020, https://www.youtube.com/watch?v=0fKBhvDjuy0.

126. Kees Dorst, *Frame Innovation: Create New Thinking by Design* (Cambridge, MA: MIT Press, 2015).

127. Bryan Lawson, *How Designers Think*, 4th ed. (New York: Architectural Press, 2005): 117.

128. Lawson, *How Designers Think*, 121.

129. Lawson, *How Designers Think*, 118.

130. Lawson, *How Designers Think*, 120.

131. Lawson, *How Designers Think*, 121.

132. Lawson, *How Designers Think*, 120.

133. Lawson, *How Designers Think*, 121.

134. Lawson, *How Designers Think*, 121.

135. Lawson, *How Designers Think*, 122.

136. Kathryn McElroy, *Prototyping for Designers* (Sebastopol, CA: O'Reilly Media, 2017).

137. Luis Perez-Breva, *Innovating, A Doer's Manifesto for Starting from a Hunch, Prototyping Problems, Scaling up, and Learning to be Productively Wrong* (Cambridge, MA: MIT Press, 2018), ch. 6.

138. Luis Perez-Breva, *Innovating, A Doer's Manifesto for Starting from a Hunch, Prototyping Problems, Scaling up, and Learning to be Productively Wrong* (Cambridge, MA: MIT Press, 2018), 174.

139. Perez-Breva, *Innovating*, 174–75.

140. Scott Doorley and Scott Witthoft, *Makespace: How to Set the Stage for Creative Collaboration* (Hoboken, NJ: Wiley, 2012).

141. Chris Anderson, *Makers: The New Industrial Revolution* (New York: Crown Business, 2012).

142. NESTA Foundation, "Proof of Concept—What's in a Name?" accessed September 21, 2020, https://www.nesta.org.uk/blog/proof-of-concept-prototype-pilot-mvp-whats-in-a-name/.

143. IDEO.org, The Field Guide to Human-Centered Design, "Methods: How Do I Assess If My Solution Is Working?" accessed September 22, 2020, https://www.designkit.org/methods#filter.

144. Curedale, *Design Thinking Process & Methods*, 479–501.

145. Jeanne Liedtka, Andrew King and Kevin Bennett, *Solving Problems with Design Thinking: Ten Stories of What Works* (New York: Columbia Business School, 2013), 142.

146. Liedtka et al., *Designing for Growth Field Book,* 78.

147. Liedtka et al., *Designing for Growth Field Book,* 78–79.

148. Perez-Breva, *Innovating*, 245.

149. See a list of resources, websites, organizations, and competitions in Warren Berger, *Glimmer: How Design Can Transform Your Life, and Maybe Even the World* (New York: Penguin Press, 2009): 311–14.

150. Berger, *Glimmer*, 211–16.

151. David Bornstein, *How to Change the World: Social Entrepreneurs and the Power of New Ideas* (Oxford: Oxford University Press, 2007).

152. Alex Daly, *The Crowdsourceress: Get Smart, Get Funded, and Kickstart Your Next Big Idea* (New York: Public Affairs, 2017); Vilius Stanislovaitis, *Your First Kickstarter Campaign* (independently published, 2019); William Eggers and Paul Macmillan, *The Solution Revolution: How Business, Government, and Social Enterprises Are Teaming up to Solve Society's Toughest Problems* (Boston: Harvard Business Review, 2013).

153. Liedtka et al., *Designing for Growth Field Book*, 10–11.

154. Katherine Best, *Design Management: Managing Design Strategy, Process, Implementation*, 2nd ed. (London: Bloomsbury, 2015).

155. Aidan Hornsby, "How Design Teams Can Avoid Bad Project Management," (October 2, 2017), accessed September 22, 2020, https://www.getflow.com/blog/project-management-for-designers.

156. Best, *Design Management*.

157. Steven Wu, "The Best Project Management Software for Designers" (May 10, 2019), accessed September 22, 2020, redirected to https://www.creativebloq.com/software/best-project -management-71515632.

158. Catapult Design, accessed September 22, 2020, https://catapultdesign.org/.

159. Elizabeth B.-N Sanders and Pieter Jan Stappers, "Co-creation and the New Landscape of Design," *Co-Design* 4, no. 1 (2008): 5–18, https://doi.org/10.1080/15710880701875068.

160. John McCarthy and Peter Wright, *Taking [A]part: The Politics and Aesthetics of Participation in Experience-Centered Design* (Cambridge, MA: MIT Press, 2015), 3.

161. McCarthy and Wright, *Taking [A]part*, 117.

162. McCarthy and Wright, *Taking [A]part*, xv.

163. McCarthy and Wright, *Taking [A]part*, xvi.

164. IDEO.org, *The Field Guide to Human-Centered Design* (2015), accessed September 19, 2020, https://www.designkit.org/resources/1.

165. Hasso Plattner Institute of Design at Stanford, *A D.School Design Project Guide*

166. Liedtka and Ogilvie, *Designing for Growth*.

167. Liedtka et al., *Designing for Growth Field Book*.

168. Michael Q. Patton, *Developmental Evaluation: Applying Complexity Concepts to Enhance Innovation and Use* (New York: Guilford Press, 2011)

Chapter 6

1. Eric Knight, Jarryd Daymond, and Sotirios Paroutis, "Design-Led Strategy: How to Bring Design Thinking into the Art of Strategic Management," *California Management Review* 62, no. 2 (February 2020): 30–52, https://doi.org/10.1177/0008125619897594. See also Tua Björklund et al., "Integrating Design in Organizations: The Coevolution of Design Capabilities," *California Management Review* 62, no. 2 (February 2020): 100–24, https://doi.org/10.1177/0008125619898245; Cara Wrigley, Erez Nusem, and Karla Straker, "Implementing Design Thinking: Understanding Organizational Conditions," *California Management Review* 62, no. 2 (February 2020): 125–43, https://doi.org/10.1177/0008125619897606.

2. James Carlopio, *Strategy by Design* (New York: Palgrave Macmillan, 2010).

3. Carlopio, *Strategy by Design*, 3.

4. Carlopio, *Strategy by Design*, 6.

5. Giulia Calabretta, Gerda Gemser, and Ingo Karpen, *Strategic Design: Eight Essential Practices Every Strategic Designer Must Master* (Amsterdam: BIS Publishers, 2006), 9. Also see Claude Diderich, *Design Thinking for Strategy: Innovating Towards Competitive Advantage* (Richterswil, Switzerland: Springer, 2020); and Ray Holland and Busayawan Lam, *Managing Strategic Design* (New York: Palgrave, 2014).

6. Brigitte Borja de Mozota, *Design Management* (New York: Allworth Press, 2003); Brigitte Borja de Mozota and Faviane Wolff, "Forty Years of Research in Design Management: A Review of the Literature and Directions for the Future," *Strategic Design Research Journal* 12, no. 1 (January–April 2019): 4–26, https://doi.org/10.4013/sdrj.2019.121.02.

7. Design Management Institute, "2015 dmi: Design Value Index Results and Commentary" 27, no. 4 (2015): 6, https://cdn.ymaws.com/www.dmi.org/resource/resmgr/design_value_index /16274RAE04.pdf.

8. Design Management Institute, "DMI Design Value Index 2005–2015," 5.

9. Design Management Institute, "2015 dmi: Design Value Index Results and Commentary," 6 (emphasis in the original).

10. Clay Chandler et al., "Fortune's 2018 Business by Design List," *Fortune*, December 22, 2017, https://fortune.com/2017/12/22/business-design-apple-airbnb-tesla/.

11. Marc Gruber et al., "Managing by Design: From the Editors," *Academy of Management Journal* 58, no. 1 (February 2015): 6.

12. Benedict Sheppard et al., "The Business Value of Design," *McKinsey Report*, October 25, 2018, https://www.mckinsey.com/business-functions/mckinsey-design/our-insights/the-business -value-of-design.

13. A design action could be adding someone to the executive board with the responsibility for design, for user experience, or both. Another action could be linking management bonuses to design quality or customer satisfaction metrics.

14. Sheppard et al., "The Business Value of Design," 5.

15. Sheppard et al., "The Business Value of Design."

16. Claudia Kotchka, "Innovation at P&G," May 2009, *Vimeo*, video, 47:02, https://vimeo.com /5203345.

17. Jennifer Reingold, "What P&G Knows about the Power of Design," *Fast Company*, June 2, 2005, https://www.fastcompany.com/53103/what-pg-knows-about-power-design. Other companies have gone through similar processes compared to P&G. See Adi Ignatius, "How Indra Nooyi Turned Design Thinking into Strategy: An Interview with PepsiCo's CEO," *Harvard Business Review*, September 2015, https://hbr.org/2015/09/how-indra-nooyi-turned-design-thinking-into-strategy; James de Vries, "PepsiCo's Chief Design Officer on Creating an Organization Where Design Can Thrive," *Harvard Business Review*, August 11, 2015, https://hbr.org/2015/08/pepsicos-chief-design -officer-on-creating-an-organization-where-design-can-thrive; Linda Tischler, "Dynamic Duos: PepsiCo's Indra Nooyi and Mauro Porcini on Design-Led Innovation," *Fast Company*, September 23, 2013, https://www.fastcompany.com/3016310/pepsico-indra-nooyi-and-mauro-porcini.

18. Public organizations, owned and operated by governments, exist to provide services for countries' citizens and other residents. Nonprofits, established to further a particular social cause or advocate a particular point of view, use their nontaxable revenue to achieve social objectives instead of distributing income to shareholders, leaders, or members.

19. Anna Meroni, "Strategic Design: Where Are We Now? Reflection around the Foundations of a Recent Discipline," *Strategic Design Research Journal* 1, no. 1 (July–December, 2008): 1–38, https://doi.org/10.4013/sdrj.20081.05. For a review of the research on small and medium-sized businesses in Denmark, see Pia G. Erichsen, *Design Integration: A Theoretical and Empirical Study of Design in Small and Medium-Sized Danish Companies* (Odense: University Press of Southern Denmark, 2014).

20. See, for example, Christian Bason, *Leading Public-Sector Innovation* (Bristol, UK: Policy Press, 2010); Christian Bason, *Leading Public Design* (Bristol, UK: Policy Press, 2017); Ray Holland and Busayawan Lam, *Managing Strategic Design* (London: Red Globe Press, 2014), ch. 9, 302–37; and Jonathan Veale's "Field Guide about Strategic Design inside Government," *Medium*, May 27, 2016, https://medium.com/@jonathanveale/a-field-guide-about-strategic-design-inside-government-9 -lessons-from-the-frontier-de50b4f1ea8e. Case studies, projects, and publications on public-sector design also can be found on the website of the Observatory of Public Sector Innovation at the Organisation for Economic Co-operation and Development (OECD), accessed September 25, 2020, https://www.oecd-opsi.org/guide/strategic-design/.

21. Jeanne M. Liedtka, Randy Salzman, and Daisy Azer, *Design Thinking for the Greater Good: Innovation in the Social Sector* (New York: Columbia Business School Press, 2017), ch. 5.

22. Wayne W. Grigsby et al., "Integrated Planning: The Operations Process, Design, and the Military Decision Making Process," *Military Review* (January/February 2011): 28–35; Grant Martin, "A Tale of Two Design Efforts (and Why They Both Failed in Afghanistan)", *Small Wars Journal* (July 2011), https://smallwarsjournal.com/blog/journal/docs-temp/809-martin.pdfsmallwarsjournal.com; See also the 2011 six-part series by Ben Zweibelson, "To Design, or Not to Design": Introduction, Part One, March 4; Part Two, March 11; Part Three, March 18; Part Four, April 5; Part Five, April 15; and Part Six, May 9, *Small Wars Journal*, https://smallwarsjournal.com/jrnl/art /to-design-or-not-to-design.

23. Espen Berg-Knutsen and Nancy C. Roberts (eds.), *Strategic Design for NORSOF 2025* (Monterey, CA: Naval Postgraduate School, 2015), https://apps.dtic.mil/sti/citations/AD1060147.

24. There are many options from which to choose. See, for example: Jay R. Galbraith, *Designing Organizations: Strategy, Structure, and Process at the Business Unit and Enterprise Levels*, 3rd ed. (San Francisco: Jossey-Bass, 2014); Jamshid Gharajedaghi, *Systems Thinking: Managing Chaos and Complexity: A Platform for Designing Business Architecture*, 3rd ed. (Amsterdam: Morgan Kaufmann, 2011).

25. Charles C. Snow, Raymond E. Miles, and Grant Miles, "A Configurational Approach to the Integration of Strategy and Organization Research," *Strategic Organization* 3, no. 4 (2005): 431–39, https://doi.org/10.1177/1476127005057965.

26. Nancy C. Roberts, "Roberts Organizational System Framework," *Coping with Wicked Problems Class Notes*, 2015.

27. A mandate is the official, legal statement that sets up an organization and defines its parameters of action. A mission defines an organization's "reason for being." It clarifies what the organization does, for whom, and how it accomplishes its goals. It also can include the

organization's distinctive competencies and driving forces. Values and beliefs describe the modes of conduct that the organization espouses. A vision gives what the organization aspires to be in the future, assuming that its strategy is successful. A strategy lays out the actions that the organization will undertake to achieve its vision. Goals are general actions to be achieved as part of the strategy, in contrast to objectives, which are specific actions to be achieve within a given time period.

28. Karl E. Weick and Robert E. Quinn, "Organizational Change and Development," *Annual Review of Psychology* 50 (1999): 361–86.

29. See the introduction for a full description of the term "VUCA."

30. Although the sources for this overview were numerous, the team used the format of the National Intelligence Council, *Global Trends 2030: Alternative Worlds* (Washington, DC: US Office of the Director of National Intelligence, December 2012), www.dni.gov/nic/globaltrends. For an updated report, see the National Intelligence Council, *Global Trends Paradox of Progress* (Washington, DC: Office of the Director of National Intelligence, January 2017), https://www.dni.gov /files/documents/nic/GT-Full-Report.pdf.

31. National Intelligence Council, *Global Trends 2030: Alternative Worlds*.

32. SR is a small unit of trained SOFs who operate behind enemy lines, avoid direct combat and detection by the enemy for the purpose of environmental reconnaissance, target acquisition, area assessment, poststrike assessment, emplacement and recovery of sensors, and support of human intelligence and signals intelligence operations.

33. DA emcompasses small-scale raids, ambushes, sabotage, or similar actions in hostile, denied, or politically sensitive environments for the purpose of seizing, destroying, capturing, exploiting, recovering, or damaging designated targets.

34. MA includes the training and development of other states' military and security forces.

35. Berg-Knutsen and Roberts, *Strategic Design for NORSOF 2025*, "Appendix B: Anti-Access/Area Denial," 82–83.

36. Members of the NORSOF Tasks subgroup in conjunction with the subgroup on the technology of warfare organized a war game at NPS in May 2015 to explore the kind of challenges that Norway and NORSOF might face in a complex warfare environment. For a description of the war game and its findings, see Berg-Knutsen and Roberts, *Strategic Design of NORSOF*, "Appendix A: Hybrid Warfare," 78–81.

37. John Arquilla and Nancy C. Roberts, *Design of Warfare* (Monterey, CA: Naval Postgraduate School, 2017), https://calhoun.nps.edu/handle/10945/62564.

38. John Arquilla, "personal communication," May 15, 2015.

39. *Jus in bello* (meaning "international humanitarian law") is the law that governs the way in which warfare is conducted.

40. Berg-Knutsen and Roberts, *Strategic Design of NORSOF*, "Appendix B."

41. Berg-Knutsen and Roberts, *Strategic Design of NORSOF*, "Appendix A."

42. William S. Lind, Keith Nightingale, John F. Schmitt, Joseph W. Sutton, and Gary I. Wilson, "The Changing Face of War: Into the Fourth Generation," *Marine Corps Gazette*, October 1989, 22–26, https://www.academia.edu/7964013/The_Changing_Face_of_War_Into_the_Fourth_Generation.

43. Berg-Knutsen and Roberts, eds. *Strategic Design for NORSOF 2025*.

44. Dean T. Spaulding, *Evaluation in Practice*, 2nd ed. (San Francisco: Jossey-Bass, 2014).

45. Espen Berg-Knutsen, "personal communication," September 15, 2015.

46. Tim Brown, *Change by Design* (New York: HarperCollins, 2009), 66–67.

Chapter 7

1. Interview of Dan Saffer, via email with Hugh Dubberly, "What Is Systems Design?" February 2006, http://www.dubberly.com/articles/what-is-systems-design.html.

2. Mieke van der Bijl-Brouwer and Bridget Malcolm, "Systemic Design Principles in Social Innovation: A Study of Expert Practices and Design Rationales," *She Ji: The Journal of Design, Economics, and Innovation* 6, no. 3 (Autumn 2020): 386–407, https://doi.org/10.1016/j.sheji.2020.06.001.

3. Peter H. Jones and Kyoichi Kijima, eds. *Systemic Design: Theory, Methods, and Practice* (Tokyo: Springer Japan, 2018).

4. Bela H. Bernathy, *Designing Social Systems in a Changing World* (New York: Plenum Publishing Co., 1996).

5. Jones and Kijima, *Systemic Design*; Peter Jones, "The Systemic Turn: Leverage for World Changing," *She Ji: The Journal of Design, Economics and Innovation* 3, no. 3 (2017): 157–63, https://doi.org/10.1016/j.sheji.2017.11.001; Peter H. Jones, "Systemic Design Principles for Complex Social Systems, in *Social Systems and Design*, ed. Gary S. Metcalf (Tokyo: Springer Japan, 2014), 91–128.

6. Pennie G. Foster-Fishman et al., "Mobilizing Residents for Action: The Role of Small Wins and Strategic Supports," *American Journal of Community Psychology*, 38 (2006): 143–52, https://doi.org/10.1007/s10464-006-9081-0.

7. Ray Ison and Ed Straw, *The Hidden Power of Systems Thinking in a Climate Emergency* (New York: Routledge, 2020).

8. Ezio Manzini, "Social Innovation and Design," *Design Issues* 30, no. 1 (Winter 2014): 57–66, https://doi.org/10.1162/DESI_a_00248.

9. In this instance, "network" is defined as links between two or more nodes (e.g., people or organizations) that are interconnected for a particular purpose.

10. Russell L. Ackoff, *Redesigning the Future: A Systems Approach to Societal Problems* (New York: Wiley, 1974), 21.

11. For a good summary of three network coordination approaches, see H. Brinton Milward and Keith G. Provan, *A Manager's Guide to Choosing and Using Collaborative Networks*, IMB Center for the Business of Government, https://www.businessofgovernment.org/sites/default/files/Collaborative Networks.pdf. For a comprehensive overview of governance networks, see Erik H. Klijn and Joop Koppenjan, *Governance Networks in the Public Sector* (New York: Routledge, 2016).

12. Klijn and Koppenjan, *Governance Networks in the Public Sector*, 200.

13. Klijn and Koppenjan, *Governance Networks in the Public Sector*, 117.

14. For references of "system change," see Foster-Fishman et al., "Mobilizing Residents for Action," 2006. And for references on large-scale systems change, see Michael Fullan, "Large-Scale

Change Comes of Age," *Journal of Educational Change* 10 (2009): 101–13, https://doi.org/10.1007/s10833-009-9108-z; Sandra Waddock et al., "The Complexity of Wicked Problems in Large-Scale Change," *Journal of Organizational Change Management* 28, no. 6 (2015): 993–1012, doi/10.1108/JOCM-08-2014-0146/full/html; and Domenico Dentoni, Steve Waddell, and Sandra Waddock, "Pathways of Transformation in Global Food and Agricultural Systems: Implications from a Large Systems Change Theory Perspective," *Current Opinion in Environmental Sustainability* 29 (December 2017): 8–13, https://doi.org/10.1016/j.cosust.2017.10.003.

15. David Bornstein, *How to Change the World* (Oxford: Oxford University Press, 2007), ch. 7. See also Ashoka Fellows, accessed October 1, 2020, https://www.ashoka.org/en-US/our-network/ashoka-fellows.

16. CHILDLINE India 1098, accessed October 1, 2020, https://www.childlineindia.org/a/about/childline-india.

17. Alex Ryan, "Transforming Community Health through Systemic Design," March 21, 2016, https://medium.com/the-overlap/transforming-community-health-through-systemic-design-5b22b9d5bf.

18. Ryan, "Transforming Community Health," figure 1.

19. Organisation for Economic Co-operation and Development (OECD), *Systems Approaches to Public-Sector Challenges: Working with Change* (Paris: OECD, 2017), ch. 2.

20. OECD, *Systems Approaches to Public Challenges*, 45. The report linked design thinking to Herbert Simon's rational-technical problem-solving logic, included a questionable description of design thinking's origins, and mislabeled design thinking's "tools and toolkits" as constituting "a reductionist approach."

21. OECD, *Systems Approaches to Public Challenges*, 85.

22. Jeanne Liedtka, Randy Salzman, and Daisy Azer, *Design Thinking for the Greater Good: Innovation in the Social Sector* (New York: Columbia Business School Publishing, 2017), 234.

23. BRAC, "Empowering People to Rise Above Poverty," accessed October 1, 2020, https://bracusa.org/.

24. To date, BRAC reaches 120 million people in eleven countries, with a total global expenditure of more than $1 billion. A total of 75 percent of its Bangladesh budget is self-financed through its own social enterprises and microfinance activities, although much of its important work—including its schools, health care, ultra-poor graduation program, and most of its programs outside Bangladesh—remains reliant on outside donors. See BRAC, *Pathways to Prosperity: BRAC USA 2017 Annual Report*, accessed February 20, 2021, https://www.brac.net/sites/default/files/annual-report/2017/BRACUSA_AnnualReport_FY2017.pdf.

25. Susan Davis, "Enabling Entrepreneurial Ecosystems," *Innovations* 7, no. 2 (2012): 7.

26. Davis, "Enabling Entrepreneurial Ecosystems," 8.

27. Davis, "Enabling Entrepreneurial Ecosystems," 9.

28. Davis, "Enabling Entrepreneurial Ecosystems," 9.

29. Davis, "Enabling Entrepreneurial Ecosystems," 4.

30. Davis, "Enabling Entrepreneurial Ecosystems," 5.

31. Davis, "Enabling Entrepreneurial Ecosystems," 6.

32. Davis, "Enabling Entrepreneurial Ecosystems," 6.

33. Davis, "Enabling Entrepreneurial Ecosystems," 9.

34. For additional references on entrepreneurial ecosystems, see Business Oregon, "Entrepreneurial Ecosystems Literature and Frameworks," accessed October 1, 2020, https://www.oregon4biz.com/assets/docs/EcoLitFrameworks.pdf.

35. For an excellent article on the latest lessons learned in social innovation, see Jocelyn Wyatt, Tim Brown, and Shauna Carey, "The Next Chapter in Design for Social Innovation," *Stanford Social Innovation Review* (Winter 2021): 41–47.

36. Frances Westley, Katharine McGowan, and Ola Tjörnbo, eds. *Social Innovation: Building Resilience through Transitions* (Cheltenham, UK: Edward Elgar, 2017); Filippo Addarii and Fiorenza Lipparini, *Vision and Trends of Social Innovation for Europe* (Brussels: European Commission, Directorate-General for Research and Innovation, 2017), https://doi.org/10.2777/08700; Bastian Pelka and Judith Terstriep, "Mapping Social Innovation Maps: The State of Research Practice across Europe," *European Public & Social Innovation Review* 1, no. 1 (June 2016): 3–16; Alex Nicholls, Julie Simon, and Madeleine Gabriel, eds. *New Frontiers in Social Innovation* (London: Palgrave Macmillan, 2015), https://doi.org/10.1057/9781137506801.

37. Geoff Mulgan, "Foreword: The Study of Social Innovation—Theory, Practice, and Progress," in *New Frontiers in Social Innovation Research*, ed. Alex Nicholls, Julie Simon, and Madeleine Gabriel (New York: Palgrave Macmillan, 2015), x, https://doi.org/10.1057/9781137506801.

38. Mulgan, "Foreword: The Study of Social Innovation," x–xi.

39. Geoff Mulgan et al., *Social Innovation: What It Is, Why It Matters and How It Can Be Accelerated* (Oxford, UK: Said Business School, Skoll Centre for Social Entrepreneurship, 2007), 7.

40. Nicholls et al., *New Frontiers in Social Innovation Research*, 1.

41. Nicholls et al., *New Frontiers in Social Innovation Research*, 6.

42. Roberto M. Unger, "Conclusion: The Task of the Social Innovation Movement," in *New Frontiers in Social Innovation Research*, ed. Alex Nicholls, Julie Simon, and Madeleine Gabriel (London: Palgrave Macmillan, 2015), 235, https://link.springer.com/chapter/10.1057/9781137506801_12#Abs1.

43. Unger, "Conclusion," 235.

44. Unger, "Conclusion," 233–234.

45. Unger, "Conclusion," 233.

46. Unger, "Conclusion," 234.

47. Unger, "Conclusion," 235.

48. Resilience: Building a World of Resilient Communities, *Design for the Other 90%*. https://www.resilience.org/stories/2007-06-10/design-other-90/.

49. Maria Rogal and Raúl Sánchez, "Codesigning for Development," in *Routledge Handbook for Sustainable Design*, ed. Rachel Beth Egenhoefer (London: Routledge, 2017) 250–62, https://doi.org/10.4324/9781315625508.

50. Bornstein, *How to Change the World*; Beverly Schwartz, *Rippling, How Social Entrepreneurs Spread Innovation throughout the World* (San Francisco: Jossey-Bass, 2012); Diana E. Wells, "From Social Entrepreneurship to Everyone a Changemaker: 40 Years of Social Innovation Point to What's Next," *Social Innovations Journal* (November 30, 2018), https://socialinnovationsjournal. org/editions/issue-52/75-disruptive-innovations/2906-from-social-entrepreneurship-to-everyone-a-changemaker-40-years-of-social-innovation-point-to-what-s-next.

51. Roger L. Martin and Sally R. Osberg, *Getting beyond Better: How Social Entrepreneurship Works* (Boston: Harvard Business Review Press, 2015).

52. Charles Leadbeater, *The Rise of the Social Entrepreneur* (London: Demos, 1997).

53. Devin Thorpe, "Father of Social Entrepreneurship Says 'Society Is at a Profound Turning Point'," *Forbes*, September 13, 2019, https://www.forbes.com/sites/devinthorpe/2019/09/13/father -of-social-entrepreneurship-says-society-is-at-a-profound-turning-point/?sh=324a6b7e4d6c

54. Wells, "From Social Entrepreneurship to Everyone a Changemaker," 14.

55. Paul N. Bloom and J. Gregory Dees, "Cultivate Your Ecosystem," *Stanford Social Innovation Review* (Winter 2008): 47–53, https://ssir.org/articles/entry/cultivate_your_ecosystem.

56. Bloom and Dees, "Cultivate Your Ecosystem," p. 47.

57. See Bloom and Dees, "Cultivate Your Ecosystem," 48–52, for a description of how to map ecosystems and change them using the example of Martin Eakes's Self-Help organization, the goal of which is "to change the landscape of low-income lending in the United States."

58. Martin and Osberg, *Getting beyond Better*, 17–20.

59. Martin and Osberg, *Getting beyond Better*, 168.

60. Schwab Foundation for Social Entrepreneurship, "Social Entrepreneur Sanjit (Bunker) Roy," accessed October 1, 2020, https://www.schwabfound.org/awardees/sanjit-bunker-roy.

61. Greg Mortenson, "Sanjit 'Bunker' Roy," *The 2010 TIME 100*, April 29, 2010, http://content .time.com/time/specials/packages/article/0,28804,1984685_1984745_1985478,00.html.

62. Bunker Roy, "Learning from a Barefoot Movement," TED Global July 2011, video, 19:07, https://www.ted.com/talks/bunker_roy/up-next?language=en.

63. Bunker Roy and Jesse Hartigan, "Empowering the Rural Poor to Develop Themselves: The Barefoot Approach," *Innovations* (Spring 2008): 70, https://www.mitpressjournals.org/doi/pdf /10.1162/itgg.2008.3.2.67.

64. Roy and Hartigan, "Empowering the Rural Poor to Develop Themselves," 71.

65. Roy and Hartigan, "Empowering the Rural Poor to Develop Themselves," 70.

66. Roy and Hartigan, "Empowering the Rural Poor to Develop Themselves," 71.

67. Roy and Hartigan, "Empowering the Rural Poor to Develop Themselves, 69.

68. Roy and Hartigan, "Empowering the Rural Poor to Develop Themselves," 72.

69. Roy and Hartigan, "Empowering the Rural Poor to Develop Themselves," 73–74.

70. Roy and Hartigan, "Empowering the Rural Poor to Develop Themselves," 74.

71. Barefoot College International, *Annual Report 2020-2022*, 5.

72. Bhanwar Jat joined Barefoot College in 1977. His initial task was transporting water to houses with his donkey. Then he worked in the fields growing food for the center, eventually taking care of chicks on the poultry farm and driving people on a tractor from the center to the night school. When he was asked to direct the building of the new center, "that didn't bother me." It was just one more job I was asked to do." Roy and Hartigan, "Empowering the Rural Poor to Develop Themselves," 76.

73. Roy, "Learning from a Barefoot Movement," TED Global.

74. Roy and Harigan, "Empowering the Rural Poor to Develop Themselves, 77.

75. Roy and Hartigan, "Empowering the Rural Poor to Develop Themselves," 92.

76. Barefoot College, "The Barefoot Story."

77. Barefoot College, "Solutions in Education," accessed October 1, 2020, https://www.barefoot college.org/solution/education-preview/.

78. Barefoot College, "Solutions in Solar," accessed October 1, 2020, https://www.barefootcollege .org/solution/solar/.

79. Barefoot College, "Where We Work," accessed October 1, 2020, https://www.barefootcollege .org/about/where-we-work/.

80. Barefoot College, "Solutions in Water," accessed October 1, 2020, https://www.barefootcollege .org/solution/water/.

81. Barefoot College, "Health Solutions," accessed October 22, 2020, https://www.barefootcollege .org/solution/health/.

82. Barefoot College, "Enriche," accessed October 1, 2020, https://www.barefootcollege.org /solution/enriche/.

83. Barefoot College, "Learn the Barefoot Approach: A Path to Development Led by Communities," accessed October 1, 2020, https://www.barefootcollege.org/approach/.

84. Roy and Hartigan, "Empowering the Rural Poor to Develop Themselves," 75.

85. Roy and Hartigan, "Empowering the Rural Poor to Develop Themselves," 75.

86. Roy and Hartigan, "Empowering the Rural Poor to Develop Themselves," 74.

87. Field centers operate in the Silora Block Ajmer in Rajasthan. Each center is situated in a village with its own campus located within a radius of fifteen to twenty-five villages.

88. Roy and Hartigan, "Empowering the Rural Poor to Develop Themselves," 74.

89. Barefoot College, "Audit Statement," accessed October 1, 2020, https://www.barefootcollege .org/wp-content/uploads/2018/11/Annexure-xii-Audit-Statement-2017-18.pdf.

90. Roy and Hartigan, "Empowering the Rural Poor to Develop Themselves," 75.

91. Barefoot College, *The Barefoot College Annual Report 2016–17*, accessed October 1, 2020, https://www.barefootcollege.org/wp-content/uploads/2018/10/Barefoot_annualreport_2016-17 _v7_online.pdf.

92. Social Action for Rural Advancement (SARA), "Sampada Network," accessed October 1, 2020, http://www.barefootsara.org/sampada-network.php.

93. Tilonia Artisans of India, accessed October 1, 2020, https://www.tilonia.com/.

94. Nancy C. Roberts, "Public Entrepreneurship and Innovation," *Review of Policy Research* 11, no. 1 (March 1992): 55–74. https://doi.org/10.1111/j.1541-1338.1992.tb00332.x; Nancy C. Roberts and Paula J. King, *Transforming Public Policy: Dynamics of Policy Entrepreneurship and Innovation* (San Francisco, Jossey-Bass, 1996).

95. Michael Mintrom and Phillipa Norman, "Policy Entrepreneurship and Policy Change," *Policy Studies Journal* 37, no. 4 (2009): 649–67, https://doi.org/10.1111/j.1541-0072.2009.00329.x.

96. Michael Mintrom and Sandra Vergari, "Advocacy Coalitions, Policy Entrepreneurs, and Policy Change," *Policy Studies Journal* 24 (1996): 420–34, https://doi.org/10.1111/j.1541-0072.1996.tb01638.x.

97. Scott E. Kalafatis and Maria C. Lemos, "The Emergence of Climate Change Policy Entrepreneurs in Urban Settings," *Regional Environmental Change* 17 (April 2017): 1791–99, https://doi.org/10.1007/s10113-017-1154-0; Michael Mintrom and Joannah Luetjens, "Policy Entrepreneurs and Problem Framing: The Case of Climate Change," *Environment and Planning C: Politics and Space* 35, no. 8 (December 2017): 1362–77, https://doi.org/10.1177/2399654417708440.

98. Eivor Oborn, Michael Barrett, and Mark Exworthy, "Policy Entrepreneurship in the Development of Public Sector Strategy: The Case of London Health Reform," *Public Administration* 89, no. 2 (June 2011): 325–44, https://doi.org/10.1111/j.1467-9299.2010.01889.x; Dayashankar Maurya and Michael Mintrom, "Policy Entrepreneurs as Catalysts of Broad System Change: The Case of Social Health Insurance Adoption in India," *Journal of Asian Public Policy* 13, no. 1 (2020): 18–34, https://doi.org/10.1080/17516234.2019.1617955.

99. Daniel R. Hammond, "Policy Entrepreneurship in China's Response to Urban Poverty," *Policy Studies Journal* 41, no. 1 (2013): 119–46, https://doi.org/10.1111/psj.12005.

100. Dave Huitema, Luis Lebel, and Sander Meijerink, "The Strategies of Policy Entrepreneurs in Water Transitions around the World," *Water Policy* 13, no. 5 (October 2011): 717–33, https://doi.org/10.2166/wp.2011.107.

101. Michael Mintrom, "Policy Entrepreneurs and Controversial Science: Governing Human Embryonic Stem Cell Research," *Journal of European Public Policy* 20, no. 3 (2013): 442–57, https://doi.org/10.1080/13501763.2012.761514.

102. Roberts and King, *Transforming Public Policy*.

103. Harold G. Nelson and Erik Stolterman, *The Design Way*, 2nd ed. (Cambridge, MA: MIT Press, 2014), 12.

104. Sabine Junginger, "Design and Innovation in the Public Sector: Matters of Design in Policy-Making and Policy Implementation," *Annual Review of Policy Design* 1, no. 1 (2013), 1–11; Michael Howlett, "From the 'Old' to the 'New' Policy Design: Design Thinking beyond Markets and Collaborative Governance," *Policy Sciences* 47, no. 3 (September 2014): 187–207, https://doi.org/10.1007/s11077-014-9199-0.

105. B. Guy Peters and Nenad Rava, "Policy Design: From Technocracy to Complexity, and Beyond," presented at the International Conference on Public Policy, Singapore, June 28–30, 2017, 20, https://www.ippapublicpolicy.org/file/paper/5932fa23369d0.pdf.

106. Mark Considine, "Thinking outside the Box? Applying Design Theory to Public Policy," *Politics & Policy* 40, no. 4 (2012): 704–24, https://doi.org/10.1111/j.1747-1346.2012.00372.x; Michael Mintrom and Joannah Luetjens, "Design Thinking in Policy Processes: Opportunities

and Challenges," *Australian Journal of Public Administration* 75, no. 3 (2016): 391–402, https://doi .org/10.1111/1467-8500.12211; Michael Mintrom and Madeline Thomas, "Policy Entrepreneurs and Collaboration Action: Pursuit of the Sustainable Development Goals," *International Journal of Entrepreneurial Venturing* 10, no. 2 (2018): 153–71, https://doi.org/10.1504/IJEV.2018.092710.

107. Michael McGann, Emma Blomkamp, and Jenny M. Lewis, "The Rise of Public-Sector Inno-vation Labs: Experiments in Design Thinking for Policy," *Policy Sciences* 51 (March 2018): 249–67, https://doi.org/10.1007/s11077-018-9315-7; Jenny M. Lewis, Michael McGann, and Emma Blom-kamp, "When Design Meets Power: Design Thinking, Public Sector Innovation, and the Politics of Policymaking," *Policy & Politics* 48, no. 1 (2020): 111–30, https://doi.org/10.1332/0305573 19X15579230420081.

108. Roberts and King, *Transforming Public Policy*, is a longitudinal case study that documents the activities of six policy entrepreneurs within the traditional phases of the policy process. In exchange for detailed information about their plans and strategies during the innovation process, we agreed to maintain their anonymity in the book. I follow the same protocol here.

109. Nelson W. Polsby, *The Politics of Policy Initiation* (New Haven, CT: Yale University Press, 1984).

110. B. Guy Peters, "Agenda Setting and Public Policy," in *American Public Policy*, 57-79. 11th ed. (Los Angeles: SAGE, 2019); Thomas A. Birkland and Kathryn L. Schwaeble, "Agenda Setting and the Policy Process, Politics: Focusing Events," in *Oxford Research Encyclopedia of Politics*, ed. W. R. Thompson, 2021, https://doi.org/10.1093/acrefore/9780190228637.013.165; Nikolaos Zaharia-dis, *Handbook of Public Policy Agenda Setting* (Cheltenham, UK: Edward Elgar, 2016).

111. Mara S. Sidney, "Policy Formulation: Design and Tools," in *Handbook of Public Policy Analy-sis: Theory, Politics, and Methods*, ed. Frank Fischer, Gerald J. Miller and Mara S. Sidney (Boca Raton, FL: CRC Press, 2007), 79–88.

112. Peters, "Legitimating Policy Choices," in *American Public Policy*, pp. 81-97.

113. Peters, "Organization and Implementation, in *American Public Policy*, 99-121.

114. Peters, "Evaluation and Policy Change, in *American Public Policy*, 159-175.

115. Gerald Zaltman, Robert Duncan, and Jonny Holbek, *Innovations and Organizations* (New York: Wiley, 1973), 10.

116. National Commission on Excellence in Education, *A Nation at Risk: The Imperative for Educa-tional Reform* (Washington, DC: US Government Printing Office, 1983), 5.

117. Citizens League, *Citizens League Report: Rebuilding Education to Make It Work* (Minneapolis: Citizens League, 1982), https://citizensleague.org/wp-content/uploads/2017/07/PolicyReport EducationMay-1982.pdf.

118. Citizens League, *Citizens League Report*, i.

119. Minnesota Business Partnership, *Educating Students for the 21st Century* (Minneapolis: Min-nesota Business Partnership, 1984).

120. Beatrice Gross and Ronald Gross, eds. *The Great School Debate: Which Way for American Edu-cation?* (New York: Simon & Schuster, 1985), 17.

121. Gross and Gross, *The Great School Debate*.

122. Thomas R. Peek, Edward L. Duren, and Lawrence C. Wells, *Minnesota K–12 Education: The Current Debate, the Present Condition*, Report No. CURA 85–3 (Minneapolis: Center for Urban and Regional Affairs, University of Minnesota, 1985), https://files.eric.ed.gov/fulltext/ED255619.pdf.

123. "The Reindustrialization of America," *Business Week, Special Issue,* June 30, 1980, 55–142, https://doi.org/10.1177/003232928001000123.

124. Minnesota Department of Education, *Planning Document No. 5* (St. Paul: Minnesota Department of Education, 1986).

125. Thomas R. Peek and Douglas S. Wilson, *Fiscal Constraints on Minnesota—Impacts and Policies: Economic Conditions and Changing Government Policies,* Report No. CURA 83–1 (Minneapolis: Center for Urban and Regional Affairs, University of Minnesota, 1983), https://conservancy.umn.edu/handle/11299/208144.

126. Patricia M. Wilhelm, *The Involvement and Perceived Impact of the Citizens League on Minnesota State School Policymaking, 1969–1984* (PhD diss., University of Minnesota, 1984), 212.

127. Roberts and King, *Transforming Public Policy,* 68.

128. Antony Downs, *Inside Bureaucracy* (Glenview, IL: Scott, Foresman, 1967).

129. Peek et al., *Minnesota K–12 Education.*

130. Peek et al., *Minnesota K–12 Education.*

131. Eric A. Hanushek, "Throwing Money at Schools," *Journal of Policy Analysis and Management* 1, no. 1 (1981): 19.

132. Citizens League, *Citizen League Report.*

133. Public School Incentives (PSI), "Nine High-Potential Ideas" (St. Paul, MN: Public School Incentives, 1984a).

134. For more details on the policy entrepreneurs' networking, cultivation of bureaucratic insiders, strategizing, coordinating, and idea dissemination during this time frame, see Nancy C. Roberts and Paula J. King, *Transforming Public Policy: Dynamics of Policy Entrepreneurship and Innovation* (San Francisco: Jossey-Bass, 1996). 71–76.

135. Public School Incentives (PSI), "What Is Public School Incentives?" (St. Paul, MN: Public School Incentives, 1984b).

136. The detailed story of the policy entrepreneurs and their impact on Minnesota education is documented in Roberts and King, *Transforming Public Policy.*

137. Jeffrey L. Bradach, "Going to Scale," *Stanford Social Innovation Review,* Spring 2003, accessed October 3, 2020, https://ssir.org/articles/entry/going_to_scale; Frances R. Westley and Nino Antadze, "Making a Difference: Strategies for Scaling Social Innovation for Greater Impact," *The Innovation Journal: The Public Sector Innovation Journal* 15, no. 2 (2010), article 2, https://www.innovation.cc/scholarly-style/2010_15_2_2_westley-antadze_social-innovate.pdf.

138. J. Gregory Dees, Beth B. Anderson, and Jane Wei-Skillern, "Scaling Social Impact: Strategies for Spreading Innovation," *Stanford Innovation Review* 1, no. 4 (Spring 2004): 24–32, https://ssir.org/articles/entry/scaling_social_impact.

Chapter 8

1. Lakna, "Difference between Ecology and Ecosystem," *PEDIAA,* accessed October 31, 2020, http://pediaa.com/difference-between-ecology-and-ecosystem/.

2. Bill Reed, "Shifting from 'Sustainability' to Regeneration," *Building Research & Information* 35, no. 6 (September 2007): 675, https://doi.org/10.1080/09613210701475753; S. D. Noam Cook,

"Design and Responsibility: The Interdependence of Natural, Artifactual, and Human Systems," in *Philosophy and Design*, eds. Peter Kroes, Pieter C. Vermaas, Andrew Light and Steven A. Moore, 259–69 (Berlin and Heidelberg, Germany: Springer, 2008), https://doi.org/10.1007/978-1-4020-6591-0_20.

3. Pamela Mang and Bill Reed, "Designing from Place: A Regenerative Framework and Methodology," *Building Research & Information* 40, no. 1 (2012): 23–38, https://doi.org/10.1080/09613218.2012.621341.

4. Bill Reed, "Shifting from 'Sustainability' to Regeneration," *Building Research & Information* 35, no. 6 (September 2007): 674, https://doi.org/10.1080/09613210701475753.

5. Read, "Shifting from 'Sustainability to Regeneration'," 676.

6. Read, "Shifting from 'Sustainability to Regeneration'," 676.

7. Read, "Shifting from 'Sustainability to Regeneration'," 677.

8. Read, "Shifting from 'Sustainability to Regeneration'," 677.

9. Read, "Shifting from 'Sustainability to Regeneration'," 677–680. A comparable term to regenerative design as it applies to nature is "Nature-Based Solutions." The International Union for Conservation of Nature has produced an excellent overview of nature-based solutions and the different approaches within the Nature-Based Solutions "family." Its ten cases of Nature-Based Solution designs and their lessons learned are also an excellent resource for regenerative designers. See E. Cohen-Shacham, G. Walters, C. Janzen, and S. Maginnis, eds., *Nature-Based Solutions to Address Global Societal Challenges* (Gland, Switzerland: International Union for Conservation of Nature, 2016), https://doi.org/10.2305/IUCN.CH.2016.13.en.

10. Daniel C. Wahl, *Designing Regenerative Cultures* (Axminster, UK: Triarchy Press, 2016), 31.

11. Wahl, *Designing Regenerative Cultures*, 195.

12. Jane Benyus, *Biomimicry: Innovations Inspired by Nature* (New York: Harper Perennial, 2002).

13. Sue L. T. McGregor, "Transdisciplinary and Biomimicry," *Transdisciplinary Journal of Engineering & Science* 4 (December 2013): 59–60.

14. McGregor, "Transdisciplinary and Biomimicry," 60–61.

15. McGregor, "Transdisciplinary and Biomimicry," 61–62.

16. McGregor, "Transdisciplinary and Biomimicry," 62.

17. Plant & Soil Sciences eLibrary, "Introduction - What is the Adaptive Cycle," 2, accessed January 27, 2021, https://passel2.unl.edu/view/lesson/b4790b02d93e/2, image courtesy of A. Garmestani, US Environmental Protection Agency (EPA).

18. Lance H. Gunderson and C. S. Holling, eds., *Panarchy: Understanding Transformations in Human and Natural Systems* (Washington, DC: Island Press, 2002).

19. Arthur Koestler, *The Ghost in the Machine* (London: Hutchinson & Co., 1967).

20. Plant and Soil Sciences eLibrary, "Panarchy, Example—Federal System," 5, accessed January 27, 2021, https://passel2.unl.edu/view/lesson/2e6e3c012632/5, image courtesy of A. Garmestani, US Environmental Protection Agency (EPA).

21. Plant and Soil Sciences eLibrary, "Panarchy Transitions, Pathway 1: Revolt," 3, https://passel2.unl.edu/view/lesson/2e6e3c012632/3, image courtesy of A. Garmestani, US Environmental Protection Agency (EPA).

22. Plant and Soil Sciences eLibrary, "Panarchy Transitions," "Pathway 2: Remember," 3, https://passel2.unl.edu/view/lesson/2e6e3c012632/3, image courtesy of A. Garmestani, US Environmental Protection Agency (EPA).

23. Wahl, *Designing Regenerative Cultures*, 110.

24. Wahl, *Designing Regenerative Cultures*, 111.

25. Wahl, *Designing Regenerative Cultures*, 209.

26. Wahl, *Designing Regenerative Cultures*, 211–212. For other sources, see Chris Martenson, a former *Fortune* 300 executive, who offers a series of short videos (four hours in total) on his website Peak Prosperity, which explores the interconnected dysfunctions of the economic system; accessed October 31, 2020, https://www.peakprosperity.com/crashcourse/.

27. Robin Murray, Julie Caulier-Grice, and Geoff Mulgan, *The Open Book of Social Innovation* (London: NESTA and the Young Foundation, 2010).

28. Murray et al., *The Open Book of Social Innovation*, 3–4.

29. Paul Hawken, Amory Lovins, and L. Hunter Lovins, *Natural Capitalism: Creating the Next Industrial Revolution* (New York: Little, Brown, 1999).

30. Ellen MacArthur Foundation, "Our Mission Is to Accelerate the Transition to a Circular Economy," accessed October 31, 2020, https://www.ellenmacarthurfoundation.org/.

31. MacArthur Foundation, *Towards the Circular Economy: An Economic and Business Rationale for an Accelerated Transition*, 2013. https://www.ellenmacarthurfoundation.org/assets/downloads/publications/Ellen-MacArthur-Foundation-Towards-the-Circular-Economy-vol.1.pdf. See also Ken Webster, *The Circular Economy: A Wealth of Flows*, 2nd ed. (Cowes, Isle of Wight, UK: Ellen MacArthur Foundation Publishing, 2016) and Walter R. Stahel, *The Circular Economy: A User's Guide* (New York: Routledge, 2019).

32. Kate Raworth, *Doughnut Economics: Seven Ways to Think Like a 21st-Century Economist* (Chelsea Green: Vermont, 2017).

33. The Democracy Collaborative, accessed October 31, 2020, https://democracycollaborative.org/.

34. Next System Project, accessed October 31, 2020. https://democracycollaborative.org/content/next-system-project.

35. James G. Speth and Kathleen Courrier, eds. *The New Systems Reader: Alternatives to a Failed Economy* (New York: Routledge, 2021).

36. John Fullerton, "Regenerative Capitalism: How Universal Principles and Patterns Will Shape the New Economy," April 2015, https://capitalinstitute.org/wp-content/uploads/2015/04/2015-Regenerative-Capitalism-4-20-15-final.pdf.

37. Ethical Markets Quality of Life Indicators (originally Calvert-Henderson Quality of Life Indicators), accessed October 31, 2020, http://ethicalmarketsqualityoflife.com/overview/.

38. David Korten, "David's Story," https://davidkorten.org/about-the-forum/davids-story/.

39. Bernard Lietaer et al., *Money and Sustainability: The Missing Link* (Charmouth, UK: Triarchy Press, 2012).

40. Ethan Roland and Gregory Landua, *Regenerative Enterprise: Optimizing for Multi-capital Abundance* (Morrisville, NC: Lulu Press, 2015), 12.

41. Carol Sanford, *The Regenerative Business* (New York: Nicholas Brealey, 2017), 2017; Carol Sanford, *The Responsible Business: Reimaging Sustainability and Success*, 2nd ed. (Edmunds, WA: InterOctave, 2020).

42. James G. Speth and Kathleen Courrier, eds. *The New Systems Reader: Alternatives to a Failed Economy* (New York: Routledge, 2021). These solutions should not be conflated with what Klaus Schwab is calling "the Fourth Industrial Revolution"—the technological revolution of disruptive technologies and trends (e.g., robotics, virtual reality, artificial intelligence (AI), machine learning and automation, high-speed mobile Internet, cloud computing, genome editing, three-dimensional printing, autonomous vehicles, the Internet of Things, and others) in the pursuit of higher productivity, new markets, lower barriers to entrepreneurship, and changes in the way that people live and work. See Klaus Schwab, *The Fourth Industrial Revolution* (New York: Crown Business, 2016).

43. Solidarity NYC, accessed November 1, 2020, http://solidaritynyc.org/. See also US Solidarity Economy Network, accessed November 1, 2020, https://ussen.org/; "What Is a Social Solidarity Economy?" accessed November 1, 2020, http://www.ripess.org/what-is-sse/what-is-social-solidarity-economy/?lang=en; Solidarity Economy: Building an Economy for People & Planet, accessed November 1, 2020, https://ccednet-rcdec.ca/en/toolbox/solidarity-economy-building-economy-people-planet; Alliance for a Responsible Plural and Solidarity Economy, accessed November 1, 2020, http://aloe.socioeco.org/; Global Transition to a New Economy—Map, accessed November 1, 2020, http://wiki.p2pfoundation.net/Global_Transition_to_a_New_Economy_-_Map.

44. Wahl, *Designing Regenerative Cultures*, 226. See also Vasilis Kostakis and Michel Bauwens, *Network Society and Future Scenarios for a Collaborative Economy* (London: Palgrave Macmillan, 2014). For additional resources on the commons, see David Bollier, "News and Perspectives on the Commons," accessed November 1, 2020, http://www.bollier.org/mybackpages/2017?order=title&sort=asc; the P2P Foundation (peer to peer, person to person, and people to people) that creates common goods through open participatory production and governance, accessed November 1, 2020, https://p2pfoundation.net/the-p2p-foundation; Commons Transition Primer, "How Does the Commons Work?" accessed November 1, 2020. https://primer.commonstransition.org/4-more/how-does-the-commons-work.

45. Community Wealth, "The Cleveland Model—How the Evergreen Cooperatives Are Building Community Wealth," accessed November 1, 2020, https://community-wealth.org/content/cleveland-model-how-evergreen-cooperatives-are-building-community-wealth.

46. Evergreen Cooperatives, "Innovations for an Emerging Green Economy," accessed November 1, 2020, http://www.evgoh.com/.

47. Robin Murray, "Danger and Opportunity Crisis and the New Social Economy," NESTA, September 1, 2009, https://www.nesta.org.uk/report/danger-and-opportunity-crisis-and-the-new-social-economy/; Murray et al., *The Open Book of Social Innovation*.

48. Gar Alperovitz, "Principles of a Pluralist Commonwealth," June 28, 2017, https://thenextsystem.org/principles; Gar Alperovitz and Keane Bhatt, "What Then Can I Do? Ten Ways to Democratize the Economy," September 24, 2013, https://www.garalperovitz.com/what-then-can-i-do/.

49. Gar Alperovitz, "Old Economy's Not Coming Back. So What's Next?" *YES!* May 26 2011, https://www.yesmagazine.org/new-economy/the-new-economy-movement.

50. Jill Bamburg, "Mondragon through a Critical Lens: Ten Lessons from a Visit to the Basque Cooperative Confederation," *Fifty by Fifty*, October 3, 2017, https://medium.com/fifty-by-fifty /mondragon-through-a-critical-lens-b29de8c6049.

51. Mondragon Corporation, "About Us," accessed November 1, 2020, https://www.mondragon-corporation.com/en/about-us/; Mondragon Corporation, "Entrepreneurship Ecosystem," accessed November 1, 2020, https://www.mondragon-corporation.com/en/; Richard Wolff, "On the Mondragon Cooperatives," March 14, 2014, YouTube, 44:35, https://www.youtube.com /watch?v=mKbukSeZ29o. The Wolff video embeds an eight-minute clip of a film called *Shift Change*, directed by Mark Dworkin and Melissa Young (2012: Basque Country, Spain, Cleveland, San Francisco, Madison, WI, Boston: Bullfrog Films, 2012), http://shiftchange.org. The film describes successful employee-owned businesses operating in a market economy that provide dignified and secure jobs in a democratic workplace; Bamburg, "Mondragon through a Critical Lens."

52. Eve Blossom, *Material Change: Design Thinking and the Social Entrepreneurship Movement* (New York: Metropolis Books, 2011).

53. Blossom, *Material Change*, 72–73.

54. Blossom, *Material Change*, 89–94.

55. Blossom, *Material Change*, 19, 28.

56. Blossom, *Material Change*, 101.

57. Blossom, *Material Change*, 147.

58. Grameen Bank, *Bank for the Poor*, accessed November 1, 2020, http://www.grameen.com/.

59. Self-Help Credit Union, "Our Story," accessed January 17, 2023, https://www.self-help.org /who-we-are/about-us/our-story.

60. Pamela Mang and Bill Reed, "Regenerative Development and Design," in *Sustainable Build Environments, Encyclopedia of Sustainability Science and Technology Series*, edited by Vivian Loftness, 115–41 (New York: Springer, 2020).

61. Regenesis, "Regenerative Development: Transforming the Way Humans Inhabit the Earth," accessed November 2, 2020, https://regenesisgroup.com/; "The Regenerative Practitioner Series," accessed November 2, 2020, https://regenerat.es/the-regenerative-practitioner-series/.

62. Regenesis, "Regenerative Development: How We Work," accessed November 2, 2020, https:// regenesisgroup.com/how-we-work/.

63. Regenesis, "Playa Viva," accessed November 2, 2020, https://regenesisgroup.com/project /playa-viva/.

64. For other examples of regenerative development, see Leah V. Gibbons, Scott A. Cloutier, Paul J. Coseo, and Ahmed Barakat, "Regenerative Development as an Integrative Paradigm and Methodology for Landscape Sustainability," *Sustainability* 10, no. 6 (June 2018), https://doi .org/10.3390/su10061910.

65. Gibbons et al., "Regenerative Development as an Integrative Paradigm."

66. Melissa Luna, *Playa Viva 2018 Social Impact Report*, 126, https://www.playaviva.com/wp -content/uploads/2018-Social-Impact-Report-Digital.pdf, accessed November 1, 2020.

67. Allan Berger, *Systemic Design Can Change the World* (Delft, Netherlands: SUN Architecture, 2009).

68. Christopher J. Rhodes, "The Imperative for Regenerative Agriculture," *Science Progress* 100, no. 1 (March 2017): 80–129, https://doi.org/10.3184/003685017X14876775256165.

69. Regeneration International, "Why Regenerative Agriculture," accessed November 2, 2020, https://regenerationinternational.org/why-regenerative-agriculture/.

70. Rodale Institute, "Regenerative Organic Agriculture and Climate Change," accessed November 2, 2020, https://rodaleinstitute.org/wp-content/uploads/rodale-white-paper.pdf; Paul Hawken, *Drawdown* (London: Penguin Books, 2017). Hawken identifies more than 100 ways to reduce atmospheric carbon concentrations, including agricultural regeneration. See Project Drawdown, "Drawdown Solutions Summary: Table of Solutions," accessed November 2, 2020, https://www.drawdown.org/solutions-summary-by-rank.

71. Project Drawdown, "Food, Agriculture, and Land Use," accessed November 2, 2020, https://www.drawdown.org/solutions/food/regenerative-agriculture.

72. Foodtank, "17 Organizations Promoting Regenerative Agriculture around the Globe," accessed November 2, 2020, https://foodtank.com/news/2018/05/organizations-feeding-healing-world-regenerative-agriculture-2/.

73. Steven Maxwell, "From Sand Quarry to Food Forest," *Organic & Wellness News*, May 31, 2017, https://www.organicwellnessnews.com/?ArticleID=638; Terra Genesis International, "Walker's Reserve: From Quarry to Food Forest, A Pathway of Regeneration," accessed November 2, 2020, http://www.terra-genesis.com/walkers-case-study/; Reconomics Institute, "Old Sand Quarry in Barbados Is Being Transformed into a Vibrant Wildlife Reserve," *Revitalization: The Journal of Urban, Rural & Environmental Resilience*, no. 7, https://revitalization.org/article/43718/.

74. Maxwell, "From Sand Quarry to Food Forest."

75. Terra Genesis International, "Cultivating the Regenerative Potential of Your Supply," accessed November 2, 2020, http://www.terra-genesis.com/.

76. André Brasser and Willem Ferwerda, *4 Returns from Landscape Restoration: A Systemic and Practical Approach to Restore Degraded Landscapes* (Amsterdam: Commonland, 2015), https://www.iucn.org/sites/dev/files/import/downloads/commonlandpublicationv1lr_269496814.pdf.

77. World Resources Institute, *Millennium Ecosystem Assessment: Ecosystems and Human Well-being: Synthesis* (Washington, DC: Island Press, 2005).

78. Luca Montanarella, Robert Scholes, and Anastasia Brainich, eds., *The Assessment Report on Land Degradation and Restoration* (Bonn, Germany: Secretariat of the Intergovernmental Science-Policy Platform on Biodiversity and Ecosystem Services (IPBES), March 24, 2018), https://doi.org/10.5281/zenodo.3237392.

79. Montanarella et al., *Assessment Report*, 30.

80. Montanarella et al., *Assessment Report*, 15.

81. Montanarella et al., *Assessment Report*, 31.

82. Brasser and Ferwerda, *4 Returns from Landscape Restoration*, 16.

83. Brasser and Ferwerda, *4 Returns from Landscape Restoration*, 8.

84. Montanarella et al., *Assessment Report*, 34.

85. Hilary Hove, Jo-Ellen Parry, and Nelson Lujara, "Maintenance of Hydropower Potential in Rwanda through Ecosystem Restoration," *World Resources Report*, Washington, DC, 2010–2011,

https://www.iisd.org/system/files/publications/maintenance_hydro_rwanda.pdf?q=sites/default/files/publications/maintenance_hydro_rwanda.pdf; Marc Ndimukaga, "Rugezi Wetland Conservation Project, Rwanda: Final Report," Conservation Leadership Programme, CLP Project ID: 0167312, https://www.conservationleadershipprogramme.org/project/rugezi-wetland-conservation-rwanda.

86. John D. Liu, "The Lessons of the Loess Plateau," accessed November 2, 2020, https://www.academia.edu/5567047/_Lessons_of_the_Loess_Plateau; John. D. Liu, "Greening China's Loess Plateau," January 30, 3013, YouTube, 1:21, https://www.youtube.com/watch?v=UAmai36XJDk.

87. Brasser and Ferwerda, *4 Returns from Landscape Restoration*.

88. Daniel Christian Wahl, "Join the Re-Generation! Designing Regenerative Cultures," *Medium*, April 27, 2016, https://medium.com/insurge-intelligence/join-the-re-generation-designing-regenerative-cultures-77f7868c63cd.

Chapter 9

1. Connie Malamed, "A Designer Addresses Criticisms of Design Thinking," *Learning Solutions*, March 16, 2018, https://learningsolutionsmag.com/articles/a-designer-addresses-criticism-of-design-thinking.

2. Tim Malbon, "The Problem with Design Thinking," *Made by Many*, February 24, 2016, https://medium.com/the-many/the-problem-with-design-thinking-988b88f1d696.

3. Sean Carney, "Design Thinking Is Dead. Long Live Design Thinking," *Phillips*, accessed October 23, 2020, https://www.philips.com/a-w/about/news/archive/blogs/innovation-matters/design-thinking-is-dead-long-live-design-thinking.html.

4. Shane Ketterman, "Exploring the Reasons for Design Thinking Criticism," *Mobile Design*, accessed October 23, 2020, https://www.toptal.com/designers/product-design/design-thinking-criticism.

5. Natasha Jen, "Design Thinking Is Bullsh*t," 99U Conference, June 7–9, 2017, *Vimeo* video, 13:26, https://vimeo.com/228126880.

6. Malamed, "A Designer Addresses Criticisms of Design Thinking."

7. Natasha Jen, "Design Thinking Is B.S.," *Fast Company*, April 9, 2018, https://www.fastcompany.com/90166804/design-thinking-is-b-s..

8. Jeffrey Tjendra, "Why Design Thinking Will Fail," *Business Innovation Design*, March 25, 2014, https://businessinnovation.design/blog/2014/3/23/why-design-thinking-will-fail.

9. Malbon, "The Problem with Design Thinking."

10. Jen, "Design Thinking Is B.S."

11. Malbon, "The Problem with Design Thinking."

12. Jen, "Design Thinking Is B.S."

13. Jen, "Design Thinking Is B.S."

14. Carney, "Design Thinking Is Dead. Long Live Design Thinking."

15. Rafiq Elmansy, "Why Design Thinking Doesn't Work," *Designorate*, September 17, 2018, https://www.designorate.com/why-design-thinking-doesnt-work/.

16. Niklaus Gerber, "A Critical Review of Design Thinking," August 20, 2018, https://medium.com/@niklausgerber/a-critical-review-of-design-thinking-44d8aed89e90.

17. Gerber, "A Critical Review of Design Thinking."

18. Jen, "Design Thinking Is B.S."

19. Kal Joffres, "Design Thinking Isn't the Problem—Here's What It Takes to Do Good Design," UX Collective, December 29, 2019, https://uxdesign.cc/design-thinking-isnt-the-problem-but-here-s-what-it-takes-to-do-good-design-eb4cf4278c63.

20. Jen, "Design Thinking Is B.S."

21. Joffres, "Design Thinking Isn't the Problem."

22. Michaela Fiasová, "Beyond Controversy: Demystifying Design Thinking," UX Collective, April 20, 2018, https://uxdesign.cc/demystifying-design-thinking-818ecd450c5a.

23. Don Norman, "Design Thinking: A Useful Myth," *CORE77*, June 25, 2010, https://www.core77.com/posts/16790/design-thinking-a-useful-myth-16790. Norman wrote a second essay, "Rethinking Design Thinking," which supported his major points but changed the conclusion. The conclusion now reads: "So three cheers for design thinking, for those practitioners and schools that are using these techniques, that encourage breakthrough thinking, and that encourage asking the stupid question. Not all schools teach design thinking in this way. Not all students learn it. Not all designers practice it. But for those who do teach, learn, and practice all of the techniques of design thinking, it can be transformative." See Don Norman, "Rethinking Design Thinking," jnd.org, December 3, 2018, https://jnd.org/rehtinking_design_thnking/.

24. Petra Badke-Schaub, Norbert Roozenburg, and Carlos Cardoso, "Design Thinking: A Paradigm on Its Way from Dilution to Meaninglessness," in *Proceedings of the 8th Design Thinking Research Symposium*, ed. Kees Dorst, Susan Stewart, Ilka Staudinger, Bec Paton, and Andy Dong, *Interpreting Design Thinking* (Sydney: DTRS, 2010), 39–49, https://www.academia.edu/33430269/Conveanor_8th_Design_Thinking_Research_Symposium_DTRS8.

25. James Woudhuysen, "The Craze for Design Thinking: Roots, a Critique, and Toward an Alternative," *Design Principles and Practices: An International Journal* 5, no. 6 (December 2011): 235–48, https://doi.org/10.18848/1833-1874/cgp/v05i06/38216.

26. Bruce Nussbaum, "Design Thinking Is a Failed Experiment. So What's Next?" *Fast Company*, April 5, 2011, https://www.fastcompany.com/1663558/design-thinking-is-a-failed-experiment-so-whats-next.

27. Thomas Wendt, "Toward Sustainable Design Thinking," Design Gym, accessed October 23, 2020, https://www.thedesigngym.com/toward-sustainable-design-thinking/.

28. Victor Papanek, *Design for the Real World: Human Ecology and Social Change* (Chicago: Chicago Review Press, 1971).

29. Tony Fry, *Design Futuring: Sustainability Ethics and New Practice* (Oxford, UK: Berg, 2008).

30. Wendt, "Toward Sustainable Design Thinking."

31. Lee Vinsel, "Design Thinking Is a Boondoggle," *Chronicle of Higher Education*, May 21, 2018, https://www.chronicle.com/article/Design-Thinking-Is-a/243472, 6. Vinsel acknowledges that he has no background in design or design thinking. He says that he conducted an "informal survey" with people who either teach at or were trained at "top art, architecture, and design schools in the United States," although he provides no references for the survey or its results.

32. Vinsel, "Design Thinking Is a Boondoggle," 6.

33. Vinsel, "Design Thinking Is a Boondoggle," 6.

34. Vinsel, "Design Thinking Is a Boondoggle," 3.

35. Vinsel, "Design Thinking Is a Boondoggle," 7.

36. Vinsel, "Design Thinking Is a Boondoggle," 5.

37. Vinsel, "Design Thinking Is a Boondoggle," 7.

38. Vinsel, "Design Thinking Is a Boondoggle," 8 (emphasis in the original).

39. Lee Vinsel, "A Response to the Stanford d.school's Defense of Design," *Noteworthy—The Journal Blog*, June 14, 2018, https://blog.usejournal.com/theres-so-little-there-there-a-response-to-the-stanford-d-school-s-defense-of-design-thinking-3cac35a1a365 (emphasis in the original).

40. Jon Kolko, "The Divisiveness of Design Thinking," *IX Interactions*, May–June 2018, https://interactions.acm.org/archive/view/may-june-2018/the-divisiveness-of-design-thinking.

41. Jon Kolko (interviewee), "Design Should Be a Liberal Art," *Unexpected Sources of Inspiration* (blog), May 11, 2016, https://blog.usievents.com/en/interview-jon-kolko-design-thinking/.

42. Natasha Iskander, "Design Thinking Is Fundamentally Conservative and Preserves the Status Quo," *Harvard Business Review* 5, September 5, 2018, https://hbr.org/2018/09/design-thinking-is-fundamentally-conservative-and-preserves-the-status-quo.

43. Iskander offers "interpretive engagement" as a contrast to design thinking and the rational-experimental approach to problem solving. However, as she describes interpretive engagement, it appears to be very compatible and consistent with the more evolving forms of design thinking practiced as illustrated in chapters 6, 7, and 8 of this book. Her point, that design has a conservative bias, is a central issue for those who explore the "politics of design" (see chapter 5) and for those who use critical theory to challenge results of government-driven policy designs, such as Jocelyn Bailey, "Governmentality and Power in 'Design for Government' in the UK, 2008–2017: An Ethnography of an Emerging Field" (PhD diss., University of Brighton, UK, 2021), https://research.brighton.ac.uk/en/studentTheses/governmentality-and-power-in-design-for-government-in-the-uk-2008.

44. Benedict Sheppard, Hugo Sarrazin, Garen Kouyoumjia, and Fabricio Dore. "The Business Value of Design." *McKinsey Report*, October 25, 2018. https://www.mckinsey.com/business-functions/mckinsey-design/our-insights/the-business-value-of-design.

45. For information on the cases of IBM, Intuit, Rotterdam Eye Hospital, Australian Tax Office, and Optican, see Hasso Plattner Institute, "This Is Design Thinking," https://thisisdesignthinking.net/why-this-site/who-we-are/. See also Lisa Carlgren, *Design Thinking as an Enabler of Innovation* (PhD diss., Chalmers University of Technology, Gothenburg, Sweden, 2013); Lisa Carlgren, Maria Elmquist and Ingo Rauth, "Design Thinking: Exploring Values and Effects from an Innovation Capability Perspective," *Design Journal* 17, no. 3 (2014): 403–24, https://doi.org/10.2752/175630614X13982745783000; Lisa Carlgren, Ingo Rauth, and Marie Elmquist, "Framing Design Thinking: The Concept in Idea and Enactment," *Creativity and Innovation Management* 25, no. 1 (March 2016): 38–57, https://doi.org/10.1111/caim.12153; Lisa Carlgren, Marie Elmquist, and Ingo Rauth, "The Challenges of Using Design Thinking in Industry-Experiences from Five Large Firms," *Creativity and Innovation Management* 25, no. 3 (September 2016): 307–426, https://doi.org/10.1111/caim.12176; Sean D. Carr et al., "The Influence of Design Thinking in Business: Some Preliminary Observations," *Design Management Review* 21, no. 3 (September 2010): 58–63,

https://doi.org/10.1111/j.1948-7169.2010.00080.x; Steven Chen and Allidi Venkatesh, "An Investigation of How Design-Oriented Organizations Implement Design Thinking," *Design Management Review* 21, no. 3 (September 2010): 58–63, https://doi.org/10.1111/j.1948-7169.2010.00080.x; Ingo Rauth, Lisa Carlgren, and Maria Elmquist, "Making it Happen: Legitimizing Design Thinking in Large Organizations," *Design Management Journal* 9, no. 1 (October 2014): 47–60: https://doi.org/10.1111/dmj.12015.

46. Marcus Jahnke, *Meaning in the Making: Introducing a Hermeneutic Perspective on the Contribution of Design Practice to Innovation* (PhD diss., University of Gothenburg, Sweden, 2013); Christophe J. Vetterli, *Embedded Design Thinking* (PhD diss., University of St. Gallen, Switzerland, 2015).

47. Jan Schmiedgen et al., *Parts without a Whole?—The Current State of Design Thinking Practice in Organizations*, Study Report no. 97 (Potsdam: Hasso-Plattner-Institut für Softwaresystemtechnik an der Universität Potsdam, 2015), https://thisisdesignthinking.net/why-this-site/the-study/. The research team from the Hasso-Plattner-Institute at Potsdam University compiled an online questionnaire and sent out a call for participants via multiple channels to those people and organizations that "consciously associate themselves with design thinking as a description for what they are doing." The survey contained both closed and open-ended questions about design thinking. Based on the survey analysis, eight experienced design thinking experts were then selected to participate in the in-depth interviews.

48. Sabine Junginger, "Design in the Organization: Parts and Wholes," *Design Research Journal* 2, no. 9 (January 2009): 23–9, https://www.academia.edu/213937/Design_in_the_Organization _Parts_and_Wholes.

49. Schmiedgen et al., *"Parts without a Whole,"* 50–52, https://thisisdesignthinking.net/why -this-site/the-study/.

50. Schmiedgen et al., *Parts without a Whole?*, 7f.

51. Schmiedgen et al., *Parts without a Whole?*, 106–12.

52. Schmiedgen et. al., Parts with a Whole?, 9.

53. Schmiedgen et al., *Parts without a Whole?* 108.

54. Schmiedgen et al., *Parts without a Whole?* 111.

55. Schmiedgen et al., *Parts without a Whole?* 112

56. Schmiedgen et al., *Parts without a Whole?* 56.

57. Schmiedgen et al., *Parts without a Whole?* 111.

58. Schmiedgen et al., *Parts without a Whole?* 9.

59. Schmiedgen et al., *Parts without a Whole?* 112.

60. Schmiedgen et al., *Parts without a Whole?* 34.

61. Schmiedgen et al., *Parts without a Whole?* 49.

62. Schmiedgen et al., *Parts without a Whole?* 8.

63. Schmiedgen et al., *Parts without a Whole?* 115.

64. Schmiedgen et al., *Parts without a Whole?* 116.

65. Schmiedgen et al., *Parts without a Whole?* 116.

66. Schmiedgen et al., *Parts without a Whole?* 116f.

67. Schmiedgen et al., *Parts without a Whole?* 116f.

68. Schmiedgen et al., *Parts without a Whole?* 116.

69. Schmiedgen et al., *Parts without a Whole?* 116.

70. Schmiedgen et al., *Parts without a Whole?* 116–17.

71. Thomas Lockwood and Edgar Papke, *Innovation by Design: How Any Organization Can Leverage Design Thinking to Produce Change, Drive New Ideas, and Deliver Meaningful Solutions* (Newbury-port, MA: Weiser, 2017); Jeanne Liedtka, Andrew King, and Kevin Bennett, *Solving Problems with Design Thinking: Ten Stories of What Works* (New York: Columbia Business School, 2013). Roger L. Martin, "The Innovation Catalysts," *Harvard Business Review* 89 (June 2011): 82–87, https://hbr.org/2011/06/the-innovation-catalysts;

72. Schmiedgen et al., *Parts without a Whole?* 117.

73. Schmiedgen et al., *Parts without a Whole?* 117.

74. Schmiedgen et al., *Parts without a Whole?* 117. These stories fill a whole book every year and includes information about the design team, challenges faced and addressed, lessons learned, solutions, and the metrics employed (e.g., cost savings, customer engagement, and revenues). For information on these stories, visit http://bit.ly/dtmetric.

75. Schmiedgen et al., *Parts without a Whole?* 114.

76. Schmiedgen et al., *Parts without a Whole?* 115. The researchers attribute this response to the fact that most respondents only recently began to engage with design thinking.

77. Schmiedgen et al., *Parts without a Whole?* 114.

78. Kate Svensson et al., "Evaluating Social Innovations for Evaluation Design," *American Journal of Evaluation* 39, no. 4 (April 2018): 459, https://doi.org/10.1177/1098214018763553.

79. Hallie Preskill and Tanya Beer, *Evaluating Social Innovation* (Washington, DC: Center for Evaluation Innovation, 2012), 2, https://www.evaluationinnovation.org/publication/evaluating-social-innovation/.

80. Preskill and Beer, *Evaluating Social Innovation*, 2.

81. Preskill and Beer, *Evaluating Social Innovation*, 5.

82. Michael Q. Patton, *Essentials of Utilization-Focused Evaluation* (Los Angeles: SAGE, 2012), 37.

83. Patton, *Essentials of Utilization-Focused Evaluation*, 37.

84. Svensson et al., "Evaluating Social Innovations for Evaluation Design."

85. Preskill and Beer, *Evaluating Social Innovation*, 3.

86. Michael Q. Patton, "What Is Essential in Developmental Evaluation?" *American Journal of Evaluation* 37, no. 2 (2016): 254, https://doi.org/10.1177/1098214015626295.

87. Patton, "What Is Essential in Developmental Evaluation?"

88. Patton, *Essentials of Utilization-Focused Evaluation*, 5.

89. Michael Q. Patton, *Developmental Evaluation: Applying Complexity Concepts to Enhance Innovation and Use* (New York: Guilford Press, 2011), 43.

90. Patton, *Developmental Evaluation*, 7.

91. Patton, *Developmental Evaluation*, 97.

92. Michael Q. Patton, *Qualitative Research and Evaluation Methods*, 4th ed. (Thousand Oaks, CA: SAGE, 2015), 302.

93. Patton, *Developmental Evaluation*, 308–13.

94. Patton, *Developmental Evaluation*, 23–25, 44–47.

95. Preskill and Beer, *Evaluating Social Innovation*, 4.

96. Patton, *Developmental Evaluation*, 97.

97. Patton, *Developmental Evaluation*, 19; see also ch. 9.

98. Patton, *Qualitative Research and Evaluation Methods*, 296.

99. Patton, *Developmental Evaluation*, 23–25.

100. Patton, *Developmental Evaluation*, 23–25; 46–47.

101. Patton uses the term "innovator." I prefer the term "designer" since we do not know whether a new design will be an innovation.

102. Patton, *Developmental Evaluation*, 46.

103. Patton, *Developmental Evaluation*, 131.

104. Patton, *Developmental Evaluation*, 162.

105. United Nations Environment Program, "Deforestation in Borneo Is Slowing, but Regulation Remains Key," February 18, 2019, https://www.unenvironment.org/news-and-stories/story/deforestation-borneo-slowing-regulation-remains-key.

106. See the interactive Special Report by Rebecca Wright et al., "Borneo Is Burning: How the World's Demand for Palm Oil Is Driving Deforestation in Indonesia," CNN, November 2019, https://www.cnn.com/interactive/2019/11/asia/borneo-climate-bomb-intl-hnk/. See also Richard C. Paddock and Muktita Suhartono, "A Blood-Red Sky: Fires Leave a Million Indonesians Gasping," September 25, 2019, https://www.nytimes.com/2019/09/25/world/asia/indonesia-red-sky-fires.html.

107. National Aeronautics and Space Administration (NASA) Earth Observatory, "Smoke Blankets Borneo," September 14, 2019, https://earthobservatory.nasa.gov/images/145614/smoke-blankets-borneo.

108. "Indonesia Haze: Why Do Forests Keep Burning?" *BBC News*, September16, 2019, https://www.bbc.com/news/world-asia-34265922.

109. Hans Nicholas Jong, "Indonesia Fires Emitted Double the Carbon of Amazon Fires, Research Shows," November 25, 2019, *Mongabay* Series, https://news.mongabay.com/2019/11/indonesia-fires-amazon-carbon-emissions-peatland/.

110. Following Ezio Manzini's lead, I do not view Willie Smits as a designer in the traditional sense, but he is a de facto designer and innovator. See Ezio Manzini, *Design When Everybody Designs* (Cambridge, MA: MIT Press, 2015), 60.

111. Willie Smits, "How to Restore a Rainforest," February 2009, TED video, 20:23.

112. The first four stages school the seven- to nine-year-old orangutans so that they can be released into the first-growth forests, where the trees are big enough and the food plentiful

enough to support them. Stage 5 is for those who are too old to be released, and stage 6 is for those who are sick and need to be close to the clinics.

113. Masarang Foundation, "Sugar Palm, A Miraculous Tree," accessed October 30, 2020, https:// masarang.nl/en/projects/sugar-palm-miracle-tree/.

114. Raymond Hartman and Daniël Nijenhuis, "Village Hub: A Sweet Sustainable Solution; a Promising Project by Willie Smits and the Masarang Foundation," accessed October 30, 2020, https://www.offgridquest.com/green/a-sweet-sustainable-solution.

115. The SPIE Engineering Group is an independent European leader that supports its customers to design, build, operate, and maintain energy-efficient and environmentally friendly facilities; see "Toward the Emergence of a Post-Carbon Economy," accessed October 30, 2020, https://www .spie.com/en#accueil. See also Willie Smits, "Sustainability Starts at the Village Level," August 30, 2012, TEDxMidwest video, 20:58, https://www.youtube.com/watch?v=gHNeVoxxYxU.

116. See Masarang Foundation, "We Restore Rainforests," accessed October 30, 2020, https:// masarang.nl/en/. It was founded by Smits in 2001.

117. "Willie Smits TED2009 Talk Challenged," accessed October 30, 2020, https://www.ted.com /about/programs-initiatives/ted-talks/willie-smits-ted-talk-challenged.

118. The bilocation of this design intervention is a reminder that evaluations need to get even more sophisticated when they span silos, borders, regions, and even countries, especially when connecting designs through micro, meso, and macro interactions and independencies. For this next generation of evaluation, see Michael Q. Patton, *Blue Marble Evaluation: Premises and Principles* (New York: Guilford Press, 2020).

119. Johan G. Redström, "Certain Uncertainties and the Design of Design Education," *She Ji Journal of Design, Economics, and Innovation*, 6, 1 (spring 2020): 99.

120. Michael W. Meyer and Don Norman, "Changing Design Education for the 21st Century," *She Ji Journal of Design, Economics, and Innovation* 6, 1 (spring 2020): 14 (emphasis added).

121. The Future of Design Education Initiative, https://www.futureofdesigneducation.org/.

122. Guillermina Noël, ed. "Design Education, Part I," *She Ji Journal of Design, Economics, and Innovation* 6, 1 (spring 2020): 1–118, https://www.sciencedirect.com/journal/she-ji-the-journal-of-design -economics-and-innovation/vol/6/issue/1; Guillermina Noël, ed., "Design Education, Part II," *She Ji Journal of Design Economics, and Innovation* 6, 2 (summer 2020): 119–274, https://www.sciencedirect .com/journal/she-ji-the-journal-of-design-economics-and-innovation/vol/6/issue/2.

123. Patton, *Developmental Evaluation*, 207.

124. Preskill and Beer, *Evaluating Social Innovation*, 3.

125. Preskill and Beer, *Evaluating Social Innovation*, 3.

126. Patton, *Blue Marble Evaluation*, 2020.

Chapter 10

1. Kees Dorst, "Frame Creation and Design in the Expanded Field," *She Ji: The Journal of Design, Economics and Innovation* 1, no. 1 (Autumn 2015): 23, https://doi.org/10.1016/j.sheji.2015.07.003.

2. Dorst, "Frame Creation and Design," 23.

3. Ezio Manzini, *Design When Everybody Designs* (Cambridge, MA: MIT Press, 2015), 60.

4. Dorst, "Frame Creation and Design," 30–31.

5. Roger L. Martin, "The Innovation Catalysts," *Harvard Business Review* 89, no. 6 (June 2011): 82–87, https://hbr.org/2011/06/the-innovation-catalysts; Jeanne Liedtka, Andrew King, and Kevin Bennett, *Solving Problems with Design Thinking: Ten Stories of What Works* (New York: Columbia Business School, 2013).

6. Manzini, *Design, When Everybody Designs*, 15.

7. Peter-Paul Verbeek, "Materializing Morality Design Ethics and Technological Mediation," *Science, Technology, & Human Values* 31, no. 3 (May, 2006): 361–80, https://doi.org/10.1177 /0162243905285847.

8. Jenny M. Lewis, Michael McGann, and Emma Blomkamp, "When Design Meets Power: Design Thinking, Public Sector Innovation and the Politics of Policymaking," *Policy & Politics* 48, no. 1 (January 2020): 111–30, https://doi.org/10.1332/030557319X15579230420081.

9. See Jocelyn Bailey, "Governmentality and Power in 'Design for Government' in the UK, 2008–2017: An Ethnography of an Emerging Field" (PhD diss., University of Brighton, UK, 2021), https:// research.brighton.ac.uk/en/studentTheses/governmentality-and-power-in-design-for-government -in-the-uk-2008.

10. Brian Boyer, "Helsinki Design Lab Ten Years Later," *She Ji: The Journal of Design, Economics, and Innovation* 6, no. 3 (Autumn 2020): 279–300, https://doi.org/10.1016/j.sheji.2020.07.001.

11. Stefanie Di Russo, *Understanding the Behavior of Design Thinking in Complex Environments*, Ph.D. diss., Swinburne University, Melbourne, Australia, 2016, https://researchbank.swin burne.edu.au/file/a312fc81-17d3-44b5-9cc7-7ceb48c7f277/1/Stefanie%20Di%20Russo%20 Thesis.pdf.

12. Di Russo, *Understanding the Behavior of Design Thinking*, 259. Also see Lisa Carlgren, Ingo Rauth, and Maria Elmquist, "Framing Design Thinking: The Concept in Idea and Enactment," *Creativity and Innovation Management* 25, no. 1 (2016): 38–57, https://doi.org/10.1111/caim.12153; Lotta Hassi and Miko Laakso, "Making Sense of Design Thinking," in IDBM Papers Vol. 1, T.-M. Karjalainen, M. Koria, and M. Salimäki, eds. (Helsinki: IDBM Program, Aalto University, 201) 1, 50–63, https://www.researchgate.net/publication/274066130_Making_sense_of_design_thinking;

13. Di Russo, *Understanding the Behavior of Design Thinking*, 262.

14. Jeanne M. Liedtka, "Perspective: Linking Design Thinking with Innovation Outcomes through Cognitive Bias Reduction," *Journal of Product Innovation Management* 32, no. 6 (March 2014): 937, https://doi.org/10.1111/jpim.12163. See also Linda N. Laursen and Louise M. Haase, "The Shortcomings of Design Thinking Compared to Designerly Thinking," *Design Journal* 22, no. 6 (September 2019): 813–32, https://doi.org/10.1080/14606925.2019.1652531. They also found the central paradigms of "design thinking" and "designerly thinking" to be "surprisingly similar" (824). However, they did put less emphasis on what they define as "design methodology," more attention to the design process, and a more expansive list of tools and techniques in design thinking compared to "designerly thinking." Since design thinking was initially developed to teach nondesigners and people from other disciplines how designers solve problems, it seems reasonable that people who first engage in design would want greater emphasis on the design process and design's tools and technologies, while their appreciation and use of the "design methodology" would evolve as they build their experience in design.

15. Pieter E. Vermaas and Udo Pesch, "Revisiting Rittel and Webber's Dilemmas: Designerly Thinking against the Background of New Social Distrust," *She Ji: The Journal of Design Economics, and Innovation* 6, no. 4 (Winter 2020): 530–45, https://doi.org/10.1016/j.sheji.2020.11.001.

16. Kipum Lee, "Critique of Design Thinking in Organizations: Strongholds and Shortcomings of the Making Paradigm," *She Ji: The Journal of Design, Economics, and Innovation* 7, no. 4 (Winter 2021): 497–515, https://doi.org/10.1016/j.sheji.2021.10.003.

17. Lee, "Critique of Design Thinking in Organizations," 510.

18. Lee, "Critique of Design Thinking in Organizations," 511.

19. David A. Kolb, *Experiential Learning: Experience as the Source of Learning and Development* (Englewood Cliffs, NJ: Prentice-Hall, 1984), 41.

20. Brian Logan and Tim Smithers, "Creativity and Design as Exploration," in *Modeling Creativity and Knowledge-Based Creative Design*, ed. John S. Gero and Mary Lou Maher (Hillsdale, NJ: Lawrence Erlbaum, 1993), 145; Charles L. Owen, "Design Research: Building the Knowledge Base," *Design Studies* 19, no. 1 (January 1998): 9–20, https://id.iit.edu/wp-content/uploads/2015/03/Design-researching-building-the-knowledge-base-Owen_desstud97.pdf.

21. Donald A. Schön, *The Reflective Practitioner: How Professionals Think in Action* (New York: Basic Books, 1983); Sara L. Beckman and Michael Berry, "Innovation as a Learning Process," *California Management Review* 50, no. 1 (Fall 2007): 25–56. https://doi.org/10.2307/41166415.

22. Liedtka, "Perspective: Linking Design Thinking with Innovation Outcomes through Cognitive Bias Reduction"; Jeanne M. Liedtka, "Why Design Thinking Works," *Harvard Business Review* 96, no. 5 (September–October 2018): 72–79, https://hbr.org/2018/09/why-design-thinking-works; Jeanne Liedtka, "Putting Technology in Its Place: Design Thinking's Social Technology at Work," *California Management Review*, 62, no. 2 (March 2020): 53–83, https://doi.org/10.1177/0008125619897391.

23. Liedtka, "Why Design Thinking Works," 75.

24. Liedtka, "Why Design Thinking Works," 74.

25. Liedtka, "Why Design Thinking Works," 78.

26. Leigh Thompson and David Schonthal, "The Social Psychology of Design Thinking," *California Management Review* 62, no. 2 (2020): 84–99, https://doi.org/10.1177/000812561989763.

27. Sara L. Beckman and Michael Barry, "Innovation as a Learning Process: Embedding Design Thinking," *California Management Review* 50, no. 1 (Fall 2007): 25–56, https://doi-org.libproxy.nps.edu/10.2307/41166415.

28. Medhanie Gaim and Nils Wålin, "In Search of a Creative Space: A Conceptual Framework of Synthesizing Paradoxical Tensions," *Scandinavian Journal of Management* 32, no. 1 (March 2016): 36, https://doi.org/10.1016/j.scaman.2015.12.002.

29. Gaim and Wålin, "In Search of a Creative Space," 34–36.

30. Gaim and Wålin. "In Search of a Creative Space," 35.

31. BOS Borneo Orangutan Survival Foundation, "BOSF Working Areas," accessed November 5, 2020, http://orangutan.or.id/bosf/#.

32. Masarang Foundation, "Our Mission and Objectives," https://masarang.eu/about/mission/.

33. Masarang Foundation, "Sugar Palm, A Miraculous Tree," https://masarang.nl/en/projects/sugar-palm-miracle-tree/; "The Role of the Sugar Palm in Masarang Projects," accessed November 5, 2020, https://masarang.nl/en/what-we-do/the-role-of-the-sugar-palm-in-masarang-projects/.

34. Wendy K. Smith and Marianne W. Lewis, "Toward a Theory of Paradox: A Dynamic Equilibrium Model of Organizing," *Academy of Management Review* 36, no. 2 (April 2011): 382, https://doi.org/10.5465/AMR.2011.59330958.

35. Gaim and Wålin, "In Search of a Creative Space," 33.

36. Timothy J. Hargrave and Andrew H. Van de Ven, "Integrating Dialectical and Paradox Perspectives on Managing Contradictions in Organizations," *Organization Studies* 38, no. 3–4 (April 2017): 319–39, https://doi.org/10.1177/0170840616640843; see table 1 on p. 323.

37. Gaim and Wålin, "In Search of a Creative Space," 35.

38. Alain Findeli, "The Methodological and Philosophical Foundations of Moholy-Nagy's Design Pedagogy in Chicago (1927–1946)," *Design Issues* 7, no. 1 (Autumn 1990): 4–19, 8, https://doi.org/10.2307/1511466.

39. Fred Collopy, "'I Think with My Hands;' On Balancing the Analytical and Intuitive Designing," in *Managing as Designing*, ed. Richard Boland and Fred Collopy (Stanford, CA: Stanford Business Books, 2004), 164–68.

40. Kees Dorst, "Design Problems and Design Paradoxes," *Design Issues* 22, no. 3 (July 2006): 4–17, 15, https://doi.org/10.1162/desi.2006.22.3.4 (emphasis in the original).

41. Kathrina Dankl, "The Paradox of Design Methods: Towards Alternative Functions," *Nordes: Nordic Design Research* no. 6 (2015): 1, https://archive.nordes.org/index.php/n13/article/view/403/381.

42. Gaim and Wålin. "In Search of a Creative Space."

43. Giovanni Innella, Craig Bremner, and Paul A. Rodgers, "Paradoxes in Design Thinking," *Design Journal* 20, Supl. 1 (September 2017): 4444–458, https://doi.org/10.1080/14606925.2017.1352941 (emphases added).

44. Hargrave and Van de Ven, "Integrating Dialectical and Paradox Perspectives," 325.

45. Gabriela Goldschmidt, "The Dialectics of Sketching," *Creativity Research Journal* 4, no. 2 (January 1991): 123, https://doi.org/10.1080/10400419109534381.

46. Jeanne Liedtka, "In Defense of Strategy as Design," *California Management Review* 42, no. 3 (Spring 2000): 19, https://doi.org/10.2307/41166040.

47. Richard Buchannan and Victor Margolis, eds. *Discovering Design* (Chicago: University of Chicago Press, 1995), 15–16, quoted in Liedtka, "In Defense of Strategy as Design," 17–18.

48. Liedtka, "In Defense of Strategy as Design," 20.

49. Liedtka, "In Defense of Strategy as Design," 20.

50. Roger L. Martin, *The Opposable Mind: How Successful Leaders Win through Integrative Thinking* (Boston: Harvard Business Review Press, 2007).

51. Roger L. Martin, *The Design of Business: Why Design Thinking Is the Next Competitive Advantage* (Boston: Harvard Business Review Press, 2009), 6 (emphasis in the original).

52. Anne Tomes and Peter Armstrong, "Dialectics of Design: How Ideas of 'Good Design' Change," *Prometheus* 28, no. 1 (March 2010): 37, https://doi.org/10.1080/08109021003694154.

53. Ian Gonsher, "On Creative Dialectics," *Articles* 13 (2015), 1–2, https://digitalcommons.risd .edu/critical_futures_symposium_articles/13.

54. Stephen J. Beckett, "The Logic of the Design Problem: A Dialectical Approach," *Design Issues* 33, no. 4 (Autumn 2017): 5–16, https://doi.org/10.1162/DESI_a_00470.

55. Richard Buchanan, "Creativity and Principles in the Enterprise," Closing Keynote of Enterprise UX 2018 June 13–15, San Francisco, https://www.youtube.com/watch?v=-Hlue5U88VU.

56. Cameron Tonkinwise, "Prototyping Risks When Design Is Disappearing," *Current* (blog), n.d., 1, https://current.ecuad.ca/prototyping-risks-when-design-is-disappearing.

57. For an overview, see Hargrove and Van de Ven, "Integrating Dialectical and Paradox Perspectives on Managing Contradictions in Organizations," 323 (table 1).

58. Gerry Stoker and Alice Moseley, "Motivation, Behavior, and the Microfoundations of Public Services," in *Public Services: A New Reform Agenda*, ed. Henry Kippin, Gerry Stoker, and Simon Griffiths (London: Bloomsbury, 2013), 17–36, https://doi.org/10.5040/9781472544872.ch-002.

59. Liedtka, "In Defense of Strategy as Design."

60. Bruce Hanington, "Empathy, Values, and Situated Action Sustaining People and Planet through Human-Centered Design," in *Routledge Handbook of Sustainable Design*, ed. Rachel Beth Egendoefer (London: Routledge, 2018), 193–205.

61. Bela Banathy, *Designing Social Systems in a Changing World* (New York: Springer Science+Business Media, 1996).

62. Jatinder Sidhu and Patrick Reinmoeller, *The Ambidextrous Organization: Management Paradox Today* (London: Routledge, 2017).

63. Steve Rayner, "How to Eat an Elephant: A Bottom-up Approach to Climate Change," *Climate Policy* 10, no. 6 (2010): 615–21; Jessica F. Green, Thomas Sterner and Gernot Wagner, "A Balance of Bottom-up and Top-down in Linking Climate Policies," *Nature Climate Change* 4 (November 2014): 1064–67, https://doi.org/10.1038/nclimate2429.

64. Connie Gersick, "Revolutionary Change Theories: A Multilevel Exploration of the Punctuated Equilibrium Paradigm, *Academy of Management Review* 16, no. 1 (January 1991): 10–36, https://doi.org/10.2307/258605; Catrien J. Termeer and Art Dewulf, "A Small Wins Framework to Overcome the Evaluation Paradox of Governing Wicked Problems," *Policy Society* 38, no. 2 (August 2018): 298–314, https://doi.org/10.1080/14494035.2018.1497933.

65. Donald A. Norman and Roberto Verganti. "Incremental and Radical Innovation: Design Research vs. Technology and Meaning Change," *Design Issues* 30, no. 1 (Winter 2014): 78–96, https://doi.org/10.1162/desi_a_00250.

66. C. West Churchman, "Wicked Problems." *Management Science* 14, no. 4 (December 1967): 142, https://www.jstor.org/stable/2628678.

67. Mark N. Wexler, "Exploring the Moral Dimension of Wicked Problems." *International Journal of Sociology and Social Policy* 29, no. 9/10 (September 2009): 536, https://doi.org/10.1108/01443330910986306 (emphases in the original).

68. Unlike philosophy, which tends not to make distinctions between ethics and morality, I separate the two in this section. "Ethics" refers to standards of right and wrong that are imposed by an outside authority, such as a professional association's code of conduct or ethics. "Morality"

refers to a designer's personal beliefs about what is right and what is wrong, not something that is imposed on the designer from the outside.

69. Michael Hardt, "Design & Ethics: Good, Bad, Innocent or Ignorant?" International Council of Design 18 (November 2009), https://www.ico-d.org/connect/features/post/353.php.

70. Harold G. Nelson and Erik Stolterman, *The Design Way: Intentional Change in an Unpredictable World,* 2nd ed. (Cambridge, MA: MIT Press, 2014), 201.

71. S. D. Noam Cook, "Design and Responsibility: The Interdependence of Natural, Artifactual, and Human Systems," in *Philosophy and Design: From Engineering to Architecture*, ed. Pieter E. Vermaas et al. (Berlin and Heidelberg, Germany: Springer, 2008), 259.

72. Cook, "Design and Responsibility," 259.

73. Nelson and Stolterman, *The Design Way*, 201.

74. Nelson and Stolterman, *The Design Way*, 201.

75. Hardt, "Design & Ethics: Good, Bad, Innocent or Ignorant?"

76. Richard Devon and Ibo Van De Pol, "Design Ethics: The Social Ethics Paradigm," *International Journal of Engineering Education* 20, no. 3 (2004): 461, https://www.researchgate.net/profile/Richard_Devon2/publication/228827371_Design_ethics_The_social_ethics_paradigm/links/00463516e95aa10d7c000000/Design-ethics-The-social-ethics-paradigm.pdf.

77. "Ethics for Designers," accessed November 6, 2020, https://www.ethicsfordesigners.com/.

78. Nelson and Stolterman, *The Design Way*, 185–86.

79. Nelson and Stolterman, *The Design Way*, 185–86.

80. Eric Katz, *Death by Design: Science, Technology, and Engineering in Nazi Germany* (London: Pearson Longman, 2006).

81. Vilém Flusser, *The Shape of Things: A Philosophy of Design* (London: Reaktion, 1999), 34.

82. American Institute of Architects, "2020 Code of Ethics and Professional Conduct," accessed January 19, 2023. https://content.aia.org/sites/default/files/2020-08/2020_Code_of_Ethics.pdf. Another example is the Design Institute of Australia, "Code of Ethics," accessed November 6, 2020, https://www.design.org.au/code-of-ethics.

83. Mike Monteiro, *A Designer's Code of Ethics*, accessed November 6, 2020, https://muledesign.com/2017/07/a-designers-code-of-ethics.

84. David Berman, *Do Good Design: How Designers Can Change the World*, accessed November 6, 2020, https://davidberman.com/social/dogood/.

85. IDEO, *The Little Book of Design Research Ethics*, accessed November 6, 2020, https://lbodre.ideo.com/.

86. "Ethics for Designers," 2020.

87. Nelson and Stolterman, *The Design Way*, 204.

88. Nelson and Stolterman, *The Design Way*, 204–8.

89. Nelson and Stolterman, *The Design Way*, 209.

90. Nelson and Stolterman, *The Design Way*, 209.

91. Nelson and Stolterman, *The Design Way*, 188.

92. Nelson and Stolterman, *The Design Way*, 210.

93. Nelson and Stolterman, *The Design Way*, 210–11.

94. Robert Nozick, *The Examined Life: Philosophical Meditations* (New York: Touchstone Books, 1989).

95. Schön, *The Reflective Practitioner*.

96. James Hillman, *The Soul's Code: In Search of Character and Calling* (New York: Random House, 1996).

97. Ben Sweeting, "Wicked Problems in Design and Ethics," in *Systemic Design: Theory, Methods, and Practice*, ed. Peter H. Jones and Kyoichi Kijima (Tokyo: Springer, 2018). The full print text also has been uploaded by the author into Research Gate (https://www.researchgate.net/profile /Ben-Sweeting/research). The pagination follows the article in Research Gate, 22.

98. Horst W. J. Rittel and Melvin W. Webber, "Dilemmas in a General Theory of Planning," *Policy Sciences* 4 (1973): 155–69.

99. Sweeting, "Wicked Problems in Design and Ethics," 14.

100. Sweeting, "Wicked Problems in Design and Ethics," 19.

101. Rittel and Webber, "Dilemmas in a General Theory of Planning," 161.

102. Normative ethical positions include consequentialism, deontology, and virtue ethics. *Consequentialism*, sometimes referred to as *teleological ethics*, explores ethics in terms of its outcomes or consequences and addresses such questions as "What consequences count as good consequences?" "Who is the prime beneficiary" of the action? "How are consequences judged and who judges them?" *Deontology* approaches ethics by focusing on the rightness or wrongness of action rather than its consequences. *Virtue ethics* puts the spotlight on people's characters rather than on their actions or the consequences of their actions. It identifies the habits and behaviors (virtues) that people employ to achieve well-being or a good life, offers practical wisdom to resolve any conflicts among the virtues, and posits that a lifetime practice of these virtues leads to or constitutes happiness and the good life.

103. Sweeting, "Wicked Problems in Design and Ethics," 13.

104. Sweeting, "Wicked Problems in Design and Ethics," 12.

105. Sweeting, "Wicked Problems in Design and Ethics," 13.

106. Sweeting, "Wicked Problems in Design and Ethics," 13, f10.

107. Caroline Whitbeck, *Ethics in Engineering Practice and Research*, 2nd ed. (Cambridge: Cambridge University Press, 2011).

108. Sweeting, "Wicked Problems in Design and Ethics," 130.

109. Whitbeck, *Ethics in Engineering Practice and Research*, 135.

110. Whitbeck, *Ethics in Engineering Practice and Research*, 136.

111. For case examples, see ch. 3, "Ethics as Design—Doing Justice to Moral Problems," in Whitbeck, *Ethics in Engineering Practice and Research*, 135–54.

112. Kees Dorst and Lambèr Royakkers, "The Design Analogy: A Model for Moral Problem Solving," *Design Studies* 27, no. 6 (November 2006): 633–36, https://doi.org/10.1016/j.destud.2006.05.002.

113. Ezio Manzini, *Design When Everybody Designs* (Cambridge, MA: MIT University Press, 2016); Terry Irwin, Cameron Tokinwise, and Gideon Kossoff, "Transition Design: An Educational Framework for Advancing the Study and Design of Sustainable Transitions," *Cuaderno 105*, Centro de Estudios en Diseño y Comunicación (2020/2021): 31–65.

114. Jeffrey L. Bradach, "Going to Scale: The Challenge of Replicating Social Programs," *Stanford Social Innovation Review* (2003): 19–25; Fred Dust and Ilya Prokopoff, "Designing Systems at Scale," *Rotman Magazine* (Winter 2009): 53–56; Nicole Fabricant, *Mobilizing Bolivia's Displaced: Indigenous Politics and the Struggle over Land* (Chapel Hill: University of North Carolina Press, 2012); Jeri Eckart-Queenan et al., "Designing for Transformative Scale: Global Lessons in What Works," *Rotman Magazine* (Winter 2015), https://www.rotman.utoronto.ca/Connect/Rotman-MAG/Issues/2015/Back-Issues---2015/Winter-2015---Wicked-Problems-III. For an elaboration of alternative governance arrangements that include both top-down and bottom-up adaptions to climate change, see Catrien Termeer et al., "Governance Arrangements for the Adaptation to Climate Change," in *Oxford Research Encyclopedia of Climate Science*, October 2017, https://doi.org/10.1093/acrefore/9780190228620.013.600.

115. Michael J. Mintrom and Joannah Luetjens, "Policy Entrepreneurs and Problem Framing: The Case of Climate Change," *Environment and Planning C: Politics and Space* 35, no. 8 (May 2017): 1362–77, https://doi.org/10.1177/2399654417708440.

116. Elinor Ostrom, "A Polycentric Approach for Coping with Climate Change," *Annals of Economics and Finance* 15, no. 1 (2014): 97–134.

117. Ostrom, "A Polycentric Approach for Coping with Climate Change," 100.

118. Ostrom, "A Polycentric Approach for Coping with Climate Change," 102.

119. Ostrom, "A Polycentric Approach for Coping with Climate Change," 103.

120. Ostrom, "A Polycentric Approach for Coping with Climate Change," 98.

121. Ostrom. "A Polycentric Approach for Coping with Climate Change," 99.

122. Ostrom, "A Polycentric Approach for Coping with Climate Change," 115–16.

123. Ostrom, "A Polycentric Approach for Coping with Climate Change," 118.

124. Ostrom, "A Polycentric Approach for Coping with Climate Change," 99.

125. Ostrom, "A Polycentric Approach for Coping with Climate Change," 121. For a fuller discussion of polycentricity, see Michael D. McGinnis and Elinor Ostrom, "Reflections on Vincent Ostrom, Public Administration, and Polycentricity," *Public Administration Review* 72, no. 1 (January/February, 2012):15–25. https://doi.org/10.1111/j.1540-6210.2011.02488.x.

126. Ostrom, "A Polycentric Approach for Coping with Climate Change," 124 (emphasis added).

127. Steven Ney and Marco Verweij, "Messy Institutions for Wicked Problems: How to Generate Clumsy Solutions," *Environment and Planning C: Government Policy* 33 (2015): 1679–96, https://doi.org/10.1177/0263774X15614450; Steven Ney and Christoph Meinel, *Putting Design Thinking to Work: How Large Organizations Can Embrace Messy Institutions to Tackle Wicked Problems* (Cham, Switzerland: Springer Nature, 2019).

128. Mary M. Douglas, "A History of Grid and Group Cultural Theory," Semiotics Institute Online, University of Toronto, http://semioticon.com/sio/courses/the-group-grid-model/.

129. Charles E. Lindblom, "The Science of Muddling Through," *Public Administration Review* 19, no. 2 (Spring 1959): 79–88, http://www.jstor.org/stable/973677.

130. Ney and Verweij, "Messy Institutions for Wicked Problems," 1683.

131. "Stanford Design Challenge 2020: Reducing the Inequity Gap," accessed November 7, 2020, https://contestwatchers.com/stanford-design-challenge-2020-reducing-the-inequity-gap/.

132. Stanford Center on Longevity, "Closing the Inequity Gap: Designing for Affordability Design Challenge Winners," April 7, 2020, Stanford, CA, http://longevity.stanford.edu/design-challenge/2020/04/07/stanford-center-on-longevity-announces-closing-the-inequity-gap-designing-for-affordability-design-challenge-winners/.

133. Ezio Manzini, "Making Things Happen: Social Innovation and Design," *Design Issues* 30, no. 1 (winter 2014): 57–66, https://doi.org/10.1162/DESI_a_00248; Corentin Girard et al., "Integrating Top-down and Bottom-up Approaches to Design Global Change Adaption at the River Basin Scale," *Global Environmental Change* 34 (September 2015): 132–46, https://doi.org/10.1016/j.gloenvcha.2015.07.002.

134. Natasha Iskander, "Design Thinking Is Fundamentally Conservative and Preserves the Status Quo," *Harvard Business Review Digital Articles* (September 5, 2018):1–9, https://hbr.org/2018/09/design-thinking-is-fundamentally-conservative-and-preserves-the-status-quo.

135. See, for example, Samuel L. Hayes and Ken Nguyen, "CA 2025: The Strategic Design of Civil Affairs" (master's thesis, Naval Postgraduate School, Monterey, CA, 2015), http://hdl.handle.net/10945/45870.

136. Liedtka, "In Defense of Strategy as Design," 21.

137. Churchman, "Wicked Problems," 141.

138. Jarmila A. Kopecka, Sicco C. Santema, and Jan A. Buijs, "Designerly Ways of Muddling Through," *Journal of Business Research* 65, no. 6 (June 2012): 729–39, https://doi.org/10.1016/j.jbusres.2010.12.009.

139. Lindblom, "The Science of Muddling Through," 81.

140. Charles E. Lindblom, "Still Muddling, Not Yet Through," *Public Administration Review* 39 (November–December 1979): 520.

141. Karl E. Weick, "Small Wins: Redefining the Scale of Social Problems," *American Psychologist* 39, no. 1 (January1984): 40–9, 43, https://doi.org/10.1037/0003-066X.39.1.40.

142. Weick, "Small Wins," 44.

143. Weick, "Small Wins," 44–47.

144. Weick, "Small Wins," 47.

145. Karl E. Weick and Robert E. Quinn, "Organizational Change and Development," *Annual Review of Psychology* 50 (1999), 361–86, 375, https://doi.org/10.1146/ANNUREV.PSYCH.50.1.361; Shona L. Brown and Kathleen M. Eisenhardt, "The Art of Continuous Change: Linking Complexity Theory and Time-Paced Evolution in Relentlessly Shifting Organizations," *Administrative Science Quarterly* 42, no. 1 (March 1997): 1–34, https://doi.org/10.2307/2393807.

146. Elizabeth Gerber, "Prototyping: Facing Uncertainty through Small Wins," in *Proceedings of ICED, Vol. 9, Human Behavior in Design*, ed. M. Norell Bergendahl et al. (Palo Alto, CA: ICED, 2009), https://www.designsociety.org/publication/28513/DS+58-9%3A+Proceedings+of+ICED+09%2C+the +17th+International+Conference+on+Engineering+Design%2C+Vol.+9%2C+Human+Behavior+in +Design%2C+Palo+Alto%2C+CA%2C+USA%2C+24.-27.08.2009.

147. Catrien J. Termeer, Art Dewulf, and Robert Biesbroek, "A Critical Assessment of the Wicked Problem Concept: Relevance and Usefulness for Policy Science and Practice," *Policy and Society* 38, no. 2 (May 2019): 167–179, https://doi.org/10.1080/14494035.2019.1617971.

148. Rittel and Webber, "Dilemmas in a General Theory of Planning," 162.

149. Termeer et al., "A Critical Assessment," 173.

150. Barbara Gray, *Collaborating: Finding Common Ground for Multiparty Problems* (San Francisco: Jossey-Bass, 1989), 5.

151. For more information, see the preface of this book. See also Nancy C. Roberts, "Wicked Problems and Network Approaches to Resolution," *International Public Management Review* 1, no. 1 (2000): 1–19. https://journals.sfu.ca/ipmr/index.php/ipmr/article/view/175.

Conclusion

1. Subcommission on Quaternary Stratigraphy, Anthropocene Working Group, "Results of a Binding Vote," May 21, 2019, accessed November 29, 2020, http://quaternary.stratigraphy.org /working-groups/anthropocene/.

2. Simon L. Lewis and Mark A. Maslin, *The Human Planet: How We Created the Anthropocene* (New Haven, CT: Yale University Press, 2018), 332.

3. Bela H. Bernathy, *Designing Social Systems in a Changing World* (New York: Springer Science+Business Media, 1996); Susan P. Besemer, *Creating Products in the Age of Design* (Stillwater, OK: New Forums Press, 2006); Rob Walker, "A Golden Age of Design," *New York Times Style Magazine*, September 28, 2014, https://www.nytimes.com/2014/09/22/t-magazine/design-golden-age .html; James Noble, "Anything Is Possible in the Age of Design," Linkedin, November 20, 2017, https://www.linkedin.com/pulse/anything-possible-age-design-james-noble.

4. Jeff Conklin, "The Age of Design," CogNexus Institute, 2001, 12, http://www.cognexus.org.

5. Sim Van der Ryn and Stuart Cowan, *Ecological Design: Tenth Anniversary Edition* (Washington, DC: Island Press, 1996), 24–25.

6. "UN Chief Issues 'Red Alert,' Urges the World to Come Together in 2018 to Tackle Pressing Challenges," *UN News*, December 31, 2018, video message by UN secretary-general António Guterres on the occasion of the 2018 New Year. https://news.un.org/en/story/2017/12/640812-un-chief-issues-red -alert-urges-world-come-together-2018-tackle-pressing.

7. Bill and Melinda Gates Foundation, "Global Grand Challenges," accessed November 29, 2020, https://grandchallenges.org/grant-opportunities.

8. USAID, "Grand Challenges for Development," accessed November 29, 2020, https://www .usaid.gov/grandchallenges.

9. XPRIZE, "$100 M Gigaton Scale Carbon Removal," accessed February 10, 2021, https://www .xprize.org/prizes/elonmusk.

10. XPRIZE, "Discover. Understand. Preserve. Rainforest," accessed November 29, 2020, https://www.xprize.org/prizes/rainforest.

11. XPRIZE, "Work Reimagined. Rapid Reskilling," accessed November 29, 2020, https://www.xprize.org/prizes/rapidreskilling.

12. XPRIZE, "Turning CO2 into Products," accessed November 29, 2020, https://www.xprize.org/prizes/carbon.

13. XPRIZE, "Creating Water from Thin Air," accessed November 29, 2020, https://www.xprize.org/prizes/water-abundance.

14. Wendy Schmidt Ocean Health XPRIZE, "Healing Our Oceans," accessed November 29, 2020, https://www.xprize.org/prizes/ocean-health.

15. Intergovernmental Panel on Climate Change (IPCC) et al., eds., *Global Warming of 1.5°C: An IPCC Special Report on the Impacts of Global Warming of 1.5°C above Pre-Industrial Levels and Related Global Greenhouse Gas Emission Pathways, in the Context of Strengthening the Global Response to the Threat of Climate Change, Sustainable Development, and Efforts to Eradicate Poverty* (Geneva, Switzerland: World Meteorological Organization, 2018). https://archive.ipcc.ch/pdf/special-reports/sr15/sr15_citation.pdf.

16. C. Otto Scharmer and Katrin Kaufer, *Leading from the Emerging Future: From Ego-System-to Eco-System* (San Francisco: Barrett-Koehler, 2013).

17. "Janus," Wikimedia Commons 4.0 International; File: Санкт-Петербург, Летний сад. Бюст_«Двуликий_Янус»_2; Author Игорь Гордеев.

18. C. Otto Scharmer. *The Essentials of Theory U* (Oakland, CA: Berrett Koehler, 2018), 4. See also Joshua C. Ramo, *The Age of the Unthinkable: Why the New World Order Constantly Surprises Us and What We Can Do about It* (New York: Little, Brown and Company).

19. Commons Transition, "About the Commons Transition, Transition Plans, Projects, Network, Stories, Book, Wiki," accessed November 29, 2020, https://commonstransition.org/about-commons-transition-2/.

20. Forum for the Future, "Who Are We, What We Do, Global Challenges, Systems Change, Understanding the Future, News and Insights," accessed November 29, 2020, https://www.forumforthefuture.org/.

21. School of System Change, "System Change, about Us, Blog, Courses, Contributors, Resources," accessed November 29, 2020, www.forumforthefuture.org/school-of-system-change.

22. Just Transition Alliance, "What Is a Just Transition?" accessed November 29, 2020, http://jtalliance.org/what-is-just-transition/.

23. Frank W. Geels et al., "The Socio-Technical Dynamics of Low-Carbon Transitions," *Joule* 1, no. 3 (November 2017): 463–79, https://www.sciencedirect.com/science/article/pii/S2542435117300922.

24. Sustainability Transitions Research Network, "About STRN," accessed November 29, 2020, https://transitionsnetwork.org/about-strn/.

25. "Great Transition Initiative: Toward a Transformative Vision and Praxis," accessed November 29, 2020, https://greattransition.org/.

26. Transition Network, "A Movement of Communities Coming Together to Reimagine and Rebuild Our World," accessed November 29, 2020, https://transitionnetwork.org/.

27. Terry Irwin, "Transition Design: A Proposal for a New Area of Design Practice, Study, and Research," *Design and Culture* 7, no. 2 (2015): 238 footnote # 1, https://doi.org/10.1080/1754707 5.2015.1051829.

28. Irwin, "Transition Design: A Proposal," 238, fn1.

29. Rob Hopkins, Michael Thomas, and the Transition Network Team, *The Essential Guide to Doing Transition: Getting Transition Started in Your Street, Community, Town or Organization*, accessed November 29, 2020, https://transitionnetwork.org/wp-content/uploads/2018/08/The-Essential-Guide-to-Doing -Transition-English-V1.2.pdf?pdf=essential-guide-to-transition-v-1; Rob Hopkins, *The Transition Movement in Global Perspective: Thomas Henfrey & Justin Kenrick*," February 2, 2016, https://transitionnetwork .org/news-and-blog/the-transition-movement-in-global-perspective-thomas-henfrey-justin-kenrick/.

30. Transition Network, "Principles," accessed November 29, 2020, https://transitionnetwork .org/about-the-movement/what-is-transition/principles-2/.

31. Ezio Manzini, *Design When Everybody Designs* (Cambridge, MA: MIT Press, 2015).

32. Manzini, *Design When Everybody Designs*, 2.

33. Manzini, *Design When Everybody Designs*, 10.

34. Manzini, *Design When Everybody Designs*, 61.

35. Manzini, *Design When Everybody Designs*, 114.

36. Manzini, *Design When Everybody Designs*, 117.

37. Manzini, *Design When Everybody Designs*, 123.

38. Manzini, *Design When Everybody Designs*, 153.

39. Manzini, *Design When Everybody Designs*, 173.

40. Manzini, *Design When Everybody Designs*, 197.

41. Manzini, *Design When Everybody Designs*, 198.

42. The redesign of design education is a complicated and challenging endeavor. See the excellent series of articles on "Design Education, Part I," ed. Guillermina Noël, *She Ji Journal of Design Economics, and Innovation* 6, no. 1 (spring 2020): 1–118, https://www.sciencedirect.com/journal/she-ji-the -journal-of-design-economics-and-innovation/vol/6/issue/1, and "Design Education, Part II," ed. Guillermina Noël, *She Ji Journal of Design Economics, and Innovation* 6, no. 2 (summer 2020): 119–274, https://www.sciencedirect.com/journal/she-ji-the-journal-of-design-economics-and-innovation/vol /6/issue/2.

43. New School, "Parsons Launches MFA in Transdisciplinary Design," February 18, 2010, https://www.newschool.edu/pressroom/pressreleases/2010/transdesign.aspx.

44. Jamer Hunt, "Letter from the Editor: Transdisciplinary Design," *Journal of Design Strategies* 5, no. 1 (April 2012): 5–10, https://issuu.com/journalofdesignstrategies/docs/the_journal_of_design _strategies_vo_bec4beb3c64ed5.

45. Hunt, "Letter from the Editor," 5–6.

46. Hunt, "Letter from the Editor," 5.

47. Hunt, "Letter from the Editor," 6.

48. Hunt, "Letter from the Editor," 6.

49. Hunt, "Letter from the Editor," 8.

50. Hunt, "Letter from the Editor," 7.

51. Hunt, "Letter from the Editor," 6.

52. Hunt, "Letter from the Editor." 8–9.

53. Human Sciences and Technologies Advanced Research Institute, Stanford University, Stanford, CA, accessed February 3, 2021, https://hstar.stanford.edu/.

54. The term "transition design" was originally proposed by Gideon Kossoff in his PhD Dissertation. See Gideon Kossoff, *Holism and the Reconstitution of Everyday Life: A Framework for Transition to a Sustainable Society* (PhD diss., University of Dundee, Scotland, 2011).

55. Terry Irwin, "Redesigning a Design Program: How Carnegie Mellon University Is Developing a Design Curricula for the 21st Century," *Solutions* 6, no. 1 (January/February 2015): 91–100, https://www.thesolutionsjournal.com/article/redesigning-a-design-program-how-carnegie-mellon-university-is-developing-a-design-curricula-for-the-21st-century.

56. Irwin, "Redesigning a Design Program," 94.

57. Irwin, "Transition Design: A Proposal," 232.

58. Irwin "Transition Design: A Proposal," 232 (emphasis in the original). For a more complete description of these four areas, see 233–237.

59. See Terry Irwin, Cameron Tonkinwise, and Gideon, Kossoff, "Transition Design: An Educational Framework for Advancing the Study and Design of Sustainable Transitions," paper presented to the Sustainability Transition Research Network Conference, Sussex University (Brighton, UK, 2015), https://www.academia.edu/15283122/Transition_Design_An_Educational_Framework_for_Advancing_the_Study_and_Design_of_Sustainable_Transitions_presented_at_the_STRN_conference_2015_Sussex.

60. Carnegie Mellon Design, "Design's Terry Irwin Developing Transition Design Institute," *Design*, July 30, 2019, https://design.cmu.edu/content/design%E2%80%99s-terry-irwin-developing-transition-design-institute.

61. For a good summary of this research, see İdil Gaziulusoy and Elif Erdğan Öztekin, "Design for Sustainability Transitions: Origins, Attitudes and Future Directions," *Sustainability* 11, no. 13, article number 3601 (June 2019): 1–16, https://doi.org/10.3390/su11133601.

62. Rethinking Design Education Initiative, https://www.futureofdesigneducation.org/.

63. Stuart Brand, *Whole Earth Catalogue*, "Statement of Purpose," 1968, https://monoskop.org/images/0/09/Brand_Stewart_Whole_Earth_Catalog_Fall_1968.pdf.

64. Tony Fry, *Design Futuring: Sustainability, Ethics and New Practice* (Oxford, UK: Berg, 2009), 248.

65. Richard Buchanan, "Wicked Problems in Design Thinking," *Design Issues* 8, no. 2 (Spring 1992), 16.

66. Daniel C. Wahl and Seaton Baxter, "The Designer's Role in Facilitating Sustainable Solutions," *Design Issues* 24, no. 2: 75, https://doi.org/10.1162/desi.2008.24.2.72.

Bibliography

Academy of Design Professionals. "2020 Code of Professional Conduct." http://designproacademy.org/code-of-professional-conduct.html.

Acaroglu, Leyla. "Disrupt Design: Post Disposable." https://www.disruptdesign.co/post-disposable.

Acaroglu, Leyla. "Disrupt Design: Post Disposable Workshops." https://www.disruptdesign.co/workshops.

Acaroglu, Leyla. "Toolkit: Free Post Disposable Activation." https://online.unschools.co/courses/post-disposable-activation-kit.

Ackerman, Spencer. "How the US's Terrorism Watchlists Work—and How You Could End Up on One." *The Guardian*, July 24, 2014. https://www.theguardian.com/world/2014/jul/24/us-terrorism-watchlist-work-no-fly-list.

Ackoff, Russell L. *Redesigning the Future: A Systems Approach to Societal Problems*. Hoboken, NJ: John Wiley & Sons, 1974.

Adams, James L. *Conceptual Blockbusting: A Guide to Better Ideas*. 4th ed. Cambridge, UK: Perseus, 2001.

Addarii, Filippo, and Fiorenza Lipparini. *Vision and Trends of Social Innovation for Europe*. Brussels: European Commission, Directorate-General for Research and Innovation, 2017. https://doi.org/10.2777/08700.

Agranoff, Robert. *Collaborating to Manage: A Primer for the Public Sector*. Washington, DC: Georgetown University Press, 2012.

Agranoff, Robert. "Inside Collaborative Networks: Ten Lessons for Public Managers." *Public Administration Review* 66, no. s1 (December 2006): 56–65. https://onlinelibrary.wiley.com/toc/15406210/2006/66/s1.

Alford, John, and Brian W. Head. "Wicked and Less Wicked Problems: A Typology and a Contingency Framework." *Policy and Society* 36, no. 3 (2017): 397–413. https://doi.org/10.1080/14494035.2017.1361634.

Alliance for a Responsible Plural and Solidarity Economy. http://aloe.socioeco.org/.

Alperovitz, Gar. "Old Economy's Not Coming Back. So What's Next?" *YES!* May 26, 2011. https://www.yesmagazine.org/new-economy/the-new-economy-movement.

Alperovitz, Gar. "Principles of a Pluralist Commonwealth." June 28, 2017. https://thenextsystem.org/principles.

Alperovitz, Gar, and Keane Bhatt. "What Then Can I Do? Ten Ways to Democratize the Economy." September 2013. https://www.garalperovitz.com/what-then-can-i-do/.

Altman, Steven, Pankaj Ghemawat, and Phillip Bastian. *DHL Global Connectedness Index 2018: The State of Globalization in a Fragile World*. Bonn, Germany: Deutsche Post DHL Group, January 2019. https://www.dhl.com/content/dam/dhl/global/core/documents/pdf/glo-core-gci-2018-full-study.pdf.

Amadeo, Kimberly. "US Economic Outlook for 2020 and Beyond." Updated August 15, 2020. The Balance, https://www.thebalance.com/us-economic-outlook-3305669.

American Institute of Architects. "Code of Ethics and Professional Conduct." https://www.aia .org/pages/3296-code-of-ethics-and-professional-conduct.

American Psychological Association. "2020 Presidential Election a Source of Significant Stress for More Americans than the 2016 Presidential Race." October 7, 2020. https://www.apa.org/news /press/releases/2020/10/election-stress.

American Sustainable Business Council. "Help Create an Economic System That Works for All." https://www.asbcouncil.org/.

Amsler, Lisa B., Janet K. Martinez, and Stephanie E. Smith. *Dispute System Design: Preventing, Managing, and Resolving Conflict*. Stanford, CA: Stanford University Press, 2020.

Anderson, Chris. *Makers: The New Industrial Revolution*. New York: Crown Business, 2012.

Anderson, Virginia, and Lauren Johnson. *Systems Thinking Basics*. Arcadia, CA: Pegasus Communication, 1997.

Ansell, Christopher K., and Martin Bartenberger. "Tackling Unruly Public Problems." In *Governance in Turbulent Times*, edited by Christopher K. Ansell, Jarle Trondal, and Morten Ogard, 107–36. Oxford: Oxford University Press, 2016.

Ansell, Christopher K., and Alison Gash. "Collaborative Governance in Theory and Practice." *Journal of Public Administration Research and Theory* 18, no. 4 (October 2008): 543–71. https://doi .org/10.1093/jopart/mum032.

Ansell, Christopher, and Jacob Torfing. "Collaborating on Design—Designing Collaboration." In *Public Innovation through Collaboration and Design*, edited by Christopher Ansell and Jacob Torfing, 229–39. London: Routledge, 2014.

Appleyard, Melissa M., Albrecht H. Enders, and Herb Velazquez. "Regaining R&D Leadership: The Role of Design Thinking and Creative Forbearance." *California Management Review* 62, no. 2 (January 2020): 12–29. https://doi.org/10.1177/0008125619897395.

Archer, Bruce. "Design as a Discipline." *Design Studies* 1, no. 1 (July 1979): 17–20. https://doi .org/10.1016/0142-694X(79)90023-1.

Arendt, Hannah. *The Human Condition*. 2nd ed. Chicago: University of Chicago Press, 1998.

Arnheim, Rudolf. *Visual Thinking*. 2nd ed. Berkeley: University of California Press, 2004.

Arquilla, John, and Nancy C. Roberts. *Design of Warfare*. Monterey. CA: Naval Postgraduate School, 2017. https://calhoun.nps.edu/handle/10945/62564.

Arquilla, John, and David Ronfeldt. *The Advent of Netwar*. Santa Monica, CA: RAND, 1996.

Ashbrook, Tom. "Time for a Guaranteed Basic Income?" *Audio: On Point*. January 19, 2016. https:// basicincome.org/news/2016/01/audio-on-point-with-tom-ashbrook-time-for-a-guaranteed-basic -income/.

Ashoka Fellows. https://www.ashoka.org/en-US/our-network/ashoka-fellows.

Atkins, Paul W. B., David S. Wilson, and Steven C. Hays. *Prosocial: Using Evolutionary Science to Build Productive Equitable, and Collaborative Groups*. Oakland, CA: Context Press/New Harbinger Publications, 2019.

Australian Public Service Commission. *Tackling Wicked Problems: A Public Policy Perspective*. Canberra: Australian Public Service Commission, 2007.

Axelrod, Robert. *The Evolution of Cooperation*. New York: Basic Books, 1984.

Axinte, Lorena F., Abid Mehmood, Terry Marsden, and Dirk Roep. "Regenerative City-Regions: A New Conceptual Framework." *Regional Studies, Regional Science* 6, no. 1 (March 2019): 117–29. https://doi.org/10.1080/21681376.2019.1584542.

Azevêdo, Roberto. "Trade Set to Plunge as COVID-19 Pandemic Upends Global Economy." Press release, World Trade Organization, April 8, 2020. https://www.wto.org/english/news_e/pres20_e /pr855_e.htm.

Bacevich, Andrew J. "Endless War in the Middle East." *CATO Institute* 14, no. 3 (Summer 2016): 1–7. https://www.cato.org/publications/catos-letter/endless-war-middle-east.

Badke-Schaub, Petra, and Ozgur Eris. "A Theoretical Approach to Intuition in Design." In *An Anthology of Theories and Models of Design*, edited by Amaresh Chakrabarti and Lucienne T. M. Blessing, 353–70. London: Springer, 2014. https://doi.org/10.1007/978-1-4471-6338-1_17.

Badke-Schaub, Petra, Norbert Roozenburg, and Carlos Cardoso. "Design Thinking: A Paradigm on Its Way from Dilution to Meaninglessness." In *Proceedings of the 8th Design Thinking Research Symposium: Interpreting Design Thinking*, Sydney, October 19–20, 2010. https://www.academia .edu/33430269/Conveanor_8th_Design_Thinking_Research_Symposium_DTRS8.

Bailey, Jocelyn. "Governmentality and Power in 'Design for Government' in the UK, 2008–2017: An Ethnography of an Emerging Field." PhD diss., University of Brighton, UK, 2021. https://research.brigh ton.ac.uk/en/studentTheses/governmentality-and-power-in-design-for-government-in-the-uk-2008.

Balint, Peter J., Ronald E. Stewart, Anand Desai, and Lawrence C. Walters. *Wicked Environmental Problems*. Washington, DC: Island Press, 2011.

Ballon, Marc. "Artificial Intelligence: Are We Facing a Future of Robots Running Wild?" *USC News*, August 31, 2016. http://news.usc.edu/106565/artificial-intelligence-for-a-better-tomorrow/.

Bamburg, Jill. "Mondragon through a Critical Lens: Ten Lessons from a Visit to the Basque Cooperative Confederation." *Fifty by Fifty*. October 3, 2017. https://medium.com/fifty-by-fifty/mondragon -through-a-critical-lens-b29de8c6049.

Banerjee, Banny. "Designer as Agent of Change: A Vision for Catalyzing Rapid Change." In *Changing the Change Conference Proceedings*, Torino, July 11–12, 2008. https://uploads-ssl.webflow .com/5a9898f92fa8fa00017acfa3/5c63e109cbc13e075f6db2aa_Banny%20Banerjee-Designer%20 as%20Agent%20of%20Change.pdf.

Baradat, Leon P., and John A. Philips. *Political Ideologies: Their Origins and Impact*. 12th ed. New York: Routledge, 2017.

Bardach, Eugene. *Getting Agencies to Work Together*. Washington, DC: Brookings Institution Press, 1998.

Barefoot College. "Audit Statement." https://www.barefootcollege.org/wp-content/uploads/2018/11 /Annexure-xii-Audit-Statement-2017-18.pdf.

Barefoot College. *The Barefoot College Annual Report 2016–17*. https://www.barefootcollege.org /wp-content/uploads/2018/10/Barefoot_annualreport_2016-17_v7_online.pdf.

Barefoot College. "The Barefoot Story." https://www.barefootcollege.org/about/.

Barefoot College. "Enriche." https://www.barefootcollege.org/solution/enriche/.

Barefoot College. "Health Solutions." https://www.barefootcollege.org/solution/health/.

Barefoot College. "Learn the Barefoot Approach: A Path to Development Led by Communities." https://www.barefootcollege.org/approach/.

Barefoot College. "Powering the Future We Believe In: Three-Year Strategic Focus 2015–2018." https://www.barefootcollege.org/wp-content/themes/barefoot-college/download/strategic-plan.pdf.

Barefoot College. "Solutions in Education." https://www.barefootcollege.org/solution/education -preview/.

Barefoot College. "Solutions in Solar." https://www.barefootcollege.org/solution/solar/.

Barefoot College. "Solutions in Water." https://www.barefootcollege.org/solution/water/.

Barefoot College. "Where We Work." https://www.barefootcollege.org/about/where-we-work/.

Barrett, David, George T. Kurian, and Todd M. Johnson, eds. *World Christian Encyclopedia: A Comparative Survey of Churches and Religions in the Modern World, Vol. 1: The World by Countries: Religionists, Churches, Ministries*. 2nd ed. Oxford: Oxford University Press, 2001.

Bartlett, Dean, and Pauline Dibben. "Public Sector Innovation and Entrepreneurship: Case Studies from Local Government," *Local Government Studies* 28, no. 4 (Winter 2002): 107–21. https://doi.org/10.1080/714004159.

Bason, Christian. "Design Attitude as an Innovation Catalyst." In *Public Innovation through Collaboration and Design*, edited by Christopher Ansell and Jacob Torfing, 209–28. London: Routledge, 2014.

Bason, Christian. *Leading Public Design*. Bristol, UK: Policy Press, 2017.

Bason, Christian. *Leading Public-Sector Innovation: Co-creating for a Better Society*. Bristol, UK: Bristol University Press, 2010.

Batie, Sandra S. "Wicked Problems and Applied Economics." *American Journal of Agricultural Economics* 90, no. 5 (December 2008): 1176–91. https://doi.org/10.1111/j.1467-8276.2008.01202.x.

Battle, Joyce, and Malcolm Byrne, eds. "The Iraq War Ten Years After." *National Security Briefing Book* No. 418, March 19, 2013. *National Security Archive*. Washington, DC: George Washington University, 2013. https://nsarchive2.gwu.edu/NSAEBB/NSAEBB418/.

Bausch, Ken. "Problematique and the Club of Rome." http://quergeist.net/Problematique_Club -of-Rome.htm.

BBC News. "Indonesia Haze: Why Do Forests Keep Burning?" September16, 2019. https://www .bbc.com/news/world-asia-34265922.

Beck, Don E., and Christophe C. Cowan. *Spiral Dynamics: Mastering Values, Leadership, and Change*. Malden, MA: Blackwell, 2006.

Beck, Don E., Teddy H. Larsen, Sergey Solonin, Rica Viljoen, and Thomas Q. Johns. *Spiral Dynamics in Action: Humanity's Master Code*. Hoboken, NJ: Wiley, 2018.

Beck, Don E., and Graham Linscott. *The Crucible: Forging South Africa's Future, in Search of a Template for the World*. Columbia, MD: Graphic Press, 1991.

Beckett, Stephen J. "The Logic of the Design Problem: A Dialectical Approach." *Design Issues* 33, no. 4 (Autumn 2017): 5–16. https://doi.org/10.1162/DESI_a_00470.

Beckman, Sara L. "To Frame or Reframe: Where Might Design Thinking Research Go Next?" *California Management Review* 62, no. 2 (March 2020): 144–62. https://doi.org/10.1177%2F0008125620906620.

Beckman, Sara L., and Michael Berry. "Innovation as a Learning Process: Embedding Design Thinking." *California Management Review* 50, no. 1 (Fall 2007): 25–57. https://doi.org/10.2307/41166415.

Ben-Dov, Yoav. "Hanoi Traffic." 2009. YouTube video, 2:34. https://www.youtube.com/watch?v=LzjifmHavAQ.

Benyus, Jane. *Biomimicry: Innovations Inspired by Nature*. New York: Harper Perennial, 2002.

Berg, Nate. "See inside a Hospital Designed by Patients." *Fast Company*, December 16, 2020. https://www.fastcompany.com/90586705/see-a-hospital-designed-by-patients.

Berger, Allan. *Systemic Design Can Change the World*. Delft, Netherlands: SUN Architecture, 2009.

Bergen, Peter, and Paul Cruickshank. "The Iraq Effect." *Mother Jones*, March 1, 2007. https://www.motherjones.com/politics/2007/03/iraq-101-iraq-effect-war-iraq-and-its-impact-war-terrorism-pg-1/.

Berger, Peter L., and Thomas Luckmann. *The Social Construction of Reality*. Garden City, NY: Doubleday, 1966.

Berger, Warren. *Glimmer: How Design Can Transform Your Life, and Maybe Even the World*. New York: Penguin Press, 2009.

Berg-Knutsen, Espen, and Nancy C. Roberts, eds. *Strategic Design for NORSOF 2025*. Monterey, CA: Naval Postgraduate School, 2015. https://apps.dtic.mil/sti/citations/AD1060147.

Berman, David B. *Do Good Design: How Design Can Change the World*. 2nd ed. Berkeley, CA: New Riders Design Press, in association with AIGA Design Press, 2013.

Bernathy, Bela H. *Designing Social Systems in a Changing World*. New York: Plenum Publishing Co., 1996.

Berry, Frances S., and Geraldo Flowers. "Public Entrepreneurs in the Policy Process: Performance-Based Budgeting Reform in Florida." *Journal of Public Budgeting, Accounting & Financial Management* 11, no. 4 (Winter 1999): 578–617.

Besemer, Susan P. *Creating Products in the Age of Design*. Stillwater, OK: New Forums Press, 2006.

Best, Kathryn. *Design Management: Managing Design Strategy, Process, and Implementation*. 2nd ed. London: Bloomsbury, 2015.

Bichl, Sandra. "Career Advice in a VUCA World." *Career Angels* (blog). https://blog.careerangels.eu/career-advice-in-a-vuca-world/.

Bill and Melinda Gates Foundation. "Global Grand Challenges." https://grandchallenges.org/grant-opportunities.

Bingham, Claire. "Inside the Growing Nexus of Politics and Design." *Architecture + Design*, November 8, 2018. https://www.architecturaldigest.com/story/political-design.

Bioneers. "Our Purpose." https://bioneers.org/.

Birkland, Thomas A., and Kathryn L. Schwaeble. "Agenda Setting and the Policy Process, Politics: Focusing Events." In *Oxford Research Encyclopedia of Politics*, 2019. https://doi.org/10.1093/acrefore/9780190228637.013.165.

Björklund, Tua, Hanna Maula, Sarah A. Soule, and Jesse Maula. "Integrating Design into Organizations: The Coevolution of Design Capabilities." *California Management Review* 62, no. 2 (January 2020): 100–24. https://doi.org/10.1177/0008125619898245.

Block, Peter. *Community: The Structure of Belonging.* 2nd ed. Oakland, CA: Barrett-Koehler, 2018.

Bloom, Paul N., and Gregory Dees. "Cultivate Your Ecosystem." *Stanford Social Innovation Review* (Winter 2008): 47–53. https://ssir.org/articles/entry/cultivate_your_ecosystem.

Blossom, Eve. *Material Change: Design Thinking and the Social Entrepreneurship Movement.* New York: Metropolis Books, 2011.

Bohm, David. *On Dialogue.* London: Routledge, 1996.

Boland, Richard J., and Fred Collopy, eds. *Managing as Designing.* Stanford, CA: Stanford Business Books, 2004.

Bollier, David. "News and Perspectives on the Commons." https://www.bollier.org/.

Borja de Mozota, Brigitte. *Design Management.* New York: Allworth Press, 2003.

Borja de Mozota, Brigitte, and Faviane Wolff. "Forty Years of Research in Design Management: A Review of the Literature and Directions for the Future." *Strategic Design Research Journal* 12, no. 1 (January–April 2019): 4–26. https://doi.org/10.4013/sdrj.2019.121.02.

Bornstein, David. *How to Change the World: Social Entrepreneurs and the Power of New Ideas.* Oxford: Oxford University Press, 2007.

BOS Borneo Orangutan Survival Foundation. "BOSF Working Areas." http://orangutan.or.id/bosf/#.

Boselli, Filippo. *Regenerative Cities in China: Roadmap for a Better Urban Future.* Hamburg, Germany: World Future Council, 2016. https://www.worldfuturecouncil.org/wp-content/uploads/2016/03/WFC_2016_Regenerative_Cities_in_China_En.pdf.

Bousbaci, Rabah. "'Models of Man' in Design Thinking: The 'Bounded Rationality' Episode." *Design Issues* 24, no. 4 (Autumn 2008): 38–52. https://doi.org/10.1162/desi.2008.24.4.38.

Boyer, Brian. "Helsinki Design Lab Ten Years Later." *She Ji: The Journal of Design, Economics, and Innovation* 6, no. 3 (Autumn 2020): 279–300. https://doi.org/10.1016/j.sheji.2020.07.001.

BRAC. "Empowering People to Rise Above Poverty." https://bracusa.org/.

BRAC. *Pathways to Prosperity: BRAC USA 2017 Annual Report.* https://www.brac.net/sites/default/files/annual-report/2017/BRACUSA_AnnualReport_FY2017.pdf.

Bradach, Jeffrey L. "Going to Scale." *Stanford Social Innovation Review.* (Spring 2003). https://ssir.org/articles/entry/going_to_scale.

Brafman, Ori, and Rom Brafman. *Sway: The Irresistible Pull of Irrational Behavior.* New York: Doubleday, 2008.

Brand, Ralf, and Frank Gaffikin. "Collaborative Planning in an Uncollaborative World." *Planning Theory* 6, no. 3 (November 2007): 282–313. https://doi.org/10.1177/1473095207082036.

Brasser, André, and Willem Ferwerda. *4 Returns from Landscape Restoration: A Systemic and Practical Approach to Restore Degraded Landscapes*. Amsterdam: Commonland, 2015. https://www.iucn.org/sites/dev/files/import/downloads/commonlandpublicationv1lr_269496814.pdf.

Brenner, Walter, Falk Uebernickel, and Thomas Abrell. "Design Thinking as Mindset, Process, and Toolbox." In *Design Thinking for Innovation*, edited by Walter Brenner and Falk Uebernickel, 3–21. Cham, Switzerland: Springer, 2016. https://doi.org/10.1007/978-3-319-26100-3.

Brilliant, Larry. "My Wish: Help Me Stop Pandemics." February 2006. TED video, 25:38. https://www.ted.com/talks/larry_brilliant_my_wish_help_me_stop_pandemics.

Brinkerhoff, Derick W. "State Fragility and Failure as Wicked Problems: Beyond Naming and Taming." *Third World Quarterly* 35, no. 2 (March 2014): 333–44. https://doi.org/10.1080/01436597.2014.878495.

Brooks, Courtney G., James M. Grimwood, and Loyd S. Swensen, Jr. *Chariots for Apollo: A History of Manned Lunar Spacecraft*. NASA Special Publication-4205 in the NASA History Series, 1979. https://www.hq.nasa.gov/office/pao/History/SP-4205/contents.html.

Brown, Chad P., and Melina Kolb. "Trump's Trade War Timeline: An Up-to-Date Guide." Peterson Institute for International Economics, December 18, 2020. https://www.piie.com/blogs/trade-investment-policy-watch/trump-trade-war-china-date-guide.

Brown, Gabe. *Dirt to Soil: One Family's Journey into Regenerative Agriculture*. White River Junction, VT: Chelsea Green Publishing, 2018.

Brown, L. David. "Planned Change in Underorganized Systems." In *Systems Theory for Organization Development*, edited by Tom G. Cummings, 181–203. New York: Wiley, 1980.

Brown, Shona L., and Kathleen M. Eisenhardt. "The Art of Continuous Change: Linking Complexity Theory and Time-Paced Evolution in Relentlessly Shifting Organizations." *Administrative Science Quarterly* 42, no. 1 (March 1997): 1–34. https://doi.org/10.2307/2393807.

Brown, Stuart, and Christopher Vaughan. *Play: How It Shapes the Brain, Opens the Imagination, and Invigorates the Soul*. New York: Penguin, 2010.

Brown, Tim. *Change by Design*. New York: HarperCollins, 2009.

Brown, Tim. "Design Thinking." *Harvard Business Review* (June 2008): 84–95. https://readings.design/PDF/Tim%20Brown,%20Design%20Thinking.pdf.

Brown, Tim. "Strategy by Design." *Fast Company*, June 1, 2005. https://www.fastcompany.com/52795/strategy-design.

Brown, Tim. "Tales of Creativity and Play." May 2008. TED video, 27:58. https://www.ted.com/talks/tim_brown_on_creativity_and_play.

Bryson, John M. *Strategic Planning for Public and Nonprofit Organizations*. San Francisco: Jossey-Bass, 1995.

Bryson, John M., Barbara C. Crosby, and Laura Bloomberg. eds. *Discerning and Assessing Public Value: Major Issues and New Direction*. Washington, DC: Georgetown University Press, 2015.

Bryson, John M., Barbara C. Crosby, and Melissa M. Stone. "The Design and Implementation of Cross-Sector Collaborations." *Public Administration Review* 66, no. s1 (December 2006): 44–55. https://onlinelibrary.wiley.com/toc/15406210/66/s1.

B Team: A Global Colective of Business and Civil Society Leaders Driving a Better Way of Doing Business for People and Planet. "Our Economic Model Is Broken: Building a New One." https://bteam.org/.

Buchanan, Ashley, and Margaret L. Kern. "The Benefit Mindset: The Psychology of Contribution and Everyday Leadership." *International Journal of Wellbeing* 7, no. 1 (June 2017): 1–11. https://doi.org/10.5502/ijw.v7i1.538.

Buchanan, Richard. "Creativity and Principles in the Enterprise." Closing Keynote of Enterprise UX 2018, June 13–15, San Francisco. https://www.youtube.com/watch?v=-Hlue5U88VU.

Buchanan, Richard. "Declaration by Design: Rhetoric, Argument, and Demonstration in Design Practice." *Design Issues* 2, no. 1 (Spring 1985): 4–22. https://www.jstor.org/stable/1511524.

Buchanan, Richard. "Design Research and the New Learning." *Design Issues* 17, no. 4 (Autumn 2001): 3–23. https://doi.org/10.1162/07479360152681056.

Buchanan, Richard. "Human Dignity and Human Rights: Thoughts on the Principles of Human-Centered Design." *Design Issues* 17, no. 3 (Summer 2001): 35–9. https://www.jstor.org/stable/1511799.

Buchanan, Richard. "Wicked Problems in Design Thinking." *Design Issues* 8, no. 2 (Spring 1992): 5–21. https://doi.org/10.2307/1511637.

Buchannan, Richard, and Victor Margolis, eds. *Discovering Design*. Chicago: University of Chicago Press, 1995.

Budiman, Abby. *Key Findings about U.S. Immigrants*. Washington, DC: Pew Research Center, 2020. https://www.pewresearch.org/fact-tank/2020/08/20/key-findings-about-u-s-immigrants/.

Bunker, Barbara B., and Billie T. Alban. *Large Group Interventions: Engaging the Whole System for Rapid Change*. San Francisco: Jossey-Bass, 1997.

Bunker, Barbara B., and Billie T. Alban, eds. *Handbook of Large Group Methods: Creating Systemic Change in Organizations and Communities*. San Francisco: Jossey-Bass, 2006.

Burke, James. *Internet Archive*. "Connections, Seasons 1–3." Updated November 7, 2018. Video, 18:57. https://archive.org/details/ConnectionsByJamesBurke/.

Burke, James. *Internet Archive*, "Connections: The Trigger Effect." 1978. Video, 49:24. http://www.dominoprinciple.com/2015/02/15/connections-trigger-effect-james-burke/.

Burke, Warner. *Organization Change: Theory and Practice*. 5th ed. Thousand Oaks, CA: SAGE, 2018.

Bush, George W. "Address to Joint Session of Congress (transcript)." CNN.com/US. September 30, 2001. http://edition.cnn.com/2001/US/09/20/gen.bush.transcript/.

Business Oregon. "Entrepreneurial Ecosystems Literature and Frameworks." https://www.oregon4biz.com/assets/docs/EcoLitFrameworks.pdf.

Calabretta, Giuila, Gerda Gemser, and Ingo Karpen. *Strategic Design: Eight Essential Practices Every Strategic Designer Must Master*. Amsterdam: BIS Publishers, 2016.

Camarota, Steven A., and Karen Zeigler. "Foreign-Born Population Hits Record in January 2022." Center for Immigration Studies, February 23, 2022. https://cis.org/.

Camillus, John C. "Strategy as a Wicked Problem." *Harvard Business Review* (May 2008): 99–106. https://hbr.org/2008/05/strategy-as-a-wicked-problem.

Campaign for an Independent Britain. "7 Reasons Why We Should Leave the EU." http://campaignforanindependentbritain.org.uk/the-economy/.

Capano, Giliberto, and Maria Tullia. "From Policy Entrepreneurs to Policy Entrepreneurship: Actors and Actions in Public Policy Innovation." *Policy and Politics* (July 2020): 321–42. https://doi.org/10.1332/030557320X15906842137162.

Carlgren, Lisa. *Design Thinking as an Enabler of Innovation: Exploring the Concept and Its Relationship to Building Innovation Capabilities.* PhD diss.. Chalmers University of Technology, Gothenburg, Sweden, 2013.

Carlgren, Lisa, Marie Elmquist, and Ingo Rauth. "The Challenges of Using Design Thinking in Industry—Experiences from Five Large Firms." *Creativity and Innovation Management* 25, no. 3 (2016): 344–62. https://doi.org/10.1111/caim.12176.

Carlgren, Lisa, Maria Elmquist, and Ingo Rauth. "Design Thinking: Exploring Values and Effects from an Innovation Capability Perspective." *Design Journal* 17, no. 3 (2014): 403–24. https://doi.org/10.2752/175630614X13982745783000.

Carlgren, Lisa, Marie Elmquist, and Ingo Rauth. "Exploring the Use of Design Thinking in Large Organizations: Towards a Research Agenda." *Swedish Design Research Journal* 11, no. 1 (June 2016): 55–63. https://svid.ep.liu.se/article/view/523.

Carlgren, Lisa, Ingo Rauth, and Maria Elmquist. "Framing Design Thinking: The Concept in Idea and Enactment." *Creativity and Innovation Management* 25, no. 1 (March 2016): 38–57. https://doi.org/10.1111/caim.12153.

Carlopio, James. *Strategy by Design: A Process of Strategy Innovation.* New York: Palgrave Macmillan, 2010.

Carnegie Mellon Design. "Design's Terry Irwin Developing Transition Design Institute." *Design,* July 30, 2019. https://design.cmu.edu/content/design%E2%80%99s-terry-irwin-developing-transition-design-institute.

Carney, Sean. "Design Thinking Is Dead. Long Live Design Thinking." *Phillips,* accessed October 23, 2020, https://www.philips.com/a-w/about/news/archive/blogs/innovation-matters/design-thinking-is-dead-long-live-design-thinking.html.

Carr, Sean D., Amy Halliday, Andrew C. King, Jeanne M. Liedtka, and Thomas Lockwood. "The Influence of Design Thinking in Business: Some Preliminary Observations." *Design Management Review* 21, no. 3 (September 2010): 58–63. https://doi.org/10.1111/j.1948-7169.2010.00080.x.

Carvalho, Lucila, Andy Dong, and Karl Maton. "Legitimating Design: A Sociology of Knowledge Account of the Field." *Design Studies* 30, no. 5 (September 2009): 483–502. https://doi.org/10.1016/j.destud.2008.11.005.

Catapult Design. https://catapultdesign.org/.

Center for the Advancement of the Steady State Economy. "Steady State Economic Definition." https://steadystate.org/discover/definition/.

Center for Geographic Analysis, Harvard University. https://gis.harvard.edu/.

Chandler, Clay, Andrew Nusca, Debbie Yong, Michal Lev-Ram, Erika Fry, Beth Kowitt, and Leigh Gallagher. "Fortune's 2018 Business by Design List." *Fortune,* December 22, 2017. https://fortune.com/2017/12/22/business-design-apple-airbnb-tesla/.

Checkland, Peter, and Jim Scholes. *Soft Systems Methodology in Action*. Chichester, UK: John Wiley, 1999.

Chen, Steven, and Alladi Venkatesh. "An Investigation of How Design-Oriented Organizations Implement Design Thinking." *Journal of Marketing and Management* 29, no. 15–16 (November 2013): 1680–1700. https://doi.org/10.1080/0267257X.2013.800898.

Childline India 1098. https://www.childlineindia.org/a/about/childline-india.

Chrislip, David D., and Carl E. Larson. *Collaborative Leadership*. New York: Wiley, 1994.

Church, George, and Ed Regis. *Regenesis: How Synthetic Biology Will Reinvent Nature and Ourselves*. New York: Basic Books, 2012.

Churchman, C. West. "Wicked Problems." *Management Science* 14, no. 4 (December 1967): B141–B142. https://www.jstor.org/stable/2628678.

Citizens League. *Citizen League Report: Rebuilding Education to Make It Work*. Minneapolis: Citizens League, 1982. https://citizensleague.org/wp-content/uploads/2017/07/PolicyReportEducation-May-1982.pdf.

Cohen, Michael D., James G. March, and Johan P. Olsen. "A Garbage Can Model of Organizational Choice." *Administrative Science Quarterly* 17, no. 1 (March, 1972): 1–25. https://doi.org/10.2307/2392088.

Cohen-Shacham, E., C. Janzen, Stewart Maginnis, and Gretchen Walters, eds. *Nature-Based Solutions to Address Global Societal Challenges*. Gland, Switzerland: International Union for Conservation of Nature, 2016. https://doi.org/10.2305/IUCN.CH.2016.13.en.

Collier, David, Jody LaPorte, and Jason Seawright. "Putting Typologies to Work: Concept Formation, Measurement, and Analytics Rigor." *Political Research Quarterly* 65, no. 1 (2012): 217–32. https://doi.org/10.1177/1065912912437162.

Collins, Terry. "Twitter Suspends Another 235,000 Terrorism-Related Accounts." C/Net, August 18, 2016. https://www.cnet.com/news/twitter-suspends-another-235000-terrorism-related-accounts/.

Collopy, Fred. "'I Think with My Hands;' On Balancing the Analytical and Intuitive Designing." In *Managing as Designing*, edited by Richard Boland and Fred Collopy, 164–68. Stanford, CA: Stanford Business Books, 2004.

Comfort, Louise K., William L. Waugh, Jr., Beverly A. Cigler, and Christine G. Springer. "Emergency Management Research and Practice in Public Administration." *Public Administration Review* 72, no. 4 (July/August 2012): 539–49. https://www.jstor.org/stable/i40073944.

Commons Transition. "About the Commons Transition, Transition Plans, Projects, Network, Stories, Book, Wiki." https://commonstransition.org/about-commons-transition-2/.

Commons Transition Primer. "How Does the Commons Work?" accessed November 1, 2020, https://primer.commonstransition.org/4-more/how-does-the-commons-work.

Community Wealth. "The Cleveland Model—How the Evergreen Cooperatives Are Building Community Wealth." https://community-wealth.org/content/cleveland-model-how-evergreen-cooperatives-are-building-community-wealth.

Conklin, Jeff. "The Age of Design." CogNexus Institute, 2001. http://www.cognexus.org.

Conklin, Jeff. *Dialogue Mapping: Building Shared Understanding of Wicked Problems*. Chichester, UK: John Wiley, 2006.

Conklin, Jeff. "Issue Mapping FAQs." CogNexus Institute. http://www.cognexus.org/issue _mapping_faqs.htm.

Conklin, Jeff, Min Basadur, and G. K. VanPatter. "Rethinking Wicked Problems: Unpacking Paradigms Bridging Universes. Part 1 of 2." *NextD Journal*, Conversation 28, February 8, 2011. https:// issuu.com/nextd/docs/conv28.

Conklin, Jeff, Min Basadur, and G. K. VanPatter. "Unpacking Paradigms, Bridging Universes Part 2 of 2." *NextD Journal*, Conversation 30, February 8, 2011. https://issuu.com/nextd/docs/conv30.

Connaughton, Jeff. *The Payoff: Why Washington Always Wins*. Westport, CT: Prospecta Press, 2012.

Considine, Mark. "Thinking outside the Box? Applying Design Theory to Public Policy." *Politics & Policy* 40, no. 4 (2012): 704–24. https://doi.org/10.1111/j.1747-1346.2012.00372.x.

Cook, S. D. Noam. "Design and Responsibility: The Interdependence of Natural, Artifactual, and Human Systems." In *Philosophy and Design: From Engineering to Architecture*, edited by P. E. Vermaas, P. Kroes, A. Light, and S. Moore, 259–69. Berlin and Heidelberg, Germany: Springer, 2008.

Cooper, Rachel F., Sabine Junginger, and Thomas Lockwood. "Design Thinking and Design Management: A Research and Practice Perspective." *Design Management Review* 20, no. 2 (June 2009): 46–55. https://doi.org/10.1111/j.1948-7169.2009.00007.x.

Crime and Justice News. "Illinois Town of 26,000 Has Nation's Highest Murder Rate." *The Crime Report*. April 24, 2019. https://thecrimereport.org/2019/04/24/e-st-louis-il-has-the-nations -highest-murder-rate/.

Christensen, Clayton M. *The Innovator's Dilemma: When New Technologies Cause Great Firms to Fail*. Boston: Harvard Business School Press, 1997.

Christensen, Clayton M., Michael E. Raynor, and Rory McDonald. "What Is Disruptive Innovation?" *Harvard Business Review Magazine*, December 2015. https://hbr.org/2015/12/what-is -disruptive-innovation.

Christakis, Alexander N., and Kenneth C. Bausch. *How People Harness Their Collective Wisdom and Power to Construct Their Future in Co-laboratories of Democracy*. Greenwich, CT: Information Age Publishers, 2006.

Crosby, Barbara B., and John M. Bryson. *Leadership for the Common Good: Tackling Public Problems in a Shared-Power World*. 2nd ed. San Francisco: Jossey-Bass, 2005.

Crosby, Ned, Janet M. Kelly, and Paul Schaefer. "Citizen Panels: A New Approach to Citizen Participation." *Public Administration Review* 46, no. 2 (March/April 1986):170–8. https://doi.org/10 .2307/976169.

Cross, Nigel. "Design as Discipline." In *Designerly Ways of Knowing*, 95–103. London: Springer-Verlag, 2006. https://link.springer.com/book/10.1007/1-84628-301-9.

Cross, Nigel. "Designerly Ways of Knowing." *Design Studies* 3, no. 4 (October 1982): 221–7. https://doi.org/10.1016/0142-694X(82)90040-0.

Cross, Nigel. "Designerly Ways of Knowing: Design Discipline Versus Design Science." *Design Issues* 17, no. 3 (Summer 2001): 49–55. https://doi.org/10.1162/074793601750357196.

Cross, Nigel, ed. *Design Participation: Proceedings of the Design Research Society Conference, 1971*. London: Academy Editions, 1972.

Cross, Nigel. *Design Thinking: Understanding How Designers Think and Work*. Oxford, UK: Berg, 2011.

Cross, Nigel. "From a Design Science to a Design Discipline: Understanding Designerly Ways of Knowing and Thinking." In *Design Research Now*, edited by Ralf Michael, 41–54. Basel, Switzerland: Birkhäuser, 2007.

Cross, Nigel, Henri Christiaans, and Kees Dorst, eds. *Analysing Design Activity*. New York: Wiley, 1997.

Crowley, Kate, and Brian W. Head. "The Enduring Challenge of 'Wicked Problems.'" *Policy Science* 50 (2017): 539–47. https://doi.org/10.1007/s11077-017-9302-4.

Crutzen, Paul J. "The 'Anthropocene.'" *Journal de Physique* 12, no. 10 (November 2002): 1–5. https://doi.org/10.1051/jp4:20020447.

Cunningham, Dan. "Social Network Map." *CORE Lab*, Naval Postgraduate School. July 17, 2017.

Curedale, Robert. *Design Thinking Process & Methods*. 4th ed. Los Angeles: DCC, 2018.

Curry, Andrew, and Anthony Hodgson. "Seeing in Multiple Horizons: Connecting Futures to Strategy." *Journal of Future Studies* 13, no. 1 (August 2008): 1–20. https://jfsdigital.org/wp-content/uploads/2014/01/131-A01.pdf.

Daly, Alex. *The Crowdsourceress: Get Smart, Get Funded, and Kickstart Your Next Big Idea*. New York: Public Affairs, 2017.

Danish Design Center. "The Design Ladder: Four Steps of Design Use." May 6, 2015. https://danskdesigncenter.dk/en/design-ladder-four-steps-design-use.

Dankl, Kathrina. "The Paradox of Design Methods: Towards Alternative Functions." *Nordes: Nordic Design Research* no. 6 (2015): 1–9. https://archive.nordes.org/index.php/n13/article/view/403/381.

Davis, Susan. "Enabling Entrepreneurial Ecosystems." *Innovations* 7, no. 2 (2012): 1–10.

Daviter, Falk. "Coping, Taming, or Solving: Alternative Approaches to the Governance of Wicked Problems." *Policy Studies* 38, no. 6 (2017): 571–88. https://doi.org/10.1080/01442872.2017.1384543.

Dawes, Sharon S., Anthony M. Cresswell, and Teresa A. Pardo. "From 'Need to Know' to 'Need to Share': Tangled Problems, Information Boundaries, and the Building of Public Sector Knowledge Networks." *Public Administration Review* 69, no. 3 (May/June 2009): 392–402. https://doi.org/10.1111/j.1540-6210.2009.01987_2.x.

de Bono, Edward. *Lateral Thinking: Creativity Step by Step*. New York: Harper & Row, 1970.

"Debunking Years of Tabloid Claims about Europe." *The Economist*, June 22, 2016. https://www.economist.com/graphic-detail/2016/06/22/debunking-years-of-tabloid-claims-about-europe.

Dees, J. Gregory, Beth B. Anderson, and Jane Wei-Skillern. "Scaling Social Impact: Strategies for Spreading Innovation." *Stanford Innovation Review* 1, no. 4 (Spring 2004): 24–32. https://ssir.org/articles/entry/scaling_social_impact.

Deming, W. Edwards. *The New Economics for Industry, Government, Education*. Cambridge, MA: MIT Center for Advanced Engineering Study, 1993.

Democracy Collaborative. https://democracycollaborative.org/.

Dentoni, Domenico, Steve Waddell, and Sandra Waddock. "Pathways of Transformation in Global Food and Agricultural Systems: Implications from a Large Systems Change Theory

Perspective." *Current Opinion in Environmental Sustainability* 29 (December 2017): 8–13. https://doi.org/10.1016/j.cosust.2017.10.003.

De Paula, Danielly, Franziska Dobrigkeit, and Kathryn Cormican. "Doing It Right—Critical Success Factors for Design Thinking Implementation." In *International Conference on Engineering Design* 1, no. 1 (August 2019): 3851–60. https://doi.org/10.1017/dsi.2019.392.

Design Council. "Introducing Design for Europe." https://www.designcouncil.org.uk/news-opinion/introducing-design-europe.

Design Institute of Australia. "Code of Ethics." https://www.design.org.au/code-of-ethics.

Design Management Institute. "2015 DMI: Design Value Index Results and Commentary." 27, no. 4 (2015). https://cdn.ymaws.com/www.dmi.org/resource/resmgr/design_value_index/16274RAE04.pdf.

de Souza Briggs, Xavier. *Democracy as Problem Solving: Civic Capacity in Communities across the Globe*. Cambridge, MA: MIT Press, 2008.

DevelopmentSeed. *Connectivity Atlas*. "Communications." https://atlas.developmentseed.org/communications/.

DevelopmentSeed, the University of Wisconsin–Madison Cartography Lab, and Dr. Parag Khanna. *Connectivity Atlas*. Last updated August 28, 2020. https://atlas.developmentseed.org/data/.

Devon, Richard, and Ibo Van De Pol. "Design Ethics: The Social Ethics Paradigm." *International Journal of Engineering Education* 20, no. 3 (2004): 461–69. https://www.researchgate.net/profile/Richard_Devon2/publication/228827371_Design_ethics_The_social_ethics_paradigm/links/00463516e95aa10d7c000000/Design-ethics-The-social-ethics-paradigm.pdf.

de Vries, James. "PepsiCo's Chief Design Officer on Creating an Organization Where Design Can Thrive." *Harvard Business Review*, August 11, 2015. https://hbr.org/2015/08/pepsicos-chief-design-officer-on-creating-an-organization-where-design-can-thrive.

Diamandis, Peter H. "Abundance Is Our Future." February 2012. TED video, 15:59. https://www.ted.com/talks/peter_diamandis_abundance_is_our_future?language=en.

Diamandis, Peter H. "Abundance—The Future Is Better Than You Think." *Singularity Hub*. June 28, 2012. https://singularityhub.com/2012/06/28/abundance-the-future-is-better-than-you-think/.

Diamandis, Peter H., and Steven Kotler. *Abundance*. New York: Free Press, 2012.

Diamond, Jared. *Collapse: How Societies Choose to Fail or Succeed*. New York: Penguin, 2006.

Diderich, Claude. *Design Thinking for Strategy: Innovating Towards Competitive Advantage*. Richterswil, Switzerland: Springer, 2020.

Di Russo, Stefanie. "Understanding the Behavior of Design Thinking in Complex Environments." PhD diss.. Swinburne University of Technology, Melbourne, Australia, 2016. https://researchbank.swinburne.edu.au/file/a312fc81-17d3-44b5-9cc7-7ceb48c7f277/1/Stefanie%20Di%20Russo%20Thesis.pdf.

DiSalvo, Carl. *Adversarial Design*. Cambridge, MA: MIT Press, 2015.

Doig, Jameson W., and Erwin C. Hargrove, eds. *Leadership and Innovation: A Biographical Perspective on Entrepreneurs in Government*. Baltimore: Johns Hopkins University Press, 1990.

Dong, Andy, Massimo Garbuio, and Dan Lovallo. "Generative Sensing: A Design Perspective on the Microfoundations of Sensing Capabilities." *California Management Review* 58, no. 4 (August 2016): 97–117. https://doi.org/10.1525/cmr.2016.58.4.97.

Donini, Antonio. "An Elusive Quest: Integration in the Response to the Afghan Crisis." *Ethics & International Affairs* 18, no. 2 (2004): 21–27.

Doorley, Scott, and Scott Witthoft. *Makespace: How to Set the Stage for Creative Collaboration.* Hoboken, NJ: Wiley, 2012.

Dörner, Dietrich. *The Logic of Failure: Recognizing and Avoiding Error in Complex Situations.* Translated by Rita and Robert Kimber. New York: Metropolitan Books, 1996.

Dorst, Kees. "Design Problems and Design Paradoxes." *Design Issues* 22, no. 3 (Summer 2006): 4–17. https://doi.org/10.1162/desi.2006.22.3.4.

Dorst, Kees. "Frame Creation and Design in the Expanded Field." *She Ji: The Journal of Design, Economics, and Innovation* 1, no. 1 (Autumn 2015): 22–33. https://doi.org/10.1016/j.sheji.2015.07.003.

Dorst, Kees. *Frame Innovation: Create New Thinking by Design.* Cambridge, MA: MIT Press, 2015.

Dorst, Kees. "Layers of Design Practice." Paper presented at the International Association of Societies of Design Research, Seoul, South Korea, October 18–22, 2009. https://opus.lib.uts.edu.au/bitstream/10453/11246/1/2009003488.pdf.

Dorst, Kees, and Nigel Cross. "Creativity in the Design Process." *Design Studies* 22, no. 5 (2001): 425–37. https://doi.org/10.1016/S0142-694X(01)00009-6.

Dorst, Kees, and Judith Dijkhus. "Comparing Paradigms for Describing Design Activity." *Design Studies* 16, no. 2 (April 1995): 261–74. https://doi.org/10.1016/0142-694X(94)00012-3.

Dorst, Kees, and Lambèr Royakkers. "The Design Analogy: A Model for Moral Problem Solving." *Design Studies* 27, no. 6 (November 2006): 633–36. https://doi.org/10.1016/j.destud.2006.05.002.

Dosi, Clio, Francesca Rosati, and Matteo Vignoli. "Measuring Design Thinking Mindset." In *Proceedings of the DESIGN 2018 15th International Design Conference*, edited by D. Marjanović, M. Štorga, S. Škec, N. Bojčetić, and N. Pavković, 1991–2002. Glasgow: Design Society, 2018. https://doi.org/10.21278/idc.2018.0493.

Douglas, Mary M. "Four Cultures: The Evolution of a Parsimonious Model." *Geojournal* 47 (March 1999), 411–415. https://DOI:10.1023/A:1007008025151.

Downs, Antony. *Inside Bureaucracy.* Glenview, IL: Scott, Foresman, 1967.

Drug Policy Alliance. "A Brief History of the Drug War." http://www.drugpolicy.org/new-solutions-drug-policy/brief-history-drug-war.

Drug Policy Alliance. "Drug War Statistics." https://www.drugpolicy.org/issues/drug-war-statistics.

Druin, Allison, and Carina Fast. "The Child as Learner, Critic, Inventor, and Technology Design Partner." *International Journal of Technology and Design Education* 12 (2002): 189–213. https://doi.org/10.1023/A:1020255806645.

Dubberly, Hugh. *How Do You Design? A Compendium of Models.* San Francisco: Dubberly Design Office, 2005. Last edited March 18, 2005. http://www.dubberly.com/articles/how-do-you-design.html.

Duffield, Mark, Patricia Gossman, and Nicholas Leader. *Review of the Strategic Framework for Afghanistan.* Islamabad: Afghanistan Research and Evaluation Unit, 2001.

Duncan, Jessica, Michael Carolan, and Johannes S. C. Wiskerke, eds. *Routledge Handbook of Sustainable and Regenerative Food Systems*. New York: Routledge, 2021.

Dunnigan, James F. "Cracked, Leaking and Limping Along." *Strategy Page*. February 24, 2012. https://www.strategypage.com/dls/articles/Cracked,-Leaking-And-Limping-Along-2-24-2012.asp.

Durant, Will, and Ariel Durant. *The Lessons of History*. New York: Simon & Schuster, 1968.

Durden, Tyler. "China Furious after US Launches Trade War 'Nuke' With 522% Duty." *Zero Hedge*, May 19, 2016. http://www.zerohedge.com/news/2016-05-19/china-furious-after-us-launches -trade-war-nuke-522-duty.

Dust, Fred, and Illya Prokopoff. "Designing Systems at Scale." *Rotman Magazine* (Winter 2009): 53–56.

Dweck, Carol S. *Mindset: The New Psychology of Success*. New York: Ballantine, 2006.

Dworkin, Mark, and Melissa Young, dirs. *Shift Change*. Basque Country, Spain, Cleveland, San Francisco, Madison WI, and Boston: Bullfrog Films, 2012. http://shiftchange.org/about/.

Eames, Charles, and Ray Eames. "IBM Mathematics Peep Show: Legend of the Chessboard." 2011. YouTube video, 1:58. https://www.youtube.com/watch?v=t3d0Y-JpRRg.

Eames, Charles, and Ray Eames. "Power of Ten." 1977. YouTube video, 9:00. https://www.youtube .com/watch?v=0fKBhvDjuy0.

Earth Overshoot Day. "Past Earth Overshoot Days." https://www.overshootday.org/newsroom /past-earth-overshoot-days/.

Eberhard, David M., Gary F. Simons, and Charles D. Fenning, eds. *Ethnologue; Languages of the World*. 23rd ed. Dallas: SIL International, 2020. https://www.ethnologue.com/.

Eckart-Queenan, Jeri, Abe Grindle, Jacquelyn Hadley, and Roger Thompson. "Designing for Transformative Scale: Global Lessons in What Works." *Rotman Magazine* (Winter 2015). https:// www.rotman.utoronto.ca/Connect/Rotman-MAG/Issues/2015/Back-Issues---2015/Winter-2015 ---Wicked-Problems-III.

EDF. "Energywise." https://www.edfenergy.com/for-home/energywise/renewable-energy-sources.

Edmondson, Amy. *Teaming: How Organizations Learn, Innovate, and Compete in the Knowledge Economy*. San Francisco: Jossey-Bass Pfeiffer, 2012.

Eggers, William D., and Paul MacMillan. *The Solution Revolution: How Business, Government, and Social Enterprise Are Teaming up to Solve Society's Toughest Problems*. Boston: Harvard Business Review Press, 2013.

Ellen MacArthur Foundation. "Towards the Circular Economy, Vol. 1: An Economic and Business Rationale for an Accelerted Transition." 2013. https://www.ellenmacarthurfoundation.org/assets /downloads/publications/Ellen-MacArthur-Foundation-Towards-the-Circular-Economy-vol.1.pdf.

Ellyatt, Holly. "US Hits China and Others with More Steep Steel Duties." CNBC, updated May 26, 2016. http://www.cnbc.com/2016/05/26/us-hits-china-and-others-with-more-steep-steel-duties.html.

Elmansy, Rafiq. "Why Design Thinking Doesn't Work." *Designorate*. September 17, 2018. https:// www.designorate.com/why-design-thinking-doesnt-work/.

Elsbach, Kimberly D., and Ileana Stigliani. "Design Thinking and Organizational Culture: A Review and Framework for Future Research." *Journal of Management* 44, no. 6 (July 2018): 2274–306. https://doi.org/10.1177/0149206317744252.

Emerson, Kirk, and Tina Nabatchi. *Collaborative Governance Regimes*. Washington, DC: Georgetown University Press, 2015.

Emerson, Kirk, Tina Nabatchi, and Stephen Balogh. "An Integrative Framework for Collaborative Governance." *Journal of Public Administration Research and Theory* 22, no. 1 (January 2012): 1–29. https://doi.org/10.2307/41342607.

Emery, Merrelyn, and Ronald E. Purser. *The Search Conference*. San Francisco: Jossey-Bass, 1996.

Enriquez, Juan, and Steve Gullans. *Evolving Ourselves: Redesigning the Future of Humanity—One Gene at a Time*. New York: Current, 2015.

Erichsen, Pia G. *Design Integration: A Theoretical and Empirical Study of Design in Small and Medium-Sized Danish Companies*. Odense: University Press of Southern Denmark, 2014.

Ethical Markets Quality of Life Indicators (originally Calvert-Henderson Quality of Life Indicators). http://ethicalmarketsqualityoflife.com/overview/.

"Ethics for Designers." Accessed November 6, 2020, https://www.ethicsfordesigners.com/.

European Movement United Kingdom. "Reasons to Remain in the European Union." May 20, 2019. http://www.proeuropa.org.uk/twelevereasons.

Evergreen Cooperatives. "Innovations for an Emerging Green Economy." http://www.evgoh.com/.

Everton, Sean F. *Disrupting Dark Networks*. New York: Cambridge University Press, 2012.

Fabricant, Nicole. *Mobilizing Bolivia's Displaced: Indigenous Politics and the Struggle over Land*. Chapel Hill: University of North Carolina Press, 2012.

Fairless, Tom. "ECB Mario Draghi Urges Central Bank to Align Monetary Policy." *Wall Street Journal*, June 28, 2016. http://www.wsj.com/articles/ecbs-mario-draghi-urges-central-banks-to-coordinate-monetary-policy-1467104849.

Fearon, James. "Ethnic and Cultural Diversity by Country." *Journal of Economic Growth* 8, no. 2 (June 2003): 195–222. https://www.jstor.org/stable/40215943?origin=JSTOR-pdf&seq=1.

Ferlie, Ewan, Louise Fitzgerald, Gerry McGivern, Sue Dopson, and Chris Bennett. *Making Wicked Problems Governable? The Case of Managed Networks in Health Care*. Oxford: Oxford University Press, 2013.

Ferrari, Ed, and Alasdair Rae. *GIS for Planning and the Build Environment: An Introduction to Spatial Analysis*. London: Red Globe Press, 2019.

Fiasová, Michaela. "Beyond Controversy: Demystifying Design Thinking." UX Collective. April 20, 2018. https://uxdesign.cc/demystifying-design-thinking-818ecd450c5a.

Fields, Gary. "White House Czar Calls for End to 'War on Drugs'." *Wall Street Journal*, updated May 14, 2009. https://www.wsj.com/articles/SB124225891527617397.

FinancesOnline.com. "Income Inequality: Views & Solutions from Experts." http://financesonline.com/income-inequality-views-solutions-from-experts/.

Findeli, Alain. "The Methodological and Philosophical Foundations of Moholy-Nagy's Design Pedagogy in Chicago (1927–1946)." *Design Issues* 7, no. 1 (Autumn 1990): 4–19. https://doi.org/10.2307/1511466.

Financial Crisis Inquiry Commission. *The Financial Crisis Inquiry Report*. Washington, DC: US Government Printing Office, 2011. http://fcic-static.law.stanford.edu/cdn_media/fcic-reports/fcic_final_report_full.pdf.

Fischer, Andreas, Samuel Greiff, and Joachim Funke. "The Process of Solving Complex Problems." *Journal of Problem Solving* 4 (2012): 19–42. https://doi.org/10.7771/1932-6246.1118.

Fischer, Gerhard, and Elisa Giaccardi. "Meta Design: A Framework for the Future of End-User Development." In *End User Development*, edited by Henry Lieberman, Fabio Pataernó, Markus Klann, and Volker Wulf, 427–57. New York: Springer, 2006.

Fishkin, James S. "Consulting the Public through Deliberative Polling." *Journal of Policy Analysis and Management* 22, no. 1 (Winter 2003): 128–33. https://doi.org/10.2307/3325851.

Flanagan, Edward. "China's 'Zombie' Steelmakers Hit with Huge U.S. Tariffs." NBC News, May 18, 2016. http://www.nbcnews.com/business/business-news/china-s-zombie-steelmakers-hit-huge-u-s-tariffs-n576006.

Flick, Deborah. *From Debate to Dialogue: Using the Understanding Process to Transform Our Conversations*. Hong Kong: Orchid Publications, 1998.

Flight, Colette. "Smallpox: Eradicating the Scourge." BBC History. Last updated February 17, 2011. http://www.bbc.co.uk/history/british/empire_seapower/smallpox_01.shtml.

Flusser, Vilém. *The Shape of Things: A Philosophy of Design*. London: Reaktion, 1999.

Folkmann, Mads Nygaard. *The Aesthetics of Imagination in Design*. Cambridge, MA: MIT Press, 2013.

Food and Agriculture Organization of the United Nations (FAO). "The Water-Energy-Food Nexus: A New Approach in Support of Food Security and Sustainable Agriculture." Rome: FAO, 2014. https://www.fao.org/3/bl496e/bl496e.pdf.

Foodtank. "17 Organizations Promoting Regenerative Agriculture around the Globe," accessed November 2, 2020, https://foodtank.com/news/2018/05/organizations-feeding-healing-world-regenerative-agriculture-2/.

Forum for the Future. "Who Are We, What We Do, Global Challenges, Systems Change, Understanding the Future, News and Insights." https://www.forumforthefuture.org/.

Foster-Fishman, Pennie G., Katie Fitzgerald, Cherise Brandell, Branda Nowell, David Chavis, and Laurie A. Van Egeren. "Mobilizing Residents for Action: The Role of Small Wins and Strategic Supports." *American Journal of Community Psychology* 38 (2006): 143–52. https://doi.org/10.1007/s10464-006-9081-0.

Freedman, Lawrence. *Strategy: A History*. Oxford: Oxford University Press, 2013.

Freeman, R. Edward, Jeffrey S. Harrison, and Stelios Zyglidopoulos. *Stakeholder Theory*. Cambridge: Cambridge University Press, 2018.

Frensch, Peter A., and Joakim Funke. "Definitions, Traditions, and a General Framework for Understanding Complex Problem Solving." In *Complex Problem Solving: The European Perspective*, edited by Peter A. Frensch and Joachim Funke, 3–25. New York: Psychology Press, 2014.

Friedman, Ken, and Erik Stolterman. "Series Foreword." Editors of *Design Thinking, Design Theory Series*. In *Making Design Theory*, edited by John Redström. Cambridge, MA: MIT Press, 2017, ix-xiv.

frog. "Design and the (Ir)Rational Mind: The Rise of Affective Sensing." May 1, 2014. https://designmind.frogdesign.com/2014/05/design-irrational-mind-rise-affective-sensing-2/.

Fry, Tony. *Design Futuring: Sustainability Ethics and New Practice*. Oxford, UK: Berg Publishers, 2008.

Fry, Tony. *Design as Politics*. Oxford, UK: Berg Publishers, 2011.

Fullan, Michael. "Large-Scale Change Comes of Age." *Journal of Educational Change* 10 (2009): 101–13. https://doi.org/10.1007/s10833-009-9108-z.

Fuller, R. Buckminster, and Kiyoshi Kuromiya. *Critical Path*. New York: St. Martin's Press, 1981.

Fullerton, John. "Regenerative Capitalism: How Universal Principles and Patterns Will Shape the New Economy." April 2015. https://capitalinstitute.org/wp-content/uploads/2015/04/2015 -Regenerative-Capitalism-4-20-15-final.pdf.

Future of Design Education Initiative. https://www.futureofdesigneducation.org/.

Gaim, Medhanie, and Niles Wålin. "In Search of a Creative Space: A Conceptual Framework of Synthesizing Paradoxical Tensions." *Scandinavian Journal of Management* 32, no. 1 (March 2016): 33–44. https://doi.org/10.1016/j.scaman.2015.12.002.

Galbraith, Jay R. *Designing Organizations: Strategy, Structure, and Process at the Business Unit and Enterprise Levels*. 3rd ed. San Francisco: Jossey-Bass, 2014.

Gallup. "Confidence in Institutions." https://news.gallup.com/poll/1597/confidence-institutions .aspx.

Garud, Raghu, Philipp Tuertscher, and Andrew H. Van de Ven. "Perspectives on Innovation Processes." *Academy of Management Annuals* 7, no. 1 (2013): 773–817. https://journals.aom.org/doi /10.5465/19416520.2013.791066.

Gastil, John, and Peter Levine, eds. *The Deliberative Democracy Handbook: Strategies for Effective Civic Engagement in the 21st Century*. New York: John Wiley and Sons, 2005.

Gates, Bill H. "What Gives Me Hope about the World's Future." Interview by Nancy Gibbs. *Time Magazine*, January 4, 2018. https://time.com/5086907/bill-gates-nancy-gibbs-interview/.

Gaziulusoy, İdil, and Elif Erdğan Öztekin. "Design for Sustainability Transitions: Origins, Attitudes and Future Directions." *Sustainability* 11, no. 13, 3601 (June 2019): 1–16. https://doi .org/10.3390/su11133601.

Geels, Frank W., Benjamin K. Sovacool, Tim Schwanen, and Steve Sorrell. "The Socio-Technical Dynamics of Low-Carbon Transitions," *Joule* 1, no. 3 (November 2017): 463–79. https://www .sciencedirect.com/science/article/pii/S2542435117300922.

Gerber, Elizabeth. "Prototyping: Facing Uncertainty through Small Wins." In *Proceedings of ICED, Vol. 9, Human Behavior in Design*, edited by M. Norell Bergendahl, M. Grimheden, L. Leifer, P. Skogstad, and U. Lindemann, 333–42. Palo Alto, CA: ICED, 2009. https://www.designsociety.org /publication/28513/DS+58-9%3A+Proceedings+of+ICED+09%2C+the+17th+International+Confe rence+on+Engineering+Design%2C+Vol.+9%2C+Human+Behavior+in+Design%2C+Palo+Alto%2 C+CA%2C+USA%2C+24.-27.08.2009.

Gerber, Niklaus. "A Critical Review of Design Thinking." August 20, 2018. https://medium.com/@ niklausgerber/a-critical-review-of-design-thinking-44d8aed89e90.

Gersick, Connie. "Revolutionary Change Theories: A Multilevel Exploration of the Punctuated Equilibrium Paradigm." *Academy of Management Review* 16, no. 1 (January 1991): 10–36. https:// doi.org/10.2307/258605.

Gharajedaghi, Jamshid. *Systems Thinking: Managing Chaos and Complexity: A Platform for Designing Business Architecture*. 3rd ed. Amsterdam: Morgan Kaufmann, 2011.

Giacomin, Joseph. "What Is Human Centred Design?" *Design Journal* 17, no. 4 (2014): 606–23. https://doi.org/10.2752/175630614X14056185480186.

Gibbons, Leah V., Scott A. Cloutier, Paul J. Coseo, and Ahmed Barakat. "Regenerative Development as an Integrative Paradigm and Methodology for Landscape Sustainability." *Sustainability* 10, no. 6 (June 2018). https://doi.org/10.3390/su10061910.

Gibbons, Paul. *Impact: 21st-Century Change Management, Behavioral Science, Digital Transformation, and the Future of Work*. Oslo: Phronesis Media, 2019.

Gibbons, Paul. *The Science of Successful Organizational Change: How Leaders Set Strategy, Change Behavior, and Create an Agile Culture*. Oslo: Phronesis Media, 2019.

Gibley, Michelle. "Currency Wars: Is a Weaker Currency Good or Bad?" Charles Schwab. September 16, 2019. http://www.schwab.com/public/schwab/nn/articles/Currency-Wars-Is-a-Weaker -Currency-Good-or-Bad.

Girard, Corentin, Manuel Pulido-Velazquez, Jean-Daniel Rinaudo, Christian Pagé, and Yvan Caballero. "Integrating Top-down and Bottom-up Approaches to Design Global Change Adaption at the River Basin Scale." *Global Environmental Change* 34 (September 2015): 132–46, https:// doi.org/10.1016/j.gloenvcha.2015.07.002.

Gladwell, Malcolm. *Blink: The Power of Thinking without Thinking*. New York: Little Brown, 2005.

Gladwell, Malcolm. *The Tipping Point: How Little Things Can Make a Big Difference*. New York: Back Bay Books, 2000.

Glanville, Ranulph. "A (Cybernetic) Musing: Wicked Problems." *Cybernetics and Human Knowing* 19, nos. 1–2 (2012): 163–73. http://ranulphglanville.org.za/publications/.

Glanville, Ranulph. "Try Again. Fail Again. Fail Better: The Cybernetics in Design and the Design of Cybernetics." *Kybernetes* 36, no. 9 (October 2007): 1173–206. https://doi.org/10.1108 /03684920710827238.

Global Alliance for Banking on Values. "Advancing Positive Change in the Banking Sector." http://www.gabv.org/.

Global Ecovillage Network. "A Growing Network of Regenerative Communities and Initiatives that Bridge Cultures, Countries, and Continents for a Regenerative World." https://ecovillage .org/about/about-gen/.

Global Footprint Network. https://data.footprintnetwork.org/?_ga=2.198581423.1472058788 .1612805772-1111178020.1612805772#/.

Global Footprint Network. "Overshoot Days 1970–2020." 2019 ed. https://www.overshootday .org/newsroom/past-earth-overshoot-days/.

Global Transition to a New Economy—Map. http://wiki.p2pfoundation.net/Global_Transition _to_a_New_Economy_-_Map.

Gloor, Peter A. *Swarm Creativity: Competitive Advantage through Collaborative Innovation Networks*. Oxford: Oxford University Press, 2006.

Goerner, Sally. "Regenerative Development: The Art and Science of Creating Durably Vibrant Human Networks." https://capitalinstitute.org/wp-content/uploads/2014/08/000-Goerner-Regene rative-Development-Sept-15-2015.pdf.

Goldschmidt, Gabriela. "The Dialectics of Sketching." *Creativity Research Journal* 4, no. 2 (January 1991): 123–43. https://doi.org/10.1080/10400419109534381.

Goleman, Daniel. *Emotional Intelligence: Why It Can Matter More Than IQ.* New York: Bantam, 1995.

Gonsher, Ian. "On Creative Dialectics." *Articles* 13 (2015): 1–2. https://digitalcommons.risd.edu /critical_futures_symposium_articles/13.

Goodspeed, Robert. "Smart Cities: Moving beyond Urban Cybernetics to Tackle Wicked Problems." *Cambridge Journal of Regions, Economy, and Society* 8, no. 1 (March 2015): 79–92. https://doi .org/10.1093/cjres/rsu013.

Goodwin, Jeff, and James M. Jasper, eds. *Rethinking Social Movements.* Lanham, MD: Rowman and Littlefield, 2004.

Grameen Bank. *Bank for the Poor,* accessed November 1, 2020, http://www.grameen.com/.

Gray, Barbara. *Collaborating: Finding Common Ground for Multiparty Problems.* San Francisco: Jossey-Bass, 1989.

Gray, Barbara, and Jill Purdy. *Collaborating for Our Future: Multi-stakeholder Partnerships for Solving Complex Problems.* Oxford: Oxford University Press, 2018.

Great Transition Initiative: Toward a Transformative Vision and Practice. https://greattransition.org/.

Green, Jessica F., Thomas Sterner, and Gernot Wagner. "A Balance of Bottom-up and Top-down in Linking Climate Policies." *Nature Climate Change* 4 (November 2014): 1064–67. https://doi. org/10.1038/nclimate2429.

Grigsby, Wayne W., Scott Gorman, Jack Marr, Joseph McLamb, Michael Stewart, and Pete Schifferle. "Integrated Planning, the Operations Process, Design, and the Military Decision Making Process." *Military Review* (January/February 2011): 28–35. https://www.armyupress.army.mil/Portals/7 /military-review/Archives/English/MilitaryReview_20110228_art007.pdf.

Grisogono, Anne-Marie. "How Could Future AI Help Tackle Global Complex Problems?" *Frontiers in Robotics and AI,* April 21, 2020, https://www.frontiersin.org/articles/10.3389/frobt.2020.00050 /full.

Gross, Beatrice, and Ronald Gross, eds. *The Great School Debate: Which Way for American Education?* New York: Simon & Schuster, 1985.

GroupMap. "Stakeholder Analysis." https://www.groupmap.com/map-templates/stakeholder -analysis/.

Gruber, Marc, Nick De Leon, Gerard George, and Paul Thomson. "Managing by Design: From the Editors." *Academy of Management Journal* 58, no. 1 (February 2015): 1–7. https://doi.org/10.5465 /amj.2015.4001.

GSMA. *The Mobile Economy 2020.* https://www.gsma.com/mobileeconomy/#key_stats.

Guilford, Joy Paul. "The Structure of Intellect." *Psychological Bulletin* 53, no. 4 (1956): 267–93. https://doi.org/10.2307/1179339.

Gunderson, Lance H., and C. S. Holling, eds. *Panarchy: Understanding Transformations in Human and Natural Systems.* Washington, DC: Island Press, 2002.

Gunn, Andrew. "Policy Entrepreneurs and Policy Formulation." In *Handbook of Policy Formulation*, edited by Michael Howlett and Ishani Mukherjee, 265–82. Cheltenham, UK: Edward Elgar, 2017. https://doi.org/10.4337/9781784719326.00024.

Hackman, J. Richard. *Collaborative Intelligence*. San Francisco: Berrett-Koehler, 2011.

Halberstam, David. *The Best and the Brightest*. New York: Ballantine Books, 1969.

Hammond, Daniel R. "Policy Entrepreneurship in China's Response to Urban Poverty." *Policy Studies Journal* 41, no. 1 (2013): 119–46. https://doi.org/10.1111/psj.12005.

Hanington, Bruce. "Empathy, Values, and Situated Action Sustaining People and Planet through Human-Centered Design." In *Routledge Handbook of Sustainable Design*, edited by Rachel Beth Egendoefer, 193–205. London: Routledge, 2018.

Hannigan, Ben, and Michael Coffey. "Where the Wicked Problems Are: The Case of Mental Health." *Health Policy* 101, no. 3 (2011): 220–27. https://doi.org/10.1016/j.healthpol.2010.11.002.

Hanushek, Eric A. "Throwing Money at Schools." *Journal of Policy Analysis and Management* 1, no. 1 (1981): 19–40.

"Happiness Website." www.authentichappiness.org.

Hardt, Michael. "Design & Ethics: Good, Bad, Innocent or Ignorant?" International Council of Design 18 (November 2009). https://www.theicod.org/resources/news-archive/design-ethics-good-bad-innocent-or-ignorant.

Hargrave, Timothy J., and Andrew H. Van de Ven. "Integrating Dialectical and Paradox Perspectives on Managing Contradictions in Organizations." *Organization Studies* 38, no. 3–4 (April 2017): 319–39. https://doi.org/10.1177/0170840616640843.

Harmon, Willis, and Howard Rheingold. *Higher Creativity: Liberating the Unconscious for Breakthrough Insights*. Los Angeles: Tarcher, 1984.

Harris, Richard. "Predicting the Crash: Tracking Tipping Points." NPR. September 16, 2009. http://www.npr.org/templates/story/story.php?storyId=112886911.

Hartman, Raymond, and Daniël Nijenhuis. "Village Hub: A Sweet Sustainable Solution; a Promising Project by Willie Smits and the Masarang Foundation." https://www.offgridquest.com/green/a-sweet-sustainable-solution.

Harvard University. *Exploring the World of Connectography*. http://worldmap.harvard.edu/maps/connectography.

Hassi, Lotta, and Miko Laakso. "Making Sense of Design Thinking." In *IDBM Papers Vol. 1*, edited by T.-M. Karjalainen, M. Koria, and M. Salimäki, 50–63. Helsinki: IDBM Program, Aalto University, 2011. https://www.researchgate.net/publication/274066130_Making_sense_of_design_thinking

Hasso Plattner Institute of Design at Stanford. *A D.School Design Project Guide*. 2016. https://static1.squarespace.com/static/57c6b79629687fde090a0fdd/t/589ba9321b10e3beb925e044/1486596453538/DESIGN-PROJECT-GUIDE-SEPT-2016-V3.pdf.

Hasso Plattner Institute of Design at Stanford. "This Is Design Thinking." https://thisisdesignthinking.net/why-this-site/who-we-are/.

Hatch, Mark. *The Maker Movement Manifesto*. New York: McGraw-Hill Education, 2014.

Hauss, Charles. *Security 2.0: Dealing with Global Wicked Problems*. New York: Rowman & Little-field, 2015.

Hawken, Paul. *Blessed Unrest: How the Largest Movement in the World Is Restoring Grace, Justice, and Beauty to the World, Came into Being and Why No One Saw It Coming*. New York: Viking Penguin, 2007.

Hawken, Paul. *Drawdown*. London: Penguin Books, 2017.

Hawken, Paul, Amory Lovins, and L. Hunter Lovins. *Natural Capitalism: Creating the Next Industrial Revolution*. New York: Little, Brown, 1999.

Hayes, Chris. *Twilight of the Elites: America after Meritocracy*. New York: Crown Publishers, 2012.

Hayes, Samuel L., and Ken Nguyen. *CA 2025: The Strategic Design of Civil Affairs*. Calhoun Institutional Archive of the Naval Postgraduate School, Monterey, CA. http://hdl.handle.net/10945/45870.

Hayes, Thomas C. "Confrontation in the Gulf; The Oilfields Lying below the Iraq-Kuwait Dispute." *New York Times*, September 3, 1990. http://www.nytimes.com/1990/09/03/world/confrontation-in-the-gulf-the-oilfield-lying-below-the-iraq-kuwait-dispute.html?pagewanted=all.

Head, Brian W. "Forty Years of Wicked Problems Literature: Forging Closer Links to Policy Studies." *Policy and Society* 38, no. 2 (April 2019): 180–97. https://doi.org/10.1080/14494035.2018.1488797.

Head, Brian W. "Wicked Problems in Public Policy." *Public Policy* 3, no. 2 (2008): 101–18.

Head, Brian W., and John Alford. "Wicked Problems: Implications for Public Policy and Management." *Administration & Society* 47, no. 6 (August 2015): 711–39. https://doi.org/10.1177/0095399713481601.

Head, Brian W., Helen Ross, and Jennifer Bellamy. "Managing Wicked Natural Resource Problems: The Collaborative Challenge at Regional Scales in Australia." *Landscape and Urban Planning* 154 (October 2016): 68–92. https://doi.org/10.1016/j.landurbplan.2016.03.019.

Heath, Chip, and Dan Heath. *Switch: How to Change Things When Change Is Hard*. New York: Broadway Books, 2010.

Heifetz, Ronald A. *Leadership without Easy Answers*. Cambridge, MA: Harvard University Press, 1994.

Held, David, Jonathan Perraton, and Anthony G. McGrew. *Global Transformations: Politics, Economics and Culture*. Stanford, CA: Stanford University Press, 1999.

Helms, Robin M. "Going International." *Higher Education Today* (blog). January 23, 2015. https://www.higheredtoday.org/2015/01/23/going-international/.

Hemenway, Toby. *The Permaculture City: Regenerative Design for Urban, Suburban, and Town Resilience*. White River Junction, VT: Chelsea Green Publishing, 2015.

Hernández, Ricardo J., Rachel Cooper, Bruce Tether, and Emma Murphy. "Design, the Language of Innovation: A Review of the Design Studies Literature." *She Ji: The Journal of Design, Economics, and Innovation* 4, no. 3 (Autumn 2018): 249–74. https://doi.org/10.1016/j.sheji.2018.06.001.

Heskett, John. *Design: A Very Short Introduction*. Oxford: Oxford University Press, 2005.

Heskett, John. *Toothpicks and Logos: Design in Everyday Life*. New York: Oxford University Press, 2002.

Heyne, Paul L., Peter J. Boettke, and David L. Prychitko. *The Economic Way of Thinking*. 13th ed. New York: Pearson, 2013.

"Highest Tariffs in U.S. History: American Businesses Pay Record $6.8 Billion in July." *Tariffs Hurt the Heartland*. September 11, 2019. https://tariffshurt.com/news/highest-tariffs-in-u-s-history-ameri can-businesses-pay-record-6-8-billion-in-july.

Hillman, James. *The Soul's Code: In Search of Character and Calling*. New York: Random House, 1996.

Hisschemöller, Maatthijs, and Robert Hoppe. "Coping with Intractable Controversies: The Case for Problem Structuring in Policy Design and Analysis." *Knowledge and Policy: The International Journal of Knowledge Transfer and Utilization* 8, no. 4 (Winter 1995–1996): 40–60.

Hitti, Natashah. "Virgin Unveils First Prototype of Hyperloop One Passenger Pod." *De Zeen*, February 26, 2018. https://www.dezeen.com/2018/02/26/virgin-unveils-first-prototype-hyperloop-one -passenger-pod/.

HMC Architects. "Regenerative Architecture Principles: A Departure from Modern Sustainable Design." https://hmcarchitects.com/news/regenerative-architecture-principles-a-departure-from -modern-sustainable-design-2019-04-12/.

Hobbes, Thomas. "Of Man, Being the First Part of Leviathan." *Harvard Classics, Vol. 34, Part 5*. New York: P. F. Collier & Son, 1909–1914. www.bartleby.com/34/5/.

Hodgson, Anthony. *Systems Thinking for a Turbulent World: A Search for New Perspectives*. London: Routledge, Taylor and Francis Group, 2020.

Holman, Peggy, Tom Devane, Steven Cady, and Associates. *The Change Handbook*. San Francisco: Berrett Koehler, 2007.

Holland, John H. "Studying Complex Adaptive Systems." *Journal of Systems Science and Complexity* 19, no. 1 (2006): 1–8. https://doi.org/10.1007/s11424-006-0001-z.

Holland, Ray, and Busayawan Lam. *Managing Strategic Design*. New York: Palgrave, 2014.

Homer-Dixon, Thomas. *The Upside of Down*. Washington, DC: Island Press, 2006.

Hopkins, Rob. *The Transition Movement in Global Perspective: Thomas Henfrey & Justin Kenrick*. February 2, 2016. https://transitionnetwork.org/news-and-blog/the-transition-movement-in-global -perspective-thomas-henfrey-justin-kenrick/.

Hopkins, Rob, Michael Thomas, and the Transition Network Team. *The Essential Guide to Doing Transition: Getting Transition Started in Your Street, Community, Town or Organization*. https:// transitionnetwork.org/wp-content/uploads/2018/08/The-Essential-Guide-to-Doing-Transition -English-V1.2.pdf?pdf=essential-guide-to-transition-v-1.

Hoppe, Robert. "Policy Analysis, Science and Politics: From 'Speaking Truth to Power' to 'Making Sense Together.'" *Science and Public Policy* 26, no. 3 (1999): 201–10. https://doi.org/10.3152 /147154399781782482.

Horn, Robert E. "Social Messes." Nautilus Institute. https://nautilus.org/gps/solving/social-messes -robert-e-horn/.

Horn, Robert E., and Robert P. Weber. 2007. "New Tools for Resolving Wicked Problems: Mess Mapping and Resolution Mapping Processes." http://www.strategykinetics.com/New_Tools_For _Resolving_Wicked_Problems.pdf.

Hornsby, Aidan. "How Design Teams Can Avoid Bad Project Management." *Accent* (blog). October 2, 2017. https://www.getflow.com/blog/project-management-for-designers.

Hove, Hilary, Jo-Ellen Parry, and Nelson Lujara. "Maintenance of Hydropower Potential in Rwanda through Ecosystem Restoration." *World Resources Report*. Washington, DC, 2010–2011. https://www.iisd.org/system/files/publications/maintenance_hydro_rwanda.pdf?q=sites/default /files/publications/maintenance_hydro_rwanda.pdf.

Howlett, Michael. "From the 'Old' to the 'New' Policy Design: Design Thinking beyond Markets and Collaborative Governance." *Policy Sciences* 47, no. 3 (September 2014): 187–207. https://doi .org/10.1007/s11077-014-9199-0.

HR Team. "Career Advice in a VUCA World." *Career Angels* (blog). August 21, 2017. https://blog .careerangels.eu/career-advice-in-a-vuca-world/, use permission granted on January 6, 2021.

Huesemann, Michael, and Joyce Huesemann. *Techno-Fix: Why Technology Won't Save Us or the Environment*. Gabriola Island, British Columbia, Canada: New Society Publishers, 2011.

Huitema, Dave, Luis Lebel, and Sander Meijerink. "The Strategies of Policy Entrepreneurs in Water Transitions around the World." *Water Policy* 13, no. 5 (October 2011): 717–33. https://doi .org/10.2166/wp.2011.107.

Human Sciences and Technologies Advanced Research Institute. Stanford University, Stanford, CA. https://hstar.stanford.edu/.

Humans of Data. https://humansofdata.atlan.com/2016/11/visualizing-time-series-data/.

Hunt, Jamer. "Letter from the Editor: Transdisciplinary Design." *Journal of Design Strategies* 5, no. 1 (April 2012): 5–10. https://issuu.com/journalofdesignstrategies/docs/the_journal_of_design _strategies_vo_bec4beb3c64ed5.

Huxham, Chris, and Siv Vangen. *Managing to Collaborate*. New York: Routledge, 2005.

IDEO. *The Little Book of Design Research Ethics*. https://lbodre.ideo.com/.

IDEO (blog). "IDEO's Human-Centered Design Process: How to Make Things People Love." December 4, 2018. https://www.usertesting.com/blog/how-ideo-uses-customer-insights-to-design -innovative-products-users-love.

IDEO.org. https://www.ideo.org/.

IDEO.org. *The Field Guide to Human-Centered Design*. https://www.designkit.org/resources/1.

IDEO. *Design Kit: Methods. "How Do I Assess If My Solution is Working?"* https://www.designkit.org /methods, accessed March 1, 2023.

Ignatius, Adi. "How Indra Nooyi Turned Design Thinking into Strategy: An Interview with PepsiCo's CEO." *Harvard Business Review*, September 2015. https://hbr.org/2015/09/how-indra-nooyi-turned -design-thinking-into-strategy.

Imperial, Mark T. "Using Collaboration as a Governance Strategy: Lessons from Six Watershed Management Programs." *Administration & Society* 37, no. 3 (July 2005): 281–320. https://doi.org /10.1177/0095399705276111.

Innes, Judith E. "Consensus Building: Clarifications for the Critics." *Planning Theory* 3, no. 1 (July 2004): 5–20. https://doi.org/10.1177/1473095204042315.

Innes. Judith E., and David E. Booher. "Collaborative Rationality as a Strategy for Working with Wicked Problems." *Landscape and Urban Planning* 154 (October 2016): 8–10. https://doi.org/10.1016/j.landurbplan.2016.03.016.

Innes, Judith E., and David E. Booher. "Collaborative Policymaking: Governance through Dialogue." In *Deliberative Policy Analysis: Understanding Governance in the Network Society*, edited by Maarten Hajer and Hendrik Wagenaar, 33–59. Cambridge: Cambridge University Press, 2003. https://doi.org/10.1017/CBO9780511490934.003.

Innes, Judith E., and David E. Booher. *Planning with Complexity: An Introduction to Collaborative Rationality for Public Policy*. Abingdon-on-Thames, UK: Routledge, 2010.

Innes, Judith E., and David E. Booher. "A Turning Point for Planning Theory? Overcoming Dividing Discourses." *Planning Theory* 14, no. 2 (2015): 195–213. https://doi.org/10.1177/1473095213519356.

Institute for Policy Studies. "New Economy Working Group (New Group)." https://ips-dc.org/ips-authors/new-economy-working-group-newgroup/.

Inter-Agency Mission to Islamabad and Afghanistan. "Draft Strategic Framework for International Assistance in Afghanistan," September–October 1997.

Intergovernmental Panel on Climate Change (IPCC) et al., eds. *Global Warming of 1.5°C: An IPCC Special Report on the Impacts of Global Warming of 1.5°C above Pre-Industrial Levels and Related Global Greenhouse Gas Emission Pathways, in the Context of Strengthening the Global Response to the Threat of Climate Change, Sustainable Development, and Efforts to Eradicate Poverty*. Geneva, Switzerland: World Meteorological Organization, 2018. https://archive.ipcc.ch/pdf/special-reports/sr15/sr15_citation.pdf.

International Civil Aviation Organization (ICAO). "Economic Impacts of COVID-19 on Civil Aviation." Updated as of December 2022. https://www.icao.int/sustainability/Pages/Economic-Impacts-of-COVID-19.aspx.

International Council of Design. "Code of Conduct." http://www.ico-d.org/database/files/library/icoD_BP_CodeofConduct.pdf.

International Geosphere-Biosphere Programme. "Global Change." http://www.igbp.net/globalchange/greatacceleration.4.1b8ae20512db692f2a680001630.html.

International Trade Center. "Trade Map–International Trade Statistics." Geneva, Switzerland: UNCTAD/WTO ITC, 2020. https://www.trademap.org/tradestat/Country_SelProduct_TS.aspx?nvpm=1%7c%7c%7c%7c%7cTOTAL%7c%7c%7c2%7c1%7c1%7c2%7c2%7c1%7c2%7c1%7c%7c1.

Internet World Stats. "Internet Growth Statistics." https://www.internetworldstats.com/emarketing.htm.

Irwin, Terry. "Redesigning a Design Program: How Carnegie Mellon University Is Developing a Design Curricula for the 21st Century." *Solutions* 6, no. 1 (January/February 2015): 91–100. https://www.thesolutionsjournal.com/article/redesigning-a-design-program-how-carnegie-mellon-university-is-developing-a-design-curricula-for-the-21st-century.

Irwin, Terry. "Transition Design: A Proposal for a New Area of Design Practice, Study, and Research," *Design and Culture* 7, no. 2 (2015): 229–46. https://doi.org/10.1080/17547075.2015.1051829.

Irwin, Terry, Cameron Tonkinwise, and Gideon Kossoff. "Transition Design: An Educational Framework for Advancing the Study and Design of Sustainable Transitions." Paper presented to the Sustainability Transition Research Network Conference, Sussex University, Brighton, UK, 2015. https://www.academia.edu/15283122/Transition_Design_An_Educational_Framework_for _Advancing_the_Study_and_Design_of_Sustainable_Transitions_presented_at_the_STRN_conference _2015_Sussex.

Isaacs, William W. *Dialogue and the Art of Thinking Together: A Pioneering Approach to Communication*. New York: Currency, 1999.

Isaacson, Walter. "Madeline's War." *Time*, May 17, 1999. http://content.time.com/time/world /article/0,8599,2054293,00.html.

Iskander, Natasha. "Design Thinking Is Fundamentally Conservative and Preserves the Status Quo." *Harvard Business Review* 5, September 5, 2018. https://hbr.org/2018/09/design-thinking-is-funda mentally-conservative-and-preserves-the-status-quo.

Ison, Ray, and Ed Straw. *The Hidden Power of Systems Thinking in a Climate Emergency*. New York: Routledge, 2020.

Jahnke, Marcy. *Meaning in the Making: Introducing a Hermeneutic Perspective on the Contribution of Design Practice to Innovation*. PhD diss., University of Gothenburg, Sweden, 2013. http://hdl .handle.net/2077/33428.

James, Paul, and Manfred B. Steger. "A Genealogy of 'Globalization': The Career of a Concept." *Globalizations* 11, no. 4 (September 2014): 417–34. https://doi.org/10.1080/14747731.2014 .951186.

Janis, Irving L. *Groupthink*. 2nd ed. Boston: Wadsworth, 1982.

"Janus." Wikimedia Commons 4.0 International. St. Petersburg, Russia, "Summer Garden Bust of Two-Faced Janus." Photographed by Igor Gordeev. September 24, 2021.

Jasper, James M. *The Art of Moral Protest*. Chicago: University of Chicago Press, 1997.

Jasper, James M. *The Emotions of Protest*. Chicago: University of Chicago Press, 2018.

Jen, Natasha. "Design Thinking Is B.S." *Fast Company*, April 9, 2018. https://www.fastcompany. com/90166804/design-thinking-is-b-s.

Jen, Natasha. "Design Thinking Is Bullsh*t." 99U Conference. June 7–9, 2017. Vimeo video, 13:26. https://vimeo.com/228126880.

Joffres, Kai. "Design Thinking Isn't the Problem—Here's What It Takes to Do Good Design." UX Collective. December 29, 2019. https://uxdesign.cc/design-thinking-isnt-the-problem-but-here-s -what-it-takes-to-do-good-design-eb4cf4278c63.

Johansson-Sköldberg, Ulla, Jill Woodilla, and Mehves Çetinkaya. "Design Thinking: Past, Present and Possible Futures." *Creativity and Innovation Management* 22, no. 2 (2013): 121–46. https://doi .org/10.1111/caim.12023.

Jones, Peter H. "Design Research Methods in Systemic Design." Paper presented at the *Design Research Methods for Systemic Design: Perspectives from Design Education and Practice*, 58th Annual Meeting of the International Society for the Systems Sciences, Washington, DC, July 27— August 1, 2014). https://www.researchgate.net/publication/289551227_Design_research_meth ods_for_systemic_design_Perspectives_from_design_education_and_practice.

Jones, Peter H. "Systemic Design Principles for Complex Social Systems." In *Social Systems and Design*, edited by Gary S. Metcalf, 91–128. Tokyo: Springer Japan, 2014.

Jones, Peter H. "The Systemic Turn: Leverage for World Changing." *She Ji: The Journal of Design, Economics, and Innovation* 3, no. 3 (2017): 157–63. https://doi.org/10.1016/j.sheji.2017.11.001.

Jones, Peter H., and Kyoichi Kijima, eds. *Systemic Design: Theory, Methods, and Practice* Tokyo: Springer Japan, 2018.

Jones, Peter H., and Kristel Van Ael. *Design Journeys through Complex Systems*. Amsterdam: BIS, 2022.

Jong, H. Nicholas. "Indonesia Fires Emitted Double the Carbon of Amazon Fires, Research Shows." *Mongabay Series*, November, 25, 2019. https://news.mongabay.com/2019/11/indonesia-fi res-amazon-carbon-emissions-peatland/.

Josephs, Leslie. "A Flood of Job Losses Looms as Airline Industry Struggles in Pandemic." CNBC, August 16, 2020. https://www.cnbc.com/2020/08/16/a-flood-of-job-losses-looms-as-airlines-industry -struggle-in-coronavirus-pandemic.html.

Junginger, Sabine. "Design and Innovation in the Public Sector: Matters of Design in Policy-Making and Policy Implementation." *Annual Review of Policy Design* 1, no. 1 (2013): 1–11.

Junginger, Sabine. "Design in the Organization: Parts and Wholes." *Design Research Journal* 2, no. 9 (January 2009): 23–9. https://www.academia.edu/213937/Design_in_the _Organization_Parts_and_Wholes.

Just Transition Alliance. "What Is a Just Transition?" http://jtalliance.org/what-is-just -transition/.

Kahneman, Daniel. *Thinking Fast and Slow*. New York: Farrar, Straus and Giroux, 2011.

Kalafatis, Scott E., and Maria C. Lemos. "The Emergence of Climate Change Policy Entrepreneurs in Urban Settings." *Regional Environmental Change* 17 (April 2017): 1791–9. https://doi .org/10.1007/s10113-017-1154-0.

Kaluza, Pablo, Andrea Kölzsch, Michael T. Gastner, and Bernd Blasius. "The Complex Network of Global Cargo Ship Movements." *Journal of the Royal Society Interface*, no. 7 (January 2010): 1093–103. https://royalsocietypublishing.org/doi/pdf/10.1098/rsif.2009.0495.

Kanter, Rossabeth M. *Men and Women of the Corporation*. New York: Basic Books, 1977.

Karnow, Stanley. "A Verdict on Vietnam." *Washington Post*, October 28, 1984. https://www .washingtonpost.com/archive/entertainment/books/1984/10/28/a-verdict-on-vietnam/ca05dbd0 -1838-4998-8be0-42c14b5ad1e5/.

Katz, Eric. *Death by Design: Science, Technology, and Engineering in Nazi Germany*. London: Pearson Longman, 2006.

Kaufman, James C., and Robert J. Sternberg, eds. *Cambridge Handbook of Creativity*. Cambridge: Cambridge University Press, 2010.

Kearney, Claudine, Robert D. Hisrich, and Frank Roche. "Public and Private Sector Entrepreneurship: Similarities, Differences, or a Combination." *Journal of Small Business and Enterprise Development*, 16, no. 1 (February 2009): 26–46. https://doi.org/10.1108/14626000910932863.

Keller, Evelyn Fox. *A Feeling for the Organism*. New York: W. H. Freeman, 1984.

Kelley, Tom, and David Kelley. *Creative Confidence: Unleashing the Creative Potential within Us All.* New York: Crown Business, 2013.

Kennedy, Carrie H., and Eric A. Zillmer. *Military Psychology: Clinical and Operational Applications.* 2nd ed. New York: Guilford Press, 2012.

Kennedy, John F. "Address at Rice University on the Nation's Space Effort." John F. Kennedy Archives, September 12, 1962. https://www.jfklibrary.org/archives/other-resources/john-f -kennedy-speeches/rice-university-19620912.

Kennedy, John F. "Special Message to Congress on Urgent National Needs." John F. Kennedy Archives, May 25, 1961. https://www.jfklibrary.org/asset-viewer/archives/JFKWHA/1961/JFKWHA -032/JFKWHA-032.

Kerner, Sean M. "Global Internet Traffic on Track to Hit 4.8 Zettabyes by 2022." *Enterprise Networking Planet.* December 7, 2018. http://www.enterprisenetworkingplanet.com/netsp/global -internet-traffic-on-track-to-hit-4.8-zettabytes-by-2022.html.

Ketterman, Shane. "Exploring the Reasons for Design Thinking Criticism." *Mobile Design,* accessed October 23, 2020, https://www.toptal.com/designers/product-design/design-thinking-criticism.

Kettl, Donald K. "Managing the Boundaries in American Administration: The Collaboration Imperative." *Public Administration Review* (December 2006):10–19. https://doi.org/10.1111/j.1540 -6210.2006.00662.x.

Khanna, Parag. *Connectography: Mapping the Future of Global Civilization.* New York: Random House, 2016.

Kilcullen, David J. *The Accidental Guerrilla: Fighting Small Wars in the Midst of the Big One.* Oxford: Oxford University Press, 2009.

Kim, Daniel H. "Using 'Tragedy of the Commons' to Link Local Action to Global Outcomes." *Systems Thinker.* https://thesystemsthinker.com/using-tragedy-of-the-commons-to-link-local-action -to-global-outcomes/.

Kim, Daniel H., and Virginia Anderson. *Systems Archetype Basics: From Story to Structure.* Waltham, MA: Pegasus Communications, 1998.

Kim, Marina. "Rethinking the Impact Spectrum." Ashoka U, April 30, 2015. https://ashokau.org /blog/rethinking-the-impact-spectrum/.

Kimbell, Lucy. "Rethinking Design Thinking: Part I." *Design and Culture* 3, no. 3 (2011): 285–306. https://doi.org/10.2752/175470811X13071166525216.

Kingdon, John W. *Agendas, Alternatives, and Public Policies.* 2nd ed. New York: Pearson, 2010.

Kirshenbaum, Sheril. "'Climate Change' or 'Global Warming'? Two New Polls Suggest That Language Matters." *Scientific American,* December 15, 2014. https://blogs.scientificamerican.com /plugged-in/climate-change-or-global-warming-two-new-polls-suggest-language-matters/.

Klein, Gary. *Sources of Power: How People Make Decisions.* Cambridge, MA: MIT Press, 1998.

Klijn, Erik Hans, and Joop Koppenjan. *Governance Networks in the Public Sector.* New York: Routledge, 2016.

Knight, Eric R.W., Jarryd Daymond, and Sotirios E. Paroutis. "Design-Led Strategy: How to Bring Design Thinking into the Art of Strategic Management." *California Management Review* 62, no. 2 (January 2020): 30–52. https://doi.org/10.1177/0008125619897594.

Knight, Eric, Sotirios E. Paroutis, and Loizos Heracleous. "The Power of PowerPoint: A Visual Perspective on Meaning Making in Strategy." *Strategic Management Journal* 39, no. 3 (March 2018): 894–921. https://doi.org/10.1002/smj.2727.

Koberlein, Brian. "Gravity." *Cradle to Grave* (blog). February, 26 2015. https://briankoberlein .com/blog/cradle-to-grave/#:~:text=In%20Einstein's%20model%2C%20gravity%20isn,tells%20 mass%20how%20to%20move.&text=Space%20really%20is%20curved%2C%20and,that%20 looks%20like%20a%20force.

Koestler, Arthur. *The Ghost in the Machine.* London: Hutchinson & Co., 1967.

Koh, J. H. L., C. S. Chai, B. Wong, and H.-Y. Hong. "Developing and Evaluating Design Thinking." In *Design Thinking for Education: Conceptions and Applications in Teaching and Learning,* 109–20. Singapore: Springer, 2015.

Kolb, David A. *Experiential Learning: Experience as the Source of Learning and Development.* Englewood Cliffs, NJ: Prentice-Hall, 1984.

Kolko, Jon. "Abductive Thinking and Sensemaking: The Drivers of Design Synthesis." *Design Issues* 26, no. 1 (Winter 2010): 15–28. https://doi.org/10.1162/desi.2010.26.1.15.

Kolko, Jon (interviewee). "Design Should Be a Liberal Art." *Unexpected Sources of Inspiration* (blog). May 11, 2016. https://blog.usievents.com/en/interview-jon-kolko-design-thinking/.

Kolko, Jon. "The Divisiveness of Design Thinking." *IX Interactions,* May–June 2018. https:// interactions.acm.org/archive/view/may-june-2018/the-divisiveness-of-design-thinking.

Kolko, Jon. *Well-Designed: How to Use Empathy to Create Products People Love.* Brighton, MA: Harvard Business Review Press, 2014.

Kopecka, Jarmila A., Sicco C. Santema, and Jan A. Buijs. "Designerly Ways of Muddling Through." *Journal of Business Research* 65, no. 6 (June 2012): 729–39.

Köppen, Eva, and Christoph Meinel. "Empathy via Design Thinking: The Creation of Sense and Knowledge." In *Design Thinking Research: Building Innovators,* edited by Hans Plattner, Christoph Meinel, and Larry Leifer, 15–28. Cham: Springer, 2015. https://link.springer.com/chapter/10.100 7%2F978-3-319-06823-7_2.

Kose, M. Ayhan, and Ezgi Ozturk. "A World of Change: Taking Stock of the Past Half Century." *Finance and Development* 51, no. 3 (September 2014): 6–11. http://www.imf.org/external/pubs/ft /fandd/2014/09/kose.htm.

Kossoff, Gideon. *"Holism and the Reconstitution of Everyday Life: A Framework for Transition to a Sustainable Society."* PhD diss., University of Dundee, Scotland, 2011.

Kostakis, Vasilis, and Michel Bauwens. *Network Society and Future Scenarios for a Collaborative Economy.* London: Palgrave Macmillan, 2014.

Kotchka, Claudia. "Innovation at P&G." May 2009. Vimeo video, 47:02. https://vimeo.com/5203345.

Kotter, John, and Dan Cohen. *The Heart of Change.* Boston: Harvard Business Review, 2012.

Kozubek, James. *Modern Prometheus: Editing the Human Genome with Crisper-Cas9.* Cambridge: Cambridge University Press, 2016.

Krause, Kerri-Lee. "Addressing the Wicked Problem of Quality in Higher Education: Theoretical Approaches and Implications." *Higher Education Research & Development* 31, no. 3 (2012): 285–97. https://doi.org/10.1080/07294360.2011.634381.

Kreuter, Marshall W., Christopher De Rosa, Elizabeth H. Howze, and Grant T. Baldwin. "Understanding Wicked Problems: A Key to Advancing Environmental Health Promotion." *Health Education & Behavior* 31, no. 4 (August 2004): 441–54. https://doi.org/10.1177/1090198104265597.

Krippendorff, Klaus. "On the Essential Contexts of Artifacts or on the Proposition That 'Design Is Making Sense (of Things)'." *Design Issues* 5, no. 2 (1989): 9–39. https://doi.org/10.2307/1511512.

Krippendorff, Klaus. *The Semantic Turn*. Boca Raton, FL: CRC Press, 2006.

Krulak, Charles C. "The Strategic Corporal: Leadership in the Three Block War." *Marine Corps Gazette* 83, no. 1 (January 1999): 18–23. www.au.af.mil/au/awc/awcgate/usmc/strategic_corporal.htm.

Kunz, Werner, and Horst W. J. Rittel. "Issues as Elements of Information Systems." In *The Universe of Design: Horst Rittel's Theories of Design and Planning*, edited by Jean-Pierre Protzen and David Harris, 181–86. London: Routledge, 2010. (Originally published as Working Paper No. 131, Berkeley: Institute of Urban and Regional Development, July 1970, reprinted in 1978.)

Kurzweil, Ray. *The Age of Spiritual Machines: When Computers Exceed Human Intelligence*. New York: Penguin, 1999.

Kurzweil, Ray. "The Law of Accelerating Returns." March 7, 2001. https://www.kurzweilai.net/the -law-of-accelerating-returns.

Labour Migration Branch. *ILO Estimates on International Migrant Workers—Results and Methodology*. Geneva, Switzerland: International Labour Organization, 2018. https://www.ilo.org/wcmsp5 /groups/public/---dgreports/---dcomm/---publ/documents/publication/wcms_652001.pdf.

Lafley, A. G., and Roger L. Martin. *Playing to Win*. Boston: Harvard Business Review Press, 2013.

Lafley, A. G., Roger L. Martin, and Jennifer Riel. "A Playbook for Strategy: The Five Essential Questions at the Heart of Any Winning Strategy." *Rotman Magazine* (Winter 2013). https:// matthewemay.com/wp-content/uploads/2014/08/Play2Win-Roger1.pdf.

Lahart, Justin. "A World of Trouble for the Fed." *Wall Street Journal*, January 22, 2016. https:// www.wsj.com/articles/the-fed-fought-the-world-and-the-world-won-1453491425.

Lakna. "Difference between Ecology and Ecosystem," *PEDIAA*, accessed October 31, 2020, http:// pediaa.com/difference-between-ecology-and-ecosystem/.

Lash, Denise, Steve Raynor, and Helen Ingram. "Taming the Waters: Strategies to Domesticate the Wicked Problems of Water Resource Management." *Water* 3, no. 1 (2005): 1–17.

Laursen, Linda N., and Louise M. Haase. "The Shortcomings of Design Thinking Compared to Designerly Thinking." *Design Journal* 22, no. 6 (September 2019): 813–32. https://doi.org/10.1080 /14606925.2019.1652531.

Lawson, Benn, and Danny Samson. "Developing Innovation Capability in Organizations: A Dynamic Capabilities Approach." *International Journal of Innovation Management* 5, no. 3 (October 2011): 377–400.

Lawson, Bryan. *How Designers Think: The Design Process Demystified*. 4th ed. London: Routledge, 2005.

Layne, Rachel. "Trump Trade War with China Has Cost 300,000 U.S. Jobs, Moody's Estimates." CBS. September 12, 2019. https://www.cbsnews.com/news/trumps-trade-war-squashed-an-estimated -300000-jobs-so-far-moodys-estimates/.

Lazarus, Richard J. "Super Wicked Problems and Climate Change: Restraining the Present to Liberate the Future." *Cornell Law Review* 94 (2009): 1153–234. https://scholarship.law.cornell.edu/cgi/viewcontent.cgi?article=3143&context=clr.

Leach, William D. "Collaborative Public Management and Democracy: Evidence from Western Watershed Partnerships." *Public Administration Review* 66, no. s1 (December 2006): 100–10. https://onlinelibrary.wiley.com/toc/15406210/66/s1.

Leadbeater, Charles. *The Rise of the Social Entrepreneur.* London: Demos, 1997.

Lee, Kipum. "Critique of Design Thinking in Organizations: Strongholds and Shortcomings of the Making Paradigm." *She Ji: The Journal of Design, Economics, and Innovation* 7, no. 4 (Winter 2021): 497–515. https://doi.org/10.1016/j.sheji.2021.10.003.

Lee, Tom, and Jacqueline Varas. "The Total Costs of Trump's Tariffs." American Action Forum. August 14, 2020. https://www.americanactionforum.org/research/the-total-cost-of-trumps-new-tariffs/.

Leicester, Graham. *Transformative Innovation.* Axminster, UK: Triarchy Press, 2016.

Levesque, Vanessa R., Kathleen P. Bell, and Aram J. K. Calhoun. "Planning for Sustainability in Small Municipalities." *Journal of Planning Education and Research* 37, no. 3 (September 2017): 322–33. https://doi.org/10.1177/0739456X16655601.

Levesque, Vanessa R., Aram J. K. Calhoun, Kathleen P. Bell, and Teresa R. Johnson. "Turning Contention into Collaboration: Engaging Power, Trust, and Learning in Collaborative Networks." *Society and Natural Resources* 30, no. 2 (February 2017): 245–60. https://doi.org/10.1080/08941920.2016.1180726.

Levin, Kelly, Benjamin Cashore, Steven Bernstein, and Graeme Auld. "Overcoming the Tragedy of Super Wicked Problems: Constraining Our Future Selves to Ameliorate Global Climate Change." *Policy Sciences* 45, no. 2 (June 2012): 123–52, https://www.jstor.org/stable/41486859.

Levin, Martin A., and Mary Bryna Sanger. *Making Government Work: How Entrepreneurial Executives Turn Bright Ideas into Real Results.* San Francisco: Jossey Bass, 1994.

Levine, Peter. "Beyond Deliberation: A Strategy for Civic Renewal." *Journal of Public Deliberation* 10, no. 1 (2014). https://doi.org/10.16997/jdd.193.

Levitsky, Steven, and Daniel Ziblatt. *How Democracies Die.* New York: Broadway Books, 2019.

Lewis, Jenny M., Michael McGann, and Emma Blomkamp. "When Design Meets Power: Design Thinking, Public Sector Innovation and the Politics of Policymaking." *Policy & Politics* 48, no. 1 (January 2020): 111–30, https://doi.org/10.1332/030557319X15579230420081.

Lewis, Simon L., and Mark A. Maslin. *The Human Planet: How We Created the Anthropocene.* New Haven, CT: Yale University Press, 2018.

Lewrick, Michael, Patrick Link, and Larry Leifer. *The Design Thinking Toolbox.* New York: Wiley, 2020.

Lieberman, J. Nina. *Playfulness: Its Relationship to Imagination and Creativity.* New York: Academic Press, 1977.

Liedtka, Jeanne M. "In Defense of Strategy as Design." *California Management Review* 42, no. 3 (April 2000): 8–30. https://doi.org/10.2307/41166040.

Liedtka, Jeanne M. "Design Process: What *Is*? What *If*? What *Wows*? What *Works*?" Image adapted from https://www.facebook.com/liedtkaj/photos/a.354796684646539/399591383500402.

Liedtka, Jeanne M. "Exploring the Impact of Design Thinking in Action." University of Virginia, Charlottesville, Darden Working Paper Series, 2018. https://designatdarden.org/app/uploads /2018/01/Working-paper-Liedtka-Evaluating-the-Impact-of-Design-Thinking.pdf.

Liedtka, Jeanne M. "Perspective: Linking Design Thinking with Innovation Outcomes through Cognitive Bias Reduction." *Journal of Product Innovation Management* 32, no. 6 (March 2014): 925–38. https://doi.org/10.1111/jpim.12163.

Liedtka, Jeanne M. "Putting Technology in Its Place: Design Thinking's Social Technology at Work." *California Management Review* 62, no. 2 (March 2020): 53–83. https://doi .org/10.1177/0008125619897391.

Liedtka, Jeanne M. "Why Design Thinking Works." *Harvard Business Review* 96, no. 5 (September/ October 2018): 72–9. https://hbr.org/2018/09/why-design-thinking-works.

Liedtka, Jeanne M., and Saul Kaplan. "How Design Thinking Opens New Frontiers for Strategy Development." *Strategy and Leadership* 47, no. 2 (March 2019): 3–10. https://doi .org/10.1177/0008125619897594.

Liedtka, Jeanne M., Andrew King, and Kevin Bennett. *Solving Problems with Design Thinking: Ten Stories of What Works.* New York: Columbia Business School, 2013.

Liedtka, Jeanne M., and Tim Ogilvie. *Designing for Growth: A Design Thinking Toolkit for Managers.* New York: Columbia Business School, 2011.

Liedtka, Jeanne M., Tim Ogilvie, and Rachel Brozenske. *The Designing for Growth Field Book.* New York: Columbia Business School, 2014.

Liedtka, Jeanne M., and John W. Rosenblum. "Teaching Strategy as Design: A Report from the Field." *Journal of Management Education* 22, no. 3 (June 1998): 285–303. https://doi.org/10.1177 /105256299802200303.

Liedtka, Jeanne M., Randy Salzman, and Daisy Azer. *Design Thinking for the Greater Good: Innovation in the Social Sector.* New York: Columbia Business School Press, 2017.

Lietaer, Bernard, Christian Arnsperger, Sally Goerner, and Stefan Brunnhuber. *Money and Sustainability: The Missing Link.* Charmouth, UK: Triarchy Press, 2012.

Lind, William S., Keith Nightengale, John F. Schmitt, Joseph W. Sutton, and Gary I. Wilson. "The Changing Face of War: Into the Fourth Generation." *Marine Corps Gazette*, October 1989, 22–26. http://www.lesc.net/system/files/4GW+Original+Article+1989.pdf.

Lindblom, Charles E. "The Science of Muddling Through." *Public Administration Review* 19, no. 2 (Spring 1959): 79–88. http://www.jstor.org/stable/973677.

Lindblom, Charles E. "Still Muddling, Not Yet Through." *Public Administration Review* 39 (November–December, 1979): 517–26. https://doi.org/10.2307/976178.

Lindgaard, Karen, and Heico Wesselius. "Once More, with Feeling: Design Thinking and Embodied Cognition." *She Ji: The Journal of Design, Economics, and Innovation* 3, no. 2 (Summer 2017): 83–92. https://ojs.unbc.ca/index.php/design/article/view/1724/1325.

Liu, John D. "Greening China's Loess Plateau." January 30, 3013. YouTube video, 1.21. https:// www.youtube.com/watch?v=UAmai36XJDk.

Liu, John D. "The Lessons of the Loess Plateau." https://www.academia.edu/5567047/_Lessons _of_the_Loess_Plateau.

Lockwood, Thomas, and Edgar Papke. *Innovation by Design: How Any Organization Can Leverage Design Thinking to Produce Change, Drive New Ideas, and Deliver Meaningful Solutions*. Newburyport, MA: Weiser, 2017.

Lockwood, Thomas, and Thomas Walton. *Building Design Strategy: Using Design to Achieve Key Business Objectives*. New York: Allworth Press, 2008.

Loevinger, Jane. *Ego Development*. San Francisco: Jossey-Bass, 1976.

Logan, Brian, and Tim Smithers. "Creativity and Design as Exploration." In *Modeling Creativity and Knowledge-Based Creative Design*, edited by John S. Gero and Mary Lou Maher, 139–73. Hillsdale, NJ: Lawrence Erlbaum, 1993.

Lönngren, Johanna, and Katrien van Poeck. "Wicked Problem: A Mapping Review of the Literature." *International Journal of Sustainable Development and World Ecology* 28, no. 6 (December 2020): 481–502. https://doi.org/10.1080/13504509.2020.1859415.

Luetjens, Joannah. "Policy Entrepreneurs and Problem Framing: The Case of Climate Change." *Environment and Planning C: Politics and Space* 35, no. 8 (2017): 1362–77. https://doi.org/10.1177/2399654417708440.

Lukensmeyer, Carolyn J., and Steven Brigham. "Taking Democracy to Scale: Creating a Town Hall Meeting for the Twenty-First Century." *National Civic Review* 91, no. 4 (Winter 2002): 351–66. https://doi.org/10.1002/ncr.91406l.

Lukensmeyer, Carolyn J., and Steve Brigham. "Taking Democracy to Scale: Large Scale Interventions—for Citizens." *Journal of Applied Behavioral Science* 41, no. 1 (March 2005): 47–60. https://doi.org/10.1177/0021886304272656.

LUMA Institute. *Innovating for People: Handbook of Human-Centered Design Methods*. Pittsburgh: LUMA Institute, 2012.

Luna, Melissa. *Playa Viva 2018 Social Impact Report*. https://www.playaviva.com/wp-content/uploads/2018-Social-Impact-Report-Digital.pdf.

Maani, Kambiz E., and Robert Y. Cabana. *Systems Thinking and Modelling*. Auckland, New Zealand: Pearson Education, 2000.

Mack, W. R., Deanna Green, and Arnold Vedlitz. "Innovation and Implementation in the Public Sector: An Examination of Public Entrepreneurship." *Review of Policy Research* 25, no. 3 (May 2008): 233–52. https://doi.org/10.1111/j.1541-1338.2008.00325.x.

Maharidge, Dale, and Michael S. Williamson. *Someplace Like America: Tales from a New Great Depression*. Berkeley: University of California Press, 2011.

Malamed, Connie. "A Designer Addresses Criticisms of Design Thinking." *Learning Solutions*. March 16, 2018. https://learningsolutionsmag.com/articles/a-designer-addresses-criticism-of-design-thinking.

Malbon, Tim. "The Problem with Design Thinking." *Made by Many*. February 24, 2016. https://medium.com/the-many/the-problem-with-design-thinking-988b88f1d696.

Malone. Thomas W., and Kevin Crowston. "The Interdisciplinary Study of Coordination." *ACM Computing Survey* 26, no. 1 (1994): 87–119.

Mang, Pamela, and Ben Haggard. *Regenerative Development and Design*. Hoboken, NJ: John Wiley, 2016.

Mang, Pamela, and Bill Reed. "Designing from Place: A Regenerative Framework and Methodology." *Building Research & Information* 40, no. 1 (2012): 23–38. https://doi.org/10.1080/09613218.2012.621341.

Mang, Pamela, and Bill Reed. "Regenerative Development and Design." In *Sustainable Build Environments, Encyclopedia of Sustainability Science and Technology Series*, edited by Vivian Loftness, 115–41. New York: Springer, 2020. https://doi.org/10.1007/978-1-0716-0684-1_303.

Manyika, James, Susan Lund, Jacques Bughin, Jonathan Woetzel, Kalin Stamenov, and Dhruv Dhingra. *Digital Globalization: The New Era of Global Flows*. New York: McKinsey Global Institute, March 2016. https://www.mckinsey.com/~/media/McKinsey/Business%20Functions/McKinsey%20Digital/Our%20Insights/Digital%20globalization%20The%20new%20era%20of%20global%20flows/MGI-Digital-globalization-Full-report.pdf.

Manzini, Enzio. *Design When Everybody Designs*. Cambridge, MA: MIT Press, 2015.

Manzini, Enzio. "Making Things Happen: Social Innovation and Design." *Design Issues* 30, no. 1 (Winter 2014): 57–66. https://doi.org/10.1162/DESI_a_00248.

Margerum, Richard D. *Beyond Consensus: Improving Collaborative Planning and Management*. Cambridge, MA: MIT Press, 2011.

Marris, Peter. *Loss and Change*. London: Routledge & Kegan Paul, 1974.

Marsh, Kevin, and Jeffrey S. Lantis. "Are All Foreign Policy Innovators Created Equal? The New Generation of Congressional Foreign Policy Entrepreneurship." *Foreign Policy Analysis* 14, no. 2 (April 2018): 212–34, https://doi.org/10.1093/fpa/orw030.

Martenson, Chris. *Peak Prosperity*. https://www.peakprosperity.com/crashcourse/.

Martin, Grant. "A Tale of Two Design Efforts (and Why They Both Failed in Afghanistan)." *Small Wars Journal* (July 2011). https://smallwarsjournal.com/blog/journal/docs-temp/809-martin.pdfsmallwarsjournal.com.

Martin, Roger L. *The Design of Business: Why Design Thinking Is the Next Competitive Advantage*. Boston: Harvard Business Review Press, 2009.

Martin, Roger L. "How Successful Leaders Think." *Harvard Business Review* 85, no. 6 (June 2007): 60–67.

Martin, Roger L. "The Innovation Catalysts." *Harvard Business Review* 89, no. 6 (June 2011): 82–87. https://hbr.org/2011/06/the-innovation-catalysts.

Martin, Roger L. *The Opposable Mind: How Successful Leaders Win through Integrative Thinking*. Boston: Harvard Business Review Press, 2007.

Martin, Roger L., and Sally R. Osberg. *Getting beyond Better: How Social Entrepreneurship Works*. Boston: Harvard Business Review Press, 2015.

Masarang Foundation. "Sugar Palm, A Miraculous Tree." https://masarang.nl/en/projects/sugar-palm-miracle-tree/.

Masarang Foundation. "The Role of the Sugar Palm in Masarang Projects." https://masarang.nl/en/what-we-do/the-role-of-the-sugar-palm-in-masarang-projects/.

Masarang Foundation. "Our Mission and Objectives." https://masarang.eu/about/mission/.

Masri, Lena. "After Brexit, Many 'Leave' Voters Express Buyer's Remorse." ABC News, June 27, 2016. http://www.todayonline.com/world/europe/buyers-remorse-brexit-sinks.

Masters, Nicole. *For the Love of Soil: Strategies to Regenerate Our Food Production System*. Waitakere, New Zealand: Printable Reality, 2019.

Mau, Bruce. "Incomplete Manifesto for Growth." *Chicago Magazine*, May 17, 2010. https://www.chicagomag.com/Chicago-Magazine/June-2010/Bruce-Mau-Manifesto-for-Growth/.

Maurya, Dayashankar, and Michael Mintrom. "Policy Entrepreneurs as Catalysts of Broad System Change: The Case of Social Health Insurance Adoption in India." *Journal of Asian Public Policy* 13, no. 1 (2020): 18–34. https://doi.org/10.1080/17516234.2019.1617955.

Maxfield, John. "25 Factors That Caused or Contributed to the Financial Crisis." *The Motley Fool*. Updated October 2, 2018. http://www.fool.com/investing/general/2015/02/28/25-major-factors-that-caused-or-contributed-to-the.aspx.

Maxwell, Steven. "From Sand Quarry to Food Forest." *Organic & Wellness News*, May 31, 2017. https://www.organicwellnessnews.com/?ArticleID=638.

Mazé, Ramia. "Politics of Designing Visions of the Future." *Journal of Future Studies* 23, no. 3 (March 2019): 23–38.

McCall, Raymond, and Janet Burge. "Untangling Wicked Problems." *Design Computing and Cognition* 30, Special Issue 2 (May 2016): 200–10. https://doi.org/10.1017/S089006041600007X.

McCann, Joseph, and John W. Selsky. *Mastering Turbulence*. San Francisco: Jossey-Bass, 2012.

McCarthy, John, and Peter Wright. *Taking [A]part: The Politics and Aesthetics of Participation in Experience-Centered Design*. Cambridge, MA: MIT Press, 2015.

McCarthy, Niall. "How Many British Euromyths Has the EU Debunked?" Statista, November 22, 2018. https://www.statista.com/chart/16181/how-many-british-euromyths-has-the-eu-debunked/.

McConnell, Allan. "Rethinking Wicked Problems as Political Problems and Policy Problems." *Policy & Politics* 46, no. 1 (2018): 165–80. https://doi.org/10.1332/030557317X15072085902640.

McElroy, Kathryn. *Prototyping for Designers*. Sebastopol, CA: O'Reilly Media, 2017.

McGann, Michael, Emma Blomkamp, and Jenny M. Lewis. "The Rise of Public-Sector Innovation Labs: Experiments in Design Thinking for Policy." *Policy Sciences* 51 (March 2018): 249–67. https://doi.org/10.1007/s11077-018-9315-7.

McGinnis, Michael, and Elinor Ostrom. "Reflections on Vincent Ostrom, Public Administration, and Polycentricity." *Public Administration Review* 72, no. 1 (January/February 2012): 15–25. https://doi.org/10.1111/j.1540-6210.2011.02488.x.

McGregor, Sue L. T. "Transdisciplinary and Biomimicry." *Transdisciplinary Journal of Engineering & Science* 4 (December 2013): 57–65. https://doi.org/10.22545/2013/00042.

McGuire, Michael. "Collaborative Public Management: Assessing What We Know and How We Know It." *Public Management Review* 66, no. s1 (December 2006): 33–43. https://onlinelibrary.wiley.com/toc/15406210/66/s1.

McGuire, Michael, and Robert Agranoff. "Networking in the Shadow of Bureaucracy." In *Oxford Handbook of American Bureaucracy*, edited by Robert F. Durant, 372–420. Oxford: Oxford University Press, 2010.

McMillan, Elizabeth, and Ysanne Carlisle. "Strategy as Order Emerging from Chaos: A Public Sector Experience." *Long Range Planning* 40 (2007): 574–93. https://doi.org/10.1016/j.lrp.2007.07.002.

McNamara, Robert. *In Retrospect: The Tragedy and Lessons of Vietnam*. New York: Times Books, 1995.

McShane, Sveta, and Jason Dorrier. "Ray Kurzweil Predicts Three Technologies Will Define Our Future." *Singularity Hub*. April 19, 2016. http://singularityhub.com/2016/04/19/ray-kurzweil -predicts-three-technologies-will-define-our-future/.

Meadows, Donella H. "Leverage Points: Places to Intervene in a System." Donella Meadows Archives. http://donellameadows.org/archives/leverage-points-places-to-intervene-in-a-system/.

Meadows, Donella H., Dennis Meadows, and Jørgen Randers. "Beyond the Limits to Growth." Donella Meadows Archives (Summer 2002). http://donellameadows.org/archives/beyond-the -limits-to-growth/.

Meadows, Donella H., Dennis L. Meadows, Jørgen Randers, and William W Behrens III. *The Limits to Growth. A Report for the Club of Rome's Project on the Predicament of Mankind*. New York: Universe Books, 1972.

Meadows, Donella H., Jørgen Randers, and Dennis L. Meadows. *Limits to Growth: The 30-Year Update*. White River Junction, VT: Chelsea Green Publishing, 2004.

Meinel, Christoph, and Larry Leifer. "Introduction—Design Thinking Is Mainly about Build-ing Innovators." In *Design Thinking Research: Building Innovators*, edited by Hasso Plattner, Christophe Meinel, and Larry Leifer, 1–11. Heidelberg, Germany: Springer, 2015. https://doi .org/10.1007/978-3-319-06823-7_1.

Melucci. Alberto. *Challenging Codes*. Cambridge: Cambridge University Press, 2009.

Melville, Keith, Taylor L. Willingham, and John R. Dedrick. "National Issues Forum: A Network of Communities Promoting Public Deliberation." In *The Deliberative Democracy Handbook: Strategies for Effective Civic Engagement in the Twenty-First Century*, edited by John Gastil and Peter Levine, 37–58. San Francisco: Jossey-Bass, 2005.

Meroni, Anna. "Strategic Design: Where Are We Now? Reflection around the Foundations of a Recent Discipline." *Strategic Design Research Journal* 1, no. 1 (July–December, 2008): 1–38. https:// doi.org/10.4013/sdrj.20081.05.

Merton, Robert K. "The Unanticipated Consequences of Purposive Social Action." *American Socio-logical Review* 1, no. 6 (December 1936): 894–904. https://doi.org/10.2307/2084615.

Meyer, Michael W., and Don Norman. "Changing Design Education for the 21st Century." *She Ji: The Journal of Design, Economics, and Innovation* 6, no. 1 (Spring 2020): 13–49. https://www .sciencedirect.com/science/article/pii/S2405872620300046.

Micheli, Petro, Helen Perks, and Michael B. Beverland. "Elevating Design in the Organization." *Journal of Product Innovation Management* 35, no. 4 (July 2018): 629–51.

Michlewski, Kamil. "Uncovering Design Attitude: Inside the Culture of Designers." *Organization Studies* 29, no. 3 (2008): 373–92. https://doi.org/10.1177/0170840607088019.

Miles, Mathew B., A. Michael Huberman, and Jonny Saldaña. *Qualitative Data Analysis*. 4th ed. Thousand Oaks, CA: SAGE, 2020.

Miller, George A. "The Magical Number Seven, Plus or Minus Two: Some Limits on Our Capac-ity for Processing Information." *Psychological Review* 63 (1956): 81–97. https://doi.org/10.1037 /h0043158.

Milm, Karl, Jacob Apkon, and Sruthi Venkatachalam. "Litigation Tracker: Pending Criminal and Civil Cases against Donald J. Trump." *Just Security*, originally published February 28, 2021, continually updated, https://www.justsecurity.org/75032/litigation-tracker-pending-criminal-and-civil-cases-against-donald-trump/.

Milward, H. Brint, and Keith G. Provan. *A Manager's Guide to Choosing and Using Collaborative Networks*. Washington, DC: IBM Center for the Business of Government, 2006.

Mink, Annemarie. *Design for Well-Being: An Approach for Understanding Users' Lives in Design for Development*. Delft, Netherlands: Delft Academic Press, 2016.

Minnesota Business Partnership. *Educating Students for the 21st Century*. Minneapolis: Minnesota Business Partnership, 1984.

Minnesota Department of Education. *Planning Document No. 5*. St. Paul: Minnesota Department of Education, 1986.

Minnesota Department of Education. *Postsecondary Enrollment Options Evaluation Report*. St. Paul: Minnesota Department of Education, 1987.

Mintrom, Michael. "Policy Entrepreneurs and Controversial Science: Governing Human Embryonic Stem Cell Research." *Journal of European Public Policy* 20, no. 3 (2013): 442–57. https://doi.org/10.1080/13501763.2012.761514.

Mintrom, Michael. "Policy Entrepreneurs and the Diffusion of Innovation." *American Journal of Political Science* 41, no. 3 (July 1997): 738–70. https://doi.org/10.2307/2111674.

Mintrom, Michael. *Policy Entrepreneurs and Dynamic Change*. Cambridge: Cambridge University Press, 2020.

Mintrom, Michael. *Policy Entrepreneurs and Social Choice*. Washington, DC: Georgetown University Press, 2000.

Mintrom, Michael, and Joannah Luetjens. "Design Thinking in Policy Processes: Opportunities and Challenges." *Australian Journal of Public Administration* 75, no. 3 (2016): 391–402. https://doi.org/10.1111/1467-8500.12211.

Mintrom, Michael, and Joannah Luetjens. "Policy Entrepreneurs and Problem Framing: The Case of Climate Change." *Environment and Planning C: Politics and Space* 35, no. 8 (December 2017): 1362–77. https://doi.org/10.1177/2399654417708440.

Mintrom, Michael, and Phillipa Norman. "Policy Entrepreneurship and Policy Change." *Policy Studies Journal* 37, no. 4 (2009): 649–67. https://doi.org/10.1111/j.1541-0072.2009.00329.x.

Mintrom, Michael, and Madeline Thomas. "Policy Entrepreneurs and Collaboration Action: Pursuit of the Sustainable Development Goals." *International Journal of Entrepreneurial Venturing* 10, no. 2 (2018): 153–71. https://doi.org/10.1504/IJEV.2018.092710.

Mintrom, Michael, and Sandra Vergari. "Advocacy Coalitions, Policy Entrepreneurs, and Policy Change." *Policy Studies Journal* 24 (1996): 420–34. https://doi.org/10.1111/j.1541-0072.1996.tb01638.x.

Mintzberg, Henry. "Five Ps for Strategy." *California Management Review* (Fall 1987): 11–24. https://doi.org/10.2307/41165263.

Mitroff, Ian I., and Richard O. Mason. "Structuring Ill-Structured Problems: Further Explorations in a Methodology for Messy Problems." *Strategic Management Journal* 1, no. 4 (1980): 331–42. https://doi.org/10.1002/smj.4250010404.

Mitroff, Ian L., and Abraham Silvers. *Dirty Rotten Strategies: How We Trick Ourselves and Others into Solving the Wrong Problems Precisely*. Stanford, CA: Stanford University Press, 2010.

Mondragon Corporation. "About Us." https://www.mondragon-corporation.com/en/about-us/.

Mondragon Corporation. "Entrepreneurship Ecosystem." https://www.mondragon-corporation.com/en/.

Montanarella, Luca, Robert Scholes, and Anastasia Brainich, eds. *The Assessment Report on Land Degradation and Restoration*. Bonn, Germany: Secretariat of the Intergovernmental Science-Policy Platform on Biodiversity and Ecosystem Services (IPBES), March 24, 2018. https://zenodo.org/record/3237393#.YDQoh-hKiMo.

Monteiro, Mike. *A Designer's Code of Ethics*. https://muledesign.com/2017/07/a-designers-code-of-ethics.

Morris, Michael H., and Foard F. Jones. "Entrepreneurship in Established Organizations: The Case of the Public Sector." *Entrepreneurship Theory and Practice* 24, no. 1 (October 1999): 331–40. https://doi.org/10.1177/104225879902400105.

Mortenson, Greg. "Sanjit 'Bunker' Roy." *The 2010 TIME 100*. April 29, 2010. http://content.time.com/time/specials/packages/article/0,28804,1984685_1984745_1985478,00.html.

Morton, Oliver. *The Planet Remade: How Geoengineering Could Change the World*. Princeton, NJ: Princeton University Press, 2016.

Mulgan, Geoff. "Forward: The Study of Social Innovation—Theory, Practice, and Progress." In *New Frontiers in Social Innovation Research*, edited by Alex Nicholls, Julie Simon and Madeleine Gabriel. New York: Palgrave Macmillan, 2015, x. https://doi.org/0.1057/9781137506801.

Mulgan, Geoff, Simon Tucker, Rushanara Ali, and Ben Sanders. *Social Innovation: What It Is, Why It Matters and How It Can Be Accelerated*. Oxford: Oxford Said Business School, Skoll Centre for Social Entrepreneurship, 2007.

Müller, Boris. "Intuition Is the Key to Good Design." *MODUS*. January 6, 2017. https://modus.medium.com/in-defence-of-intuition-f924ab82f76b.

Murray, Robin. "Danger and Opportunity Crisis and the New Social Economy." NESTA. September 1, 2009. https://www.nesta.org.uk/report/danger-and-opportunity-crisis-and-the-new-social-economy/.

Murray, Robin, Julie Caulier-Grice, and Geoff Mulgan. *The Open Book of Social Innovation*. London: NESTA and the Young Foundation, 2010.

Nabatchi, Tina, and Matt Leighninger. *Public Participation for 21st-Century Democracy*. Hoboken, NJ: Wiley, 2015.

National Aeronautics and Space Administration (NASA). "Project Apollo: A Retrospective Analysis." Updated April 21, 2014, https://history.nasa.gov/Apollomon/Apollo.html.

National Aeronautics and Space Administration (NASA) Earth Observatory. "Smoke Blankets Borneo." September 14, 2019. https://earthobservatory.nasa.gov/images/145614/smoke-blankets-borneo.

National Commission on Excellence in Education. *A Nation at Risk: The Imperative for Educational Reform*. Washington, DC: US Government Printing Office, 1983.

National Consortium for the Study of Terrorism and Responses to Terrorism (START). Global Terrorism Database. https://www.start.umd.edu/gtd/.

National Intelligence Council. *Global Trends 2030: Alternative Worlds*. Washington, DC: US Office of the Director of National Intelligence, December 2012. www.dni.gov/nic/globaltrends.

National Intelligence Council. *Global Trends Paradox of Progress*. Washington, DC: Office of the Director of National Intelligence, January 2017. https://www.dni.gov/files/documents/nic/GT -Full-Report.pdf.

Nature Conservancy. "Beyond Sustainable: A Food System to Restore the Planet." https://www .nature.org/en-us/what-we-do/our-insights/perspectives/regenerative-agriculture-food-system -restore-planet/.

Ndimukaga, Marc. "Rugezi Wetland Conservation Project, Rwanda: Final Report." Conservation Leadership Programme, CLP Project ID: 0167312. https://www.conservationleadershipprogramme .org/project/rugezi-wetland-conservation-rwanda.

Nelson, Harold G., and Erik Stolterman. *The Design Way: Intentional Change in an Unpredictable World*. 2nd ed. Cambridge, MA: MIT Press, 2012.

NESTA Foundation. "Proof of Concept—What's in a Name?" https://www.nesta.org.uk/blog/proof -of-concept-prototype-pilot-mvp-whats-in-a-name/.

New Economics Institute (NEI). "Resource Website of Social and Solidarity Economy." http:// www.socioeco.org/bdf_organisme-297_en.html.

Newell, Allen, and Herbert Simon. *Human Problem Solving*. Englewood Cliffs, N.J.: Prentice-Hall, 1972.

Newman, Damian. "Design Squiggle." thedesignsquiggle.com.

New School. "Parsons Launches MFA in Transdisciplinary Design." February 18, 2010. https:// www.newschool.edu/pressroom/pressreleases/2010/transdesign.aspx.

Next System Project. https://democracycollaborative.org/content/next-system-project.

Next System Project. "System Problems Require Systemic Solutions." https://thenextsystem.org /about-next-system-project.

Ney, Steve, and Christoph Meinel. *Putting Design Thinking to Work: How Large Organizations Can Embrace Messy Institutions to Tackle Wicked Problems*. Cham, Switzerland: Springer Nature, 2019.

Ney, Steven, and Marco Verweij. "Messy Institutions for Wicked Problems: How to Generate Clumsy Solutions." *Environment and Planning C: Government Policy* 33 (December 2015): 1679–96. https://doi.org/10.1177/0263774X15614450.

Nicholls, Alex, Julie Simon, and Madeleine Gabriel, eds. *New Frontiers in Social Innovation*. London: Palgrave Macmillan, 2015. https://doi.org/10.1057/9781137506801.

Nixon, Richard M. "Special Message to the Congress on Drug Abuse Prevention and Control." June 17, 1971. https://www.presidency.ucsb.edu/documents/special-message-the-congress-drug -abuse-prevention-and-control.

"Nixon's Views on Presidential Power: Excerpts from a 1977 Interview with David Frost." May 19, 1977. https://ilearn.marist.edu/access/content/user/10043047@marist.edu/my%20documents /EDAC631/Lesson%20Presentation%20Final%20Project/Nixon%20interview.pdf.

Noble, James. "Anything Is Possible in the Age of Design." Linkedin, November 20, 2017. https:// www.linkedin.com/pulse/anything-possible-age-design-james-noble.

Noël, Guillermina, ed. "Design Education, Part I." *She Ji: The Journal of Design, Economics, and Innovation* 6, no. 1 (Spring 2020): 1–118. https://www.sciencedirect.com/journal/she-ji-the -journal-of-design-economics-and-innovation/vol/6/issue/1.

Noël, Guillermina, ed. "Design Education, Part II." *She Ji: The Journal of Design, Economics, and Innovation* 6, 2 (Summer 2020): 119–274. https://www.sciencedirect.com/journal/she-ji-the -journal-of-design-economics-and-innovation/vol/6/issue/2.

Noordegraaf, Mirko, Scott Douglas, Karin Geuijen, and Martijn van der Steen. *Policy and Society* 38, no. 2 (2019): 293–95, 278. https://doi.org/10.1080/14494035.2019.1617970.

Norman, Donald A. *The Design of Everyday Things*. New York: Basic Books, 2013.

Norman, Don. "Design Thinking: A Useful Myth." *CORE77*. June 25, 2010. https://www.core77. com/posts/16790/design-thinking-a-useful-myth-16790.

Norman, Donald A. *The Psychology of Everyday Things*. New York: Basic Books, 1988.

Norman, Don. "Rethinking Design Thinking. jnd.org. December 3, 2018. https://jnd.org/rehtinking _design_thnking/.

Norman, Donald A., and Roberto Verganti. "Incremental and Radical Innovation: Design Research vs. Technology and Meaning Making." *Design Issues* 30, no. 1 (Winter 2014): 78–96. https://doi.org/10.1162/DESI_a_00250.

NOVA Science Now. "Emergence: Everyday Examples." http://www.pbs.org/wgbh/nova/sciencenow /3410/03-ever-nf.html.

Nozick, Robert. *The Examined Life: Philosophical Meditations*. New York: Touchstone Books, 1989.

Nussbaum, Bruce. "Design Thinking Is a Failed Experiment. So What's Next?" *Fast Company*, April 5, 2011. https://www.fastcompany.com/1663558/design-thinking-is-a-failed-experiment -so-whats-next.

Nussbaum, Bruce. "How Serious Play Leads to Breakthrough Innovation." *Fast Company*, March 4 2013. https://www.fastcompany.com/1671971/how-serious-play-leads-to-breakthrough-innovation.

Oborn, Eivor, Michael Barrett, and Mark Exworthy. "Policy Entrepreneurship in the Development of Public-Sector Strategy: The Case of London Health Reform." *Public Administration* 89, no 2 (June 2011): 325–44. https://doi.org/10.1111/j.1467-9299.2010.01889.x.

Observatory of Public Sector Innovation, Organisation for Economic Co-operation and Development (OECD). https://www.oecd-opsi.org/guide/strategic-design/.

Ockuly, Marta Davidovich. *Joy of Quotes*. http://www.joyofquotes.com/inspirational-quotes-by -author.html#R.

Office of the Historian, Department of State. "280 Memorandum from the President's Assistant for National Security Affairs (Kissinger) to President Ford," May 12, 1975. *Foreign Relations of the United States, 1969–1976, Volume X, Vietnam*, January 1973–July 1975. https://history.state.gov /historicaldocuments/frus1969-76v10/d280.

O'Flynn, Janine. "The Cult of Collaboration in Public Policy." *Australian Journal of Public Administration* 68, no. 1 (2009): 112–16. https://doi.org/10.1111/j.1467-8500.2009.00616.x.

Okhuysen, Gerardo A., and Beth A. Bechky. "Coordination in Organizations: An Integrative Perspective." *Academy of Management Annals* 3, no. 1 (2009): 463–502. https://doi.org/10.5465 /19416520903047533.

OpenIDEO. "Design Thinking Defined." Facebook. May 4, 2020. https://www.facebook.com/openideo/photos/a.157018881007518/3839137512795618/?type=3.

Ophuls, William. *Immoderate Greatness: Why Civilizations Fail.* North Charleston, SC: Create Space Independent Publishing Platform, 2012.

Organisation for Economic Co-operation and Development (OECD). *Systems Approaches to Public Sector Challenges: Working with Change.* Paris: OECD, 2017.

Orloff, Judith. *Second Sight.* New York: Three Rivers Press, 2010.

Orr, David. "Architecture, Ecological Design, and Human Ecology." 89th ACSA Annual Meeting, Baltimore, March 16–20, 2001: 23.

Osnos, Evan. *Wildland: The Making of America's Fury.* New York: Farrar, Straus and Giroux, 2021.

Ostrom, Elinor. "A Polycentric Approach for Coping with Climate Change." *Annals of Economics and Finance* 15, no. 1 (2014): 97–134.

Owen, Charles L. "Considering Design Fundamentally." *Design Processes Newsletter* 5, no. 3 (1993): 2.

Owen, Charles L. "Design Research: Building the Knowledge Base." *Design Studies* 19, no. 1 (January 1998): 9–20. https://id.iit.edu/wp-content/uploads/2015/03/Design-researching-building-the-knowledge-base-Owen_desstud97.pdf.

Özbekhan, Hasan. "The Predicament of Mankind: Quest for Structured Responses to Growing World-Wide Complexities and Uncertainties: A Proposal (to the Club of Rome)." 1970. https://www.futureworlds.eu/wiki/The_Predicament_of_Mankind.

P2P Foundation. https://p2pfoundation.net/the-p2p-foundation.

Packer, George. *The Unwinding: An Inner History of the New America.* New York: Farrar, Straus and Giroux: 2013.

Paddock, Richard, and Muktita Suhartono. "A Blood-Red Sky: Fires Leave a Million Indonesians Gasping." *New York Times*, September 25, 2019. https://www.nytimes.com/2019/09/25/world/asia/indonesia-red-sky-fires.html.

Pahl, Gerhard, Wofgang Beitz, Jörg Feldhusen, and Karl-Heinrich Grote. *Engineering Design: A Systematic Approach.* 3rd ed. Translated by Ken Wallace and Luciënne T. M. Blessing. London: Springer-Verlag, 2007.

Papanek, Victor. *Design for the Real World: Human Ecology and Social Change.* 2nd ed. London: Thames & Hudson, 1985.

Papanek, Victor. "The Politics of Design." Exhibition at the Vitra Design Museum. https://metropolismag.com/profiles/victor-papanek-politics-design-vitra-museum/.

Pape, Robert, Keven Ruby, Vincent Everton, and Gentry Jenkins. "How to Fix the Flaws in the Global Terrorism Database and Why It Matters." *Washington Post*, August 11, 2014. https://www.washingtonpost.com/news/monkey-cage/wp/2014/08/11/how-to-fix-the-flaws-in-the-global-terrorism-database-and-why-it-matters/.

Pater, Ruben. *CAPS LOCK: How Capitalism Took Hold of Graphic Design and How to Escape From It.* Amsterdam: Valiz, 2021.

Pater, Ruben. *Politics of Design: A (Not So) Global Manual for Visual Communication*. London: Laurence King Publishing, 2016.

Patton, Michael Q. *Blue Marble Evaluation: Premises and Principles*. New York: Guilford Press, 2020.

Patton, Michael Q. *Developmental Evaluation: Applying Complexity Concepts to Enhance Innovation and Use*. New York: Guilford Press, 2011.

Patton, Michael Q. *Essentials of Utilization-Focused Evaluation*. Los Angeles: SAGE, 2012.

Patton, Michael Q. *Qualitative Research and Evaluation Methods*. 4th ed. Thousand Oaks, CA: SAGE, 2015.

Patton, Michael Q. "What Is Essential in Developmental Evaluation?" *American Journal of Evaluation* 37, no. 2 (2016): 250–65. https://doi.org/10.1177/1098214015626295.

Peek, Thomas R., Edward L. Duren, and Lawrence C. Wells. *Minnesota K–12 Education: The Current Debate, the Present Condition*. Report No. CURA 85–3. Minneapolis: Center for Urban and Regional Affairs, University of Minnesota, 1985. https://files.eric.ed.gov/fulltext/ED255619.pdf.

Peek, Thomas R., and Douglas S. Wilson. *Fiscal Constraints on Minnesota—Impacts and Policies: Economic Conditions and Changing Government Policies*. CURA 83–1. Minneapolis: Center for Urban and Regional Affairs, University of Minnesota, 1983. https://conservancy.umn.edu /handle/11299/208144.

Peirce, Charles S. *The Collected Works of Charles Sanders Peirce*. Cambridge, MA: Harvard University Press, 1958.

Pelka, Bastian, and Judith Terstriep. "Mapping Social Innovation Maps: The State of Research Practice across Europe." *European Public & Social Innovation Review* 1, no. 1 (June 2016): 3–16. https://doi.org/10.31637/epsir.16-1.1.

Pendleton-Julian, Ann, and John Seely Brown. *Pragmatic Imagination*. San Francisco: Blurb, 2016.

Pennington, Deana D. "Cross Disciplinary Collaboration and Learning." *Ecology and Society* 13, no. 2 (December 2008). http://www.jstor.org/stable/26267958.

Perez-Breva, Luis. *Innovating: A Doer's Manifesto for Starting from a Hunch, Prototyping Problems, Scaling up, and Learning to be Productively Wrong*. Cambridge, MA: MIT Press, 2018.

Perks, Helen, Rachel Cooper, and Cassie Jones. "Characterizing the Role of Design in New Product Development: An Empirically Derived Taxonomy." *Journal of Product Innovation Management* 22, no. 2 (February 2005): 111–27. https://doi.org/10.1111/j.0737-6782.2005.00109.x.

Perrow, Charles. *Normal Accidents: Living with High-Risk Technologies*. New York: Basic Books, 1984.

Peters, B. Guy. "Agenda Setting and Public Policy." In *American Public Policy*, 57–79. 11th ed. Los Angeles: SAGE, 2019.

Peters, B. Guy. "Evaluation and Policy Change." In *American Public Policy*, 159–75. 11th ed. Los Angeles: SAGE, Los Angeles: 2019.

Peters, B. Guy. "Legitimating Policy Choices." In *American Public Policy*, 81–97. 11th ed. Los Angeles: SAGE, 2019.

Peters, B. Guy. "Organization and Implementation." In *American Public Policy*, 99–121. 11th ed. Los Angeles: SAGE, Los Angeles: 2019.

Peters, B. Guy. "What Is so Wicked about Wicked Problems? A Conceptual Analysis and a Research Program." *Policy and Society* 36, no. 3 (2017): 385–96. https://doi.org/10.1080/14494035 .2017.1361633.

Peters, B. Guy, and Nenad Rava. "Policy Design: From Technocracy to Complexity, and Beyond." Presentation at the International Conference on Public Policy, Singapore, June 28–30, 2017. https://www.ippapublicpolicy.org/file/paper/5932fa23369d0.pdf.

Pfeffer, Jeffrey. *Managing with Power*. Boston: Harvard Business Press, 1992.

Pfeffer, Jeffrey. *Power in Organizations*. New York: Harper Business, 1981.

Pham, Peter. "China's Steel Industry Is Dominating the Global Market—But Will It Last?" *Forbes*, April 27, 2016. http://www.forbes.com/sites/peterpham/2016/04/27/chinas-steel-industry-is -dominating-the-global-market-but-will-it-last/#ceeed04380b1.

Pinker, Steven. *The Better Angels of Our Nature: Why Violence Has Declined*. New York: Penguin Books, 2012.

Plant and Soil Sciences eLibrary. "Introduction—What Is the Adaptive Cycle?" https://passel2 .unl.edu/view/lesson/b4790b02d93e/2. Image courtesy of A. Garmestani, US Environmental Protection Agency (EPA).

Plant and Soil Sciences eLibrary. "Panarchy, Example—Federal System." https://passel2.unl.edu/ view/lesson/2e6e3c012632/5. Image courtesy of A. Garmestani, US Environmental Protection Agency (EPA).

Plant and Social Sciences eLibrary. "Panarchy Transitons, Pathway 1: Revolt." https://passel2.unl .edu/view/lesson/2e6e3c012632/3. Image courtesy of A. Garmestani, US Environmental Protection Agency (EPA).

Plant and Social Sciences eLibrary. "Panarchy Transitons, Pathway 2: Remember." https://passel2 .unl.edu/view/lesson/2e6e3c012632/3. Image courtesy of A. Garmestani, US Environmental Protection Agency (EPA).

Plattner, Hasso, Christoph Meinel, and Larry Leifer, eds. *Design Thinking Research: Making Design Thinking Foundational*. Heidelberg, Germany: Springer, 2016.

Plattner, Hasso, Christopher Meinel, and Larry Leifer, eds. *Design Thinking: Understand, Improve, Apply*. Berlin: Springer, 2011. https://doi.org/10.1007/978-3-642-13757-0.

Plotkin, Bill. *Nature and the Human Soul: Cultivating Wholeness and Community in a Fragmented World*. Novato, CA: New World Library, 2007.

Polsby, Nelson W. *The Politics of Policy Initiation*. New Haven, CT: Yale University Press, 1984.

Poole, Marshall S., and Andrew H. Van de Ven. *Oxford Handbook of Change and Innovation*, 2nd ed. Oxford: Oxford University Press, 2021.

Porter, Eduardo. "Finding Common Ground on Poverty." *New York Times*, February, 3 2016. http:// www.nytimes.com/2016/02/03/business/finding-common-political-ground-on-poverty.html.

Porter, Michael E. *Competitive Advantage*. New York: Free Press, 1985.

Preskill, Hallie, and Tanya Beer. *Evaluating Social Innovation*. Washington, DC: Center for Evaluation Innovation, 2012. https://www.evaluationinnovation.org/publication/evaluating-social -innovation/.

Prigogine, Ilya, and Isabelle Stengers. *Order out of Chaos: Man's New Dialogue with Nature*. Portsmouth, NH: William Heinemann, 1984.

Project Drawdown. "Drawdown Solutions Summary: Table of Solutions," accessed November 2, 2020, https://www.drawdown.org/solutions-summary-by-rank.

Project Drawdown. "Food, Agriculture, and Land Use" accessed November 2, 2020, https://www.drawdown.org/solutions/food/regenerative-agriculture.

Protzen, Jean-Pierre, and David Harris. *The Universe of Design: Horst Rittel's Theories of Design and Planning*. London: Routledge, 2010.

Public School Incentives (PSI). "Nine High-Potential Ideas." St. Paul, MN: Public School Incentives, 1984a.

Public School Incentives (PSI). "What Is Public School Incentives?" St. Paul, MN: Public School Incentives, 1984b.

Puiman. Rosalie. *The Mindful Guide to Conflict Resolution: How to Thoughtfully Handle Difficult Situations, Conversations, and Personalities*. New York: Adams Media, 2019.

Putnam, Robert D., Lewis M. Feldstein, and Don Cohen. *Better Together: Restoring the American Community*. New York: Simon & Schuster, 2003.

Raiffa, Howard, John Richardson, and David Metcalfe. *Negotiation Analysis: The Science and Art of Collaborative Decision Making*. Cambridge, MA: Harvard University Press, 2002.

Ramo, Joshua C. *The Age of the Unthinkable: Why the New World Disorder Constantly Surprises Us and What We Can Do about It*. New York: Little, Brown and Company, 2009.

Randall, Ruth E., and Keith Geiger. *School Choice: Issues and Answers*. Bloomington, IN: National Education Service, 1991.

Rauth, Ingo, Lisa Carlgren, and Maria Elmquist. "Making It Happen: Legitimizing Design Thinking in Large Organizations." *Design Management Journal* 9, no. 1 (October 2014): 47–60. https://doi.org/10.1111/dmj.12015.

Raworth, Kate. "A Doughnut for the Anthropocene: Humanity's Compass in the 21st Century." *The Lancet Planetary Health* 1, no. 2 (May 2017): e48–e49. https://doi.org/10.1016/S2542-5196(17)30028-1.

Raworth, Kate. *Doughnut Economics: Seven Ways to Think Like a 21st-Century Economist*. White River Junction, VT: Chelsea Green Publishing, 2017.

Raworth, Kate. "A Safe and Just Space for Humanity: Can We Live within the Doughnut?" Oxfam discussion paper (February 2012). https://www-cdn.oxfam.org/s3fs-public/file_attachments/dp-a-safe-and-just-space-for-humanity-130212-en_5.pdf.

Rayner, Steve. "How to Eat an Elephant: A Bottom-up Approach to Climate Change." *Climate Policy* 10, no. 6 (2010): 615–21.

Reaves, Thom. "Eric Gibbons: Reflecting Our Humanity, Beauty, and Imperfections." *Thom Reaves' Studio Tour Magazine: The Artists behind the Art*. August 28, 2016. https://www.studiotourmagazine.com/single-post/2016/08/27/Eric-Gibbons-Reflecting-Our-Humanity-Beauty-Imperfections.

Reconomics Institute. "Old Sand Quarry in Barbados Is Being Transformed into a Vibrant Wildlife Reserve." *Revitalization: The Journal of Urban, Rural & Environmental Resilience*, no. 7. https://revitalization.org/article/43718/.

Redström, Johan G., "Certain Uncertainties and the Design of Design Education." *She Ji: The Journal of Design, Economics, and Innovation* 6, no. 1 (Spring 2020): 83–100. https://www.diva-portal.org/smash/get/diva2:1469973/FULLTEXT01.pdf.

Reed, Bill. "Shifting from 'Sustainability' to Regeneration." *Building Research & Information* 35, no. 6 (September 2007): 674–80. https://doi.org/10.1080/09613210701475753.

Regenerative International. *Why Regenerative Agriculture?* https://regenerationinternational.org/why-regenerative-agriculture/.

Regeneration International, "Why Regenerative Agriculture," accessed November 2, 2020, https://regenerationinternational.org/why-regenerative-agriculture/.

Regenesis. "Playa Viva." https://regenesisgroup.com/project/playa-viva/.

Regenesis. "Regenerative Development: How We Work." https://regenesisgroup.com/how-we-work/.

Regenesis. "Regenerative Development: Transforming the Way Human Inhabit the Earth." https://regenesisgroup.com/.

Regenesis. "The Regenerative Practitioner Series." https://regenerat.es/the-regenerative-practitioner-series/.

Reich, Robert B. "Big Tech Has Become Way Too Powerful." *New York Times*, September 18, 2015. http://www.nytimes.com/2015/09/20/opinion/is-big-tech-too-powerful-ask-google.html.

Reil, Jennifer, and Roger L. Martin. *Creating Great Choices: A Leader's Guide to Integrative Thinking.* Boston: Harvard Business School Press, 2017.

"Reindustrialization of America." *Business Week, Special Issue*, June 30, 1980: 55–142. https://doi.org/10.1177/003232928001000123.

Reingold, Jennifer. "What P&G Knows about the Power of Design." *Fast Company*, June 2, 2005. https://www.fastcompany.com/53103/what-pg-knows-about-power-design.

Resnick, Paul, and Sara Kiesler. *Building Successful Online Communities: Evidence-Based Social Design.* Cambridge, MA: MIT Press, 2016.

Rethinking Design Education Initiative. https://www.futureofdesigneducation.org/.

Rhodes, Christopher J. "The Imperative for Regenerative Agriculture." *Science Progress* 100, no. 1 (March 2017): 80–129. https://doi.org/10.3184/003685017X14876775256165.

Rhodes, James Melvin. "An Analysis of Creativity." *Phi Delta Kappan* 42, 1961: 305–10.

Rice, Keith E. "vMemes #4." *Integrated Socio-Psychological Blog.* https://www.integratedsociopsychology.net/theory/vmemes/vmemes-3/.

Ries, Charles P., Marco Hafner, Troy D. Smith, Frances G. Burwell, Daniel Egel, Eugeniu Han, Martin Stepanek, and Howard J. Shatz. *After Brexit: Alternative Forms of Brexit and Their Implications for the United Kingdom, the European Union, and the United States.* Santa Monica, CA: RAND Corporation, 2017. https://www.rand.org/randeurope/research/projects/brexit-economic-implications.html.

Rigotti, Nancy A., and Robert B. Wallace. "Using Agent-Based Models to Address 'Wicked Problems' Like Tobacco Use: A Report from the Institute of Medicine." *Annals of Internal Medicine* 163, no. 6 (September 2015): 469–71. https://doi.org/10.7326/M15-1567.

Ritchey, Tom. "Wicked Problems: Modelling Social Messes with Morphological Analysis." *ACTA Morphologica Generalis* 2, no. 1 (2013): 1–8. https://vdocuments.net/amp/wicked-problems-modelling-social-messes-with-morphological-analysis.html.

Ritchey, Tom. *Wicked Problems—Social Messes*. Berlin: Springer, 2011.

Rittel, Horst W. J. "The Structure and Usefulness of Planning Information Systems." In *The Universe of Design: Horst Rittel's Theories of Design and Planning*, edited by Jean-Pierre Protzen and David Harris, 171–80. London: Routledge, 2010.

Rittel, Horst W. J., and Melvin M. Webber. "Dilemmas in a General Theory of Planning." *Policy Sciences* 4 (June 1973): 155–69. doi.org/10.1007/BF01405730.

Roam, Dan. *The Back of the Napkin: Solving Problems and Selling Ideas with Pictures*. New York: Portfolio/Penguin, 2013.

Roberts, Nancy C. "Public Entrepreneurship and Innovation." *Review of Policy Research* 11, no. 1 (March 1992): 55–74. https://doi.org/10.1111/j.1541-1338.1992.tb00332.x.

Robert, Nancy C. "Roberts Organizational System Framework." *Coping with Wicked Problems Class Notes*. (2015).

Roberts, Nancy C. "Wicked Problems and Network Approaches to Resolution." *International Public Management Review* 1, no. 1 (2000): 1–19.

Roberts, Nancy C. "Wicked Problem Territory and the Design Strategy." Paper presented to the International Public Policy Workshop on Wicked Problems and Agenda Setting, June 26–28, 2018: 15–20. IPPA—IWPP, Pittsburgh 2019, Policy (ippapublicpolicy.org).

Roberts, Nancy C., and Raymond T. Bradley. "Stakeholder Collaboration and Innovation: A Study of Public Policy Initiation at the State Level." *Journal of Applied Behavioral Science* 27, no. 2 (1991): 209–27. https://doi.org/10.1177/0021886391272004.

Roberts, Nancy C., and Sean F. Everton. "Monitoring and Disrupting Dark Networks: A Bias toward the Center and What It Costs Us." In *Eradicating Terrorism from the Middle East*, edited by Alexander R. Dawoody, 29–42. Berlin: Springer, 2016. https://doi.org/10.1007/978-3-319-31018-3_2.

Roberts, Nancy C., and Paula J. King. *Transforming Public Policy: Dynamics of Policy Entrepreneurship and Innovation*. San Francisco: Jossey-Bass, 1996.

Robinson, Sir Ken. "Do Schools Kill Creativity?" TED video, 19:12. Filmed in February 2006 in Monterey, CA. https://www.ted.com/talks/sir_ken_robinson_do_schools_kill_creativity.

Rockström, Johan, W. et al. "A Safe Operating Space for Humanity." *Nature* 461, no. 24 (September 2009): 472–75. https://doi.org/10.1038/461472a.

Rodale Institute. "Regenerative Organic Agriculture and Climate Change," accessed November 2, 2020, https://rodaleinstitute.org/wp-content/uploads/rodale-white-paper.pdf.

Rodgers, Paul A., Giovanni Innella, and Craig Bremner. "Paradoxes in Design Thinking." *Design Journal* 20, sup1 (September 2017): 4444–58. https://doi.org/10.1080/14606925.2017.1352941.

Rogal, Maria, and Raúl Sánchez. "Codesigning for Development." In *Routledge Handbook for Sustainable Design*, edited by Rachel Beth Egenhoefer, 250–62. London: Routledge, 2017. https://doi.org/10.4324/9781315625508.

Rogers, Simon. "The McChrystal Afghanistan PowerPoint Slide: Can You Do Any Better?" *The Guardian*, April 29, 2010. https://www.theguardian.com/news/datablog/2010/apr/29/mcchrystal-afghanistan-powerpoint-slide.

Roland, Ethan, and Gregory Landua. *Regenerative Enterprise: Optimizing for Multi-capital Abundance*. Morrisville, NC: Lulu Press, 2015.

Rosati, Clio, Francesca Rosati, and Matteo Vignoli. "Measuring Design Thinking Mindset." Paper presented to *DS 92: Proceedings of the Design 2018*, 15th International Design Conference, Dubrovnik, Croatia, May 21–24, 2018: 1991–2002. https://doi.org/10.21278/idc.2018.0493.

Rosensweig, Ryan R. *Elevating Design: Building Design as a Dynamic Capability.* PhD diss. University of Cincinnati, 2011.

Roser, Max. "Research and Data to Make Progress against the World's Largest Problems." *Our World in Data.* https://ourworldindata.org/.

Rosling, Hans. "The Best Stats You've Ever Seen." February 2006. TED video, 19:38. https://www.ted.com/talks/hans_rosling_the_best_stats_you_ve_ever_seen.

Rowe, Peter G. *Design Thinking.* Cambridge, MA: MIT Press, 1991.

Roy, Bunker. "Learning from a Barefoot Movement." TED Global July 2011. TED video, 19:07. https://www.ted.com/talks/bunker_roy/up-next?language=en.

Roy, Bunker, and Jesse Hartigan. "Empowering the Rural Poor to Develop Themselves: The Barefoot Approach." *Innovations* (Spring 2008): 68–93. https://www.mitpressjournals.org/doi/pdf/10.1162/itgg.2008.3.2.67.

Ruhl, Jack, and Diane Ruhl. "NCR Research: Costs of Sex Abuse Crisis to US Church Underestimated." *National Catholic Reporter*, November 2, 2015. https://www.ncronline.org/news/accountability/ncr-research-costs-sex-abuse-crisis-us-church-underestimated.

Rusk, Reuben, and Lea Waters. "Tracing the Size, Reach, Impact, and Breadth of Positive Psychology." *Journal of Positive Psychology* 8, no. 3 (2013): 207–21. https://doi.org/10.1080/17439760.2013.777766.

Russ, Sandra W. "Pretend Play and Creative Processes." *American Journal of Play* 6, no. 1 (Fall 2013): 136–48.

Ryan, Alex. "Transforming Community Health through Systemic Design." March 21, 2016. https://medium.com/the-overlap/transforming-community-health-through-systemic-design-5b22b9d5bf.

Saggar, Manish, et al. "Developing Novel Methods to Assess Long-Term Sustainability of Creative Capacity Building and Applied Creativity." In *Design Thinking Research. Understanding Innovation*, edited by Hasso Plattner, Christoph Meinel, and Larry Leifer, 29–39. Cham, Switzerland: Springer, 2015. https://doi.org/10.1007/978-3-319-06823-7_3.

Saint-Onge, Hubert, and Debra Wallace. *Leveraging Communities of Practice for Strategic Advantage.* Amsterdam: Butterworth/Heinmann, 2003.

Sanders, Elizabeth B.-N., and Pieter J. Stappers. "Co-creation and the New Landscapes of Design." *CoDesign* 4, no. 1 (March 2008): 5–18. https://doi.org/10.1080/15710880701875068.

Sanford, Carol. *The Regenerative Business.* New York: Nicholas Brealey, 2017.

Sanford, Carol. "The Regenerative Education System and Practice—Part 1." Medium.com. https://medium.com/@carolsanford/the-regenerative-education-system-and-practice-part-1-23ffcc86326e.

Sanford, Carol. "The Regenerative Education System and Practice—Part 2." Medium.com. https://medium.com/@carolsanford/the-regenerative-education-system-and-practice-part-2-d6c07a7beac5.

Sanford, Carol. "The Regenerative Education System and Practice—Part 3." Medium.com. https://medium.com/@carolsanford/the-regenerative-education-system-and-practice-part-3 -c4e7d04cde11.

Sanford, Carol. *The Regenerative Life: Transform Any Organization, Our Society, and Your Destiny*. Boston: Nicholas Brealey, 2020.

Sanford, Carol. *The Responsible Business: Reimaging Sustainability and Success*. 2nd ed. Edmunds, WA: InterOctave, 2020.

Scharmer, C. Otto. *The Essentials of Theory U: Core Principles and Applications*. Oakland, CA: Berrett-Koehler Publishers, 2018.

Scharmer, C. Otto. "Leading from the Future: A New Social Technology for Our Times." *Systems Thinker*. Based on a Creative Commons ShareAlike 4.0 license. https://thesystemsthinker.com /leading-from-the-future-a-new-social-technology-for-our-times/.

Scharmer, C. Otto, and Katrin Kaufer. *Leading from the Emerging Future: From Ego-System-to Eco-System*. San Francisco: Barrett-Koehler, 2013.

Schilling, David R. "Knowledge Doubling Every 12 Months, Soon to Be Every 12 Hours." *Industry Tap*. April 19, 2013. http://www.industrytap.com/knowledge-doubling-every-12-months-soon-to -be-every-12-hours/3950.

Schmiedgen, Jan., Holger Rhinow, Eva Köppen, and Christoph Meinel. *Parts without a Whole?— The Current State of Design Thinking Practice in Organizations*. Technical Report No. 97. Potsdam: Hasso-Plattner-Institut für Softwaresystemtechnik an der Universität Potsdam, 2015. https:// thisisdesignthinking.net/why-this-site/the-study/.

Schmitt, Neal, ed. *The Oxford Handbook of Personnel Assessment and Selection*. Oxford: Oxford University Press, 2012.

Schmitt, Neal. "Personality and Cognitive Ability as Predictors of Effective Performance at Work." *Annual Review of Organizational Psychology and Organizational Behavior* 1, no. 1 (March 2014): 45–65. https://www.annualreviews.org/doi/abs/10.1146/annurev-orgpsych-031413-091255.

Schneider, Mark, Paul Teske, and Michael Mintrom. *Public Entrepreneurs: Agents for Change in American Government*. Princeton, NJ: University Press, 2011.

Schön, Donald A. *The Reflective Practitioner*. New York: Basic Books, 1983.

Schön, Donald A., and Martin Rein. *Frame Reflection: Toward the Resolution of Intractable Policy Controversies*. New York: Basic Books, 1994.

School of System Change. "System Change, about Us, Blog, Courses, Contributors, Resources." www.forumforthefuture.org/school-of-system-change.

Schwab Foundation for Social Entrepreneurship. "Social Entrepreneur Sanjit (Bunker) Roy." https://www.schwabfound.org/awardees/sanjit-bunker-roy.

Schwab, Klaus. *The Fourth Industrial Revolution*. New York: Crown Business, 2016.

Schwartz, Beverly. *Rippling: How Social Entrepreneurs Spread Innovation throughout the World*. San Francisco: Jossey-Bass, 2012.

Schwartz, Judith D. *Water in Plain Sight: Hope for a Thirsty World*. White River Junction, VT: Chelsea Green Publishing, 2019.

Schweitzer, Jochen, Lars Groeger, and Leanne Sobel. "The Design Thinking Mindset: An Assessment of What We Know and What We See in Practice." *Journal of Design, Business & Society* 2, no. 1 (March 2016): 71–94. https://doi.org/10.1386/dbs.2.1.71_1.

ScienceDaily. "Human-Machine Superintelligence Can Solve the World's Most Dire Problems." January 4, 2016. https://www.sciencedaily.com/releases/2016/01/160104080041.htm.

Searle, John R. *The Construction of Social Reality*. New York: Free Press, 1995.

Security Council. "Alarmed by Continuing Syria Crisis, Security Council Affirms Its Support for Special Envoy's Approach in Moving Political Solution Forward." *United Nations Coverages and Press Releases*. August 17, 2015. http://www.un.org/press/en/2015/sc12008.doc.htm.

Seed Communities. "The Regenerative Educator Community." https://seed-communities.com /regeneducatorfounders/.

Seelig, Tina. *inGenius: A Crash Course in Creativity*. New York: HarperOne, 2012.

Seidel, Victor P., and Sabastian K. Fixson. "Adopting Design Thinking in Novice Multidisciplinary Teams: The Application and Limits of Design Methods and Reflexive Practices." *Journal of Product Innovation Management* 30, no. S1 (December 2013): 19–33. https://doi.org/10.1111/jpim.12061.

Self-Help Credit Union. "Who We Are," accessed November 1, 2020, https://www.self-help.org /who-we-are.

Seligman, Martin. *Flourish*. New York: Free Press, 2011.

Seligman, Martin. *Learned Optimism: How to Change Your Mind and Your Life*. New York: Vintage Books, 2006.

Sen, Amartya. *Development as Freedom*. Oxford: Oxford University Press, 1999.

Senge, Peter M. *The Fifth Discipline: The Art and Practice of the Learning Organization*. 2nd ed. New York: Currency, 2006.

Shapiro, Eddie, and Debbie Shapiro. *The Unexpected Power of Mindfulness and Meditation*. Mineola, New York: IXIA Press, 2019.

Sharpe, Bill. *Three Horizons: Patterning of Hope*. Axminster, UK: Triarchy Press, 2013.

Sharpe, Bill, A. Hodgson, G. Leicester, A. Lyon, and I. Fazey. "Three Horizons: A Pathways Practice for Transformation." *Ecology and Society* 21, no. 2 (June 2016). https://doi.org/10.5751 /ES-08388-210247.

Shea, William R., and Mariano Artigas. *The Rise and Fall of a Troublesome Genius*. Oxford: Oxford University Press, 2003.

Sheppard, Benedict, Hugo Sarrazin, Garen Kouyoumjia, and Fabricio Dore. "The Business Value of Design." *McKinsey Report*, October 25, 2018. https://www.mckinsey.com/business-functions /mckinsey-design/our-insights/the-business-value-of-design.

Shepard, Mark. *Restoration Agriculture: Real World Permaculture for Farmers*. Austin, TX: Acres USA, 2013.

Shore, Zachary. *Blunder: Why Smart People Make Bad Decisions*. New York: Bloomsbury, 2008.

Sibbet, David. *Visual Meetings: How Graphics, Sticky Notes, and Idea Mapping Can Transform Group Productivity*. Hoboken, NJ: Wiley, 2010.

Sidhu, Jatinder, and Patrick Reinmoeller. *The Ambidextrous Organization: Management Paradox Today*. London: Routledge, 2017.

Sidney, Mara S. "Policy Formulation: Design and Tools." In *Handbook of Public Policy Analysis: Theory, Politics, and Methods*, edited by Frank Fischer, Gerald J. Miller, and Mara S. Sidney, 79–88. Boca Raton, FL: CRC Press, 2007.

Siegel, Ethan. "Yes, The Multiverse Is Real, But It Won't Fix Physics." *Forbes*, January 25, 2018. https://www.forbes.com/sites/startswithabang/2018/01/25/yes-the-multiverse-is-real-but-it-wont -fix-physics/#132b47e33a67.

Simon, Herbert A. "Forecasting the Future or Shaping It?" Complex Information Processing, Working Paper # 550. Presented at the Carnegie Mellon University Earthware Symposium, sponsored by the Department of Computer Science, Carnegie Mellon University, Pittsburgh, October 19, 2000.

Simon, Herbert A. *Models of Man*. New York: Wiley, 1957.

Simon, Herbert A. *The Sciences of the Artificial*. Cambridge, MA: MIT Press, 1969.

Simon, Herbert A. *The Sciences of the Artificial*, 2nd ed. Cambridge, MA: MIT Press, 1982.

Simon, Herbert A. *The Sciences of the Artificial*. 3rd ed. Cambridge, MA: MIT Press, 1996.

Simon, Herbert A. "The Structure of Ill-Structured Problems." *Artificial Intelligence* 4, no. 3–4 (Winter 1973): 181–201. https://doi.org/10.1016/0004-3702(73)90011-8.

Simon, Herbert A., and Allen Newell. *Human Problem Solving*. Englewood, NJ: Prentice Hall, 1972.

Simonsen, Jesper, Connie Svabo, Sara M. Strandvad, Kristine Samson, Morten Hertzum, and Ole E. Hansen, eds. *Situated Design Methods*. Cambridge, MA: MIT Press, 2014.

Skaburskis, Andrejs. "The Origin of 'Wicked Problems.'" *Planning Theory and Practice* 9, no. 2 (June 2008): 277–80.

Slaughter, Richard, and Chris Riedy. "Understanding and Resolving the Global Problematique: Assessing the Balance between Progressive and Socially Conservative Foresight." *Foresight* 11, no. 5 (August 2009): 21–39.

Smith, Wendy K., and Marianne W. Lewis. "Toward a Theory of Paradox: A Dynamic Equilibrium Model of Organizing." *Academy of Management Review* 36, no. 2 (April 2011): 381–403. https://doi.org/10.5465/AMR.2011.59330958.

Smithsonian Natural Museum of Natural History. "What Does It Mean To Be Human?" Last updated January 6, 2001. http://humanorigins.si.edu/evidence/human-family-tree.

Smits, Willie. "How to Restore a Rainforest." February 2009. TED video, 20:24, https://www.ted .com/talks/willie_smits_how_to_restore_a_rainforest?language=en.

Smits, Willie. "Sustainability Starts at the Village Level." August 30, 2012. TEDxMidwest video, 20:58. https://www.youtube.com/watch?v=gHNeVoxxYxU.

Snow, Charles C., Raymond E. Miles, and Grant Miles. "A Configurational Approach to the Integration of Strategy and Organization Research." *Strategic Organization* 3, no. 4 (2005): 431–39. https://doi.org/10.1177/1476127005057965.

Social Action for Rural Advancement (SARA). "Sampada Network," accessed October 1, 2020, http://www.barefootsara.org/sampada-network.php.

Solidarity Economy: Building an Economy for People & Planet. https://ccednet-rcdec.ca/en/toolbox/solidarity-economy-building-economy-people-planet.

Solidarity NYC. Accessed November 1, 2020, http://solidaritynyc.org/.

Spaulding, Dean T. *Evaluation in Practice*. 2nd ed. San Francisco: Jossey-Bass, 2014.

Speth, James G., and Kathleen Courrier, eds. *The New Systems Reader: Alternatives to a Failed Economy*. New York: Routledge, 2021.

SPIE Engineering Group, "Toward the Emergence of a Post-Carbon Economy," accessed October 30, 2020, https://www.spie.com/en#accueil.

Stahel, Walter R. *The Circular Economy: A User's Guide*. New York: Routledge, 2019.

Stahl, Cynthia H. "Out of the Land of Oz: The Importance of Tackling Wicked Environmental Problems without Taming Them." *Environment Systems and Decisions*, 34, no. 4 (2014): 473–77.

Stanford's Bootcamp Bootleg. "Method: Interview Preparation." https://static1.squarespace.com/static/57c6b79629687fde090a0fdd/t/58890239db29d6cc6c3338f7/1485374014340/METHODCARDS-v3-slim.pdf.

Stanford Center on Longevity. "Closing the Inequity Gap: Designing for Affordability Design Challenge Winners." April 7, 2020. Stanford, CA, http://longevity.stanford.edu/design-challenge/2020/04/07/stanford-center-on-longevity-announces-closing-the-inequity-gap-designing-for-affordability-design-challenge-winners/.

"Stanford Design Challenge 2020: Reducing the Inequity Gap," accessed November 7, 2020, https://contestwatchers.com/stanford-design-challenge-2020-reducing-the-inequity-gap/.

Stanford dSchool. "Design Thinking Bootleg." https://dschool.stanford.edu/resources/design-thinking-bootleg.

Stanford dSchool. "How to Kick Off a Crash Course." April 2020. https://dschool.stanford.edu/resources/gear-up-how-to-kick-off-a-crash-course.

Stanford dSchool. "Method: Interview Preparation," *Bootcamp Bootleg*, 9–16. https://static1.squarespace.com/static/57c6b79629687fde090a0fdd/t/58890239db29d6cc6c3338f7/1485374014340/METHODCARDS-v3-slim.pdf.

Stanford dSchool. "Stanford Design Thinking Virtual Crash Course." October 21, 2019. YouTube 1:20:04. https://www.youtube.com/watch?v=pmjyZPibH14.

Stanislovaitis, Vilius. *Your First Kickstarter Campaign*. Independently published, 2019.

Statista Research Department. "Terrorism—Facts and Statistics." Statista. http://www.statista.com/topics/2267/terrorism/.

Steffen, Will, Wendy Broadgate, Lisa Deutsch, Owen Gafney, and Cornelia Ludwig. "The Trajectory of the Anthropocene: The Great Acceleration." *Anthropocene Review* 2, no. 1 (April 2015): 81–98. doi.org/10.1177/2053019614564785.

Steffen, Will W., et al. *Global Change and the Earth System: A Planet under Pressure*. Berlin: Springer, 2004.

Sternberg, Robert J. "Creativity as a Decision:" Comment. *American Psychologist* 57, no. 5 (2002): 376. https://doi.org/10.1037/0003-066X.57.5.376a.

Stiehm, Judith H., and Nicholas W. Townsend. *The U.S. Army War College: Military Education in a Democracy*. Philadelphia: Temple University Press, 2002.

Stiglitz, Joseph E., Nell Abernathy, Adam Hersh, Susan Homberg, and Mike Konczal. *Rewriting the Rules of the American Economy: An Agenda for Growth and Shared Prosperity*. New York: Roosevelt Institute, 2015. https://rooseveltinstitute.org/wp-content/uploads/2015/05/RI-Rewriting-the -Rules-201505.pdf.

Stiglitz, Joseph E., Amartya Kumar Sen, and Jean-Paul Fitoussi. *Report by the Commission on the Measurement of Economic Performance and Social Progress*. Paris: Commission on the Measurement of Economic Performance and Social Progress, 2009. https://www.cpc.unc.edu/projects/rlms-hse /publications/1921.

Stockholm Resilience Centre, Stockholm University. "The Nine Planetary Boundaries." https:// www.stockholmresilience.org/research/planetary-boundaries/planetary-boundaries/about-the -research/the-nine-planetary-boundaries.html.

Stoker, Gerry, and Alice Moseley. "Motivation, Behavior, and the Microfoundations of Public Services." In *Public Services: A New Reform Agenda*, edited by Henry Kippin, Gerry Stoker, and Simon Griffiths, 17–36. London: Bloomsbury, 2013. https://doi.org/10.5040/9781472544872.ch-002.

Stracker, David. *Rapid Problem Solving with Post-it Notes*. Boston: Da Capo Press, 1997.

Stratfor Worldview. "How Many Countries Are There in the World in 2019?" April 15, 2019. https://worldview.stratfor.com/article/how-many-countries-are-there-world-2019.

Straus, David. *How to Make Collaboration Work*. San Francisco: Berrett-Koehler, 2002.

Subcommission on Quaternary Stratigraphy, Anthropocene Working Group. "Results of a Binding Vote," May 21, 2019. http://quaternary.stratigraphy.org/working-groups/anthropocene/.

Sullivan, Walter. "The Enstein Papers: A Man of Many Parts." *New York Times*, March 29, 1972: 1.

Sunstein. Cass R. *How Change Happens*. Cambridge, MA: MIT Press, 2019.

Susskind, Lawrence, Sarah McKearnan, and Jennifer Thomas-Larmer. eds. *The Consensus Building Handbook*. Thousand Oaks, CA.: SAGE, 1999.

Sustainability Transitions Research Network. "About STRN." https://transitionsnetwork.org /about-strn/.

Svensson, Kate, Barbara Szijarto, Peter Milley, and J. Bradley Cousins. "Evaluating Social Innovations for Evaluation Design." *American Journal of Evaluation* 39, no. 4 (April 2018): 459–77. https://doi.org/10.1177/1098214018763553.

Sweeting, Ben. "Wicked Problems in Design and Ethics." In *Systemic Design: Theory, Methods, and Practice*, edited by Peter H. Jones and Kyoichi, 119–43. Tokyo: Springer, 2018. https://doi .org/10.1007/978-4-431-55639-8.

Systems Innovation. "Complex Adaptive Systems," 2015. YouTube video, 10:22. https://www .youtube.com/watch?v=IWhkUne8T68.

Systems Innovation. "Complex Adaptive Systems Overview." 2014. YouTube video, 4:53. https:// www.youtube.com/watch?v=rl0yFwcGx_o.

Systems Innovation. "Self-Organization Overview." 2014. YouTube video, 5:53. https://www .youtube.com/watch?v=BTR17I_Eb_o.

Tainter, Joseph. *The Collapse of Complex Societies*. New York: Cambridge University Press, 1990.

Taleb, Nassim N. *Black Swans*. 2nd ed. New York: Random House, 2010.

Tapscott, Don, and Anthony Williams. "Innovating the 21st-Century University: It's Time!" *Educause Review* 45, no. 1 (January/February 2010): 16–29. https://er.educause.edu/articles/2010/2/innovating-the-21stcentury-university-its-time.

Taylor, Jill Bolte. *My Stroke of Insight*. New York: Viking, 2006.

Tenner, Edward. *Why Things Bite Back: Technology and the Revenge of Unintended Consequences*. New York: Vintage, 1996.

Termeer, Catrien J., and Art Dewulf. "A Small Wins Framework to Overcome the Evaluation Paradox of Governing Wicked Problems." *Policy Society* 38, no. 2 (August 2018): 298–314. https://doi.org/10.1080/14494035.2018.1497933.

Termeer, Catrien J., Art Dewulf, and Robert Biesbroek. "A Critical Assessment of the Wicked Problem Concept: Relevance and Usefulness for Policy Science and Practice." *Policy and Society* 38, no. 2 (May 2019): 167–79. https://doi.org/10.1080/14494035.2019.1617971.

Termeer, Catrien J., Art Dewulf, and Gerard Breeman. "Governance of Wicked Climate Adaptation Problems." In *Governance of Wicked Climate Adaptation Problems*, edited by J. Knieling and Filho W. Leal, 27–39. Heidelberg, Germany: Springer, 2013. https://doi.org/10.1007/978-3-642-29831-8_3.

Termeer, Catrien J., Arwin van Buuren, Art Dewulf, Dave Huitema, Heleen Mees, Sander Meijerink, and Marleen van Rijswick. "Governance Arrangements for the Adaptation to Climate Change." In *Oxford Research Encyclopedia of Climate Science*, October 2017. https://doi.org/10.1093/acrefore/9780190228620.013.600.

Terra Genesis International. "Cultivating the Regenerative Potential of Your Supply." http://www.terra-genesis.com/.

Terra Genesis International. "Walker's Reserve: From Quarry to Food Forest, A Pathway of Regeneration," accessed November 2, 2020, http://www.terra-genesis.com/walkers-case-study/.

Teske, Paul, and Mark Schneider. "The Bureaucratic Entrepreneur: The Case of City Managers." *Public Administration Review* 54, no. 4 (July/August, 1994): 331–40. https://doi.org/10.2307/977380.

Tetlock, Philip E., and Dan Gardner. *Superforecasting: The Art and Science of Prediction*. New York: Crown Publishers, 2015.

Tharp, Bruce M., and Stephanie M. Tharp. *Discursive Design: Critical, Speculative, and Alternative Things*. Cambridge, MA: MIT Press, 2018.

Thayer, Robert L. "Leadership/Communication: A Critical Review and a Modest Proposal." In *Handbook of Organizational Communication*, edited by Gerald M. Goldhaber and George A. Barnett, 231–263. Norwood, NJ: Ablex, 1988.

Thibault, John. *How to Change a Law*. Menlo Park, CA: iLobby, 2016.

Thompson, Leigh, and David Schonthal. "The Social Psychology of Design Thinking." *California Management Review* 62, no. 2 (January 2020): 84–99. https://doi.org/10.1177/0008125619897636.

Thomson, Ann M., and James L. Perry. "Collaboration Processes: Inside the Black Box." *Public Administration Review*, 66 (December 2006): 20–32. https://doi.org/10.1111/j.1540-6210.2006.00663.x.

Tietjen, Anne, and Gertrud Jørgensen. "Translating a Wicked Problem: A Strategic Planning Approach to Rural Shrinkage in Denmark." *Landscape & Urban Planning*, 154 (October 2016): 29–43. https://doi.org/10.1016/j.landurbplan.2016.01.009.

Tilonia Artisans of India. Accessed October 1, 2020, https://www.tilonia.com/.

Tischler, Linda. "Dynamic Duos: PepsiCo's Indra Nooyi and Mauro Porcini on Design-Led Innovation." *Fast Company*, September 23, 2013. https://www.fastcompany.com/3016310/pepsico -indra-nooyi-and-mauro-porcini.

Tjendra, Jeffrey. "Why Design Thinking Will Fail." *Business Innovation Design*, March 25, 2014. https://businessinnovation.design/blog/2014/3/23/why-design-thinking-will-fail.

Toesland, Finbarr. "Five Futuristic Modes of Transport Transforming Travel." *Racontour*, May 31, 2018. https://www.raconteur.net/business-innovation/five-futuristic-transport-modes.

Tomes, Anne, and Peter Armstrong. "Dialectics of Design: How Ideas of 'Good Design' Change." *Prometheus* 28, no. 1 (March 2010): 29–39.

Tonkinwise, Cameron. "Prototyping Risks When Design Is Disappearing." *Current* (blog), n.d., 1. https://current.ecuad.ca/prototyping-risks-when-design-is-disappearing.

Torbert, Bill, and Associates. *Action Inquiry: The Secret of Timely and Transforming Leadership*. San Francisco: Barrett Koehler, 2004.

Torfing, Jacob. *Collaborative Innovation in the Public Sector*. Washington, DC: Georgetown University Press, 2016.

Torfing, Jacob. "Collaborative Innovation in the Public Sector: The Argument." *Public Management Review* 21, no. 1 (2019): 1–11. https://doi.org/10.1080/14719037.2018.1430248.

Transition Network. "A Movement of Communities Coming Together to Reimagine and Rebuild Our World," accessed November 29, 2020, https://transitionnetwork.org/.

Transition Network. "Principles." Accessed November 29, 2020, https://transitionnetwork.org /about-the-movement/what-is-transition/principles-2/.

Turchin, Peter. *Ages of Discord: A Structural-Demographic Analysis of American History*. Chaplin, CT: Beresta Books, 2016.

Turnbull, Nick, and Robert Hoppe. "Problematizing 'Wickedness:' A Critique of the Wicked Problem Concept, from Philosophy to Practice." *Policy and Society* 38, no. 2 (2019): 315–37. doi.org/10 .1080/14494035.2018.1488796.

Turnpenny, John, Irene Lorenzoni, and Mavis Jones. "Noisy and Definitely Not Normal: Responding to Wicked Issues in the Environment, Energy and Health." *Environmental Science & Policy* 12, no. 3 (2009): 347–58. https://doi.org/10.1016/j.envsci.2009.01.004.

Tushman, Michael L., and Charles A. O'Reilly III. "Ambidextrous Organizations: Managing Evolutionary and Revolutionary Change." *California Review* 38, no. 4 (Summer 1996): 8–30. http:// web.mit.edu/curhan/www/docs/Articles/15341_Readings/Organizational_Learning_and_Change /Tushman_&_OReilly_1996_Ambidextrous_Organizations.pdf.

Unger, Roberto M. "Conclusion: The Task of the Social Innovation Movement." In *New Frontiers in Social Innovation Research*, edited by Alex Nicholls, Julie Simon and Madeleine Gabriel, 233–251. London: Palgrave Macmillan, 2015. https://link.springer.com/chapter/10.1057/978113 7506801_12#Abs1.

United Nations. "Strategic Framework for Afghanistan: Towards a Principled Approach to Peace and Reconstruction." September 15, 1998.

United Nations, Department of Economic and Social Affairs. *Population Facts*. New York: Population Division, 2019. https://www.un.org/en/development/desa/population/migration /publications/populationfacts/docs/MigrationStock2019_PopFacts_2019-04.pdf.

United Nations, Department of Economic and Social Affairs. "World Population Prospects: The 2015 Revision." https://www.un.org/en/development/desa/publications/world-population -prospects-2015-revision.html.

United Nations, Department of Economic and Social Affairs, Population Division. *Population Facts*. "Migration and Population Change—Drivers and Impacts." No. 2017/8, December 2017. https://www.un.org/en/development/desa/population/migration/publications/populationfacts /docs/MigrationPopFacts20178.pdf.

United Nations Development Program. *2018 Statistical Update: Human Development Indices and Indicators*. New York: UNDP, 2018. http://hdr.undp.org/en/content/human-development-indices -indicators-2018-statistical-update.

United Nations Environment Program. "Deforestation in Borneo Is Slowing, but Regulation Remains Key." February 18, 2019. https://www.unenvironment.org/news-and-stories/story/defo restation-borneo-slowing-regulation-remains-key.

United Nations Humanitarian Crisis Response. "Syria Refugee Response." *Operational Portal Refugee Situations*. Last updated January 19, 2023. https://data2.unhcr.org/en/situations/syria.

United Nations World Tourism Organization. "UNWTO World Tourism Barometer and Statistical Annex. January 2019." eLibrary. https://www.e-unwto.org/doi/abs/10.18111/wtobarometereng .2019.17.1.1.

UN News. "UN Chief Issues 'Red Alert, Urges the World to Come Together in 2018 to Tackle Pressing Challenges." December 31, 2018. https://news.un.org/en/story/2017/12/640812-un-chief-issues-red -alert-urges-world-come-together-2018-tackle-pressing.

USAID. "Grand Challenges for Development." https://www.usaid.gov/grandchallenges.

US Army Heritage and Education Center. "Origin of the Term VUCA." Updated May 7, 2019. https://usawc.libanswers.com/faq/84869.

US Census Bureau. "Trade in Goods with China." https://www.census.gov/foreign-trade/balance /c5700.html.

US Census Bureau. "U.S. and World Population Clock." http://www.census.gov/popclock/.

US Department of Transportation, February 14, 2019. https://www.bts.gov/newsroom/estimated -january-2019-us-airline-traffic-data.

US Department of Transportation, Bureau of Transportation Statistics. "Estimated January 2019 U.S. Airline Traffic Data." Washington, DC

US Department of Treasury Office of International Affairs. *Foreign Exchange Policies of Major Trading Partners of the United States*. April 29, 2016. https://www.treasury.gov/resource-center /international/exchange-rate-policies/Documents/2016-4-29%20(FX%20Pol%20of%20Major%20 Trade%20Partner)_final.pdf.

US Solidarity Economy Network. https://ussen.org/.

US Special Operation Command (USSOCOM). "SOF Truths.," https://www.socom.mil/about/sof-truths#:~:text=Humans%20are%20more%20important%20than%20hardware&text=People%20%E2%80%93%20not%20equipment%20%E2%80%93%20make%20the,lack%20of%20the%20right%20people.

University of Southampton. "Scientists Identify Climate 'Tipping Points'." *Science Daily*, October 15, 2015. https://www.sciencedaily.com/releases/2015/10/151015084348.htm.

Vaillancourt, Allison M. *The Organizational Politics Playbook: 50 Strategies to Navigate Power Dynamics at Work*. Tucson, AZ: Wheatmark, 2021.

van der Bijl-Brouwer, Mieke, and Bridget Malcolm. "Systemic Design Principles in Social Innovation: A Study of Expert Practices and Design Rationales." *She Ji: The Journal of Design, Economics, and Innovation* 6, no. 3 (Autumn 2020): 386–407. https://doi.org/10.1016/j.sheji.2020.06.001.

Van der Ryn, Sim, and Stuart Cowan. *Ecological Design: Tenth Anniversary Edition*. Washington, DC: Island Press, 1996.

Van Patter, G. K. "Design 1.0, 2.0. 3.0. 4.0." *NextD Journal: ReRe Thinking Design*. March 2009. https://pdfslide.net/documents/design-10-20-30-40-the-rise-of-visual-sensemaking.html.

Vaughan, Frances. *Awakening Intuition*. Garden City, NY: Anchor Books, 1979.

Veale, Jonathan. "Field Guide about Strategic Design inside Government." *Medium*, May 27, 2016. https://medium.com/@jonathanveale/a-field-guide-about-strategic-design-inside-government-9-lessons-from-the-frontier-de50b4f1ea8e.

Verbeek, Peter-Paul. "Materializing Morality Design Ethics and Technological Mediation." *Science, Technology, & Human Values* 31, no. 3 (May 2006): 361–80. https://doi.org/10.1177/0162243905285847.

Verganti, Roberto. *Design-Driven Innovation*. Boston: Harvard Business School Press, 2009.

Vermaas, Pieter E., and Udo Pesch. "Revisiting Rittel and Webber's Dilemmas: Designerly Thinking against the Background of New Social Distrust," *She Ji: The Journal of Design, Economics, and Innovation* 6, no. 4 (Winter 2020): 530–45. https://doi.org/10.1016/j.sheji.2020.11.001.

Verweij, Marco. "Wicked Problems, Clumsy Solutions, and Messy Institutions in Transnational Governance." In *The Problem-Solving Capacity of the Modern State: Governance Challenges and Administrative Capacity*, edited by Martin Lodge and Kai Wegrich, 183–97. Oxford: Oxford University Press, 2014.. https://doi.org/10.1093/acprof:oso/9780198716365.003.0010.

Vetterli, Christophe J. *Embedded Design Thinking*. PhD diss., University of St. Gallen, Switzerland, 2015.

Vigota, Eran. "From Responsiveness to Collaboration: Governance, Citizens, and the New Generation of Public Administration." *Public Administration Review* 62, no. 5 (September/October 2002): 527–60. https://doi.org/10.1111/1540-6210.00235.

Vinsel, Lee. "Design Thinking is a Boondoggle." *Chronicle of Higher Education*, May 21, 2018. https://www.chronicle.com/article/Design-Thinking-Is-a/243472.

Vinsel, Lee. "A Response to the Stanford d.school's Defense of Design." *Noteworthy—The Journal Blog*, June 14, 2018. https://blog.usejournal.com/theres-so-little-there-there-a-response-to-the-stanford-d-school-s-defense-of-design-thinking-3cac35a1a365.

Vygotsky, Lev S. "Imagination and Creativity in Childhood." *Journal of Russian and East European Psychology* 42, no. 1 (January/February 2004): 7–97. https://doi.org/10.1080/10610405.2004.110 59210.

Waddock, Sandra, Greta M. Meszoely, Steve Waddell, and Domenico Dentoni. "The Complexity of Wicked Problems in Large-Scale Change." *Journal of Organizational Change Management* 28, no. 6 (2015): 993–1012. doi/10.1108/JOCM-08-2014-0146/full/html.

Wahl, Daniel C. *Designing Regenerative Cultures*. Axminster, UK: Triarchy Press, 2016.

Wahl, Daniel C. "Human and Planetary Health." *Resilience*, December 5, 2018. https://www .resilience.org/stories/2018-12-05/human-and-planetary-health-ecosystem-restoration-at-the -dawn-of-the-century-of-regeneration/.

Wahl, Daniel C. "Meta-Design for Whole Systems Health." *Age of Awareness*, April 8, 2017. https://medium.com/age-of-awareness/design-for-whole-systems-health-e700f1f030c6.

Wahl, Daniel C. "Planetary Health and Regeneration Resource Compilation." September 11, 2018. http://newstoryhub.com/2018/09/planetary-health-and-regeneration-resource-compilation -daniel-wahl/.

Wahl, Daniel C. "'Regeneration Hits the Mainstream." *Medium*, November 1, 2018. https:// medium.com/age-of-awareness/regeneration-hits-the-mainstream-but-what-about-the-deeper -practice-746c4aa7ea1b.

Wahl, Daniel C. "Regenerative (R)evolution: Reclaiming Humanity's Oneness with Nature." *Medium*, May 2, 2017. https://medium.com/insurge-intelligence/regenerative-r-evolution-f1058a975e96.

Wahl, Daniel C., and Seaton Baxter. "The Designer's Role in Facilitating Sustainable Solutions." *Design Issues* 24, no. 2 (2008). https://doi.org/10.1162/desi.2008.24.2.72.

Walker, Rob. "A Golden Age of Design." *New York Times Style Magazine*, September 28, 2014. https://www.nytimes.com/2014/09/22/t-magazine/design-golden-age.html.

Walter, Barbara, F. *How Civil Wars Start*. New York: Crown, 2022.

Ward, Antonia, Ellie Runcie, and Lesley Morris. "Embedding Innovation: Design Thinking for Small Enterprises." *Journal of Business Strategy* 30, no. 2–3 (February 2009): 78–84. https://doi .org/10.1108/02756660910942490.

Ware, Colin. *Visual Thinking for Design*. Amsterdam: Morgan Kaufmann, 2008.

Watzlawick, Paul, John Weakland, and Richard Fisch. *Change: Principles of Problem Formulation and Problem Resolution*. New York: W. W. Norton, 1974.

Weber, Edward P., and Anne M. Khademian. "Wicked Problems, Knowledge Challenges, and Collaborative Capacity Builders in Network Settings." *Public Administration Review* 68, no. 2 (March/April 2008): 344–9. https://doi.org/10.1111/j.1540-6210.2007.00866.x.

Webster, Ken. *The Circular Economy: A Wealth of Flows*. 2nd ed. Cowes, Isle of Wight, UK: Ellen MacArthur Foundation Publishing, 2016.

Webster, Steven W. *American Rage: How Anger Shapes Our Politics*. Cambridge: Cambridge University Press, 2020.

Weick, Karl E. *Sensemaking in Organizations*. Thousand Oaks, CA: SAGE, 1995.

Weick, Karl E. "Small Wins: Redefining the Scale of Social Problems." *American Psychologist* 39, no. 1 (January 1984): 40–9. https://doi.org/10.1037/0003-066X.39.1.40.

Weick, Karl E., and Robert E. Quinn. "Organizational Change and Development." *Annual Review of Psychology* 50 (1999): 351–86. https://doi.org/10.1146/ANNUREV.PSYCH.50.1.361.

Weick, Karl E., and Kathleen M. Sutcliffe. *Managing the Unexpected: Resilient Performance in an Age of Uncertainty.* 2nd ed. San Francisco: Jossey-Bass, 2007.

Weick, Karl E., Kathleen M. Sutcliffe, and David Obstfeld. "Organizing and the Process of Sensemaking." *Organization Science* 16, no. 4 (July-August 2005): 409–21. https://doi.org/10.1287/orsc.1050.0133.

Weisbord, Marvin R., and Sandra Janoff. *Future Search: Getting the Whole System in the Room for Vision, Commitment, and Action.* San Francisco: Berrett-Koehler, 2010.

Wells, Diana E. "From Social Entrepreneurship to Everyone a Changemaker: 40 Years of Social Innovation Point to What's Next." *Social Innovations Journal* (November 30, 2018). https://socialinnovationsjournal.org/editions/issue-52/75-disruptive-innovations/2906-from-social-entrepreneurship-to-everyone-a-changemaker-40-years-of-social-innovation-point-to-what-s-next.

Wendt, Thomas. "Toward Sustainable Design Thinking." Design Gym. https://www.thedesigngym.com/toward-sustainable-design-thinking/.

Wendy Schmidt Ocean Health XPRIZE. "Healing Our Oceans." https://www.xprize.org/prizes/ocean-health.

Wenger, Etienne C., and William M. Snyder. "Communities of Practice: The Organizational Frontier." *Harvard Business Review* (January/February 2000): 139–45. https://hbr.org/2000/01/communities-of-practice-the-organizational-frontier.

Westley, Frances R., and Nino Antadze. "Making a Difference: Strategies for Scaling Social Innovation for Greater Impact." *The Innovation Journal: The Public Sector Innovation Journal* 15, no. 2 (2010), 1–19. https://www.innovation.cc/scholarly-style/2010_15_2_2_westley-antadze_social-innovate.pdf.

Westley, Frances R., Katharine McGowan, and Ola Tjörnbo, eds. *Social Innovation: Building Resilience through Transitions.* Cheltenham, UK: Edward Elgar, 2017.

Wexler, Mark N. "Exploring the Moral Dimensions of Wicked Problems." *International Journal of Sociology and Social Policy* 29, nos. 9–10 (2009): 531–542. https://doi.org/10.1108/0144333091098630.

"What Is Problem Solving?" *Cognitive Psychology.* Last edited April 14, 2009. http://cognitivepsychology.wikidot.com/cognition:problem-solving.

"What Is a Social Solidarity Economy?" Accessed November 1, 2020, http://www.ripess.org/what-is-sse/what-is-social-solidarity-economy/?lang=en.

Whitbeck, Carol. "Ethics as Design-Doing Justice to Moral Problems." In *Ethics in Engineering Practice and Research* (135–153). 2nd ed. chapter 3. Cambridge University Press, 2011.

Whitbeck, Caroline. "Ethics as Design-Doing Justice to Moral Problems." In *Ethics in Engineering Practice and Research,* 2nd ed., 135–153. Cambridge: Cambridge University Press, 2011.

White, Rachael E. "The Power of Play: A Research Summary on Play and Learning." http://www.childrensmuseums.org/images/MCMResearchSummary.pdf.

Wilber, Ken. *A Brief History of Everything: 20th Anniversary Edition*. Boulder, CO: Shambhala, 2017.

Wilber, Ken. *A Theory of Everything: An Integral Vision for Business, Politics, Science, and Spirituality*. Boston: Shambala, 2001.

Wildavsky, Aaron. *Speaking Truth to Power*. Boston: Little, Brown and Company, 1979.

Wilhelm, Patricia M. *The Involvement and Perceived Impact of the Citizens League on Minnesota State School Policymaking, 1969–1984*. PhD diss., University of Minnesota, 1984.

Williams, Paul. *Collaboration in Public Policy and Practice: Perspectives on Boundary Spanners*. Bristol, UK: Bristol University Press, 2012.

"Willie Smits TED2009 Talk Challenged." https://www.ted.com/about/programs-initiatives/ted-talks/willie-smits-ted-talk-challenged.

WikiDiff. "What Is the Difference between Imagination and Image?" https://wikidiff.com/imagination/image.

Wikimedia Commons. "Linear, Cubic, and Exponential Growth." Last modified October 10, 2020. https://commons.wikimedia.org/wiki/File:Exponential.png.

Wikipedia. "Cobra Effect." Last modified January 14, 2023. https://en.wikipedia.org/wiki/Cobra_effect.

Wikipedia, "David Korten," Last modified January 20, 2023. https://en.wikipedia.org/wiki/David_Korten.

Wikipedia. "Design." Last modified January 30, 2023. https://en.wikipedia.org/wiki/Design.

Wikipedia. "List of Religious Leaders Convicted of Crimes." Last modified December 30, 2022. https://en.wikipedia.org/wiki/List_of_religious_leaders_convicted_of_crimes.

Wikipedia. "World War I Casualties." Last modified Jauary 19, 2023. https://en.wikipedia.org/wiki/World_War_I_casualties.

Wikipedia. "World War II Casualties." Last modified January 1, 2023. https://en.wikipedia.org/wiki/World_War_II_casualties.

Windrum, Paul, and Per Koch, eds. *Innovation in Public Sector Services: Entrepreneurship, Creativity and Management*. Cheltenham, UK: Edward Elgar, 2008.

Wittgenstein, Ludwig. *Philosophical Investigations*. Translated by G. E. M Anscombe. 4th ed. Hoboken, NJ: Wiley-Blackwell, 1998.

Wolff, Richard. "On the Mondragon Cooperatives." March 14, 2014. YouTube video, 44:35. https://www.youtube.com/watch?v=mKbukSeZ29o.

Wolfle, Dael. "The Administration of NASA." *Science* 162, no. 3855 (November 15, 1968): 753. https://www.jstor.org/stable/1725721.

Wood, Donna J., and Barbara Gray. "Toward a Comprehensive Theory of Collaboration." *Journal of Applied Behavioral Science* 27, no. 2 (June 1991): 139–62. https://doi.org/10.1177/0021886391272001.

World Bank. "Restoring China's Loess Plateau." March 15, 2007. http://www.worldbank.org/en/news/feature/2007/03/15/restoring-chinas-loess-plateau.

World Bank. "World Bank Forecasts Global Poverty to Fall below 10% for First Time; Major Hurdles Remain in Goal to End Poverty by 2030." October 4, 2015. https://www.worldbank.org /en/news/press-release/2015/10/04/world-bank-forecasts-global-poverty-to-fall-below-10-for-first -time-major-hurdles-remain-in-goal-to-end-poverty-by-2030.

World Economic Forum. "Circular Economy and Material Value Chains." https://www.weforum .org/projects/circular-economy/.

World Health Organization (WHO). *The Global Eradication of Smallpox: The Final Report of the Global Commission for the Certification of Smallpox Eradication.* Geneva, Switzerland: WHO, 1980. http://apps.who.int/iris/bitstream/10665/39253/1/a41438.pdf.

World Resources Institute. *Millennium Ecosystem Assessment: Ecosystems and Human Well-being: Synthesis.* Washington, DC: Island Press, 2005.

Woudhuysen, James. "The Craze for Design Thinking: Roots, a Critique, and Toward an Alternative." *Design Principles and Practices: An International Journal* 5, no. 6 (December 2011): 235–48. https://doi.org/10.18848/1833-1874/cgp/v05i06/38216.

Wrigley, Cara, Erez Nusem, and Karla Straker. "Implementing Design Thinking: Understanding Organizational Conditions." *California Management Review* 62, no. 2 (January 2020): 125–43. https://doi.org/10.1177/0008125619897606.

Wright, Rebecca, Evan Watson, Tom Booth, and Masrur Jamaluddin. "Borneo Is Burning: How the World's Demand for Palm Oil Is Driving Deforestation in Indonesia." CNN, November 2019. https://www.cnn.com/interactive/2019/11/asia/borneo-climate-bomb-intl-hnk/.

Wu, Steven. "The Best Project Management Software for Designers." May 10, 2019. https://www .creativebloq.com/software/best-project-management-71515632.

Wyatt, Jocelyn, Tim Brown, and Shauna Carey. "The Next Chapter in Design for Social Innovation." *Stanford Social Innovation Review* (Winter 2021): 41–7.

XPRIZE. "$100 M Gigaton Scale Carbon Removal." https://www.xprize.org/prizes/elonmusk.

XPRIZE. "Creating Water from Thin Air." https://www.xprize.org/prizes/water-abundance.

XPRIZE. "Discover. Understand. Preserve. Rainforest." https://www.xprize.org/prizes/rainforest.

XPRIZE. "Turning CO2 into Products." https://www.xprize.org/prizes/carbon.

XPRIZE. "Work Reimagined. Rapid Reskilling." https://www.xprize.org/prizes/rapidreskilling.

XPRIZE. "XPRIZE Rapid COVID Testing." https://www.xprize.org/prizes/covidtesting.

Zahariadis, Nikolaos. *Handbook of Public Policy Agenda Setting.* Cheltenham, UK: Edward Elgar, 2016.

Zaltman, Gerald, Robert Duncan, and Jonny Holbek. *Innovations and Organizations.* New York: Wiley, 1973.

Zari, Maibritt Pedersen. *Regenerative Urban Design and Ecosystem Biomimicry.* London: Routledge, 2018.

Zweibelson, Ben. "To Design, or Not to Design": Introduction, Part One, March 4, 2011; Part Two, March 11, 2011; Part Three, March 18, 2011; Part Four, April 5, 2011; Part Five, April 15, 2011; and Part Six May 9, 2011. *Small Wars Journal.* https://smallwarsjournal.com/jrnl/art/to -design-or-not-to-design.

Index

Page numbers followed by *t* indicate tables and *f* indicate figures.